P9-APY-727

BRIEF CONTENTS

v

Writers' Roles

Enactments of the Process

WRITERS' ROLES

Enactments of the Process

NONDITA MASON
Hunter College, The City University of New York

GEORGE OTTE
Baruch College, The City University of New York

Harcourt Brace College Publishers

Fort Worth   Philadelphia   San Diego   New York   Orlando   Austin   San Antonio
Toronto   Montreal   London   Sydney   Tokyo

PUBLISHER	Ted Buchholz
ACQUISITIONS EDITOR	Stephen T. Jordan
DEVELOPMENTAL EDITOR	Karl Yambert
PROJECT EDITOR	Kelly Riche/Deanna Johnson
PRODUCTION MANAGER	Erin Gregg
ART DIRECTOR	Peggy Young
PERMISSIONS EDITOR	Julia C. Stewart

Cover Illustration and Icons: Catherine Denvir, London, U.K.

Address for editorial correspondence
Harcourt Brace College Publishers
301 Commerce Street, Suite 3700
Fort Worth, Texas 76102

Address for orders
Harcourt Brace & Company
6277 Sea Harbor Drive
Orlando, Florida 32887
1-800-782-4479; in Florida 1-800-433-0001

Copyright acknowledgments begin on p. 555 and constitute a continuation of the copyright page.

ISBN: 0-15-500160-4

Library of Congress Catalog Card Number: 93-77914

Printed in the United States of America

3 4 5 6 7 8 9 0 1 2   016   9 8 7 6 5 4 3 2 1

DETAILED CONTENTS

PROCESS FOCUS
Invention and
Peer Dialogue

STUDENT ESSAY
Hugh Melvin Robinson
"Being Wrong
Was a Habit"

PROCESS FOCUS
Revision and
Peer Review

STUDENT ESSAY
Nikki Pearson
"A Journey to
Kindergarten"

PROCESS FOCUS
Surveying

STUDENT ESSAY
Julio Olivencia
"Reversal of Gender Roles
in Popular TV Shows"

PROCESS FOCUS
Item Analysis

STUDENT ESSAY
Melissa Schmeelk
"Why More Students
Should Participate in
Extracurricular Activities"

PROCESS FOCUS
Rhetorical Reading

STUDENT ESSAY
Thomas Lorentzen
"Woman by Profession"

PROCESS FOCUS
Double-Entry Journal

STUDENT ESSAY
Mikhael Yanko
"Education of the Fittest"

STUDENT ESSAY
Alexandra Cruz
"My Own Understanding
of 'A Rose for Emily'"

STUDENT ESSAY
Missole Louizaire
"Role of Women and
Children in Family
Relationships in Haiti"

STUDENT ESSAY
Valentina Fedorovsky
"IQ Tests:
Are They Fair?"

TO THE INSTRUCTOR

Textbooks don't teach courses; teachers do. It follows that a textbook should supplement rather than supplant the role of the instructor, and that's just what we've designed this book to do.

Writers' Roles offers more than a dozen enactments of the writing process (since we know it is not a single process) in the form of student essays written in response to specific writing assignments. Each chapter presents a sustained example of a student's response to an assignment, following the student's efforts through successively refined drafts of an essay. We consistently present, not just sample pieces of student writing and accounts of how they came to be, but an enacted response to each piece: where it works, how it works, why it works.

Thinking of what we would want a textbook to do for us—and of what our own students would like to see—we realized the best approach to a writing assignment would be neither a blow-by-blow recipe nor a recitation of generalizations about, say, the importance of being specific. Instead, it would be the presentation of a student's successful response to the assignment and a teacher's explanation of why it was successful. To accomplish this, we needed distinctive student voices, not just for the sake of engaging interest, but also for the sake of provoking thought.

The students' pieces, at least, fit this bill even better than we expected. We can confidently say that the student writing here is inimitable without being at all intimidating. If the students' essays in some sense defy imitation, it's not because they are exhibitions of singular talent. It surely has much to do with the students' remarkably various cultural and ethnic backgrounds, but it also has to do with the plan of the book, with our conviction that students should write about what they know, what interests them, what they feel strongly about. Besides having an unmistakable personal stamp, such writing tends to be more interesting to the reader as well as to the writer. And this interest has more to do with the way the writing is situated than with what type of writing it is. Consequently, *Writers' Roles* is not organized according to a taxonomy of writing types or tasks but rather ranges through writing situations that are charged with purpose and that are attuned increasingly to the academic context.

Accordingly, the progression of the chapters is meant to seem logical without being lockstep. Each three-chapter section maps out an arena of writerly authority the students have access to, with the progression moving from authority already available to the students to authority that must be earned and deployed according to academic conventions.

The first section of *Writers' Roles*, then, treats writing about past experience, in part so the importance of making connections between personal and general significance can be stressed from the start. Here the students are introduced to invention and revision strategies, peer-group work, causal and comparative analysis, and relevant examples of professional as well as student writing. Trial Run and Checklist sections are interspersed throughout every chapter as practical invitations for students to apply to their own writing projects the techniques and strategies they read about in the sustained student examples.

Section Two invites students to consider their present circumstances, particularly as they figure in the academic context. As in each chapter of Sections One through Five, "Reading the Writing Assignment" sections teach students to focus on the principal issues posed by the assignment, and to break it into manageable writing tasks. Students are introduced to observation and data-gathering techniques in Section Two, as well as to the principles of induction and the basics for formal argumentation. Here, too, the students have professional as well as student writing to ponder.

Writing essays about published writing, the focus of Section Three, may also be considered an introduction to deduction as the students evaluate authors' premises and strategies in chapters that highlight analysis, relevance-testing, and evaluative comparison, specifically by such means as rhetorical reading, the double-entry journal, and Burke's pentad. Section Four, building on what has gone before, presents sustained examples of three research papers: one primarily inductive, one primarily deductive, and one primarily transactional. Section Five, the not-quite-final-section (it precedes Section Six, on special writing situations and matters of form and convention) considers disciplinary variations on researched argumentation, with sustained examples of student essays in literature, sociology, and science.

Ultimately a textbook should be tested against the goal it sets for itself: our goal is to make students rhetorically versatile writers. They should have access to certain strategies and techniques, certainly, but they should be readers of situations, modulators of their voices, adaptable as well as capable. We want them to analyze purpose as well as technique, to think about why something is written as well as how it is written. Doing this with other authors' texts, especially texts produced by student authors situated like themselves, is a proven way of stimulating students to think critically about their own texts. Teaching students to think about how they write is also teaching them to think about how they think—a tall order, to be sure. But we feel certain many writing instructors share this goal.

ACKNOWLEDGMENTS

Putting together a text like this one means incurring many debts along the way. Telling stories of how writing gets written, we know our greatest debt is to the writers whose stories are told—our students. Our grateful thanks, then, to all the students who, quite literally, made this book possible.

We thank also the many reviewers of the various drafts of this book; their comments have been enlightening, and much appreciated: Chris Anderson (Oregon State University), Chris Anson (University of Minnesota—Twin Cities), Poonam Arora (University of Michigan—Dearborn), Stuart C. Brown (New Mexico State University), Christine Cetrulo (University of Kentucky), Ramola Gereben (University of San Francisco), Joan Gilson (University of Missouri—Kansas City), Richard L. Larson (Lehman College—CUNY), Robert K. Mittan (University of Arizona), Pat Morgan (Louisiana State University), Virginia Nees-Hatlen (University of Maine), Donnalee Robin (Salem State College), Lucille M. Schultz (University of Cincinnati), Judith Shushan (Cabrillo College), Jeff Sommers (Miami University—Middletown Campus), and J. Randall Woodland (University of Michigan—Dearborn).

We should also thank the several others who have helped shape the text as it now stands: Nina Straus, Marlane Miriello, and Karen Allanson for their invaluable help in the early stages; Kelly Riche and Deanna Johnson for their accommodating and efficient supervision of proofs; Julia Stewart for her work on permissions; Peggy Young for the book's design and Erin Gregg for supervision of production; Stephen Jordan and Karl Yambert for their indispensable editorial guidance; and finally Bryant and Dee for their all-enduring patience and support.

TO THE STUDENT

This is a book about purposeful writing, about having (or finding) something to say. But that's only half the battle. That "something to say" must be worth attending to—and that means you have to think about the person who's receiving your transmission. When we were students writing for college instructors (and that wasn't so long ago that we can't remember), thinking about that meant asking the question "What does the teacher want?"

Actually, writing teachers answer that question all the time with terms like "development," "coherence," and "authority." But these are abstractions, and concrete realizations of them can't be had by following easy, step-by-step recipes. What's more, a favorite term for what teachers want is "originality," which really means that teachers don't entirely know what they want until they see it—and are pleasantly surprised.

We know. We're teachers. And what we're talking about here is not the evasiveness of teachers, but their honesty, especially their honesty about the complexity of written communication. Not only are readers not sure what they want from writers until they see it, writers are not sure what they have to say until they write it. It's all a wonderful kind of groping for meanings that can be effectively expressed and understood, shared and responded to.

WHY THIS BOOK GOT WRITTEN

How can a textbook help if there aren't easy recipes and tidy categories (and there aren't)? We found our answer to that question the hard way. For a long time, we did what many writing teachers do. We designed assignments we hoped would tap into the interests and abilities the students brought to the course but would also challenge them, force them to stretch a bit. Students' responses to those assignments were often so good we shared them with the class—photocopying them, using overhead projectors to display them, sometimes just reading them. Doing this made sense, but it also made us wonder if the students weren't thinking, as we showcased these jobs well done, "*Now* you tell us...."

What we needed was a way of putting the showcasing up front, concretely demonstrating our standards and expectations **before** we put our students to work on a project. So we began collecting essays and also what went into them—journal entries, drafts, peer evaluations. What would be especially instructive, we thought, would be to preview an assignment by unpacking all the expectations that might be invested in it, then follow that with a student's successful response to it and an explanation of why we found that response successful—and provide all that in a context allowing other instructors to modify what we said, add to it, tailor it to their own purposes. That context is this textbook, and that, briefly, is why we wrote it.

THE MORALS OF STORIES OF THE WRITING PROCESS

Writers' Roles does other things, to be sure, but what it does most is tell tales, stories of how writing gets written, of how stuck students get unstuck, of how good writing gets better, of how teachers get what they want—even when they're not sure what that is until they see it. These are success stories, and the success seems to have relatively little to do with following generalizations about what makes good writing good or a certain type of writing true to type. Experience has taught us that success lies mostly in making the most of a writing situation, first by gauging it carefully, then by making use of a host of abilities and resources, things writing teachers (or textbooks) call audience analysis, invention heuristics, organizational strategies, collaborative review, and revision techniques. The product of the writing process may be praise-worthy for a long list of reasons, reasons writing teachers might specify as the shrewd implication of the reader here, a telling metaphor there, a subtle manipulation of chronology, a striking paradox, an opening with a narrative hook, a conclusion that resists closure. All of these things—and they are just the tip of the iceberg—may seem intimidating in jargonistic shorthand. They would surely be tedious to generalize about. But they're easy to exemplify. And the exemplifications keep returning us to the one great truth about good writing: it's so hard to generalize about because what makes it good is not general but specific, not one thing, but many things.

THE DANGERS OF OVERSIMPLIFICATION

People who boil writing down to one thing are not just mistaken; they're in trouble. One crippling myth is that writing is all a matter of following rules and formulas. Too many people don't see writing—especially writing in college writing courses—as communication at all; instead, they think it's a chore whose object is to avoid making mistakes. For those people, writing becomes something like sweatshop work: the product of uninspired toil, it's piecework turned over to the teacher-as-taskmaster, who in turn dispenses grades as pay or punishment. You can assume that any instructor who would assign this text would not subscribe to such a bleak view of writing instruction. This is not to say that what are defined as "errors" or "grammatical mistakes" or "violations of usage conventions" don't matter: they matter as distractions disturbing the reception of what's transmitted, and we have a whole portion of this book devoted to helping you keep such distractions to a minimum. But what's transmitted is what matters most. And that's what you have to say, what you think. Writing is essentially thought on paper, and thinking is a process it would be wrong to oversimplify.

Realizing this does much to dispel other myths: that writing ability is a matter of inborn talent, for instance, and that if you don't have that gift, you need instruction in certain forms and patterns so you can stuff your thoughts into these pre-assembled boxes. Actually, the complexity of thought teaches a simple lesson: there is no easy way, no quick fix. What's more, the complexity of thought is very nearly matched by the variety of circumstance. Writing situations vary, and so writers must adjust. Constantly.

HOW THIS BOOK IS ORGANIZED

Working through this book means walking through a number of writing situations. Your instructor will probably not insist on an exhaustive tour of every chapter, but we do hope you at least visit each section. If you do, you'll find a sequence that has worked for us and for our students.

In **Section One**, there's the invitation to write from experience, tapping memories and interests that are already there, just waiting to be used. This isn't necessarily all that easy: writing needs a reader, and so you need to excite interest, make sense to someone else, look for connections, build bridges—just what you'll find exemplified in Mel Robinson's paper on his addiction and recovery, Nikki Pearson's on kindergarten in Guyana, and Rafael Matos's on the differences in his experiences of private and public education.

Section Two treats attempts to investigate, describe, and even argue about the circumstances you find yourself in—attempts like Guneet Kaur's definition of what it's like to be an Indian student, Julio Olivencia's survey of responses to gender roles, and Melissa Schmeelk's call for greater involvement in extracurricular activities. This chance to say something important about what's going on in your school, your peer group, your outward rather than your inner life is like on-the-job writing in the so-called real world. It tests your powers of observation, your capacity to do on-site data gathering (rather than library research), and your ability to make sense of (and perhaps recommend changing) what's going on around you.

Section Three looks at texts by authors who have done just that (though maybe on a wider scale) and asks you, as you are so often asked in college, to make something of those texts: to analyze them, respond to them, evaluate them—just as Tom Lorentzen analyzes Virginia Woolf, Mikhael Yanko responds to Paolo Freire, and Hideaki Kazeno evaluates arguments on both sides of the "U.S. English" controversy. The assumption, and it's a well-grounded one, is that you will not simply become skilled at writing about reading; you'll also become more skilled at looking at your own writing with a reader's eyes, and gauging your audience's responses and evaluations even as you write.

In **Section Four**, you're given examples and discussions of different kinds of researched arguments, kinds that differ because of the approach to the subject and the relation to the reader. The examples are research papers on different subjects—Kooheon Chung's paper on Koreans' attitudes toward abortion, Ruby Huang's on the rape victim's right to privacy, and Jennifer Leung's on increasing access to a course in her major—but they have more basic, instructive differences because, fundamentally, they are arguing on the basis of facts or values or a need to negotiate with the opposition. It will be useful to strike up an acquaintance with each of these approaches; one should prove especially useful to your own purpose in researched writing.

Section Five is still more specific, going into detail about something you probably already know (or suspect): even if we're talking about a particular kind of paper, the research paper, that paper does not take the same shape in different courses. There are special expectations for the use of sources in a literature paper (like Alexandra Cruz's on a Faulkner short story); a sociology paper (like Missole Louizaire's on changing family roles in Haiti); or science paper (like Valentina Fedorovsky's on intelligence testing) pose research problems in different ways. The fifth section says why, doing just as the rest of the book does, explaining primarily by way of examples rather than generalizations.

Section Six focuses on special applications (like note taking and essay exams) and matters of convention (ranging from the citation of sources to the issue of correct usage). We hope it will do much to dispel the mystery and anxiety associated with satisfying the expectations for writing in the academic context. Here, as elsewhere, we teach by example, doing without rules and recipes, preferring instead to give you the whys behind the hows. That way, we believe, you'll have carefully considered reasons rather than memorized rules for how to proceed, whether you're tackling a midterm or a research project or the editing of a paper.

WHAT YOU NEED TO DO

However much time you spend with any one chapter or section, we hope you will spend time with your writing, time to realize the possibilities of whatever writing situations in which you find yourself. Any piece of writing is the issue of something far less tight and tidy than that piece itself is: it is only the end of attempts to give it form and the outgrowth of circumstances helping to shape it. It's important to realize that process is necessary and context inescapable. A writer's preliminary notes and drafts, like a sculptor's sketches and models or a major-league baseball player's batting practice, are the opposite of inefficient: they're indispensable. You need to work your way toward success. You need to realize that each new situation requires new thinking. We never produce writing exactly the same way twice or in exactly the same circumstances. There can be no secret formulas, no surefire shortcuts. Thought on paper always calls for thinking things through.

Because that is indisputably true, the examples we give you are not models for you to imitate. You can't learn to be a good writer by imitating good writing because you can't let someone else's experience substitute for your own. That word *experience* comes from the Latin *experientia* for "act of trying," and we have created plenty of opportunities for you to try some of the techniques and strategies that have worked for the students whose writing is on display.

These "trial runs" are crucial, but they are not enough. Again, this is a book about purposeful writing, about having (or finding) something to say. The writers in *Writers' Roles* all have their purposes; their motives, which shape their methods, can't be yours. You'll have to come up with your own. This book is designed to help; you supply the subjects—and the confidence to write about them. It shouldn't be too hard. Your thoughts are indeed worthy of an audience—particularly the audience your teacher represents. You can indeed write with real authority and expertise—particularly if you will take a shot at trying to teach the teacher. And why not? Who's to say you don't have plenty to say that's well worth listening to? If you don't feel prepared to write with authority right off the top of your head (and almost no one does), perhaps all you need to do is realize the virtue of a little preparation: some time spent remembering, observing, reading, researching. If you don't feel instantly inclined to take the time, perhaps all you need to do is consider the alternative: writing that doesn't try to interest and impress your reader isn't going to be very interesting to you either.

HOW WE CAN WORK TOGETHER

For our part, we propose to give you examples of the writing process to experience as well as observe, always changing the subject, altering the context, upping the ante by increasing the challenge. But we also try to give you chances to build on what you've done, not just in terms of specific strategies or techniques, but in terms of whole projects—so that something done for Section One or Two might be the foundation for a paper done after you've reached Section Four or Five. You make all the important decisions: defining your purpose, gauging your situation and your audience, putting the pieces together. We offer readings as examples of writers who made the same sorts of decisions. Again, neither imitation nor inspiration is our object: these are simply writers who realized their possibilities. Now it's your turn, and it's worth considering how high the stakes might be. We're not just talking about finding your voice here. You have as many voices as you allow yourself to speak with. You have as many kinds of authority as you choose to cultivate. You have citizenship in as many worlds as you apply yourself to. Whatever the writing situation, give yourself what no one else can give you: a higher purpose than just getting the thing done. Give your reader something more to do than simply reading the thing through. Have (or find) something to say. Think on paper. Excite some interest. Write.

WRITERS' ROLES

Enactments of the Process

WRITING ABOUT WHAT YOU'VE EXPERIENCED

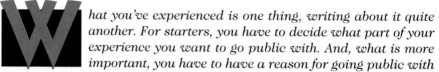

What you've experienced is one thing, writing about it quite another. For starters, you have to decide what part of your experience you want to go public with. And, what is more important, you have to have a reason for going public with it. Writing is communication—not just putting things on paper, but also turning that paper over to a reader, someone who is not you, who lacks your chief reason for being interested in your experience (because it's your experience.)

This shouldn't be too intimidating. Think of all the great writing that came out of personal experience. As a matter of fact, all writing is in some sense personal. What people tend to call "personal writing" is simply the sort that is most obviously personal. What is rather less obvious, but no less important, is that this sort of writing also wrestles with the great question all writing must answer: Why should a reader be interested?

The three chapters in this section give three general answers. The first chapter treats the kind of personal experience that is self-defining, distinctive, even unique. Here the special challenge is to make that experience seem generally significant, perhaps because it represents an extreme most are unwilling or unable to go to, perhaps because recounting it requires rigorous honesty, perhaps because it presents a chance to learn from especially good or bad fortune. Writing that makes such a case tends to take courage.

Different as we all are, there is much that we have in common. The second chapter is devoted to writing that offers distinctive perspectives on shared experience. We all come from families, we all go through school, we all come of age—but we don't all look at these experiences in the same way. A writer can cover common ground in a way that allows the reader to identify ("Yes, I've been through something like that") and also to learn, to rethink, to find new light falling on old memories. The watch-word for writing that manages this is probably thoughtfulness.

Looking back need not mean dwelling on freeze-frames of the past. It also affords the opportunity to trace connections between then and now. Writing that does just that is the focus of the third chapter. The interest excited by such writing tends to be double-visioned: there is interest in how the past differs from the present but also in how the past caused the present. The capacity to compare and contrast (to trace out similarities and differences) and the capacity for causal analysis (for working out agents and effects) are two of the more useful and impressive abilities of the human intellect. It can be a pleasure to watch them in action. And we will have the pleasure of watching them in action well beyond the realm of "personal writing."

CHAPTER ONE

GENERALIZING YOUR PERSONAL EXPERIENCE

Writing that excites us as readers must have been exciting for the writer who created it. The end result shows the energy and enthusiasm that the writer invested in the work. But people who get pleasure from the act of writing usually write about what interests them, and not necessarily about what someone else requires them to write. They do not have to work within the constraints of the college classroom with such directives as "Your essay based on the reading in Chapter 3 is due this Thursday." How can we, as college writers, become engaged enough in our writing that writing becomes a challenging and exciting process?

The word *process* is our clue. To become more invested in our writing and to have some fun, we might shift our focus from the finished product—the final paper—to the writing *process* that happens in the time between receiving an assignment and producing a final draft. To make college writing our own, we can creatively infuse the written activities that *precede* the final draft with our own energy and enthusiasm, turning what writing teacher Janet Emig calls "school-sponsored writing" into "self-sponsored writing." Such **prewriting** exercises, or writings on the way to the final draft, enable us first to discover the multiple possibilities offered by an assigned topic and then to match those possibilities to our personal experiences.

When student Hugh Melvin Robinson was asked to write about a significant event that made a difference in his life, he was confronted with the many different emotions and impressions that he associated with the event. As Mel pondered his writing assignment, he felt bogged down by his conflicting emotions. He decided to talk about his assignment with his friend Mike to try him as a sounding board for his ideas. This chapter shows how Mel's **dialogue** with Mike helped Mel both to generate a variety of ideas and to select from within that variety to find a direction for his assignment.

His dialogue with a friend as a prewriting activity enabled Mel to sort through his emotional experiences to arrive at some insight about his own thoughts on the assigned writing topic. He gained focus not only on *what* he wanted to write about but also, more significantly, on *why*. He realized that the lesson he learned from the events might set an example for others.

In addition to the writer's ability to find and define a subject, the reader or the audience often determines the effectiveness of writing. Every writer has the need to write for someone: you will need to know who your audience is, even if that means inventing one by thinking of your audience in generalized terms according to the human values we all share. That was perhaps the audience that Mel had in mind when he gave his very personal experience a general significance. If he had been overly concerned about the individual responses of his readers—his classmates and his teacher—he might have been too intimidated to write. At the same time, the knowledge that others who shared his feelings would understand his story gave him confidence to write. By choosing to write about an intensely personal experience, Mel demonstrated courage and honesty, and a desire to share his life so others might learn.

Like Mel, the two professional writers in this chapter, Langston Hughes and Mike Rose, recount significant events in their lives. Hughes tells of a painful acknowledgment of deceit and disillusionment; Rose finds revelation in a high-school student's disarmingly casual statement that sums up the humiliation and frustration experienced by "vocational" students. Though we do not see the prewriting activities that preceded the published works, we know from their own accounts that Hughes and Rose were participants in the events they recall, events that were especially significant in their lives. To focus their narratives, they each had to select a point of view and organize and communicate to their readers the significance of the events. By doing so, they were able to extend a vision of their personal experiences to include others around them.

As you prepare to write about a significant event in your own life, some of the prewriting activities that helped Mel may help you get started. Read the essays by Mel, Hughes, and Rose carefully for encouragement before embarking on your own writing project.

WRITING ASSIGNMENT

Write an essay in which you focus on a significant event that made a difference in your life. Your challenge is to bring out the general significance of the personal event while making the writing interesting for both you and your reader.

READING THE WRITING ASSIGNMENT

On the surface, the assignment requires you to tell a story that will capture a reader's interest. So you first must write a coherent narrative in which you arrange the events according to their occurrence or importance and bring them to a logical conclusion. But the key words, "bring out the general significance of the personal event," signal that this is storytelling as a purposeful exercise for a defined audience (your instructor and/or class-mates), and not just a chronological stringing together of events. For example, you may recount how you almost drowned while swimming in the ocean during a summer vacation. If you simply narrate the events in the order they occurred, your readers' response may be, "So what? You're alive now!" On the other hand, if you also show how you precipitated the near-fatal accident by being careless, and if you relate the steps you took to rescue yourself, your readers may see how your personal experience could also touch their lives, and they may learn something from your lesson.

Your purpose is to forge meaning out of your individual event and then relate it to the universal human experience. A good storyline is the basic framework to capture your readers' interest; then, as they are caught up in your narrative, show them why the event is significant for you and may also be for them.

DISCOVERING IDEAS

When you get a writing assignment, the most important challenge is to gather and organize information about the subject into a logical structure. An efficient way to confront this challenge is to break it into smaller tasks. A carpenter does not build a cabinet all at once but starts with the individual parts: the frame, the drawers, the shelves, and the hinges. Similarly, instead of attempting to write the whole paper at one time, set yourself smaller goals and begin to coax writing out of yourself.

Even before composing his first draft, Mel had to choose an appropriate topic by talking with his friend, Mike. He also brainstormed, a process that records on paper the spontaneous explosion of ideas in the writer's mind. Then he organized his ideas about the topic by examining his feelings, arranging details, and determining the event's significance. Each of these methods may help you write the first draft of your own personal story. The Trial Run sections may also stimulate ideas.

Talk with a Friend

Talk with a friend, a classmate, or a teacher to help you generate and organize ideas for an assignment. Your talk will help most if it is not a haphazard one but a guided conversation that may lead you to a suitable topic or an approach to the topic.

When Mel received his personal writing assignment, he had some vague ideas of what he wanted to write about. He could remember the event that most affected his life, of course, but there were so many aspects to it that he didn't quite know how to sort through them. Then there was the added problem of self-revelation: Did he really want to put so much about himself on paper? Mel felt he could confide in his friend, Mike, who was in a drug and alcohol rehabilitation program with him, because they had many shared experiences. One of the first discovery techniques Mel used for his writing project, therefore, was to talk with Mike. Mel tape-recorded their talk and later transcribed it on paper.

Mel and Mike's Dialogue

Mike: You've been talking about writing about your new life. What *is* your new life?

Mel: I have a new life in college that is very different from my past. I used to be a drug and alcohol abuser—more alcohol than drugs—and never looked at it as a problem. I hung out with the guys and drank beer and alcohol, never thinking I had a problem. Everybody else I knew was doing the same thing. So what was the problem? My addiction led me to crime because I needed money to support it. I want to write about this. I want to see for myself clearly what got me where I am today. I might have been lost.

Mike: Are you going to write about all the things you used to do in the past?

Mel: No, I can't write about everything. I want to zero in on some of the things I remember clearly.

Mike: Can you give me an example?

Mel: I think I'll focus on what happened the day I got arrested.

Mike: You mention wanting to be an alcoholism counselor. How does this fit in with your story?

Mel: I want to help people like myself, who have a problem and need help.

Mike: Have you been helped by counseling?

Mel: I've been helped a lot in group therapy—alcohol and drug abuse.

Mike: How do you feel writing about it?

Mel: It's hard for me to talk about it because I'm not proud of my past. I feel badly about the time I've wasted.

Mike: Why do you want to write about your past? Have you been asked to write about it?

Mel: It's part of an assignment, but I don't have to write about my arrest. I want to write about it because it will help me to face it. I want to face it. Also I might help others in a similar situation.

Mike: What's the hardest thing to face?

Mel: The fact that I hurt people, my mom, my friends, myself.

Mike: Does your Mom know you're planning to write this?

Mel: I might let her see it.

Mike: When you get an assignment to write from a personal experience, are you afraid to expose yourself to the teacher? Does it give you writer's block?

Mel: Yes, I think the teacher and students might look at me as different from everybody else. I don't want it to be held against me.

Mike: But are you going to try it anyway?

Mel: I'll give it a try.

Mike: Try your first sentence out on me.

Mel: I'll begin with my life of crime.

For most of us, talking seems more effortless than writing. So one way to help your ideas flow is to talk about them with a friend. You could talk into a tape recorder, but the advantage of talking with a friend is that your friend's questions may probe into areas of your mind that you might not look at otherwise. It helps to talk to a friend rather than a stranger, because a friend knows something about your background and is therefore more likely to ask the right questions to guide you through your own ideas as Mike was able to do for Mel.

Mike picked up on ideas expressed by Mel and encouraged him to elaborate on them. As they continued to talk, Mel's answers became more expansive and more specific. Mike's questions made Mel think creatively about the writing task at hand and made him face some of the problems he might have to deal with in writing about a personal situation. The conversation helped Mel decide what he wanted to focus on in his writing. Although, as you will see, much that was revealed in the dialogue does not appear in the finished essay, the dialogue served its main purpose, which is to stimulate the writer's thoughts at the outset of writing. The dialogue should help the writer broaden the search for potential writing topics and then help narrow the focus. For example, by answering Mike's questions, Mel expanded his list of potential topics by remembering the day he went to jail, and then he narrowed his topic again when he decided to make that day the center of his writing about his "new life." In addition, talking to a friend helps you recall conversations and other details that can make your writing lively, specific, and immediate. Mike's questions were spontaneous and yet to the point because of his shared experience with Mel. While the spontaneity is important, it is also important to avoid haphazard and far-flung questions. To ensure some control and guidance, you may prepare a list of questions in collaboration with your partner and have your instructor check the questions before you begin the dialogue.

▋RIAL RUN

For your own personal writing assignment, ask a classmate to interview you. Let the interviewer know the topic of your writing assignment so that he or she can ask probing questions to help you expand or narrow the topic. You may help the interviewer draft some questions and ask your instructor to examine the list of questions prepared by your interviewer in collaboration with you.

CHECKLIST: TALKING WITH A FRIEND

- How well do I know the person I want to talk with?
- Do we have shared experiences?
- If my experience is unusual, will the interviewer understand it?
- How much am I willing to reveal myself to this person?
- How do I feel about other people asking me personal questions?
- What do I expect from this talk?

Brainstorm

Talking with Mike gave Mel a general idea about the incident that would be the focus of his writing. The problem he faced was to develop a plan to organize the many details he might mention about the episode. What was he going to say, and how did he want his readers to react to his writing? Feeling overwhelmed, Mel went to his instructor for help, who suggested that Mel, for the time being, disregard the organization and direction of his paper and just put whatever came to his mind on paper.

This technique, often referred to as *brainstorming*, helps a writer open the mind's door so that all the thoughts—complete, incomplete, silly, outrageous, serious, and profound—pour on to the paper. The purpose of brainstorming is not to produce a draft of a paper but simply to discover what ideas lurk in the front and back of the writer's mind that seem to have some connection to the topic. Then, when the thoughts are written down visibly on paper, the writer can select those that best fit the topic. Here are Mel's brainstorming notes:

the evening of the arrest
the planning ended in our arrest
maybe the arrest was good for me
the car, the reefer smoke, the darkness of
the night, the highway near the East River
the excitement for Leroy, Jimmy and me
the thought of stealing a whole tractor trailer
— frightening but the money was good
the deserted parking lot — the eerie silence

things went wrong - the truck started
with an explosion - the noise attracted
the cops
feeling of isolation and fear - thought of
mom and Dad
wish I could look into the future to see
what I had to face.

By putting together the ideas generated by brainstorming, Mel produced about one-and-a-half handwritten pages about his topic: the night of his arrest.

That evening we were going to
steal a truck for a man who paid
us for the job. We had done this
(Leroy, Jimmy, and I) many times
before, but we were still nervous.
We started to smoke reefer and
get ready for the job. Everything
went wrong that evening. Maybe I
should have listened to Mike. That
might have prevented the arrest but
maybe the arrest was good for me.
I didn't see it that way then, though.
If only I could look into the future.

If only I could see mom and Dad in the picture. Anyway, with the windows of the car rolled up, we smoked a few joints when Leroy suggested that we drive around and case the docks where the truck was to be placed for us. We slowly passed the truck in the darkness under the highway near the East River. The reefer made me very alert and I was eager to get this over with and collect my share of the money. We drove the car back to the parking lot and turned off the motor. The game plan was set and we were ready to make our move. Jimmy and I walked out of the parking lot together while Leroy locked up the car. Jimmy said he was afraid of taking the whole tractor trailer. I told him I was thinking about the money and that took my shakes away. Leroy at this point was no longer in sight but we knew he would be there after we were set up. I walked toward the left end of the pier as Jimmy walked to the right. We had to keep track of anyone coming and going to ensure that no one saw Leroy as he hotwired the truck to get it started. The truck started with an explosion and we had started to run towards it when I spotted a car coming towards us.

Brainstorming can be in any form, including jotted fragments, scrawled sentences, or long or short passages produced on a typewriter or word processor. In brainstorming, the writer does not have to worry about structure (beginning, middle, and end) or grammar or spelling. As long as the ideas keep returning somehow to your central focus, the prose does not have to be polished—in fact, the key idea in brainstorming is *not* to take time to polish your prose, because that would interrupt your flow of ideas.

In his dialogue with Mike, Mel was not sure what he was going to write about, though he had some general ideas. He wanted to write about the evening he got arrested, but he mentioned few details. The brainstorming helped him burrow into his mind and dredge out details about the evening of his arrest. He stayed close to his subject, particularly the details of the action, without straying too far. If brainstorming takes you off on a tangent, follow it for a while in case you find useful ideas, but then work your way back to your goal.

TRIAL RUN

To help you recall details and emotions about the incident you want to focus on, brainstorm on your topic through uncensored sentences, through fragments of ideas, through lists of events, people, or feelings, or through anything that comes to your mind in connection with the subject. Write quickly everything you can possibly remember without stopping to think twice.

CHECKLIST: BRAINSTORMING

- Have I quickly put on paper the ideas that came into my head?
- Have I valued only the ideas, disregarding grammar and sentence structure?
- Have I listed things that came to mind regardless of my initial judgment or opinion about them?
- Have I written down absolutely everything that may be useful?
- Have I focused on quantity rather than quality?

COMPOSING THE FIRST DRAFT

Examine Your Feelings

As most aspects of experience are constantly changing, so are our feelings and assumptions about them. In his dialogue with Mike, Mel wasn't sure he could face the past to write about it. He wasn't certain about revealing his personal feelings and situation to other people. He only said he'd give it a try. After recalling the major details, Mel wanted to examine his feelings to clarify for himself his present perspective about his past experience. He wrote the following paragraph:

The arrest really was the best thing that could happen to me. At that time though it looked like the worst. Then I was more concerned about the police, my parents, family, and friends than I was about what led to my arrest. Now, looking back, I know I would have continued a life of drugs and crime if the arrest had not put an end to it. For a long time I blamed myself for the poor planning of the heist. If only we had planned it right, we might not have been caught. Everytime I thought about it, I went crazy. I became angry and frustrated. It took me a while to realize that the punishment I received straightened me out. Now I can look back and tell my story without anger or shame. I feel my life could have been much worse. I want to talk about my experience to people like myself so they may know that it is possible to change. We hear a lot of talk about why we should stay away from drugs and crime. But I think my story will show my readers a real situation and I hope they see its importance.

TRIAL RUN

Use the checklist below to examine your own perspective about a personal writing assignment by asking yourself a series of questions about how you felt at the time of your experience, how you feel now, and why your feelings have changed, if they have. Write a short paragraph summarizing your initial response to your feelings.

CHECKLIST: EXAMINING YOUR FEELINGS

- What does the incident reveal about me as a person?
- Am I the same person now? Would I do the same things now? How have I changed and why?
- What are my emotions about the way I acted then? Am I angry, bitter, ashamed, resigned, or indifferent?
- How do I feel now? Do I feel the same most of the time, or do my feelings change a lot when I look back on this segment of my life?
- Have my emotions settled, and do I have the necessary calm to write about them?
- Will my readers identify with some of the ways I feel?

Arrange Details

Your main objective is to tell in detail a dramatic personal story with a main point to it. The way you select, emphasize, and arrange details will strengthen the idea you wish to convey in your story. Most writers generally use chronological order, the order in which the event actually took place, but the best way to begin is to put down the details as you remember them or as they happened. Langston Hughes' essay, for example, detailed the events in the order they happened, while Mike Rose wrote events as he remembered them and saw how important they were to him.

Before working on your first draft, try any of these general orderings:

- **Chronological order.** Write down the details as they come to your mind. Then rearrange them following a logical time order.
- **Specifics first, generalizations last.** Introduce specific persons, places, or things in your first paragraph, use the body of the paper to tell your story, and *generalize* about the ideas in the body in your last paragraph. This arrangement—specifics first, generalizations last—is common in personal writings.
- **Generalizations first, specifics last.** Use the reverse organizational structure—generalizations first, specifics last—when you have a "big" idea you want to illustrate through your own experience.
- **Climactic order.** Arrange your writing in order of climax: start with less important details and move toward a climactic "scene" that occurs in your last or next-to-last paragraph.

Mel arranged his details following the specifics first, generalizations last structure, particularly in his final draft. The first draft began with Mel's reflections on the events, which later he felt detracted from the action and slowed down the narrative. So in the final draft, he went straight to the action at the beginning, followed the events in the order in which they happened, and saved his reflections and generalizations for the end.

RIAL RUN

Using any of the general orderings discussed above, write a paragraph in which you arrange the main details of a personal account so that they effectively support your purpose. Do not be concerned about including all the details but concentrate instead on shaping the general order of your narrative.

CHECKLIST: ARRANGING DETAILS

- Have I identified my purpose in describing this particular event?
- Have I arranged the details in the order that will reinforce the feeling or idea? Would my story have a stronger impact if I rearranged the details according to a different general ordering?
- Have I included only those details that would make the story believable?
- Have I cut out the irrelevant and repetitious details, and retained the most appropriate and interesting details in the most effective order?

Determine the Significance of Your Story

The significance of the story takes it beyond the "what happened" level. It reveals what you or others have gained or lost in course of the episode. In Mel's case, the night of his arrest turned his life around.

Writers can use several ways to convey the significance of their narrative. They can show the reader, through dramatized action, how the event or the situation affected their lives. Many narratives rely simply on showing the events to illustrate their significance. They let the actions speak for themselves, with little or no commentary. But showing is more commonly accompanied by telling, which comments on the action to emphasize its significance. As you will see when you read Mel's first draft below, his dramatic account of the events of the evening of his arrest is complemented by his own statements about the events' tremendous impact on his life.

A commentary can be your own reflections—some meditative thoughts on why the event is so important in your life. Hughes reflects on the hypocrisy in his own life, and Rose explores the hypocrisy in the vocational education system. The pitfall in doing this is the risk of sounding preachy or moralistic, which a writer can avoid, as Hughes and Rose do, with honesty and candor. Mel's beginning and ending in his first draft seemed artificial, as if they had been tacked on to the narrative to give it added importance. They gave the narrative a tone of self-importance and self-pity at the same time. Mel sensed this while reviewing the draft and tried, though not with complete success, to eliminate that tone in his final draft.

TRIAL RUN

At this stage in planning your own narrative, you should be certain that your story has more to it than just "what happened." Why do you think the story is worth telling? Write your responses in one paragraph.

CHECKLIST: DETERMINING THE SIGNIFICANCE OF YOUR STORY

- What is my story about?
- Why is my story important now as I look back?
- Why do I think my story will appeal to others?
- Have I learned anything from the events?
- Will others benefit by reading my story?
- Have I taken care both to show and tell about the events?
- Have I taken care to avoid preaching or moralizing?
- Do I want to reflect and comment on the action?
- Do I want to return from the closing to the beginning to remind readers of my purpose?
- Have I avoided tying up all loose ends into neat generalizations?

Mel used two invention methods—talking with a friend and brainstorming—to generate ideas. He then planned his first draft by examining feelings, arranging details, and determining the significance of the story. These activities moved Mel closer to his main purpose, which was to write about the night of his arrest and how it affected his life. The dialogue with Mike started him thinking about the demands of the assignment and the focus of his writing. Brainstorming stirred up his memory and helped him recollect the details of the events. He was concerned about reader identification—would his readers understand or blame him for what he did? As he sorted through the events in his own mind, he felt confident that his readers would understand his actions because of the positive and corrective effects on him. He felt ready to put his thoughts on paper. As he began to write, much to his surprise, one word began to follow another, and he was on his way to the first draft of his assignment.

PRESENTING MEL'S FIRST DRAFT

1   My life today is very different from my past. My desire to be at peace with myself and live within society's laws has enabled me slowly to start a new life. I used to always want everything to go my way. I was raised in a household where selfishness was a way of life, and I carried that attitude outside in dealing with others. I didn't know any better. I

set my own rules and constantly fought with people if they did not accept things my way. This attitude always got me into trouble.

2   At a young age, I started to steal things. By the age of 16, I was quite a pro. Then I, along with a couple of my friends, Jimmy and Leroy, started to get into more serious stealing. Leroy was an expert driver and he could always borrow his father's car. That set us on a crime spree that ended in my arrest. Leroy knew a man who paid us good money for stealing trucks and tractor trailers from the dock areas. We started to steal big trucks for the man who sold their contents and paid us for the job. We needed the money to pay for drugs and alcohol. Everything was fine until the evening when all went wrong.

3   As we approached the truck, the laughing and joking ceased. The atmosphere became serious as the time for action got near. "There's the truck," Leroy said, as he slowly drove past the place where the truck with all its contents was standing in the dark, under the highway near the East River. The reefer had us very alert to the darkness. I was eager to get this over with and collect the money. Leroy set out the plans. He wanted us to walk to the truck in the dark, start it up, and drive it away. But I had other plans. I suggested that Jimmy and I stand on either end of the dock to make sure nobody came as Leroy started up the truck. I wasn't about to take orders from any-one. I insisted, "Your way will only put the cops on our trail. Someone must be on the lookout for the cops while you get the truck started. If you want things your way, do the job with someone else." Leroy reluctantly accepted my plan.

4   Jimmy and I stood in the darkness to see if anyone was approaching from either end of the dock. As Leroy started up the truck and started to drive it away, Jimmy and I started running toward it to jump on the running boards on each side of the door. As we ran towards the truck, a car turned the corner and started to come our way. Somehow it just didn't look right. My feeling told me it was a cop car, so I took off after warning Jimmy. I heard someone yell, "Halt!" and a shot was fired from the spot I had taken off from. As I was turning the corner in full stride, a bullet hit the wall and fragments of brick hit me on the side of my face. I kept running without looking back.

5   I thought everything was okay when I looked through the peephole after hearing a knock on the door. It was about 8:30; I had been home about half an hour, watching a baseball game with my father, who was surprised to see me home so early. I opened the door after seeing Jimmy through the peephole, only to be collared by a detective. The detectives did not need

much proof. They heard Jimmy say in front of my parents that I was present at the scene of the crime. My mother, in shock, protested, but my father said, "Take him away because he did it." As the detective handcuffed me and led me away, I saw the tears in my mother's eyes. I knew how much I hurt her. I felt terrible.

6   After serving time, I got into a rehab program for alcohol and drug abusers. I used my experience to tell other young people to stay away from drugs and alcohol. Going into a rehab program helped me to assume responsibilities for my own actions. I no longer blame the world for my situations or my parents for not having enough. I accept life on life's terms, not always demanding to have my way. Things that happen today are not easier to handle; I just approach them in a different way and try to remain positive about my life. If there's doubt in anyone's mind that they cannot change, let me say you are wrong. There's help for those who are willing to give themselves a chance. You have to be willing to accept yourself for who you are. Now I approach life with pride and self-esteem. I try to set an example, try to make people, especially young people, realize that a good and productive life doesn't have to be put on hold. I tell them that we can all learn from our mistakes and achieve a new and rewarding life.

Thinking Critically about Mel's First Draft

1. Are you surprised or shocked at the writer's personal disclosures? Could you write about things that you've done that you are not proud of? How do Langston Hughes and Mike Rose handle similar situations in their writings at the end of the chapter?

2. Do you think Mel's first sentence is an effective way to begin his personal narrative? Why or why not? How does Mel's beginning compare with those of Hughes and Rose?

3. Paragraphs 3 through 4 are packed with dramatic action. How does the writer create drama and tension? What moves the story forward?

4. What motivated Mel, Hughes, and Rose to tell their stories? What are the predominant emotions in the stories—anger, bitterness, calm, resignation, euphoria? What indications can you find that these writers do or do not have enough emotional distance from the events to tell their stories?

5. Comment on Mel's use of language. Look for the techniques he uses to create suspense, his use of similes and metaphors, his pacing of sentences, and his use of dialogue.

6. Is there a transition between paragraphs 4 and 5? How does the writer take us from the scene of the crime to his living room at home? Does this help to continue the suspense and drama?

7. What is at the center of the writer's desire to change his life—his arrest? his mother? his cellmates? Why is Mel telling his story? What is the significance of his story to Mel and to his readers?

8. Comment on the way Mel concludes his narrative. Is it effective? Could you write it any other way?

RETHINKING AND REVISING

Revision continues throughout the writing process instead of merely providing damage control to a weak paper. The focus of revision should be both on details and the larger picture, local and global, terms used by the writing teacher, Maxine Hairston. Mel made a number of changes in his final draft, in reference to details and the larger picture, after a careful review of his first draft. One of the major changes involved the structure of the paper. While his first draft began with more generalizations and later focused on the particulars, the final draft begins directly with the details of his life of crime. This gives his paper more immediacy and adds drama. The generalizations, which are relocated at the end of the paper in the final draft, are more terse, condensed, more honest, and less sentimental than in the first draft. The final draft also eliminates most of the background information and focuses more on descriptive details of the event itself. Mel adds to the existing details and introduces a new paragraph in the final draft that captures the frenzied excitement of the evening. A more vivid picture of life in jail, absent in the first draft, makes Mel's desire to change his way of life more convincing for his readers.

The way you revise your paper is your own. Here is a checklist Mel used as he revised his first draft.

CHECKLIST: REVISING YOUR DRAFT

- Is there a clear purpose to my story? Did I achieve what I set out to achieve?
- Have I made clear the relationships between the others in the story and me, between the different places, the different times, and the different events?
- Have I used concrete sensory language that shows, not just tells?
- Have I juxtaposed events in a way that they highlight the contrasts?
- Have I examined the order of my narrative? Events need not necessarily be in a chronological order, but have I cued the reader if I have changed the order?

For a more comprehensive discussion on revising and editing, turn to the guidelines for revision beginning on p. 43 in Chapter 2.

PRESENTING MEL'S FINAL DRAFT

Being Wrong Was a Habit

Hugh Melvin Robinson

Mel deletes his first draft intro. Begins directly with his life of crime to add drama.

1   My life of crime began when I was 16 years old. A group of us started stealing trucks for a man who paid us for the job and sold their contents. A friend's father allowed him to drive his car, and we used it to stake out our jobs. Leroy had been driving since he was 13, and everyone knew of his ability to handle himself behind the wheel. Having a good driver with us was the beginning of a series of crime sprees, which supported our drug and alcohol habits. I was totally self-absorbed and cared only about how I felt, without any concern for others. I was raised in a household where there wasn't much, and whatever little I had I guarded very strictly. I carried that attitude outside in my dealings with other people. I never shared what I had with others but felt what other people had belonged rightfully to me. I wanted to set the rules in everything I did with people and constantly fought if people did not accept my way. This attitude got me into trouble as I got older, and finally culminated in the night of my arrest.

He accepts more responsibility for his action than he was willing to in the first draft.

Mel provides more condensed background information than in the first draft.

2   Leroy, Jimmy, and I were sitting in the car drinking beer and smoking reefer. We were getting our plans together for the evening job, which was supposed to be very simple. The windows of the car were rolled up. Inside the sweet smell of reefer was heavy, and the cloud of smoke within the car seemed as if a thick fog had set in. On this particular evening, like many others before it, we were going to steal a truck and sell the goods to the man for a lot of money. We badly needed the money to replenish our dwindling supply of drugs and alcohol. We drove around the docks to case the place until we spotted a truck that we could work on.

Mel pays more attention to descriptive details than in first draft.

3   As we approached the truck, the laughing and joking ceased. The atmosphere became serious as the time for action got near. "There's the truck," Leroy said, as he slowly drove past the place where the truck with all its contents was standing in the dark, under the highway near the East River. The reefer had us very alert to the darkness; we moved with the

cautiousness of a feline on the prowl. I was tense and nervous, eager to get this over with and collect my money. Leroy set out the plans. He wanted us to walk to the truck in the dark, start it up, and drive it away. But I had other plans. I suggested that Jimmy and I stand on either end of the dock to make sure nobody came as Leroy started up the truck. I wasn't about to take orders from anyone. I insisted, "Your way will only put the cops on our trail. Someone must be on the lookout for the cops while you get the truck started. If you want things your way, do the job with someone else." Leroy reluctantly accepted my plan.

4   Jimmy and I stood in the darkness to see if anyone was approaching from either end of the dock. I could see Leroy easing into the truck. In the silence of the night on that deserted dock, the noise of the truck starting up sounded like an explosion. I jumped with fear. The guard must have been paid off because after all that noise, we were still the only ones moving around. As the truck slowly crept away from its parking place, Jimmy and I started running toward it to jump on the running boards on each side of the doors. The time it was taking us to catch up with the truck seemed an eternity.

5   As we ran through the darkness towards the truck, a car turned the corner and started to come our way. Somehow it just didn't look right. I knew instinctively that it was not the man coming to take over the truck and pay us for the job. My feeling told me that this was a cop car, so I took off, after warning Jimmy. I heard someone yell, "Halt!" and a shot was fired from the spot I had taken off from. As I was turning the corner in full stride, a bullet hit the wall and fragments of brick hit me on the side of my face. I kept running without looking back.

Mel introduces new paragraph not included in first draft—new details to add drama and excitement to action.

6   I thought everything was okay when I looked through the peephole, after hearing a knock on the door. It was about 8:30; I had been home about half an hour, watching a baseball game with my father, who was surprised to see me home so early. I opened the door after seeing Jimmy through the peephole, only to be collared by a detective. The detectives did not need much proof. They heard Jimmy say in front of my parents that I was present at the scene of the crime. My mother, in shock, protested, but my father said, "Take him away because he did it." As the detective handcuffed me and led me away, I saw the tears in my mother's eyes. I knew how much I hurt her. I felt terrible.

Mel shifts his locale from action-packed crime scene to deceptive calm of living room.

Admission of emotion and guilt absent in first draft.

7   This arrest woke me up to the reality of the dark side of life in jail. Sitting in an overcrowded filthy cell, I realized what freedom meant. I missed being able to walk down my

Mel gives detailed description of time spent in jail not included in first draft. Mel adds new information on how life in jail made him change his life.

block in the sunlight, greeting friends, talking to people. I was thrown in with hardened criminals, tough men who were not about to change. All day these guys talked about their plans to get out and resume their life of crime. Only this time they wouldn't make the mistake of getting caught. None of these men had any regrets about what they had done to be in jail. This lack of concern for themselves and for others shocked me. It jolted me into realizing that I had to do something to change the way I had been living or I feared I would become like my jailmates. I knew I got a charge out of doing things I wasn't supposed to do. It made my peers look up to me. But in jail I realized this was no way to get attention. I had to do things that would be rewarding for me in a positive way. I couldn't go through life hurting people.

Shorter and more focused conclusion than in first draft—less preachy and moralizing—shows Mel now more willing to accept responsibility for his own actions.

8   After serving time, I got into a rehab program for alcohol and drug abuse. I used my experience to tell other young people to stay away from drugs and alcohol, which pave the way for a life of crime. Going into a rehab program helped me to assume responsibilities for my own actions. I no longer blame the world or my parents for my situation.

Commentary on Mel's Final Draft

The tighter organization of Mel's final draft quickens the pace and adds more drama and excitement to the opening paragraph, compared to his first draft. Mel writes a completely new introductory paragraph, which goes straight to the event. The introduction in the first draft reveals Mel's hesitancy to come to terms with his own life and his desire to blame others for his actions. The writer's voice in the new introduction is more confident as, in the process of writing, Mel begins to accept his own involvement in the action. He omits the second paragraph in the first draft as he includes the background information necessary for the reader in the new opening paragraph.

Mel's personal narrative focuses on an intensely dramatic and suspenseful event. He states at the beginning that his life of crime started when he was 16 years old. Now, as a college freshman, he looks back with a sense of relief on a way of life that he is happy to have left behind. There are several levels of conflict in the story. First there is the conflict between Mel and the world around him in paragraph 1. Then he is in conflict with his peers in paragraph 3. Paragraph 5 focuses on the dramatic conflict between him and the policeman, and Mel's conflict with his parents is revealed in paragraph 6. Paragraph 7 begins with Mel's conflict with his cellmates and culminates in his conflict with himself. This last one is perhaps the most important conflict, and the writer gradually builds toward it. It is the resolving of this conflict in the last paragraph that brings out the insight and the significance of the story. As a change from his draft, Mel uses more action details and descriptive language in the final draft. And to accommodate them, he breaks paragraph 4 in the first draft into paragraphs 4 and 5 in the final draft. We understand why the writer goes into such details about the event: because it transforms his life.

Mel's story creates suspense and drama through carefully selected descriptive language. The last sentence in the first paragraph points directly to action, which is picked up and continued in the second paragraph. Through an effective use of simile, he creates the mood of tension and suspense. There are several examples: "the cloud of smoke within the car seemed as if a thick fog had set in," "the truck starting up sounded like an explosion" (anticipating the gun shots that follow), and "the cautiousness of a feline on the prowl." This last image adds to the overall image of the darkness, the urban jungle, the hunter, and the prey.

Paragraph 6 in the final draft is an important addition. It provides more dramatic details of the arrest that Mel might not have felt comfortable including in the first draft. There is a sudden shift of locale from the scene of the crime to Mel's parents' living room. The calm at the beginning of paragraph 6 is deceptive because the readers do not anticipate the arrival of the detectives and the dramatic arrest.

In the first draft, Mel had skipped over the description of the time he spent in jail and moved quickly to the rehab center he attends after serving time in jail. This was perhaps the most difficult time for Mel and it must have been painful for him to document it. But while working on the final draft, he decided to write about it because he realized that the seamy side of life he experienced in jail contributed greatly to his transformation and might help his readers' understanding.

In revising the conclusion, Mel sensed that in the first draft, while he was cautioning his readers to avoid the path his life had taken, he sounded too much like a preacher. On the advice of his instructor, he omitted most of the last paragraph in the final draft, retaining only the section that focused on how he benefited from the rehabilitation program. In his final draft, he accepted more responsibility for his actions than he did while composing the first draft. While shifting through his memories and putting the events in their perspective to write his paper, Mel stopped blaming others for his actions and resolved the conflict within himself. This is one of the main reasons Mel's final draft is less sentimental, more focused, and more mature than his first draft.

Questions for Further Thought

1. In a story as dramatic as Mel's, it is possible to lose sight of its focus and purpose. Does Mel's narrative have a clear focus and purpose? What are they and where does he state them?

2. When we write about ourselves, our tendency is to present ourselves in the best possible light to earn our readers' admiration. But Mel takes a risk and shares some of the darkest moments of his life with his readers. Does this earn him his readers' admiration? What saves his story from being just a self-disclosure?

3. Autobiographical writing is often like persuasive writing because the writer wants the readers to accept and identify with his or her opinion. Does Mel succeed in influencing his readers' opinions? With what aspects of the narrative can the reader, in general, identify?

4. Self-disclosure in writing often leads to self-discovery. What does Mel discover about himself through writing his story? Is there anything the readers learn about themselves by reading Mel's story?

PROFESSIONAL ESSAYS

Langston Hughes

SALVATION

"I was saved from sin when I was going on thirteen. But not really saved."

ONE OF THE MOST IMPORTANT FIGURES IN twentieth-century American literature, Langston Hughes (1902–67) wrote poems, plays, short stories, satirical sketches, and novels, most of them devoted to giving voice to the African-American experience. Among his works of nonfiction are two autobiographies, The Big Sea *(1940) and* I Wonder as I Wander *(1956). Each contains many short, focused, individually titled anecdotes.* "Salvation" *is one of these from* The Big Sea.

Before he came to New York and made it big in what came to be known as the Harlem Renaissance, Hughes was just a "colored" boy growing up in Kansas. While his father traveled outside the United States, searching for a place "where a colored man could get ahead and make money quicker," Hughes was raised by his mother, then his grandmother, then two friends of hers he came to know as Auntie and Uncle Reed. "For me, there have never been any better people in the world," he writes in The Big Sea.

His affection for his Auntie Reed helps to explain the hypocrisy Hughes finds himself guilty of in "Salvation." Nevertheless, this tale of disillusionment and dishonesty cannot have been an easy one to tell. Few things are harder to get honest about than dishonesty. As you read, look for indications that Hughes has managed to get some emotional distance from his experience, some perspective on it, even some benefit from it.

ON THE WAY INTO THE READING

1. *The Big Sea,* from which "Salvation" is excerpted, was published in 1940. As you read it more than 50 years later, try to think of parallel situations in your own life or in the lives of those you know.

2. This is a tale of hypocrisy told by a boy of twelve who is full of remorse for his act of dishonesty. Do you sympathize with him? As you read, try to identify others who you think act dishonestly and examine your feelings about them. How do their actions compare with that of the young protagonist?

3. Besides telling a good story, why else does Hughes select this particular incident to write about? What purposes does it serve for the writer?

1   I was saved from sin when I was going on thirteen. But not really saved. It happened like this. There was a big revival at my Auntie Reed's church. Every night for weeks there had been much preaching, singing, praying, and shouting, and some very hardened sinners had been brought to Christ, and the membership of the church had grown by leaps and bounds. Then just before the revival ended, they held a special meeting for children, "to bring the young lambs to the fold." My aunt spoke of it for days ahead. That night I was escorted to the front row and placed on the mourners' bench with all the other young sinners, who had not yet been brought to Jesus.

2   My aunt told me that when you were saved you saw a light, and something happened to you inside! And Jesus came into your life! And God was with you from then on! She said you could see and hear and feel Jesus in your soul. I believed her. I had heard a great many old people say the same thing and it seemed to me they ought to know. So I sat there calmly in the hot, crowded church, waiting for Jesus to come to me.

3   The preacher preached a wonderful rhythmical sermon, all moans and shouts and lonely cries and dire pictures of hell, and then he sang a song about the ninety and nine safe in the fold, but one little lamb was left out in the cold. Then he said: "Won't you come? Won't you come to Jesus? Young lambs, won't you come?" And he held out his arms to all us young sinners there on the mourners' bench. And the little girls cried. And some of them jumped up and went to Jesus right away. But most of us just sat there.

4   A great many old people came and knelt around us and prayed, old women with jet-black faces and braided hair, old men with work-gnarled hands. And the church sang a song about the lower lights are burning, some poor sinners to be saved. And the whole building rocked with prayer and song.

5   Still I kept waiting to *see* Jesus.

6   Finally all the young people had gone to the altar and were saved, but one boy and me. He was a rounder's son named Westley. Westley and I were surrounded by sisters and deacons praying. It was very hot in the church, and getting late now. Finally Westley said to me in a whisper: "God damn! I'm tired o' sitting here. Let's get up and be saved." So he got up and was saved.

7   Then I was left all alone on the mourners' bench. My aunt came and knelt at my knees and cried, while prayers and songs swirled all around me in the little church. The whole congregation prayed for me alone, in a mighty wail of moans and voices. And I kept waiting serenely for Jesus, waiting, waiting—but he didn't come. I wanted to see him, but nothing happened to me. Nothing! I wanted something to happen to me, but nothing happened.

8   I heard the songs and the minister saying: "Why don't you come? My dear child, why don't you come to Jesus? Jesus is waiting for you. He wants you. Why don't you come? Sister Reed, what is this child's name?"

9   "Langston," my aunt sobbed.

10   "Langston, why don't you come? Why don't you come and be saved? Oh, Lamb of God! Why don't you come?"

11   Now it was really getting late. I began to be ashamed of myself, holding everything up so long. I began to wonder what God thought about Westley, who certainly hadn't seen Jesus either, but who was now sitting proudly on the platform, swinging his knickerbockered legs and grinning down at me, surrounded by deacons and old women on their knees praying. God had not struck Westley dead for taking his name in vain or for lying in the temple. So I decided that maybe to save further trouble, I'd better lie, too, and say that Jesus had come, and get up and be saved.

12   So I got up.

13   Suddenly the whole room broke into a sea of shouting, as they saw me rise. Waves of rejoicing swept the place. Women leaped in the air. My aunt threw her arms around me. The minister took me by the hand and led me to the platform.

14   When things quieted down, in a hushed silence, punctuated by a few ecstatic "Amens," all the new young lambs were blessed in the name of God. Then joyous singing filled the room.

15   That night, for the last time in my life but one—for I was a big boy twelve years old—I cried. I cried, in bed alone, and couldn't stop. I buried my head under the quilts, but my aunt heard me. She woke up and told my uncle I was crying because the Holy Ghost had come into my life, and because I had seen Jesus. But I was really crying because I couldn't bear to tell her that I had lied, that I had deceived everybody in the church, that I hadn't seen Jesus, and that now I didn't believe there was a Jesus any more, since he didn't come to help me.

CRITICAL READING

1. The piece begins with a statement that is immediately contradicted. How does this set you up for what follows? How serious, for instance, do you

expect Hughes to be? Do you already know what will happen as you read—or at least have some suspicions? If your interest is piqued by the contradiction, if one reason you read on is because you want to see it resolved, *is* it resolved?

2. One important way Hughes sets up his readers is the description of the way Auntie Reed set *him* up. How is her enthusiasm for what she expects to happen communicated? What is young Langston's response? Why is his response important in explaining his behavior later on?

3. Did you find Hughes' account at all humorous? Can you identify what struck you as amusing and why? Are there any indications that Hughes might want you to find some things funny? What might humor suggest about Hughes' perspective on his experience?

4. Of all his younger self's peers, Hughes chooses to characterize only one. Why? What is Westley's importance? How does he help make the attitudes of the young Langston more obvious? Of the two boys' attitudes, which seems more sensible to you? Which seems more attractive?

5. The story concludes on a note of bitter disillusionment. Take a look at that conclusion. In the long last sentence, Hughes explains why he wept that night—but is the explanation adequate from the adult's as well as the child's perspective? How can you tell between them, if in fact you can?

6. The story's ending raises questions about Hughes' purpose. A story with such an ending would hardly be told just to amuse. What might we be expected to learn from this account? Is there some way in which the title, "Salvation," is not merely ironic?

Mike Rose

"I JUST WANNA BE AVERAGE"

"School can be a tremendously disorienting place. No matter how bad the school, you're going to encounter notions that don't fit with the assumptions and beliefs you grew up with."

MIKE ROSE, BORN IN 1954, IS CURRENTLY Associate Director of Writing Programs at the University of California at Los Angeles. He has published a number of books and articles for and about the "educationally underprepared"—students who are relegated to remedial classes, vocational tracks of instruction, or programs for problem students. In Lives on the Boundary *(1989), from which our selection comes, Rose recalls that he was once classified as just such a student. When his parents, Italian-American immigrants, enrolled their son in a Catholic high school, he was given a battery of placement tests and, he explains, "somehow the results of my tests got confused with those of another student named Rose.... The error went undetected, and I remained in the vocational track for two years. What a place."*

He describes what it was like mainly by describing his fellow class-mates in "vocational education" ("a euphemism for the bottom level") at the all-boys school: their distaste for academics, their untapped potential, the disciplinary problems they created, their means of coping with bottom-level placement. This makes Rose more of a spectator than a participant in his own account. Even the remark that he uses for his title—"I just wanna be average"—is not uttered by him. Still, Rose has a very important role to play in his account, less as an actor than as commentator. In contrast to the essays by Mel and by Langston Hughes in this chapter, commentary in Rose's essay actually outweighs the recounted action. As you read, think about why this is so and what your reactions are.

ON THE WAY INTO THE READING

1. Rose makes a distinction in the first paragraph between "vocational education" and "vocational track." It is essential to understand this in order to see Rose's purpose in this story. What do these words mean to you? Do you agree with Rose's explanation?

2. Like most writers, Rose would want his readers to identify with his view. He uses small stories or anecdotes as supportive evidence for his case against Voc. Ed. How effective do you think this is as a writing technique? What other kinds of evidence could he have used? How would they compare with the anecdotal approach?

3. Who is the "I" in "I Just Wanna Be Average?" Whose story is it? How does the writer feature in the story? Do you think he identifies with the "I"? Can you?

4. From the biographical information, we know Mike Rose did not become one of the Voc. Ed. disaster statistics. As you read, try to figure out what saved him. Is that stated implicitly in the story? Why or why not?

1   Students will float to the mark you set. I and the others in the vocational classes were bobbing in pretty shallow water. Vocational education has aimed at increasing the economic opportunities of students who do not do well in our schools. Some serious programs succeed in doing that, and through exceptional teachers—like Mr. Gross in *Horace's Compromise*—students learn to develop hypotheses and troubleshoot, reason through a problem, and communicate effectively—the true job skills. The vocational

track, however, is most often a place for those who are just not making it, a dumping ground for the disaffected. There were a few teachers who worked hard at education; young Brother Slattery, for example, combined a stern voice with weekly quizzes to try to pass along to us a skeletal outline of world history. But mostly the teachers had no idea of how to engage the imaginations of us kids who were scuttling along at the bottom of the pond.

2   And the teachers would have needed some inventiveness, for none of us was groomed for the classroom. It wasn't just that I didn't know things— didn't know how to simplify algebraic fractions, couldn't identify different kinds of clauses, bungled Spanish translations—but that I had developed various faulty and inadequate ways of doing algebra and making sense of Spanish. Worse yet, the years of defensive tuning out in elementary school had given me a way to escape quickly while seeming at least half alert. During my time in Voc. Ed., I developed further into a mediocre student and a somnambulant problem solver, and that affected the subjects I did have the wherewithal to handle: I detested Shakespeare; I got bored with history. My attention flitted here and there. I fooled around in class and read my books indifferently—the intellectual equivalent of playing with your food. I did what I had to do to get by, and I did it with half a mind.

3   But I did learn things about people and eventually came into my own socially. I liked the guys in Voc. Ed. Growing up where I did, I understood and admired physical prowess, and there was an abundance of muscle here. There was Dave Snyder, a sprinter and halfback of true quality. Dave's ability and his quick wit gave him a natural appeal, and he was welcome in any clique, though he always kept a little independent. He enjoyed acting the fool and could care less about studies, but he possessed a certain maturity and never caused the faculty much trouble. It was a testament to his independence that he included me among his friends—I eventually went out for track, but I was no jock. Owing to the Latin alphabet and a dearth of Rs and Ss, Snyder sat behind Rose, and we started exchanging one-liners and became friends.

4   There was Ted Richard, a much-touted Little League pitcher. He was chunky and had a baby face and came to Our Lady of Mercy as a seasoned street fighter. Ted was quick to laugh and he had a loud, jolly laugh, but when he got angry he'd smile a little smile, the kind that simply raises the corner of the mouth a quarter of an inch. For those who knew, it was an eerie signal. Those who didn't found themselves in big trouble, for Ted was very quick. He loved to carry on what we would come to call philosophical discussions: What is courage? Does God exist? He also loved words, enjoyed picking up big ones like *salubrious* and *equivocal* and using them in our conversations—laughing at himself as the word hit a chuckhole rolling off his tongue. Ted didn't do all that well in school—baseball and parties and testing the courage he'd speculated about took up his time. His textbooks were *Argosy* and *Field and Stream,* whatever newspapers he'd find on the bus stop—from *The Daily Worker* to pornography—conversations with uncles or hobos or businessmen he'd meet in a coffee shop, *The Old Man*

and the Sea. With hindsight, I can see that Ted was developing into one of those rough-hewn intellectuals whose sources are a mix of the learned and the apocryphal, whose discussions are both assured and sad.

5   And then there was Ken Harvey. Ken was good-looking in a puffy way and had a full and oily ducktail and was a car enthusiast...a hodad. One day in religion class, he said the sentence that turned out to be one of the most memorable of the hundreds of thousands I heard in those Voc. Ed. years. We were talking about the parable of the talents, about achievement, working hard, doing the best you can do, blah-blah-blah, when the teacher called on the restive Ken Harvey for an opinion. Ken thought about it, but just for a second, and said (with studied, minimal affect), "I just wanna be average." That woke me up. Average?! Who wants to be average? Then the athletes chimed in with the clichés that make you want to laryngectomize them, and the exchange became a platitudinous melee. At the time, I thought Ken's assertion was stupid, and I wrote him off. But his sentence has stayed with me all these years, and I think I am finally coming to understand it.

6   Ken Harvey was gasping for air. School can be a tremendously disorienting place. No matter how bad the school, you're going to encounter notions that don't fit with the assumptions and beliefs that you grew up with— maybe you'll hear these dissonant notions from teachers, maybe from the other students, and maybe you'll read them. You'll also be thrown in with all kinds of kids from all kinds of backgrounds, and that can be unsettling—this is especially true in places of rich ethnic and linguistic mix, like the L.A. basin. You'll see a handful of students far excel you in courses that sound exotic and that are only in the curriculum of the elite: French, physics, trigonometry. And all this is happening while you're trying to shape an identity, your body is changing, and your emotions are running wild. If you're a working-class kid in the vocational track, the options you'll have to deal with this will be constrained in certain ways: You're defined by your school as "slow"; you're placed in a curriculum that isn't designed to liberate you but to occupy you, or, if you're lucky, train you, though the training is for work the society does not esteem; other students are picking up the cues from your school and your curriculum and interacting with you in particular ways. If you're a kid like Ted Richard, you turn your back on all this and let your mind roam where it may. But youngsters like Ted are rare. What Ken and so many others do is protect themselves from such suffocating madness by taking on with a vengeance the identity implied in the vocational track. Reject the confusion and frustration by openly defining yourself as the Common Joe. Champion the average. Rely on your own good sense. Fuck this bullshit. Bullshit, of course, is everything you—and the others—fear is beyond you: books, essays, tests, academic scrambling, complexity, scientific reasoning, philosophical inquiry.

7   The tragedy is that you have to twist the knife in your own gray matter to make this defense work. You'll have to shut down, have to reject intellectual stimuli or diffuse them with sarcasm, have to cultivate stupidity, have to

convert boredom from a malady into a way of confronting the world. Keep your vocabulary simple, act stoned when you're not or act more stoned than you are, flaunt ignorance, materialize your dreams. It is a powerful and effective defense—it neutralizes the insult and the frustration of being a vocational kid and, when perfected, it drives teachers up the wall, a delightful secondary effect. But like all strong magic, it exacts a price.

CRITICAL READING

1. "Students will float to the mark you set." What does this opening sentence suggest about Rose's audience? Does it make you, the reader, feel included or excluded? Does it help to justify the commentary provoked by Ken Harvey's remark later on?

2. The second paragraph is the only one where Rose turns the focus on himself. Does it bear out the opening sentence? Can you identify with the problematic strategies and behaviors described here? Do you think they are to be found only at this level of instruction?

3. Rose's next step is to provide three fairly detailed portraits. Why would he give his readers such thorough renderings of Dave Snyder, Ted Richard, and Ken Harvey? How would you evaluate the relevance of the many things said about, say, Ted Richard? What are your standards for determining relevance?

4. Can Ken Harvey's five-word remark bear the weight of all the commentary Rose devotes to it? Have you known students like Ken Harvey? Does what Rose says in the last two paragraphs seem to ring true?

5. Notice how those last two paragraphs use the pronoun *you,* but not in the same way as it was used in the opening statement. Who might *you* be in statements like "You'll be thrown in with all kinds of kids"? What is Rose's strategy here? Do you find it effective?

6. Having just considered the way Rose implicates the reader at the beginning and the end of his essay, you might consider also how this strategy bears on Rose's own role as a teacher who was once a Voc. Ed. student. Does Rose's double role have anything to do with the way he talks about others more than about himself? Does it help explain why commentary bulks out of proportion to action in this piece?

CHAPTER TWO

PERSONALIZING A COMMON EXPERIENCE

The popularity of the love story is no doubt due in part to recognition that, while love is a common experience, no two experiences of it are exactly the same. Life is full of shared patterns of experience—growing up, fitting in, knowing loss, growing old—that admit of infinite variations. Writers dwell on these patterns because of the double-edged fascination they exert (the familiar spiced with the new and unique) but also because of the challenge they present: age-old patterns need new light, fresh insight, if they are to seem worth looking at yet again. For readers, such accounts offer chances to look down old paths with new eyes, to feel both the fellowship and the uniqueness that make each of us human.

If you would write such an evocative account, you must first tap into that reservoir of stored-up experience called memory—and leave the tap on for a while. The test is making your account of a common experience distinctive. And when it comes to being distinctive, nothing helps so much as attention to details. They're indispensable, yet you don't want exhaustive (and thus exhausting) specifics. Which details do you select? And how do you know when you've been detailed enough?

You know the answers only by knowing your audience. Since we are considering a kind of personal writing that invites writer and reader to reflect on how their experiences are both similar and different, in this chapter we bring peer review into play as an aid to marshalling details to good effect. But even with such feedback, critical decisions are still left to the writer: the choices about what to cut, what to add, what to recast. The focus of this chapter is therefore the process of revision, as exemplified in this chapter by Nikki Pearson's "Journey to Kindergarten." We also discuss revision more generally, not in terms of a discrete stage of completing a writing task, but rather in terms of overarching principles and guidelines that you can apply whenever you write.

Each essay in this chapter ("Graduation" by Maya Angelou and "Heat and Rain" by Denise Chávez, as well as the featured piece of student writing by Nikki Pearson) treats something all of us have gone through (something we might loosely describe as growing up), but the details are different, the perspective distinctive, the experience unique—as they no doubt will be in your own case.

WRITING ASSIGNMENT

Write an essay treating an event or experience that you share with many of your peers (registration day, for instance, or graduation day) but that you also have a distinctive angle on, either because of some different aspect of the experience itself or because of a unique perspective you bring to the experience. Write for an audience of your peers, remembering that their response to what you write will largely determine how distinctive your angle truly is.

READING THE WRITING ASSIGNMENT

Before forming your purpose for writing, give some thought to the purposes behind the writing assignment. Like the previous chapter's writing assignment, this one is an invitation to reveal what makes you distinctive, but this time the distinctiveness lies less in the experience itself than in the perspective that you bring to it. Speaking of perspective, you may find it useful to consider your instructor's angle. For writing teachers, essays like the one in this chapter typically serve two purposes. First, they help introduce students to an instructor who wants (and needs) to know students more intimately than most instructors in other disciplines. Second, the use of personal experience in the academic context is a first step toward bridging personal and general significance, toward moving beyond private to public meanings and connections. This second purpose of the writing assignment represents the real test for you. You really can't fail in your first goal, to communicate some sense of yourself in the assigned essay, but your overall success depends on how well you accomplish your second goal, to communicate something important and familiar and distinctive to others.

It will probably occur to you early on that it is easier to hit upon a shared experience than it is to find and reveal a genuine insight about it. Remembering that you are writing for an audience of your peers (from the Latin *par* meaning "equal") should make this challenge seem less intimidating and mysterious. Think of your classmates as you seek a common experience you can bring some insight to.

At this point, we might also stress what's easy about the assignment. The authority, the expertise you can bring to this exercise is beyond question. There's no need to do research, to study up, to make ready. Instead, you must find a way to mine the ore of your experience and smelt it into the precious metal of a worthwhile read. Make things as easy—but also as interesting—for yourself as possible.

DISCOVERING IDEAS

Find a Subject

When the class was given the writing assignment of "finding a personal angle on a common experience," Nikki Pearson was initially at a loss. The instructor had used the example of registration day—an ordeal students had complained about at the outset of the term—but that hardly struck Nikki as a compelling possibility. What's more, the instructor had stressed two expectations that made her a little anxious. One was that her paper (and everyone's else's) would be scrutinized by a classmate, tested for common ground as well as for distinctiveness. Nikki appreciated the idea in principle—a reader's response would be an important measure of success for an essay like this—but the actual prospect intimidated her. She was even more nervous about the other point the instructor had stressed: the paper she wrote would somehow have to address not just the *what* of the experience but *why* it was worth writing (and reading) about.

That's perhaps not a hard task when you're asked to write about a defining moment in your life, just one of the very few events that are clearly of extraordinary significance to you, as in Chapter 1's writing assignment. But now you're being asked to think about experiences you have in common with others, and the possible topics might seem both limitless and commonplace.

Nikki Pearson found her specific focus by gazing at a scar on her leg while she was lost in thought—until she found her thoughts dwelling on how she got that scar. Since there's no "right" topic, there's no right way to hit upon the right topic, but we can offer some helpful advice.

 **T**RIAL RUN

Make a list of "firsts"—first times that you experienced things that happen to just about everyone: your first day of school or college, your first experience behind the wheel, your first date or first kiss, your first day on the job, and so on. Make a list of possibilities.

While you're at it, make another list—this one of "landmark" events that may happen only once in a lifetime but that happen in almost everyone's lifetime, such as a wedding or graduation, the death or funeral of a loved one, the birth of a child, or the move to a new town or country.

In a matter of minutes, you should have five or six items in each list, so that you're looking at about a dozen rich possibilities. As you contemplate which to choose, consider this checklist:

CHECKLIST: TESTING A TOPIC'S SUITABILITY

1. **Does one possibility seem especially rich?** Do you find yourself feeling amused or moved just thinking about it? If that's the case, you probably not only have a rich topic but at least the beginnings of a distinctive angle on it.

2. **Does one possible topic seem memorable for a particular reason?** When you look over your lists of experiences, does one come back to you as an event you learned something from or could crystallize by recounting a specific moment or incident? If so, then you have the beginnings of a clarifying focus for your account.

3. **Does one topic surpass the others in the details it invites you to draw on?** Memories of some events—and not always those of recent events—are especially clear and numerous. Using one of your listed possibilities that calls up such memories is likely to result in an especially vivid and particularized account.

Explore Your Subject

This is the key: the subject of your essay isn't as important as saying something distinctive about it. This is why careful revision of your first draft will be so important: you will refine your purpose during revision, perhaps even discovering your real purpose only *after* you have written that first draft. Nikki Pearson, writing about her earliest memories of school, believed that being a kindergartner *in Guyana* was all the distinctiveness she needed, but her paper ultimately had a much more powerful and general appeal due to the distinctive perspective she adopted toward her experience.

Sometimes, however, it is not your perspective but the experience itself that will have its own built-in distinctiveness. Maya Angelou's account of her graduation is a case in point. It is because Angelou's experience was superficially the same as that of others but also fundamentally different—because she and her classmates were treated by the speaker as white children never would have been—that her account is so moving, so powerful, so worthy of our attention.

How do you decide what will make your account distinctive and worthy of a reader's attention? The interviewing and dialoguing Mel Robinson did with his friend Mike in the previous chapter would be useful here, especially since a listener's (or a reader's) opinion is so important in determining what's distinctive and interesting. When Nikki told her friend Melissa that she was going to write about kindergarten in Guyana, she was a little distressed to find that Melissa didn't think that Guyanese kindergarten sounded all that distinctive. The details were different, to be sure, but the difference wasn't the sort to suggest that new ground and common ground were being covered at the same time.

Nikki's paper ultimately did communicate both commonality and distinctiveness, but not because a sense of purpose came to her in a flash of inspiration. She found it only after she had begun writing, and she found it in the writing she had done, mining and refining that ore in her final version. In the meantime, though, there's *your* subject and *your* purpose to think about. Let's see if some exploratory work can give sharper definition to both.

TRIAL RUN

If your experience seems to crystallize in a single moment or incident, try freewriting your way through that point in time. Let the writing flow from you without censoring or editing what comes. Let details give rise to more details. Let the phrases fall out as they may. Don't be at all concerned about the degree of polish: for the moment, you are mining raw ore. Refining and polishing the gold you uncover will come later.

Another possibility is to give a full account—orally—to a friend or classmate, as Nikki told hers to Melissa. Remember that your ability to get an audience to identify with you and to appreciate your own distinctive angle is very much at issue, so be open to questions about particular points (or even to questions about what the overall point of your story is).

CHECKLIST: GIVING YOUR TOPIC A DISTINCTIVE ANGLE

1. **Can you regard your experience in a way that runs against the grain?** Was your response to an experience different than the stock response? Did you turn an outward defeat into an inner victory? Were you nervous when others tend to be calm—or calm when they tend to be nervous? Did (or can) you resist sentimentalizing something others get all choked up about?

2. **Does your experience itself have an unusual twist to it?** Did you have an uncommon sort of common experience? Were people having fun at a funeral or feeling sorrow at a wedding? Was a date more like hate-at-first-sight than the perfect match?

3. **Do you see something in an experience that others might have missed?** Does mature reflection make an event from your childhood take on another meaning? Does hard-nosed honesty allow you to be glad you're past something others might simply feel nostalgia for? Does one experience provide a clue or suggest a pattern to other experiences?

COMPOSING THE FIRST DRAFT

It is attention to detail that is sure to make the account of a common experience distinctive. While the big patterns of experience are shared, our individuality—our distinctiveness—appears in little (but crucial) differences. Like the rest of her classmates, Nikki Pearson was encouraged to do a minimum of planning for this assignment. Once a topic was chosen, writing the first draft was to be mainly recording the memories as they came, making the piece rich in details. The idea was to get something on paper, then work with it.

Consider Your Motives

Before you launch into a draft, though, you may find it useful to consider the kind of writing you are being asked to generate. It's a personal narrative, to be sure, but so was Mel Robinson's "Being Wrong Was a Habit" in Chapter 1. In giving an account of his arrest and reformation, Mel could hardly expect from a reader an interest based on sharing essentially the same experience. Mel's piece is instead an opportunity for the reader to sympathize with and learn from a life that had taken a turn that the lives of most college students don't take.

Nikki Pearson's piece, by contrast, covers ground we've all traveled. Specific details and circumstances differ, of course, but we've all gone off to first days of school, all been exposed to life and regulation outside the home for the first time, all felt the fears and joys of that point in childhood. Where Mel invited the reader to enter his world, Nikki invites the reader to consider how her world and the reader's intersect. "We're not so different, you and I," she is saying. "We've had similar experiences. Telling you about my memories and feelings might light up yours, so that you learn about yourself by hearing about me."

We all need reasons to write as well as reasons to read. Think about your reasons before you compose your first draft. And remember that a first draft is just a first draft.

PRESENTING NIKKI'S FIRST DRAFT

Kindergarten

(as I remember it, while living in Anna Regina, Guyana)

1   Surprisingly enough I seem to remember my days in kindergarten rather perceptibly. I remember walking into the schoolyard clinging onto my mother's hand, frightened and nervous because this was a new experience for me and because I

was intimidated by the height and size of the older children. I remember walking up the three little steps to the kindergarten which was situated horizontally between two elementary schools. It was here that our trip together ended and my new journey began. I remember crying, feeling that my mother had abandoned me with a curious bunch of strangers, who simultaneously stopped playing with their blocks and crayons to stare at the whimpering girl wearing a hideous brown and green uniform with matching green socks and brown shoes. I remember the embarrassment of sinking into my chair as my teacher Ms. Ettis (a short, round, black woman) tried to pronounce my real name (it is Xavarine) and she never quite pronounced it right. It was at this young and tender age of five that I realized that I was not going to like kindergarten, or at least not for the first few days.

2   The walk to Anna Regina kindergarten school was a long but pleasant one, and I would make that trip every weekday with three of the neighborhood children. The first attraction we would come upon was the cinema, the only real form of entertainment in the community of Anna Regina. Further up was the market, which was more than just a place to buy groceries. It was a place where the young and old dressed in proper attire would come to socialize and gossip. Among them was my grandmother, a small and feisty East Indian woman who knew every grocer in the marketplace and haggled with every one of them for any little thing she bought. She not only lived close to the market, she also lived close to my school, which was across the street from the marketplace. On returning from her daily shopping or browsing, my grandmother would pick me up to have lunch with her. So, while other children got to eat peanut butter and jelly sandwiches for lunch, I was having a homecooked meal, prepared by my grandmother, a woman who ruled her household with an iron fist and a woman I was terrified of. When she tells someone to take their elbows off the table, or to eat everything on their plate, one better do so because she wouldn't hesitate to slap one's face. Sometimes I think I would have rather spent my lunch hour in school learning the alphabet since having lunch with Grandma was the equivalent of doing chores.

3   Kindergarten took on a new ambience in the afternoon. Once the bell rang, everyone had to form a line and those who were late had to suffer the consequences. Since physical discipline played an important part in the Guyanese education system it was common to see these children get two lashes in each palm from Ms. Ettis. After that the rest of the day brisks by

and even the work gets easier. It was probably because many children are tired after running around and playing, as the sun beat down on their skin, and drained them of their energy. The temperature in Guyana is so hot in the afternoon that people often used umbrellas to shelter them from the sun more than they would the rain. However, there were cots in the kindergarten, reserved for children who got sick, but exceptions were made for children who were exhausted because they couldn't cope with the heat. Once this happened, it is unlikely Ms. Ettis will let that child go outside for lunch ever again. While those children napped, Ms. Ettis' two assistants would go around each table teaching students how to use the abacus. I enjoyed playing with the abacus, mainly because of the fancy beads that made it fun to learn with. Sometimes, if we were lucky, Ms. Ettis herself would read us a brief story to end our day.

4   I would wait patiently or anxiously (depending on the mood I was in) for my neighbors Patrick and Tony and my best friend (to this day) Simone to take me home. My mother placed enough trust in them to get me home safe and sound, and they did, except for that one day when my three chaperones stood helpless over the fatal situation I was destined for. It began when the school's crossguards got their signals confused and one of them allowed a motorcyclist to pass, while at the same time the other one was sending me across the main road. It resulted in an accident that scarred me for life and one that nearly terminated it as well.

5   Looking back on my days in kindergarten, I cannot help thinking about what a task it was for Ms. Ettis to try and pronounce my name. I laugh at it now, thinking how unfortunate for me and for her that the nickname "Nikki" didn't come into use until I moved to the United States. It is also hard to believe that my sweet and gentle grandmother was once someone I thought of as Genghis Khan. Nowadays, it would be my pleasure to have lunch with Granny and sometimes I long to see her because she still lives in Guyana. It is in these present times that we are truly grandmother and grandchild and perhaps even pals.

6   I remember the accident more vividly than I do anything else about kindergarten and I didn't accentuate it because it is an experience I wish to forget. But it was because of the visible scar on my lower right leg that I first thought of the accident and which spewed a vision that took me down memory lane to earlier days during kindergarten.

Thinking Critically about Nikki's First Draft

1. Nikki's personal narrative begins with the statement "Surprisingly enough I seem to remember my days in kindergarten [in Anna Regina, Guyana] rather perceptibly." Does what follows bear this statement out, make it seem true? Does she give a reason for being able to remember so well? When does she give it?

2. What is this personal narrative about besides Nikki's experience in kindergarten? Are the other memories she includes clearly related? If so, what makes them seem integral? If not, how could they be more effectively integrated?

3. Nikki's narrative eventually moves beyond introduction to kindergarten to a series of impressions about kindergarten on a day-to-day basis. Are these impressions mostly favorable or unfavorable? If you find them mixed, do you also find them leaning more in one direction than another? How would you characterize Nikki's experience of kindergarten? Does it seem all of a piece? Should it? Why or why not?

4. Is Nikki speaking from her current perspective or trying to evoke the child's perspective? Can you cite a passage to support either choice?

5. Nikki's personal narrative has a story-within-a-story: the story of the accident. What purpose does it serve? Is it simply an interruption of the routines she had been describing? Or does it have real connections with the circumstances and impressions she has been communicating?

6. Consider how the narrative ends. What does it suggest about the motivation behind this piece? Do you feel it is an honest ending? Does it leave things too unresolved? Does it give you anything to take away from your reading experience beyond a sense of what life in kindergarten was like for Nikki Pearson?

RETHINKING AND REVISING

Do Your Own Stocktaking

On the day the drafts were due, the students were asked to write for ten minutes on what they thought the strengths and weaknesses of their drafts were. Here's what Nikki wrote:

> I like the way my paper begins, mainly because I *am* surprised at how well I remember kindergarten. Once I started to remember, things came flooding—so much more than I got in the paper.
>
> I don't think my paper is organized well though. The memories didn't seem to come in any particular order. I feel that the draft is all over the place. This is what needs work on most.

RIAL RUN

A popular myth about writing courses is that evaluation is the teacher's responsibility. But writing teachers will disappear from your life before writing does, so you need to get in the habit of *self*-assessment. Do what Nikki did: write two short paragraphs on what you see as your first draft's strengths and weaknesses.

Get Feedback

In Nikki's class, each student reviewed another student's draft with the help of a prepared form. Figure 2-1 shows what Nikki got back from her reviewer.

RIAL RUN

Exchange drafts with a classmate so that the two of you can review each other's drafts. Try to make your criticisms constructive and to take the criticisms made of your work in good grace. You can address the questions listed on the peer-review sheet from Nikki's class, or questions devised by your instructor, or questions you and your partner decide you want answered about each other's drafts.

Re-envision Your Draft

The word *revision* means just what it looks like it should mean: a re-seeing, a re-conceptualization. Fixing a word here and there is editing, not full-scale revision. For true revision, you have to look at your work with fresh eyes and be ready to make big changes on the basis of second thoughts—even if second thoughts later confirm that you don't need to make big changes after all.

We don't know what you've drafted, so we can't give you particular advice on just how you might re-envision it. But we can tell you what Nikki did, and follow that with some general guidelines for revision you might find helpful.

At first Nikki didn't know how to take her reviewer's comments. Initially, it almost seemed as if the only good thing about her draft was the very first paragraph. But when she took another look at the comments the next day, she saw the justice of some of the criticisms. For one thing, though she had not quite put her finger on the problem, she herself had said the draft was not especially well organized. She had called it "Kindergarten," but much of it read like a paper titled "Grandmother."

Figure 2-1

Peer Assessment of Assignment #2
(A Distinctive Angle on a Generally Shared Experience)

BEFORE YOU READ THE PAPER THROUGH identify the subject: Kindergarten (in Guyana)

What would you expect from a paper on this subject? (What do you expect to be told? What will be emphasized? What sort of point do you imagine the writer will try to make?) I would expect to be told about all the fun she had and childish things she did and about adjusting to life away from home at a school full of kids. Since the subject is kindergarten in Guyana, I would also expect to be told how kindergarten there is different from kindergarten other places.

AFTER YOU HAVE READ THE PAPER THROUGH answer the following questions.

Do the writer's expectations of your reactions seem correct? Did you indeed have a similar experience? Do you think the writer's angle on it can be called distinctive? If you answer yes, give examples. If you answer no, explain where the writer is off-track. My experience of kindergarten was similar (what I remember of it). The angle is distinctive in that her memories (of what she wore, etc) are clearer than mine. But I was sort of lost in parts of the paper I had trouble relating to, parts that didn't seem to have much to do with kindergarten.

What do you think of the writer's use of details? Are there places where you feel specifics are lacking? Are there places where you think the writer gets bogged down in particulars? Please be specific. The writer uses a lot of details very well. I would like to read more about her experience in kindergarten itself, less about her grandmother.

Do you think the writer either implicitly or explicitly makes a case for the significance of the account? If so, say what it is. If not, suggest how the author might make such a case. If she does make a case about the significance of her experience in kindergarten, I feel she is too implicit about it. She makes an explicit case about her grandmother (the old lady isn't as horrible as she seemed to be then). Maybe she could do something like that with kindergarten.

What part of the paper did you like best? Why? I liked the opening paragraph best. It has good descriptions and also I identified my experience in kindergarten with hers.

What part of the paper seems weakest? How might it be strengthened? The part that seems weakest is in the middle as she drifts away from her subject and describes her grandmother.

Acting on her reviewer's comment that she wanted to know more about Nikki's experience in kindergarten, Nikki deleted the parts of her essay about her grandmother and then followed the description of her walk to school with accounts of the mornings, the afternoons, and the accident (which, after all, happened after school). Excited that she had solved her organization problem, Nikki wrote another draft, thinking it might well be the final version.

At first things went swimmingly. Nikki kept the first paragraph just the way it was (the reviewer had singled that out for praise—no point in fixing what wasn't broken). She also kept the beginning of the next paragraph nearly the same, but she replaced the introduction of her grandmother with a description of the children arriving at school. This gave her a chance to bring out what was different about school in Guyana: the poverty of many of the children, their ethnic diversity (including Nikki's own special case), and the physical punishments at the school.

Still, there was a problem: the conclusion. When it came time to end the second version, this is what Nikki wrote:

> I remember the accident more vividly than I do anything else about kindergarten and I didn't accentuate it because it is an experience I wish to forget. But it was because of the visible scar on my lower right leg that I first thought of the accident and which spewed a vision that took me down memory lane to earlier days during kindergarten. Just like a roller-coaster ride, those days too had their ups and downs. The first few days were painful because I was parted from my home, but in the long run it was worth it. I was introduced to a whole new environment and was taught many lessons which helped prepare me for the years that followed.

As Nikki read through to the end of her second version, her heart sank. Much of what preceded her conclusion seemed to her some of the best writing she had ever done, but that last paragraph seemed to fall flat, and she wasn't sure why.

She showed her second version to her instructor, who agreed that the conclusion was weak. The word the instructor used was "platitudinous"—which was just a big word for flat, dull, trite—which Nikki already knew. Nikki admitted she wasn't sure what her thoughts and feelings added up to, she wasn't sure what effect her paper was building toward, and that made it difficult to arrive at a fitting culmination. The instructor pointed out that Nikki did seem sure of one thing—her uncertainty—and suggested that Nikki work with that thought.

Before beginning her final version, Nikki returned to her reviewer's comments and noticed two things that hadn't seemed significant before: First, the reviewer had recorded her expectation that the paper would be about "all the fun" Nikki had in kindergarten, and, second, the reviewer suggested that Nikki give her account more explicit significance by saying kindergarten had been better than it seemed at first. Taken together, the expectation and the suggestion could help create a sense of complexity that Nikki's conclusion had utterly lacked.

It also struck Nikki that her organization really seemed to work. It made her paper seem like a journey—through a town, through a day, through a period of life—and she decided she would call her paper "A Journey to Kindergarten." Saying the phrase over, Nikki also realized that it was a journey she made somewhat reluctantly. Some of the recollections were hardly happy, and in any case she was writing about a world she could never go back to except in her memories. With these thoughts in mind, she drafted a new concluding paragraph:

> Today as I remember those formative years of my child-hood, a picturesque view comes rushing to my mind's eye of a naive girl meandering on the cobblestone road to school. The faces and places she took for granted are now lost to her. She yearns to see the little government school and the little town of Anna Regina where people (no matter how poor) always seemed to be content. Yet she is afraid to make the real trip back home, afraid to think how much must have changed. She is even afraid to look too closely at the memories, to think how much needed to change, how much there was to be afraid of even then. Still, the memories remain.

This is essentially the concluding paragraph of the final version. Once she had reached the end of that version, once she had made the few changes in the above paragraph that would make it fit in and sound right, Nikki Pearson was done. She had completed her journey.

CHECKLIST: GUIDELINES FOR REVISION

Each piece of writing is unique. Your own experience of revision, even if it is on an assignment or a subject very like Nikki's, will not be the same. Still, Nikki's experience of revision suggests some general thoughts and guidelines that may prove useful to you.

1. **Plan to revise to *save* time.**

   Too often we try to save time by making everything perfect on the first attempt—and end up actually costing ourselves considerable time and effort. There's no better way to get writer's block than to decide that the first sentence you write will not only be perfect but will also be the first sentence your reader reads. Resolving to revise frees you from anxiety about the flow of words and ideas. You know you can always go back later and fill in the blanks and fine-tune your phrases.

2. **Be open to discovery even *as* you write.**

The writer E. M. Forster once said, "How will I know what I think until I see what I say?" He was making the point that, once we start writing, our words and thoughts often take us to unexpected places, revealing unforeseen possibilities, uncovering ore we didn't know was there to be mined, disclosing perspectives we hadn't planned to adopt. As long as we embrace the opportunity to revise, it's quite all right to take off from a strong start in search of a conclusion—which is just what Nikki did.

She didn't start work on her essay because of any burning desire to communicate her childhood memories; she began drafting it because a paper was due. Only in revision did she discover a deeper, better sense of purpose, a chance to make her readers feel rewarded, edified, touched. Her draft would have satisfied the assignment, but her revised version gave Nikki a shot of pride and a sense that she was growing as a writer.

3. **Plan to revise, not just edit.**

Just changing a word here and there is editing, not revising. As the word itself suggests, *re-vision* entails looking with new eyes at both your essay and the purpose behind it. Doing justice to that purpose may mean making drastic changes, just the sort made by Nikki as she slashed big chunks, added completely new material, and repeatedly rewrote her ending. No one else could have done that for her. Other people can edit your writing, but only you can revise it.

4. **Consider the reactions of others.**

Written communication is an attempt to make contact, to cultivate understanding, to get a response. You can't think only about the transmission; think about the reception as well. A reader's thoughts are invaluable, even if you just try to imagine them instead of actually soliciting them. The input you do get from others—from a friend, from a classmate who serves as a peer reviewer, from your instructor—cannot dictate your purpose, but it can tell you a great deal about how successful you have been in realizing that purpose.

Nikki certainly found feedback helpful. She was worried about organization, but it took a classmate to see that the digressions about grandma had to go. Nikki was unsure about how to sum things up until her instructor hinted that saying she was unsure might be an honest way to conclude. Suggestions are not instructions, but if they are in tune with the writer's own intuitions they can give helpful pushes in the right direction.

5. **Remember that writers are readers too.**

Most people find it far easier to give constructive criticisms of other people's writing than their own. One reason, surely, is that they apply different criteria in the two different cases. For the writing of others, they apply the criteria they use as readers: they think about what interests or bores them, what sort of style they enjoy, and so on. As writers, they apply other criteria: what seems pertinent to their purpose, what taps their expertise, what gets the appointed task done. Those are certainly relevant criteria, but so are the "readerly" considerations of what turns readers off or on.

When Nikki went into detail about her grandmother, she was acting on her "writerly" purpose of getting memories from that period of her life on paper. But she wasn't thinking like a reader; she wasn't wondering if this stood in the way of a reader's ability to appreciate her recounted experience. The comments of her peer reviewer helped her to see this, but she could have seen it for herself. She only had to look at her writing, not just as the author of it, but also as the audience for it.

6. **Give yourself enough time to revise.**

The best way to give yourself some objective distance from your writing, to look at it as the reader might, is to put it aside for a while. The Roman poet Horace recommended nine years, but a day or two is enough time in this busy world of due dates and deadlines.

When Nikki brought her draft to class for peer review, she had read it over only once, quickly, but once was enough to see (and say, on that quick self-assessment) that the organization was weak. If she had handed in that draft as her final paper, it's easy to imagine what would have happened: her teacher's comments would have confirmed that her organization did indeed need improvement, and the teacher might even have given specific suggestions for improvement. But we don't usually learn from suggestions for improvement unless we act upon them. While the criticisms by Nikki's teacher on her second draft may have told Nikki that she wasn't doing what the teacher wanted, it was only by taking the time to revise thoughtfully that Nikki learned how to make her writing seem better to *her,* how to satisfy herself.

7. **Carefully analyze the structure of your draft.**

The injunction to revise often seems an unhelpful, unfocused demand to make things better without saying what, why, or how. But one always-useful procedure is to scrutinize the organization of your draft. You can outline the organization of your draft by stating, in a single sentence, what each paragraph is about. (If one sentence won't do, you probably need to turn that paragraph into more than one paragraph—something Nikki would have discovered about the second paragraph in her draft had she tried outlining.) The process of building an outline from one-sentence summaries of paragraphs helps uncover the skeleton of structure beneath the flesh of detail. If an "arm" of your draft is joined to a "hip," it will seem odd or grotesque no matter how well-muscled your writing is otherwise.

Although it is not always easily seen, structure is crucial because its effects on the reader are profound. In Nikki's draft, her memories were so rich she had trouble seeing the forest for the trees. Her reviewer's comments that she felt "sort of lost in parts" confirmed Nikki's fears that the piece was poorly organized. Nikki didn't know what a patterned and purposeful paper she had till she uncovered its structure. She might then have seconded and extended E. M. Forster's maxim: "How do I know what I think until I see what I say—and outline it?" Outlines are usually taught as plans, roadmaps for roads not yet traveled. They're actually much more useful as maps to territory you've already staked out—but need to get more familiar with.

8. **Be ruthless.**

Writers are always a little in love with their creations, however malformed. Sometimes this love takes the shape of almost absolute resistance to change: "I went to all the trouble of writing that sentence, and it's going to stay whether it belongs there or not." But more often the reluctance to cut derives from the fondness for the discoveries that writing sometimes turns up. Nikki's draft was an unexpected chance to get reacquainted with her grandmother; her conclusion stressed the affection and amusement those details had awakened. She found it hard to banish her grandmother from her paper. Nikki's second version preserves two sentences about her, but, in preparing the final version, even these seemed more of an interruption than a contribution and they, too, were cut.

It may seem odd that writing is as often improved by cuts as by additions, but Virginia Woolf was on to something when she said, "You must put it all in before you can take it all out." The challenge for the writer is to provide enough material—and only enough—to make the reader feel "fully" informed without giving the reader too much to get through.

9. **Be complete.**

This is not a contradiction of the guideline to be ruthless, but its logical complement. "Completeness" in writing is always an illusion: writers of all kinds learn that they can—and must—leave certain aspects of their topics entirely aside. In a sense, Nikki Pearson's account of kindergarten is incomplete if it leaves out the lunches with her grandmother—they were very much a part of Nikki's whole kindergarten experience—but what the reader doesn't know about, the reader won't miss. However, when Nikki says "Kindergarten took on a new ambience in the afternoon" and says nothing about the mornings, that's clearly a gap that needs filling.

If completeness is a matter of appearances, there's an important corollary: it's all a matter of how things appear *to the reader*. The writer knows too much—knows things left unsaid that may need saying, knows things that aren't really worth going into but that perhaps are brought up anyway, knows too much to put it all in words and perhaps too much to choose just what needs to be said. This is one reason why thinking like a reader—or getting a reader's input—is so important.

10. **Be true to your vision.**

For all the importance of keeping the reader in mind, revision is the writer's job, and the writer is the final arbiter. Polonius (of Shakespeare's *Hamlet*) may have been a bore, but he gave good advice: "To thine own self be true." For a writer, this entails more than honesty. It means being accurate, coherent, and logically consistent. When Nikki started off with a walk to school and then skipped to lunches with her grandmother, she was not being true to one way of making her self-representation hold together, a way she had set up but then failed to follow through on. She realized this in her revised drafts, which follow her walk to school with her arrival in the schoolyard. Likewise, the logic of Nikki's initial conclusion was not quite consistent with what preceded it, for she spoke there of a "sweet and gentle grandmother" who in earlier paragraphs had seemed anything but. Nikki solved that inconsistency by eliminating all references to her grandmother in her final draft.

It's hard to say what is more remarkable about Nikki Pearson's revision: how much better her final version is than her first draft, or how much of that first draft was good enough to keep or recast. Revision really is efficient, not just because it allows you to polish what you've already written, but especially because the very prospect of revision can give you the freedom to mine good material to work with in the first place. Promise yourself that you'll take advantage of that freedom and you may be surprised by the gems you get to polish.

PRESENTING NIKKI'S FINAL DRAFT

A Journey to Kindergarten

Nikki Pearson

Nikki sets the scene and tone with an account of first impressions—not especially pleasant ones.

1   Surprisingly enough I seem to remember my days in kindergarten (in Anna Regina, Guyana) quite well. I remember walking into the schoolyard clinging onto my mother's hand, frightened and nervous because this was a new experience for me and because I was intimidated by the height and size of the older children. I remember walking up the three little steps to the kindergarten, which was situated between two elementary schools. I remember crying, feeling that my mother had

abandoned me with a curious bunch of strangers, all stopping their play with blocks and crayons to stare at the whimpering girl wearing a hideous brown and green uniform with matching green socks and brown shoes. I remember the embarrassment of sinking into my chair as my teacher Ms. Ettis tried to pronounce my real name (Xavarine) and never quite pronounced it right. It was at this young and tender age of five that I realized I was not going to like kindergarten, at least not for the first few days.

2   The walk to Anna Regina kindergarten school was a long but pleasant one, and I would make that trip every weekday with three of the neighborhood children. The first attraction we would come upon was the Paragon Cinema, the only real form of entertainment in the community of Anna Regina. The cinema was of immense size and dwarfed all the other buildings in the vicinity. I was scared of its dark interior; whenever I attended a show with my parents, I always hustled them out, making certain we were not the last ones remaining since I was sure lurking demons were waiting to devour anyone who stayed behind. Further up was the market, which was more than just a place to buy groceries. It was a place where young and old, dressed in proper attire, would come to socialize and gossip. Across the street from the marketplace was the entrance to the school grounds. Since there were no traffic lights in Anna Regina, we would join the noisy crowd to cross the main road. To make matters more chaotic several minibuses packed like sardine cans would unload hoards of children from the nearby communities of Sparta and Belliance. These children huddled off the minibuses to join the snaking mass rounding its way into the schoolyard. Some were dressed neatly, carrying a school bag and perhaps a pocket piece to buy lunch, but more wore mended uniforms and beat up sandals and carried lunch pails and slates. These represented the economic slump the country of Guyana was in and the suffering most of its people endured.

3   It was quite difficult to fit in with the other children. I found myself the only child of mixed parentage in a class of Chinese, Black, and East Indian students. As I took my place at one of several round tables, I could not help feeling like an outcast. Racial tension was mainly to be blamed since parents did not want their children to associate with offspring of interracial marriages. But children, largely unaware of societal problems, are likely to ignore one's race, color, or creed, and eventually they accepted me.

4   A typical day started with the bell ringing. Everyone had to form a line before entering the classroom, and those who were

She steps back from that specific moment to walk us (literally) through the context, giving us a general sense of setting, customs, living conditions.

The discomfort Nikki felt as a kindergartner had social causes she now can understand (and happily, did not have to suffer long then).

Two paragraphs paint the morning and afternoon of a typical day. (And there is no long intervening lunch with Grandma—as there was in the first draft.)

late suffered the consequences. Since corporal punishment played an important part in the Guyanese education system, it was common to see children get two lashes in each palm from Ms. Ettis. Once seated in an orderly manner, the class was allowed to explore the childhood realms of architecture, sculpture, and painting, using clay, crayons, and building blocks to create little masterpieces.

The post-luncheon period took on a whole new ambience so that the afternoon brisked away. Many children were tired after running around and playing, as the sun beat down on their skin and drained them of their energy. The temperature in Guyana is so hot in the afternoon that people often use umbrellas to shelter themselves from the sun more than they would from the rain. There were cots in kindergarten for children who got sick; they were most often used by those who succumbed to heat exhaustion. While those children napped, Ms. Ettis' two assistants would go around each table teaching students how to use the abacus. I enjoyed playing with the abacus, mainly because the fancy beads made the contraption fun to learn with. Sometimes, if we were lucky, Ms. Ettis would read us a brief story to end our day.

The end of the generalized school day is followed by one specific day's afterschool climax: Nikki's accident.

I would wait patiently or anxiously (depending on the mood I was in) for my neighbors Patrick and Tony and my best friend Simone to take me home. My mother placed enough trust in them to get me home safe and sound, and they did, except for that one day when, as destiny would have it, my three chaperones stood helpless as a nearly fatal situation unfolded before them. It began when the school's crossguards got their signals confused and one of them allowed a motorcyclist to pass while the other one was sending me across the main road. The result was an accident that forever scarred my right leg and my young mind.

Like the scar, Nikki's memories bear witness to a childhood past she regards with profound ambivalence—something missed but also feared.

I remember the accident more vividly than anything else about kindergarten, though it is an experience I wish to forget. It was the sight of the scar on my lower right leg that took me on this journey back to kindergarten. What first came rushing to my mind's eye was a picturesque view of a little girl meandering on the cobblestone road to school. The faces and places she took for granted are now lost to her. She yearns to see the little government school and the little town of Anna Regina where people (no matter how poor) always seemed to be content. Yet she is afraid to make the real trip back home, afraid to think how much it must have changed. She is even afraid to look too closely at the memories, to think how much needed to change, how much there was to be afraid of even then. Still, the memories remain.

Commentary on Nikki's Final Draft

With a piece as rich in details as this one, it may be useful first to take a step back and examine the larger structure. After a framing opening statement, we get a brief but remarkably concrete account of what Nikki's very first moments in kindergarten were like. The next paragraph is a kind of enactment of the title: a journey to kindergarten—with a few landmarks along the way pointed out until we reach the school grounds. As Nikki actually sits down at her table (third paragraph), she feels shunned by her peers as the child of an interracial couple. (Guyana was settled by peoples from throughout the British commonwealth: Nikki's father was half-African, half-Chinese, and a lukewarm Christian; her mother, East Indian and a practicing Hindu.) After explaining that her "outcast" status was by no means permanent, Nikki gives, in the next two paragraphs, a general sense of kindergarten activities, devoting the first of these two paragraphs to the morning and the second to the afternoon. After this, we learn of the afterschool accident, and the piece concludes. In term of structure, then, the piece follows the pattern of a school day: going to school, getting there and getting settled, what happens after lunch, what happens on the way home.

The structure is as useful as it is because Nikki's narrative is essentially a record of ambivalence. She doesn't have a "main idea" to organize her narrative, an idea like "kindergarten was basically wonderful" or "kindergarten was basically awful." As a matter of fact, she suggests that saying something like that, either way, would mean falsifying her experience. If the details don't all speak to the same idea, though, she's faced with another problem: how do they connect and add up?

Nikki has found several ways to answer that question. One fits with the overarching chronological structure: she's telling a story, a story of routine that is gradually established and then interrupted by a cataclysmic event, the accident. This gives her piece a climax and a sense of ending, and it also makes certain details add up—the early, quiet observation, for instance, that "there were no traffic lights in Anna Regina."

Nikki's journey is not just a journey through a story but a journey back in time, a recreation of her younger self and the world that little girl knew. Many of the details she gives have the purpose of establishing her authority as someone with firsthand knowledge of Anna Regina (and, by extension, of ddGuyana generally) and a good memory of what it feels like to be five. This task of hers means that some seemingly irrelevant details are really quite relevant. Five-year-olds do not draw distinct lines between the experience of getting to kindergarten and kindergarten itself. The Paragon Cinema belongs in this paper, as do its "lurking demons." We need to hear, not just of the abacus used to teach the children, but of the appeal (irrelevant to an adult) that the "fancy beads" had for one child. (It might be noted that this perspective limits the paper's possibilities even as it expands them; Nikki cannot go into much detail about "racial tension," for instance, without leaving for too long the perspective of a child "largely unaware" of such concerns.)

Yet another means Nikki uses to give her account coherence is to frame many of the incidents in a recurring pattern: things aren't always as bad as they seem at first. Her first exposure to kindergarten was almost traumatic, but she settled in. Chaos on the schoolground became order as the students entered the classroom. Her schoolmates were cold to her initially, but then warmed to her. The mornings may have dragged, but the afternoons "brisked away." Ms. Ettis greeted latecomers with lashes, but she might also dispense a small blessing before sending her students away: "Sometimes, if we were lucky, Ms. Ettis would read us a brief story to end our day." Even the accident is part of this pattern: "nearly fatal," it is something Nikki obviously survived, something that may even have helped her to remember her kindergarten days so "surprisingly" well.

This pattern is not really all that subtle because it is a variation on another pattern that may well be responsible for most of the narrative's force and power. A popular myth in American culture is that childhood is a happy, carefree time, untroubled by the cares and burdens of the adult world; children are innocent and merry and cute. This is a notion the whole of Nikki's narrative resists: it is an account of fears, prejudice, harsh discipline, brutal rigors, even a life-threatening incident. So when Nikki suggests that things aren't as bad as they might seem, she is also suggesting that they seem bad because the rosy picture of childhood is not as true as we would like to think. She explodes the cliché and yet remembers her hardly happy-go-lucky life with fondness as well as regret. Especially at the end, she acknowledges her ambivalence and refuses to resolve it. Her gift to her readers is a refusal to pretty things up, to moralize, to oversimplify. She has made her account seem true enough to make us wonder if our first exposure to school wasn't painful as well as helpful, disciplining as well as nurturing, scary as well as fun—if, in other words, her ambivalence isn't ours as well. If that's the case, she has made us see we have more in common with respect to this common experience than we may have known before we read her essay—no mean feat.

Questions for Further Thought

1. It's a truism that each individual is unique. Is there really such a thing as a common experience? Or are we talking about common incidents or events that everyone experiences differently? Is it possible that such experiences, honestly and fully rendered, would be so individualized, so different, that they might be incomparable and even incomprehensible?

2. Let's look at the flip side of that. It's also a truism that we aren't so different after all. Is there really such a thing as a unique perspective? Is what seems distinctive defined by standards or conventions? What might they be?

3. Nikki thought an account of kindergarten in *Guyana* would suffice to make her account distinctive, but Melissa didn't. Is "distinctiveness" something the writer imparts—or is it in the eye of the beholder? Is it something writer and reader collaborate on somehow? If so, how?

PROFESSIONAL ESSAYS

Maya Angelou
GRADUATION

"Graduation, the hush-hush magic time of frills and gifts and congratulations and diplomas, was finished for me before my name was called. The accomplishment was nothing."

WHEN SHE WAS THREE AND HER BROTHER four, Maya Angelou (born Marguerite Johnson in 1928) and brother Bailey went to the little town of Stamps, Arkansas, to live with their grandmother. There "Momma" (as they called her) ran the William Johnson General Merchandise Store "in the heart of the Negro area." Growing up in "the Black area of Stamps which in childhood's narrow measure seemed a whole world," Angelou hardly had a sheltered existence. Raped at eight, an unwed mother at sixteen, she became a widely traveled dancer, singer, actor, writer, and (at the invitation of Martin Luther King, Jr., himself), a coordinator of Dr. King's Southern Christian Leadership Conference.

She has published a number of memoirs, most recently All God's Children Need Traveling Shoes *(1986). Her first, a memoir of her childhood titled* I Know Why the Caged Bird Sings *(1969), contains the present selection. Number 23 of 36 numbered but untitled selections, it's an account for which "Graduation" seems an apt but not quite adequate title. For this piece recounts a shared experience in a double sense. Most people have had the experience of going through graduation. But Angelou's experience was an unusual one of solidarity shattered and reaffirmed after an unwelcome presence belittled the celebrants at the ceremony. The way this personal narrative is also the account of a sense of community is something to watch for as you read—and to think about afterwards.*

ON THE WAY INTO THE READING

1. Take a moment to remember your experience of graduation—the anticipation, the pride, the relief. What was it like for you? How do you expect Angelou's account to be similar or different?

2. We all have experienced moments at ceremonies or sporting events or concerts when we felt everyone was feeling the same thing. What

continued

continued

accounts for such moments? Do you think you could describe or explain one in writing?

3. As preparation for life, education is often thought of as something separate from the real world, a sheltered existence. And graduation is the last moment in that sheltered existence or the first step away from it. At your graduation, was there a sense that the real world was intruding, that there was a sense of loss mixed in with the sense of relief and pride? What did you think you might be losing? What did you think you might be moving out into?

1   The children in Stamps trembled visibly with anticipation. Some adults were excited too, but to be certain the whole young population had come down with graduation epidemic. Large classes were graduating from both the grammar school and the high school. Even those who were years removed from their own day of glorious release were anxious to help with preparations as a kind of dry run. The junior students who were moving into the vacating classes' chairs were tradition-bound to show their talents for leadership and management. They strutted through the school and around the campus exerting pressure on the lower grades. Their authority was so new that occasionally if they pressed a little too hard it had to be overlooked. After all, next term was coming, and it never hurt a sixth grader to have a play sister in the eighth grade, or a tenth-year student to be able to call a twelfth grader Bubba. So all was endured in a spirit of shared understanding. But the graduating classes themselves were the nobility. Like travelers with exotic destinations on their minds, the graduates were remarkably forgetful. They came to school without their books, or tablets or even pencils. Volunteers fell over themselves to secure replacements for the missing equipment. When accepted, the willing workers might or might not be thanked, and it was of no importance to the pregraduation rites. Even teachers were respectful of the now quiet and aging seniors, and tended to speak to them, if not as equals, as beings only slightly lower than themselves. After tests were returned and grades given, the student body, which acted like an extended family, knew who did well, who excelled, and what piteous ones had failed.

2   Unlike the white high school, Lafayette County Training School distinguished itself by having neither lawn, nor hedges, nor tennis court, nor climbing ivy. Its two buildings (main classrooms, the grade school and home economics) were set on a dirt hill with no fence to limit either its boundaries or those of bordering farms. There was a large expanse to the left of the school which was used alternately as a baseball diamond or a basketball court. Rusty hoops on the swaying poles represented the permanent recreational equipment, although bats and balls could be borrowed from the P. E. teacher if the borrower was qualified and if the diamond wasn't occupied.

3   Over this rocky area relieved by a few shady tall persimmon trees the graduating class walked. The girls often held hands and no longer bothered to speak to the lower students. There was a sadness about them, as if this old world was not their home and they were bound for higher ground. The boys, on the other hand, had become more friendly, more outgoing. A decided change from the closed attitude they projected while studying for finals. Now they seemed not ready to give up the old school, the familiar paths and classrooms. Only a small percentage would be continuing on to college—one of the South's A & M (agricultural and mechanical) schools, which trained Negro youths to be carpenters, farmers, handymen, masons, maids, cooks and baby nurses. Their future rode heavily on their shoulders, and blinded them to the collective joy that had pervaded the lives of the boys and girls in the grammar school graduating class.

4   Parents who could afford it ordered new shoes and readymade clothes for themselves from Sears and Roebuck or Montgomery Ward. They also engaged the best seamstresses to make the floating graduating dresses and to cut down secondhand pants which would be pressed to a military slickness for the important event.

5   Oh, it was important, all right. Whitefolks would attend the ceremony, and two or three would speak of God and home, and the Southern way of life, and Mrs. Parsons, the principal's wife, would play the graduation march while the lower-grade graduates paraded down the aisles and took their seats below the platform. The high school seniors would wait in empty classrooms to make their dramatic entrance.

6   In the Store I was the person of the moment. The birthday girl. The center. Bailey had graduated the year before, although to do so he had to forfeit all pleasures to make up for his time lost in Baton Rouge.

7   My class was wearing butter-yellow piqué dresses, and Momma launched out on mine. She smocked the yoke into tiny crisscrossing puckers, then shirred the rest of the bodice. Her dark fingers ducked in and out of the lemony cloth as she embroidered raised daisies around the hem. Before she considered herself finished she had added a crocheted cuff on the puff sleeves, and a pointy crocheted collar.

8   I was going to be lovely. A walking model of all the various styles of fine hand sewing and it didn't worry me that I was only twelve years old and merely graduating from the eighth grade. Besides, many teachers in Arkansas Negro schools had only that diploma and were licensed to impart wisdom.

9   The days had become longer and more noticeable. The faded beige of former times had been replaced with strong and sure colors. I began to see my classmates' clothes, their skin tones, and the dust that waved off pussy willows. Clouds that lazed across the sky were objects of great concern to me. Their shiftier shapes might have held a message that in my new happiness and with a little bit of time I'd soon decipher. During that period I looked at the arch of heaven so religiously my neck kept

a steady ache. I had taken to smiling more often, and my jaws hurt from the unaccustomed activity. Between the two physical sore spots, I suppose I could have been uncomfortable, but that was not the case. As a member of the winning team (the graduating class of 1940) I had outdistanced unpleasant sensations by miles. I was headed for the freedom of open fields.

10   Youth and social approval allied themselves with me and we trammeled memories of slights and insults. The wind of our swift passage remodeled my features. Lost tears were pounded to mud and then to dust. Years of withdrawal were brushed aside and left behind, as hanging ropes of parasitic moss.

11   My work alone had awarded me a top place and I was going to be one of the first called in the graduating ceremonies. On the classroom black-board, as well as on the bulletin board in the auditorium, there were blue stars and white stars and red stars. No absences, no tardinesses, and my academic work was among the best of the year. I could say the preamble to the Constitution even faster than Bailey. We timed ourselves often: "WethepeopleoftheUnitedStatesinordertoformamoreperfectunion…" I had memorized the Presidents of the United States from Washington to Roosevelt in chronological as well as alphabetical order.

12   My hair pleased me too. Gradually the black mass had lengthened and thickened, so that it kept at last to its braided pattern, and I didn't have to yank my scalp off when I tried to comb it.

13   Louise and I had rehearsed the exercises until we tired out ourselves. Henry Reed was class valedictorian. He was a small, very black boy with hooded eyes, a long, broad nose and an oddly shaped head. I had admired him for years because each term he and I vied for the best grades in our class. Most often he bested me, but instead of being disappointed I was pleased that we shared top places between us. Like many Southern Black children, he lived with his grandmother, who was as strict as Momma and as kind as she knew how to be. He was courteous, respectful and soft-spoken to elders, but on the playground he chose to play the roughest games. I admired him. Anyone, I reckoned, sufficiently afraid or sufficiently dull could be polite. But to be able to operate at a top level with both adults and children was admirable.

14   His valedictory speech was entitled "To Be or Not to Be." The rigid tenth-grade teacher had helped him write it. He'd been working on the dramatic stresses for months.

15   The weeks until graduation were filled with heady activities. A group of small children were to be presented in a play about buttercups and daisies and bunny rabbits. They could be heard throughout the building practicing their hops and their little songs that sounded like silver bells. The older girls (nongraduates, of course) were assigned the task of making refreshments for the night's festivities. A tangy scent of ginger, cinnamon, nutmeg and chocolate wafted around the home economics building as the budding cooks made samples for themselves and their teachers.

16   In every corner of the workshop, axes and saws split fresh timber as the woodshop boys made sets and stage scenery. Only the graduates were left out of the general bustle. We were free to sit in the library at the back of the building or look in quite detachedly, naturally, on the measures being taken for our event.

17   Even the minister preached on graduation the Sunday before. His subject was, "Let your light so shine that men will see your good works and praise your Father, Who is in Heaven." Although the sermon was purported to be addressed to us, he used the occasion to speak to backsliders, gamblers and general ne'er-do-wells. But since he had called our names at the beginning of the service we were mollified.

18   Among Negroes the tradition was to give presents to children going only from one grade to another. How much more important this was when the person was graduating at the top of the class. Uncle Willie and Momma had sent away for a Mickey Mouse watch like Bailey's. Louise gave me four embroidered handkerchiefs. (I gave her three crocheted doilies.) Mrs. Sneed, the minister's wife, made me an underskirt to wear for graduation, and nearly every customer gave me a nickel or maybe even a dime with the instruction "Keep on moving to higher ground," or some such encouragement.

19   Amazingly the great day finally dawned and I was out of bed before I knew it. I threw open the back door to see it more clearly, but Momma said, "Sister, come away from that door and put your robe on."

20   I hoped the memory of that morning would never leave me. Sunlight was itself still young, and the day had none of the insistence maturity would bring it in a few hours. In my robe and barefoot in the backyard, under cover of going to see about my new beans, I gave myself up to the gentle warmth and thanked God that no matter what evil I had done in my life He had allowed me to live to see this day. Somewhere in my fatalism I had expected to die, accidentally, and never have the chance to walk up the stairs in the auditorium and gracefully receive my hard-earned diploma. Out of God's merciful bosom I had won reprieve.

21   Bailey came out in his robe and gave me a box wrapped in Christmas paper. He said he had saved his money for months to pay for it. It felt like a box of chocolates, but I knew Bailey wouldn't save money to buy candy when we had all we could want under our noses.

22   He was as proud of the gift as I. It was a soft-leather-bound copy of a collection of poems by Edgar Allan Poe, or, as Bailey and I called him, "Eap." I turned to "Annabel Lee" and we walked up and down the garden rows, the cool dirt between our toes, reciting the beautifully sad lines.

23   Momma made a Sunday breakfast although it was only Friday. After we finished the blessing, I opened my eyes to find the watch on my plate. It was a dream of a day. Everything went smoothly and to my credit. I didn't have to be reminded or scolded for anything. Near evening I was too jittery to attend to chores, so Bailey volunteered to do all before his bath.

24   Days before, we had made a sign for the Store, and as we turned out the lights Momma hung the cardboard over the doorknob. It read clearly: CLOSED. GRADUATION.

25   My dress fitted perfectly and everyone said that I looked like a sunbeam in it. On the hill, going toward the school, Bailey walked behind with Uncle Willie, who muttered, "Go on, Ju." He wanted him to walk ahead with us because it embarrassed him to have to walk so slowly. Bailey said he'd let the ladies walk together, and the men would bring up the rear. We all laughed, nicely.

26   Little children dashed by out of the dark like fireflies. Their crepe-paper dresses and butterfly wings were not made for running and we heard more than one rip, dryly, and the regretful "uh uh" that followed.

27   The school blazed without gaiety. The windows seemed cold and unfriendly from the lower hill. A sense of ill-fated timing crept over me, and if Momma hadn't reached for my hand I would have drifted back to Bailey and Uncle Willie, and possibly beyond. She made a few slow jokes about my feet getting cold, and tugged me along to the now-strange building.

28   Around the front steps, assurance came back. There were my fellow "greats," the graduating class. Hair brushed back, legs oiled, new dresses and pressed pleats, fresh pocket handkerchiefs and little handbags, all homesewn. Oh, we were up to snuff, all right. I joined my comrades and didn't even see my family go in to find seats in the crowded auditorium.

29   The school band struck up a march and all classes filed in as had been rehearsed. We stood in front of our seats, as assigned, and on a signal from the choir director, we sat. No sooner had this been accomplished than the band started to play the national anthem. We rose again and sang the song, after which we recited the pledge of allegiance. We remained standing for a brief minute before the choir director and the principal signaled to us, rather desperately I thought, to take our seats. The command was so unusual that our carefully rehearsed and smooth-running machine was thrown off. For a full minute we fumbled for our chairs and bumped into each other awkwardly. Habits change or solidify under pressure, so in our state of nervous tension we had been ready to follow our usual assembly pattern: the American national anthem, then the pledge of allegiance, then the song every Black person I knew called the Negro National Anthem. All done in the same key, with the same passion and most often standing on the same foot.

30   Finding my seat at last, I was overcome with a presentiment of worse things to come. Something unrehearsed, unplanned, was going to happen, and we were going to be made to look bad. I distinctly remember being explicit in the choice of pronoun. It was "we," the graduating class, the unit, that concerned me then.

31   The principal welcomed "parents and friends" and asked the Baptist minister to lead us in prayer. His invocations was brief and punchy, and for a second I thought we were getting back on the high road to right action. When the principal came back to the dais, however, his voice had changed.

Sounds always affected me profoundly and the principal's voice was one of my favorites. During assembly it melted and lowed weakly into the audience. It had not been in my plan to listen to him but my curiosity was piqued and I straightened up to give him my attention.

32   He was talking about Booker T. Washington, our "late great leader," who said we can be as close as the fingers on the hand, etc.... Then he said a few vague things about friendship and the friendship of kindly people to those less fortunate than themselves. With that his voice nearly faded, thin, away. Like a river diminishing to a stream and then to a trickle. But he cleared his throat and said, "Our speaker tonight, who is also our friend, came from Texarkana to deliver the commencement address, but due to the irregularity of the train schedule, he's going to, as they say, 'speak and run.'" He said that we understood and wanted the man to know that we were most grateful for the time he was able to give us and then something about how we were willing always to adjust to another's program, and without more ado—"I give you Mr. Edward Donleavy."

33   Not one but two white men came though the door off-stage. The shorter one walked to the speaker's platform, and the tall one moved over to the center seat and sat down. But that was our principal's seat, and already occupied. The dislodged gentleman bounced around for a long breath or two before the Baptist minister gave him his chair, then with more dignity than the situation deserved, the minister walked off the stage.

34   Donleavy looked at the audience once (on reflection, I'm sure that he wanted only to reassure himself that we were really there), adjusted his glasses and began to read from a sheaf of papers.

35   He was glad "to be here and to see the work going on just as it was in the other schools."

36   At the first "Amen" from the audience I willed the offender to immediate death by choking on the word. But Amens and Yes, sir's began to fall around the room like rain through a ragged umbrella.

37   He told us of the wonderful changes we children in Stamps had in store. The Central School (naturally, the white school was Central) had already been granted improvements that would be in use in the fall. A well-known artist was coming from Little Rock to teach art to them. They were going to have the newest microscopes and chemistry equipment for their laboratory. Mr. Donleavy didn't leave us long in the dark over who made these improvements available to Central High. Nor were we to be ignored in the general betterment scheme he had in mind.

38   He said that he had pointed out to people at a very high level that one of the first-line football tacklers at Arkansas Agricultural and Mechanical College had graduated from good old Lafayette County Training School. Here fewer Amen's were heard. Those few that did break through lay dully in the air with the heaviness of habit.

39   He went on to praise us. He went on to say how he had bragged that "one of the best basketball players at Fisk sank his first ball right here at Lafayette County Training School."

40   The white kids were going to have a chance to become Galileos and Madame Curies and Edisons and Gauguins, and our boys (the girls weren't even in on it) would try to be Jesse Owenses and Joe Louises.

41   Owens and the Brown Bomber were great heroes in our world, but what school official in the white-goddom of Little Rock had the right to decide that those two men must be our only heroes? Who decided that for Henry Reed to become a scientist he had to work like George Washington Carver, as a bootblack, to buy a lousy microscope? Bailey was obviously always going to be too small to be an athlete, so which concrete angel glued to what country seat had decided that if my brother wanted to become a lawyer he had to first pay penance for his skin by picking cotton and hoeing corn and studying correspondence books at night for twenty years?

42   The man's dead words fell like bricks around the auditorium and too many settled in my belly. Constrained by hard-learned manners, I couldn't look behind me, but to my left and right the proud graduating class of 1940 had dropped their heads. Every girl in my row had found something new to do with her handkerchief. Some folded the tiny squares into love knots, some into triangles, but most were wadding them, then pressing them flat on their yellow laps.

43   On the dais, the ancient tragedy was being replayed. Professor Parsons sat, a sculptor's reject, rigid. His large, heavy body seemed devoid of will or willingness, and his eyes said he was no longer with us. The other teachers examined the flag (which was draped stage right) or their notes, or the windows which opened on our now-famous playing diamond.

44   Graduation, the hush-hush magic time of frills and gifts and congratulations and diplomas, was finished for me before my name was called. The accomplishment was nothing. The meticulous maps, drawn in three colors of ink, learning and spelling decasyllabic words, memorizing the whole of *The Rape of Lucrece*—it was for nothing. Donleavy had exposed us.

45   We were maids and farmers, handymen and washerwomen, and anything higher that we aspired to was farcical and presumptuous.

46   Then I wished that Gabriel Prosser and Nat Turner had killed all white folks in their beds and that Abraham Lincoln had been assassinated before the signing of the Emancipation Proclamation, and that Harriet Tubman had been killed by that blow on her head and Christopher Columbus had drowned in the *Santa María*.

47   It was awful to be Negro and have no control over my life. It was brutal to be young and already trained to sit quietly and listen to charges brought against my color with no chance of defense. We should all be dead. I thought I should like to see us all dead, one on top of the other. A pyramid of flesh with the whitefolks on the bottom, as the broad base, then the Indians with their silly tomahawks and teepees and wigwams and treaties, the Negroes with their mops and recipes and cotton sacks and spirituals sticking out of their mouths. The Dutch children should all stumble in their wooden shoes and break their necks. The French should choke to death on the Louisiana

Purchase (1803) while silkworms ate all the Chinese with their stupid pigtails. As a species, we were an abomination. All of us.

48 Donleavy was running for election, and assured our parents that if he won we could count on having the only colored paved playing field in that part of Arkansas. Also—he never looked up to acknowledge the grunts of acceptance—also, we were bound to get some new equipment for the home economics building and the workshop.

49 He finished, and since there was no need to give any more than the most perfunctory thank-you's, he nodded to the men on the stage, and the tall white man who was never introduced joined him at the door. They left with the attitude that now they were off to something really important. (The graduation ceremonies at Lafayette County Training School had been a mere preliminary.)

50 The ugliness they left was palpable. An uninvited guest who wouldn't leave. The choir was summoned and sang a modern arrangement of "Onward, Christian Soldiers," with new words pertaining to graduates seeking their place in the world. But it didn't work. Elouise, the daughter of the Baptist minister, recited "Invictus," and I could have cried at the impertinence of "I am the master of my fate, I am the captain of my soul."

51 My name had lost its ring of familiarity and I had to be nudged to go and receive my diploma. All my preparations had fled. I neither marched up to the stage like a conquering Amazon, nor did I look in the audience for Bailey's nod of approval. Marguerite Johnson, I heard the name again, my honors were read, there were noises in the audience of appreciation, and I took my place on the stage as rehearsed.

52 I thought about colors I hated: ecru, puce, lavender, beige and black.

53 There was shuffling and rustling around me, then Henry Reed was giving his valedictory address, "To Be or Not to Be." Hadn't he heard the white-folks? We couldn't *be*, so the question was a waste of time. Henry's voice came out clear and strong. I feared to look at him. Hadn't he got the message? There was no "nobler in the mind" for Negroes because the world didn't think we had minds, and they let us know it. "Outrageous fortune"? Now, that was a joke. When the ceremony was over I had to tell Henry Reed some things. That is, if I still cared. Not "rub," Henry, "erase." "Ah, there's the erase." Us.

54 Henry had been a good student in elocution. His voice rose on tides of promise and fell on waves of warnings. The English teacher had helped him to create a sermon winging through Hamlet's soliloquy. To be a man, a doer, a builder, a leader, or to be a tool, an unfunny joke, a crusher of funky toadstools. I marveled that Henry could go through with the speech as if we had a choice.

55 I had been listening and silently rebutting each sentence with my eyes closed; then there was a hush, which in an audience warns that something unplanned is happening. I looked up and saw Henry Reed, the conservative,

the proper, the A student, turn his back to the audience and turn to us (the proud graduating class of 1940) and sing, nearly speaking,

> "Lift ev'ry voice and sing
> Till earth and heaven ring
> Ring with the harmonies of Liberty…"*

It was the poem written by James Weldon Johnson. It was the music composed by J. Rosamond Johnson. It was the Negro national anthem. Out of habit we were singing it.

56   Our mothers and fathers stood in the dark hall and joined the hymn of encouragement. A kindergarten teacher led the small children onto the stage and the buttercups and daisies and bunny rabbits marked time and tried to follow:

> "Stony the road we trod
> Bitter the chastening rod
> Felt in the days when hope, unborn, had died.
> Yet with a steady beat
> Have not our weary feet
> Come to the place for which our fathers sighed?"

57   Every child I knew had learned that song with his ABC's and along with "Jesus Loves Me This I Know." But I personally had never heard it before. Never heard the words, despite the thousands of times I had sung them. Never thought they had anything to do with me.

58   On the other hand, the works of Patrick Henry had made such an impression on me that I have been able to stretch myself tall and trembling and say, "I know not what other course others may take, but as for me, give me liberty or give me death."

59   And now I heard, really for the first time:

> "We have come over a way that with tears
> has been watered,
> We have come, treading our path through
> the blood of the slaughtered."

60   While echoes of the song shivered in the air, Henry Reed bowed his head, said "Thank you," and returned to his place in the line. The tears that slipped down many faces were not wiped away in shame.

61   We were on top again. As always, again. We survived. The depths had been icy and dark, but now a bright sun spoke to our souls. I was no longer simply a member of the proud graduating class of 1940; I was a proud member of the wonderful, beautiful Negro race.

62   Oh, Black known and unknown poets, how often have your auctioned pains sustained us? Who will compute the lonely nights made less lonely by your songs, or the empty pots made less tragic by your tales?

---

* "Lift Ev'ry Voice and Sing"—words by James Weldon Johnson and music by J. Rosamond Johnson. Copyright by Edward B. Marks Music Corporation. Used by permission.

63   If we were a people much given to revealing secrets, we might raise monuments and sacrifice to the memories of our poets, but slavery cured us of that weakness. It may be enough, however, to have it said that we survive in exact relationship to the dedication of our poets (include preachers, musicians and blues singers).

CRITICAL READING

1. Angelou doesn't turn the focus on herself—doesn't even use the pronoun "I"—until the sixth paragraph. Why does she spend so much time on general expectations, on shared experience? How do these first five paragraphs help to prepare the reader for what happens later in the narrative?

2. Angelou's account of everything prior to the actual ceremony seems wholly positive. Did this leave you just a little incredulous, maybe even give you a sense of foreboding—as if all this seemed "too good to be true"? Can you pinpoint particular parts of this part of the narrative that gave you that impression?

3. What, exactly, are the first things to go or seem wrong? Identify specific words and phrases that suggest a change in atmosphere, in tone, in expectation. Does any one of them strike you as especially important?

4. When Angelou has "a presentiment of worse things to come" (in paragraph 30) she is "explicit in the choice of pronoun. It was 'we,' the graduating class, the unit, that concerned me then." Why is this an important choice? What has Angelou done up to this point to show that she can feel with and speak for the others?

5. Angelou's reaction to Donleavy's appearance and remarks is strong, to say the least. What does she do, not just during but even before and after describing his speech, to suggest that her reaction is not excessive, that others share it?

6. What happens to those assembled when Henry Reed begins singing "Lift Ev'ry Voice and Sing"? What happens to Angelou? Is there a new, unexpected sense in which this is a graduation, a commencement for her?

Denise Chávez

HEAT AND RAIN

"I grew up solitary in the midst of noise, a quality I didn't know then was essential to my work as a writer."

BORN IN LAS CRUCES, NEW MEXICO, IN 1948, *Denise Chávez still makes her home there; the spirit of the Southwest is important to her writing. A Chicana (or Mexican-American), she belongs to a people often considered immigrants, yet they inhabited the Southwest even before the United States was a country. (As the Chicano writer Luis Valdez has remarked, "We did not, in fact, come to the United States at all. The United States came to us.") A poet, fiction writer, and playwright, Chávez wrote a play (Novenas Narrativas) and a novel* (Face of an Angel) *the year she wrote "Heat and Rain" (1987). Her heritage has made her bilingual, and an occasional Spanish word—* cuentistas *(storytellers),* viejitas *(little old ladies)—salts her narrative.*

As for "Heat and Rain" itself, it is a testimonio, *a Latin American form defined by Renato Prada Oropeza as having the "explicit intention to provide proof of or truth to a social fact that has already occurred. Its interpretation is guaranteed by the speaker while declaring her/himself actor/witness to the events s/he narrates." The shared experience Chávez recounts, the "social fact," is growing up—something we all go through and yet all experience differently. Chávez's twist is to make her own account a map of her destiny, an account of why she became what she became: a writer. As you'll see, she writes it the way she writes everything, not as a march-through-time tale but as "an assemblage of parts, a phrase here, an image there."*

ON THE WAY INTO THE READING

1. If you were going to write an account of growing up, particularly one that accounted for who you are today, what would you focus on? How much would other people figure in this account? Would you be more of an actor or someone acted upon? Would any one person or event or circumstance have a decisive role? How much would a sense of group identity (racial or ethnic or national or whatever) contribute to your personal identity?

2. Education is supposed to have an important role to play. Did it in your case? Do you expect it to in Chávez's case? How much of what educates us lies outside the bounds of formal, institutionalized education? How much of that do we choose or control?

3. Chávez's piece is called "Heat and Rain." How much did your developing sense of your place in the world have to do with the natural world—the climate, the landscape, the cycle of the seasons? What does her title of this piece about herself suggest to you about the kind of person Chávez is, the kind of writer she is?

1   My first childhood recollection is of heat. Perhaps because I was born in the middle of August in Southern New Mexico, I have always felt the burningly beautiful intensity of my dry, impenetrable land. Land not often relieved by the rain—that wet, cleansing, and blessed catharsis. I remember as a little girl sitting waist-deep in the cool, grassy water that had been channeled from the irrigation ditch behind our house. The heat, then the rain, and the water were my first friends.

2   My other friend was my imagination that invented an extended family of loving, congenial spirits who wandered with me nighttimes in my dreams—into the other worlds I inhabited as vividly and completely as I did my own waking existence as middle daughter in a family of three girls, one mother, Delfina Rede Faver Chávez, a teacher divorced by my father, E. E. "Chano" Chávez, one lawyer, long gone.

3   These friendships with spirits were real to me, and still are. The spirits were voices of people, people I'd known and not known, feelings I felt and couldn't at the time conceive of feeling. I had no way to explain my creative world to anyone, could not even explain it to myself. All I know is that my life was rich and deep and full of wonder.

4   I always felt advanced for my age, somehow different, I always thought I *thought* more than people my own age. My imagination was a friend at first, and later a lover, a guide, a spirit teacher.

5   I grew up in a house of women. That is why I often write about women, women who are without men. My father divorced us early on; he was a brilliant lawyer, but an alcoholic. My mother was incredibly intelligent, with a keen curiosity and love of life and people. Their minds were compatible, their spirits and hearts were not. I grew up knowing separation as a quality of life—and this sorrow went hand in hand with extensions—for despite the fact my parents were apart, both families were an everpresent part of my life. So I grew up solitary in the midst of noise, a quality I didn't know then was essential to my work as a writer.

6   People always ask me how and when I started writing. The answer never varies. From an early age I kept diaries, some with locks, locks I kept losing or misplacing, others with no locks. I'm sure my mother read my diary. I'm positive my younger sister did.

DIARY

A Page a Day for 1958

New Year's Day, Wednesday January 1, 1958
1st Day—364 Days to Follow
Dear Diary,
   Today is New Year and the old year is gone and the new one here. Today school starts. I can't wait to go.

Sunday June 15, 1958
166th Day—199 Days to Follow
Dear Diary,
   Today I didn't go to Mass, I must tell the priest my sin. I'm not to happy about it.

Friday, August 15, 1958
227th Day—138 Days to Follow
Dear Diary,
   Today is my birthday. I am ten in a few years I'll be twenty. Boy oh boy ten years old.

Tuesday, November 11, 1958
315 Day—50 Days to Follow
Dear Diary,

School was fun, But I forgot to do my homework. I'm praying for daddy to come home, I hope so. He did. Thank god. Bless us all.

Thursday, November 20, 1958
324th Day—41 Days to Follow
Dear Diary,

I did not go to school today because we stayed home with Mama. She is heart sick (broken heart) She feels bad, I hope she gets well. I missed school but I loved to stay home. You know why! Don't you?

All wrong. I did go to school. drat.

Somehow, looking back on myself in these diary entries, I am aware of myself, even then, as an observer of life. Without my diaries, I don't think I'd ever have become a writer. I now see that 1958 was a hard year, the breakup of my parents' marriage, a devastating time for all of us. I see the order I began to put into my life, the need to account for, evaluate, assess. Time was of significance, my life of value. Religion was important then as spirituality is to me now. I wanted to grow up so badly, to be an adult, to understand. My life was rich then, I see that too, with much experience that was to feed me for years to come.

7   I see that I was not a good student, ever. I rarely did homework. I would study in bed, usually lying down, waking up the next morning, the light on, in my clothes, very hot a clammy, dry mouthed, Mother yelling for me to wake up, to find the History or Math book mashed into my face. I would race to school, then fly back to enter the latest news into my diary. Painful accounts were entered, then torn. Did *I* tear them, and if not me, who? My mother, my sister? Or that other girl, the me who wanted to be happy? I note with interest my early stream of consciousness technique (not a technique then), my disinterest in chronological time (critics take note), I see the roots of my still poor grammar and spelling, and observe the time I begin to sign my writing—Denise. The writing had become a statement for someone other than me. What I had to say, suddenly, to me "mattered."

8   I see also the many gaps between entries, and that too is of significance. I see that I wrote on sad, happy, elated, and depressed days. The regular days were entry-less. Writing was a gauge of my personal life. It was a record of my physical, spiritual, and emotional ups and down. I enjoyed writing, always have, the actual physical movement of pen or pencil across a piece of paper. I enjoyed/enjoy the mind-eye-to-hand-acting-out-delineation of internalness. I practiced my handwriting constantly:

a B C D E 7 G H I
9 K L M O P Q R S
T U V W X Y Z

a b c d e f g h i j
k l m n O o p q r
s t u v w x y z

9   I see now that I was training myself unconsciously to "write" efficiently, quickly. A sort of "scales" for the writing self/hand. Rolling letters, moving them through space, limbering up mechanically so that later I could use my hand like a tool, limbered, unrestrained. I still find myself practicing the alphabet on random sheets of paper, testing letter style, still looking for a more effective fluid line. Much flight time on the white canvas of my constantly emerging movement toward my work as a writer. I didn't know it then. I didn't know it when I got a notebook and started copying other people's poems, songs. But this was later, because first there were books, books, and more books to read, like my favorite childhood book called *Poems of Childhood* by Eugene Field, with scary-wonderful poems like "Seein' Things."

10   I was a voracious reader. Anything. Everything. I went on binges. My mother would hide our books in the summertime so we would help her with the housework. My sister would lock herself in the bathroom with a book, heedless of my mother's cries. It never occurred to me to do that. Every day my book would be missing, I'd find it, read awhile, then find it missing. It went on like that. I read fairy tales. Mysteries. Nancy Drew. You name it. Later on it was Ian Fleming's James Bond, D. H. Lawrence, Thomas Mann, Thomas Wolfe, Chekhov, Eugene O'Neill, Samuel Beckett. Now it's the *Enquirer*. I love the scandal sheets and movie mags and bowling and soap operas in the middle of the day, and so much of what everyone else considers pedestrian, sub-mainstream culture. Director John Waters calls Baltimore the Hairdo capital of the world. New Mexico/Texas was and is Character Capital of the Universe. Unbelievable stories, lives. I have always been a talker, friendly to strangers, and so invariably people tell me about their lives. It's a gift to listen to so many of these stories. The *Enquirer* has nothing over New Mexico/Texas or the world I see every day!

11   But this sense of wonder came early. I began to copy my favorite passages, poems. One of the earliest was a cowboy song. I loved the rhythm. Sang it to myself. Later on I copied Gibran and the Black poets, wrote angry poems to the nuns at Madonna High School, where I attended school for four years, poems they refused to publish in the *Mantle*, the school newspaper. Once, as a joke, I invented a quote for the "Quote of the Day" for World Literature class: "Christmas is the flowing of honey on a mound of cold, white snow." Mrs. Baker, lovely, frail, intelligent, and wispy-haired, loved it. I didn't know what the hell it meant. I was playing the rebellious know-it-all, making up my own poems and quotes. I didn't know writing was becoming a facile thing. Then it was just a joke. The other day I heard a writer say, "All those lies, writing all those lies—I love it!" I didn't say anything. For me, writing is no longer a facile joke, a prank to be played on a well-meaning and unsuspecting reader, nor is it a lie. I have said to writers I have taught: Don't lie. And to myself: You may lie in other things, but never in this. It's a sacred covenant I have with myself. Honesty. And no meanness. Sometimes it's been hard. Lies always surface, don't you know?

12   I never thought of lying in my writing. It would have been like hiding in the bathroom to read.

13   I could never lie to those voices, to those spirits, to those voices I hear clearly. Voices like my mother, who always spoke in Spanish, or my father, who mostly spoke in English. Mother grew up in West Texas, moved to New Mexico as a widow and met and married my father. My father, as a child, was punished for speaking Spanish in the schoolyard. He decided to beat the Anglos at their game. He went and got a law degree from Georgetown during the Depression. And he became, in his mind, more Anglo than those Anglos who had punished him. I remember my mother saying, "I never think of your father as Mexican." My mother was, though, in her heart and soul. She studied in Mexico for thirteen summers, was a student of Diego Rivera. She'd been widowed for nine years, all that time wearing black, when she met my father, just returned from the Big City. Both my parents were very intelligent, perceptive, sensitive people. My mother's grandparents were the first Spanish-speaking graduates of Sul Ross State College in West Texas. All of them became teachers. Both my grandfathers were miners, all-around men, carpenters, teamsters, fixer-uppers, workers with their hands. They used their brains and their hands to support their large families. The women were independent, creative, and did most of the child-rearing, alone. The Chávez men are painters now, artists with canvas and paint, or architects, builders of some kind. The Rede Family (my mother's clan) are educators, fighters for human rights, communicators, and believers in the equality of all people.

14   I grew up between and in the middle of two languages, Spanish and English, speaking my own as a defense. My mother always said I "made up words." Speaking Spanish to the Redes or English to the get-ahead Chávezes and Spanish to the traditional Chávezes and English to my Rede cousins was all taken in stride. We went back and forth, back and forth. My mother taught Spanish and she was always correcting, in any language. When I asked how to spell a word, she would tell me to sound out the syllables, and to find a dictionary. "There she goes again," I'd think, "teacher-ing me." I was lazy, still am. My English needs work and so does my Spanish. I can't spell, punctuate or understand the possessive. My multiplication is a mess and I can't tell time. I was absent the day we kids learned the 7, 8, and 9 multiplication tables. I have gaps—huge ones. But I've taught myself what little grammar I know, what math I know, and how to type. I can take any vacuum cleaner apart and fix it and my pen hand is very fast at the draw. I really write according to what I hear—sometimes English, sometimes Spanish, sometimes both. As a writer, I have tried to capture as clearly as I am able *voices,* intonation, inflection, mood, timbre, pitch. I write about characters, not treatises, about life, not make-believe worlds. If my characters don't work, I will go back and make them work. Without them, robust and in the living flesh, there is no story for me. Readers should stop looking for traditional stories, ABC. Writing, to me, is an assemblage of parts, a phrase here, an image there, part of a dialogue.

15   Suddenly it occurs to me that Jesusita Real, the not-so-mousy spinster in my play, *Novenas Narrativas,* should wear green tennis shoes, and so I add them to the script. When she finally does walk, it will be in comfort, with support from the ground up. I work with my characters in the way an actress or actor assumes a role, slowly, carefully, with attention to physical, emotional, and spiritual detail. I may read the material out loud, speak it into a tape recorder, play it back, rewrite it, and then tape it again. My years as a theatre person have helped me immensely. I have acted, directed, and written for the theatre. I have done props, hung lights, performed for all types of audiences, young, old, handicapped, drunk, aging, for prisoners, in Spanish and English. My work has always been for alternative groups, the people who never get much, for the poor, the forgotten. My writing as well is about the off-off Main street type of characters. My short stories are really scenes and I come from the tradition of the traveling *cuentista.* I believe stories should captivate, delight, move, inspire, and be downright funny, in a way. The "in a way" is what I try to do with all my heart. But always, I go back to the characters and their voices. I see them: flat feet, lagañas, lonjas, lumps, spider veins, and all. From the feet up and back down and around the other side. And I love them. Dearly. But I don't excuse them nor will I lie for them.

16   I write for you. And me. And Jesusita with the green tennies, spinster owner of Rael's Tiendita de Abarrotes, active member of the Third Order of St. Francis, and for the people: Anglo, Hispanic, Black, you name it: anybody out there who doesn't know Jesusita is alive, inside her little store, swatting flies, and wondering aloud about Prudencio Sifuentes, the only man who asked her to marry him.

17   I write for the viejitas at the Save-And-Gain in black scarves, for the tall blond man testing tomatoes, for the Vietnamese cashier, and for the hot dog man outside the electric door. For me, it is a joy to carry my bag full of stories.

18   Naturally I write about what I know, who I am. New Mexico. Texas. Chicanismo. Latinismo. Americanismo. Womanismo. Mujerotismo. Peopleismo. Worldismo. Peaceismo. Loveismo.

19   Writing has been my heat, my accounting, my trying to understand; and rain has been my prayer for peace, for love, and mercy. August in Southern New Mexico is very hot, for many, unbearable. It has been my blessing in this life of mine to share that heat. And to remember the rain.

CRITICAL READING

1. Chávez mentions her "first friends"—heat and rain and imagination—before she mentions her parents. She is likely to seem different to you before she says (in the fourth paragraph) that she herself felt "somehow different." How different? Does she simply seem weird to you? Or does her "creative world" of imagined spirits seem credible, something you can identify with, if only vicariously?

2. Selected diary entries from the year 1958 are given. What is the personal significance of this year? What significance does Chávez say writing took on in her life? What added significance does it take on when she begins signing her name to it?

3. A popular (and quite possibly false) saying has it that "writers are born, not made." Where does Chávez seem to come down on this issue? How much is nature, how much nurture, and how much plain hard work?

4. The shortest paragraph in the piece contains only two sentences, the first of which is "I never thought of lying in my writing." Why is honesty so important to Chávez? Does it contradict the importance she accords her imagination?

5. That shortest paragraph is followed by the two longest. The first expands on the importance of honesty by thinking of the "voices" or "spirits"— then ranges back through both sides of Chávez's family. The next treats Chávez's bilingualism, her spotty education, her techniques as a writer. Are these paragraphs as rambling as they seem? Or do they have a deeper unifying principle than straightforward chronology or topic-centeredness?

6. Chávez ends as she began, by speaking of the heat and the rain. These have become more than just aspects of the New Mexico climate. What symbolic values are they now charged with?

CHAPTER THREE

MEASURING THE DISTANCE BETWEEN YOUR PAST AND YOUR PRESENT

This chapter, the third in the section on using personal experience as a source of writing, looks back at "then" from the vantage point of "now." Distance from the past often transforms experience into a vague, nostalgic longing, but the three selections in this chapter have nothing nostalgic or sentimental about them. Reflections about their school and university days for Rafael Matos, the student writer in this chapter, and for Winston Churchill and James Thurber, professional writers included at the end of the chapter, yield surprises, incongruities, and contradictions.

The three pieces, written at different times and from divergent backgrounds, share a remarkably similar sensibility. In writing about the educational institutions they attended, the authors recall the struggle between people in authority (teachers and generals) and themselves as students who rebelled against authority. The judgments and the generalizations that their personal reactions lead to highlight the commonality of our experiences.

Rafael's account of his life in public and parochial schools shares many features with the personal writing of Mel and Nikki in Chapters 1 and 2, respectively, such as narrative action, detailed descriptions, personal stories or anecdotes, and dialogue. In spite of their shared features, though, Rafael's "My Life" is less private and personal than Mel and Nikki's accounts. This distancing of himself from his subject may have made the task somewhat less complicated for Rafael by helping him feel less exposed or vulnerable when he considered his classmates as his audience. In addition, his classmates shared many of Rafael's experiences, as most of them came from either public or parochial schools, and that common ground helped Rafael select the details and particularly the humor that he felt might appeal to his fellow students. The strategies you learned in the earlier chapters, along with Rafael's technique of listing and clustering, may help you write your own paper on looking at "then" from the vantage point of "now."

WRITING ASSIGNMENT

Write a narrative in which you compare "then" and "now" in your life. You may choose to write about how your life is different now from the way it was earlier, or how your attitude toward life is different now. For example, you might write about how you feel about high school now that you are beyond it, how your neighborhood has changed since you have lived in it, or how you would do something differently from the way you went about it earlier.

READING THE WRITING ASSIGNMENT

For the above assignment, which requires you to compare then with now, your main strategy will probably be to use comparison and contrast to look back at your life (then) from the vantage point of the present (now). To accomplish this, you will have to remember and record details, show similarities and differences between them, and finally reflect on your recollections. Comparison/contrast as the organizing principle will help you achieve your goal.

Comparison of the past with the present in personal narrative usually involves linking two or more ideas, subjects, or angles of vision. For example, Rafael's observations contrast his parochial school with his public school, and Churchill and Thurber reflect on their schools from adult perspectives. Such narratives often call for descriptive details to set off the topics and differentiate between them.

You may not plan to evaluate your items of comparison when you begin to write, but may end up doing so nonetheless. That is because when we compare items, we almost necessarily make some judgments, however implied, about them. Conversely, because judgments are relative, we turn to comparison to examine one idea or item relative to another. Which is better or which is worse? Which one do I prefer? Rafael evaluates the two schools he attended to indicate his preference for one over the other, while acknowledging the contributions of both in shaping his life. Churchill's is a chilling account of the tyranny in the exclusive British "public" school from which he was transferred to the more tolerant atmosphere of the school at Brighton. Looking back at his days as a student at Ohio State University, Thurber finds it was run much like the military, with little respect and freedom for the individual student. The tying together of the various points of comparison at the end is particularly important because it clarifies your purpose by revealing your judgment about the items you are comparing and contrasting.

DISCOVERING IDEAS

The discovery techniques used by Rafael for this assignment are **listing** and **clustering.** Though Rafael worked on his own, both of these methods of generating ideas may be used in collaboration with others. They can be particularly helpful when you are recollecting and exploring a personal topic for which you are the most important source of information.

List Details

For his paper comparing the two schools he had attended, Rafael made two separate lists of details as they came to his mind:

Parochial School	Public School
1. my parents chose it	my own choice
2. teachers mostly nuns	not nuns and many men teachers
3. strict discipline in	little discipline
4. couldn't use slang	everyone used slang
5. no freedom even in lunchroom and playground	free to do what I want
6. rigid rules for writing assignments	not required to do much writing
7. going to church compulsory	not required to go to church
8. fear and respect for the teacher	few care to listen to the teacher
9. nuns seem to care more for the students	teachers do not care much about students
10. gave me no freedom	had too much of freedom
11. didn't have much fun	enjoyed the freedom
12. learned discipline	learned to be responsible for myself

Rafael lists a few characteristic features of his parochial school, which he contrasts with those of his high school. Putting his list into two columns helps him first to remember details and then to oppose contrasting ideas across the columns. This technique is particularly effective for an assignment that requires you to write about two things or two ideas. To avoid confusion later, Rafael adds a title to each list.

TRIAL RUN

When you have selected two items to compare, jot down their characteristics in separate columns. At this stage, do not be concerned with complete thoughts or sentences. Write down the ideas as they come to you. (Only make sure that you write the details in their appropriate columns.)

CHECKLIST: LISTING DETAILS

- Have I given my list a title?
- Have I included a dozen or so ideas (or as many as I could think of)?
- Have I used short phrases (rather than complete sentences) to speed up the process?
- Have I considered all aspects of the topic—even if they seem somewhat farfetched?
- Have I looked for unusual or unfamiliar details to spark the reader's interest?
- Have I been spontaneous in recording my thoughts, or have I been slowed down by concern for order?

Use Clustering to List Ideas

Clustering, a variation of listing, is the most visual of prewriting activities. To make a cluster, write your main topic at the center of a large sheet of paper, and circle it. Then write down other related ideas: circle them and draw lines to link the ideas that go together. In this way you will create a graphic chart that enables you to see clearly the different parts of the topic and how they relate to the main idea. Figure 3-1 shows Rafael's use of clustering to generate ideas related to his topic.

TRIAL RUN

Following Rafael's lead, make your own cluster of ideas related to your topic. Write the main idea in the middle of the page. As related thoughts come to your mind, write them down, circle them, and join them to each other and to the main idea. When you feel you have put down most of what you know about the topic, you can start to narrow your focus by eliminating those ideas that connect most remotely to the main idea. If you are not satisfied with your first effort, create another cluster, which may turn out to be very different from your first effort.

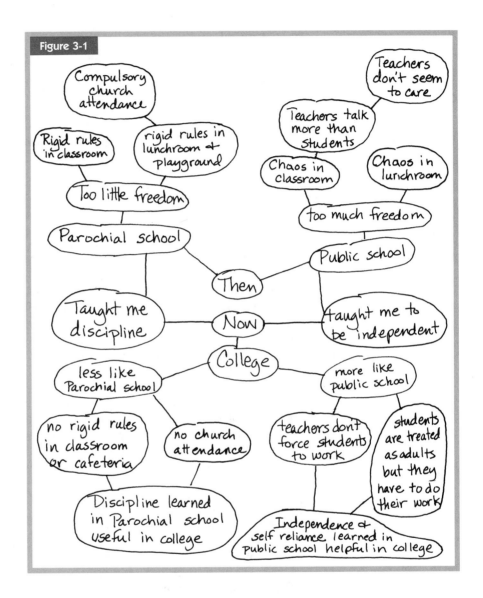

Figure 3-1

CHECKLIST: CLUSTERING

- Do I have a large sheet of paper for spreading out the cluster?
- Have I written down my main idea at the center of the page and circled it?
- Have I put down related ideas around the main idea?
- Have I circled the related ideas and drawn lines to join them to each other and to the main idea?

- Have I exhausted my thoughts on the topic?
- After creating the cluster, have I weeded out thoughts that do not relate to the main idea?

COMPOSING THE FIRST DRAFT

Arrange the Details

Before he sat down to write the first draft, Rafael had to figure out a pattern for arranging his thoughts. Should he follow a **block** method of organization in which he would discuss topic A, his parochial school, in the first few paragraphs and then shift the focus in the later paragraphs to topic B, his public school? Or should he use a **point-by-point** comparison that would discuss a point or issue relevant to both topics? For example, he might first discuss the discipline at both schools, then respect for teachers at both schools, then rules for writing assignments at both schools, and so on.

Rafael's two-column list of details about his topic contained a dozen contrasting pairs, which he considered a manageable number to raise and remember at one time. So Rafael decided to give the block method a try in his first draft, with the first half of the paper devoted to one school and the second half to the other.

Such a block pattern would have been unwieldy if, for example, Rafael had fifty points of difference between the two schools. By the time the readers got to topic B, they might have forgotten the corresponding points in topic A. A more appropriate arrangement in that situation would have been a point-by-point comparison, discussing one aspect of topic A followed immediately by a similar or contrasting aspect of topic B.

Block Method

I. Catholic school [TOPIC A]
    A. Rigid Rules
    B. Compulsory church attendance
    C. Fear and respect for teacher
    D. Learned Discipline

II. Public school [TOPIC B]
    A. More freedom
    B. Church attendance not required
    C. Not much fear or respect for teacher
    D. Learned to be responsible for myself

Point-by-Point Method

I. Rules and discipline
    A. Catholic school too rigid [TOPIC A]
    B. Public school too relaxed [TOPIC B]

    II.   Church attendance
        A.   Compulsory in Catholic school [TOPIC A]
        B.   Not required in public school [TOPIC B]
   III.   Teachers
        A.   Caring in Catholic school [TOPIC A]
        B.   Not caring in public school [TOPIC B]
   IV.   Lessons learned
        A.   Learned discipline in Catholic school [TOPIC A]
        B.   Learned to be responsible for myself
           in public school [TOPIC B]

Because Rafael's essay included two main items of comparison—the parochial and public schools—and, to a lesser degree, his college, he had to make sure that the ideas relating to them were kept separate from each other so as not to confuse his readers. For this he needed clear guideposts or transition words to show similarities and differences. For example, to show the contrast between his expectations of the Catholic school and what the school turned out to be, Rafael used the transition sentence, "But the bliss was shortlived," to begin paragraph 2 in the final draft.

Another transition technique used by Rafael is using words at the beginning of a paragraph that refer to the ideas in the preceding paragraph. For example, the opening sentence in paragraph 4 in the final draft is, "The same tyranny followed us into the lunch room and the playground." The word "same" refers to the context in paragraph 3 and provides a smooth transition between the two paragraphs.

The guideposts you use to indicate movement from one idea to another will depend on your own preference. Some commonly used words to show contrast are *but, yet, however, nevertheless, nonetheless, in contrast,* and *contrary to.* Similarity is often indicated by the use of: *also, too, in addition, furthermore, moreover, likewise,* and *besides.*

 # TRIAL RUN

Examine the information you have generated on your topic. Make sure you have appropriate ideas that relate to all the specific points of comparison. Based on the nature and amount of information, decide which form of organization will be most beneficial for you. You may wish to experiment with both block and point-by-point comparison in outline form before deciding on one or the other method.

CHECKLIST: ARRANGING DETAILS

- How many items or ideas am I comparing or contrasting?
- Depending on the information gathered, will a block or a point-by-point pattern of organization be most suitable for my purpose?

- Have I selected examples that enhance my main discussion?
- Are my examples lively, engaging, and credible for my readers?
- Do I have enough examples to illustrate all the items of comparison? Am I saying too much about one while not saying enough about the others?
- Have I separated the different items of comparison by using clear transitions?

Working from his list and cluster of ideas, Rafael began the first draft of the essay. He asked himself once again *why* he was comparing the schools he had attended. What did he wish to achieve by the comparison? At this point, he tried to imagine his readers and how much they might or might not know about his topic. Raphael expected some empathy from his readers because they all had been through high school and might have had similar experiences. But he was aware that each experience was different and he made sure he included enough details to present a clear picture. He also considered the tone of the paper. Some of his experiences were quite funny. But he did not want to sound frivolous, because his readers might not consider his observations seriously. But neither did he want to sound grim or preachy and lose his readers. He decided to include some humor while discussing the merits and shortcomings of the schools he attended.

PRESENTING RAFAEL'S FIRST DRAFT

1   I remember clearly the first day of school. I held my mother's hand tightly as I stood in my new school, surrounded by nervous kids, anxious parents, and smiling nuns. A Catholic school was the natural choice for my parents. They believed, with the permissive atmosphere in the public schools, I would be better off in an institution which respected traditional values. I played no part in choosing the school in which I spent six years of my life. If I had a choice, I doubt if I would have opted for a parochial school even though I acquired some important values: discipline and respect for others. But as soon I finished eighth grade, I made it clear to my parents that I wanted to go to a public high school. I wanted to be in an atmosphere which would allow me to make some of my own decisions and not tell me at every step what I should do. As I look back at the years I spent in a parochial school and public high school, I believe both the experiences contributed towards making me the person I am today.

2   During my eight years at St. Peter and Paul Catholic School, one of the most difficult tasks was to follow orders while maintaining my cool because I learned quickly the price for disobedience. It was a long walk to school, but I could not be a minute late. So I trudged along each morning, wearing the same old drab uniform. The Pledge of Allegiance and the Hail Mary which we had to recite every morning pretty much set the tone of the day. My English class comes to mind as a typical class. Writing was something I enjoyed so I would in a way look forward to the class. But the writing assignment with its rigid instructions would stifle all desire in me to put my thoughts on paper. "Don't use any slang," the teacher would forewarn us. But everything I wrote seemed to be "slang" in her opinion. My classmates, too, added to the tension. When I looked around, I saw most of them chewing on their fingernails and staring at blank pages. And in front of us, like a specter, stood the sister in her habit, rigid and unbending. We had a name for these classes; we called them a clash of religion and communism.

3   The same tyranny followed into the lunch room and the playground. We had to eat all the food on the plate, rinse our hands and leave the room. I often got into trouble because I wanted to wait for a friend to finish before I left the room. Throughout those eight years, I felt a clash of will between me and the nuns who were my teachers: their desire to control me, and my refusal to be controlled. I think the practice that I resented most and that stands out in my mind was when we were asked, all of a sudden, to freeze in the playground. We would be running around playing whatever we happened to be playing at that time and all of a sudden a shrill whistle would pierce our ears. Automatically we would have to stand still in our position. If we so much as turned our heads to see which sister it was with the whistle that day, we would be punished by being detained after school. I also had to go to church every week. Not that I did not have faith in God, still I questioned some of the things I heard at church. But I kept them inside me in silence. Even at that young age I questioned the dictatorial system. So when it came time for me to go to high school, I naturally chose a public school.

4   What a relief it was to be in an atmosphere which allowed me to be who I was. My first act was to discard the drab uniform and grow my hair. In my light blue jeans and a T-shirt I felt I was walking on air. Gone were the days when I had to obey orders in the classroom and not speak out of turn. Everyone around me was talking so loudly in groups and to each other that the teacher's voice was drowned by the noise. In fact the

students did more talking than the teacher. Not only that, they did not hesitate to talk back at the teacher. What a privilege, I thought! How much fun I missed during those dull rigid years in my Catholic school! I looked forward to my writing class. This would be the time when all my stifled creativity would surge through in my writing. I could express my feeling in my own language, without someone labeling my language as slang. Though I admit the atmosphere seemed a bit chaotic, I attributed it to my own inadequacies. Having come from a parochial school, I didn't know what a real classroom was meant to be. I was going to settle in comfortably in this atmosphere where liberty reigned.

5   But I soon learned that independence came with a price. Many students didn't go to class, didn't do their assignments, and the teachers didn't seem to care. Weeks went by when I wasn't required to do any writing. Students had better attendance in the lunchroom than in the classroom. Lunch time was very different from the Catholic school. Students went in and didn't come out. Many of my classmates stayed in there all day. It was always packed. I soon realized if I didn't watch out for myself, I would never graduate out of high school. It was this fear that drove me back to the classroom and to the books.

6   As much as I complained about the strict rules in my parochial school, it was the discipline I acquired there that gave me the strength to survive in the jungle of the public school. I must acknowledge most of my desire to succeed came from my junior high school days. It is strange that I can admit that even the clash of communism and religion, as we called our Catholic school, contributed to building my character. Sometimes I wonder if I made the right decision when I chose a public high school against my parents' wishes.

7   Yet I feel both institutions are responsible for the person I am today. If my parochial school taught me discipline, the public school gave me my first taste of independence and the responsibility that came with it. Without the nuns to watch over me, I learned to watch out for myself. That is a lesson that I think has helped me a lot in my college work. College, in many ways, is like my public school, only without the chaos and the lack of discipline. Now in college I can sit in the cafeteria all day without anyone forcing me to attend classes. The professors give us help and guidance but pretty much leave us alone to do our own work. For this I have my high school to thank. It made me independent and gave me the will to succeed, even in difficult circumstances.

Thinking Critically about Rafael's First Draft

1. Examine the organization of the essay. Is the block method effective, or should Rafael have used another method? Explain your reasoning.

2. Which sentence or paragraph tells the reader the intent of the writer? What do you think of its location? Would you have preferred a different location? Why or why not?

3. List the positive and negative aspects of the two school systems Rafael discusses in his essay. Do you see a pattern in the way he arranges the details?

4. Paragraphs 2 and 3 detail Rafael's distaste for the rigid atmosphere of the parochial school, and paragraph 4 presents the permissive atmosphere of the public school. What is the purpose of paragraph 5? How does it relate to the conclusion?

5. Conclusions, in general, do not introduce new ideas. Rafael's concluding paragraph, however, introduces a third element in the comparison, college. How does this affect the conclusion and the overall structure of the essay?

RETHINKING AND REVISING

Rafael worked on several drafts between the first and the final one. In the first draft, the introductory paragraph ended in a neat thesis statement, "As I look back at the years I spent in a parochial school and public high school, I believe both the experiences contributed towards making me the person I am today." In rereading, Rafael felt this statement interfered with the flow of the narrative. The only place he could fit it smoothly into his final draft was in the last paragraph, in modified form.

Removing the thesis statement from the first to the last paragraph is a rather radical relocation of the main idea. It may not work in every writing situation. But certain important aspects of personal writing—the story line, the element of suspense, the autobiographical significance—are often enhanced without a declarative statement at the beginning. (Nevertheless, beginning writers often state the main points early to guide them through their writing.)

Rafael's final draft began with a clear word picture of his first day in school. Instead of the clichéd beginning, "I remember clearly," he plunged right into action to capture his reader's interest with immediate action: "I held my mother's hand tightly." He introduced more visually descriptive words to create images of "nuns in their black and white clothes" who "looked like penguins," of the "reassuring smile and comforting pat" of a nun, and of parochial school as a "dungeon." The use of direct speech also added more immediacy to the narrative.

The addition of "But the bliss was shortlived" as the opening sentence in paragraph 2 of the final draft creates a deliberately abrupt contrast between the expectations of the child and the grim reality depicted in the subsequent paragraphs. Elsewhere, where it seemed that a smoother transition between action and reflection was called for, Rafael inserted paragraph 6 in the final draft: "Looking back, I realize that it was my parochial school background and the discipline I acquired there that gave me the strength to survive in the jungle of the public school."

The changes in the final draft improved the style and structure of the essay. In the concluding paragraph, Rafael explained the analogy, "College, in many ways, is like my public school," by adding a couple more sentences. But one of the weaknesses of the first draft, the neat and simplified generalizations based on limited personal experiences, remained in the final draft. Instead of the general comments on the different schools he had attended, Rafael could have highlighted one of the several levels of contrast in the essay, particularly the contrast between expectations and reality. He introduced this idea in the second paragraph of the final draft and he could have returned to it in the conclusion to show that neither parochial school nor high school had been as first impressions had suggested, so why should college? This skepticism and knowledge that things didn't often turn out as expected might have been the lesson Rafael learned from his experiences. His readers would have been more willing to believe him because instead of making generalizations based on a few personal observations, he would have been speaking out of his own convictions.

As Rafael worked on each draft, he made changes to improve the paper. The process of revision takes place simultaneously with the writing process. This does not mean that revision should hinder or interfere with the writing itself. What we mean by revision is not just mechanical error detection. Revision should mean having your critical eye open as you write, and when you've completed the writing, to possible additions, deletions, and changes to make your writing even better. While revising, you may also refer to the list of 10 detailed guidelines for revision in Chapter 2.

CHECKLIST: REVISING YOUR DRAFT

- Have I made my purpose clear to the readers? Why am I comparing two or more ideas or items? Where have I located the thesis statement?
- Have I alternated between the items of comparison, giving each equal space and attention?
- Have I marked the movements between different ideas or times by appropriate signposts or transitional words?
- Have I changed the verb tense when moving from "then" to "now"?
- Have I developed my paragraphs so that the readers are not left with unanswered questions about the topic?
- Have I clearly connected one paragraph to another?

RAFAEL'S FINAL DRAFT **85**

- Have I checked for paragraphs that can be combined or that should be separated based on their content?
- Have I checked for grammar and usage to make sure the sentences clearly express my thoughts?

TRIAL RUN

Look over the revision checklist above while composing your first draft and again after you complete the first draft. Keep in mind that the method of comparison that you choose should suit your purposes best. You may decide against dividing the essay into two halves devoted to each topic of comparison. Ask yourself why you are comparing and contrasting A, B, or C. What do you wish to accomplish?

PRESENTING RAFAEL'S FINAL DRAFT

My School Days: Then and Now

Rafael Matos

1

Rafael's new introduction is less reflective than in the first draft. He provides more descriptive details and action.

I held my mother's hand tightly as I arrived at my new school. Around me were children like myself, clinging to their anxious parents. The nuns, in their black and white outfits that covered them from head to foot and with their brightly scrubbed faces, looked like penguins. They gave the nervous children a reassuring smile and a comforting pat. When one of them came towards me, I tightened my grip on my mother's hand. A smiling face bent close to me and said, "Would you like to come with me and meet your friends?" I looked skeptically at my mother who whispered, "See how friendly your teachers are? You've nothing to be frightened of." I slowly let go of mother and followed the nun to my classroom. She seemed friendly enough, I thought. The tales of dungeons that I had heard from my friends about Catholic schools were perhaps creations of their imaginations.

2

Rafael adds a new paragraph to contrast expectation and reality.

But the bliss was shortlived. I soon realized the tales I had heard were not all myths. During my eight years at St. Peter and Paul Catholic School, one of the most difficult tasks was to follow strict orders while maintaining my cool because I learned quickly the price for disobedience.

3

It was a long walk to school, but I couldn't be a minute late. So I trudged along each morning, wearing the same old drab uniform. The Pledge of Allegiance and the Hail Mary which we had to recite every morning pretty much set the tone of the day. The English class comes to mind as a typical class. I enjoyed writing, so I would in a way look forward to the class. But the writing assignments with their rigid instructions would stifle my desire to write. "Don't use any slang," the teacher would admonish us. But everything I wrote seemed to be "slang" in her opinion. My classmates, too, added to the tension. When I looked around, I saw many of them chewing on their fingernails, and staring at blank pages. And in front of the class, like a specter, stood the sister, rigid and unbending. We had a name for these classes; we called them a clash of religion and communism.

4   The same tyranny followed us into the lunch room and the playground. We had to eat all the food on the plate. (We were reminded about all the hungry children around the world as though if we cleaned our plates, somehow they wouldn't go hungry any more!) We had to leave the lunch room as soon as we finished our meals. I often got into trouble because I wanted to wait for my friend who was a slow eater. Throughout these eight years, I felt a clash of will between me and the nuns who were my teachers: their need to control my life and my refusal to be controlled.

5   The practice that I resented most and that stands out in my

Rafael creates a new paragraph to include more details.

mind was when we were asked, all of a sudden, to freeze in the playground. At the sound of a shrill whistle, we would have to stop everything and stand still in our position. If we so much as turned our heads to see who was blowing the whistle, we would be punished by being detained after school. I also had to go to church every week. Not that I didn't have faith in God, but I questioned some of the things I heard at church. But I kept them inside me in silence. Even at that young age I questioned the dictatorial system. So when it came time for me to go to high school, I naturally chose a public school.

6   What a relief it was to be in an atmosphere that allowed me to be myself. My first act was to discard the drab uniform and grow my hair. In my light blue jeans and T-shirt, I felt I was walking on air. Gone were the days when I had to obey orders in the classroom and not speak out of turn. Everyone around me was talking so loudly in groups and to each other that the teacher's voice was drowned out by the noise. In fact the students did more talking than the teacher, and they did not hesitate to talk back at the teacher. What a privilege, I thought! How much freedom I missed during those dull rigid years in the Catholic school! I looked forward to my writing class to express my feelings in my own language, without someone labeling it as slang. Though the atmosphere in the

public school seemed somewhat chaotic, I attributed it to my own inadequacies. Having come from a parochial school, I didn't know what a real classroom was meant to be. I was going to settle in comfortably in this place where liberty reigned.

7   But I soon learned that independence came with a price. Many students didn't go to class, didn't do their assignments, and the teachers didn't seem to care. Weeks went by when I wasn't required to do any writing. Students had better attendance in the lunchroom than in the classroom. Lunch time was very different from the Catholic school. Students went in and didn't come out. Many of my classmates stayed there all day. I soon realized if I didn't watch out for myself, I would never graduate. It was this fear that drove me back to the classroom and to the books.

He adds more information and new descriptive details.

8   Looking back, I realize that it was my parochial school background and the discipline I acquired there that gave me the strength to survive in the jungle of the public school. Now I acknowledge that the clash of communism and religion, as we called our Catholic school, contributed to building my character and helped me to get an education in the chaos that was my high school.

Rafael replaces paragraph 6 of first draft with new paragraph more focused on benefits of parochial school.

9   Yet I feel both institutions are responsible for the person I am today. If the parochial school taught me discipline, the public school gave me my first taste of independence and the responsibility that came with it. Without the nuns to watch over me, I learned to watch over myself. This experience has certainly helped me in my college work. Many students tend to misuse the freedom they get in college, where the professors give them help and guidance but expect them to be responsible for their work. They can sit in the cafeteria all day without anyone forcing them to attend classes. The discipline I acquired in my parochial school taught me not abuse the freedom during my high school years. I hope both the schools have given me values that will see me through college.

Rafael adds reflections to make personal experience more general.

Commentary on Rafael's Final Draft

In the personal narratives in Chapters 1 and 2, Mel captures the drama and the trauma of the event that transforms his life, and Nikki makes an inward journey into her past to rediscover the girl that she was. Rafael's narrative, on the other hand, turns more outward. He does not risk as much personal disclosure as the earlier narrators but instead centers his writing on the two institutions that left their imprint on his life.

The purpose of Rafael's essay is to look back at the two institutions to see how they contributed to making him the person he is now. There are several levels in this narrative structure. On one level, Rafael looks back at his life and compares it to his life now as a college student. On another level, he looks for similarities and differences between the two institutions that he attended as a young person. A third level is the comparison between the two schools and the college Rafael is attending now. Finally, there is a contrast between expectation and reality, between what school is supposed to be and what it turns out to be. To present these different levels, Rafael uses a strategy of comparison and contrast. Paragraphs 2 through 5 focus on the Catholic school, while paragraphs 6 and 7 delineate Rafael's life as a student in a public high school. This block method of comparison considers the details of one of the subjects of comparison before moving on to the details of the other (parochial school first, followed by high school). When the details are not too many, as in Rafael's essay, this form of arrangement is often convenient. However, writers with a large number of details, where one large cluster of details followed by another might confuse the reader, often choose the point-by-point method of comparison over the block method.

While commenting on Mel's story in Chapter 1, we noted how a writer can quicken or reduce the narrative pace to tighten or slacken the tension. Rafael's story about his school days follows an even pace because it does not have the dramatic intensity of Mel's narrative. Even so, if you compare Rafael's first draft with his final draft, you will notice that the earlier version began with more reflection than action. In rewriting, Rafael decided to go directly to the action and leave the reflection for the concluding paragraph. This tightened the narrative and made it more interesting for the reader.

Writers often use humor as a weapon because they can say something important without sounding too serious. But you don't have to search hard for the outrageous to be funny; something commonplace can be humorous if you see it with conviction in a new light. Rafael's description of his parochial school as a combination of communism and religion is amusing because of the unusual coupling of the two systems generally considered antagonistic to each other. His aside on the fate of the hungry children while he is force-fed by his teachers is humor that has its source in irony. Irony can be an amusing way of making a serious point by showing a discrepancy between the ideal and the real.

Rafael's conclusion, reflecting on the influence of the parochial and public school in shaping his life, is perhaps the weakest segment of his story. The generalizations about the two school systems seem oversimplified and somewhat preachy in tone. His conclusion loses effectiveness because he attempts to tie everything into a neat package. You are not expected to have answers to all questions. If situations or events are unresolved in your own mind, it is better to be honest with the reader, who will sympathize more readily with your uncertainty than with your pretending to have all the right answers.

Questions for Further Thought

1. A common purpose of comparison/contrast is evaluative judgment. What's to prevent such a comparison from becoming a fixed fight, one that's loaded in favor of one or the other items being compared?

2. Representations of past experiences have to rely on selected details. How can you be sure, either as author or reader, that the details are fairly selected and representative?

3. Rafael's conclusion has been identified as the essay's weak point. How might you conclude an essay like Rafael's without seeming platitudinous or preachy? How would you avoid wrapping things up too neatly?

4. How can you gauge a reader's ability to agree and identify with what you write? How much should differences among individual readers be taken into account?

PROFESSIONAL ESSAYS

Winston Churchill
SCHOOL DAYS

"Where my reason, imagination or interest were not engaged, I would not or I could not learn."

SIR WINSTON LEONARD SPENCER CHURCHILL was born in 1874, eldest son of Lord Randolph Churchill. He spent much of his youth away from home at boarding schools. He lost his father when he was a student at the Sandhurst military school, entered the army in 1895 and served in Cuba, India, Egypt, and the Sudan. He was elected twice as the prime minister of England, serving from 1940 to 1945 and from 1951 to 1955.

Most of Churchill's ancestors had been involved with politics, so history to him was of absorbing interest if only because it was the story of his own family. Even though he had written five books before his twenty-sixth birthday, Churchill's first full-scale historical book was the life of his father. What many consider to be his best book, Life and Times of Marlborough, *was also a tribute to an ancestor. The others of his historical books—*The River War, The World Crisis, The Second World War*—centered on his own personal experiences. For this body of extraordinary writings, he was awarded the Nobel Prize for Literature in 1953, indeed an unusual honor for a man who spent most of his life as a soldier and politician.*

Because of his love for toy soldiers and war stories in his youth, his parents chose a military education for him. Later in his life he expressed regret that he had not attended college. It is said that he seriously considered going to college after he left the army but the idea of memorizing Latin prose again made him change his mind. Winston Churchill was too individualistic and obstinate to accept the form of education that was provided for him, as you will note in this short excerpt from his book A Roving Commission: My Early Life, *published in 1930.*

Like Rafael, who looks back at his life at the parochial and public schools, Churchill in "School Days" describes the two private schools he attended and expresses his preference for the second, Brighton. It was the first school, St. James's, that Churchill was forced to leave, much to his relief, because of ill health. As a fiercely independent individual, he found the "hateful servitude" at St. James's, which he exemplifies through the Latin lesson, quite intolerable. His intelligent and curious question, "But why O table?" is stifled by the teacher, who labels his young ward "impertinent." Looking back at his school days Churchill concludes that he rebelled in the first school because it oppressed him. The environment in the second school, however, was quite different. "Not being resisted or ill-treated, I yielded myself complacently, to a broad-minded tolerance and orthodoxy." As he describes his life in the two schools, Churchill shows the difference between expectation and reality and between appearance and reality. We sympathize with him because we may feel the same way when we look back at our life. We also derive pleasure out of reading "School Days," which is alive with rich details, lively dialogue, and a touch of humor.

ON THE WAY INTO THE READING

1. Churchill attended a "public" school in England. What is meant by public school in the United States? How does it differ from the British "public" school? How would you describe the school you attended?

2. A classroom that does not acknowledge students as individuals and ignores their imagination and interests can destroy all incentives for learning, as in Churchill's situation. Were you, as a student, able to bring your own imagination and interests into the classroom? In this regard, do you find college to be similar to or different from high school?

3. Despite his courage in challenging some of the tyrannical ways of his school, Churchill must have been aware that he might run into trouble with the authorities. Would the situation be much different today? Do today's students have more freedom than students in Churchill's time? To what effect?

1 The school my parents had selected for my education was one of the most fashionable and expensive in the country. It modelled itself upon

Eton and aimed at being preparatory for that Public School above all others. It was supposed to be the very last thing in schools. Only ten boys in a class; electric light (then a wonder); a swimming pond; spacious football and cricket grounds; two or three school treats, or "expeditions" as they were called, every term; the masters all M.A.'s in gowns and mortarboards; a chapel of its own; no hampers allowed; everything provided by the authorities. It was a dark November afternoon when we arrived at this establishment. We had tea with the Headmaster, with whom my mother conversed in the most easy manner. I was preoccupied with the fear of spilling my cup and so making "a bad start." I was also miserable at the idea of being left alone among all these strangers in this great, fierce, formidable place. After all I was only seven, and I had been so happy in my nursery with all my toys. I had such wonderful toys: a real steam engine, a magic lantern, and a collection of soldiers already nearly a thousand strong. Now it was to be all lessons. Seven or eight hours of lessons every day except half-holidays, and football or cricket in addition.

2   When the last sound of my mother's departing wheels had died away, the Headmaster invited me to hand over any money I had in my possession. I produced my three half-crowns which were dully entered in a book, and I was told that from time to time there would be a "shop" at the school with all sorts of things which one would like to have, and that I could choose what I liked up to the limit of the seven and sixpence. Then we quitted the Headmaster's parlour and the comfortable private side of the house, and entered the more bleak apartments reserved for the instruction and accommodation of the pupils. I was taken into a Form Room and told to sit at a desk. All the other boys were out of doors, and I was alone with the Form Master. He produced a thin greeny-brown-covered book filled with words in different types of print.

3   "You have never done any Latin before, have you?" he said.

4   "No, sir."

5   "This is a Latin grammar." He opened it at a well-thumbed page. "You must learn this," he said, pointing to a number of words in a frame of lines. "I will come back in half an hour and see what you know."

6   Behold me then on a gloomy evening, with an aching heart, seated in front of the First Declension.

Mensa	a table
Mensa	O table
Mensam	a table
Mensae	of a table
Mensae	to or for a table
Mensa	by, with or from a table

7   What on earth did it mean? Where was the sense of it? It seemed absolute rigmarole to me. However, there was one thing I could always do: I

could learn by heart. And I thereupon proceeded, as far as my private sorrows would allow, to memorise the acrostic-looking task which had been set me.

8   In due course the Master returned.

9   "Have you learnt it?" he asked.

10   "I think I can *say* it, sir," I replied; and I gabbled it off.

11   He seemed so satisfied with this that I was emboldened to ask a question.

12   "What does it mean, sir?"

13   "It means what it says. Mensa, a table. Mensa is a noun of the First Declension. There are five declensions. You have learnt the singular of the First Declension."

14   "But," I repeated, "what does it mean?"

15   "Mensa means a table," he answered.

16   "Then why does mensa also mean O table," I enquired, "and what does O table mean?"

17   "Mensa, O table, is the vocative case," he replied.

18   "But why O table?" I persisted in genuine curiosity.

19   "O table,—you would use that in addressing a table, in invoking a table." And then seeing he was not carrying me with him, "You would use it in speaking to a table."

20   "But I never do," I blurted out in honest amazement.

21   "If you are impertinent, you will be punished, and punished, let me tell you, very severely," was his conclusive rejoinder.

22   Such was my first introduction to the classics from which, I have been told, many of our cleverest men have derived so much solace and profit.

23   The Form Master's observations about punishment were by no means without their warrant at St. James's School. Flogging with the birch in accordance with the Eton fashion was a great feature in its curriculum. But I am sure no Eton boy, and certainly no Harrow boy of my day ever received such a cruel flogging as this Headmaster was accustomed to inflict upon the little boys who were in his care and power. They exceeded in severity anything that would be tolerated in any of the Reformatories under the Home Office. My reading in later life has supplied me with some possible explanations of his temperament. Two or three times a month the whole school was marshalled in the Library, and one or more delinquents were hauled off to an adjoining apartment by the two head boys, and there flogged until they bled freely, while the rest sat quaking, listening to their screams. This form of correction was strongly reinforced by frequent religious services of a somewhat High Church character in the chapel. Mrs. Everest was very much against the Pope. If the truth were known, she said, he was behind the Fenians. She was herself Low Church, and her dislike of ornaments and ritual, and generally her extremely unfavourable opinion of the Supreme Pontiff, had prejudiced me strongly against that personage and all religious practices supposed to be associated with him. I therefore did not derive much comfort from the spiritual side of my education at this

juncture. On the other hand, I experienced the fullest applications of the secular arm.

24   How I hated this school, and what a life of anxiety I lived there for more than two years. I made very little progress at my lessons, and none at all at games. I counted the days and the hours to the end of every term, when I should return home from this hateful servitude and range my soldiers in line of battle on the nursery floor. The greatest pleasure I had in those days was reading. When I was nine and a half my father gave me *Treasure Island,* and I remember the delight with which I devoured it. My teachers saw me at once backward and precocious, reading books beyond my years and yet at the bottom of the Form. They were offended. They had large resources of compulsion at their disposal, but I was stubborn. Where my reason, imagination or interest were not engaged, I would not or I could not learn. In all the twelve years I was at school no one ever succeeded in making me write a Latin verse or learn any Greek except the alphabet. I do not at all excuse myself for this foolish neglect of opportunities procured at so much expense by my parents and brought so forcibly to my attention by my Preceptors. Perhaps if I had been introduced to the ancients through their history and customs, instead of through their grammar and syntax, I might have had a better record.

25   I fell into a low state of health at St. James's School, and finally after a serious illness my parents took me away. Our family doctor, the celebrated Robson Roose, then practised at Brighton; and as I was now supposed to be very delicate, it was thought desirable that I should be under his constant care. I was accordingly, in 1883, transferred to a school at Brighton kept by two ladies. This was a smaller school than the one I had left. It was also cheaper and less pretentious. But there was an element of kindness and of sympathy which I had found conspicuously lacking in my first experiences. Here I remained for three years; and though I very nearly died from an attack of double pneumonia, I got gradually much stronger in that bracing air and gentle surroundings. At this school I was allowed to learn things which interested me: French, History, lots of Poetry by heart, and above all Riding and Swimming. The impression of those years makes a pleasant picture in my mind, in strong contrast to my earlier schoolday memories.

26   My partiality for Low Church principles which I had acquired from Mrs. Everest led me into one embarrassment. We often attended the service in the Chapel Royal at Brighton. Here the school was accommodated in pews which ran North and South. In consequence, when the Apostles' Creed was recited, everyone turned to the East. I was sure Mrs. Everest would have considered this practice Popish, and I conceived it my duty to testify against it. I therefore stood stolidly to my front. I was conscious of having created a "sensation." I prepared myself for martyrdom. However, when we got home no comment of any kind was made upon my behaviour. I was almost disappointed, and looked forward to the next occasion for a further demonstration of my faith. But when it came, the school was shown into

different pews in the Chapel Royal facing East, and no action was called for from any one of us when the Creed was said. I was puzzled to find my true course and duty. It seemed excessive to turn away from the East. Indeed I could not feel that such a step would be justified. I therefore became willy-nilly a passive conformist.

27   It was thoughtful and ingenious of these old ladies to have treated my scruples so tenderly. The results repaid their care. Never again have I caused or felt trouble on such a point. Not being resisted or ill-treated, I yielded myself complacently to a broad-minded tolerance and orthodoxy.

CRITICAL READING

1. Explain Churchill's statement, "It was supposed to be the very last thing in schools." Describe some of the characteristics of St. James's School. How similar or different is it from the school you attended?

2. What does the writer achieve by contrasting the "comfortable private side" of the school house and "the more bleak apartments reserved for instruction and accommodation of the pupils"?

3. Describe the Latin lesson. Was Churchill justified in being called impertinent by his teacher? How would you have acted under the circumstances?

4. Comment on the dialogue between Churchill and his Latin teacher. Is the account of the lesson enhanced by the dialogue? Explain how and why.

5. In two separate columns list the similarities and differences between the two schools Churchill attended. How does the list compare with Rafael's list? What method does Churchill use to organize his material?

6. Does Churchill reflect and evaluate as he recollects his impressions about the two schools? Point out the passages that you think show his opinion or judgment. How does his method of evaluation differ from Rafael's or Thurber's?

7. Why did Churchill accept authority more willingly at the second school?

James Thurber
UNIVERSITY DAYS

"Looking back on it now I can see that he meant me although he was looking at a fly, but I just stood there."

THE WRITINGS OF JAMES THURBER, ONE OF the best humorists of our time, are tempered by warmth, insight, and irony. Born in 1894 in Columbus, Ohio, Thurber started his career as a journalist. In 1927 he gave up his newspaper career to join the staff of the New Yorker magazine and remained there for thirty years. Among his many short stories, the best known is probably "The Secret Life of Walter Mitty," (1932) which describes the colorful escapist fantasies of a docile man.

Like "School Days," the focus of "University Days," from My Life and Hard Times *(1933), is the conflict and tension between youth and people in positions of authority. It is about miscommunication between students and teachers, army cadets and generals. By dividing the narrative between the classroom and the army training ground, Thurber may also be suggesting how the classroom is similar to the regimented routine of the army.*

The anecdotes, while funny, are critical comments on the education system at his university. The botany teacher demands that students not look for beauty in flowers. The economics teacher is not concerned by the football tackle's failure in his class as long as the boy helps his team to win the biggest game of the season. The army, too, did not prepare the young men for serious combat. With characteristic humor, Thurber comments, "It was good training for the kind of warfare that was waged in Shiloh but it had no connection with what was going on in Europe." Humor in this piece, as in Rafael's essay, acts as a foil for the harsh criticism of the academic system as good funny writing often hides a serious message.

Unlike Rafael and to some extent Churchill, Thurber does not analyze or comment directly on what is wrong with his university. He shows, through dramatized action, some of the blatant deficiencies in the system. You have to read carefully to see the significance of his story.

ON THE WAY INTO THE READING

1. Two years of military drill was compulsory at Thurber's school while a war was being fought in Europe. Do you support compulsory military or other compulsory training such as gymnastics in college? What are your reasons for supporting or not supporting such training?

2. Thurber refers to his school days as a period of decline in higher education in the Middle West. What is your impression of the state of higher education in your time? Do you find any parallels between your own time and that of Thurber?

3. As you read about the student who was on the football team, think about the preferential treatment of star athletes on some college campuses. How do you feel about such treatment for athletes even if they do not meet the academic requirements?

1   I passed all the other courses that I took at my University, but I could never pass botany. This was because all botany students had to spend

several hours a week in a laboratory looking through a microscope at plant cells, and I could never see through a microscope. I never once saw a cell through a microscope. This used to enrage my instructor. He would wander around the laboratory pleased with the progress all the students were making in drawing the involved and, so I am told, interesting structure of flower cells, until he came to me. I would just be standing there. "I can't see anything," I would say. He would begin patiently enough, explaining how anybody can see through a microscope, but he would always end up in a fury, claiming that I could *too* see through a microscope but just pretended that I couldn't. "It takes away from the beauty of flowers anyway," I used to tell him. "We are not concerned with beauty in this course," he would say. "We are concerned solely with what I may call the *mechanics* of flars." "Well," I'd say, "I can't see anything." "Try it just once again," he'd say, and I would put my eye to the microscope and see nothing at all, except now and again a nebulous milky substance—a phenomenon of maladjustment. You were supposed to see a vivid, restless clockwork of sharply defined plant cells. "I see what looks like a lot of milk," I would tell him. This, he claimed, was the result of my not having adjusted the microscope properly, so he would readjust it for me, or rather, for himself. And I would look again and see milk.

2   I finally took a deferred pass, as they called it, and waited a year and tried again. (You had to pass one of the biological sciences or you couldn't graduate.) The professor had come back from vacation brown as a berry, bright-eyed, and eager to explain cell-structure again to his classes. "Well," he said to me, cheerily, when we met in the first laboratory hour of the semester, "we're going to see cells this time, aren't we?" "Yes, sir," I said. Students to right of me and to left of me and in front of me were seeing cells; what's more, they were quietly drawing pictures of them in their notebooks. Of course, I didn't see anything.

3   "We'll try it," the professor said to me, grimly, "with every adjustment of the microscope known to man. As God is my witness, I'll arrange this glass so that you see cells through it or I'll give up teaching. In twenty-two years of botany, I—" He cut off abruptly for he was beginning to quiver all over, like Lionel Barrymore, and he genuinely wished to hold onto his temper; his scenes with me had taken a great deal out of him.

4   So we tried it with every adjustment of the microscope known to man. With only one of them did I see anything but blackness or the familiar lacteal opacity, and that time I saw, to my pleasure and amazement, a variegated constellation of flecks, specks, and dots. These I hastily drew. The instructor, noting my activity, came back from an adjoining desk, a smile on his lips and his eyebrows high in hope. He looked at my cell drawing. "What's that?" he demanded, with a hint of a squeal in his voice. "That's what I saw," I said. "You didn't, you didn't, you *did*n't" he screamed, losing control of his temper instantly, and he bent over and squinted into the microscope. His head snapped up. "That's your eye!" he shouted. "You've fixed the lens so that it reflects! You're drawn your eye!"

*He was beginning to quiver all over
like Lionel Barrymore.*

5   Another course that I didn't like, but somehow managed to pass, was economics. I went to that class straight from the botany class, which didn't help me any in understanding either subject. I used to get them mixed up. But not as mixed up as another student in my economics class who came there direct from a physics laboratory. He was a tackle on the football team, named Bolenciecwcz. At that time Ohio State University had one of the best football teams in the country, and Bolenciecwcz was one of its outstanding stars. In order to be eligible to play it was necessary for him to keep up in his studies, a very difficult matter, for while he was not dumber than an ox he was not any smarter. Most of his professors were lenient and helped him along. None gave him more hints, in answering questions, or asked him simpler ones than the economics professor, a thin, timid man named Bassum. One day when we were on the subject of transportation and distribution, it came Bolenciecwcz's turn to answer a question. "Name one means of transportation," the professor said to him. No light came into the big tackle's eyes. "Just any means of transportation," said the professor. Bolenciecwcz sat staring at him. "That is," pursued the professor, "any medium, agency, or method of going from one place to another."

Bolenciecwcz was trying to think.

Bolenciecwcz had the look of a man who is being led into a trap. "You may choose among steam, horse-drawn, or electrically propelled vehicles," said the instructor. "I might suggest the one which we commonly take in making long journeys across land." There was a profound silence in which everybody stirred uneasily, including Bolenciecwcz and Mr. Bassum. Mr. Bassum abruptly broke this silence in an amazing manner. "Choo-choo-choo," he said, in a low voice, and turned instantly scarlet. He glanced appealingly around the room. All of us, of course, shared Mr. Bassum's desire that Bolenciecwcz should stay abreast of the class in economics, for the Illinois game, one of the hardest and most important of the season, was only a week off. "Toot, toot, too-toooooooot!" some student with a deep voice moaned, and we all looked encouragingly at Bolenciecwcz. Somebody else gave a fine imitation of a locomotive letting off steam. Mr. Bassum himself rounded off the little show. "Ding, dong, ding, dong," he said, hopefully. Bolenciecwcz was staring at the floor now, trying to think, his great brow furrowed, his huge hands rubbing together, his face red.

6   "How did you come to college this year, Mr. Bolenciecwcz?" asked the professor. "*Chuffa* chuffa, *chuffa* chuffa."

7   "M'father sent me," said the football player.

8   "What on?" asked Bassum.

9   "I git an 'lowance," said the tackle, in a low, husky voice, obviously embarrassed.

10   "No, no," said Bassum. "Name a means of transportation. What did you *ride* here on?"

11   "Train," said Bolenciecwcz.

12   "Quite right," said the professor. "Now, Mr. Nugent, will you tell us——"

13   If I went through anguish in botany and economics—for different reasons—gymnasium work was even worse. I don't even like to think about it. They wouldn't let you play games or join in the exercises with your glasses on and I couldn't see with mine off. I bumped into professors, horizontal bars, agricultural students, and swinging iron rings. Not being able to see, I could take it but I couldn't dish it out. Also, in order to pass gymnasium (and you had to pass it to graduate) you had to learn to swim if you didn't know how. I didn't like the swimming pool, I didn't like swimming, and I didn't like the swimming instructor, and after all these years I still don't. I never swam but I passed my gym work anyway, by having another student give my gymnasium number (978) and swim across the pool in my place. He was a quiet, amiable blond youth, number 473, and he would have seen through a microscope for me if we could have got away with it, but we couldn't get away with it. Another thing I didn't like about gymnasium work was that they made you strip the day you registered. It is impossible for me to be happy when I am stripped and being asked a lot of questions. Still, I did better than a lanky agricultural student who was cross-examined just before I was. They asked each student what college he was in—that is, whether Arts, Engineering, Commerce, or Agriculture. "What college are you in?" the instructor snapped at the youth in front of me. "Ohio State University," he said promptly.

14   It wasn't that agricultural student but it was another a whole lot like him who decided to take up journalism, possibly on the ground that when farming went to hell he could fall back on newspaper work. He didn't realize, of course, that that would be very much like falling back full-length on a kit of carpenter's tools. Haskins didn't seem cut out for journalism, being too embarrassed to talk to anybody and unable to use a typewriter, but the editor of the college paper assigned him to the cow barns, the sheep house, the horse pavilion, and the animal husbandry department generally. This was a genuinely big "beat," for it took up five times as much ground and got ten times as great a legislative appropriation as the College of Liberal Arts. The agricultural student knew animals, but nevertheless his stories were dull and colorlessly written. He took all afternoon on each of them, on account of having to hunt for each letter on the typewriter. Once in a while he had to ask somebody to help him hunt. "C" and "L," in particular, were hard letters for him to find. His editor finally got pretty much annoyed at the farmer-journalist because his pieces were so uninteresting. "See here, Haskins," he snapped at him one day, "Why is it we never have anything hot from you on the horse pavilion? Here we have two hundred head of horses on this campus—more than any other university in the Western Conference except Purdue—and yet you never get any real low down on them. Now shoot over to the horse barns and dig up something lively." Haskins shambled out and came back in about an hour; he said he had something. "Well, start it off snappily," said the editor. "Something

people will read." Haskins set to work and in a couple of hours brought a sheet of typewritten paper to the desk; it was a two-hundred word story about some disease that had broken out among the horses. Its opening sentence was simple but arresting. It read: "Who has noticed the sores on the tops of the horses in the animal husbandry building?"

15   Ohio State was a land grant university and therefore two years of military drill was compulsory. We drilled with old Springfield rifles and studied the tactics of the Civil War even though the World War as going on at the time. At 11 o'clock each morning thousands of freshmen and sophomores used to deploy over the campus, moodily creeping up on the old chemistry building. It was good training for the kind of warfare that was waged at Shiloh but it had no connection with what was going on in Europe. Some people used to think there was German money behind it, but they didn't dare say so or they would have been thrown in jail as German spies. It was a period of muddy thought and marked, I believe, the decline of higher education in the Middle West.

16   As a soldier I was never any good at all. Most of the cadets were glumly indifferent soldiers, but I was no good at all. Once General Littlefield, who was commandant of the cadet corps, popped up in front of me during regimental drill and snapped, "You are the main trouble with this university!" I think he meant that my type was the main trouble with the university but he may have meant me individually. I was mediocre at drill, certainly—that is, until my senior year. By that time I had drilled longer than anybody else in the Western Conference, having failed at military at the end of each preceding year so that I had to do it all over again. I was the only senior still in uniform. The uniform which, when new, had made me look like an interurban railway conductor, now that it had become faded and too tight made me look like Bert Williams in his bellboy act. This had a definitely bad effect on my morale. Even so, I had become by sheer practise little short of wonderful at squad maneuvers.

17   One day General Littlefield picked our company out of the whole regiment and tried to get it mixed up by putting it through one movement after another as fast as we could execute them: squads right, squads left, squads on right into line, squads right about, squads left front into line, etc. In about three minutes one hundred and nine men were marching in one direction and I was marching away from them at an angle of forty degrees, all alone. "Company, halt!" shouted General Littlefield, "That man is the only man who has it right!" I was made a corporal for my achievement.

18   The next day General Littlefield summoned me to his office. He was swatting flies when I went in. I was silent and he was silent too, for a long time. I don't think he remembered me or why he had sent for me, but he didn't want to admit it. He swatted some more flies, keeping his eyes on them narrowly before he let go with the swatter. "Button up your coat!" he snapped. Looking back on it now I can see that he meant me although he was looking at a fly, but I just stood there. Another fly came to rest on a paper in front of the general and began rubbing its hind legs together. The

general lifted the swatter cautiously. I moved restlessly and the fly flew away. "You startled him!" barked General Littlefield, looking at me severely. I said I was sorry. "That won't help the situation!" snapped the General, with cold military logic. I didn't see what I could do except offer to chase some more flies toward his desk, but I didn't say anything. He stared out the window at the faraway figures of co-eds crossing the campus toward the library. Finally, he told me I could go. So I went. He either didn't know which cadet I was or else he forgot what he wanted to see me about. It may have been that he wished to apologize for having called me the main trouble with the university; or maybe he had decided to compliment me on my brilliant drilling of the day before and then at the last minute decided not to. I don't know. I don't think about it much any more.

CRITICAL READING

1. Thurber begins his story in the college classroom and ends in the general's office. What do you think is the purpose of this arrangement?
2. What is the effect of Thurber being a character in the story? What would it have been like if he were only an observer instead of an observer who also participated? Would the story have been more or less credible?
3. What is the central conflict in the narrative? What are the opposing forces?
4. Make a list of the events that stand out in the writer's mind both as a student and a soldier. Do you notice similarities and differences between them?
5. Comment on Thurber's description of the economics and journalism students. What purpose does it serve in the essay?
6. Why does the fly feature so prominently in the last paragraph? In what way does it help Thurber figure out the reason for his presence in the general's office?

SECTION TWO

WRITING ABOUT WHAT'S GOING ON AROUND YOU

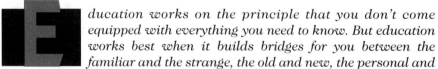

ducation works on the principle that you don't come equipped with everything you need to know. But education works best when it builds bridges for you between the familiar and the strange, the old and new, the personal and the general. This section is about conducting a self-education along those lines. You begin with you—your sense of self, your goals and interests and values—and turn that loose on your immediate circumstances. How, for example, do your goals and interests and values mesh with those of others? What do other people think about things of real interest to you? How well served are you by the context in which you currently learn and live?

In addressing such questions, you'll find that your own personal authority is still a crucial resource, as it was throughout Section 1, but now you are asked to earn (and not just tap) your authority by doing a little fact gathering (by way of observing and surveying and informal research).

This section's first chapter, Chapter 4, asks you to define a type of person, preferably the type of person you yourself are. But this is an exercise in social (not just self) definition. Can you account for differences as well as similarities within the group you are defining? On what evidence do you base your statements? How much can you speak for others? How well can you bridge the gap between personal and general or genuinely social characterizations?

In Chapter 5 you need to worry less about speaking for others, more about getting others to speak to you. In collaboration with classmates or on your own, you are invited to define an area of inquiry or concern, then to get the opinions of others. The basic principles of induction and adequate sampling are not hard to grasp, but some questions you must answer for yourself, and the answers aren't easy. How do you frame questions so as to get people to say what you want to know? How much can you trust their answers? How much can you conclude and extrapolate from your results?

On the basis of investigations along lines laid down in Chapters 4 and 5—or in response to other research, your instructor's proddings, or your own interests and concerns—you reach a point where the time has come to argue, and that is what Chapter 6 is about. You know the status quo: do you want to defend it or change it? You have your knowledge and your beliefs: on that basis what claim would you like to make? Once you answer such questions, others arise: what is the relation between opinion and evidence, between the writer of an argument and its reader?

The questions addressed in each of the chapters are so important, not least of all to so-called real-world writing as well as academic writing, that our examples in each chapter include full accounts of the process, from first thoughts to final touches.

CHAPTER FOUR

DEFINING YOUR IMMEDIATE CIRCUMSTANCES

Reflections on past experiences tell your reader more than who you were; a look back also says much about who you are. But now we turn to what may be the most interesting question: who are you becoming? That question tends to be tied up with another: what sort of circumstances do you find yourself in now? We are all shaped by circumstances, but we also have the capacity to adjust ourselves and our situations to our advantage. Understanding our real and potential relation to our surroundings requires getting beyond the purely personal perspective. It means seeing that there are other participants in the process, other members of the community, other actors in the play. Where do we fit in? How do we fit in? These are questions we will be asking ourselves all our lives. Asking them now, in writing, may make us conscious of things we had not considered and heighten our awareness of what needs to be done. Attempts to answer them can also fascinate our readers because, for all our circumstantial differences, we undeniably have so many of these questions—and answers—in common.

If the subject is "fitting in," students are likely to be even more knowledgeable about it than the instructor. This chapter taps that knowledge by highlighting journal keeping and peer work during both the invention and revision stages. The means of going beyond a strictly personal perspective include, in addition to observation and peer review, the informal survey (surveying as a research technique is treated more extensively in the chapter immediately following this one).

The professional pieces in this chapter are Paula Gunn Allen's "Where I Come From Is Like This" and Richard Rodriguez's "Mr. Secrets." The featured piece of student writing, Guneet Kaur's "Being an Indian Student in an American College," is like them in reflecting on how cultural assimilation and institutionalized education can threaten one's cultural heritage. But it does so more tentatively, from the perspective of a student whose formal education is still very much in process.

The process of writing that paper was itself a history of adjustments and accommodations. The temptation in writing on a topic of this kind is to take the easy way out, resorting to labels and stereotypes. But Guneet resisted this temptation, realizing that so many of the things that define us, the affiliations and identifications, can pull us in contrary directions. Feeling such tensions herself, she was able to be honest and thoughtful about them, and thus to define a type of person in a way that can teach us about the ways such types are defined.

WRITING ASSIGNMENT

Write an essay in which you define a type of student—not just any type, but one with whom you identify because you share a common predicament, a common cause, a common set of concerns or attitudes. Keeping in mind your instructor as your primary audience, feel free to tap your own experience, but also make sure you go beyond it. As you work on this assignment, train your thoughts on these three general questions:

1. What gives you the authority to write on this type?
2. What makes this type distinctive?
3. What makes this type significant?

READING THE WRITING ASSIGNMENT

Realizing what the assignment asks for involves realizing what it does not ask for. You are being asked to engage in an exercise in definition, not in argument. Definition is a form of analytical writing, and analytical writing provides information or enhances understanding; argumentative writing, on the other hand, attempts to convince or persuade the reader. Too many college writers suppose their writing must always be argumentative, especially if it's to seem impressive and forceful. Actually, analytical writing more often has priority: a good argument always rests on analysis, for you must inform and explain before you can convince or persuade. You can certainly let analysis become a foundation for argument (as Guneet did in a follow-up paper). However, for the time being, define (so as to give grounds for forming an opinion) rather than argue (so as to sway opinion).

Your goal, then, is to be informative, interesting, and illuminating. The best way to do that is to keep your thoughts trained on the three questions in the writing assignment above. You should be able to write with authority because you're asked to define a type with whom you identify, but that authority will be damaged by a subjective, this-is-what-it's-like-to-be-me account. You need some objective distance. Balancing what it's like to be that type with how that type is perceived by others will also help in showing what makes the type distinctive. Remember that you're not writing about students generally but about a certain kind of student, a type you can delineate with distinctive examples and identifying characteristics. This is sometimes done in an attempt to entertain: the nerd or jock or social butterfly is defined in terms that are stereotypical; the result is crude rather than sophisticated, merely amusing rather than genuinely edifying, trivial rather than significant. The real test of significance is to justify your claim on your reader's attention. What makes your type significant is not really its innate social or psychological importance but the thoughtfulness you bring to your definition. With the instructor as your audience, think of this assignment as an invitation to teach the teacher, and you're likely to do just that.

DISCOVERING IDEAS

Find a Subject

Guneet Kaur knew right away what she would write about, at least in a general way. This was just her second year in the United States: she had come here from India just before her last year of high school. As she had discovered during certain early rites of college—freshman orientation, registration day, and the like—there were other Indian students on campus, though the ones she had met had been in this country longer than she had. She would define the Indian student as a student type.

Guneet found her subject almost instantly, then, and perhaps it seems the choice was made for her by her circumstances. But her friend and classmate Priya Jani, also Indian—and in the United States only a year more than Guneet—chose a different type: the working student. It isn't hard to see the lesson for her choice: assimilation wasn't the problematic issue for Priya that it was for Guneet, and Priya had just entered the world of work-for-pay. Priya had to juggle college coursework with the demands of her job, and she was interested in how similarly circumstanced students were handling such conflicts.

Both Priya and Guneet focused on central issues in their lives. They found labels for themselves—the Indian student, the working student—that gave them each a starting point for their writing assignments.

 **T**RIAL RUN

None of us can be adequately defined by a label, yet we are all labeled in countless ways by a society obsessed with categories and classifications. What are your labels? Are you defined, however inadequately, by your ethnic background or your economic circumstances, your academic specialization or your career goals, your sexual orientation or your physical type? Make a list of the labels applicable to you—not just labels you are proud of but also ones you resist.

CHECKLIST: PICKING A LABEL

- Of the labels you listed, does one seem central to your self-definition? (A label that goes right to the roots of your sense of self could allow you to write with real authority.)
- Does one of the labels raise issues that need to be tackled? (A focus that allows you to shed light not just on a type but on an important issue—much as Guneet's choice led her to a consideration of cultural assimilation—could do much to imbue your paper with significance.)
- Is one label shrouded in ignorance that your paper could dispel? (Remember that your primary audience is your instructor; then, consider how much the treatment of any one label could allow you to teach the teacher.)

Keep a Journal

Most of us have resolved, at one time or another, to keep a diary or journal of some kind—and most of us have given up after a few entries. Like other forms of writing, journal writing needs to be purposeful, to serve some useful function. To show you how useful a journal can be to a writer, let's return to Guneet.

Pleased that she decided on a subject so quickly, Guneet tried to imagine what her essay would be like. The extremely tentative outlines it assumed in her mind didn't amount to much more than a list of characteristics: hardworking, polite, shy—attributes she suspected would apply to other groups as well. Her instructor was fond of saying that any problem with writing a paper was really a problem with finding a reason for writing it—especially a reason beyond doing it just because it was assigned. Guneet had assumed her quick choice of a subject had given her a reason for writing; it had really only given her a subject.

To find a reason, she consulted the journal she had been keeping for class. (Since the first day, the students had been asked to write entries at least twice a week on their writing class in particular and student life in general.) Reading over the first entry, Guneet had a sense that if she hadn't yet found a reason, she had at least found a good source of material.

There were, in fact, a number of relevant entries. For instance, a class discussion on the way certain usages and styles were frowned upon in the academic context had prompted this reflection:

> English not being my mother tongue has sometimes erected barriers which I've tried to tear down. And even my kind of English can cause problems. I know I sometimes get into trouble with my writing because I tend to follow British patterns rather than American ones. There is not a tremendous difference between them, but some British expressions confuse Americans or offend them.

Such material would no doubt prove useful, but Guneet did not really have an organizing purpose until she came upon this, a journal entry giving her response to a reading for class:

> I am not sure I like the piece by Richard Rodriguez. I admire his writing skill, and he has a fine formal education. But he is isolated and lost about his cultural heritage. Reading about that made me nervous. I suppose I want to avoid the same fate.

What happened to Guneet's thinking about the impending assignment when she re-encountered that entry in her journal? As an answer, we have another journal entry:

> I just read what I said about Rodriguez. I had not thought about this before, but now I think my next paper and maybe my research paper will be about cultural assimilation. This is why I will write on Indians as a student type. Being a member of the category myself, I have some sense of the problems they have in adjusting to the American lifestyle, and I have some questions about how much they should adjust. Writing about this will be my main purpose. My secondary purpose is to help me get started on my research project.

Just looking at selected entries from Guneet's journal gives us an impressive sense of how much that journal allowed her to accomplish before she began writing—even before she decided on a subject. If you haven't been keeping a journal, you obviously won't have previous entries to look back over, but you may still find keeping a journal enormously useful. We invite you to try it.

We don't want to beset you with a lot of instructions for journal writing, but we do have a few pieces of advice. First, journal writing works best when it's focused and task-oriented. Guneet was asked to write, not about life in general, but about her experiences as a student. If you're just starting a journal, why not make your focus this assignment? Jot down ideas as they come to you, or record your observations of students who seem to fit the type you're defining.

The other thing that makes journal writing work is making a habit of it. Give yourself a schedule—say, ten minutes of writing every other day—and stick to it. When the time comes, write whether or not you feel like it. If your topic doesn't excite you, try to say why; if you're stuck, try to write your way out of the block.

TRIAL RUN

Select a likely candidate from your list of labels and write a journal entry on it—nothing formal, just ten minutes or so of thinking on paper. What motives would you have for writing about it? What motives would your instructor have for reading about it? All writing for readers is an appeal for understanding, but what kind of understanding would you be looking for—recognition, sympathy, admiration, grudging respect? What special demands would your subject place on you? Would it strain your knowledge, your honesty, your interest, your discretion?

Go Beyond the Personal

When Guneet announced her subject and purpose to her best friend, Priya Jani, Priya was approving but wary. "I hope you don't explain things just from your own point of view," she said. "You're very conservative, you know." Recording the remark in her journal, Guneet felt taken aback, but she also felt that Priya had a point. Priya wore makeup, had a stylish haircut, dated, knew all about popular music. Guneet, on the other hand, was a Sikh: bound by her people's traditions, she was not even supposed to cut her hair or to talk to members of the opposite sex. Even as a representative of a culturally distinct group, she was culturally distinct, maybe even unrepresentative.

Temporarily at a loss, Guneet recollected hearing something in her writing class about the next assignment being a survey. That was it: she would interview other Indian students, get their opinions. She resolved to interview males as well as females—even if that meant bending the rules a bit.

Whether you follow Guneet's resolve to do interviews, you do need to follow her impulse to explore the subject in a way that gets beyond your own experience and opinions. This assignment is not an exercise in autobiography. You have to realize how important it is to bridge personal and general experience. You are locating yourself in a double sense: you are identifying yourself as a member of some distinctive group, and you are identifying yourself as a distinctive voice within that group, someone able to say something significant.

How do you go about expanding your limited store of knowledge? First, you could do as Guneet did: do an informal survey, realizing that the object is not to conduct a statistically valid survey but to say something that rings with authority and accuracy. You may also tap an authority who is not a member of the group, yet has wide acquaintance with such students—as a coach has with athletes, a placement officer has with job candidates, or a special-services counselor has with disabled students. Your school's office of admissions or student services may keep useful data on students. (Priya, focusing on the working student, used an existing survey of entering freshmen to determine how many had part-time or full-time jobs.) We could go on, but you get the idea: there are all sorts of sources of information besides those gathered in the library.

▉RIAL RUN

Make a list of places and people you could go to for information. (It may help to imagine yourself a reporter interested in doing an article on your type: you don't want library sources so much as a sense of current trends and impressions.) Establish priorities based on ease of access and the value of the information you could obtain. (Remember that you are interested not just in representatives of a certain type but also how that type is perceived.) Could you benefit from talking to students (or instructors) you have classes with? Could potentially rich sources be just a phone call or a visit away? If so, why not tap them now?

Get Feedback

One way of going beyond the personal is to expose your preliminary thoughts on your subject and purpose to someone else. In Guneet's case, students were asked to interview one another in class on their chosen topics. Guneet paired off with Priya because she regarded Priya's remark of the other day as a challenge she wanted to answer. Their interview sheet consisted of three questions:

1. What is the subject?
2. What is the purpose?
3. What needs more thought or attention?

Priya already knew the answer to the first question. When it came to the second question, Guneet emphasized that her primary purpose was to find out how *other* Indian students had coped with cultural change, and that she proposed to interview no less than ten students. Prompted by her journal entries, she also noted that she would be particularly interested in such problems as language barriers, differences in school systems, and difficulty establishing or maintaining relationships with family and friends. Finally she added that she expected this assignment to help her lay the groundwork for a later research paper, which would treat cultural assimilation. Priya was apparently impressed: the completed interview sheet seemed to have almost no empty space left on it—except after the third question, where Priya seemed to draw a blank.

All that took just twenty minutes. The next twenty minutes Guneet spent interviewing Priya on her topic. Then the instructor collected the interview sheets and read to the class from them, without giving names. The students commented on how focused each interview seemed—or on how far some of the projects had yet to go in defining a workable purpose. Guneet's plan, though, was singled out as especially well thought out and purposeful.

RIAL RUN

Try doing what Guneet and Priya did. Find a classmate who can probe your preliminary ideas. This needn't involve a formal interview sheet, but it should address several questions, such as the three that Guneet and Priya used (just above) or the three that you were asked to keep in mind when reading the writing assignment. You could ask such questions of yourself, of course—and you should—but another party will be able to see gaps in your thinking or points of interest you hadn't thought to pursue. If this other person shares your knowledge of the type you're defining, you stand the chance of adding to your expertise, and to do so when it's most likely to benefit you: before you begin writing.

COMPOSING THE FIRST DRAFT

Consider Definition as a Pattern

Sentence-length definitions tend to follow a pattern:

$$\text{thing to be defined} \quad = \quad \begin{array}{c} \text{general type to which it belongs} \\ + \\ \text{distinguishing characteristics} \end{array}$$

Thus, a hammer (thing to be defined) is a tool (general type) used for driving nails (distinguishing characteristic), just as economics (thing) is the science (type) treating the production, distribution, and consumption of goods and services (distinction), or just as oolong (thing) is a kind of tea (type) grown in China and partially fermented before being dried (distinction). Note that the general class or type to which the thing defined belongs must be known to the reader; these definitions would do no good to anyone who didn't know what a tool, a science, or a tea was.

   Good as that pattern for defining is, though, it won't organize an essay for you. In fact, organizationally, essay-length definitions may be anything-goes propositions. You can define by telling a story, giving examples, explaining a process, tracing causes to effects (or vice versa), dividing and classifying, comparing and contrasting—using just about every pattern of organization known to humankind.

Consider Definition as a Task

So let's return to your purpose and context. You're defining a type of student, and your audience is your instructor. It may be useful to refer to that standard pattern for sentence-length definitions here. Since the general type is *student* and since your reader obviously doesn't need to be filled in on what a student is, your chief task will be to elucidate distinguishing characteristics. Two important conclusions follow from this. First, information should be given on a need-to-know basis: your instructor will be more knowledgeable about some things (like what goes on in the classroom) than about others (like what goes on outside), and you should pitch your evidence accordingly. Second, giving distinguishing characteristics inevitably means that you will be doing some comparing and contrasting. In fact, given your assignment and your audience's general knowledge of students, your paper will probably be largely a comparison-contrast paper. Guneet, defining the Indian student in America, found her point of comparison in native-born students. Priya, defining the working student, compared that type with its logical foil: the type of student who didn't have to work.

TRIAL RUN

A good way to work out a tentative plan for your draft would be to list those features that distinguish your type of student. This won't necessarily be an outline—you may choose not to pursue certain of the subtopics—but it will be a beginning. When you have a list of, say, half a dozen characteristics, consider them in light of the following checklist.

CHECKLIST: EVALUATING SUBTOPICS

- Which characteristics promise to hold the most interest for your reader or to play best to your knowledge and experience?
- What are the best grounds for comparison—another distinctive type of student? Some assumed "average" student?
- What does your reader need to be told about the types you are comparing? (Consider, for instance, how little Guneet might need to tell her reader about native-born American students.)
- What would be the best way of ordering your type's distinguishing features in the draft?

Try Climactic Ordering

Very broadly, there are two kinds of organizational patterns: those that rely on chronology, and those that don't. Certain types of writing are essentially accounts of what unfolds in time: narrative, process explanation, causal analysis. For the others, you simply have your intentions, the requirements of your subject, and the needs of your reader to consider.

But writing, as it is read, also unfolds in time, and this gives us a clue to organizing writing that is not otherwise organized by time. Think of your paper as an experience your reader goes through. Ideally, reading point 1 of your paper should empower the reader to understand or appreciate points 2 or 3 as the reader could not if their order were changed. What's more, the encounter with point 3 is an encounter anticipated and worth waiting for if suspense is created at the outset, sustained throughout points 1 and 2, and satisfied by point 3 and the conclusion.

To build such a climactic progression of expanding knowledge and heightening interest requires that you think of the experience of reading the paper as a reader's adventure: you can't come up with a good plot without constantly considering your reader. That necessarily means experiencing your draft as a reader once you've written it, so we'll have occasion to return to considerations of building to a climax when we turn to revision.

PRESENTING GUNEET'S FIRST DRAFT

1   How would you define an Indian student that has come to the United States, to this college, for undergraduate study? Well, being a member of the above category, I think I could answer the question. But in order to do that I would need some feedback from other members so that I might gather support to corroborate my definition. The purpose behind doing this is for me to find out how well these students have adjusted to the American lifestyle. Secondly, it would help me in the research paper which too will be based on cultural assimilation. My feedback will come from ten Indian students.

2   I interviewed the students before and after class, mostly in the cafeteria. I made sure I interviewed them quickly since some of them felt their teacher would be in shock if they went to their next class only 4 and 3/4 minutes early instead of the usual 5 minutes.

3   The results were not surprising as the responses to some questions were all alike and quite consistent with what I had expected. All of them felt excluded and isolated from American society when they first came to the States. They found a major difference between the school systems, and they had no problem with grades. The American school system was found to be simpler, the teachers more concerned and eager to teach, and there was greater independence with few restrictions in forming a program. Only a fifth of the students found a language barrier since the rest of them came from Indian schools in which English was the medium in teaching. Half of them had difficulty in making friends as American students had a problem in understanding what they were saying. Thus, they had to adopt the American accent in order for them to feel part of society.

4   Surprisingly none of them found any incidence of discrimination. You can hardly pick up a newspaper and not find talk of discrimination which is repeatedly seen in big cities. I have

been subject to all sorts of discrimination because of the color of my skin, my ethnic and cultural background, and even my success in school.

5   After interviewing some members I can now give a better and well represented definition. From personal experience, when I think of an Indian student, I think of intelligence yet not confidence. I see a meek, kind and hardworking person, with a not-so-generous character, but with respect towards all. I found out that most Indian students did not have a problem assimilating with American society after a couple of months in the United States. But sadly from observation I see us students turning American and starting to forget our cultural heritage. To make sure that we are accepted into this society we are discarding our long-worshipped morals and traditions and are replacing them by sharply contradicting Western thoughts. It is not that we are deliberately trying to split our ties with these traditions but instead it is our insecurity which is a victim of these two very different cultures. We students are fairly insecure as we are not totally American or even totally Indian.

6   Life in America has not been easy but so far I have managed it and I don't know for how long. There is certainly more pressure and responsibility here than compared to India where I lived a fairly carefree life. The pressure surrounding me could at any moment encircle me and then I might lose all control. I can only ask for God's help to keep me from giving in to this pressure. Well, I can say I have assimilated into this society, but at what cost?

Thinking Critically about Guneet's First Draft

1. Considering climactic ordering, how well does Guneet's paper build? Do you see ways she might improve her organization?

2. Guneet's paper is essentially an exercise in definition, and, as we have seen, one means of defining something is by comparing and contrasting it with other things. What are Guneet's points of comparison? What effects are achieved by her comparisons? How clear are they to you?

3. One challenge in this assignment is to balance objective evidence with subjective experience. How successfully has Guneet done this? What adjustments do you think she might make?

4. Consider Guneet's final paragraph. How well integrated does it seem with what precedes it? Are there other effects to consider here besides overall coherence—like honesty or intensity? What might be done to make the conclusion more consistent with the rest of the paper (or the rest of the paper more consistent with the conclusion)?

RETHINKING AND REVISING

Get Feedback

When Guneet brought her draft in for peer review, she again paired off with Priya. Here are the questions each was asked to answer with respect to the other's draft:

1. Before you read the essay, give your initial reactions to the type being described. (Are you inclined to think the type is, say, insignificant or all too familiar?)

2. Once you've read the essay, does the type seem significant in a way you hadn't expected? What has the writer done to establish the significance of the type? What more can or should be done?

3. What has been done to establish the writer's authority to define the type? What more can or should be done?

4. What do you think about the use of examples and evidence? Do any details seem to you more or less extraneous? What would you like to know more about?

5. Is the conclusion truly earned—that is, does it follow from what preceded it?

Critical of Guneet's initial idea, Priya was no less critical of her draft in peer review. Though she found it "well-researched and interesting," she also said, in response to question 4 on her peer-review sheet,

> Use of evidence is good, but sometimes the evidence doesn't say what Guneet wants to say, and she says it anyway. The part on discrimination is not backed up. The other part I found a little disturbing is when she talks about giving up traditional morals in order to assimilate. This could be handled differently. It is unclear whether the students (besides Guneet) are really caught between cultures or really wanting to assimilate.

What's more, in response to question 5, "Is the conclusion truly *earned*— that is, does it follow from what preceded it?" Priya wrote:

> No. Not really. I'm not sure Guneet is talking about the Indian students she talked to. I think she is just talking about herself.

Usually, the only feedback on a draft was from a fellow classmate, but this draft also got the following comment from the instructor:

> This is purposeful, almost passionate (especially at the end), and I can say I found it genuinely enlightening. I think, though, that you don't do justice to what you have to say about what you discovered. After the paragraph that begins by saying there were no real surprises, you have a paragraph beginning with "Surprisingly...." After the paragraph reporting that "most Indian students did not have a problem assimilating" comes the

paragraph where the Indian student we're most concerned with wonders aloud if she can stand the pressure anymore, if she "might lose all control." These may be apparent rather than real contradictions, bits of evidence that good material has been insufficiently digested or organized. What you have to say remains compelling, but that is more in spite of than because of the way you present things.

Put yourself in Guneet's place for a moment, and it's not hard to see how comments like these might take the wind out of your sails. When someone says something's wrong with something you've done, you may feel, at first, as if they've said something is wrong with you. You just have to let that initial sting pass and then see what you want to do about the criticisms made. After all, the expectation is that you'll improve on the first draft; the whole point of criticisms is to show you where and how.

If you are lucky enough, as Guneet was, to have a peer reviewer who knows your student type as you do, peer review on this assignment is a chance for two experts to confer on the best way to brief the uninitiated. Such a peer reviewer can test the validity of your statements in a way your instructor cannot—just as Priya wondered if Guneet's casting of cultural assimilation as a problem was indeed the problem for other Indian students that it was for Guneet.

Even if you pair off with someone who doesn't know your student type as you do, your peer reviewer has another kind of expertise that may be indispensable to your success: you're both writers for the same audience. Even when you try to see your writing through the eyes of your reader, you may miss things your peer reviewer can catch. Priya was an Indian student challenging Guneet's conclusions about Indian students, but she did as anyone else in the class might have done: she pointed out that Guneet's conclusions did not seem supported by her evidence.

Either way, peer review can be useful to you. See if you can get written comments on your draft—written responses will allow for second looks (and second thoughts) after that first sting of criticism passes.

Do Self-Assessment

You don't have to wait for feedback from others to give you cues for revision: you can have second opinions of your own. Specifically, you may benefit from an easy exercise that her instructor's comment suggests would have been especially useful to Guneet: generate a version of your paper that eliminates everything but the first sentence of each paragraph. Had Guneet done this, she would have seen that her draft followed the paragraph beginning "The results are not surprising" with one beginning "Surprisingly." Coherence is more than a matter of first sentences and transitional words and phrases, but this stripped-down view should help you see how your organization stacks up—and whether your climactic ordering is really building to a climax.

Be Efficient—Work with What You Have

You begin revising the moment you begin writing. You consider, reconsider, and reject possible topics or approaches. You frame statements and then reframe them before they ever get on paper. You probably entertain three or four different ways of beginning before your draft is even begun. Realizing as much, you should also realize that revising your draft, crucial as it is, is but one part of an on-going process of thinking about how well you're meeting your goals and your reader's needs. And so it often involves less work than you might think. The success of Guneet's revision was in no small part due to her determination to keep work for herself at a minimum.

For example, Priya's comments seemed to suggest that there were problems with the evidence Guneet presented, or, more accurately, with the sense that Guneet is straying from the evidence—"the evidence doesn't say what Guneet wants to say, and she says it anyway." Like the instructor, Priya suggests not going back to the drawing board, but resolving apparent contradictions. Like so many first drafts, Guneet's could benefit from reorganization as well as rewording. That is precisely what she gave it— along with a little more material taken from her journal, the very thing that had helped her so much at the very beginning.

Like Guneet, you may find that a first draft—however flawed it seems to you, however many criticisms it's subjected to—can give you most of what you need for a fine final version. Don't run from the problems your draft poses; think them through.

CHECKLIST: REVISING YOUR DRAFT

- Have you adequately addressed the questions of authority, distinctiveness, and significance posed by the assignment?
- Have you kept in mind that you are being asked for analysis and not argument, that your overarching goal is to inform and explain, not to convince or persuade?
- Have you balanced your own experience and opinions with careful observation and samplings of the views of others?
- Have you drawn the distinguishing characteristics of your specific type with reference to a more general or familiar type?
- Have you provided information on a need-to-know basis, being careful to include what is genuinely interesting and informative, and being no less careful to exclude all that might be extraneous?
- Have you ordered the details of your presentation so that they build to climactic effect?

• Have you made sure that what you say in your conclusion is justified, that the claims or statements of the conclusion are supported by the evidence you've presented?

PRESENTING GUNEET'S FINAL DRAFT

Being an Indian Student in an American College

Guneet Kaur

In her first two paragraphs, Guneet introduces a question and her two means of answering it: she is going to draw on her own knowledge and experience and also on informal research.

1   How would you define an Indian student who has come to the United States for undergraduate study? As one such student, I could begin to answer that question. But in order to give a full answer I would need some feedback to corroborate my definition. I could thereby learn how well these students have adjusted to the American lifestyle. I could also see how well I have assimilated in comparison with other Indian students.

2   I interviewed ten Indian students before and after class, mostly in the overcrowded cafeteria. Most of them felt excited to know that someone was actually interested in knowing about them and readily agreed to be questioned.

Noting that her interviews held one surprise for her, she begins with what wasn't surprising: first a sense of exclusion and isolation. (Note here and in the next several paragraphs how Guneet interweaves her interviewee's observations with her own experience.)

3   The students' responses were quite consistent with what I had expected--except in one instance. I was not surprised to learn that all of them, like me, had felt excluded and isolated when they first came to the States. They found major differences between the school systems, but they had no problems with grades. American schools seemed easier for them; in fact, they did better here than in India. They observed that teachers here were more concerned and eager to teach and treated them as mature students, whereas in India the teachers had no time for them and treated them as mere adolescents. The teachers I knew in India each taught a minimum of five to six classes a day, each of which included a minimum of fifty students. Therefore it was extremely hard to establish a one-to-one relationship with a teacher.

4   The interviewees confirmed my own experience when they pointed out that they were given greater independence in forming a school program here in the United States; in India, most decisions were made for them. In fact, as one interviewee suggested, this difference between the two school systems is also a difference between the two societies. One feels less constrained by conventions in America.

She notes curricular differences, but not so great as to pose major problems of adjustment.

5   Only two of the ten students found the English language a barrier since the rest of them came from Indian schools where

Similarly, language differences are not seen as major impediments by most, though accommodations had to be made.   6

Guneet gets to the one surprise: no one claimed discrimination. Guneet notes how this conflicts with her own experience, though she understands her interviewees' responses.

7

What Guneet has learned and reported all seems to her to point to one thing: what's at issue is not the ability to assimilate, but the extent of assimilation.

8

Guneet does not resolve the issue, which she has shown to be a complex one. It is enough for her to present it.

the teaching was done in English. Still, several of these had difficulty making friends as American students seemed to have trouble understanding what they were saying. Thus, they had to adopt an American accent in order to feel part of American society. I myself consciously eliminated certain British expressions from my speech and writing since such expressions seem puzzling or affected to some Americans.

The one surprise for me was that none of the interviewees reported any incidence of discrimination. In my opinion, giving the question further thought would reveal that they all were subject to some type of discrimination, directly or indirectly. I know that I have felt ridiculed on those occasions when I wore my native dress to school here in the States. Also, I was not chosen to be on my high school's academic team even though I scored higher than anyone else on the general knowledge test; presumably, it was thought that I did not know enough about American culture. Still, I understand the interviewees' reticence on the subject of discrimination; sometimes it is hard to tell the difference between feeling different and being made to feel different.

Overall, I found that most Indian students do not have a problem assimilating with American society after a fairly short time in the United States. But, sadly, I see us Indian students turning American and starting to turn away from our cultural heritage. To make sure we are accepted into this society we are discarding venerated morals and traditions and replacing them with Western habits that do not jibe with these traditions. We are not deliberately trying to sever our ties with these traditions, but instead, because of our insecurity, we are torn between two very different cultures. We are only made that much more insecure because we are not totally American or even totally Indian anymore. This is the reason why there is such a sense of exclusion and a drive for assimilation even if language, school, and discrimination are not seen to be problems.

Integration into American society is not just physical but also emotional. I can say that I have assimilated physically, but mentally and emotionally I don't know how long it will take. My truly Indian parents want the assimilation process to go only so far, as further absorption into American society would lead me to forget my cultural heritage. Most Indian students who have come recently to the States have to make this choice: to what extent does one want to assimilate?

Commentary on Guneet's Final Draft

One way of getting at the difference between Guneet's draft and her final version is to consider the difference between two sentences found in those two versions. In paragraph 3 of the draft, we are told this of the Indian students Guneet interviewed:

> They found a major difference between the school sys-
> tems, and they had no problems with grades.

This is the sentence's counterpart in paragraph 3 of the final version:

> They found major differences between the school sys-
> tems, but they had no problem with grades.

Think for a moment of how the two small but significant changes—making *differences* plural, and using *but* in place of *and*—result in very different signals sent to the reader. In the draft, one "major difference" is mentioned but not identified. Actually, the reader expects there to be a number of differences between the school systems, so in her final version Guneet speaks of "major differences"—and goes on to enumerate them. The other little change also has the big effect of satisfying an expectation rather than thwarting it. Guneet saw that her emphasis on difference hardly implied "no problem with grades"—on the contrary—and so she acknowledged the sense of contradiction by using *but* rather than *and*.

These little changes are worth pausing over because the important thing is not the extent of the change, but the reason it's made. In this case, the draft's sentence raises questions it does not answer. The revised sentence anticipates the reader's questions and forecasts the author's answers. And that, essentially, is the difference between the original and final versions: consideration for the reader that is typically shown by those little changes that go a long way.

Guneet abandons the superfluous remarks in the opening paragraph of her draft about her plans for her research paper and the size of her sample. She also gives her revised opening paragraph a last sentence that promises to use Guneet herself as a touchstone and point of comparison. The draft had suggested that what Guneet thought would be checked against the ideas of other Indian students. The revision suggests that what they think, in turn, will be checked against Guneet. This will be crucial when we come to that part of the paper where, in draft form, Guneet had seemed to leave the evidence behind.

But before we get to that there's some more setting up to do. The short (transitional) second paragraph contains just two sentences in both versions, but here, too, we see consequential changes. Adding one word ("ten") to the first in the revision makes the whole last sentence in the draft's first paragraph unnecessary. The second sentence in both versions gives a casual introduction to these students, generalizing about them in an offhand way. But note how differently that's done. The draft's slightly amusing characterization of Indian students as hyperpunctual also implies that their answers to Guneet's questions may well have been hasty and undeveloped. Her final version characterizes them, instead, as being especially open—and a bit touched that someone's interested in what they have to say. The suggestion of an eagerness to please and a kind of loneliness sets up the drift of the whole paper.

The setting-up in the third paragraph is still more crucial. The final version of this paragraph opens by saying what the draft had failed to say—had even seemed to deny: that what Guneet got from her respondents was surprising in one respect. That said, the final version tells in three paragraphs (paragraph 3–5) what the draft had attempted to tell in one (paragraph 3): what was *not* surprising about the responses. These three paragraphs create a progression of information where the draft had simply had a lump of ideas. First, there are differences in school systems, then a difference in societies with respect to degrees of independence, and then differences in language. In each paragraph, Guneet inserts herself as someone who shares in the experiences and perceptions of her respondents: in paragraph 3, "I was not surprised to learn that all of them, like me,...."; in paragraph 4, "The interviewees confirmed my own experience when..."; in paragraph 5, "I myself...."

Then comes paragraph 6, which begins with "The one surprise for me...." In making her readers wait several paragraphs for it, Guneet has engaged in climactic ordering: she has suggested that she has an especially interesting point, and she has held her reader in suspense about it while she treated other points. Now, and only now, she delivers on her promise by unveiling her surprise. There are obvious advantages to this pattern of organization, but the possible perils are scarcely less obvious. The climax can turn out to be anticlimactic; the surprise can fall flat.

We don't think this happens to Guneet for reasons that may be instructive. First of all, unlike her draft, her final version has established how very much she is a member of the group she is defining, how much she identifies with what they have gone through. Now that we reach a point of divergence, the difference she represents is not a mere difference—as it was in the draft, where what she says amounts to something like, "They say they weren't discriminated against; I say I was." No, Guneet questions what her respondents have said so as to suggest that they, too, might have answered differently had they thought more deeply. And this time, she does not merely claim she has been discriminated against, she gives examples. These, in turn, also support her summary claim: "sometimes it is hard to tell the difference between feeling different and being made to feel different."

This is a fine stroke, a careful balancing of personal and more general experience, and Guneet has earned the right to begin to wrap up. Sparing her reader her draft's list of adjectives—"meek," "kind," "hardworking," and so on—she moves directly to the problem of assimilation, suggesting that the problem really isn't difficulty in assimilating so much as *ease* of assimilating—with the loss that may accompany that transformation. Such an implication, however, poses a problem for Guneet, for none of the people she interviewed complained about losing their cultural heritage.

She addresses the problem in her thoroughly rewritten concluding paragraph. Here the focus is on Guneet—but in ways that make her seem more representative than distinctive. She stresses that assimilation is not an event but a process, one that is on-going for her (and, presumably, for everyone she talked to). She notes a generation gap we can suppose many Indian students like her are experiencing. And she ends with a question that explicitly applies to others as well as herself, that poses assimilation as a choice—but, like so many choices in life, a choice accompanied by pressures to choose one way or the other. Once again, Guneet carefully negotiates a way, not of transcending the personal perspective, but of locating the perspective in a more general scheme, making it seem significant, representative, and generally edifying.

Questions for Further Thought

1. It is generally thought that labels are unfortunate; that they are simplifications that highlight our differences and obscure both what makes each of us unique and what makes all of us similar. Can an assignment like defining a student type avoid reducing its subjects to stereotypes? Is the examination of labels just a form of relabeling?

2. This chapter stresses the assignment's invitation to "teach the teacher" and the importance of providing information on a "need-to-know" basis. Unless one's a telepath, who's to say what the instructor wants or needs to know? If the answers to such questions are a matter of guesswork, what will make those guesses *educated* guesses?

3. This chapter also emphasizes the importance of both subjective authority and objective distance; the challenge is to balance objective evidence with subjective experience. But isn't what passes for objectivity just a consensus of subjective viewpoints? Asked "to bridge personal and general experience," how can you tell where one leaves off and the other begins? Do you actually need to be able to draw a line between one and the other?

PROFESSIONAL ESSAYS

Paula Gunn Allen

WHERE I COME FROM
IS LIKE THIS

"Most Indian women I know are in the same bicultural bind: we vacillate between being dependent and strong, self-reliant and powerless, strongly motivated and hopelessly insecure."

BORN IN 1939 IN CUBERO, NEW MEXICO, OF Laguna Pueblo-Sioux ancestry, Paula Gunn Allen is one of the foremost Native American scholars, poets, novelists, and literary critics. Gunn Allen, who holds a doctorate from the University of New Mexico, became increasingly aware in her academic career that writings by Native Americans, particularly women like her, had been excluded from the traditional literary canon. Her own life and writings have been devoted to remedying this situation. She is the author of Skins and Bones *and six other books of poetry, a novel titled* The Woman Who Owned the Shadows, *and an essay collection,* The Sacred Hoop: Recovering the Feminine in American Indian Traditions. *In "Where I Come From Is Like This," excerpted from* The Sacred Hoop, *Gunn Allen uses the vital storytelling tradition of the Native Americans as a backdrop to examine the link between ethnic identity and contemporary feminist ideology.*

In the introduction to The Sacred Hoop, *Paula Gunn Allen cautions her readers to be aware that Native American life does not function according to Western assumptions. Native American women have to be viewed in traditional as well as modern terms. Gunn Allen's East Indian counterpart, Guneet Kaur, in "Being an Indian Student in an American College" faces a similar situation in defining herself as an East Indian student in a large urban American college. Both Gunn Allen and Guneet Kaur have first to define themselves as culturally different before defining their places with respect to the dominant culture. And they remind us that the cultures they come from are as rich and complex as the cultures they at once move toward and resist.*

ON THE WAY INTO THE READING

1. Like Guneet, Gunn Allen is concerned about preserving her distinct cultural heritage. How do you feel about cultural difference? Does it enrich a society? Or does it exacerbate division and misunderstanding? What is it that makes one's cultural heritage worth preserving?

2. Cultures do not just define themselves. They are also defined by other cultures. Do you have roots in a culture that has been misrepresented or misunderstood, stereotyped or otherwise

continued

continued

diminished? Do you have hope for a greater understanding between cultures? Why or why not?

3. The roles we play are, to a considerable extent, culturally defined. Gunn Allen's special emphasis is on the roles of women in Native American and Anglo-European cultures. What would you want to change about the ways women's roles are defined by the dominant culture? What would you want to keep?

I

1   Modern American Indian women, like their non-Indian sisters, are deeply engaged in the struggle to redefine themselves. In their struggle they must reconcile traditional tribal definitions of women with industrial and postindustrial non-Indian definitions. Yet while these definitions seem to be more or less mutually exclusive, Indian women must somehow harmonize and integrate both in their own lives.

2   An American Indian woman is primarily defined by her tribal identity. In her eyes, her destiny is necessarily that of her people, and her sense of herself as a woman is first and foremost prescribed by her tribe. The definitions of woman's roles are as diverse as tribal cultures in Americas. In some she is devalued, in others she wields considerable power. In some she is a familial/clan adjunct, in some she is as close to autonomous as her economic circumstances and psychological traits permit. But in no tribal definition is she perceived in the same way as are women in western industrial and postindustrial cultures.

3   In the west, few images of women form part of the cultural mythos, and these are largely sexually charged. Among Christians, the madonna is the female prototype, and she is portrayed as essentially passive: her contribution is simply that of birthing. Little else is attributed to her and she certainly possesses few of the characteristics that are attributed to mythic figures among Indian tribes. This image is countered (rather than balanced) by the witch-goddess/whore characteristics designed to reinforce cultural beliefs about women, as well as western adversarial and dualistic perceptions of reality.

4   The tribes see women variously, but they do not question the power of femininity. Sometimes they see women as fearful, sometimes peaceful, sometimes omnipotent and omniscient, but they never portray women as mindless, helpless, simple, or oppressed. And while the women in a given tribe, clan, or band may be all these things, the individual woman is provided with a variety of images of women from the interconnected supernatural, natural, and social worlds she lives in.

5   As a half-breed American Indian woman, I cast about in my mind for negative images of Indian women, and I find none that are directed to

Indian women alone. The negative images I do have are of Indians in general and in fact are more often of males than of females. All these images come to me from non-Indian sources, and they are always balanced by a positive image. My ideas of womanhood, passed on largely by my mother and grandmothers, Laguna Pueblo women, are about practicality, strength, reasonableness, intelligence, wit, and competence. I also remember vividly the women who came to my father's store, the women who held me and sang to me, the women at Feast Day, at Grab Days, the women in the kitchen of my Cubero home, the women I grew up with; none of them appeared weak or helpless, none of them presented herself tentatively. I remember a certain reserve on those lovely brown faces; I remember the direct gaze of eyes framed by bright-colored shawls draped over their heads and cascading down their backs. I remember the clean cotton dresses and carefully pressed hand-embroidered aprons they always wore; I remember laughter and good food, especially the sweet bread and the oven bread they gave us. Nowhere in my mind is there a foolish woman, a dumb woman, a vain woman, or a plastic woman, though the Indian women I have known have shown a wide range of personal style and demeanor.

6   My memory includes the Navajo woman who was badly beaten by her Sioux husband; but I also remember that my grandmother abandoned her Sioux husband long ago. I recall the stories about the Laguna woman beaten regularly by her husband in the presence of her children so that the children would not believe in the strength and power of femininity. And I remember the women who drank, who got into fights with other women and with the men, and who often won those battles. I have memories of tired women, partying women, stubborn women, sullen women, amicable women, selfish women, shy women, and aggressive women. Most of all I remember the women who laugh and scold and sit uncomplaining in the long sun on feast days and who cook wonderful food on wood stoves, in beehive mud ovens, and over open fires outdoors.

7   Among the images of women that come to me from various tribes as well as my own are White Buffalo Woman, who came to the Lakota long ago and brought them the religion of the Sacred Pipe which they still practice; Tinotzin the goddess who came to Juan Diego to remind him that she still walked the hills of her people and sent him with her message, her demand and her proof to the Catholic bishop in the city nearby. And from Laguna I take the images of Yellow Woman, Coyote Woman, Grandmother Spider (Spider Old Woman), who brought the light, who gave us weaving and medicine, who gave us life. Among the Keres she is known as Thought Woman who created us all and who keeps us in creation even now. I remember Iyatiku, Earth Woman, Corn Woman, who guides and counsels the people to peace and who welcomes us home when we cast off this coil of flesh as huskers cast off the leaves that wrap the corn. I remember Iyatiku's sister, Sun Woman, who held metals and cattle, pigs and sheep, highways and engines and so many things in her bundle, who went away to the east saying that one day she would return.

II

8   Since the coming of the Anglo-Europeans beginning in the fifteenth century, the fragile web of identity that long held tribal people secure has gradually been weakened and torn. But the oral tradition has prevented the complete destruction of the web, the ultimate disruption of tribal ways. The oral tradition is vital; it heals itself and the tribal web by adapting to the flow of the present while never relinquishing its connection to the past. Its adaptability has always been required, as many generations have experienced. Certainly the modern American Indian woman bears slight resemblance to her forebears—at least on superficial examination—but she is still a tribal woman in her deepest being. Her tribal sense of relationship to all that is continues to flourish. And though she is at times beset by her knowledge of the enormous gap between the life she lives and the life she was raised to live, and while she adapts her mind and being to the circumstances of her present life, she does so in tribal ways, mending the tears in the web of being from which she takes her existence as she goes.

9   My mother told me stories all the time, though I often did not recognize them as that. My mother told me stories about cooking and childbearing; she told me stories about menstruation and pregnancy; she told me stories about gods and heroes, about fairies and elves, about goddesses and spirits; she told me stories about the land and the sky, about cats and dogs, about snakes and spiders; she told me stories about climbing trees and exploring the mesas; she told me stories about going to dances and getting married; she told me stories about dressing and undressing, about sleeping and waking; she told me stories about herself, about her mother, about her grandmother. She told me stories about grieving and laughing, about thinking and doing; she told me stories about school and about people; about darning and mending; she told me stories about turquoise and about gold; she told me European stories and Laguna stories; she told me Catholic stories and Presbyterian stories; she told me city stories and country stories; she told me political stories and religious stories. She told me stories about living and stories about dying. And in all of those stories she told me who I was, who I was supposed to be, whom I came from, and who would follow me. In this way she taught me the meaning of the words she said, that all life is a circle and everything has a place within it. That's what she said and what she showed me in the things she did and the way she lives.

10   Of course, through my formal, white, Christian education, I discovered that other people had stories of their own—about women, about Indians, about fact, about reality—and I was amazed by a number of startling suppositions that others made about tribal customs and beliefs. According to the un-Indian, non-Indian view, for instance, Indians barred menstruating women from ceremonies and indeed segregated them from the rest of the people, consigning them to some space specially designed for them. This showed that Indians considered menstruating women unclean and not fit to enjoy the company of decent (nonmenstruating) people, that is, men. I

was surprised and confused to hear this because my mother had taught me that white people had strange attitudes toward menstruation: they thought something was bad about it, that it meant you were sick, cursed, sinful, and weak and that you had to be very careful during that time. She taught me that menstruation was a normal occurrence, that I could go swimming or hiking or whatever else I wanted to do during my period. She actively scorned women who took to their beds, who were incapacitated by cramps, who "got the blues."

11   As I struggled to reconcile these very contradictory interpretations of American Indians' traditional beliefs concerning menstruation, I realized that the menstrual taboos were about power, not about sin or filth. My conclusion was later borne out by some tribes' own explanations, which, as you may well imagine, came as quite a relief to me.

12   The truth of the matter as many Indians see it is that women who are at the peak of their fecundity are believed to possess power that throws male power totally out of kilter. They emit such force that, in their presence, any male-owned or -dominated ritual or sacred object cannot do its usual task. For instance, the Lakota say that a menstruating woman anywhere near a yuwipi man, who is a special sort of psychic, spirit-empowered healer, for a day or so before he is to do his ceremony will effectively disempower him. Conversely, among many if not most tribes, important ceremonies cannot be held without the presence of women. Sometimes the ritual woman who empowers the ceremony must be unmarried and virginal so that the power she channels is unalloyed, unweakened by sexual arousal and penetration by a male. Other ceremonies require tumescent women, others the presence of mature women who have borne children, and still others depend for empowerment on postmenopausal women. Women may be segregated from the company of the whole band or village on certain occasions, but on certain occasions men are also segregated. In short, each ritual depends on a certain balance of power, and the positions of women within the phases of womanhood are used by tribal people to empower certain rites. This does not derive from a male-dominant view; it is not a ritual observance imposed on women by men. It derives from a tribal view of reality that distinguishes tribal people from feudal and industrial people.

13   Among the tribes, the occult power of women, inextricably bound to our hormonal life, is thought to be very great; many hold that we possess innately the blood-given power to kill—with a glance, with a step, or with a judicious mixing of menstrual blood into somebody's soup. Medicine women among the Pomo of California cannot practice until they are sufficiently mature; when they are immature, their power is diffuse and is likely to interfere with their practice until time and experience have it under control. So women of the tribes are not especially inclined to see themselves as poor helpless victims of male domination. Even in those tribes where something akin to male domination was present, women are

perceived as powerful, socially, physically, and metaphysically. In times past, as in times present, women carried enormous burdens with aplomb. We were far indeed from the "weaker sex," the designation that white aristocratic sisters unhappily earned for us all.

14   I remember my mother moving furniture all over the house when she wanted it changed. She didn't wait for my father to come home and help—she just went ahead and moved the piano, a huge upright from the old days, the couch, the refrigerator. Nobody had told her she was too weak to do such things. In imitation of her, I would delight in loading trucks at my father's store with cases of pop or fifty-pound sacks of flour. Even when I was quite small I could do it, and it gave me a belief in my own physical strength that advancing middle age can't quite erase. My mother used to tell me about the Acoma Pueblo women she had seen as a child carrying huge ollas (water pots) on their heads as they wound their way up the tortuous stairwell carved into the face of the "Sky City" mesa, a feat I tried to imitate with books and tin buckets. ("Sky City" is the term used by the Chamber of Commerce for the mother village of Acoma, which is situated atop a high sandstone table mountain.) I was never very successful, but even the attempt reminded me that I was supposed to be strong and balanced to be a proper girl.

15   Of course, my mother's Laguna people are Keres Indian, reputed to be the last extreme mother-right people on earth. So it is no wonder that I got notably nonwhite notions about the natural strength and prowess of women. Indeed, it is only when I am trying to get non-Indian approval, recognition, or acknowledgment that my "weak sister" emotional and intellectual ploys get the better of my tribal woman's good sense. At such times I forget that I just moved the piano or just wrote a competent paper or just completed a financial transaction satisfactorily or have supported myself and my children for most of my adult life.

16   Nor is my contradictory behavior atypical. Most Indian women I know are in the same bicultural bind: we vacillate between being dependent and strong, self-reliant and powerless, strongly motivated and hopelessly insecure. We resolve the dilemma in various ways: some of us party all the time; some of us drink to excess; some of us travel and move around a lot; some of us land good jobs and then quit them; some of us engage in violent exchanges; some of us blow our brains out. We act in these destructive ways because we suffer from the societal conflicts caused by having to identify with two hopelessly opposed cultural definitions of women. Through this destructive dissonance we are unhappy prey to the self-disparagement common to, indeed demanded of, Indians living in the United States today. Our situation is caused by the exigencies of a history of invasion, conquest, and colonization whose searing marks are probably ineradicable. A popular bumper sticker on many Indian cars proclaims: "If You're Indian You're In," to which I always find myself adding under my breath, "Trouble."

III

17   No Indian can grow to any age without being informed that her people were "savages" who interfered with the march of progress pursued by respectable, loving, civilized white people. We are the villains of the scenario when we are mentioned at all. We are absent from much of white history except when we are calmly, rationally, succinctly, and systematically dehumanized. On the few occasions we are noticed in any way other than as howling, bloodthirsty beings, we are acclaimed for our noble quaintness. In this definition, we are exotic curios. Our ancient arts and customs are used to draw tourist money to state coffers, into the pocketbooks and bank accounts of scholars, and into support of the American-in-Disneyland promoters' dream.

18   As a Roman Catholic child I was treated to bloody tales of how the savage Indians martyred the hapless priests and missionaries who went among them in an attempt to lead them to the one true path. By the time I was through high school I had the idea that Indians were people who had benefited mightily from the advanced knowledge and superior morality of the Anglo-Europeans. At least I had, perforce, that idea to lay beside the other one that derived from my daily experience of Indian life, an idea less dehumanizing and more accurate because it came from my mother and the other Indian people who raised me. That idea was that Indians are a people who don't tell lies, who care for their children and their old people. You never see an Indian orphan, they said. You always know when you're old that someone will take care of you—one of your children will. Then they'd list the old folks who were being taken care of by this child or that. No child is ever considered illegitimate among the Indians, they said. If a girl gets pregnant, the baby is still part of the family, and the mother is too. That's what they said, and they showed me real people who lived according to those principles.

19   Of course the ravages of colonization have taken their toll; there are orphans in Indian country now, and abandoned, brutalized old folks; there are even illegitimate children, though the very concept still strikes me as absurd. There are battered children and neglected children, and there are battered wives and women who have been raped by Indian men. Proximity to the "civilizing" effects of white Christians has not improved the moral quality of life in Indian country, though each group, Indian and white, explains the situation differently. Nor is there much yet in the oral tradition that can enable us to adapt to these inhuman changes. But a force is growing in that direction, and it is helping Indian women reclaim their lives. Their power, their sense of direction and of self will soon be visible. It is the force of the women who speak and work and write, and it is formidable.

20   Through all the centuries of war and death and cultural and psychic destruction have endured the women who raise the children and tend the fires, who pass along the tales and the traditions, who weep and bury the dead, who are the dead, and who never forget. There are always the women, who make pots and weave baskets, who fashion clothes and cheer their

children on at powwow, who make fry bread and piki bread, and corn soup and chili stew, who dance and sing and remember and hold within their hearts the dream of their ancient peoples—that one day the woman who thinks will speak to us again, and everywhere there will be peace. Meanwhile we tell the stories and write the books and trade tales of anger and woe and stories of fun and scandal and laugh over all manner of things that happen every day. We watch and we wait.

21   My great-grandmother told my mother: Never forget you are Indian. And my mother told me the same thing. This, then, is how I have gone about remembering, so that my children will remember too.

CRITICAL READING

1. According to Gunn Allen, images of women in the Western world are either the passive madonna or the witch-goddess/whore, whereas the Native American tribes see women variously. In two separate columns list the characteristic features of Western and Native American women as seen by Gunn Allen. Do you agree with her characterizations? Can you identify what it is that she does to win or lose your assent?

2. From the outset, Gunn Allen notes that in the Native American tradition women are defined differently, but she also notes that those definitions are changing. How are the women's roles defined in your culture? How do they compare with those in your mother's or grandmother's time? How much control in defining such roles is left to the individual? Does your answer seem to be the same as or different from Gunn Allen's?

3. One of the subjects of the essay is the "bicultural bind, the phenomenon of having a foot in each of two distinct, even opposing cultures. Can you point to specific evidence of this bicultural bind in the essay's content? Do you think it has any bearing on the essay's form?

4. Who is Gunn Allen's audience? Is she writing to people like her? People who need to understand people like her? Women generally? People who might be in analogous circumstances though they are neither women nor Native Americans? Can you point to evidence in the text to support whatever answer you give?

5. Contending with images of women, Gunn Allen also contends with images of Native Americans—people perceived as bloodthirsty savages or as quaint but ignorant, redeemed only by embracing Western values. How does Gunn Allen counter such superficial generalizations? Doesn't she also generalize herself? What does she do to prevent her generalizations from seeming simplistic or misinformed?

6. It is important for Gunn Allen never to forget that she is of native American ancestry. She implies that the loss of memory about cultural heritage is harmful to one's being. Do you agree? Are your own cultural roots important to you? Why or why not?

Richard Rodriguez

MR. SECRETS

"I write for a reader who exists in my mind only phantasmagorically. Someone with a face erased; someone of no particular race or sex or age or weather. A gray presence."

WHAT MAKES RICHARD RODRIGUEZ A CONtroversial figure in American education is his insistence that bilingual education is not the panacea for nonnative speakers of English. He believes that assimilation into the mainstream culture should be the aim of all education, and in order to achieve it, linguistic minorities must relinquish their native language to embrace English. His opposition to bilingualism rests on his deep conviction that anyone who wants to experience a culture fully must move from the merely private life to one that is both public and private and be able to convey events of personal significance to an audience outside the barrio.

Born to Mexican-American parents in San Francisco in 1944, Richard Rodriguez learned to speak English in elementary school. He graduated from Stanford University and earned a Ph.D. in Renaissance literature from the University of California at Berkeley. Disillusioned with the status of minorities in the education system, Rodriguez declined several offers to teach in many of America's prestigious universities, including Yale. Currently he is a writer and lecturer living in California.

"Mr. Secrets" (taken from Rodriguez's 1982 autobiography, The Hunger of Memory: The Education of Richard Rodriguez) *has as its main focus the conflicting demands of Spanish and English, home and school, family and strangers. The writer wrestles with the present difficulties of writing about his past. Explicitly, writing becomes choosing a voice and so defining oneself. This definition conflicts with other definitions, other affiliations, other possibilities for being understood by others and oneself.*

ON THE WAY INTO THE READING

1. Growing up can also mean growing away from the world that shaped and nurtured us. Have ties to the world of your childhood home been loosened or cut? Can you identify gains that help to compensate for such losses?

2. Rodriguez feels his education transformed him into a person his parents could no longer entirely understand. Even if you are not coming to academic culture from a radically different home culture (as Rodriguez was), do you think your education may have changed you in ways your parents could not foresee and may not endorse? How might you describe the change from your perspective? How might you describe it from theirs?

3. How much of who you are is a matter of chosen associations? How much is by chance? Can you imagine yourself as being essentially

continued

continued

the same if you were born to parents with different economic or cultural circumstances? How do you imagine Rodriguez might answer that question?

1   I am writing about those very things my mother has asked me not to reveal. Shortly after I published my first autobiographical essay seven years ago, my mother wrote me a letter pleading with me never again to write about our family life. 'Write about something else in the future. Our family life is private.' And besides: 'Why do you need to tell the *gringos* about how "divided" you feel from the family?'

2   I sit at my desk now, surrounded by versions of paragraphs and pages of this book, considering that question.

3   When I decided to compose this intellectual autobiography, a New York editor told me that I would embark on a lonely journey. Over the noise of voices and dishes in an East Side restaurant, he said, 'There will be times when you will think the entire world has forgotten you. Some mornings you will yearn for a phone call or a letter to assure you that you still are connected to the world.' There *have* been mornings when I've dreaded the isolation this writing requires. Mornings spent listless in silence and in fear of confronting the blank sheet of paper. There have been times I've rushed away from my papers to answer the phone; gladly gotten up from my chair, hearing the mailman outside. Times I have been frustrated by the slowness of words, the way even a single paragraph never seemed done.

4   I had known a writer's loneliness before, working on my dissertation in the British Museum. But that experience did not prepare me for the task of writing these pages where my own life is the subject. Many days I feared I had stopped living by committing myself to remember the past. I feared that my absorption with events in my past amounted to an immature refusal to live in the present. Adulthood seemed consumed by memory. I would tell myself otherwise. I would tell myself that the act of remembering is an act of the present. (In writing this autobiography, I am actually describing the man I have become—the man in the present.)

5   Times when the money ran out, I left writing for temporary jobs. Once I had a job for over six months. I resumed something like a conventional social life. But then I have turned away, come back to my San Francisco apartment to closet myself in the silence I both need and fear.

6   I stay way from late-night parties. (To be clearheaded in the morning.) I disconnect my phone for much of the day. I must avoid complex relationships—a troublesome lover or a troubled friend. The person who knows me best scolds me for escaping from life. (*Am* I evading adulthood?) People I know get promotions at jobs. Friends move away. Friends get married. Friends divorce. One friend tells me she is pregnant. Then she has a baby. Then the baby has the formed face of a child. Can walk. Talk. And still I sit

at this desk laying my words like jigsaw pieces, a fellow with ladies in housecoats and old men in slippers who watch TV. Neighbors in my apartment house rush off to work about nine. I hear their steps on the stairs. (They will be back at six o'clock.) Somewhere planes are flying. The door slams behind them.

7   'Why?' My mother's question hangs in the still air of memory.

8   The loneliness I have felt many mornings, however, has not made me forget that I am engaged in a highly public activity. I sit here in silence writing this small volume of words, and it seems to me the most public thing I ever have done. My mother's letter has served to remind me: I am making my personal life public. Probably I will never try to explain my motives to my mother and father. My mother's question will go unanswered to her face. Like everything else on these pages, my reasons for writing will be revealed instead to public readers I expect never to meet.

I

9   It is to those whom my mother refers to as the *gringos* that I write. The *gringos*. The expression reminds me that she and my father have not followed their children all the way down the path to full Americanization. They were changed—became more easy in public, less withdrawn and uncertain—by the public success of their children. But something remained unchanged in their lives. With excessive care they continue today to note the difference between private and public life. And their private society remains only their family. No matter how friendly they are in public, no matter how firm their smiles, my parents never forget when they are in public. My mother must use a high-pitched tone of voice when she addresses people who are not relatives. It is a tone of voice I have all my life heard her use away from the house. Coming home from grammar school with new friends, I would hear it, its reminder: My new intimates were strangers to her. Like my sisters and brother, over the years, I've grown used to hearing that voice. Expected to hear it. Though I suspect that voice has played deep in my soul, sounding a lyre, to recall my 'betrayal,' my movement away from our family's intimate past. It is the voice I hear even now when my mother addresses her son- or daughter-in-law. (They remain public people to her.) She speaks to them, sounding the way she does when talking over the fence to a neighbor.

10   It was, in fact, the lady next door to my parents—a librarian—who first mentioned seeing my essay seven years ago. My mother was embarrassed because she hadn't any idea what the lady was talking about. But she had heard enough to go to a library with my father to find the article. They read what I wrote. And then she wrote her letter.

11   It is addressed to me in Spanish, but the body of the letter is in English. Almost mechanically she speaks of her pride at the start. ('Your dad and I are very proud of the brilliant manner you have to express yourself.') Then the matter of most concern comes to the fore. 'Your dad and I have only one objection to what you write. You say too much about the family. . . . Why do

you have to do that?…Why do you need to tell the *gringos?*…Why do you think we're so separated as a family? Do you really think this, Richard?'

12 A new paragraph changes the tone. Soft, maternal. Worried for me she adds, 'Do not punish yourself for having to give up our culture in order to "make it" as you say. Think of all the wonderful achievements you have obtained. You should be proud. Learn Spanish better. Practice it with your dad and me. Don't worry so much. Don't get the idea that I am mad at you either.

13 'Just keep one thing in mind. Writing is one thing, the family is another. I don't want *tus hermanos* hurt by your writings. And what do you think the cousins will say when they read where you talk about how the aunts were maids? Especially I don't want the *gringos* knowing about our private affairs. Why should they? Please give this some thought. Please write about something else in the future. Do me this favor.'

14 Please.

15 To the adult I am today, my mother needs to say what she would never have needed to say to her child: the boy who faithfully kept family secrets. When my fourth-grade teacher made our class write a paper about a typical evening at home, it never occurred to me actually to do so. 'Describe what you do with your family,' she told us. And automatically I produced a fictionalized account. I wrote that I had six brothers and sisters, I described watching my mother get dressed up in a red-sequined dress before she went with my father to a party, I even related how the imaginary baby sitter ('a high school student') taught my brother and sisters and me to make popcorn and how, later, I fell asleep before my parents returned. The nun who read what I wrote would have known that what I had written was completely imagined. But she never said anything about my contrivance. And I never expected her to either. I never thought she *really* wanted me to write about my family life. In any case, I would have been unable to do so.

16 I was very much the son of parents who regarded the most innocuous piece of information about the family to be secret. Although I had, by that time, grown easy in public, I felt that my family life was strictly private, not to be revealed to unfamiliar ears or eyes. Around the age of ten, I was held by surprise listening to my best friend tell me one day that he 'hated' his father. In a furious whisper he said that when he attempted to kiss his father before going to bed, his father had laughed: 'Don't you think you're getting too old for that sort of thing, son?' I was intrigued not so much by the incident as by the fact that the boy would relate it to *me.*

17 In those years I was exposed to the sliding-glass-door informality of middle-class California family life. Ringing the doorbell of a friend's house, I would hear someone inside yell out, 'Come on in, Richie; door's not locked.' And in I would go to discover my friend's family undisturbed by my presence. The father was in the kitchen in his underwear. The mother was in her bathrobe. Voices gathered in familiarity. A parent scolded a child in front of me; voices quarreled, then laughed; the mother told me something about her son after he had stepped out of the room and she was sure he

couldn't overhear; the father would speak to his children and to me in the same tone of voice. I was one of the family, the parents of several good friends would assure me. (Richie.)

18   My mother sometimes invited my grammar school friends to stay for dinner or even to stay overnight. But my parents never treated such visitors as part of the family, never told them they were. When a school friend ate at our table, my father spoke less than usual. (Stray, distant words.) My mother was careful to use her 'visitor's voice.' Sometimes, listening to her, I would feel annoyed because she wouldn't be more herself. Sometimes I'd feel embarrassed that I couldn't give to a friend at my house what I freely accepted at his.

19   I remained, nevertheless, my parents' child. At school, in sixth grade, my teacher suggested that I start keeping a diary. ('You should write down your personal experiences and reflections.') But I shied away from the idea. It was the one suggestion that the scholarship boy couldn't follow. I would not have wanted to write about the minor daily events of my life; I would never have been able to write about what most deeply, daily, concerned me during those years: I was growing away from my parents. Even if I could have been certain that no one would find my diary, even if I could have destroyed each page after I had written it, I would have felt uncomfortable writing about my home life. There seemed to me something intrinsically public about written words.

20   Writing, at any rate, was a skill I didn't regard highly. It was a grammar school skill I acquired with comparative ease. I do not remember struggling to write the way I struggled to learn how to read. The nuns would praise student papers for being neat—the handwritten letters easy for others to read; they promised that my writing style would improve as I read more and more. But that wasn't the reason I became a reader. Reading was for me the key to 'knowledge'; I swallowed facts and dates and names and themes. Writing, by contrast, was an activity I thought of as a kind of report, evidence of learning. I wrote down what I heard teachers say. I wrote down things from my books. I wrote down all I knew when I was examined at the end of the school year. Writing was performed after the fact; it was not the exciting experience of learning itself. In eighth grade I read several hundred books, the titles of which I still can recall. But I cannot remember a single essay I wrote. I only remember that the most frequent kind of essay I wrote was the book report.

21   In high school there were more 'creative' writing assignments. English teachers assigned the composition of short stories and poems. One sophomore story I wrote was a romance set in the Civil War South. I remember that it earned me a good enough grade, but my teacher suggested with quiet tact that next time I try writing about 'something you know more about—something closer to home.' Home? I wrote a short story about an old man who lived all by himself in a house down the block. That was as close as my writing ever got to my house. Still, I won prizes. When teachers suggested I contribute articles to the school literary magazine, I did so. And

when I was asked to join the school newspaper, I said yes. I did not feel any great pride in my writings, however. (My mother was the one who collected my prize-winning essays in a box she kept in her closet.) Though I remember seeing my by-line in print for the first time, and dwelling on the printing press letters with fascination: RICHARD RODRIGUEZ. The letters furnished evidence of a vast public identity writing made possible.

22   When I was a freshman in college, I began typing all my assignments. My writing speed decreased. Writing became a struggle. In high school I had been able to handwrite ten- and twenty-page papers in little more than an hour—and I never revised what I wrote. A college essay took me several nights to prepare. Suddenly everything I wrote seemed in need of revision. I became a self-conscious writer. A stylist. The change, I suspect, was the result of seeing my words ordered by the even, impersonal, anonymous typewriter print. As arranged by a machine, the words that I typed no longer seemed mine. I was able to see them with a new appreciation for how my reader would see them.

23   From grammar school to graduate school I could always name my reader. I wrote for my teacher. I could consult him or her before writing, and after. I suppose that I knew other readers could make sense of what I wrote—that, therefore, I addressed a general reader. But I didn't think very much about it. Only toward the end of my schooling and only because political issues pressed upon me did I write, and have published in magazines, essays intended for readers I never expected to meet. Now I am struck by the opportunity. I write today for a reader who exists in my mind only phantas-magorically. Someone with a face erased; someone of no particular race or sex or age or weather. A gray presence. Unknown, unfamiliar. All that I know about him is that he has had a long education and that his society, like mine, is often public (*un gringo*).

II

24   'What is psychiatry?' my mother asks. She is standing in her kitchen at the ironing board. We have been talking about nothing very important. ('Visiting.') As a result of nothing we have been saying, her question has come. But I am not surprised by it. My mother and father ask me such things. Now that they are retired they seem to think about subjects they never considered before. My father sits for hours in an armchair, wide-eyed. After my mother and I have finished discussing obligatory family news, he will approach me and wonder: When was Christianity introduced to the Asian continent? How does the brain learn things? Where is the Garden of Eden?

25   Perhaps because they consider me the family academic, my mother and father expect me to know. They do not, in any case, ask my brother and sisters the questions wild curiosity shapes. (That curiosity beats, unbeaten by age.)

26   Psychiatry? I shrug my shoulders to start with to tell my mother that it is very hard to explain. I go on to say something about Freud. And analysis.

Something about the function of a clinically trained listener. (I study my mother's face as I speak to see if she follows.) I compare a psychiatrist to a Catholic priest hearing Confession. But the analogy is inexact. My mother can easily speak to a priest in a darkened confessional; can easily make an act of self-revelation using the impersonal formula of ritual contrition: 'Bless me, father, for I have sinned. . . .' It would be altogether different for her to address a psychiatrist in unstructured conversation, revealing those events and feelings that burn close to the heart.

27   'You mean that people tell a psychiatrist about their personal lives?'

28   Even as I begin to respond, I realize that she cannot imagine ever doing such a thing. She shakes her head sadly, bending over the ironing board to inspect a shirt with the tip of the iron she holds in her hand. Then she changes the subject. She is talking to me about one of her sisters, my aunt, who is seriously ill. Whatever it is that prompted her question about psychiatry has passed.

29   I stand there. I continue thinking about what she has asked me—and what she cannot comprehend. My parents seem to me possessed of great dignity. An aristocratic reserve. Like the very rich who live behind tall walls, my mother and father are always mindful of the line separating public from private life. Watching a celebrity talk show on television, they listen for several minutes as a movie star with bright teeth recounts details of his recent divorce. And I see my parents grow impatient. Finally, my mother dgets up from her chair. Changing the channel, she says with simple disdain, 'Cheap people.'

30   My mother and my father are not cheap people. They never are tempted to believe that public life can also be intimate. They remain aloof from the modern temptation that captivates many in America's middle class: the temptation to relieve the anonymity of public life by trying to make it intimate. They do not understand, consequently, what so pleases the television audience listening to a movie star discuss his divorce with bogus private language. My father opens a newspaper to find an article by a politician's wife in which she reveals (actually, renders merely as gossip) intimate details of her marriage. And he looks up from the article to ask me, 'Why does she do this?'

31   I find his question embarrassing. Although I know that he does not intend to embarrass me, I am forced to think about this book I have been writing. And I realize that my parents will be as puzzled by my act of self-revelation as they are by the movie star's revelations on the talk show. They never will call me cheap for publishing an autobiography. But I can well imagine their faces tightened by incomprehension as they read my words.

32   (Why does he do this?)

33   Many mornings at my desk I have been paralyzed by the thought of their faces, their eyes. I imagine their eyes moving slowly across these pages. That image has weakened my resolve. Finally, however, it has not stopped me. Despite the fact that my parents remain even now in my mind a critical,

silent chorus, standing together, I continue to write. I do not make my parents' sharp distinction between public and private life. With my mother and father I scorn those who attempt to create an experience of intimacy in public. But unlike my parents, I have come to think that there is a place for the deeply personal in public life. This is what I have learned by trying to write this book: There are things so deeply personal that they can be revealed only to strangers. I believe this. I continue to write.

34   'What is psychiatry?' my mother asks. And I wish I could tell her. (I wish she could imagine it.) 'There are things that are so personal that they can only be said to someone who is not close. Someone you don't know. A person who is not an intimate friend or a relation. There are things too personal to be shared with intimates.'

35   She stands at the ironing board, her tone easy because she is speaking to me. (I am her son.) For my mother that which is personal can only be said to a relative—her only intimates. She makes the single exception of confessing her sins to a Catholic priest. Otherwise, she speaks of her personal life only at home. The same is true of my father—though he is silent even with family members. Of those matters too jaggedly personal to reveal to intimates, my parents will never speak. And that seems to me an extraordinary oppression. The unspoken may well up within my mother and cause her to sigh. But beyond that sigh nothing is heard. There is no one she can address. Words never form. Silence remains to repress them. She remains quiet. My father in his chair remains quiet.

36   I wonder now what my parents' silence contains. What would be their version of the past we once shared? What memories do they carry about me? What were their feelings at many of the moments I recollect on these pages? What did my father—who had dreamed of Australia—think of his children once they forced him to change plans and remain in America? What contrary feelings did he have about our early success? How does he regard the adults his sons and daughters have become? And my mother. At what moments has she hated me? On what occasions has she been embarrassed by me? What does she recall feeling during those difficult, sullen years of my childhood? What would be her version of this book? What are my parents unable to tell me today? What things are too personal? What feelings so unruly they dare not reveal to other intimates? Or even to each other? Or to themselves?

37   Some people have told me how wonderful it is that I am the first in my family to write a book. I stand on the edge of a long silence. But I do not give voice to my parents by writing about their lives. I distinguish myself from them by writing about the life we once shared. Even when I quote them accurately, I profoundly distort my parents' words. (They were never intended to be read by the public.) So my parents do not truly speak on my pages. I may force their words to stand between quotation marks. With every word, however, I change what was said only to me.

38   'What is new with you?' My mother looks up from her ironing to ask me. (In recent years she has taken to calling me Mr. Secrets, because I tell her

so little about my work in San Francisco—this book she must suspect I am writing.)

39   Nothing much, I respond.

40   I write very slowly because I write under the obligation to make myself clear to someone who knows nothing about me. It is a lonely adventure. Each morning I make my way along a narrowing precipice of written words. I hear an echoing voice—my own resembling another's. Silent! The reader's voice silently trails every word I put down. I reread my words, and again it is the reader's voice I hear in my mind, sounding my prose.

41   When I wrote my first autobiographical essay, it was no coincidence that, from the first page, I expected to publish what I wrote. I didn't consciously determine the issue. Somehow I knew, however, that my words were meant for a public reader. Only because of that reader did the words come to the page. The reader became my excuse, my reason for writing.

42   It had taken me a long time to come to this address. There are remarkable children who very early are able to write publicly about their personal lives. Some children confide to a diary those things—like the first shuddering of sexual desire—too private to tell a parent or brother. The youthful writer addresses a stranger, the Other, with 'Dear Diary' and tries to give public expression to what is intensely, privately felt. In so doing, he attempts to evade the guilt of repression. And the embarrassment of solitary feeling. For by rendering feelings in words that a stranger can understand—words that belong to the public, this Other—the young diarist no longer need feel all alone or eccentric. His feelings are capable of public intelligibility. In turn, the act of revelation helps the writer better understand his own feelings. Such is the benefit of language: By finding public words to describe one's feelings, one can describe oneself to oneself. One names what was previously only darkly felt.

43   I have come to think of myself as engaged in writing graffiti. Encouraged by physical isolation to reveal what is most personal; determined at the same time to have my words seen by strangers. I have come to understand better why works of literature—while never intimate, never individually addressed to the reader—are so often among the most personal statements we hear in our lives. Writing, I have come to value written words as never before. One can use *spoken* words to reveal one's personal self to strangers. But *written* words heighten the feeling of privacy. They permit the most thorough and careful exploration. (In the silent room, I prey upon that which is most private. Behind the closed door, I am least reticent about giving those memories expression.) The writer is freed from the obligation of finding an auditor in public. (As I use words that someone far from home can understand, I create my listener. I imagine her listening.)

44   My teachers gave me a great deal more than I knew when they taught me to write public English. I was unable then to use the skill for deeply personal purposes. I insisted upon writing impersonal essays. And I wrote always with a specific reader in mind. Nevertheless, the skill of public writing was gradually developed by the many classroom papers I had to compose. Today

I *can* address an anonymous reader. And this seems to me important to say. Somehow the inclination to write about my private life in public is related to the ability to do so. It is not enough to say that my mother and father do not want to write their autobiographies. It needs also to be said that they are unable to write to a public reader. They lack the skill. Though both of them can write in Spanish and English, they write in a hesitant manner. Their syntax is uncertain. Their vocabulary limited. They write well enough to communicate 'news' to relatives in letters. And they can handle written transactions in institutional America. But the man who sits in his chair so many hours, and the woman at the ironing board—'keeping busy because I don't want to get old'—will never be able to believe that any description of their personal lives could be understood by a stranger far from home.

III

45   When my mother mentioned seeing my article seven years ago, she *wrote* to me. And I responded to her letter with one of my own. (I wrote: 'I am sorry that my article bothered you...I had not meant to hurt...I think, however, that education has divided the family...That is something which happens in most families, though it is rarely discussed...I had meant to praise what I have lost...I continue to love you both very much.') I wrote to my mother because it would have been too difficult, too painful to hear her voice on the phone. Too unmanageable a confrontation of voices. The impersonality of the written word made it the easiest means of exchange. The remarkable thing is that nothing has been spoken about this matter by either of us in the years intervening. I know my mother suspects that I continue to write about the family. She knows that I spend months at a time 'writing,' but she does not press me for information. (Mr. Secrets.) She does not protest.

46   The first time I saw my mother after she had received my letter, she came with my father to lunch. I opened the door to find her smiling slightly. In an instant I tried to gather her mood. (She looked as nervous and shy as I must have seemed.) We embraced. And she said that my father was looking for a place to park the car. She came into my apartment and asked what we were having for lunch. Slowly, our voices reverted to tones we normally sound with each other. (Nothing was said of my article.) I think my mother sensed that afternoon that the person whose essay she saw in a national magazine was a person unfamiliar to her, some Other. The public person— the writer Richard Rodriguez—would remain distant and untouchable. She never would hear his public voice across a dining room table. And that afternoon she seemed to accept the idea, granted me the right, the freedom so crucial to adulthood, to become a person very different in public from the person I am at home.

47   Intimates are not always so generous. One close friend calls to tell me she has read an essay of mine. 'All that Spanish angst,' she laughs. 'It's not really you.' Only someone very close would be tempted to say such a thing—only a person who knows who I am. From such an intimate one must sometimes

escape to the company of strangers, to the liberation of the city, in order to form new versions of oneself.

48   In the company of strangers now, I do not reveal the person I am among intimates. My brother and sisters recognize a different person, not the Richard Rodriguez in this book. I hope, when they read this, they will continue to trust the person they have known me to be. But I hope too that, like our mother, they will understand why it is that the voice I sound here I have never sounded to them. All those faraway childhood mornings in Sacramento, walking together to school, we talked but never mentioned a thing about what concerned us so much: the great event of our schooling, the change it forced on our lives. Years passed. Silence grew thicker, less penetrable. We grew older without ever speaking to each other about any of it. Intimacy grooved our voices in familiar notes; familiarity defined the limits of what could be said. Until we became adults. And now we see each other most years at noisy family gatherings where there is no place to stop the conversation, no right moment to turn the heads of listeners, no way to essay this, my voice.

49   I see them now, my brother and sisters, two or three times every year. We do not live so very far from one another. But as an entire family, we only manage to gather for dinner on Easter. And Mother's Day. Christmas. It is usually at our parents' house that these dinners are held. Our mother invariably organizes things. Well before anyone else has the chance to make other arrangements, her voice will sound on the phone to remind us of an upcoming gathering.

50   Lately, I have begun to wonder how the family will gather even three times a year when she is not there with her phone to unite us. For the time being, however, she presides at the table. She—not my father, who sits opposite her—says the Grace before Meals. She busies herself throughout the meal. 'Sit down now,' somebody tells her. But she moves back and forth from the dining room table to the kitchen. Someone needs more food. (What's missing?) Something always is missing from the table. When she is seated, she listens to the conversation. But she seems lonely. (Does she think things would have been different if one of her children had brought home someone who could speak Spanish?) She does not know how or where to join in when her children are talking about Woody Allen movies or real estate tax laws or somebody's yoga class. (Does she remember how we vied with each other to sit beside her in a movie theatre?) Someone remembers at some point to include her in the conversation. Someone asks how many pounds the turkey was this year. She responds in her visitor's voice. And soon the voices ride away. She is left with the silence.

51   Sitting beside me, as usual, is my younger sister. We gossip. She tells me about her trip last week to Milan; we laugh; we talk about clothes, mutual friends in New York.

52   Other voices intrude: I hear the voices of my brother and sister and the people who have married into our family. I am the loudest talker. I am the

one doing most of the talking. I talk, having learned from hundreds of cocktail parties and dinner parties how to talk with great animation about nothing especially. I sound happy. I talk to everyone about something. And I become shy only when my older sister wonders what I am doing these days. Working in Los Angeles? Or writing again? When will she be able to see something I've published?

53   I try to change the subject.

54   'Are you writing a book?'

55   I notice, out of the corner of my eye, that my mother is nervously piling dishes and then getting up to take them out to the kitchen.

56   I say yes.

57   'Well, well, well. Let's see it. Is it going to be a love story? A romance? What's it about?'

58   She glances down at her thirteen-year-old son, her oldest. 'Tommy reads and reads, just like you used to.'

59   I look over at him and ask him what sort of books he likes best.

60   'Everything!' his mother answers with pride.

61   He smiles. I wonder: Am I watching myself in this boy? In this face where I can scarcely trace a family resemblance? Have I foreseen his past? He lives in a world of Little League and Pop Warner. He has spoken English all his life. His father is of German descent, a fourth-generation American. And he does not go to a Catholic school, but to a public school named after a dead politician. Still, he is someone who reads...

62   'He and I read all the same books,' my sister informs me. And with that remark, my nephew's life slips out of my grasp to imagine.

63   Dinner progresses. There is dessert. Four cakes. Coffee. The conversation advances with remarkable ease. Talk is cheerful, the way talk is among people who rarely see one another and then are surprised that they have so much to say. Sometimes voices converge from various points around the table. Sometimes voices retreat to separate topics, two or three conversations.

64   My mother interrupts. She speaks and gets everyone's attention. Some cousin of ours is getting married next month. (Already.) And some other relative is now the mother of a nine-pound baby boy. (Already?) And some relative's son is graduating from college this year. (We haven't seen him since he was five.) And somebody else, an aunt, is retiring from her job in that candy store. And a friend of my mother's from Sacramento—Do we remember her after all these years?—died of cancer just last week. (Already!)

65   My father remains a witness to the evening. It is difficult to tell what he hears (his hearing is bad) or cannot understand (his English is bad). His face stays impassive, unless he is directly addressed. In which case he smiles and nods, too eagerly, too quickly, at what has been said. (Has he really heard?) When he has finished eating, I notice, he sits back in his chair. And his eyes move from face to face. Sometimes I feel that he is looking at me. I look over to see him, and his eyes dart away the second after I glance.

66   When Christmas dinner is finished, there are gifts to exchange in the front room. Tradition demands that my brother, the oldest, play master of ceremonies, 'Santa's helper,' handing out presents with a cigar in his hand. It is the chore he has come to assume, making us laugh with his hammy asides. 'This is for Richard,' he says, rattling a box next to his ear, rolling his eyes. 'And this one is for Mama Rodriguez.' (There is the bright snap of a camera.)

67   Nowadays there is money enough for buying useless and slightly ludicrous gifts for my mother and father. (They will receive an expensive backgammon set. And airplane tickets to places they haven't the energy or the desire to visit. And they will be given a huge silver urn—'for chilling champagne.')

68   My mother is not surprised that her children are well-off. Her two daughters are business executives. Her oldest son is a lawyer. She predicted it all long ago. 'Someday,' she used to say when we were young, 'you will all grow up and all be very rich. You'll have lots of money to buy me presents. But I'll be a little old lady. I won't have any teeth or hair. So you'll have to buy me soft food and put a blue wig on my head. And you'll buy me a big fur coat. But you'll only be able to see my eyes.'

69   Every Christmas now the floor around her is carpeted with red and green wrapping paper. And her feet are wreathed with gifts.

70   By the time the last gift is unwrapped, everyone seems very tired. The room has become uncomfortably warm. The talk grows listless. ('Does anyone want coffee or more cake?' Somebody groans.) Children are falling asleep. Someone gets up to leave, prompting others to leave. ('We have to get up early tomorrow.')

71   'Another Christmas,' my mother says. She says that same thing every year, so we all smile to hear it again.

72   Children are bundled up for the fast walk to the car. My mother stands by the door calling good-bye. She stands with a coat over her shoulders, looking into the dark where expensive foreign cars idle sharply. She seems, all of a sudden, very small. She looks worried.

73   'Don't come out, it's too cold,' somebody shouts at her or at my father, who steps out onto the porch. I watch my younger sister in a shiny mink jacket bend slightly to kiss my mother before she rushes down the front steps. My mother stands waving toward no one in particular. She seems sad to me. How sad? Why? (Sad that we all are going home? Sad that it was not quite, can never be, the Christmas one remembers having had once?) I am tempted to ask her quietly if there is anything wrong. (But these are questions of paradise, Mama.)

74   My brother drives away.

75   'Daddy shouldn't be outside,' my mother says. 'Here, take this jacket out to him.'

76   She steps into the warmth of the entrance hall and hands me the coat she has been wearing over her shoulders.

77   I take it to my father and place it on him. In that instant I feel the thinness of his arms. He turns. He asks if I am going home now too. It is, I realize, the only thing he has said to me all evening.

CRITICAL READING

1. Much of "Mr. Secrets" treats Rodriguez's becoming a writer. Do you identify with any of the stages or circumstances he recounts? How does he distinguish his writing in school from his writing as a professional writer? How clear is the distinction? Are there aspects of his writing that you would not think possible or appropriate for a college writing class?

2. In paragraph 23 Rodriguez talks about progressing from writing for a known to an unknown audience of "no particular race or sex or age or weather." What effect does this impersonal audience have on him? For you, is it easier or more difficult to write about personal feelings for an audience whom you know?

3. Guneet, you may recall, did not respond favorably to Rodriguez, finding him "isolated and lost about his cultural heritage." How do you respond to Rodriguez? Can you point to specific points in the text to help explain your responses?

4. Guneet Kaur, Paula Gunn Allen, and Richard Rodriguez all in their own way confront the dilemma of the culturally split self: the East Indian/American, the Native American/white Western, Chicano/Gringo. How are their approaches similar or different?

5. Paragraphs 34 to 42 may seem a disjointed ramble, but in retrospect they work through a progression of importantly related topics: psychiatry, confession, the benefits of writing autobiography. What does Rodriguez mean when he claims in paragraph 42, "By finding public words to describe one's feelings, one can describe oneself to oneself?" How important is the world "public" there?

6. Does Rodriguez succeed in reconciling the private and the public? What purpose does the long Christmas dinner episode (paragraphs 49 to 77) serve in the essay? How much do you think things have been resolved by the end? How much should or could they be resolved?

7. Do you feel a formal education leads to a loss of what is distinctive and different about one's own cultural values? Even those who feel themselves thoroughly American (whatever that means) feel themselves moving away from the values of home and family as they are initiated into what is often called the "academic culture." Have you felt this way? How easy or difficult has it been for you to maintain ties with your own culture and family while assimilating into the academic world?

CONDUCTING INFORMAL SURVEYS

In becoming who you are—a college student—you have to adjust to the special circumstances in which you find yourself. These changes, while offering new choices and opening new horizons, frequently require enormous sacrifices and even painful compromises. But if getting a college education is such a traumatic experience, why do students go through the process?

Each individual may have a different response to the question above. To arrive at a general consensus, you would have to include the opinions of a number of college students. An effective instrument to sample other people's opinions, ideas, or points of view is a *survey,* which seeks answers to the questions raised by the surveyor. It is important to note here that the focus of this chapter is on informal surveys to generate ideas for writing. While it introduces you to some basic and informal survey methods, it does not pretend to train you in scientifically and statistically valid sampling or extrapolation of data. But as this chapter illustrates, even an informal survey allows us to move beyond the personal to a better understanding of our environment and, in the process, to a better understanding of ourselves.

If you take a poll on your campus asking what motivated many of the students to attend college in spite of the hardship, some of them may say college will enable them to earn a better living, to have job satisfaction, to be better informed about themselves and others, or to be more productive citizens. These may also be your own reasons for coming to college, but by identifying with the responses of others, you both shape your environment and are shaped by it. Because answers to the survey questions enable you to see what other people have to say about a given topic, it is an excellent method for generating ideas outside of library research. The student writing in this chapter illustrates that you do not have to be a statistician or an expert pollster to prepare an informal survey questionnaire.

The writing by Julio Olivencia stemmed from a class discussion on gender-role stereotypes. The students were aware of the stereotypes—men are aggressive and women are passive; men are high achievers and women are underachievers. A class discussion focused on traditional gender roles and the reversal of those roles, particularly as they are portrayed in popular television shows. What happens when a man takes on a role traditionally played by women or when a woman takes on a male role? As the class broke into smaller groups to try their ideas on each other, Julio began by first brainstorming with his own group to collect ideas. When they felt they had something to report, the groups put their ideas together, and with help of the instructor, designed an informal survey questionnaire to give to 20 friends or acquaintances outside the classroom. Each student tallied the results to get a general idea about how the people surveyed felt about the reversal of gender roles. In the example essay in this chapter, Julio first reports the findings of the informal survey and then comments on them.

The two professional essays in this chapter reveal some of the techniques, problems, and benefits of writing based on information gathered through questionnaires and surveys. Elisabeth Bumiller's more informal questionnaire administered to the semiliterate women in a village in northern India yields different kinds of results and poses different kinds of problems than the sampling of opinions by Andrew N. Rowan in a more homogeneous and controlled situation. Yet all three writers, Julio Olivencia included, were able to gather information through surveys, however informal, that would not have been obtained otherwise.

WRITING ASSIGNMENT

Think about something that touches our lives—in college, at work, or at home—that people may be interested in talking about. Is the grading system fair? Should college professors take attendance in class? Is there sexual harassment in college or in the workplace? Select an issue that interests you and that might interest the group you survey. Following the guidelines for the survey, prepare a list of questions to administer to the group you have selected. Based on the survey results of the informal survey, write an essay that states your findings and your conclusions.

READING THE WRITING ASSIGNMENT

This assignment depends to a great extent on prewriting activities—the survey and its results. To get enthusiastic responses to the survey, you need to select issues that touch people's lives and ask thought-provoking questions, answers to which will be essential for your essay. As vital as the survey is to your assignment, however, your essay will not include the survey itself, but its results, which remain only a small part of the essay. For example, the results of a survey of 30 people about taking attendance in college classes and not the survey itself, which may be a list of any number of questions, will be the focus of your essay.

Because the results of a survey are such a small part of the essay, the onus is on you to inform your reader about the intent and purpose of the study. What made you investigate the issue? Were you challenged, provoked, or curious about finding answers to some questions? Was there a need for the study? It is pertinent to remember that your readers do not have access to the survey itself, so you need to provide a brief review of the questions, focusing on the results.

The discussion segment toward the end of the essay that states the significance of your findings is the most important challenge for you. Was the survey worth the work involved? What did you learn? What are the implications of the results? Are the results applicable to broader issues? The answers may not be clear cut, but don't let that stop you. Try to remember that survey results are often unpredictable and may take the researcher by surprise. In addition, professional writers and researchers sometimes have to admit that their surveys did not work for various reasons. The best approach in reporting and discussing the results is to be honest. If the survey works for you, let your readers know why it worked; if it doesn't work, say why not. Before you embark on your own writing project, read the three essays based on survey results in this chapter. Were the results predictable? Did the researchers experience frustration or disappointment? Then go about working on your project with an open mind. You may be pleasantly surprised!

SURVEYS AND INDUCTIVE REASONING

The method of arriving at some general conclusions from the observation of particular items, responses, or instances is **induction**. Inductive reasoning, also referred to as scientific reasoning, often reaches conclusions such as these:

1. Smoking is a major cause of lung cancer.
2. Children learn violent behavior by watching television.
3. Ray's pizza is the best in town.
4. Vitamin C helps prevent colds.
5. Deciduous trees shed their leaves in autumn.

All five of these inductive conclusions are results of some kind of observation, but some of the conditions are more reliable than the others. For example, the fact that all deciduous trees lose their leaves in the fall rests on the observation of a natural phenomenon that occurs, without fail, every year. We are therefore confident that statement 5 is a highly valid generalization. But when we claim that Ray's pizza is the best in town or that TV violence is the source of violent behavior in children, we are on less certain ground. The shedding of leaves is a more observable, more objectively measurable phenomenon than is the "betterness" of Ray's pizza, no matter how good we think his pizza is. Other people may think another pizza is better, for reasons of their own. "Better" is a matter of taste, so to speak, and it is therefore a quality that is difficult to measure with certainty. Likewise, what is negatively "violent" behavior to one person will be acceptable and even admirable behavior to another. Thus, inductive statements commonly need to be qualified by "usually," "generally," or "often" when the results have some elements of doubt and when they do not cover all members of the group. Some people, in spite of taking lots of vitamin C, still catch colds. Some heavy smokers do not develop lung cancer. Most generalizations are true only to some extent. Surveying is a technique for determining what that extent is.

RIAL RUN

Form a small group and have each member write down six statements that may be conclusions of inductive reasoning. Discuss the accuracy of the statements. Are they reliable? Why or why not? Report your findings to other groups or to your instructor for comments.

DISCOVERING IDEAS

Prepare a Survey Questionnaire

As a preparation for a paper on the reversal of gender roles, Julio's class first decided to examine some of their own ideas and observations about the traditional roles assigned by society to men and women.

The students broke into smaller groups for discussion. Julio's group included Alberto Castane and Hilda Reyes. The members of the group discussed their own assumptions about men and women and talked about how society had portrayed men as aggressive and women as passive. Alberto, who was from Costa Rica in Central America, was surprised that this assumption was not very different in the United States from what it was in Costa Rica. Though Julio and Hilda grew up in the United States, they, too, had come to accept the idea that men had the "killer instinct" to get ahead in a competitive world. Women fell behind because they just did not have the aggressiveness necessary to get ahead. Hilda acknowledged that she had almost come to believe this because men were always shown to be more aggressive in the images she saw around her, but she was not absolutely convinced. She believed that a survey of gender behavior might generate conclusions that would challenge some of these assumptions.

Julio's group decided to write papers based on a survey of public opinion about gender roles on popular TV shows. Led by their instructor, the students considered the following issues while constructing a survey questionnaire.

1. First the students had to figure out the purpose of the survey, which was to arrive at some generalizations about the viewing public's attitudes towards roles, both traditional and nontraditional, played by men and women in popular television shows.

   The students selected three popular television situation comedies, "Who's the Boss," "Three's Company," and "The Brady Bunch," that portrayed men and women in both traditional and nontraditional roles. (These shows are quite old and seen mostly on reruns now. But of course many current shows address gender issues.) Next they decided to determine how they were perceived by the general viewing public. Did the public feel that the roles assigned to the characters reflected real-life situations and did they approve or disapprove of them?

2. Then the students had to set a limit to the survey by deciding:
   a. What group is going to be surveyed?
   b. How many responses would be necessary for a representative sample?
   c. What exactly is the survey intended to investigate?
   d. What part does demography (age, gender, race, class, and so on) play in the current survey?

   Students in the different groups agreed that they would each administer the survey to at least 10 men and 10 women outside the class, people who might include other students in the cafeteria, neighbors, or coworkers.

3. The next task at hand was to work on the survey questions. It is much more complicated to analyze open questions that require brief written responses than to tally closed or multiple-choice questions that reveal specific information.

   As an invention process for their writing assignment, students opted for closed questions. However, to ensure they had enough details in the survey for their writing assignment based on it, they decided to include a few open-ended questions at the end of the survey.

4. It is usually advisable to check survey questions carefully to help avoid problems of confusion with regard to directions or misreading of questions.

   The entire class collaborated in selecting the most appropriate questions for the survey. Finally, they checked to see if the questions met the following requirements:
   a. Can the questions be asked the way they are written?
   b. Can they be answered?
   c. Will people be willing to answer them?
   d. Will they mean different things to different people?

Reasonably satisfied, the class constructed the survey shown in Figure 5-1 (next page).

Figure 5-1

A Survey of Gender Roles on Popular TV Shows

Sex_____   Age_____

1. Which of these shows do you think are offensive to your gender?
   a. Who's the Boss?   b. Three's Company   c. The Brady Bunch   d. None

2. Which of these shows reveal a bias against one sex?
   a. Who's the Boss?   b. Three's Company   c. The Brady Bunch   d. None

3. In which of these shows do you think attitudes toward gender roles are the same as in real life?
   a. Who's the Boss?   b. Three's Company   c. The Brady Bunch   d. None

4. In which of these shows do you find the stereotypes not offensive?
   a. Who's the Boss?   b. Three's Company   c. The Brady Bunch   d. None

5. Which of these shows portray actual reversals of gender roles?
   a. Who's the Boss?   b. Three's Company   c. The Brady Bunch   d. None

6. Do you find the personal relationship between the employer and the employee in "Who's the Boss" unethical?
   a. Yes   b. No

7. Do you approve of their business/personal relationship?
   a. Yes   b. No

8. Do you find "Three's Company" homophobic or demeaning to homosexuals?
   a. Yes   b. No

9. Do you find some characters in "Three's Company" offensive to women?
   a. Yes   b. No

10. Do you find the portrayal of Mrs. Brady offensive to women?
    a. Yes   b. No

11. Do you find the role of Alice, the housekeeper in "The Brady Bunch," offensive to women?
    a. Yes   b. No

12. Do you believe Mrs. Brady should have had a job outside the house?
    a. Yes   b. No

13. In a few words, state your opinions about gender roles in the real world today.

14. In a few words, state your opinion about the ways gender roles are portrayed on television.

⬛RIAL RUN

Following the survey questionnaire above as a guide, collaborate with your classmates and design an informal survey on a topic that is familiar to the group you want to survey and that generates interest, discussion, and controversy. Make sure you include some open-ended questions in addition to the multiple-choice ones. Administer the survey to a group at school, at your place of work, or in your neighborhood. Report the results in a short paragraph.

COMPOSING THE FIRST DRAFT

Each student then had to tally the multiple-choice responses and summarize the two short answers to write an essay based on the results. Julio surveyed 15 men and 15 women in his neighborhood and at his place of work. He tallied up the 12 multiple-choice responses, summarized the last two short responses, and started working on his first draft to report his findings.

Before beginning the first draft, it is important to remember that the focus of an essay based on a survey is not the survey itself but what you learn from it. As a form of research away from the library, a survey helps you generate ideas. Reporting the results alone, however, without stating what they suggest to you about the topic, does not constitute an essay. Your audience—the instructor or classmates—will want to know the purpose of the survey. What did you set out to achieve? Did the results conform to your expectations or did they surprise you?

As you compose the first draft, have the survey questions and the results close at hand, for you will need to refer to them constantly as you write. Remember that this is only the first draft and that good writing is rewriting. Read Julio's first draft with a critical eye and think of changes you could recommend for improvement.

PRESENTING JULIO'S FIRST DRAFT

1   I distributed about equal numbers of questionnaires to females and males around where I live and at the food-processing factory where I work after school. I will discuss the three comedies separately to show how the people surveyed responded to them. My biggest surprise was that almost all the men and women, with the exception of only two women and one man, did not find anything particularly offensive in the three comedies when answering the multiple-choice questions. But these same people had very different things to say in answering questions 13 and 14. This raised some serious questions in my own mind about the nature of surveys.

2   In "Who's the Boss," Angela is a successful, well-educated woman, perhaps in her late thirties, who owns an advertising agency. She is a lousy cook with no time or desire for household work. This is where Tony comes into the picture. He is a handsome and charming young man, apparently younger than Angela, who is hired to cook, take care of her son, and clean the house. Though it is never made very explicit, underneath the employer/employee relationship there are many suggestions of a romantic involvement between Angela and Tony in several of the episodes. By far the majority of the men and women surveyed were not unhappy with the reversal of the traditional gender roles in this comedy. Nor did they feel that the show discriminated against one sex, since both Tony and Angela were generally satisfied with their work. A large majority of the respondents did not find the personal relationship between Angela and Tony unethical or their work relationship unusual.

3   The three main characters in "Three's Company" are Jack, Chrissy, and Janet. There is gender reversal at more than one level in this comedy. First, Jack, who is heterosexual, has to pretend to be homosexual in order for the landlord to allow him to share an apartment with Janet and Chrissy. Like Tony in "Who's the Boss," Jack is an excellent cook, and he works as a chef in a restaurant. Chrissy and Janet both have jobs, are poor cooks, and are not particularly good at housework. The viewers did not find this reversal offensive. What some women viewers did find offensive, however, was the stereotypical portrayal of Chrissy and Janet as the dumb blonde and bright brunette, respectively. Some also found the character Larry, a playboy who lives in the same building and treats women as objects of his pleasure, pretty obnoxious. The men, on the other hand, had no negative comments on Larry.

4   The responses to the questions on "The Brady Bunch," were mixed. Many did not circle the letter next to it, mostly, I think, because they have not seen the show. This show, about a perfect American family, mother, father, six kids, and a live-in housekeeper, has been off the air for quite some time, though it is sometimes rerun on some stations. To the question about how they felt about Mrs. Brady having a maid, most people thought it was an acceptable lifestyle at that time, especially because Mrs. Brady had six children. Most thought she needed the help and was not a lazy woman.

5   The answers to question 13 revealed a substantial difference of opinion between men and women. The men expressed general satisfaction with the way gender roles are played out in real life--man as the basic wage earner and the woman substituting his salary or staying home to take care of the chil-

dren. The women, however, pointed to the deep gender biases in real life. Women often face discrimination in hiring and often do not receive equal pay with men for equal work. Many women also said that men often hired women for the way they looked rather than for their abilities. They felt men are threatened by qualified women.

6   Question 14 brought out quite humorous responses from the men. Some men expressed dissatisfaction with Tony as the housekeeper in "Who's the Boss." But most showed almost a sense of relief that this was only a TV sitcom, not likely to happen very often in real life. Some men also felt that Tony was really the boss because Angela was secretly in love with him, hence the ambiguity in the title of the show. In "Three's Company" most men found it offensive that a heterosexual man was forced to be identified as a homosexual, yet most of these respondents answered "no" to question 8, which asked if they found the show offensive to homosexuals.

7   The women's responses to question 14 were predictably different. Many were pleased that a successful businesswoman hired a man as her housekeeper, but some also expressed their reservations about the nature of the relationship, which is unlike most in the real world. Most women bosses, they felt, did not flirt with their male subordinates. Some women also complained about the character of Angela's mother, who is like a meddling mother-in-law. The women surveyed were concerned about the role of the men and women not being clear-cut in "Who's the Boss," which added to the confusion. Most women did not find it offensive that Jack Tripper in "Three's Company" had to pretend to be gay to get an apartment. Many, on the other hand, objected to the stereotype of the dumb blonde, which was mentioned only in three male responses, and they also found Jack and Larry's comments offensive to women in general.

8   Why were the responses between men and women so similar in the multiple-choice part and so different in the brief-answer section? My guess is that people do not think too hard when they answer the yes/no questions, at least that has been my own experience in taking multiple-choice exams. The brief answers required more concentrated thinking that brought out what the people really felt and not just quick reactions.

Thinking Critically about Julio's First Draft

1. Comment on Julio's introductory paragraph. Is there adequate background information for the audience to understand the purpose of the essay?

2. Who are the people Julio selected to answer the survey questions? If you had to administer the same questionnaire, would your group be different from Julio's? How?

3. Do the readers have adequate information on the group surveyed? For example, do they know the age, occupation, or the economic status of the people surveyed? How does this affect the survey results?

4. What, according to Julio, are some of the disadvantages of multiple-choice surveys? Do you agree with his views? What concerns, if any, do you have about the multiple-choice tests that you have had to take?

5. Why do you think the men's and women's responses to questions 13 and 14 were so different? Would your own responses be different from those Julio received? Why?

6. Comment on Julio's last paragraph. Are his conclusions plausible? Did his survey results add to your knowledge in any way?

RETHINKING AND REVISING

The first people to view and comment on Julio's draft were his original group partners, Alberto and Hilda. They gave the draft a thorough reading together and found many aspects of Julio's first draft promising. First, the responses from the men and women were tallied quite effectively. Julio did not just attach numbers to the responses but gave the reader a general idea about how the majority of the men and women surveyed felt about the issues. And he offered a plausible analysis of the causes of the difference between the responses to the two open-ended questions and to the multiple-choice questions.

A problem area, however, was the lack of focus in Julio's essay. What exactly did Julio want to do with the information generated by the survey? Looking back on the discussion on the inductive method, Julio remembered that the purpose of gathering data was to arrive at some general conclusion. What was the general conclusion he was trying to arrive at in his essay? He was not sure, nor were his readers at this point.

Though Julio's comments on the nature of multiple-choice questions, in general, and his reactions in the concluding paragraph, in particular, were extremely insightful, his readers questioned their location. Were these comments a logical conclusion to the essay on gender roles in society and on television shows? Julio realized that, valid though his feelings were about multiple-choice surveys and questionnaires, they did not belong in the conclusion. He knew he had to work on revising the conclusion.

His group helped Julio see a few other items that he had overlooked. For example, the survey questions asked for both the sex and age of the people surveyed. Why was there no mention of age? Did age play any part on the nature of the responses? This was another area, Julio realized, that needed some thought. In addition to their age, could Julio add some information about the kind of people he surveyed in the food-processing factory? How many of them had a high school or college education? What about the people in the neighborhood? How much would the professional and educational status of the people surveyed influence the results? Answers to these might give the reader a more accurate picture. Following these suggestions, Julio went to work on the next draft.

CHECKLIST: REVISING YOUR DRAFT

- Do the answers to the survey questions tell me what the people think about the issues under discussion?
- Does my essay focus on the ideas generated by the survey?
- Do I use the survey data to arrive at some general conclusions about the topic?
- Have I prevented my own biases from interfering with the opinions gathered by the survey?
- Do I include my own opinions, feelings, or conclusions about the results of the survey?

PRESENTING JULIO'S FINAL DRAFT

Reversal of Gender Roles in Popular TV Shows

Julio Olivencia

Julio makes the new introduction less abrupt and adds necessary background information. He raises questions his essay will address—an effective way to arouse interest.

Julio describes the population for his survey, giving his essay and his report a credible content.

1   The involvement of women in every aspect of life has brought about many changes in the American way of life. Even in the 1950s life was very different from what it is today. Most households included two parents, with dad as the wage earner, and women stayed home to rear children. But all that has changed. The nuclear family has been replaced by single-parent households, often headed by working women. The high rate of divorce has also forced men to adopt roles traditionally ascribed to women. Popular media, TV in particular, have focused on these changes in the American family. How accurately have these changes been incorporated into the popular television shows? How do male and female viewers feel about TV's portrayal of gender roles or the reversal of the traditional gender roles? To find out, I surveyed 15 men and women from my neighborhood and at the food-processing plant where I work for their impressions of three popular TV programs, ''Who's the Boss,'' ''Three's Company,'' and ''The Brady Bunch.''

2   "Who's the Boss" is a departure from the traditional man/woman relationship. The female main character, Angela, is a successful, well-educated woman, perhaps in her late thirties, who owns an advertising agency. She is a lousy cook, with no time or desire for household work. This is where Tony comes into the picture. He is a handsome and charming young man, apparently younger than Angela, who is hired by her to cook, take care of her son, and clean the house. By far the majority of the men and women surveyed were not unhappy with the reversal of the gender roles. Nor did they feel the show discriminated against one sex since both Tony and Angela were generally satisfied with the situation. Though it is never made very explicit, underneath the employer/employee relationship are many suggestions of a romantic involvement between Angela and Tony in several of the episodes. Still a large number of the respondents did not find the personal relationship between Angela and Tony unethical or their work relationship unusual.

He moves from summary to reporting results of survey.

3   The three main characters in "Three's Company" are Jack, Chrissy, and Janet. Reversal of gender roles takes place at more than one level in this comedy. First, Jack, who is heterosexual, has to pretend to be homosexual in order to get the landlord's permission to share the apartment with Janet and Chrissy. Like Tony in "Who's the Boss," Jack is an excellent cook, and he works as a chef in a restaurant. The women have jobs outside the home and do not know much about cooking or housework. The viewers did not find these gender reversals offensive. What some women viewers did find offensive, however, was the stereotypical portrayal of Chrissy and Janet as the dumb blonde and the smart brunette, respectively. Many women also found Larry, the playboy who lives in the same building and treats women as objects of his pleasure, pretty obnoxious. Few men, on the other hand, had anything negative to say about Larry.

Julio provides second plot summary to create content.

He moves from summary to reporting results of survey.

4   The responses to the questions on "The Brady Bunch" were insufficient, perhaps because the people surveyed were not very familiar with it. Centered on a perfect American family, mother, father, six children, and a live-in housekeeper, the show has been off the air for quite some time, though there are reruns. To the question of how they felt about Mrs. Brady having a maid, most people thought it was an acceptable lifestyle at that time, especially because Mrs. Brady had six children. Most said she needed the help and was not a lazy woman.

5

Julio devotes two
paragraphs to
discussing
answers to the
two open-
ended questions
that required
brief written
responses. These
are important as
they help him to
set up his conclu-
sions beginning
with paragraph 7.

6

Questions 13 and 14 brought out quite humorous responses from the men. In "Who's the Boss," some men expressed dis-satisfaction with Tony as the housekeeper. But most showed almost a sense of relief that the situation in a television comedy was not likely to be repeated too often in real life. Some men also felt that Tony was really the boss because Angela was secretly in love with him, hence the ambiguous title. In "Three's Company," however, many men found it offensive that a heterosexual man was forced to be identified as a homosexual, yet most of these respondents answered "no" to question 8, which asked if they found the show offensive to homosexuals.

The women's responses to questions 13 and 14 were predict-ably different. Many were pleased that a successful busi-nesswoman hired a man as her housekeeper, but some also expressed their reservations about the nature of the rela-tionship, which is unlike most in the real world. Most women bosses, they felt, did not desire sexual involvement with their male subordinates. Some women also complained about the character of Angela's mother, who is like a meddling mother-in-law. The women surveyed expressed their concern about male and female roles not being clear-cut in "Who's the Boss," which added to the confusion. Most women did not find it offensive that Jack in "Three's Company" had to pretend to be gay to get an apartment. Many, on the other hand, objected to the stereotype of the dumb blonde, which was picked up by few males. Women, in general, found Jack and Larry's comments about women offensive.

7

Julio uses
his personal
observations
to set up his
conclusion.
Again he begins
with a question
to arouse his
reader's interest
and curiosity.

Why were the responses from men and women so similar in the multiple-choice part and so different in the brief-answer section? My guess is that people do not think too hard when they answer the yes/no questions, at least that has been my own experience in taking multiple-choice exams. The brief-answer questions required more concentrated thinking that brought out what the people really felt and not just quick reactions. Judging by the response to the multiple-choice questions, both women and men found the traditional and the reversal of the gender roles in the three comedies generally satisfying, with few exceptions. But given more time to think through their answers, the women had more to complain about these shows than men.

8

Julio begins his
own commentary

In addition to time constraints, there might have been other factors that influenced the responses. Age, for exam-ple, may have played a part. Most of the men and women surveyed and analysis of survey results instead of just reporting them.

9

Julio comments on the nature and reliability of his survey. This is a change from his first draft, which ends with a discussion of the differences between multiple-choice and open-ended questions.

were between the ages of 18 and 30, many of them students, and some who worked full time in the food-processing plant. None were college graduates yet or had a profession. Would an older professional group or a group that included gay men and women have given different answers? I am inclined to believe so.

While I was aware all the time that a survey of 30 men and women was not adequate to arrive at general truths, in the end I did arrive at some generalizations within the context of the people surveyed. I found out that my colleagues at school and at work were not outraged by the reversal of traditional male/female roles on some TV sit-coms. Both men and women might have felt negatively about certain aspects of male/female relationships as portrayed in these shows. But, in general, they accepted the role reversals, which might indicate that they would be willing to accept gender role reversals in their real lives. That, to me, is an improvement from the attitudes of thirty or forty years ago, though I am aware that whenever one deals with human responses, one is bound to run into trouble with regard to certainties. Still, the survey enabled me to sample opinions, limited as they might be, to reach some conclusions about the feelings of men and women with regard to gender roles in television.

Commentary on Julio's Final Draft

In contrast to the abrupt beginning of the first draft, the final draft provides some necessary background information. Television shows have changed from the 1950s to the 1990s to accommodate the changes in real life in the country. The gender roles portrayed on television also reflect these changes in recent years. To add the focus that the first draft lacked, Julio needed to state his purpose based on the results of a survey. In place of a declarative thesis or purpose statement in the first draft, Julio raises questions that the body of the essay attempts to answer. This is an effective way to introduce the reader to your writing, because questions arouse interest and curiosity that motivate the reader to probe further. In addition, it was difficult for Julio to come up with a strong thesis statement because there were no clear-cut answers to the survey questions. Therefore, questions allowed him the flexibility he needed to discuss the results of the survey with all their variables.

Alberto and Hilda's comments had made Julio see the flaws in his conclusion in the first draft. Yet he was convinced that his personal observations on the problems posed by multiple-choice questions were valid enough to be included in the essay, though perhaps not in the conclusion. In order to make the transition smoother, Julio posed another question toward the end of the essay with regard to the kinds of answers he received for the multiple-choice and short answer questions. Why were they so clearly different? The answer allowed Julio to comment on the effectiveness of the two kinds of questions used in his survey and bring the essay to a logical conclusions.

Because Julio felt that two short-answer questions brought out the people's true feelings about gender issues in real life and on television, he based his conclusions of the survey more on them than on the yes/no answers. Yet, through the probings of his group mates, he had become aware that there were several other variables that had to be considered before he could arrive at a broad generalization. The surveyed population did not include people of different ages, education, economic background, or sexual preference. He had neglected to mention this in the first draft. So he worked on the conclusion to make it clear that his survey results were far from the well-known Harris or Gallup polls that are more formal and include large numbers of people from diverse backgrounds. Still, though localized and limited, his conclusions based on the survey had credibility within a particular context.

Questions for Further Thought

1. So much of the survey paper depends on the survey itself. Would your survey questionnaire on a similar theme differ significantly from Julio's? What would you include that Julio's group did not, or what would you delete to make it more effective?

2. Julio has some strong opinions about open and closed questions. Is your opinion similar to Julio's or significantly different? What kinds of questions would you rather be asked and why?

3. Julio's survey was not able to come up with clear-cut answers to the questions about reversal of traditional gender roles. Did that disappoint you? How reliable are surveys? What are some conditions the reader of an essay should be aware of while trying to make meaning out of an essay's survey results?

4. Julio's introductory paragraph does not boldly state the purpose of the essay in the form of a thesis statement. Instead, he raises questions, answers to which are found in the essay. Comment on the efficacy of beginning with questions. Why is such a beginning particularly suitable for Julio's essay?

PROFESSIONAL ESSAYS

Elisabeth Bumiller

BEYOND THE VEIL:
THE WOMEN OF THE
VILLAGE OF KHAJURON

"The artificial situation I had constructed—an interview—was not the best way to learn the truth about rural women's lives. And yet it was a beginning."

THE TITLE OF THE BOOK BY ELISABETH Bumiller from which this segment has been excerpted is May You Be the Mother of a Hundred Sons. *Bestowed upon Hindu women at the time of marriage, these words are more a curse than a blessing and signify much that is wrong with the status of women in India. Ms. Bumiller traveled to a small village in northern India to talk to the women about their lives. Because most of these women were not literate, she interviewed them orally instead of handing out survey questions. Bumiller's study concurs with the fact that though Indian women have been glorified as goddesses, the reality of their lives seems to indicate otherwise. Though she is a professional writer, her account reveals the kinds of problem situations surveyors often run into, not unlike those encountered by the student writer in this section, Julio Olivencia.*

Elisabeth Bumiller was born in Aalborg, Denmark, in 1956, and grew up in Cincinnati. Since 1979, she has worked for The Washington Post *in Washington, D.C., New Delhi, and Tokyo.*

ON THE WAY INTO THE READING

1. Think about the title of the book, *May You Be the Mother of a Hundred Sons,* and the chapter title, "Beyond the Veil." What do they say about the culture Bumiller is writing about? What are the similarities and differences between this culture and the culture in which you grew up?

2. Surveys, even informal ones (as Julio Olivencia's situation illustrates), may be quite complicated and often frustrating even when conducted among people whose cultural values are familiar to the surveyor. What difficulties would you anticipate if you had to conduct a survey among people whose culture was very different from yours? How would you deal with those situations?

3. Almost every illiterate woman Bumiller spoke with said she would have liked an education. How do you think education empowers people? Why do women in particular need to be educated? What thoughts on the education of women in the United States can you bring to this essay?

1 The physical plan of the village was an indication of the complex social structure that lay underneath. The most powerful landlord, a mild-mannered college-educated Kshatriya farmer named Shardul Singh, lived in a large brick house on the highest spot in the village; around him were clustered tiny communities of houses belonging to the different castes and subcastes. There are four main castes in India, the highest being the Brahmins, who were traditionally teachers and priests. Next are the Kshatriyas, the warriors. Below them are the Vaisyas, who were traders and merchants, and after them come the Sudras, the farmers. The Harijans have no caste at all—hence they are considered outcastes. For thousands of years they were called Untouchables, but during the independence struggle Mahatma Gandhi gave them the name Harijans—"Children of God"—which paved the way for reform, including affirmative action quotas for Harijans and other low castes in jobs and education. Harijans, however, are still among the most impoverished and degraded people in India.

2 Within each caste are hundreds of subcastes, which change from region to region, and, like the main castes, were originally connected with specific professions. The Indian Constitution did not abolish caste, but it did outlaw discrimination on the basis of caste. In the cities, caste is to some extent disappearing, and people generally do not have to make their livings according to the accident of birth. But in the villages, caste was as insidious as ever and in large part predetermined the course of a person's life. The education of the younger generation was only slowly changing things.

3 The subcaste of mustard-oil makers in Khajuron, for example, lived together in their own little grouping of mud huts and still, for the most part, made oil from mustard seeds. The clay-pot makers still made clay pots and lived in a little community near one of the village hand pumps. The Kurmis, or large farmers, lived in relatively sizable houses not far from Shardul Singh's gates; most of them still worked the land for a living, although some of their sons had found jobs in Lucknow. The Pasis, who traditionally had been pig tenders, were farmers, too, although with smaller holdings. They were one group whose occupation had changed, yet their former calling would forever classify them as Harijans. This had not prevented them, however, from creating castes within their outcaste. Those Pasis who had been born in Khajuron—the old families—lived in the heart of the Harijan section, called Pasitolla; those who had arrived only in the last few decades lived on the outskirts of he village, closer to the dirt road. The two Pasi groups did not mix much and even supported different candidates in the election for village pradhan.

4 Steve and I arrived in Khajuron to begin our work in September 1987, four months after I first met Dr. Singh. (A year later, even after sharing a shed with him, and putting our charpoys side by side under the stars, we never called him anything but Dr. Singh. We were always "Mrs. Elisabeth" and "Mr. Steve.") Dr. Singh and three of his daughters stayed with us at the home of his brother, who turned out to be the second-largest landowner in the village. Without our ever requesting it, the entire Singh family had

become involved in our project. There were, I think, several reasons for this. Most of all, Dr. Singh wanted to make absolutely certain that his American guests were comfortable and stayed out of trouble. But I also think our research interested him and gave him a fresh glimpse of his roots.

5   Unfortunately, staying with the Singhs aligned us with the upper-caste landlords in the eyes of the rest of the villagers, and in the beginning I had trouble talking with some of the Harijan women because of our living arrangements. Rameshwar Prasad, the Harijan leader and, I later learned, a blood enemy of the landlords, actually went so far as to report Steve and me to the local police as possible American spies. It is difficult to know what the CIA might have learned in Khajuron, and, needless to say, nothing ever came of Prasad's harassment. Yet I fretted about our decision to live with the village landlords, even though I never figured out an alternative. Living with the Harijans would simply have aligned me with them, against the landlords, whose good graces I needed to remain in the village. Beyond that, it was unrealistic to think of living with anyone but a family that had space for us and could afford to feed us. Eventually it worked out. In the end, I was able to talk with plenty of Harijan women, I made peace with Prasad, and Bhabhiji and her husband could not have been more generous hosts.

6   Their house was one of the largest in Khajuron, built so that all family activity occurred in the central courtyard open to the sky. Once a week, the mud floor was smoothed with fresh greenish-brown cow dung, believed to be a disinfectant. In the hot weather, Bhabhiji and her husband slept in their charpoys in the courtyard; in the cold weather, they slept in one of the enclosed storage rooms off this courtyard, which contained five-foot-tall mud urns that held wheat and rice. Bhabhiji's mud stove, or chulha, was built into the floor of the courtyard in a protected corner. There was no electricity, and at night we ate by the light of an oil lamp.

7   In the mornings after breakfast (fried Indian bread and potatoes for Dr. Singh; omelettes and white bread for us, because that is the sort of breakfast Americans were supposed to eat), Steve would leave with Dr. Singh for Gurha. I would go with one, two or three of Dr. Singh's five daughters—different ones came along on each trip—to begin my interviews in Khajuron. My Hindi was passable for Bhabhiji's house, but the lower castes spoke a local dialect and could scarcely understand me. I had an easier time understanding them, but I still needed Dr. Singh's daughters to translate. I selected the women by caste, so that I would have a representative sampling. I would arrive at a woman's house, tell her I was writing a book about women in India and ask if she would answer a few questions for me. The "few questions" claim was not exactly accurate, but I needed to get my foot in the door. The truth was that I had prepared a somewhat nightmarish list of 193 questions with my Hindi teacher in Delhi, covering work, education, living conditions, family relationships, health, education, religion, politics, popular culture and knowledge of the world outside Khajuron and India. Only rarely had I written out questions for interviews before, but then, I had

never tried to interview so many uneducated women, in a foreign language, and in depth.

8 Every single interview was excruciatingly slow and difficult. Many lasted for two hours, the limit of my patience, and considerably beyond the limits of patience of many of the women. Although a few were amazed that someone was actually interested in their opinions, and appeared ready to talk all day, most were shy and nervous. Many times a woman had to breast-feed her baby and peel potatoes while she was talking to me. Sometimes her husband would try to speak for her, although I usually asked the husbands to leave. Other times friends would wander in and offer their opinions, or a swarm of kids would stand around giggling. They called me "the Ameriki poochnee wallee," which means "the American question-asking woman." The weather was usually suffocatingly hot, and flies buzzed incessantly around my head.

9 At times I lost heart and decided the questionnaire was a bad idea and was not getting me anywhere. I knew a lot of the answers were made up, and that the artificial situation I had constructed—an interview—was not the best way to learn the truth about rural women's lives. And yet it was a beginning, a way of getting to know them. The interviews allowed me to sit in their houses for hours. I watched them knead the chapati dough, saw how they massaged their babies with mustard oil and listened to them fight with their mothers-in-law. The women were poor, but this did not mean they all had inhibited personalities. When I asked the village pradhan's daughter-in-law, Santosh Kumari, if she had any say in her arranged marriage, she laughed and gestured toward the mud floor and crumbling brick walls of her home. "If they had asked me, I wouldn't have come to this house," she said. "I would have gone to a much better place." When I asked if her mother-in-law treated her well, she laughed again. "If my mother-in-law is bad," she said, "will you bring me a nice one?"

10 People I knew in rural development had advised me to be as specific as possible in my questions. I would get nowhere, they said, dealing in abstract concepts like fairness and equality. So I devised my questions as simple building blocks on basic themes. For example: "What is your education?" "Would you like to know how to read and write?" "Why did you not go to school?" "Do your children go to school?" "Who is it more important to educate—your son or your daughter?" Invariably, the sons were sent to school and the daughters stayed at home.

11 I also asked the women to tell me precisely how they had spent the day before, from the moment they got up to the time they went to bed. The minutiae always led me to the same onclusion: the women worked harder than the men. Phula, for example, was forty years old, a mother of four, the wife of a prosperous Pasi farmer who had lived in Khajuron all his life. He grew sugarcane, potatoes, rice, coriander and wheat. During the harvest, he employed up to fifteen people a day, and he made close to $1,000 each year. In the government census, a man like Phula's husband would be listed as

the head of household, which he was, but a wife like Phula would be considered a nonworking dependent. And yet consider what she did all day: "Yesterday I got up at five in the morning," she told me as we sat in a dark, cramped room off her central courtyard. After rising, Phula walked half an hour into the fields, because the family had no latrine, then half an hour back. When she returned, she cleaned the pots used for the meal the night before. Soap was a luxury, so she used mud and water, scraping with her bare hands. She swept the floor of the house, squatting over a short-handled broom, then walked back to the fields to collect tall grasses for her cows to eat. This took several hours because she had to remove all the thorns. She fed the animals, then went into the house to make lunch for herself and her husband—the lentil stew called dal, and chapaties and rice. She rested during the heat of the afternoon, then got up to wash the pots before dinner. A dozen times during the day she had to fetch water from the well outside her house; she also had to make cow-dung cakes for fuel. And this was a leisurely time of year. In a few weeks, when the wheat was ready for harvesting, she would have to spend most of her time in the fields, managing her household chores in between. She felt her husband treated her well, although he was, after all, entitled to certain rights as the head of the family. "Sometimes he beats me if I make a mistake, or if I forget to give fodder to the animals," she said matter-of-factly. Phula had been married at seven and had begun living with her husband at fourteen. She had never learned to read and write because her parents had not sent her to school. "If I had been educated," she said, "I would have done some work." By "work" she meant paid work; she did not take into account the hard physical labor that she did all day.

12   Of the twenty-five women I interviewed, nineteen had never been to school. The other six had at least a grade-school education; three of them were Brahmins, and three were from prosperous middle-caste farming families. Almost all of the men had more education, however rudimentary, than the women, which meant they could at least read the local Hindi newspapers and participate in discussions about politics and other issues affecting their lives. It was almost always the men who went shopping, either by foot or bicycle, at the wooden stalls that lined the main road through Gurha, and so it was the men who dealt quite literally in the ideas of the marketplace. Even the lower-caste women who ignored purdah rarely went to the market. When I asked why, they usually said they did not want to go, either because it was too far, or because they did not like the way the men treated them. Whatever the reason, it further isolated the women from society, and from each other.

13   Almost every illiterate woman I spoke to said she would have liked an education, and when I took that a step further and asked each woman what she thought an education might have done for her, a large number firmly believed that schooling would have pulled them out of the village and saved them from a life of drudgery. "If I had been educated, I would be a big person and I would not be doing all of this," said Sada Vati, the forty-year-

old wife of a middle-caste farmer. I asked her what a "big person's" job would be. "Service," she replied, which was the village description for work in government service in an office in a town or city, perhaps even Lucknow, typically as a low-level clerk behind a desk with a salary guaranteed for life. In the village, any work that did not involve hard physical labor was considered almost glamorous. "I want to sit on a chair and do work," said Rajban, a tailor and the mother of five. It was naïve, of course, for the women to think education would have guaranteed them a job. One of India's biggest problems was its millions of young men with high school and college educations who could not find work.

14   The one encouraging sign was that the women of Khajuron were beginning to send their daughters to school, however sporadically. There were ninety-three boys and eighty-eight girls registered at the village's two-room schoolhouse. "At first, girls were not educated," Cheta Lal, the headmaster, told me. "But now they are coming a little more." That was just grade school, however; 80 percent of the boys went on to the high school in Gurha, but only 20 percent of the girls did. And although almost every woman I spoke to said it was important to educate sons and daughters equally—I am sure they said this because they thought it was what I wanted to hear—the reality, when I pressed, was that the boys were sent to school more often than the girls. It was practical economics in a country with no social security system. When money was scarce in a family, it made more sense to educate the boy, who would remain with his parents and support them in their old age. A girl was a wasted investment because she would leave her parents after her marriage and live at her in-laws' house. As Sada Vati, the farmer's wife who wanted to do "service," explained about her son and daughter: "The boy will live here, but my girl will go." Sada Vati had complained about her lack of education, and yet she was not sending her seven-year-old daughter to school, just as her mother had not sent her.

15   One of the more serious problems of the women in the village was their lack of access to adequate medical care. Although there was a government-trained midwife assigned to the village, she lived in Gurha and was so overburdened with her work there and in one other village that she rarely got to Khajuron. Only a third of the women I interviewed used her, even though her services were free. Most of them went to a Dr. Kamlesh in Gurha, who charged more than one dollar—two days' wages for field work—per visit. On his wall he displayed a photograph of himself standing next to a cadaver in medical school. Those seriously ill had to go all the way to Bachharawan, or even Lucknow. Most women delivered their babies on the floors of their huts, and at least half had lost one or more children during childbirth or in the first few years of the baby's life. Three women I interviewed admitted they were trying to limit the size of their families, but two of them were doing it by only now and then taking birth control pills. The other woman, a Brahmin, had been given an IUD by a doctor in Bachharawan after the birth of her fifth child. The average number of living children per family appeared to be three or four, but Sheela, the

thirty-year-old wife of the village silversmith, had eight. She was more than ready to stop, but her husband refused to allow her to have a government-funded sterilization operation. "There is no need," he insisted. Sheela, who was sitting on a nearby charpoy, just shrugged. "He is afraid it will make me weak," she said.

16   Not surprisingly, the women knew almost nothing about the village council, or panchayat, although they generally voted in elections, following their husbands' instructions. Seven claimed never to have heard of the panchayat. Of those who had, about half said it did some good. The rest complained. "There is no justice," said Rama Devi, a Harijan woman who served as one of the village midwives. "Only the rich people are given the facilities and we are not." Although the Uttar Pradesh state government had reserved places on every panchayat for women, the provision was widely ignored. As elsewhere, no woman served in Khajuron, and no women went to the meetings. But the women were clearly aware of where the real power lay in the village. When I asked who was the most powerful person in Khajuron, only one said it was Shri Ram Choudhary, the incumbent pradhan. Almost everyone else said it was Shardul Singh, the largest landlord. When I asked why, the answer was simple. "He has the most money and the most land," said Vidhya Devi, a thirty-five-year-old field laborer.

17   A number of women had never heard of Rajiv Gandhi, and of those who had, there was some confusion about who he was. Most identified him not as prime minister but as Indira Gandhi's son, and most were unable to say whether he was good or bad. Indira Gandhi, however, was widely viewed as good. "She helped the poor people," several women told me. Some clearly identified with her as a woman and said that being a woman helped her become a good leader.

18   At the end of each interview, I asked each woman what her biggest problem was. The answers included not having enough money, worries about marrying off a daughter, needing a better house and fears about a husband's illness. Many women complained that the water from the wells and hand pumps was brackish, which it was, and that they did not have enough land. Only one woman owned land in her own name. The rest did not even own it jointly with their husbands. The pradhan's daughter-in-law complained that she did not have enough nice saris. Susheela Bajpai, the Brahmin landowner's wife, wanted better schools for her children. Sudevi, the widow, said she did not have enough money. But by far the most obvious, pressing problem, more than education and medical care, was lack of paid work. The women had no way to earn a living, no skills, no training. At the most, they could find field work only six months of the year. Every single woman I interviewed wanted to be taught a skill, but there was no factory near Khajuron, and no accessible market for goods she might produce in her home.

19   I also asked each woman this question: "If you could be anyone in the world you wanted, or have any job that you wanted, what would it be?" This stumped everyone—it was one of those abstractions I had been advised to

avoid—but I was curious, and the answers were revealing. The immediate response of almost every woman was, "But I am not educated, so I cannot do anything." Then I would say, "No, imagine"—and "imagine" was the difficult word—"that anything is possible. What would you be?" It was nearly impossible for the women to make that leap. Finally, after prompting, a woman usually said she would like to be a teacher. It was one job they knew about. Teachers were usually Brahmins, and respected. Susheela Bajpai, the Brahmin landowner's wife, wanted to be a teacher, and so did Sudevi. Three women wanted to be doctors, and two wanted to do sewing at home. My favorite answer came from Phula, the prosperous Pasi farmer's wife. She wanted to be the village pradhan, which I took as a sign of great progress.

20   I often went back to the women who had been the most receptive to me and talked about other things. Susheela, the Brahmin landowner's wife, always liked to hear the news from Delhi and insisted I sit with her and have tea. Unlike the others, Susheela could talk to me about Indian film stars because she saw three or four movies a year during her trips to Lucknow. Sudevi, the widow, had never seen a movie in her life. When I went to see Sudevi again during Holi, the spring harvest festival in early March, she was in the middle of her hut, up to her knees in mud, at last repairing the crumbling wall of her house. The more exciting news was that her daughter-in-law had given birth to a little boy, who was now four months old. Amazingly, he looked plump and healthy. I asked Sudevi and her daughter-in-law to come outside with the baby, and I took a picture of all three of them in the afternoon light. I promised I would bring them a copy on my next trip.

21   At the end of each day in the village, just as it was getting dark, I would walk back to Bhabhiji's house, completely exhausted. Bhabhiji always gave me a cup of her sweet, milky tea and invited me to relax on the charpoy near her mud stove. So much smoke came out of it that I found it difficult to breathe—I suppose Bhabhiji, in all her years of cooking, had somehow become used to it—but I would sit there anyway, watching as she chopped onions for dinner on a small wooden board on the floor. As the guest, I was never allowed to help, but Bhabhiji was always interested to hear about my day. So I told her, and related just a little of what the women had said. I think she found my compilation of the obvious details of the women's lives quite odd; she must have wondered what possible use it was for me to know that Phula had spent several hours collecting fodder for her cows that morning. I imagined reversing the situation: Bhabhiji's daughter (her only child, who was married and living in another village) turning up at my mother's house in Cincinnati and interviewing my mother's friends about how long it took each of them to drive to the supermarket.

22   As Bhabhiji and I talked, her husband was outside supervising either the slaughter of the chickens or the plucking of the waterfowl that had been shot in a nearby marshland that afternoon. I never learned what kind of birds they were. Every time I asked, I was told they were "local birds," and

from what I could see, they looked to be about the size of pigeons. Bhabhiji's husband brought them in, their bright red flesh all cut up, and Bhabhiji put them in a brass pot of onions, mustard oil and spices simmering on the stove. The spices—cinnamon, coriander, red chilies, bay leaf, cloves and cardamom—had been ground by one of her servants that afternoon. Because she was the wife of Khajuron's second-largest landowner, Bhabhiji had two or three servants who turned up a few hours each day to help her wash clothes, clean pots and, in this case, grind spices by crushing them with a cylinder-shaped stone used like a rolling pin over a flat slab of rock. It was miserable work, and Bhabhiji rarely did it herself. She made certain, however, to select the combination of spices for each meal herself.

23   While Bhabhiji cooked, the men gathered under the neem tree for the evening's conversation. Steve and Dr. Singh were usually back by this time, exhausted, too. Dr. Singh would go into the house to get a cup of tea from his sister-in-law, and Steve and I would go into the shed to compare notes on the day. Often we were overcome with frustration. "This is the hardest thing I've ever done," Steve said every evening. He was collecting, at what seemed to him a glacial pace, material for what eventually became a five-part series on caste, village politics, family planning, religion and the pressures of change in Gurha. I usually complained that I had just spent six hours in three interviews and had uncovered nothing more startling than the fact that my subjects had all eaten chapaties for lunch. On other days, Steve and I could only marvel at the elliptical evasions of the villagers. In one typical exchange, a man told Steve and Dr. Singh that he had no wife and children, but then excused himself a short time later because he said his wife and children were waiting for him at home. Steve pointed out the discrepancy in English to Dr. Singh, "Yes, first he was saying one thing," Dr. Singh said diplomatically," and now he is saying this thing." That ended the discussion. Dr. Singh was above all an eternally polite man, who in any case had learned that there were some things in villages that took much effort to understand.

24   By twilight the men had built the fire under the neem tree. It was by far the most pleasant time of day. Sometimes, when we sat around the fire, Dr. Singh would tell us a little about his childhood growing up in the village, including the story, my favorite, about the monkey that kidnapped him. When he first told us, we laughed, but Dr. Singh swore it was true. When he was a baby, he said, a female monkey had grabbed him from the house and escaped all the way up to the top of the neem tree with him in her arms. The family was beside itself. "They called to the monkey but she would not come down," Dr. Singh said. "Fruits and allurements were given, but still she remained in the tree." Finally, after some time, the monkey relinquished the baby, returning him safe and sound on her own. "Yes," said Dr. Singh, pleased and amused, "she loved me." On other nights, the village pradhan from Gurha turned up, full of questions about the United States. "Are widows allowed to remarry in your country?" he once wanted to know. "Do villages in America have electricity? Do the rich people exploit the

poor?" Dr. Singh had some questions of his own. "In America," he asked, "if a person is a cobbler,"—cobblers in India were Harijans—"and he makes a lot of money, is he respected, despite his profession?"

25   If the conversation lagged, or bogged down too heavily in Gurha politics, I would go into the house to see how Bhabhiji was doing with dinner. One of Dr. Singh's daughters was always helping her, usually by rolling out the chapati dough. About nine or ten, we were called in to eat. Dr. Singh, Steve and I sat cross-legged on a grass mat in the middle of the courtyard while Bhabhiji and Sheo Singh served us bird, chicken or goat in little bowls. There were steaming chapaties to scoop up the sauce, and rice on the side. It was hot, spicy and utterly delicious.

CRITICAL READING

1. Describe Bumiller's methods of collecting data. What does she mean by "The 'few questions' claim was not exactly accurate, but I needed to get my foot in the door?" Why did she have to use this ploy? Do you disapprove? What might you be required to do in administering surveys to get a foot in the door?

2. How many women did Bumiller interview? Was the number adequate? How did the composition of this group differ from the group of people surveyed by Julio Olivencia for his paper?

3. Why did she feel at times that the questionnaire was a bad idea? Have you had to face similar disheartening situations while gathering information? How did you overcome them?

4. Why was Bumiller advised not to use abstract concepts like fairness and equality in her survey questionnaire? Comment on the kinds of problems they would pose for any audience, not just the uneducated village women in India.

5. Analyze and comment on the life of the woman, Phula, described in paragraph 11. What light does it throw on the social and economic status of women in India? What were some of the major problems in their lives? List some of the inequities between the lives of men and women in the village? Why were sons more desirable than daughters?

6. "Imagine," says Bumiller in paragraph 19, was a difficult word for the women. Why did they find it difficult to imagine situations other than their current lives? Do you find it difficult to imagine life other than your own? Think of what some of your own impressions and responses would be if you were to find yourself in the same village that Bumiller writes about.

7. In paragraph 24, the villagers ask Bumiller some questions about the United States. How would you answer similar questions about the United States by a person unfamiliar with this country? Imagine a dialogue between yourself and someone who wants to learn about your country and culture.

Andrew N. Rowan

ANIMALS IN EDUCATION

"Animals are sentient beings and we have a duty to portray them as something other than disposable biological tools."

ANDREW N. ROWAN HAS BEEN ASSOCIATED with the Institute for the Study of Animal Problems in Washington, D.C., and Tufts School of Veterinary Medicine. He is the author of Mice, Models, and Men: A Critical Evaluation of Animal Research *and has coedited* The Use of Alternatives in Drug Research. *Animal rights advocates often focus their attention on the use of animals in research laboratories. In this article, Andrew N. Rowan points to the abuse of animals in education, particularly in teaching biology. Rowan's survey, conducted in a controlled situation with professional people, is quite different from the relatively unstructured situations in Julio Olivencia's and Elisabeth Bumiller's surveys.*

ON THE WAY INTO THE READING

1. Writings based on sampled opinions require topics that are somewhat controversial and elicit strong responses, emotional or intellectual. Examine the topics in the three writings based on surveys in this section. Do you think they are debatable? Can you think of other topics that would work well for surveys and some that would not?

2. For the survey results to be credible, the population sampled must also have credibility. What, according to you, is the ideal survey population? As you read this essay, think of the people surveyed. How do they compare with the people in the other surveys in this section? Is any one ideal? Why or why not? How credible are they?

3. What part does morality play in the way humans treat animals? Do people act immorally when they conduct experiments involving animals? Is experimenting with animals essential for scientific research? What are your thoughts on this issue?

1   A number of different views of the moral status of animals exist in today's society; some have been entrenched for many years. Two of the most widely held views are the humanitarian—humans should treat animals kindly and with consideration and should not be cruel; and the dominionistic—humans have been given dominion over other animals and we may do what we want with them provided that the consequences are not unfavorable to human beings (Kellert 1980). However, these attitudes are being called into question with increasing frequency.

2   The current resurgence of interest in animal "rights" (Singer 1975; Regan and Singer 1976; Clark 1977; Frey 1980) has resulted in much greater attention being paid to the distinction between warranted and unwarranted exploitation of animals as opposed to the simpler and more emotive concepts of kindness and cruelty (Fox and Rowan 1980). While it is important to foster behavior favoring kindness and discouraging cruelty, these concepts are not particularly useful in helping to resolve conflicts between human and animal interests, such as the use of animals in biomedical research and education. For example, we are not being kind to a frog when we pith it for a classroom demonstration, but are we being cruel? For a small but vocal minority, the answer in an unequivocal "yes." For the majority, the answer is not so clear-cut, and this is where the concept of justified and unjustified exploitation is more useful in making social cost-benefit decisions. Education plays an important role in developing social consensus on such value-laden issues (Hoskins 1979; Kieffer 1979); but, to date, most educational efforts present very limited concepts of human/animal interactions. Animals are illustrated in their role in nature, or as anthropomorphized beings that behave and act very much like humans, or as useful didactic tools, especially in interactive situations between student and animal. Live animal studies are popular with teachers and students because the animal's immediate reaction to a stimulus provides positive reinforcement of learning and serves to stimulate interest and hold attention. However, maintenance of the animals in the classroom is not so welcome a past time and neglect, particularly over holiday periods, can be a problem.

3   There is a difference between the study of animals in humane education curricula in elementary grades and the use of animals in biology classes. In humane education classes, the animals are used to develop positive feelings and a humanitarian ethic (be kind, do not be cruel) towards our fellow creatures. In the biology classroom, the animal is perceived as a model of living processes and the prevailing attitude is that one should maintain a distance from the object of study so that emotions and sentiment do not interfere with accurate observation and the collection of data. Unfortunately, it is all too easy for the student to confuse scientific and humane purposes. Some students perceive the mere manipulation of an animal as "scientific" and the presence of an ethical concern for the animal's fate as emotional, unscientific, and, hence, undesirable.

4   Because many students become preoccupied with the mechanical elements of animal experimentation—rather than developing the self-critical and intuitive skills that are the basis of top-flight research—animal welfare advocates have raised questions about the use of vertebrates in school projects that do (or could) involve pain and/or distress. In contrast, the supporters of animal research point to the need to motivate, encourage, and nurture students who show an interest in animal research so that they will pursue biomedical careers. Unfortunately, many of the arguments for or against the use of vertebrates in such projects are anecdotal and scattered.

Well-designed studies to determine the truth or falsity of these assertions are few and far between. In an attempt to clarify the issues and, perhaps elucidate a few answers, a conference was organized on the use of vertebrates in secondary school and science fairs by the Institute for the Study of Animal Problems in connection with the Myrin Institute (McGiffin and Brownley 1980).

5   There were approximately forty invited participants, representing all viewpoints and including teachers, education researchers, biomedical scientists, science education administrators, and animal welfare advocates. In spite of the range of viewpoints and professions, the conference reached a relatively broad consensus when all present agreed that the study of live animals is an essential feature of biology education. This was perhaps best expressed by Mayer (1980) when he stated that he believed "in using animals to inculcate the kind of affective objectives that will stand the students in good stead, not only in the classroom, but what is more important outside the classroom as well. Only then will they come to develop that respect for all living things we must have if our current environment is to remain unscathed for future generations to possess and enjoy."

6   Another speaker stressed that animal studies involving hands-on experience provided a quality of perception that could not be obtained by other teaching methods but stressed that little evidence exists to demonstrate that this qualitative experience is necessary to develop biological literacy (Kelly 1980). Because few high school students will go on to further biological studies, the school biology curriculum should aim more at providing the general populace with an understanding of and respect for living things than the development of such inert knowledge as techniques for dissecting rats or frogs. In fact, it is important that students are taught not only biological concepts, but also the place animals play in human psychological and cultural experiences. For example, the cultivation of empathy for animals does not simply mean describing what an animal does, one must also be able to predict what it might do in given circumstances (Kelly 1980). This requires a perspective on the animal that combines realism with respect and that is neither cold-bloodedly scientific nor overly emotional.

7   The participants seemed to agree in general terms with much of the argument relating to the objectives of biology education and the place of live animals within those objectives, though pleas were made for in-service training in animal care for biology teachers. The major disagreements came in the last part of the conference in the discussion on science fairs and extra-curricular biology projects. Those involved in the organization and operation of the International Science and Engineering Fair (ISEF) program strongly supported the right of accomplished students to explore more sophisticated techniques in animal research. On the other side, many of the participants argued that high school students too rarely understood what they were doing to be allowed to conduct unsupervised research projects on animals. In fact, it was the question of supervision that was central to the

whole debate because the ISEF program relies so heavily on adult supervisors. Unfortunately, several of the participants with extensive experience in biology education and science fairs disagreed strongly with the ISEF organizers that the quality of adult supervision was adequate or that supervision safeguards against abuse (Mayer 1980; Rowsell 1980). For example, Mayer commented that a good deal of "animal experimentation is not only beyond the skill of the student but frequently beyond the skill of the teacher. It ends up teaching no lesson except that animals suffer and die in inexperienced hands."

8   Several attempts were made to reach a compromise position regarding projects for science fairs that involved significant manipulation of the animal or its environment. However, the suggestion that such research projects should only be conducted in registered research facilities under the direct supervision of a trained biomedical research scientist did not find favor with the ISEF organizers. They believed this would discriminate against students who were not close to, and hence unable to use, such facilities. However, recent developments in the National Association of Biology Teachers may well render such debate academic. The Executive Board of the NABT adopted a policy that included an admonition that students doing projects with vertebrate animals should not undertake experimental procedures that would subject animals to pain or discomfort or interfere with their health in any way (NABT 1980). The National Science Teachers Association has also adopted a new code of practice on live animals that includes similar wording. If these codes are widely publicized and strictly enforced, the Dr. Kildare syndrome should disappear from the biology classroom.

9   However, a number of pressing problems remain that the conference could not address. For example, there is a need for research on the development of student attitudes and the extent to which, and manner in which, animal studies affect such attitudes. Perhaps the most pressing need at this point, is for teachers and educational organizations to recognize that animals are sentient beings and that we have a duty to portray them as something other than disposable biological tools, especially when they are being used in the biology classroom.

REFERENCES*

Clark, S. R. L. 1977. *The moral status of animals.* Oxford: Oxford University Press.
Fox, M. W., and Rowan, A. N. 1980. A background to the journal and delineation of its scope and goals. *International Journal for the Study of Animal Problems* 1(1):2.

---

* This essay uses the author–date system for documentation recommended by the University of Chicago. It is very similar to the APA author–year system. The differences are that Chicago–style parenthetical references do not have a comma between the author and date. For works with more than one author, "and" takes the place of the ampersand. In the reference list, Chicago does not require parentheses around the date of publication. Also, the volume and issue number are separated from the page reference by a colon rather than a comma.

Frey, R. G. 1980. *Interests and rights: The case against animals.* Oxford: Clarendon Press.

Hoskins, B. B. 1979. Sensitizing introductory biology students to bioethics issues. *American Biology Teacher* 41(3):151.

Kelly, P. J. 1980. Understanding and attitudes derived from the use of animals in schools. In McGiffin, H. L., and Brownley, N. L., *Animals in education.*

Kieffer, G. H. 1979. Can bioethics be taught? *American Biology Teacher* 41(3):176.

McGiffin, H. L. and Brownley, N. L. 1980. *Animals in education: The use of animals in high school biology classes and science fairs.* Washington, D.C.: Institute for the Study of Animal Problems.

Mayer, W. V. 1980. Objectives of animal use in biology classes. In McGiffin, H. L., and Brownley, N. L. *Animals in education.*

National Association of Biology Teachers. 1980. NABT guidelines for the use of live animals at the pre-university level. *American Biology Teacher* 41(7):426.

Regan, T. and Singer, P. (eds.) 1976. *Animal rights and human obligations.* Englewood Cliffs, New Jersey: Prentice-Hall.

Rowsell, H. C. 1980. High school science fairs: Evaluation of live animal experimentation—the Canadian experience. In McGiffin, H. L., and Brownley, N. L., *Animals in education.*

Singer, P. 1975. *Animal liberation.* New York: New York Review.

CRITICAL READING

1. Point to the sentence that states the purpose of this essay. Does the sampling of opinions help the author achieve the stated goal of the essay? What supportive evidence does he offer?

2. Examine the structure of the essay. How is Rowan's method of reporting opinions similar to or different from those used by Julio Olivencia and Elisabeth Bumiller?

3. Animal advocates question methods of laboratory testing that cause pain to the animals while the supporters of animal research point to its necessity in biomedical research. What does Rowan mean when he says that the opinions for and against this issue are "anecdotal and scattered?" In what ways would anecdotal and scattered information affect the conclusions?

4. Paragraph 5 introduces the opinions gathered to find some answers to issues for and against animal research. Comment on the number of participants and the diversity of the group. How does this group compare with the people surveyed by Julio Olivencia and Elisabeth Bumiller? How would the conclusions of this group differ from theirs in terms of reliability?

5. List the positions of the people expressing views for and against animal research. Where do you stand in the controversy?

6. Dr. Kildare was a humane young doctor in a television show in the 1960s called "Dr. Kildare." What does Rowan mean by the "Dr. Kildare syndrome" in paragraph 8?

7. Are there other issues relating to use of animals in classrooms and laboratories that you would have liked to see discussed in this article? What are they? What are your sources of information?

8. To find out how your classmates feel about use of animals in classrooms and labs, design a questionnaire following the instructions in this chapter. Write up the results and discuss them with the participants.

MAKING AN ARGUMENT

In the midst of a heated exchange, two parents are surprised by their young child. "Why are you arguing?" the child asks. "This isn't an argument," one of the parents is quick to say. "We're just having a discussion."

The very notion of argument can make us uneasy. It suggests anger and disputation. But associations with other words—words like *rational, logical, well-reasoned, persuasive*—make us realize that an argument is not necessarily the same thing as a dispute: it is also a time-honored way of resolving a dispute with the powers of reason and persuasion.

What an argument is above all, at least in this context, is a special kind of claim on your reader's attention. If what you are offering is essentially some form of information or explanation, you are adding to your reader's store of knowledge, and you can presume your reader will be predisposed to hear you out. But when you attempt to convince or persuade your reader of something, when you're offering not just food for thought but an invitation to accept your own way of thinking on an issue, the stakes go up, and so do the rhetorical challenges.

Yet we want to take stands, make claims, argue. Looking at the way things are around us, we inevitably find ourselves thinking (and often speaking and writing) about the way things should be. The challenges are real—after all, making an argument means holding the quality of our thinking up to scrutiny—but so are the rewards. Rational argument is our chief way of winning allies and converts to our way of thinking. Changing minds is our chief way of making changes in the world around us.

The featured argument in this chapter, by Melissa Schmeelk, is about why more students should participate in extracurricular activities. Not a burning issue for you, perhaps, it was nevertheless one of special importance to her. A mother as well as a student, Melissa saw participation in extracurricular activities as a once-cherished opportunity she had lost, an opportunity students all around her simply dismissed. With that sense of loss as her impetus, Melissa fleshed out her reasons by means of item analysis (or the journalistic questions) and tested her success by self-assessment. Like the professional pieces at the end of the chapter—Caroline Bird's "Where College Fails Us" and Robert Pattison's "The New Literacy"—Melissa's argument demonstrates that arguing is not so much a particular stance or method as an especially intent and conscientious way of discussing an issue. Because, ideally, that discussion sways the reader, everything from the choice of words to the choice of evidence is vital. In revision, Melissa found herself reconsidering such things as her use of pronouns and her mode of organization from her audience's perspective; she ultimately found the changes she made for her reader's sake crucial to her success.

WRITING ASSIGNMENT

Take a stand on an issue that has immediate bearing on you and your classmates—and have those classmates in mind as the audience for the argument you write. Compose an argumentative essay that is logical, persuasive, and rhetorically effective.

READING THE WRITING ASSIGNMENT

Rhetorical tradition has long divided discourse into four basic categories: **narration** (telling a story), **description** (painting a verbal picture), **exposition** (explaining something), and **argumentation** (establishing a position). The first three tend to be exercises in communicating to an audience what that audience doesn't yet know. In argumentation, however, writer and reader can have essentially the same knowledge base; the issue is not so much what you know as how you think about it.

That being the case for an argument, you have to do more than state your position. You have to let your reader see the reasoning that leads to your position. Though you may add to your reader's knowledge along the way, your goal is to get your reader to see and share the logic of your position. In argumentation, logic is the key to success.

Aristotle argued, in his *Rhetoric,* that logical appeals were the most powerful and universal—more powerful than playing on the audience's emotions or claiming a special authority for the speaker. History since has shown that audiences are vulnerable to emotional appeals and leader-worship. Still, appeals to logic are seen as the most valid, not least of all in places (like courts of law) where argumentation is a way of life.

But what does it mean to be logical? Aristotle's idea of logic as the universal form of appeal includes the assumption that being logical doesn't depend on your circumstances or your personality; it depends on a sense of reasonableness so plainly evident we call it common sense. It's this general sense of what's sensible—not charisma or an especially manipulable audience—that generally ensures success in argumentation.

Your argument should certainly take the special characteristics of your audience into account—tact (as consideration of your audience) is important as well as logic—but your appeal shouldn't be restricted to a particular kind of individual or perspective. It should be an appeal to reason. That expands your possibilities instead of limiting them. One feature of reason is the capacity to imagine yourself in circumstances that you haven't actually experienced, to imagine what should be and not just what is. Most logical, persuasive arguments turn on such imaginings—the more thoroughly imagined, the more logical and persuasive.

DISCOVERING IDEAS

Build on Existing Knowledge or Interests

Ideally, you would come to this assignment with ideas and evidence for an argument drawn from assignments done earlier (for example, those suggested in Chapter 4 or 5). We encourage you to build on such a foundation because the focus for this assignment should not be the preliminaries of topic development or evidence gathering so much as careful, persuasive reasoning. If your work in defining or surveying has indeed uncovered an issue you would like to reason your way through, you can go to the next heading.

However, if you aren't sure of your subject, you're no worse off than Melissa Schmeelk was. The assignment of taking a stand on some issue or concern encountered in a previous paper didn't seem to hold much promise for Melissa. Caught up in the trials of being a new mother, she had had to cancel the survey she had planned to do. Pleading special circumstances, she got her instructor's permission to do an essay based on the annual survey of entering students done by her school. The point of that essay had been that, despite the appearance of radical diversity, entering students at Baruch College were actually the same in a number of respects: age, economic status, educational background, career plans, and so on. But how could you build an argument on that? Where was there an issue to press, and controversy to engage?

The instructor had suggested building the argument on an earlier assignment to save effort; it was not a requirement. But Melissa didn't want to go back to the drawing board. There wasn't time. After all, as she had noted in a personal narrative, there was an enormous difference between life before and after the recent birth of her daughter. At first, the demands of caring for the baby made Melissa put off going to college for a term. Once enrolled, she had to cope not just with the baby but with a time-consuming commute from home in Staten Island to college in Manhattan (a commute aggravating enough to become the subject of her eventual research paper). Thanks to motherhood and a long commute, Melissa had gone from being a high school student with a rich social life to a college student with scarcely enough time for her classwork.

As she knew from the student survey she had used for her most recent paper, her circumstances made her different from her peers. Staten Island is New York's only borough without subway connections, and most Baruch students who didn't live in Manhattan lived in Brooklyn or Queens. The vast majority of them were single. And yet—it was the one big surprise for Melissa in all the data she reviewed—less than a third planned to partake in any extracurricular activity.

Baruch offered plenty of opportunities for social interaction, all supported by student fees: student government, publications, sports, preprofessional clubs, religious groups, ethnic organizations, special interest groups, and a radio station. Most students opted out of this array of activities, activities Melissa would love to avail herself of—if only she had the time. They should think twice, thought Melissa, and that, on reflection, seemed the germ of a decent argument.

So if, like Melissa, you're not sure at first of a subject, consider situations you share with your classmates. Is there a cause for concern about new course requirements or textbook prices, the use of alcohol and drugs on campus, an emphasis on or lack of intercollegiate athletics, a campus parking or security problem? Above all, is there an issue you have hard knowledge of or a special angle on? Some time brainstorming should quickly give you several possibilities and allow you to pick one you really want to focus on. Don't pick something you'll need to do much research on. Remember that your job is to reason through a position. The deciding factor in your choice of subject, then, should be the opportunity to spend your time doing just that.

Explore Your Subject

Once she had a general sense of the subject of her argument, Melissa did an exercise in item analysis the instructor provided. Item analysis is simply a way of breaking down a subject into its constituent considerations. In this case, this was done by means of the journalistic questions (so called because they are supposed to be answered in the first paragraph of a newspaper article): Who? What? Where? When? Why? How? Figure 6-1 is a printed version of the exercise sheet Melissa filled out.

Once you have a general idea of what your subject will be, explore that subject by means of item analysis. Again, the initial prompts are the journalistic questions (Who? What? When? Where? Why? How?), questions a good reporter can answer in a single sentence like "Yesterday, Prof. Dryasdust was machine-gunned in his classroom by a distraught student, Tumanian Allnighter, who told police, 'It was either him or me.' " But you are treating an issue, not an event, so in Figure 6-2 we've added some secondary, fleshing-out questions, more even than Melissa's instructor gave.

Figure 6-1

WHO? Who are the people you're writing about? Who is your audience?

students who don't participate in extracurricular activities but should (I guess my audience is the same)

WHAT? What is your subject? What are the essential details?

students should participate --reasons:
1) socializing; 2) relaxation;
3) educational benefits

WHERE? Are you treating a particular place or context? How does it bear on your subject?

Baruch-- not a traditional campus (no dorms, students have to commute, etc.)

WHEN? Are you treating a particular time or space of time? How does it bear on your subject?

college years (should be time of socializing, personal growth)

WHY? Why are you writing? Why do you find your subject significant?

I wish I had the time, think students who do have the time and don't participate are foolish

HOW? How are you treating your subject? How are people affected?

I want to sound reasonable; students need to see reasons

TRIAL RUN

Thinking through those questions may be all the prompting you need, but we recommend that you write just those initial one-word journalistic questions on a blank sheet and, cued by the questions that follow them in Figure 6-2, do some thinking with a pen or pencil. You may discover, as Melissa did, that even sketchy responses will prove useful in the revising as well as in the drafting stages. Once you have written out your responses, take a

---

Figure 6-2

WHO? Who are the people involved? What is their stake in your argument? What is your attitude toward them? Who is your intended audience? How might that audience's knowledge and understanding of the issue at hand differ from yours?

WHAT? What are you writing about? What motivated your choice of subject? What reasons or subissues do you want to stress in arguing your overarching point? What does your reader need to know? What does your reader not need to be told?

WHERE? Are you treating a localized situation or a particular place? How does the consideration of context bear on the relevance your argument has for your audience or for you? What contextual details seem crucial?

WHEN? How is what you're planning to discuss tied to a particular time in a person's life or in the life of society? Do you need to talk about roots in the past or consequences for the future? Is the issue you're treating a sign of the times?

WHY? Why does the subject seem significant to you? Why should it seem so to your audience? Why do you look at it in the way you do? Why argue rather than simply inform or explain?

HOW? How are people affected by your subject? How will you treat it? How will you organize your thoughts? How will you reach your reader? How will your reader respond to your argument?

---

look at the full list of questions again. Are there things you want to add, things you need to think about further? Take the time to do what you can, but also realize that a clearer sense of purpose might make some of these questions easier to answer, and for that you need to do some thesis definition.

Come Up with a Thesis

In an argument, the point that's being argued is called the **thesis** (from the Greek for "something set down"). A thesis is not the same thing as a subject. It's a proposition about that subject, a claim, a contention. **Contention** might be the most useful word, in fact, since there has to be some contentiousness to a thesis. It's not just a point; it's a debatable point. A fact can't be a debatable point, but a conclusion drawn from it can be. A question can't be a debatable point, but an answer to it can be. And even when we think of bona fide debatable points, we can see that some are more debatable than others. The argument that child abuse is bad might be only theoretically debatable (how many people actually think that child abuse is good?), but arguments claiming to identify the primary cause of child abuse or to offer the best means of reducing it—these would presumably turn on genuinely debatable points.

How do you know when you've got a good thesis, a debatable and worthwhile point to argue? There is no sure-fire formula, but common sense helps. Common sense will tell you that if your thesis is something your audience doesn't need to be convinced of, arguing it will be a waste of time. Melissa knew she had an arguable point, a viable thesis, because she knew most students weren't following the advice she had to offer.

 # TRIAL RUN

You've probably come up with at least some idea of the point you plan to argue. Now put it into a thesis statement. Try different ways of wording it so as to make it more forceful or focused. Once you have satisfied yourself, think how others might respond. You might test the waters with your prospective thesis by asking some friends, maybe even conducting an informal poll. Some instructors invite students to hand in prospective theses (yes, that's the plural) for feedback. Here are the questions you want answered, if only in your own mind:

CHECKLIST: TESTING THE VIABILITY OF A THESIS STATEMENT

- Is the thesis statement <u>clear and focused</u>? (It will function as your principle of selection, telling you what you need to say and what you don't need to say—but only if it is not too fuzzy or global in its formulation.)
- Is the thesis statement <u>significant</u>? (Focus is important, but so is an element of ambition. A trivial or utterly safe thesis will make for a boring argument.)
- Is the thesis statement supportable by reasoning and evidence? (Some debatable points are matters of faith or personal taste. Your thoughts about a supreme being or the world's greatest rock band might be both focused and significant without giving you adequate grounds for a compelling, communicative argument.)

A working thesis is the engine that drives the drafting process for arguments. Once you have a thesis you can work with, it's time to begin writing.

COMPOSING THE FIRST DRAFT

Don't Organize by Formula

This probably isn't the first argument you've been asked to write, so you've probably already been treated to advice on how to put one together. Perhaps you've been given the sermon method: "Tell me what you're going to tell me; tell me; tell me what you told me." (If that isn't a formula for being boring, what is?) Perhaps you've been asked to outline, alternating Roman numerals, uppercase letters of the alphabet, Arabic numerals, and lowercase letters as you get further and further into subdivisions of thought. (That's not a bad way to break things down, but it's not a good way to build something like an argument up.) Most likely, you've been taught the five-paragraph theme: an introduction stating the three subpoints of your big point, those three subpoints in three paragraphs ("First,..." and "Second, ..." and "Last,..."), and then a paragraph of rehash. As you can guess, we're not especially fond of the five-paragraph theme.

The problem with the five-paragraph theme is that it's prefabricated. It's a bunch of preassembled boxes for your thoughts. They may not be the right kind or the right number. Why three? The adage has it that "a stool needs three legs to stand on," but whoever came up with that saw more profound connections between stools and arguments than we do.

As you'll see, Melissa's first draft is very close to being a five-paragraph theme, so a preview of it may prove instructive. One problem, later noted by Melissa herself, is that the separate reasons may not be all that distinct: she has one paragraph on extracurricular activities as "a way to have fun and relax" and another on them as a way for a student "to enjoy himself." Why are these separate paragraphs? Sometimes the suspicion arises that it's because the writer has been told that three reasons (or legs) are a must—even if only two come to mind.

Whatever their number, a list of reasons is just that: a list, not a line of reasoning followed through, not a progression of thought. As Melissa eventually realized, the idea is not to tick off reasons as if the reader's chief interest is in keeping some sort of count or score; it's to make connections, follow ideas through, build a case.

Let Your Purpose Determine Your Organization

OK, then: if the five-paragraph theme isn't the best formula for organizing arguments, what is? The answer is that there isn't one. You actually have to figure out the best way to organize your argument. How do you get your organization to suit your purpose and content? It helps if you're willing to do a *true* rough draft—typically a piece of writing begun while ideas are still forming. You can see what you have to say, and only then decide how best to organize it. For instance, you can do what Melissa did: write out the argument according to a familiar formula (like the five-paragraph theme), then scrutinize your points for clues to how they might be best organized.

If this seems inefficient (it really wasn't for Melissa; she used a word processor), you might try a different kind of outline. Don't do a formal one complete with Roman and Arabic numerals; you'll just get lost in a thicket of subdivisions of subpoints and supporting details. Instead, sketch out a few ideas, beginning with the overarching point that is your thesis. With that statement in mind, think, not just of how you want your argument to begin, but where you want it to wind up. Then see if you can't trace a trajectory between those two points, some pattern that seems the best route between starting point and destination. Time is often a straightforward ordering principle, especially if you are dealing in causes and effects. Climactic ordering places least important things first and most important things last. Melissa, in her final version, traced a movement from the general benefits of participation in extracurricular activities to personal considerations and rewards. Whatever pattern you hit upon, see to it that it's a pattern cut to fit, not a preestablished mold. Your thoughts deserve better than the cookie-cutter approach.

TRIAL RUN

Imagine that you are going to give your classmates your argument as a extemporaneous speech instead of a paper. In an extemporaneous speech, you may use a few notes, but you can't simply read from a written text. On 3" × 5" cards or small slips of paper, write out your thesis and then the points you want to cover, each written out as a single sentence. Also prepare a concluding statement of a sentence or two. Take some time shuffling the cards (and perhaps rewriting what's on some of them) until you have an effective sequence.

CHECKLIST: ORGANIZING YOUR DRAFT

- Is your thesis a debatable and significant point?
- Do your other points clearly relate to this overarching point—and to each other?
- Are you sure that these points are distinct thoughts, that one isn't just a rephrasing of another?
- Is their order a logical pattern and not just a list?
- Do you have a sense of how to conclude as well as how to begin?

PRESENTING MELISSA'S FIRST DRAFT

1   In defining the freshmen of this college, it was discovered that not many of them would participate in extracurricular

activities. In my opinion, more students should join clubs, sports and other activities, although many of these students have good reason for not doing so. The only reasons I see why a student should exclude himself from these activities are he doesn't have the time or spending time on extracurricular activities might have a bad effect on his schoolwork. Many students use the excuses that they just don't want to or that nothing offered interests them. It is hard to believe either of these excuses.

2   Extracurricular activities serve several purposes. I see them as a way to have fun and to relax. They relieve pressures that school puts on a student. One can forget about one's schoolwork for a few hours and just enjoy oneself. Another purpose these activities serve is that they are designed with the student in mind. Many of the organizations at Baruch College are started by students themselves. A lot of these clubs are focused on the students' interests. Attending club meetings might help the student learn more about his interests. Students sharing these same interests can exchange information.

3   If for no other reason, every student should participate in extracurricular activities because he wants to enjoy himself. When I was in high school, I was very outgoing and joined several after-school activities. Some I liked and some I disliked, but I joined them not because I felt obligated to, but for the sole purpose of enjoying myself and relieving the pressures of schoolwork. It was amazing how much I could enjoy myself when several times I was in school from eight o'clock in the morning until almost six o'clock at night. This might be explained when I say that several of those hours were spent doing something other than boring, repetitive schoolwork.

4   Another good reason for joining activities and clubs is that they "broaden your horizons." This is a cliche that just about everyone has heard and is tired of hearing, but it perfectly describes one of the best reasons for taking part in extracurricular activities. Although many activities are school-oriented, they provide pleasure mixed with learning. The clubs range from sports clubs for the athletic individual to business clubs for the business-minded individual. This does not mean that these clubs are exclusively for these types of people, only that they were created with them in mind.

5   All of these reasons are good for joining extracurricular activities. I realize that many students don't have the time to join as I am one of them. Everyone should participate if at all possible. At these clubs, people find interests that they never knew they had. They find new friends who share their

interests. A student can't expect his interests to find him--
he must find them. If there is no club or activity that caters
to his interests, which is highly unlikely, there is nothing
stopping him from starting his own club.

6   Extracurricular activities might not make a student
smarter so that he gets straight A's, and they might not make
him healthier in a physical sense. What they will do, though,
is make that student smarter as a person and healthier in his
mind and spirit. What I mean is that the student will learn
more about himself which I think is one of the most important
ways that a person can help himself and others. In essence, it
is finding himself in his own right. A student can do this by
participating in extracurricular activities and he deserves
anything that he gets out of them.

Thinking Critically about Melissa's First Draft

1. The great test of an argument is logic. We could apply this test to the whole draft, but let's just consider the beginning for a moment. How logical does Melissa seem to you there? Do you see room for improvement? Where and how?

2. One great concern in composing and revising arguments is organization. Can you see a strategy informing the way Melissa's revised paper is organized? If so, can you think of a way of clarifying that strategy? If not, can you think of alternative strategies for organizing it?

3. In her draft, Melissa takes a stand, arguing that students should participate in extracurricular activities. Does her argument work for you? Do you find it persuasive? If not, why not? Are there gaps in evidence or reasoning that need to be filled? If you do find the draft persuasive, is there any particular point that seems to clinch things for you?

4. One challenge the assignment places on the writer is to seem purposeful by being clear about the reasons for making the argument. How has Melissa attempted to respond to that challenge? Where does she give her reasons for feeling and arguing as she does? Could she do this more effectively? If so, how?

RETHINKING AND REVISING

Do Some Self-Assessment

Self-assessment is something that writers always do, but a formal written exercise of the kind Melissa did might be especially useful. Her responses to a self-assessment prompt sheet helped her to see what to focus on in revision. You might try responding to the same prompts yourself. As we said

Figure 6-3

Self-Assessment Sheet

Let's assume (it's a fair assumption) that your paper isn't perfect. Please identify, as specifically as possible (e.g., by noting the page number and the specific paragraph or paragraphs on that page), weaknesses in your:

1. ORGANIZATION (Do you have weak, illogical, or nonexistent transitions? Are you guilty of disproportionate development? Do your points merely succeed--rather than build on--one another? Is your introduction interesting and informative? Is your conclusion conclusive? Does your essay, as a whole, really hold together?) *From reading my essay, I got the impression that I was jumping around a lot on specific points. In my second paragraph, I discussed the reasons for participating in after-school activities to enjoy oneself. In the next paragraph, I talk about "broadening your horizons," and then I shift back to enjoying yourself. The ideas don't seem to connect.*

2. DEVELOPMENT (Have you provided adequate elaboration and substantiation? Have you kept your reader sufficiently in mind when providing examples, evidence, and background information? Have you defined relative, technical, and/or crucial terms? Are you guilty of overelaboration or oversimplification, particularly when making casual explanations?) *I don't see any real problems in my development except maybe in my concluding paragraph where I talk about a student being smarter in his own self. When I think about it, those are a bad choice of words because they aren't exactly clear as to what that expression means.*

3. EXPRESSION (Is your tone appropriate and inoffensive? Have you chosen your words carefully? Have you varied your sentence structures? Have you held any unfortunate tendencies sufficiently in check, e.g., trying to say too much with too little or being wordy and longwinded? Have you tried to be interesting and original as well as informative and persuasive?) *This is what I believe to be the better part of my paper. Reading it as if I were the reader reading it for the first time, I found it short and to the point, but simultaneously informative and persuasive.*

Finally, please specify where you think you did especially well. And spare me any false modesty.

As I said for number 3 (expression), I found this to be one of the best parts of the paper. I think I explained my points clearly. I think that my reasons were fairly reasonable and they made sense. Although I had some problems with organization, my points all tied together in some way.

at the outset of this chapter, arguing is a way of holding the quality of your thinking up to scrutiny, and perhaps the best person to give you some constructive criticism on your initial success in this endeavor would be yourself. Give it a try. Be honest, but don't confuse honesty with self-flagellation. Give credit where credit is due, but don't turn self-assessment into an exercise in self-congratulation. Melissa's self-assessment is shown in Figure 6-3.

Melissa's self-assessment made organization the chief concern. She felt that her points were related—"all tied together in some way"—but she also felt she was "jumping around" rather than building a case progressively and logically. This represented perhaps her greatest challenge in revision. She addressed it by distilling each paragraph to a single sentence, then re-examining the order of those points. Here's another good use for those 3" × 5" cards we recommended for planning your organization: you can use them now to analyze that organization's effectiveness—and perhaps shuffle up a few alternatives.

Get (or Imagine) Feedback from a Reader

Your instructor may or may not want to conduct organized peer review sessions. If you yourself want to take the initiative, try the time-honored, unorganized approach: read your draft to (or have it read by) a friend. Ask for a frank response, one that is especially attentive to your use of details and your sense of purpose. You might have the three questions for testing your thesis statement (p. 185) serve as a test of your argument as a whole. If you want something more elaborate, try the peer review worksheet shown in Figure 6-4.

In Melissa's class, this assignment was the first on which there was no collaborative work: no interviewing, no sharing of drafts, no peer review of any kind. Each student had to be his or her sole critic throughout the writing process. The instructor told the class that the major deficiencies authors might miss in their own work—but other readers would not—were insufficient elaboration and insufficient purposefulness. Writers, themselves well aware of their subjects' specifics and their reasons for writing, may forget to communicate that awareness to their readers. The instructor invited Melissa and her classmates to look at their work with their readers' eyes. For help in looking at her paper through the eyes of a reader, Melissa returned to her item analysis. Where it asked for details, she had listed abstractions (like "socializing"). Had her draft been similarly abstract? She knew what she had in mind by "extracurricular activities," but would her reader have the same thing in mind? What's more, the question WHERE? had prompted her to note a crucial, impetus-giving detail she had left out of the draft: that Baruch was a special sort of campus, one students commute to, thus making extracurricular activities that much more important. She had also noted on that sheet that her purpose in writing had much to do

---

Figure 6-4

Peer Review Worksheet

Reviewer's Name_____

Reviewee's Name_____

Briefly state what you take to be the thesis. Does it seem to you a purposeful, tenable position? Why or why not?

Briefly state the argument's points (in the order presented).

Do you question the logic of any of these? Does their order seem logical? Can you suggest improvements in organization?

How well are the points substantiated? Where do you see the need for more support or a different kind of support? Are you given any details you <u>don't</u> need?

How about the tone of the argument? Are there places where you think the author should be more or less emphatic, less chummy or less formal? Were you put off as a reader at any point?

Identify what you see as the essay's strength as it stands.

Identify what most needs attention in revision.

---

with her own situation. Had that been played down in the draft? Could playing it up give more force and purpose to her conclusion, even her whole organization? Could reviewing your responses to an item analysis raise similar questions in your own mind about your own draft?

Be Sensitive to Nuances and Implications

We have stressed that revising isn't simply a matter of changing a word here and there. And it isn't: the discussions of how to think and (rethink) about the organization of your draft should testify to that. But, given the importance of tone in an argument, changing words here and there may well be significant. Does your wording make your position seem more extreme than it really is? Do your statements approximate rather than spell out just what you mean? (In her self-assessment, this was Melissa's concern about her draft's conclusion.) Are you sensitive to the connotations as well as the denotations of the words you use? Do you appeal to reason and not emotions? Do you ask for assent or demand it? Do you seem reasonable instead of self-righteous?

You can't possibly answer such questions with absolute certainty. Once again, though, you can attempt to envision your reader. We mean this literally. Imagine the face of your reader as that (real or hypothetical) person reads certain statements. Does that person scowl? Look incredulous or bored? Raise an eyebrow? Nod in agreement? Don't dismiss the exercise. A social transaction like arguing takes a careful choice of words.

One aspect of Melissa's paper illustrates the effect of even an apparently subtle word choice. Shortly after she had prepared her draft, Melissa's class had a lesson on the consequences of pronoun choice. Among other things, the instructor urged students to resist using *he/him/his* for general reference (as in "the generic individual ... he") because the usage may be sexist, to prefer *they/them/their(s)* or *he or she/him or her/his or her(s)*. The instructor also noted two other alternatives for general reference: *she/her/her(s)* (though this alternative might also be thought sexist) and *you/your(s)* (though this alternative involves the reader, maybe too closely for the reader's comfort). As in other aspects of revision, there is no "right" choice—just a choice that seems right for the reader. You may have noticed, as Melissa did, that using *he/him/his* in her draft stood in the way of her reader connecting her generic student with the author, a young woman who had recently become a mother. Envisioning her reader, she saw someone who might not see her as the sort of student she spoke of—and thus might miss some of her paper's purpose and poignance. So she rethought her pronoun choices in revision. As the sort of reader she was trying to envision, see if Melissa's choices seem right for you.

CHECKLIST: REVISING YOUR DRAFT

- Have you laid out your reasoning, making your reasons for adopting your position clear and fully elaborated?
- Have you reviewed your organization, determining the best possible order of presentation?
- Have you made your overarching purpose and supporting details clear and sufficient to your reader?
- Have you been sensitive to matters of tone and style, conscious that your presentation needs to be tactful as well as logical?

PRESENTING MELISSA'S FINAL DRAFT

Why More Students Should Participate in Extracurricular Activities

Melissa Schmeelk

1

**Melissa intro-
duces not just her
subject but her
position. Identify-
ing reasons she
will and will not
accept for not
participating
allows her to
define her
position with
real precision.**

Researching the interests, plans, and backgrounds of the freshmen of this college, I discovered that not many of them would participate in extracurricular activities, and I imagine this might also be true for other schools. In my opinion, more students should join clubs, sports, and other extracurricular activities, although many of these students may think they have good reasons for not doing so. I can see only two good reasons why students should exclude themselves from these activities. One is that they don't have the time because of employment, children, or some other pressing demand on their time. The other is that spending time on extracurricular activities might have a bad effect on schoolwork. But many students use the excuses that they just don't want to or that nothing offered interests them. It is hard to accept either of these excuses.

2

**She begins to
build her case
with the general
importance of
extracurricular
activities as a
means of socializ-
ing—especially
important at her
particular
campus.**

Extracurricular activities serve several purposes. Most obviously, they are a way of socializing, which is supposed to be such an important part of the college experience. They are particularly important at a college like Baruch, which is not a typical college or university. Because most of the students live in the other boroughs, they must commute to Manhattan to get to the campus. And the campus is not a traditional campus but a number of highrise buildings separated in some instances by three or four city blocks. The pressures and stress that one gets from commuting to classes and from being apart from friends because there is no traditional campus can be relieved through extracurricular activities. They offer a chance for the students to get together on the students' own terms, away from the stresses of commuting and classwork.

**Extracurricular
activities, notes 3
Melissa, are
tailored to
the students'
interests. (She
gives examples.)**

It is important to remember that extracurricular activities are designed with the student in mind. Many of the organizations at Baruch and other schools were started by students themselves. They offer a chance to share one's interests with others. Organizations like the Chess Club and the Fencing Club create the opportunity to improve skills by practicing with those who are perhaps as good or better. A number of religious organizations give devout students a chance to participate in a fellowship of faith. Such extracurricular activities give students a means of enhancing whatever it is that makes them special while at the same time making them feel less isolated.

4

They can also extend or create interests, she argues.

Extracurricular activities don't just serve present interests and abilities. Another good reason for joining activities and clubs is that they "broaden your horizons." This is a cliche, of course, but it is also something almost everyone is apt to say if asked to give a reason for attending college. Although many activities are school-oriented, they provide learning mixed with pleasure. Some of the clubs organized around specific majors, like the accounting and international marketing clubs, are able to bring famous speakers and even corporate recruiters to campus. Few students know very much about their majors and future careers when they first begin a program of study, but such clubs create an opportunity to learn.

5

Melissa gives a clincher, a bottom-line ("If for no other reason") argument: students will enjoy themselves. She draws on her own experience to flesh this argument out.

If for no other reason, students should participate in extracurricular activities because they want to enjoy themselves. When I was in high school, I was very outgoing and joined several after-school activities. Some I liked and some I disliked, but I joined them not because I felt obligated to, but for the sole purpose of enjoying myself and relieving the pressures of schoolwork. It was amazing how much I could enjoy a day that lasted from eight o'clock in the morning until almost six o'clock at night. That only makes sense when you realize that the last several hours of such a day were spent doing something utterly different from boring, repetitive schoolwork. Even while I was at school, I could forget about schoolwork for a few hours and just enjoy myself. Students who participate in extracurricular activities can be doing things that are organized, purposeful, educational, and they can relax and have fun in the process.

6

Melissa notes that the opportunity she is encouraging others to take is one she no longer has.

Despite all of these good reasons for joining extracurricular activities, I realize that many students don't have the time to join as I am one of them. I travel long distances to and from school, and I also have a baby to look after. This doesn't leave me with much spare time. When I see a posted notice about the activities of some club or organization that speaks to my interests, I find myself envying the people who can take the time to go. And when I learned that most students don't participate in extracurricular activities at all, it made me

Just as she opened by weighing good and bad excuses, Melissa concludes by weighing dishonest claims for extracurricular activities against honest ones. Ultimately, she argues, extracurricular activities offer an extracurricular education.

feel puzzled and sad. These students are missing an opportunity to find new friends who share their interests and to discover interests they never knew they had. You can't expect your interests to find you--you must find them. If there is absolutely no club or activity that caters to your interests, which is highly unlikely, there is nothing stopping you from starting your own club.

7 Extracurricular activities might not make you smarter so that you get straight A's, and they might not make you healthier in a physical sense. What they will do, though, is make you smarter socially and healthier in mind and spirit. In essence, they allow you to find yourself in your own right. When you go to college classes, you learn about academic subjects. When you get involved in extracurricular activities, you learn about yourself.

Commentary on Melissa's Final Draft

Over a page has been added in revision, mostly through increased specificity, yet the first paragraph focuses on something Melissa did *not* get more specific about: in both versions she says that "not many" students plan to get involved in extracurricular activities. This seems curious because, after all, Melissa knew the actual number from that survey of entering students, and she could have given it. That might not have been a bad idea—far be it from us to encourage a lack of specificity—but the number of students isn't the issue here. Given her inclinations and circumstances, Melissa thought it appalling that two-thirds of the entering students wouldn't be engaging in extracurricular activities. Yet someone with other priorities might think the involvement of a third of the students in such activities was quite enough. Almost any number might seem too many or too few depending on the perceptions of the reader; it was those perceptions Melissa was out to adjust by arguing that students (not a certain number of students) should participate.

Melissa did get more specific about what acceptable excuses students might have for not participating. In her draft, the excuse that a student "doesn't have the time" passes muster, but in her final draft that's a catchall excuse Melissa won't accept. She gives specific, "pressing" reasons a student may not have the time, including, significantly, her own: "children."

Save for its first sentence, the entire second paragraph is new—and quite specific. In both the draft and the final version the second paragraph addresses the same general theme: extracurricular activities as a means of relieving stress. But just what is "stress" and how is it relieved? In the draft, these are blurry matters, but Melissa's revision brings them into focus by being specific about the forms of stress as well as relief. She emphasizes the special nature of her college as a campus students have to commute to. Once there, they have no dorm halls or frat houses to congregate in, no quads or playing fields to sun and play frisbee on. They have to dash across busy streets and up and down elevators in the inner city. Hence the pressure, but extracurricular activities are cast as more than respite from this: they are opportunities to socialize, to schmooze, to commune after the commute.

Melissa's revision points up something amazing about her first draft: it never identified one specific extracurricular activity. It spoke of "interests" without ever giving one example of what an "interest" is. The revision makes no such mistake. Specific organizations and kinds of organizations are named. An exhaustive list of available activities would be a bore, but Melissa economically names enough, and with enough variety, to suggest a whole array, like a magician who flashes a few cards to show he's holding a whole deck.

Perhaps the most impressive details are the ones given when Melissa gets personal. The revision is much more specific about how her present circumstances shape her perspective on the issue she's arguing: after three paragraphs detailing reasons why participating in extracurricular activities is wise, she has a paragraph stressing how much she once enjoyed them, followed by one noting she no longer has the chance. Like sweepstakes advertisers who warn viewers not to throw away that winning number, Melissa makes the option she's advocating seem sweeter by having her reader imagine missing it. This particular point is also, of course, her motive for writing.

That outline in miniature reminds us that Melissa has not simply been more specific, more personal, more purposeful in her revision; she has also changed her organization. In her draft, Melissa's recollection of her own experience of extracurricular activities begins as it does in her revision: "If for no other reason...." This looks like a last-ditch argument. But in the draft this invitation to enjoy oneself came in the middle, before the "broadening your horizons" paragraph—and after a paragraph billing extracurricular activities as "a way to have fun and relax." (Isn't that enjoying oneself? No wonder Melissa was worried about jumping around and repeating ideas.)

To see how much Melissa improved her organization, we have to get a sense of the structure of the essay as a whole. She begins by identifying her position—more students should participate in extracurricular activities—and shows that she's not an absolutist, that she grants some excuses for not participating, but not others. Her second paragraph gives the first reason supporting her position: extracurricular activities are an opportunity to socialize, an opportunity her own nontraditional campus makes especially precious (though she does note, as she didn't in her draft, that her reasoning applies to other schools as well). The next paragraph homes in on activities that let students pursue interests they already have; here Melissa mentions sports, games, religious groups. The fourth paragraph moves beyond keeping up with existing interests to broadening interests (or developing new ones); here Melissa cites preprofessional or career-oriented clubs. Thereafter, she stresses sheer enjoyment and gives her own account about how much she once enjoyed such activities, testimony the sixth paragraph makes more poignant by noting that motherhood has ruled out this option for Melissa, if not for other students. Here we are again considering extracurricular activities generally, not any specific one or any specific type. Melissa presumably is inviting the reader to fill in the blanks at this point, to imagine whatever his or her interests dictate. Melissa's conclusion returns to reasons for participating in extracurricular activities. She singles out one that completes the movement of the argument as a whole, a movement in which the stress gradually shifts from socializing to self-discovery.

This shift in emphasis is supported by a pronoun shift. Melissa's draft, you'll remember, was characterized by statements like this: "The only reasons I see why a student should exclude himself from these activities are he doesn't have the time or spending time on extracurricular activities might have a bad effect on his schoolwork." Urged to resist using the masculine pronoun when the point of reference is as apt to be feminine, Melissa found her cue for what to do in the draft's next sentence: "Many students use the excuses that they just don't want to or that nothing offered interests them." The plural clearly worked just as well as the singular (and without requiring her to specify gender).

But this was true only up to a point. At the end of the paper, talking of "students" generally just wouldn't do. There was a need to conjure up one particular student, one for whom perhaps no existing extracurricular activity would suit, one who might have to start a new group or club, one, above all, for whom the special benefit of self-discovery could be posed.

At this point, the instructor's invitation to consider the alternative of "you" came to mind, and its use does seem especially appropriate in context. Melissa's audience is the student who needs to be persuaded by her argument; such a reader has seen Melissa talk about herself. Now addressing the reader seems fair, not least of all because Melissa is stressing options and benefits, not unwelcome impositions. The effect is to draw the reader in just as the argument is winding up, to make more intimate contact, to close the distance.

Readers don't always like to be at the close quarters that the second-person pronoun creates, but there are occasions when the use of "you" seems to be just the thing. They occur, for instance, when "you" the reader are being asked to imagine something, try on a role or an idea, see "yourself" in a scenario created by the writer. And that, essentially, is what an argument almost always does, second-person pronoun or no. Consequently, though choosing the "right" pronoun isn't an ever-present issue, involving your reader is.

Questions for Further Thought

1. How often are our minds truly changed by an argument we read or hear? Do we have to be predisposed (or at least uncommitted) to be swayed by an argument? Can an argument be of any use to us if we are already predisposed to accept it?

2. Another, rather more negative, term for common sense is received wisdom. Does an appeal to generally accepted notions of what seems reasonable mean an appeal to old, tried-and-true ideas? Are there occasions that call for *uncommon* sense? How do we make a case for innovative thinking?

3. People often argue about logic itself. What's logical to one person may not seem so to another. Is logic really the universal basis of argument Aristotle believed and hoped? If not, what (if anything) keeps the universe of discourse from being an anarchy of opposing opinions and competing interests?

PROFESSIONAL ESSAYS

Caroline Bird
WHERE COLLEGE FAILS US

"Whatever college graduates *want* to do, most of them are going to wind up doing what *there is* to do."

BORN IN NEW YORK CITY IN 1915, CAROLINE Bird was primarily a journalist (working for Newsweek, Fortune, *and other magazines) until she published a book on the lingering effects of the Great Depression in 1966. Since then, she has been primarily a book author (with a special focus on the status of women), though she has also taught, done lecture tours, and written journalistic pieces for magazines like* Ms. *Her books include* Born Female *(1970) and* The Two-Paycheck Marriage *(1979).*

    Bird's case against college, at least as the ideal destination of every teenager, is reasoned but unsparing. Typical of her argument is one of her parting shots: "College is an ideal place for those young adults who love learning for its own sake, who would rather read than eat, and who like nothing better than writing research papers. But they are a minority...." Bird's article, published in Signature *in 1975, belongs to the same period as the book-length project* The Case Against College *(1975). Obviously, then, it is a dated argument, and one of the things you want to think about as you read it is how much the relevance and accuracy and persuasive force have leached away in the passing years. (Perhaps less than you might hope.)*

ON THE WAY INTO THE READING

1. The success of a college education has to be measured against the goals set for it. How would you define those goals? Do you think they are defined differently by your instructors, your parents, your future employers? Who has the most say? Who should have the most say, to your mind?

2. Bird spends much of her argument considering college (and especially the money spent on tuition) as an investment. Whose investment is it—and on whose behalf? Can there be returns on that investment that extend beyond you personally? (Is furthering your education a way of contributing to the social good, for instance?) Are there any guaranteed returns? Should there be? How might they be managed?

3. How much was coming to college a conscious decision on your part? Was it one of several options afforded you? Or did it seem the only thing to do? If you were influenced by others, how did they exert that influence? How were their expectations for you shaped? Would you change anything about the decision-making process if you could go through it all over again? Would you want anything to be different when it's your children's turn?

---

1 The case *for* college has been accepted without question for more than a generation. All high school graduates ought to go, says Conventional Wisdom and statistical evidence, because college will help them earn more money, become "better" people, and learn to be more responsible citizens than those who don't go.

2 But college has never been able to work its magic for everyone. And now that close to half our high school graduates are attending, those who don't fit the pattern are becoming more numerous, and more obvious. College graduates are selling shoes and driving taxis; college students sabotage each other's experiments and forge letters of recommendation in the intense competition for admission to graduate school. Others find no stimulation in their studies, and drop out—often encouraged by college administrators.

3 Some observers say the fault is with the young people themselves—they are spoiled, stoned, overindulged, and expecting too much. But that's mass

character assassination, and doesn't explain all campus unhappiness. Others blame the state of the world, and they are partly right. We've been told that young people have to go to college because our economy can't absorb an army of untrained eighteen-year-olds. But disillusioned graduates are learning that it can no longer absorb an army of trained twenty-two-year-olds, either.

4   Some adventuresome educators and campus watchers have openly begun to suggest that college may not be the best, the proper, the only place for every young person after the completion of high school. We may have been looking at all those surveys and statistics upside down, it seems, and through the rosy glow of our own remembered college experiences. Perhaps college doesn't make people intelligent, ambitious, happy, liberal, or quick to learn new things—maybe it's just the other way around, and intelligent, ambitious, happy, liberal, and quick-learning people are merely the ones who have been attracted to college in the first place. And perhaps all those successful college graduates would have been successful whether they had gone to college or not. This is heresy to those of us who have been brought up to believe that if a little schooling is good, more has to be much better. But contrary evidence is beginning to mount up.

5   The unhappiness and discontent of young people is nothing new, and problems of adolescence are always painfully intense. But while traveling around the country, speaking at colleges, and interviewing students at all kinds of schools—large and small, public and private—I was overwhelmed by the prevailing sadness. It was as visible on campuses in California as in Nebraska and Massachusetts. Too many young people are in college reluctantly, because everyone told them they ought to go, and there didn't seem to be anything better to do. Their elders sell them college because it's good for them. Some never learn to like it, and talk about their time in school as if it were a sentence to be served.

6   Students tell us the same thing college counselors tell us—they go because of pressure from parents and teachers, and stay because it seems to be an alternative to a far worse fate. It's "better" than the Army or a dead-end job, and it has to be pretty bad before it's any worse than staying at home.

7   College graduates say that they don't want to work "just" for the money: They want work that matters. They want to help people and save the world. But the numbers are stacked against them. Not only are there not enough jobs in world-saving fields, but in the current slowdown it has become evident that there never were, and probably never will be, enough jobs requiring higher education to go around.

8   Students who tell their advisers they want to help people, for example, are often directed to psychology. This year the Department of Labor estimates that there will be 4,300 new jobs for psychologists, while colleges will award 58,430 bachelor's degrees in psychology.

9 Sociology has become a favorite major on socially conscious campuses, but graduates find that social reform is hardly a paying occupation. Male sociologists from the University of Wisconsin reported as gainfully employed a year after graduation included a legal assistant, sports editor, truck unloader, Peace Corps worker, publications director, and a stockboy—but no sociologist per se. The highest paid worked for the post office.

10 Publishing, writing, and journalism are presumably the vocational goal of a large proportion of the 104,000 majors in Communications and Letters expected to graduate in 1975. The outlook for them is grim. All of the daily newspapers in the country combined are expected to hire a total of 2,600 reporters this year. Radio and television stations may hire a total of 500 announcers, most of them in local radio stations. Nonpublishing organizations will need 1,100 technical writers, and public-relations activities another 4,400. Even if new graduates could get all these jobs (they can't, of course), over 90,000 of them will have to find something less glamorous to do.

11 Other fields most popular with college graduates are also pathetically small. Only 1,900 foresters a year will be needed during this decade, although schools of forestry are expected to continue graduating twice that many. Some will get sub-professional jobs as forestry aides. Schools of architecture are expected to turn out twice as many as will be needed, and while all sorts of people want to design things, the Department of Labor forecasts that there will be jobs for only 400 new industrial designers a year. As for anthropologists, only 400 will be needed every year in the 1970s to take care of all the college courses, public-health research, community surveys, museums, and all the archaeological digs on every continent. (For these jobs graduate work in anthropology is required.)

12 Many popular occupations may seem to be growing fast without necessarily offering employment to very many. "Recreation work" is always cited as an expanding field, but it will need relatively few workers who require more special training than life guards. "Urban planning" has exploded in the media, so the U.S. Department of Labor doubled its estimate of the number of jobs to be filled every year in the 1970s—to a big, fat 800. A mere 200 oceanographers a year will be able to do all the exploring of "inner space"— and all that exciting underwater diving you see demonstrated on television—for the entire decade of the 1970s.

13 Whatever college graduates *want* to do, most of them are going to wind up doing what *there is* to do. During the next few years, according to the Labor Department, the biggest demand will be for stenographers and secretaries, followed by retail-trade salesworkers, hospital attendants, bookkeepers, building custodians, registered nurses, foremen, kindergarten and elementary-school teachers, receptionists, cooks, cosmetologists, private-household workers, manufacturing inspectors, and industrial machinery repairmen. These are the jobs which will eventually absorb the surplus archaeologists, urban planners, oceanographers, sociologists, editors, and college professors.

14   Vocationalism is the new look on campus because of the discouraging job market faced by the generalists. Students have been opting for medicine and law in droves. If all those who check "doctor" as their career goal succeed in getting their MDs, we'll immediately have ten times the target ratio of doctors for the population of the United States. Law schools are already graduating twice as many new lawyers every year as the Department of Labor thinks we will need, and the oversupply grows annually.

15   Specialists often find themselves at the mercy of shifts in demand, and the narrower the vocational training, the more risky the long-term prospects. Engineers are the classic example of the "Yo-Yo" effect in supply and demand. Today's shortage is apt to produce a big crop of engineering graduates after the need has crested, and teachers face the same squeeze.

16   Worse than that, when the specialists turn up for work, they often find that they have learned a lot of things in classrooms that they will never use, that they will have to learn a lot of things on the job that they were never taught, and that most of what they have learned is less likely to "come in handy later" than to fade from memory. One disillusioned architecture student, who had already designed and built houses, said, "It's the degree you need, not everything you learn getting it."

17   A diploma saves the employer the cost of screening candidates and gives him a predictable product: He can assume that those who have survived the four-year ordeal have learned how to manage themselves. They have learned how to budget their time, meet deadlines, set priorities, cope with impersonal authority, follow instructions, and stick with a task that may be tiresome without direct supervision.

18   The employer is also betting that it will be cheaper and easier to train the college graduate because he has demonstrated his ability to learn. But if the diploma serves only to identify those who are talented in the art of school-work, it becomes, in the words of Harvard's Christopher Jencks, "a hell of an expensive aptitude test." It is unfair to the candidates because they themselves must bear the cost of the screening—the cost of college. Candidates without the funds, the academic temperament, or the patience for the four-year obstacle race are ruled out, no matter how well they may perform on the job. But if "everyone" has a diploma, employers will have to find another way to choose employees, and it will become an empty credential.

19   (Screening by diploma may in fact already be illegal. The 1971 ruling of the Supreme Court in *Griggs v. Duke Power Co.* contended that an employer cannot demand a qualification which systemically excludes an entire class of applicants, unless that qualification reliably predicts success on the job. The requiring of a high school diploma was outlawed in the *Griggs* case, and this could extend to a college diploma.)

20   The bill for four years at an Ivy League college is currently climbing toward $25,000; at a state university, a degree will cost the student and his family about $10,000 (with taxpayers making up the difference).

21   Not many families can afford these sums, and when they look for financial aid, they discover that someone else will decide how much they will actually have to pay. The College Scholarship Service, which establishes a family's degree of need for most colleges, is guided by noble principles: uniformity of sacrifice, need rather than merit. But families vary in their willingness to "sacrifice" as much as the bureaucracy of the CSS thinks they ought to. This is particularly true of middle-income parents, whose children account for the bulk of the country's college students. Some have begun to rebel against this attempt to enforce the same values and priorities on all. "In some families, a college education competes with a second car, a color television, or a trip to Europe—and it's possible that college may lose," one financial-aid officer recently told me.

22   Quite so. College is worth more to some middle-income families than to others. It is chilling to consider the undercurrent of resentment that families who "give up everything" must feel toward their college-age children, or the burden of guilt children must bear every time they goof off or receive less than top grades in their courses.

23   The decline in return for a college degree within the last generation has been substantial. In the 1950s, a Princeton student could pay his expenses for the school year—eating club and all—on less than $3,000. When he graduated, he entered a job market which provided a comfortable margin over the earnings of his agemates who had not been to college. To be precise, a freshman entering Princeton in 1956, the earliest year for which the Census has attempted to project lifetime earnings, could expect to realize a 12.5 percent return on his investment. A freshman entering in 1972, with the cost nearing $6,000 annually, could expect to realize only 9.3 percent, less than might be available in the money market. This calculation was made with the help of a banker and his computer, comparing college as an investment in future earnings with other investments available in the booming money market of 1974, and concluded that in strictly financial terms, college is not always the best investment a young person can make.

24   I postulated that a young man (the figures are different with a young woman, but the principle is the same) whose rich uncle would give him, in cash, the total cost of four years at Princeton—$34,181. (The total includes what the young man would earn if he went to work instead of to college right after high school.) If he did not spend the money on Princeton, but put it in the savings bank at 7.5 percent interest compounded daily, he would have, at retirement age sixty-four, more than five times as much as the $199,000 extra he could expect to earn between twenty-two and sixty as a college man rather than a mere high school graduate. And with all that money accumulating in the bank, he could invest in something with a higher return than a diploma. At age twenty-eight, when his nest egg had reached $73,113, he could buy a liquor store, which would return him well over 20 percent on his investment, as long as he was willing to mind the

store. He might get a bit fidgety sitting there, but he'd have to be dim-witted to lose money on a liquor store, and right now we're talking only about dollars.

25   If the young man went to a public college rather than Princeton, the investment would be lower, and the payoff higher, of course, because other people—the taxpayers—put up part of the capital for him. But the difference in return between an investment in public and private colleges is minimized because the biggest part of the investment in either case is the money a student might earn if he went to work, not to college—in economic terms, his "foregone income." That he bears himself.

26   Rates of return and dollar signs on education are a fascinating brain teaser, and, obviously, there is a certain unreality to the game. But the same unreality extends to the traditional calculations that have always been used to convince taxpayers that college is a worthwhile investment.

27   The ultimate defense of college has always been that while it may not teach you anything vocationally useful, it will somehow make you a better person, able to do anything better, and those who make it through the process are initiated into the "fellowship of educated men and women." In a study intended to probe what graduates seven years out of college thought their colleges should have done for them, the Carnegie Commission found that most alumni expected the "development of my abilities to think and express myself." But if such respected educational psychologists as Bruner and Piaget are right, specific learning skills have to be acquired very early in life, perhaps even before formal schooling begins.

28   So, when pressed, liberal-arts defenders speak instead about something more encompassing, and more elusive. "College changed me inside," one graduate told us fervently. The authors of a Carnegie Commission report, who obviously struggled for a definition, concluded that one of the common threads in the perceptions of a liberal education is that it provides "an integrated view of the world which can serve as an inner guide." More simply, alumni say that college should have "helped me to formulate the values and goals of my life."

29   In theory, a student is taught to develop these values and goals himself, but in practice, it doesn't work quite that way. All but the wayward and the saintly take their sense of the good, the true, and the beautiful from the people around them. When we speak of students acquiring "values" in college, we often mean that they will acquire the values—and sometimes that means only the tastes—of their professors. The values of professors may be "higher" than many students will encounter elsewhere, but they may not be relevant to situations in which students find themselves in college and later.

30   Of all the forms in which ideas are disseminated, the college professor lecturing a class is the slowest and most expensive. You don't have to go to college to read the great books or learn about the great ideas of Western

Man. Today you can find them everywhere—in paperbacks, in the public libraries, in museums, in public lectures, in adult-education courses, in abridged, summarized, or adapted form in magazines, films, and television. The problem is no longer one of access to broadening ideas; the problem is the other way around: how to choose among the many courses of action proposed to us, how to edit the stimulations that pour into our eyes and ears every waking hour. A college experience that piles option on option and stimulation on stimulation merely adds to the contemporary nightmare.

31   What students and graduates say that they did learn on campus comes under the heading of personal, rather than intellectual, development. Again and again I was told that the real value of college is learning to get along with others, to practice social skills, to "sort out my head," and these have nothing to do with curriculum.

32   For whatever impact the academic experience used to have on college students, the sheer size of many undergraduate classes in the 1970s dilutes faculty-student dialogue, and, more often than not, they are taught by teachers who were hired when colleges were faced with a shortage of qualified instructors, during their years of expansion and when the big rise in academic pay attracted the mediocre and the less than dedicated.

33   On the social side, colleges are withdrawing from responsibility for feeding, housing, policing, and protecting students at a time when the environment of college may be the most important service it could render. College officials are reluctant to "intervene" in the personal lives of the students. They no longer expect to take over from parents, but often insist that students—who have, most often, never lived away from home before— take full adult responsibility for their plans, achievements, and behavior.

34   Most college students do not live in the plush, comfortable country-club-like surroundings their parents envisage, or, in some cases, remember. Open dorms, particularly when they are coeducational, are noisy, usually overcrowded, and often messy. Some students desert the institutional "zoos" (their own word for dorms) and move into run-down, overpriced apartments. Bulletin boards in student centers are littered with notices of apartments to share and the drift of conversation suggests that a lot of money is dissipated in scrounging for food and shelter.

35   Taxpayers now provide more than half of the astronomical sums that are spent on higher education. But less than half of today's high school graduates go on, raising a new question of equity: Is it fair to make all the taxpayers pay for the minority who actually go to college? We decided long ago that it is fair for childless adults to pay school taxes because everyone, parents and nonparents alike, profits by a literate population. Does the same reasoning hold true for state-supported higher education? There is no conclusive evidence on either side.

36   Young people cannot be expected to go to college for the general good of mankind. They may be more altruistic than their elders, but no great

numbers are going to spend four years at intellectual labor, let alone tens of thousands of family dollars, for "the advancement of human capability in society at large," one of the many purposes invoked by the Carnegie Commission report. Nor do any considerable number of them want to go to college to beat the Russians to Jupiter, improve the national defense, increase the Gross National Product, lower the crime rate, improve automobile safety, or create a market for the arts—all of which have been suggested at one time or other as benefits taxpayers get for supporting higher education.

37   One sociologist said that you don't have to have a reason for going to college because it's an institution. His definition of an institution is something everyone subscribed to without question. The burden of proof is not on why you should go to college, but why anyone thinks there might be a reason for not going. The implication—and some educators express it quite frankly—is that an eighteen-year-old high school graduate is still too young and confused to know what he wants to do, let alone what is good for him.

38   Mother knows best, in other words.

39   It had always been comfortable for students to believe that authorities, like Mother, or outside specialists, like educators, could determine what was best for them. However, specialists and authorities no longer enjoy the credibility former generations accorded them. Patients talk back to doctors and are not struck suddenly dead. Clients question the lawyer's bills and sometimes get them reduced. It is no longer self-evident that all adolescents must study a fixed curriculum that was constructed at a time when all educated men could agree on precisely what it was that made them educated.

40   The same with college. If high school graduates don't want to continue their education, or don't want to continue it right away, they may perceive more clearly than their elders that college is not for them.

41   College is an ideal place for those young adults who love learning for its own sake, who would rather read than eat, and who like nothing better than writing research papers. But they are a minority, even at the prestigious colleges, which recruit and attract the intellectually oriented.

42   The rest of our high school graduates need to look at college more closely and critically, to examine it as a consumer product, and decide if the cost in dollars, in time, in continued dependency, and in future returns, is worth the very large investment each student—and his family—must make.

CRITICAL READING

1. Bird begins by noting that she's writing against the grain, that "Conventional Wisdom" argues the opposite case. How does this acknowledgement affect your initial reaction to what she has to say? How does it help to determine the way she proceeds with her argument?

CHAPTER SIX / MAKING AN ARGUMENT

2. Bird also says at the outset that her point seems to be contradicted by "statistical evidence." What kind of evidence does she use? How convincing does it seem to you? How much evidence from the opposing view does she incorporate into her argument?

3. Bird cites a college graduate who says, "It's the degree you need, not everything you learn getting it." How true do you suspect this will be in your own case? Is Bird considering the importance of college education too exclusively as a job credential? How important is it for her to consider it otherwise?

4. Bird spends a number of paragraphs on the high cost of going to college. Her figures are mid-seventies figures and need to be revised upwards fairly considerably. But you're probably well acquainted with college costs. How have you and your family calculated or weighed college tuition as a kind of investment? How do you respond to this part of Bird's argument?

5. What does Bird characterize as the "ultimate defense of college"? How (and how well) does she counter it?

6. Arguing, for the most part, about the burden college amounts to for students and their families, Bird saves the point about the burden it is to taxpayers till near the end. What do you think of her organization? Why do you think she arranges her points as she does?

7. Bird concludes by stressing the choice that deciding to go—or *not* to go—to college amounts to. Since you have made the choice already, how do you respond to her conclusion?

Robert Pattison
THE NEW LITERACY

"The new media will not produce a population of non-readers or non-writers. They will, though, change fundamentally the way people regard reading and writing...."

ROBERT PATTISON IS AN ENGLISH PROFESSOR at Southampton College, out on the east end of Long Island in New York. But he might be considered a renegade English professor, one resisting the teaching (or enforcing) of correctness, choosing instead to wonder why "the doctrine of correctness" came to be and how much it really mattered. Here's how Pattison opens his preface to the book from which our selection comes, a book called On Literacy: The Politics of the Word from Homer to the Age of Rock *(1982):*

We are inadequately literate in part because we have inadequate ideas about literacy. This book seeks to improve our literacy by defining the term accurately.

My interest in defining literacy began while teaching freshman English in community colleges around New York. Interest is too mild a word. Freshman writing is a barrage of intellectual and social challenges masquerading as prose. Do these students write less literately than earlier generations? Are their mechanical errors symptomatic of a cultural decline? Are they errors at all? Has television warped their capacity for literate behavior? How seriously will their deviation from the accepted norms of literate behavior affect their hopes for employment and advancement? In short, what does it mean to be literate?

Nowhere does Pattison provide more concentrated answers to these questions than in "The New Literacy," the last section of his book before he begins his general conclusion.

ON THE WAY INTO THE READING

1. Look over those questions just cited from Pattison's introduction. How are you inclined to answer them? Do you feel your generation is not up to standards of literacy set by previous generations? Why or why not? How would you answer that last question Pattison poses: "...what does it mean to be literate?"

2. Who are the arbiters of "proper" language use besides teachers? How important is language propriety in your chosen field? Are there levels and kinds of literacy that differ according to your profession or your place in the organization? If literacy itself is changing, would it change at different paces and in different ways in different places?

3. Pattison is writing about "The New Literacy." What do you expect that to be? Do you think it represents a change for the better or the worse? Do you expect a new literacy to supplant the old or to co-exist with it?

1   The doctrine of correct English in both its practical and quasi-religious aspects has had much to contend with in the last half-century. The natural evolution of language, the introduction and triumph of electronic media, and the democratic process that has increasingly elevated those unskilled in the approved forms of language to positions of popular influence have all worked against it. It survives at all because its benefits for organization outweigh the frustration occasioned by conforming to its

restraints. Its continued authority, however, cannot help but give rise to a new, radical literacy, just as occurred in the Roman empire. Then, formal Latin became a written language of imperial power while another literacy, with its roots in the Christian message, grew up beside it and finally absorbed it. We too confront a new, popular brand of literacy, but one that has not yet found a dynamic ideology to give it purpose or direction.

2   The new popular literacy expresses itself in Americans' almost universal resistance to certain forms of correct English. Correct English, and the mechanical literacy of the middle classes that spawned it, have alienated the writing population just as it was alienated in the Hellenistic age. Today a universal system of mechanical language use according to inflexible rules has helped create two literacies. One is the established literacy taught in schools. The other is a popular literacy keyed to the spoken language of the people. We have one literacy of power and business and another still-forming literacy of popular vigor. This great development reveals itself in small examples. So far as I can judge, for instance, only Americans over forty or those educated in the select few schools that propagate the most exact habits still employ apostrophes with habitual conformity to the established rules. In the population at large, apostrophes to indicate either possession or contraction are an anachronism, and without constant pressure from the educational system, they would have passed out of usage long ago. The *New York Times* now frequently misses the apostrophe in possessives on back pages. Outside New York it disappears on front and back pages. In freshman essays it is nearly extinct. Even threats of corporal punishment could not induce college students to understand the logic or practice the use of the apostrophe. In the evolutionary scheme of the language, the apostrophe is a dodo.

3   Possessives have always vexed writers of English, and the apostrophe is an artificial solution to the problem of distinguishing between contractions, genitives, and plurals. The question of apostrophes is only one example among many. Punctuation, spelling, syntax, and grammar are all slowly suffering an evolution in their popular usage that, unhindered by the restraints of correct English, would soon revolutionize the language.

4   This revolution, were it to succeed, would have been due in part to sloth. It is easier to ignore apostrophes than to trouble with their correct use. Sloth, while always a potent force for simplification in language, is nevertheless not the only force at work in the formation of a new, popular literacy. The same students who resolutely remain in darkness about the niceties of correct English grammar are as capable of intelligence as any previous generation. They are only selective about what niceties they choose to observe. Months of exercises will not shake their nonchalance about commas, but few are likely to misspell the name Led Zeppelin. The new literacy is not a byproduct of cultural delinquency but a felt need among its users. It has evolution on its side, and its claims will be heard.

5   Heard is the right word, for like its Roman counterpart the new popular literacy is one of the ear more than the eye. The development of electronic

media has facilitated its growth, and it finds its readiest means of ideological expression in music. Radio, television, and other sound-carrying electronics systems like tape and record players have been widely blamed for the collapse of literacy. This view is of course highly biased. Literacy from the time of the pharaohs forward has never collapsed but only changed. Those who denounce the new electronic media for corrupting literacy really mean to say that these innovations menace the middle-class literacy approved by the American establishment.

6   Electronic media are a powerful stimulant to the development of a literacy centered on the spoken word. They threaten established literacy by offering a continuous stream of vernacular raised to the level of popular art—an art without the restraints of correct English. The seemingly disparate programming that fills so much airtime on radio—rock'n'roll and religious revivalism—has in common an appeal beyond the established mechanical literacy. Both reject the prevailing doctrine that language at best suggests but never itself contains truth. American evangelism's alliance with radio and television could have been predicted from the long fundamentalist Christian tradition that emphasizes the enlightening power of the spoken word. Religious revivalism and rock music both assert the primacy of language and the immediacy of its inherent truth:

> I listened and I heard
> Music in the word,

says Peter Townshend's lyric, "Pure and Easy." Though this particular song evokes Eastern mysticism, it shares common ground with the Protestant ministry of the Christian Broadcasting Corporation. Rock and popular religion are alike fed by the desire of the people at large for a literacy that credits the power of language to capture and express the fullness of life.

7   Established American literacy, with its emphasis on mechanical skills and its assertion of the limitations of language, thwarts man's desire to feel himself fully represented in words. Evangelism and rock seek to provide the satisfaction of full representation in language, one by the traditional message of the living Word, the other by reviving, in the context of new electronic media, the primal appeal of lyric poetry. Rock demands respect as the first art form of the new literacy. Its lyricism is full of vigor and wit. Like the artistic output of any generation, most of it is trite, but its successes are dazzling. The opponents of rock condemn it by the aesthetic canons of the old literacy which it is the point of rock to reject. Implicit in rock is a new set of standards of beauty and language. The best rock is not just imitation Romantic or contemporary poetry. It is a form that asks to be judged by its own new values. Those who venerate the principles of the old print literacy will likely abominate rock, and indeed rock invites their abomination.

8   Like earlier popular literacies founded on the apotheosis of speech, it scorns formal language structures for the rapture of the Word:

> Don't know nothin' 'bout no Rise and Fall
> Don't know nothin' 'bout nothin' at all.

The new man, like the first Christians, is proud to be *rudis et indoctus,* uncouth and unlearned. This pride is in part the result of the Romantic aspect of current literacy. Words are suspect and counterfeit. Feeling is spontaneous and genuine. The less I know the more real I am. But the new generations of Americans are not without enthusiasm for language. The pride they take in their ignorance of correct English arises from the passion with which they have devoted themselves to a new type of literacy.

9   Classes of college freshmen, bored by literature anthologies and wary of traditional poetry, can nevertheless recite whole stanzas of The Who's lyrics from memory and discuss them with zeal. Critics of the new literacy claim that memorization is a lost talent among contemporary students, but in fact their memories are fine. Their ability to retain lyrics, commercials, and other forms of oral expression is capacious. Increasingly, however, they resist memorizing dates and literature associated with the established norms of language. They link this kind of memorization with the mechanical view of language against which their new literacy is engaged. Their supposed failure of memory is highly selective, and their ennui is not a response to all literacy, only to the prevailing literacy. Bruce Springsteen (another difficult spelling few students will ever miss) describes the literate man in rock culture:

> the poets down here
> don't write nothing at all.
> They just stand back and let it all be.

The conjunction of incorrect grammar with immediacy in the apprehension of life is no accident in rock lyricism. It is the essence of the new literacy.

10   The desire for a vital literacy is not new. As we have seen its roots are in the doctrine of the Logos in the early Church, in the popular aspects of the Protestant Reformation. No matter how refined its pedigree, however, this new literacy is not likely to win friends among the adherents of the old. By its nature it follows the early churchmen in finding the man who is *rudis et indoctus* praiseworthy for this nearness to the truth contained in speech. By its nature, it rejects the structures of formal written English in favor of the enthusiasm of the spoken word. The new literacy, however, is not a polar opposite of the old. The two are already inextricable. Television, that scorned object of smug contempt to the guardians of the existing literacy, does not replace reading and writing so much as alter their practice. The experience of the Renaissance with the introduction of print elucidates the process. Then, print did not dislodge the popular literacy of speech and enthusiasm. Instead it blended with it in ways that modified the destinies both of print and of literacy. A recent study of television viewing among American teenagers indicates that those who at an early age watch the most television programming will at a later age read the greatest number of books. Many of us are familiar with the habit of reading while watching

television. The man propped up in front of the TV with an open book in hand is an emblem of the new literacy, which is slowly incorporating the mechanics of the old.

11   We can hear the process at work in expressions like "record library" or "tape library." Television and film strive for literary polish—their concession to established literacy. Authors constantly use TV or radio to promote their work, and script writers dream of publishing novels. Print meanwhile has become the handmaiden of the electronic media. Screenplays are prolegomena to novels. Even avant-garde writing is often little more than transcribed monologue or dialogue. The best selling magazine in America is *TV Guide.* The papers with mass circulation like the *Star* and the *National Enquirer* retail gossip about electronic-media stars.

12   The new media will not produce a population of non-readers or non-writers. They will, though, change fundamentally the way people regard reading and writing, first, by fostering an attitude toward language that believes in the real, inherent power of the Word and, second, by providing new mechanical means for the expression of literacy.

13   The new literacy, operating through the electronic media, will compel the established literacy of middle-class authority to become looser and more idiomatic. At the same time the established literacy will assert its claim that it alone provides the social and economic cohesion necessary for a productive society. Each brand of literacy will modify the other while purists of each camp watch in horror at the slow contamination of both. If we are lucky, the resulting mongrel product will be a literacy effective enough to serve the needs of social organization and technological development but sensible enough to maintain rapport with the vitality of spoken language and the need of the population for a sublime sense of language. If we are unlucky, the Edwin Newmans and John Simons will prevail. We will have two literacies, one of authority operating through print and known only to an elect handful of scribes trained at elite universities, the other propagated through electronic media and embodying the people's aspirations for an incarnation of the Word in the daily affairs of life. This second result would represent a severing of the body from the soul of our culture. It would pit class against class as well as literacy against literacy. It would be the end of the American experiment.

CRITICAL READING

1. Pattison begins his discussion of the "new literacy" with a brief definition of the old. Does what he says conform to what you know or suspect about the "doctrine of correct English"? Does it set up certain expectations of what the "new literacy" will be?

2. The "new literacy" is not simply all that lies outside the old. It's important to Pattison's argument that the "new literacy" be something coherent if diversely manifested. What are its distinguishing features?

3. Early in the process of defining the "new literacy," Pattison spends no less than nine sentences on the apostrophe. How useful and edifying do you find this example? Is it a revealing synecdoche—a part for the whole—that throws the "doctrine of correct English" into relief?

4. Pattison describes, not just differences between the old and new literacies, but real tensions between them. To what extent do you experience such tensions in your own life?

5. According to Pattison, an especially vital representative of the "new literacy" is rock, but the most recent example he gives is Springsteen's "Jungleland" (1975). Can you update his examples? Do you find that what has happened in rock bears him out?

6. Pattison is giving both explanations (about what is, was, and will be) and judgments (about what should be). How well does he balance these two? Does he explain enough to get you to accept his judgements?

7. Particularly in light of the almost apocalyptic note on which he ends, how successful does Pattison seem to you in the predictions he makes? More than a decade has passed since he published his argument. How much has he been borne out?

SECTION THREE

WRITING IN RESPONSE TO READING

houghtful, attentive, responsive reading—the sort of reading so crucial to success in college—is in a very real sense making meaning, not just getting meaning someone else made. It's vital for you to see that you have many options in reading a text besides (or beyond) those two crude alternatives known as "getting it" and "not getting it."

What more to reading could there possibly be? Plenty, apparently, if you think for a moment of the very different interpretations so many written texts generate. Whether the context is legal or literary, whether the field is politics or advertising, whether the reader is out for entertainment or edification, what a text has to say has much to do with who's doing the listening. Why? Because reading, like writing, is a purposeful activity. Purposes vary, and so do kinds of reading (or should we say kinds of reading**s**?).

Chapter 7 puts the focus on analysis—analysis not just of what a text is saying, but how and why. Such analysis is by no means an exception to the rule that reading is the construction of meaning. Analysis addresses what a text does to its audience and what the author had in mind in having it do that. These are not things that you "get." You experience them imaginatively. And various people imagine them variously, so your answers to the questions posed by analysis are very much your own.

Chapter 8 is also an invitation to analyze, but then to go beyond analysis to response, to say something about the reading that is not mere agreement or disagreement but a point that you can own. When a text says something to you, what do you say back? And how does that get translated from something that happens in your head or your reading notes to something that is itself written for a responsive reader?

Chapter 9 treats playing two texts off each other. When two texts differ, what is your comparative evaluation? Do you simply agree with one text and disagree with the other? Or do you see something both texts miss, another position between or beyond those two? Those and other possibilities depend, of course, on the texts involved, but they also depend on you. The texts will actually help you see how: thinking about other authors' methods and motives will get you thinking about your own.

Because the context we are primarily concerned with throughout this text (and in this section especially) is the academic context, we include accounts of class discussions of texts as part of the process that resulted in the sample student essays. Nothing focuses the quest for that elusive quality teachers call originality like the way class discussion is trumped by insights in an individual student's paper.

CHAPTER SEVEN

WRITING AN ANALYTICAL ESSAY

Somewhere between comprehension ("Do you follow what the author is saying?") and response ("Do you agree, find it interesting, see its relevance?") lies the forgotten step of analysis ("Can you reason through what the author is doing?"). Admittedly, analysis isn't always necessary. Sometimes purpose and technique are transparent: an ad uses sex to try to sell you something; a politician smears his opponent to get your vote; a recipe shows you step-by-step how to make a better meatball. But attempts at communicating do not have to be crassly suggestive or overtly directive to have designs on you. When you think about it, all texts are manipulative to some extent. Authors almost always ask you to be attentive and impressed, and they often ask you to change your mind or take some action. You owe it to yourself to analyze what they are up to.

You should do this out of respect for the text as well as for yourself. We may smile if someone says a drawing by Picasso is something "a three-year-old could do" or if Orson Welles' cinematic classic *Citizen Kane* is dismissed as "not half as good as an Arnold Schwarzenegger movie," but skipping past analysis to response could betray us into the same sort of misreading of purpose and technique. Texts should be approached with some humility as well as some suspicion. They can, after all, be complex things.

Our featured example of analysis is Thomas Lorentzen's reading of Virginia Woolf's "Professions for Women." Like the other professional pieces in this chapter—Mary Wollstonecraft's preface to *A Vindication of the Rights of Woman* and "The World of the Unborn" from Samuel Butler's satirical fantasy *Erewhon*—Woolf's piece was written in another time, for another audience. Complicated by historical distance and irony, the text places ample challenges on the analytical reader. Tom's reading was helped by a checklist and a questionnaire as well as by class discussion, but it is finally his own distinctive reading. It *has* to be distinctively his own because an analysis is inescapably one reader's personal interaction with a text, a *re*-construction of what is said and meant, an interpretation absolutely identical to no one else's.

In short, reading (like writing) is a process. And since the process of reading a text is so crucial to the writing of a paper on that text, we depart from our usual practice of offering a student's complete first draft as well as a final version. Instead, we give accounts of the class discussion and individual work that feed into the final paper. We are now dealing with a writing situation for which the best evidence of the process of thinking and writing is less a first draft than the partly collective, partly personal input represented by remarks made in class, jottings in journals, and responses on prompt sheets. We invite you to compare these with what happens in your own class—and in your own head.

WRITING ASSIGNMENT

Write an essay analyzing authorial purpose and technique in one of the two pieces at the end of this chapter—or any other piece assigned by your instructor. Remember to keep your essay an exercise in analysis, not a summary of the chosen text or a response to it.

READING THE WRITING ASSIGNMENT

The key word, the one that designates the job you have to do, is obviously *analyzing*. What does it mean to analyze an author's purpose and technique? To a considerable extent, you already know because you already analyze all the time. As you read, questions come up. Why is the author saying this? How does this relate to what was said just a paragraph ago? Does this evidence or example really bear on the point being made?

Because it addresses questions like these, analysis is important and useful. Texts tend to pose problems for the reader, and analysis works out solutions. It makes connections. It enhances understanding. It sheds light. But the questions analysis addresses also show that considerations of *purpose* and considerations of *technique* are interrelated: your task is not so much to distinguish between them as to show their interrelation. Thinking about your own purpose and technique will help, as will remembering that both are always determined with your audience in mind. For instance, reflecting on your task and your audience should help you see that your analysis must not become a summary or a response. Summaries are for people who haven't done the reading you have; that's not the case here. Assume that your reader (especially your instructor) has read the text and wants illumination, not reiteration. Responses usually proceed from analysis and are not so easily distinguished from it, but here, too, thinking of your task and your audience will help. The expectation is that you will make the assigned text the subject of your essay, not a point of departure for airing opinions or personal associations the text stirs within you. In your analysis of a text, star billing goes neither to the text nor to you. It goes to the understanding of the text you convey—an understanding of the methods it uses, the intentions it reveals, the questions it raises.

As you get ready to begin thinking about your analysis, perhaps with the help of your classmates, we invite you to follow along with the thinking Tom Lorentzen and his classmates did in analyzing Virginia Woolf's "Professions for Women," a text that (like yours, no doubt) can pose real problems an analysis needs to address.

DISCOVERING IDEAS

Read the Rhetorical Situation

As you read a text, you need to realize that you are not just reading a text: you are reading a whole rhetorical situation. You either know or infer the author's relationship to the audience, to the subject, to the context. Pondering an author's intentions means pondering the people for whom those intentions were shaped and the (social, historical, personal) circumstances that helped to shape those intentions.

Reading not just the text but the context can sound more difficult than it really is. In her essay below, Virginia Woolf mentions the invitation of the women's society to speak of her professional experiences; her audience is addressed directly and is sometimes even characterized or defined by her remarks.

Woolf's piece, in retaining the form of a speech before an assembly of women, gives us a stronger, more immediate sense of context and audience than many texts do. Yet all texts, in one way or another, characterize both the author and the audience; all texts let us visualize not just what is being said, but who is doing the talking—and to whom. (One of Tom's classmates, cued by the extensive use of "you" in Woolf's piece, focused her analysis on how Woolf represented her audience to themselves.)

Nor does the visualization of author and audience have to be an imaginative stretch, a strained exercise in inference and extrapolation. Let's be obvious for a moment: all the texts in this book come with some discussion of their contexts. It's our job to see to that; after all, we took them out of their original contexts so that we could use them in our textbook. And we're hardly unique in this. So you usually have some supplementary information to help you gauge the rhetorical situation. Use it.

Just what—specifically—does it mean to "do a rhetorical reading"? Here's one way to proceed:

- **Sniff out the context.** Are you given an introduction or headnote (like the ones provided in this book) describing when, why, and for whom the text was written? Does your instructor give you some contextual information? Are there clues to the context in the text itself?

- **Make educated guesses.** Even before you begin reading, take stock of your expectations. What does the title suggest to you? Do you know the author at all, even if only by reputation? Does the subject call up specific associations, attitudes, controversies?

- **Keep track of your reactions.** Before reading, make note of your expectations. As you read, record the questions you find the text raises for you. (You might try wondering about the text out loud as you read it; anything you feel moved to say you might also be moved to write down.) Do you feel confused or lost at any point? Do you sense the author is contradicting what was said earlier? Do you find the evidence given and the strategies used adequate, interesting, odd, inappropriate?

- **Consider what the text doesn't do (as well as what it does).** As a prompt to analysis, you might want to use the checklist of techniques Tom was given (see Figure 7-1, p. 229). When you look through this list of authorial stances and strategies, are you struck by any options the author *didn't* take (as Tom was struck by Woolf's diffidence where he might have expected assertiveness or anger)?

- **Characterize the text.** You might also want to use the second prompt Tom was given (Figure 7-2, p. 231), which invites written responses. Write down your sense of the subject of the text, the author's purpose, predominant techniques, apparent contradictions, and so on. In lieu of this, or in addition to it, you might simply sketch a list of words that describe the text. It is angry, amusing, hesitant, ponderous, regimented, desperate, confident, scatterbrained—or what? Try to come up with a good dozen descriptive terms. Does one seem especially apt? Why? (Words are little storehouses of meaning; pry one open and do a little ransacking.)

 # TRIAL RUN

Let's try this out on Virginia Woolf's "Professions for Women." You have already been given much of the context Tom and his classmates were given: the piece is the published version of a speech this famous writer (born 1882, died 1941) gave to an audience of women some time ago—specifically the London/National Society for Women's Service in 1931. The students were also told that, besides her novels—notably *Mrs. Dalloway* (1925), *To the Lighthouse* (1929), and *The Waves* (1931)—Woolf is esteemed for her sustained reflections on the status of women: *A Room of One's Own* (1929) and *Three Guineas* (1938).

Knowing that doesn't mean you're done sniffing out the context and making educated guesses about the text. Now that we have a specific text—and you'll want to keep this in mind as you go to work on the text you'll be writing on—we can get specific about the kinds of questions we can ask before reading:

- Do you know this author's works or reputation? Have you read a novel, story, or essay by Woolf? Do you know or suspect what sort of writer Woolf is—what, for instance, feminists might feel about her?
- Do you know something about her career's historical context—the period between the two world wars? How might a speech titled "Professions for Women" given in 1931 differ from one delivered today? Why might one given then be worth reading now?
- What do you expect a piece titled "Professions for Women" will be about? What do you think Woolf's original audience expected? Would that wholly female audience get a different speech than a mixed audience or an audience of men?

With such thoughts and questions in mind, let's look at the text.

PROFESSIONS FOR WOMEN

Virginia Woolf

1   When your secretary invited me to come here, she told me that your Society is concerned with the employment of women and she suggested that I might tell you something about my own professional experience. It is true I am a woman; it is true I am employed; but what professional experiences have I had? It is difficult to say. My profession is literature; and in that profession there are fewer experiences for women than in any other, with the exception of the stage—fewer, I mean, that are peculiar to women. For the road was cut many years ago—by Fanny Burney, by Aphra Behn, by Harriet Martineau, by Jane Austen, by George Eliot—many famous women, and many more unknown and forgotten, have been before me, making the path smooth, and regulating my steps. Thus, when I came to write, there were very few material obstacles in my way. Writing was a reputable and harmless occupation. The family peace was not broken by the scratching of a pen. No demand was made upon the family purse. For ten and sixpence one can buy paper enough to write all the plays of Shakespeare—if one has a mind that way. Pianos and models, Paris, Vienna and Berlin, masters and mistresses, are not needed by a writer. The cheapness of writing paper is, of course, the reason why women have succeeded as writers before they have succeeded in the other professions.

2   But to tell you my story—it is a simple one. You have only got to figure to yourselves a girl in a bedroom with a pen in her hand. She had only to move that pen from left to right—from ten o'clock to one. Then it occurred to her to do what is simple and cheap enough after all—to slip a few of those pages into an envelope, fix a penny stamp in the corner, and drop the envelope into the red box at the corner. It was thus that I became a journalist; and my effort was rewarded on the first day of the following month—a very glorious day it was for me—by a letter from an editor containing a cheque for one pound ten shillings and sixpence. But to show you how little I deserve to be called a professional woman, how little I know of the struggles

and difficulties of such lives, I have to admit that instead of spending that sum upon bread and butter, rent, shoes and stockings, or butcher's bills, I went out and bought a cat—a beautiful cat, a Persian cat, which very soon involved me in bitter disputes with my neighbours.

3   What could be easier than to write articles and to buy Persian cats with the profits? But wait a moment. Articles have to be about something. Mine, I seem to remember, was about a novel by a famous man. And while I was writing this review, I discovered that if I were going to review books I should need to do battle with a certain phantom. And the phantom was a woman, and when I came to know her better I called her after the heroine of a famous poem, The Angel in the House. It was she who used to come between me and my paper when I was writing reviews. It was she who bothered me and wasted my time and so tormented me that at last I killed her. You who come of a younger and happier generation may not have heard of her—you may not know what I mean by the Angel in the House. I will describe her as shortly as I can. She was intensely sympathetic. She was immensely charming. She was utterly unselfish. She excelled in the difficult arts of family life. She sacrificed herself daily. If there was chicken, she took the leg; if there was a draught she sat in it—in short she was so constituted that she never had a mind or a wish of her own, but preferred to sympathize always with the minds and wishes of others. Above all—I need not say it—she was pure. Her purity was supposed to be her chief beauty—her blushes, her great grace. In those days—the last of Queen Victoria—every house had its Angel. And when I came to write I encountered her with the very first words. The shadow of her wings fell on my page; I heard the rustling of her skirts in the room. Directly, that is to say, I took my pen in my hand to review that novel by a famous man, she slipped behind me and whispered: "My dear, you are a young woman. You are writing about a book that has been written by a man. Be sympathetic; be tender; flatter; deceive; use all the arts and wiles of our sex. Never let anybody guess that you have a mind of your own. Above all, be pure." And she made as if to guide my pen. I now record the one act for which I take some credit to myself, though the credit rightly belongs to some excellent ancestors of mine who left me a certain sum of money—shall we say five hundred pounds a year?—so that it was not necessary for me to depend solely on charm for my living. I turned upon her and caught her by the throat. I did my best to kill her. My excuse, if I were to be had up in a court of law, would be that I acted in self-defence. Had I not killed her she would have killed me. She would have plucked the heart out of my writing. For, as I found, directly I put pen to paper, you cannot review even a novel without having a mind of your own, without expressing what you think to be the truth about human relations, morality, sex. And all these questions, according to the Angel of the House, cannot be dealt with freely and openly by women; they must charm, they must conciliate, they must—to put it bluntly—tell lies if they are to succeed. Thus, whenever I felt the shadow of her wing or the radiance of her halo upon my page, I took up the inkpot and flung it at her. She died hard. Her

fictitious nature was of great assistance to her. It is far harder to kill a phantom than a reality. She was always creeping back when I thought I had despatched her. Though I flatter myself that I killed her in the end, the struggle was severe; it took much time that had better have been spent upon learning Greek grammar; or in roaming the world in search of adventures. But it was a real experience; it was an experience that was bound to befall all women writers at that time. Killing the Angel in the House was part of the occupation of a woman writer.

4   But to continue my story. The Angel was dead; what then remained? You may say that what remained was a simple and common object—a young woman in a bedroom with an inkpot. In other words, now that she had rid herself of falsehood, that young woman had only to be herself. Ah, but what is "herself"? I mean, what is a woman? I assure you, I do not know. I do not believe that you know. I do not believe that anybody can know until she has expressed herself in all the arts and professions open to human skill. That indeed is one of the reasons why I have come here—out of respect for you, who are in process of showing us by your experiments what a woman is, who are in process of providing us, by your failures and successes, with that extremely important piece of information.

5   But to continue the story of my professional experiences. I made one pound ten and six by my first review; and I bought a Persian cat with the proceeds. Then I grew ambitious. A Persian cat is all very well, I said; but a Persian cat is not enough. I must have a motor car. And it was thus that I became a novelist—for it is a very strange thing that people will give you a motor car if you will tell them a story. It is a still stranger thing that there is nothing so delightful in the world as telling stories. It is far pleasanter than writing reviews of famous novels. And yet, if I am to obey your secretary and tell you my professional experiences as a novelist, I must tell you about a very strange experience that befell me as a novelist. And to understand it you must try first to imagine a novelist's state of mind. I hope I am not giving away professional secrets if I say that a novelist's chief desire is to be as unconscious as possible. He has to induce in himself a state of perpetual lethargy. He wants life to proceed with the utmost quiet and regularity. He wants to see the same faces, to read the same books, to do the same things day after day, month after month, while he is writing, so that nothing may break the illusion in which he is living—so that nothing may disturb or disquiet the mysterious nosings about, feelings round, darts, dashes and sudden discoveries of that very shy and illusive spirit, the imagination. I suspect that this state is the same both for men and women. Be that as it may, I want you to imagine me writing a novel in a state of trance. I want you to figure to yourselves a girl sitting with a pen in her hand, which for minutes, and indeed for hours, she never dips into the inkpot. The image that comes to my mind when I think of this girl is the image of a fisherman lying sunk in dreams on the verge of a deep lake with a rod held out over the water. She was letting her imagination sweep unchecked round every rock and cranny of the world that lies submerged in the depths of our

unconscious being. Now came the experience, the experience that I believe to be far commoner with women writers than with men. The line raced through the girl's fingers. Her imagination had rushed away. It had sought the pools, the depths, the dark places where the largest fish slumber. And then there was a smash. There was an explosion. There was foam and confusion. The imagination had dashed itself against something hard. The girl was roused from her dream. She was indeed in a state of the most acute and difficult distress. To speak without figure she had thought of something, something about the body, about the passions which it was unfitting for her as a woman to say. Men, her reason told her, would be shocked. The consciousness of what men will say of a woman who speaks the truth about her passions had roused her from her artist's state of unconsciousness. She could write no more. The trance was over. Her imagination could work no longer. This I believe to be a very common experience with women writer—they are impeded by the extreme conventionality of the other sex. For though men sensibly allow themselves great freedom in these respects, I doubt that they realize or can control the extreme severity with which they condemn such freedom in women.

6   These then were two very genuine experiences of my own. These were two of the adventures of my professional life. The first—killing the Angel in the House—I think I solved. She died. But the second, telling the truth about my own experiences as a body, I do not think I solved. I doubt that any woman has solved it yet. The obstacles against her are still immensely powerful—and yet they are very difficult to define. Outwardly, what is simpler than to write books? Outwardly, what obstacles are there for a woman rather than for a man? Inwardly, I think, the case is very different; she has still many ghosts to fight, many prejudices to overcome. Indeed it will be a long time still, I think, before a woman can sit down to write a book without finding a phantom to be slain, a rock to be dashed against. And if this is so in literature, the freest of all professions for women, how is it in the new professions which you are now for the first time entering?

7   Those are the questions that I should like, had I time, to ask you. And indeed, if I have laid stress upon these professional experiences of mine, it is because I believe that they are, though in different forms, yours also. Even when the path is nominally open—when there is nothing to prevent a woman from being a doctor, a lawyer, a civil servant—there are many phantoms and obstacles, as I believe, looming in her way. To discuss and define them is I think of great value and importance; for thus only can the labour be shared, the difficulties be solved. But besides this, it is necessary also to discuss the ends and the aims for which we are fighting, for which we are doing battle with these formidable obstacles. Those aims cannot be taken for granted; they must be perpetually questioned and examined. The whole position, as I see it—here in this hall surrounded by women practising for the first time in history I know not how many different professions—is one of extraordinary interest and importance. You have won rooms of your own in the house hitherto exclusively owned by men. You are able,

though not without great labour and effort, to pay the rent. You are earning your five hundred pounds a year. But this freedom is only a beginning; the room is your own, but it is still bare. It has to be furnished; it has to be decorated; it has to be shared. How are you going to furnish it, how are you going to decorate it? With whom are you going to share it, and upon what terms? These, I think are questions of the utmost importance and interest. For the first time in history you are able to ask them; for the first time you are able to decide for yourselves what the answers should be. Willingly would I stay and discuss those questions and answers—but not to-night. My time is up; and I must cease.

Consider Specific Questions

Having given some thought to it even before you began reading it, what do you now make of Virginia Woolf's "Professions for Women"? That, of course, is an absurdly general question. It must be brought into focus by the sorts of questions asked during class discussion in Tom's class:

- Does this piece sound like the Virginia Woolf you knew or imagined?
- Does the piece live up to its title? If so, how so? If not, why not?
- Does the piece seem consistent throughout? If it does, can you identify what that consistency resides in? If not, can you point to contradictions or digressions?
- Can you identify or characterize the purpose of the piece? If you can, can you say how Woolf goes about achieving that purpose? If you can't, can you identify the techniques or methods used—and perhaps consider them as clues to her purpose?
- Does the piece pose questions for you that you would like answered, problems you would like solved? How would someone go about addressing them?

When considering questions like these, two (or twenty) heads are better than one, so they are best addressed in class discussion. Useful and thought-provoking as it can be, class discussion is really just a starting point for your writing about reading. Let's see what was said about Woolf's piece in Tom's class.

Make Something of Class Discussion

The discussion of "Professions for Women" in Tom's class revealed that the students found the text both easy and difficult. It seemed accessible enough, even pleasant in terms of tone and a certain humor. But the students also found the text perplexing, especially as they considered that their job was to analyze Woolf's means and motives. They knew—and the text reminded them—that she had been invited to give her speech as a writer of some stature, but she seemed strangely self-dismissive. Her life was a success story; why didn't her account of it sound like one? Students knew she was associated with feminism, yet her speech seemed to lack the righteous anger against male oppression some feminists convey. She seemed to be describing a problem, yet how clear was she about its cause or a solution? Why was she saying what she was saying?

The title, often an important initial clue to the purpose and content of a piece, did not provide much help. Why call something "Professions for Women" that focuses so exclusively on one profession and on one woman? How informative was Woolf being about either writing or womanhood? How seriously should one take a comment like "The cheapness of writing paper is, of course, the reason why women have succeeded as writers before they have succeeded in the other professions"? What was one to make of an author who, purportedly writing about professions for *women*, followed a posed question like "What is a woman?" with "I assure you, I do not know"? Especially when the focus was on her title, Woolf seemed to raise more questions than she answered.

But there were points of agreement among the students. Her title aside, Woolf was telling her story. And in telling her story—several stories, really—she was being thought-provoking, the students felt. The invitation, it seemed to them, was to draw one's own conclusions, not to come to those dictated by the author.

The students also agreed that in this text, as in so many others, proportion is a way of gauging significance. The two longest paragraphs (the third and the fifth) treat two sustained anecdotes—the story of the Angel in the House and the story of the mermaid imagination. These seemed pivotal in positioning, length, and import. The students agreed that these were not accounts of real-life experiences, that they were instead pointed fictions, fables of the condition of the woman writer (or at least one woman writer).

One student suggested that the fictions were both about self-censorship, and the others assented to this, though not without qualifications or reservations. For instance, just how much of the censorship, asked one student, was really done by the self and not by outside forces? Discussion eventually focused on whether the second story was consistent with the first. Sure, why not? shrugged one student. Another insisted that if Woolf had really killed the Angel in the first story she wouldn't have had to reel in her imagination in the second. Yet another suggested that the two stories treated two different subjects and kinds of writing: review of men's books in the first, imaginative writing about the passions in the second. And so it went: it seemed that everybody had a slightly different account of the relation between the two anecdotes and their relation to Woolf's overall purpose. Students might have gone on arguing the point for much longer, but the class period was soon over. Their time was up; they had to cease.

Thinking Critically about the Class Discussion

The class discussion of a text you'll be writing about can be something like a very rough draft—but you need the vision to see how revision should take you beyond it. Here are some questions you might address as you do so. You can answer them either with respect to the class discussion we've just recounted or a class discussion of the text you will be writing about.

1. When a class comes to a general conclusion about a text—as Tom's class did when they decided Woolf meant to be thought-provoking—why isn't it a good idea to write a paper that simply reiterates that conclusion? What more would you have to do and why?

2. When a point of agreement is reached, is it dangerous to dispute it in your paper? Could it be a virtue to dispute it? Does it depend on the kind of point?

3. When a controversy emerges, must you resolve it? If you choose to, must that be a matter of taking the sides that emerged in class discussion? Would it help to imagine the author as part of that discussion, maybe denying or admitting an apparent contradiction?

4. Class discussion tends to focus on certain points in the text. What if your interests lie elsewhere? What if, like the student who analyzed the way Woolf portrayed her audience, you choose to focus on something scarcely glanced at in class discussion? What are the virtues or dangers of such an approach?

Just how you answer such questions depends on you—and on what's expected of you. You might benefit, then, from discussing these questions with your instructor and your classmates. But remember: just as simply restating what the text says won't do, neither will simply restating what's said about the text in class. How much of class discussion you use (and how you use it) will vary according to your own sense of the text, the quality of the discussion, and your instructor's expectations.

TRIAL RUN

If your class discusses the text you'll be analyzing, here are some questions to help you see how to use the discussion:

- Did important points of agreement emerge? Did they tally with your own reading? If so, do they suggest how you might save time by by-passing what seems obvious to everybody? If not—if you feel agreement was reached too quickly and easily—how might you suggest the need for further thought?

- Did anything about the discussion surprise you? Was much made of something you scarcely noted? Was little made of something that struck you as important? In either case, don't suppose you missed or misread something: return to the text and explore reasons for the divergence. These reasons may become the key to making your analysis distinctive and interesting.

• Did some part or aspect of the text emerge as the focus of most of the discussion? Take some time to sketch out what was said. Do you see a way of synthesizing those statements, of adding to them, of identifying something they all missed?

Focus on *How,* Not Just *Why*

As their own discussion session concluded, Tom's instructor congratulated the class on a fruitful discussion—told them, in fact, that they seemed to have gone to the heart of the matter in focusing on the two stories, their morals, and their interrelation. But the instructor also said the discussion might have focused more on technique. To avoid letting their papers devolve into summaries, the students needed to remember their audience (in this case, the instructor) had already read the text and so did not want an account of *what* Woolf had said, but rather *how* and *why* she had said it. Because the discussion had focused on *why,* the papers needed to give a little more attention to *how.* To help in this, the instructor distributed the Checklist of Techniques shown in Figure 7-1.

TRIAL RUN

As you look over the Checklist of Techniques, note the terms and phrases that help you characterize the text you're analyzing. Note not just those that seem appropriate but those that seem inappropriate. As you ponder what the author chose to do—and chose not to do—wonder about ways the *how* leads back to the *why.*

This first checklist was just something for the students to read over and consider. No written responses were called for. As the instructor pointed out, the usefulness of such a prompt lies in the wide range of possibilities posed. Its general applicability may make it seem unwieldy when applied to any given case, Woolf's piece or your own text, for example. But it's useful to ponder what Woolf didn't do as well as what she did. Let's suppose for just a moment that the only thing you know about that piece is its title: "Professions for Women." It isn't hard to imagine a piece with that title as being a sustained exercise in the classification of the varieties of professional employment open to women, assertively supported by facts and statistics, exhaustively and straightforwardly presented, and quite possibly not just informative but even declamatory in its call for change or political action. How different this imaginary text is from the piece Woolf actually wrote! What that checklist helps us see, then, are the roads not taken.

Figure 7-1

Checklist of Techniques

How does the author treat the reader? (as an expert? underling? equal?)

How does the author come across? (as hesitant? assertive? friendly? funny?)

What does the author ask of the reader? (understanding? change of mind? action?)

How does the author organize the material?
  by narration?
  by comparison?
  by repetition?
  by casual analysis?
  by accumulation of detail?
  by division and classification?
  by association?

What kind of evidence is presented?
  facts?
  stories?
  expert opinions?
  descriptions?
  definitions?
  principles?
  appeals to emotion, imagination, common sense?

How is the material presented? (simply? complexly? carefully? casually?)

How would you characterize the author's style?
  formal?
  informal?
  angry?
  amusing?
  technical?
  straightforward?
  elliptical?

What does the author emphasize? What is ignored or summarized or simplified?

What holds the piece together as a whole? Is it a whole? Or are there contradictions, inconsistencies, digressions?

Still, the crucial thing is what a text says and does, not what it doesn't do and doesn't say, and so the instructor distributed a second prompt (see Figure 7-2)—one that, once completed, could be considered a kind of first draft. The time has come then, to draw the (always somewhat arbitrary) line between discovering ideas and composing the draft.

COMPOSING THE FIRST DRAFT
Answer Crucial Questions about the Text

Useful as class discussion can be in illuminating a text, you finally have to take your own stand with regard to the crucial questions about purpose and technique. At this point in the process of analyzing the text, you have given thought to the text even before reading it and further reflection after reading it. You have had the benefit of responses and thoughts of others aired in class discussion. Like the students in Tom's class, you might even be told that rereading is as important to good reading as revision is to good writing, and a second look at the text may have clarified certain matters for you. In any case, you have reached the point where you now need to begin developing your own angle, an analytical perspective on the text you can claim as your own.

TRIAL RUN

To flesh out your perspective, try answering the questions the students in Tom's class were given on the prompt sheet shown in Figure 7-2 (here filled out by Tom). The students were to fill out the sheet and turn it in with their drafts and final version. (Your text may not be the same, but we can assure you that the questions will remain applicable.) Given the way the questions were arranged, the instructor went so far as to say that the responses might be considered a very rough first draft.

Tom's response to the first question—"What is the piece about?"—may not be the same response that you would give. Even identifying the subject of a text is to some extent an exercise in interpretation. Whether you agree with Tom's first response or not, you can see that subject and purpose are so intertwined that proving or disproving what he says there would require knowing Woolf's intention, which is impossible.

That doesn't mean an author's intention or purpose should not be pursued; on the contrary, even though certainty eludes us in complex texts, as in most things, a reader has to make educated guesses about what an author is up to in order to make a real beginning, much less come to some conclusions. Tom's own beginning suggests that there is an exploratory quality to Woolf's text that implies lack of certainty, even on her part: "She

Figure 7-2

What is the piece about? The essay (speech) is about Woolf's own discovery of herself: how she thinks about men and women, how she feels about sexuality vs. how she is supposed to feel about her body, etc. She is discovering that the truths laid out for her (truths laid out for women by men?) may not be right.

What is the author's purpose? How explicit is it? Are there other or ulterior purposes?
I think she wants to be a humble example to the women she is speaking to. She makes several references that lead me to believe that her "angel" is very much alive — [when she buys a cat with her first pay, she says that this is the reason — "how little I deserve to be called a professional woman" (as if being herself could come with a job description); and she does not feel justified in taking credit for killing her "angel."

What are the important techniques used? (See the accompanying checklist.)
The essay is written in a friendly straight forward tone. She seems to be speaking to a familiar audience. The piece does, however, seem a bit scattered, partly because she does a great deal of 'jumping' from one idea to the next, almost a stream of consciousness.

Does any one or more seem especially important? Why? Possibly the tone that implies she's humble, maybe too humble. I think she wants to be seen by her audience as someone who has been through a struggle with sexism and still has the by-products of it hanging around.

Is there any sense of contradiction or lopsidedness? Is the author at cross purposes?
Does technique diverge from purpose?

Can you "solve" a sense of contradiction or insufficiency by redefining the essay's sense of purpose?
The contradiction of the reappearance of her "angel" is used by Virginia to show that these stumbling blocks, or censors, cannot be killed.

is discovering that the truths laid out for her (*truths laid out for women by men?*) *may* not be right."

Tom's subsequent responses bear out this sense that Woolf is in the process of discovering as well as revealing what she says, that she raises questions not quite answered, that she is more tentative than assertive, more inclined to say *may* than *must*. Asked to identify her purpose, he stresses the appearance of humility, humility that seems to undercut the few accomplishments Woolf claims for herself, notably the killing of the Angel in the House. This humble tone is also the technique he singles out, even suggesting that it is "maybe too humble." In any case, Woolf depicts herself as emerging from a struggle by no means unscathed: "she still has the by-products of it hanging around." Tom leaves the space after the question about any "sense of contradiction" blank; presumably filling it in seemed unnecessary, what with so much of the class discussion turning on the question of whether one of Woolf's accounts of herself contradicted another. Tom's position with respect to that controversy is made clear enough: "The contradiction of the reappearance of her 'Angel' is used by Virginia to show that these stumbling blocks or censors cannot be killed." Here as throughout his response to the questions on the prompt, a sense of Woolf's purpose informs Tom's analysis.

Thinking Critically about Tom's Responses

Tom's instructor suggested that completing the questionnaire would give the students something like a first draft. How close does Tom's completed questionnaire come? Try answering these questions about his responses— or, better yet, about your own responses to the questionnaire.

1. Do you see something like a thesis? Where does it occur? Where should it occur in the paper? What would be needed to substantiate it?

2. Imagine the responses as very short paragraphs. What could be done to create transitions between them? What would be the best way to arrange them?

3. Are there contradictions in Tom's responses (or yours)? What could be done to resolve them? Should some remarks be eliminated? Should others be pursued?

Make an Issue Out of Something

If you were to turn directly from exploratory thinking to the process of drafting, your draft would likely be disorganized. If you follow the outline of a questionnaire, you aren't thinking for yourself; its organization may not suit the line of thought you want to pursue. Worse still is simply following the analyzed text ("Here's what the author says first, and here's what I make of it; here's what the author says next, and here's what I make of it").

As with all writing, so it is with the essay of analysis: the first principle of organization needs to be your own sense of purpose.

What is your purpose? The analysis of a text? What you will be writing is not *the* analysis but *your* analysis. What will make it yours? We recommend that you give yourself a problem to solve. Do you sense a contradiction in the text, some inconsistency or discrepancy? If so, do you want to resolve the conflict or just highlight it? If you don't see an outright contradiction, do you sense other problems? Thwarted expectations? Suppressed evidence? Were there interesting points of disagreement when the text was discussed in class? Ask yourself, "What seems to be the big question a reader would have about the text I'm analyzing? What can I do to answer it?"

TRIAL RUN

Pose the "big question" emerging from your reading or your class's discussion. Answer it. Give some thought to making that answer your tentative thesis. Now, how would you develop it?

Organize Your Analysis

Once you've given your analysis a problem to solve, you will probably find that your thoughts will begin to fall into place. If this isn't the case—or if you just want some scaffolding to hang your thoughts on initially—you might look again at the questionnaire in Figure 7-2. Remember Tom's instructor said that, given the order of the questions, the responses to them could constitute an effective rough draft. In essence, that questionnaire asks for the text's subject, the author's purpose, the techniques used (particularly those that seem especially important), any sense of contradiction or insufficiency, and any resolution of that sense by reconceiving the author's purpose.

Tom's own organization, evolving through two drafts, turned out to be rather different. The first draft had the same scattered feel Tom ascribed to Woolf when he said that "she does a great deal of 'jumping' from one idea to the next, almost a stream of consciousness." Tom analyzed his own purpose and technique and reordered sections of his paper so that his second draft had this arrangement: a definition of subject, purpose, and context at the outset; a long look at acknowledged and unacknowledged conflicts in the text (concentrated in the two stories); a compilation of clues in Woolf's own techniques that she was experiencing as well as discussing such conflicts; and a conclusion holding that the effect of the speech was to show just that: Woolf was not above the fray but down in it, conscious of social pressures rather than victorious over them. Tom's organization was specifically designed for working through a certain text, but the general pattern is clear enough: after a general introductory overview, work from the *what* (subject or contents) to the *how* (techniques and means), and the *why* (motives and purpose) of an author's communication—never forgetting that these matters are all intertwined. But that's just a very general sense of how to proceed. As always, your organization should be determined by your own sense of focus and purpose.

Be Selective

In your analytical essay, you are not reporting on the text to somebody who hasn't read it; you're showing a reader of the text how thoughtful and insightful your own reading can be. By not being selective, you risk boring such a reader, but by being too selective, you may make your own reading seem spotty or cursory.

So what do you select? Well, what are your priorities? Do you find something problematic about the text, something to home in on? Has discussion or controversy generated by the text identified an issue for you to tackle? Are there subtleties or nuances that might be missed if you do not point them out? Do you want to redress an imbalance? Correct a first impression? Search for a missing link? You may be analyzing another author's text, but your own text needs to be governed by your own sense of purpose. That sense of purpose is not just your principle of organization; it is also your principle of selection.

 **T**RIAL RUN

Return to the text you're analyzing and do some highlighting or underlining. (If you already did this previously, do it again in a different color now.) What phrases and statements and passages strike you as especially important? Why? Keep your answers to these questions in mind as you draft.

CHECKLIST: THE DRAFTING PROCESS

- Have I answered crucial questions about the text? Can I characterize the author's purpose and techniques?

- Have I made an issue of something about the text, a problem I can address, an uncertainty I can elucidate?

- Does my general organization proceed from the *what* of the text to the *how* and the *why*? Does my purpose justify the order in which things are taken up?

- Am I being sufficiently selective, aware that my reader has read the text? Am I economical in using summary, paraphrase, and quotation, yet generous enough with such evidence to make myself clear?

RETHINKING AND REVISING
Strive for Balance

The Chinese philosopher Confucius recommended moderation in all things. It certainly seems the key to any essay analyzing an author's purpose and technique. You don't want to go to extremes here, with two of those extremes being summary and response. Take a look at your draft. Is your account of your chosen text too much like a recounting of that text? Or, on the contrary, do you use that text only as a point of departure, something to agree with or refute? If either case holds true for your first draft, you probably need a second draft from which to draw your final version; you've strayed too far from the business of analysis. If your draft can't be described as too much of a summary on the one hand or too much of a response on the other, you may still find you need to strike a balance between the following:

1. **Description and Interpretation.** Some of your statements will be primarily matters of accuracy, others of insight or judgment. Learn to alternate paraphrase with inference. Show you can both follow the text you're analyzing and make something of it.

2. **Fidelity and Originality.** Earlier we advised approaching a text with both skepticism and humility. Too much skepticism and your essay becomes an exercise in attitude, not analysis, and the text does not get fair treatment. Too much humility and you'll be doing obeisance to the text, not analysis of it, and you'll shortchange yourself. Balance your responsibility to the text with your responsibility to yourself.

3. **Detail and Economy.** You want to draw evidence from the text—that's indispensable—but avoid belaboring the obvious. Remember that your reader has read the text you're analyzing. What do you need to say and cite to pave the way for your conclusions? Hold it down to that. But do no less than that.

CHECKLIST: REVISING YOUR DRAFT

One last thought. Revision is based on an analysis of your own purpose and technique. You're primed for that. As you look over your draft, ask yourself:

- Is my purpose clear? Do I seem purposeful throughout? Is my purpose distinct from that of the author whose text I am analyzing?

- Am I staying close to the text but not too close? Am I avoiding the extremes of summary and response?

- Do I sample the text enough to show the reader how and why it supports my analysis? Have I laid out enough of my reasoning as well as enough textual evidence?

PRESENTING TOM'S FINAL DRAFT

Woman by Profession

Thomas F. Lorentzen

1

After a very brief bit of setting up, Tom introduces his focal point (about a conflict between the roles of woman and writer).

In 1931, the London/National Society for Women's Service chose Virginia Woolf, a noted author, to speak to its members. Asked to speak of her professional experiences, Woolf was to share her thoughts with these women about her career as well as present them with a positive role model. What she talked about was her experience as a writer. What she revealed was her experience as a woman. The stories and language she used illustrate the conflict between the two roles and ultimately the conflict of simply being a woman in a man's world.

2

His first example is the story of the Angel in the House. Note that he does not simply retell the story but interprets it— as in his explanation of what the Angel represents.

One of the first stories she tells in her speech is that of her phantom, the Angel in the House. The Angel, who tries to tame her writing, represents the force instilled in women to conform to ideas about how they should behave and think. Woolf's first writing assignments were reviews of books by men. It was not proper, she was taught, to be over-critical of men. A woman had to be "sympathetic" and "tender." But these qualities were in direct conflict with the task at hand, namely writing about what she saw to be the truth about these books and the attitudes they contained. It was unacceptable for a woman to speak her mind, yet to refrain from doing so would have prevented her from being a successful writer. The tale of the Angel ends with the killing of that phantom, the decision to seek and say truth instead of bowing to the social pressure of remaining "lady-like." There was a kind of censorship being employed by her own mind to keep her from thinking for herself. This type of mental constraint does not occur naturally, but is rather reared and nurtured along with the child. The growth of the mind is guided by how elders think things "should be."

The idea of censorship (imposed or "ingrained") is introduced.

3

Tom relates the second story to the first—in part by suggesting that the Angel really wasn't killed after all.

Her second story is one of imagination running wild. The scene is of someone letting the fishing line of mental curiosity out into the waters of her own imagination. But she can only let it out so far. She must abruptly halt her line of thought because her own passions and thoughts of sexuality are off limits. It is as if the Angel has returned to impose limitations. If she is to be a proper, acceptable woman, she must apparently avoid thoughts of sex. She certainly must avoid being frank and forthright about them.

4

Tom homes in on how Woolf represents herself throughout the piece. The accumulation of details is no mere recounting. Each is carefully selected and presented to contribute to the impression that Woolf is deferential, self-effacing, perhaps not even entirely in control of her own presentation.

The suggestion of an "outside force" controlling Woolf concludes her speech—and leads into the conclusion of Tom's analysis.

5

Tom ends by reflecting on what can be learned from Woolf's predicament (as he sees it): if it is not a success story, it can nevertheless achieve a kind of success for the thoughtful reader.

Virginia Woolf's accounts of her experiences gave her audience a glimpse of the conflicts she faced in her career in writing. She also gives some insight into how these conflicts shaped who she was through her example. She tells the women in her audience that she killed her Angel, only to have the censoring force it represents appear in the next story she tells. She states that she little deserves to be called a professional because she chose to buy a cat (rather than something more practical) with her first earnings as a writer. She does not feel she can take credit for killing her Angel because that credit "rightly belongs to some excellent ancestors of mine who left me a certain sum of money." Throughout her speech, she approaches her topics not like someone who has conquered outside pressures on her way to self-actualization, but as someone who still feels their presence. Her wonder at the idea that "people will give you a motor car if you will tell them a story" stresses how naive she was. Her declaration that she must "obey" the secretary of the Society concerning her material is certainly not made with a voice of assertiveness. Even the way she ends her speech--"My time is up; and I must cease"--seems guided by some unseen outside force she must bend before. Through her examples and her manner of expression she shows her audience a woman who has tried to reconcile the conflicts of two professions, being a writer and being a woman, yet she does not represent herself as a success. Saying she is unsure of what a woman even is, she may come close to being the sort of woman that society says she should be--submissive rather than assertive, questioning rather than confident, polite rather than emphatic.

Virginia Woolf's "Professions for Women" is clearly not a victory speech. She does, however, bring to light the double bind of every professional woman who is asked to fit expectations of that career and the expectations of what a woman should be. Through her professional experiences, Woolf shows how she was taught to conform to society's expectations. If she does not entirely resist those pressures, she is at least conscious of them and their power. If she does not entirely vanquish the Angel, she at least gives others a look at why they should try.

Commentary on Tom's Final Draft

Do you agree with what Tom says in his analysis? You undoubtedly have an interesting answer, but the question itself is interesting. Why ask it? Shouldn't the fruits of careful analysis be beyond dispute?

Not necessarily. And it's not just that an author's intention can never be entirely ascertained. There are other complications. Reading is a matter of reception as well as transmission, of an audience's expectations as well as an author's purpose, of convention as well as invention. Tom's first paragraph notes as much by suggesting that Woolf's speech is a response to an assignment of sorts (though he also suggests she fulfilled that assignment in a way that may have somewhat thwarted or subverted expectations):

> Asked to speak of her professional experiences, Woolf was to share her thoughts with these women about her career as well as present them with a positive role model. What she talked about was her experience as a writer. What she revealed was her experience as a woman.

In Tom's reading, Woolf is not just illustrating "the conflict between the two roles" (of writer and woman); she's also enacting a role before an audience. She is, as Tom began by noting, "a noted author," and knowing that might conjure up expectations—that she will be especially eloquent, that she will adopt an "admire me" or "do as I have done" stance, that she will tell amusing stories, that she will use the occasion to thank her many fans, etc. Clearly, an author facing an audience's expectations still has plenty of choices to make, and the analytical reader has a fair amount of room to interpret how she made them. According to Tom, Woolf enacts the role he stressed on his prompt sheet, that of one who is friendly, familiar, humble. How much is this a conscious choice? How sure is Woolf of herself and what she says? Tom implies a difference between "what she talked about" and "what she revealed," one that hints at unintentional self-revelation, but that is only a hint, at least at this point.

Tom goes on to discuss one of the stories, the story of the Angel in the House. It's not the first story Woolf tells. After introducing herself as someone with a long line of important precursors, other women writers, Woolf tells the story of posting her first piece of writing-for-pay and buying a cat with the proceeds. What justifies Tom's skipping past the first two paragraphs of the text he's analyzing? Remember that an analysis of a text of some length is going to need to be selective; the thing is to have a sensible principle of selection. Tom has already let us know that the keynote of his reading is going to be a conflict between roles; he selects two stories he reads as illustrations of this conflict—stories, moreover, that he feels are in conflict with one another. And that conflict—the sense that self-censorship vanquished in the first story returns to quash imaginative exploration in the second—is Tom's reading of the great point of interest and controversy in his class's discussion of the text. The focus on these two paragraphs does indeed seem justified.

Tom's second (and, to a lesser extent, his third) paragraph may merit a close look for the way they mingle interpretation, paraphrase, and summary. At times, what he says seems close to what the text says: "A woman had to be 'sympathetic' and 'tender.' " At other times, he is clearly interpreting the text, trying to put what Woolf is saying figuratively into his own terms: "The Angel...represents the force instilled in women to conform to ideas about how they should behave and think." There are even times when he seems to be extending Woolf's ideas, saying what she doesn't actually say but does suggest to him: "This type of mental constraint does not occur naturally, but is rather reared and nurtured along with the child." Many different interpretations of what Tom is analyzing here are possible, yet his own analysis seems exemplary for the balance achieved between registering Woolf's thinking and displaying his own: he never gets bogged down in mere rehash of the text, nor does he stray far from the details in it that anchor his thoughts about it.

His next paragraph, the one treating Woolf's story about fishing with her imagination, is less thoroughly anchored and developed. The key sentence is only an "as if" statement: "It is as if the Angel has returned to impose limitations." It would not have been too difficult to give more substance to this posed possibility. For instance, even Woolf's declaration that she killed the Angel leaves an opening for Tom's interpretation: "Though *I flatter myself* that I killed her in the end, the struggle was severe...." Nevertheless, Tom needn't insist on the connection (or discrepancy) between the two stories because he makes it clear enough that, even after the episode with the Angel, Woolf is still suggesting that she can't say all that she might in her writing because she is a writer who is also a woman.

The next paragraph, the longest, finds this sense of constraint to be a feature of the text itself. Tom ranges through the piece, culling examples of modesty, humility, even self-deprecation. His clinchers (perhaps because they imply deference to authority, a supposedly "ladylike" trait) are Woolf's remarks that she's enjoined to "obey" the society's secretary and that her "time is up." These may also be playful twists on the conventions of speech-making, but they do speak to Tom's point.

That point, as it's made in his conclusion, is that Woolf herself—not just her stories but the entire enacted self-characterization her speech represents—illustrates the conflicts and stresses society's expectations for the professional woman. "If she does not entirely resist those pressures, she is at least conscious of them and their power. If she does not entirely vanquish the Angel, she at least gives others a look at why they should try." If that repeated "at least" seems to minimize what someone else might consider an impressive feat, it is in keeping with Woolf's unassuming tone throughout her speech. But this is not Woolf. This is Tom. Or is it? How, finally, do we draw the line between the text and the thoughts it provokes?

Questions for Further Thought

1. The last remarks in the commentary seem to blur the lines so carefully drawn between analysis on the one hand and summary and response on the other. Are there clear distinctions? How would you define them? How would your instructor define them?

2. If analysis is finally interpretation, a matter of opinion, how do we tell a good analysis from one that's not so good? Is that, too, just a matter of opinion? What are the criteria that apply, the standards that are used?

3. Techniques have been identified both with conscious writing strategies for achieving the author's purpose and with standard writing conventions that are followed almost out of habit. How do we know when a technique is one or the other?

4. In the commentary and throughout the chapter, words like *purpose* and *intention* have been used as near synonyms, but it has also been stressed that an author's intention is ultimately unknowable. How fruitful is an attempt to discern it then? If intention is something you can come close to knowing, if only tentatively, how do you know when you're getting close?

PROFESSIONAL ESSAYS

Mary Wollstonecraft
LETTER TO TALLEYRAND

"I call upon you, therefore, now to weigh what I have advanced respecting the rights of women and national education, and I call with the firm tone of humanity."

LIKE THE DAUGHTER SHE NEVER KNEW—SHE died in 1797 shortly after giving birth to Mary Godwin Shelley, author of Frankenstein—*Mary Wollstonecraft wrote many works (novels, stories, histories, translations) but is remembered for one:* A Vindication of the Rights of Women (1792). *Born in 1759, Mary Wollstonecraft lived during the American and French revolutions. Talk of "the rights of man" was in the air (the phrase was also the title of a 1792 book by Tom Paine), and Mary Wollstonecraft decided it was time someone spoke up for the rights of women.*

Being more revolutionary than revolutionaries can be a tricky business, especially when you need to get others to listen to what you have to say. Reading a pamphlet on education reform by Talleyrand, a minor French revolutionary who would become a major diplomat in the 19th century, Wollstonecraft decided to address the preface of her Vindication *to him. She thus gave her general audience a particular face and attitude: liberal-thinking but all-too-blind to women's rights, empowered but not inclined to do women good, cosmopolitan, well-educated, male. If you replace the male/female antagonisms and inequalities with any other lopsided dichotomy of power (minority/ majority, child/adult, poor/rich, perhaps even student/teacher), you get a sense of the general importance of such an argument as Wollstonecraft's —and the importance of making sure it's heard.*

ON THE WAY INTO THE READING

1. What do you expect the argument of an eighteenth-century feminist to be like? How might it be similar to or different from the arguments of present-day feminists?

2. The introduction has already suggested that addressing a specific individual was probably a strategic choice, but what considerations did that choice entail? What tone would you expect Wollstonecraft to adopt? Since she published this "letter" to Talleyrand, how do you think she would want the many readers who were not Talleyrand to respond—by identifying with him, by sympathizing with her, by feeling themselves eavesdroppers on an overheard conversation?

3. You were asked to think about how Wollstonecraft might compare with her present-day counterparts. How might you compare with Wollstonecraft's contemporary readers? As you read, wonder whether your reactions at some points might be essentially the same as theirs or quite different.

1   Sir,—Having read with great pleasure a pamphlet which you have lately published, I dedicate this volume to you—the first dedication that I have ever written, to induce you to read it with attention; and, because I think that you will understand me, which I do not suppose many pert witlings will, who may ridicule the arguments they are unable to answer. But, sir, I carry my respect for your understanding still farther; so far that I am confident you will not throw my work aside, and hastily conclude that I am in the wrong, because you did not view the subject in the same light yourself. And, pardon my frankness, but I must observe, that you treated it in too cursory a manner, contented to consider it as it had been considered formerly, when the rights of man, not to advert to woman, were trampled on as chimerical—I call upon you, therefore, now to weigh what I have advanced respecting the rights of woman and national education; and I call with the firm tone of humanity, for my arguments, sir, are dictated by a disinterested spirit—I plead for my sex, not for myself. Independence I have long considered as the grand blessing of life, the basis of every virtue; and independence I will ever secure by contracting my wants, though I were to live on a barren heath.

2   It is then an affection for the whole human race that makes my pen dart rapidly along to support what I believe to be the cause of virtue; and the same motive leads me earnestly to wish to see woman placed in a station in which she would advance, instead of retarding, the progress of those glorious principles that give a substance to morality. My opinion, indeed,

respecting the rights and duties of woman seems to flow so naturally from these simple principles, that I think it scarcely possible but that some of the enlarged minds who formed your admirable constitution will coincide with me.

3   In France there is undoubtedly a more general diffusion of knowledge than in any part of the European world, and I attribute it, in a great measure, to the social intercourse which has long subsisted between the sexes. It is true—I utter my sentiments with freedom—that in France the very essence of sensuality has been extracted to regale the voluptuary, and a kind of sentimental lust has prevailed, which, together with the system of duplicity that the whole tenor of their political and civil government taught, have given a sinister sort of sagacity to the French character, properly termed *finesse,* from which naturally flow a polish of manners that injures the substance by hunting sincerity out of society. And modesty, the fairest garb of virtue! has been more grossly insulted in France than even in England, till their women have treated as *prudish* that attention to decency which brutes instinctively observe.

4   Manners and morals are so nearly allied that they have often been confounded; but, though the former should only be the natural reflection of the latter, yet, when various causes have produced factitious and corrupt manners, which are very early caught, morality becomes an empty name. The personal reserve, and sacred respect for cleanliness and delicacy in domestic life, which French women almost despise, are the graceful pillars of modesty; but, far from despising them, if the pure flame of patriotism have reached their bosoms, they should labour to improve the morals of their fellow-citizens, by teaching men, not only to respect modesty in women, but to acquire it themselves, as the only way to merit their esteem.

5   Contending for the rights of woman, my main argument is built on this simple principle, that if she be not prepared by education to become the companion of man, she will stop the progress of knowledge and virtue; for truth must be common to all, or it will be inefficacious with respect to its influence on general practice. And how can woman be expected to cooperate unless she knows why she ought to be virtuous? unless freedom strengthens her reason till she comprehends her duty, and see in what manner it is connected with her real good. If children are to be educated to understand the true principle of patriotism, their mother must be a patriot; and the love of mankind, from which an orderly train of virtues spring, can only be produced by considering the moral and civil interest of mankind; but the education and situation of woman at present shuts her out from such investigations.

6   In this work I have produced many arguments, which to me were conclusive, to prove that the prevailing notion respecting a sexual character was subversive of morality, and I have contended, that to render the human body and mind more perfect, chastity must more universally prevail, and that chastity will never be respected in the male world until the person of a woman is not, as it were, idolised, when little virtue or sense embellish it

with the grand traces of mental beauty, or the interesting simplicity of affection.

7   Consider, sir, dispassionately these observations, for a glimpse of this truth seemed to open before you when you observed, "that to see one-half of the human race excluded by the other from all participation of government was a political phenomenon that, according to abstract principles, it was impossible to explain." If so, on what does your constitution rest? If the abstract rights of man will bear discussion and explanation, those of woman, by a parity of reasoning, will not shrink from the same test; though a different opinion prevails in this country, built on the very arguments which you use to justify the oppression of woman—prescription.

8   Consider—I address you as a legislator—whether, when men contend for their freedom, and to be allowed to judge for themselves respecting their own happiness, it be not inconsistent and unjust to subjugate women, even though you firmly believe that you are acting in the manner best calculated to promote their happiness? Who made man the exclusive judge, if woman partake with him of the gift of reason?

9   In this style argue tyrants of every denomination, from the weak king to the weak father of a family; they are all eager to crush reason, yet always assert that they usurp its throne only to be useful. Do you not act a similar part when you *force* all women, by denying them civil and political rights, to remain immured in their families groping in the dark? for surely, sir, you will not assert that a duty can be binding which is not founded on reason? If, indeed, this be their destination, arguments may be drawn from reason; and thus augustly supported, the more understanding women acquire, the more they will be attached to their duty—comprehending it—for unless they comprehend it, unless their morals be fixed on the same immutable principle as those of man, no authority can make them discharge it in a virtuous manner. They may be convenient slaves, but slavery will have its constant effect, degrading the master and the abject dependent.

10   But if women are to be excluded, without having a voice, from a participation of the natural rights of mankind, prove first, to ward off the charge of injustice and inconsistency, that they want reason, else this flaw in your NEW CONSTITUTION will ever show that man must, in some shape, act like a tyrant, and tyranny, in whatever part of society it rears its brazen front, will ever undermine morality.

11   I have repeatedly asserted, and produced what appeared to me irrefragable arguments drawn from matters of fact to prove my assertion, that women cannot by force be confined to domestic concerns; for they will, however ignorant, intermeddle with more weighty affairs, neglecting private duties only to disturb, by cunning trick, the orderly plans of reason which rise above their comprehension.

12   Besides, whilst they are only made to acquire personal accomplishments, men will seek for pleasure in variety, and faithless husbands will make faithless wives; such ignorant beings, indeed, will be very excusable when,

not taught to respect public good, nor allowed any civil rights, they attempt to do themselves justice by retaliation.

13   The box of mischief thus opened in society, what is to preserve private virtue, the only security of public freedom and universal happiness?

14   Let there be then no coercion *established* in society, and the common law of gravity prevailing, the sexes will fall into their proper places. And now that more equitable laws are forming your citizens, marriage may become more sacred; your young men may choose wives from motives of affection, and your maidens allow love to root out vanity.

15   The father of a family will not then weaken his constitution and debase his sentiments by visiting the harlot, nor forget, in obeying the call of appetite, the purpose for which it was implanted. And the mother will not neglect her children to practise the arts of coquetry, when sense and modesty secure her the friendship of her husband.

16   But, till men become attentive to the duty of a father, it is vain to expect women to spend that time in their nursery which they, "wise in their generation," choose to spend at their glass; for this exertion of cunning is only an instinct of nature to enable them to obtain indirectly a little of that power of which they are unjustly denied a share; for, if women are not permitted to enjoy legitimate rights, they will render both men and themselves vicious to obtain illicit privileges.

17   I wish, sir, to set some investigations of this kind afloat in France; and should they lead to a confirmation of my principles when your constitution is revised, the Rights of Woman may be respected, if it be fully proved that reason calls for this respect, and loudly demands JUSTICE for one-half of the human race.

I am, Sir

Yours respectfully,

M.W.

CRITICAL READING

1. The preface begins like a complimentary dedication, but soon Wollstonecraft is saying things like "And, pardon my frankness, but I must observe, that you treated it in too cursory a manner...." Is this a lapse of tact or a calculated tactic? If such remarks are risky, why might they be worth the risk?

2. The same combination of praise and censure directed at Talleyrand is also directed at France—and by an English author. Why is national character an issue for Wollstonecraft? Is she straying from her main subject? Or is she developing it?

3. In the fifth paragraph Wollstonecraft gives her "main argument" its basis in a "simple principle." What is it? Is she founding her argument on a sense of fairness, utility or common good, human progress or destiny? What, fundamentally, does she suggest is the appeal of the argument she is advancing?

4. Wollstonecraft argues that the equality she is seeking is first and fore-most equality of education. Why is this primary? What effects does she ascribe to education—or the lack of it?

5. As her argument proceeds, man is cast as a tyrant (especially in paragraph 9). What motivates his tyranny? Does the characterization seem fair and explicable? If it insults Talleyrand the male, may it also appeal to Talleyrand the revolutionary?

6. Wollstonecraft does not restrict the benefits of equality to women. How would men also benefit, according to her? What will the consequences be if they persist in their tyranny?

7. One way to throw what is distinctive about Wollstonecraft's methods and motives into relief is to think of her argument in light of those advanced by feminists today. How does she seem dated or different? How does she seem prophetic and vindicated?

Samuel Butler
THE WORLD OF THE UNBORN

"Remember also, that if you go into the world you will have free will, that you will be obliged to have it, that there is no escaping it...."

BORN THE SON AND GRANDSON OF CLERGY-men in 1835, Samuel Butler rebelled against that profession, raising sheep in New Zealand till he won financial independence and returned to England. Best known now for his autobiographical novel The Way of All Flesh, *posthumously published in 1903, Butler earned fame in his own lifetime for* Erewhon (1872). *In the tradition of Swift's* Gulliver's Travels *and More's* Utopia (Latin *for "nowhere"—for which "Erewhon" is an anagram), this book is the tale of a Mr. Higgs, who, led by a Maori (or New Zealand aborigine) named Chowbok, discovers and describes a society whose customs—treating illness as a crime, attending the Colleges of Unreason, believing in a world of the unborn—seem bizarre-yet-telling reflections of aspects of Victorian society.*

Our selection from Erewhon *is heralded in the chapter preceding it by Higgs' remark, "From the book of their mythology about the unborn I made the extracts which will form the following chapter." Because Higgs is himself a conventional Victorian, and because he endorses as well as questions Erewhonian society, the precise point of Butler's satire here and elsewhere is not always easy to specify. Is he satirizing the beliefs of the Erewhonians, the reasoning they use to support those beliefs, analogous beliefs in Victorian society, the very conditions of human existence itself? It's hard to say—but analysis of purpose and technique can and should confront such a challenge.*

ON THE WAY INTO THE READING

1. As the introduction notes, casting social criticism in the form of a fantasy is unusual but hardly unprecedented. What would motivate the choice of such a form? What do you expect would be its advantages and disadvantages?

2. "The World of the Unborn" focuses on the burden children are to their parents—and vice versa. Are there aspects of the parent-child relation you suspect are universal rather than functions of specific cultural conditions? What might they be?

3. Surely some aspects of the parent-child relation *are* culturally determined. What do you expect Butler, as a Victorian, would focus on? How do you expect your own sense of parental duties or filial obligations might compare with his? Do you think you believe more or less in individual self-determination than he might have?

1   The Erewhonians say that we are drawn through life backwards; or again, that we go onwards into the future as into a dark corridor. Time walks beside us and flings back shutters as we advance; but the light thus given often dazzles us, and deepens the darkness which is in front. We can see but little at a time, and heed that little far less than our apprehension of what we shall see next; ever peering curiously through the glare of the present into the gloom of the future, we presage the leading lines of that which is before us by faintly reflected lights from dull mirrors that are behind, and stumble on as we may till the trap-door opens beneath us and we are gone.

2   They say at other times that the future and the past are as a panorama upon two rollers; that which is on the roller of the future unwraps itself on to the roller of the past; we cannot hasten it, and we may not stay it; we must see all that is unfolded to us whether it be good or ill; and what we have seen once we may see again no more. It is ever unwinding and being wound; we catch it in transition for a moment, and call it present; our flustered senses gather what impression they can, and we guess at what is coming by the tenor of that which we have seen. The same hand has painted the whole picture, and the incidents vary little, rivers, woods, plains, mountains, towns and peoples, love, sorrow, and death: yet the interest never flags, and we look hopefully for some good fortune, or fearfully lest our own faces be shown us as figuring in something terrible. When the scene is past we think we know it, though there is so much to see, and so little time to see it, that our conceit of knowledge as regards the past is for the most part poorly founded; neither do we care about it greatly, save in so far as it may affect the future, wherein our interest mainly lies.

3   The Erewhonians say it was by chance only that the earth and stars and all the heavenly worlds began to roll from east to west, and not from west to

east, and in like manner they say it is by chance that man is drawn through life with his face to the past instead of to the future. For the future is there as much as the past, only that we may not see it. Is it not in the loins of the past, and must not the past alter before the future can do so?

4   Sometimes again they say that there was a race of men tried upon the earth once, who knew the future better than the past, but that they died in a twelvemonth from the misery which their knowledge caused them; and if any were to be born too prescient now, he would be culled out by natural selection, before he had time to transmit so peace-destroying a faculty to his descendants.

5   Strange fate for man! He must perish if he get that, which he must perish if he strive not after. If he strive not after it he is no better than the brutes, if he get it he is more miserable than the devils.

6   Having waded through many chapters like the above, I came at last to the unborn themselves, and found that they were held to be souls pure and simple, having no actual bodies, but living in a sort of gaseous yet more or less anthropomorphic existence like that of a ghost; they have thus neither flesh nor blood nor warmth. Nevertheless they are supposed to have local habitations and cities wherein they dwell, though these are as unsubstantial as their inhabitants; they are even thought to eat and drink some thin ambrosial sustenance, and generally to be capable of doing whatever mankind can do, only after a visionary ghostly fashion as in a dream. On the other hand, as long as they remain where they are they never die—the only form of death in the unborn world being the leaving it for our own. They are believed to be extremely numerous, far more so than mankind. They arrive from unknown planets, full grown, in large batches at a time; but they can only leave the unborn world by taking the steps necessary for their arrival here—which is, in fact, by suicide.

7   They ought to be an exceedingly happy people, for they have no extremes of good or ill fortune; never marrying, but living in a state much like that fabled by the poets as the primitive condition of mankind. In spite of this, however, they are incessantly complaining; they know that we in this world have bodies, and indeed they know everything else about us, for they move among us whithersoever they will, and can read our thoughts, as well as survey our actions at pleasure. One would think that this would be quite enough for them; and most of them are alive to the desperate risk which they will run by indulging themselves in that body with "sensible warm motion" which they so much desire; nevertheless, there are some to whom the *ennui* of a disembodied existence is so intolerable that they will venture anything for a change; so they resolve to quit. The conditions which they must accept are so uncertain, that none but the most foolish of the unborn will consent to take them; and it is from these, and these only, that our own ranks are recruited.

8   When they have finally made up their minds to leave, they must go before the magistrate of the nearest town and sign an affidavit of their desire to quit their then existence. On their having done this, the magistrate reads them the conditions which they must accept, and which are so long that I

can only extract some of the principal points, which are mainly the following:—

9 First, they must take a potion which will destroy their memory and sense of identity; they must go into the world helpless, and without a will of their own; they must draw lots for their dispositions before they go, and take it, such as it is, for better or worse—neither are they to be allowed any choice in the matter of the body which they so much desire; they are simply allotted by chance, and without appeal, to two people whom it is their business to find and pester until they adopt them. Who these are to be, whether rich or poor, kind or unkind, healthy or diseased, there is no knowing; they have, in fact, to entrust themselves for many years to the care of those for whose good constitution and good sense they have no sort of guarantee.

10 It is curious to read the lectures which the wiser heads give to those who are meditating a change. They talk with them as we talk with a spendthrift, and with about as much success.

11 "To be born," they say, "is a felony—it is a capital crime, for which sentence may be executed at any moment after the commission of the offence. You may perhaps happen to live for some seventy or eighty years, but what is that, in comparison with the eternity which you now enjoy? And even though the sentence were commuted, and you were allowed to live on for ever, you would in time become so terribly weary of life that execution would be the greatest mercy to you. Consider the infinite risk; to be born of wicked parents and trained in vice! to be born of silly parents, and trained to unrealities! of parents who regard you as a sort of chattel or property, belonging more to them than to yourself! Again, you may draw utterly unsympathetic parents, who will never be able to understand you, and who will thwart you as long as they can to the utmost of their power (as a hen when she has hatched a duckling), and then call you ungrateful because you do not love them, or parents who may look upon you as a thing to be cowed while it is still young, lest it should give them trouble hereafter by having wishes and feelings of its own.

12 "In later life, when you have been finally allowed to pass muster as a full member of the world, you will yourself become liable to the pesterings of the unborn—and a very happy life you may be led in consequence! For we solicit so strongly that a few only—nor these the best—can refuse us; and yet not to refuse is much the same as going into partnership with half a dozen different people about whom one can know absolutely nothing before-hand—not even whether one is going into partnership with men or women, nor with how many of either. Delude not yourself with thinking that you will be wiser than your parents. You may be an age in advance of *them,* but unless you are one of the great ones you will still be an age behind your children.

13 "Imagine what it must be to have an unborn quartered upon you, who is of an entirely different temperament and disposition to your own; nay, half a dozen such, who will not love you though you have stinted yourself in a

thousand ways to provide for their comfort and well-being, who will forget all your self-sacrifice, and of whom you may never be sure that they are not bearing a grudge against you for errors of judgment into which you may have fallen, though you had hoped that such had been long since atoned for. Ingratitude such as this is not uncommon, yet fancy what it must be to bear! It is hard upon the duckling to have been hatched by a hen, but is it not also hard upon the hen to have hatched the duckling?

14   "Consider it again, we pray you, not for our sake but for your own. Your initial character you must draw by lot; but whatever it is, it can only come to a tolerably successful development after long training; remember that over that training you will have no control. It is possible, and even probable, that whatever you may get in after life which is of real pleasure and service to you, will have to be won in spite of, rather than by the help of, those whom you are now about to pester, and that you will only win your freedom after years of a painful struggle in which it will be hard to say whether you have suffered most injury, or inflicted it.

15   "Remember also, that if you go into the world you will have free will; that you will be obliged to have it, that there is no escaping it, that you will be fettered to it during your whole life, and must on every occasion do that which on the whole seems best to you at any given time, no matter whether you are right or wrong in choosing it. Your mind will be a balance for considerations, and your action will go with the heavier scale. How it shall fall will depend upon the kind of scales which you may have drawn at birth, the bias which they will have obtained by use, and the weight of the immediate considerations. If the scales were good to start with, and if they have not been outrageously tampered with in childhood, and if the combinations into which you enter are average ones, you may come off well; but there are too many "ifs" in this, and with the failure of any one of them your misery is assured. Reflect on this, and remember that should the ill come upon you, you will have yourself to thank, for it is your own choice to be born, and there is no compulsion in the matter.

16   "Not that we deny the existence of pleasures among mankind; there is a certain show of sundry phases of contentment which may even amount to a very considerable happiness; but mark how they are distributed over a man's life, belonging, all the keenest of them, to the fore part, and few indeed to the after. Can there be any pleasure worth purchasing with the miseries of a decrepit age? If you are good, strong, and handsome, you have a fine fortune indeed at twenty, but how much of it will be left at sixty? For you must live on your capital; there is no investing your powers so that you may get a small annuity of life for ever: you must eat up your principal bit by bit, and be tortured by seeing it grow continually smaller and smaller, even though you happen to escape being rudely robbed of it by crime or casualty. Remember, too, that there never yet was a man of forty who would not come back into the world of the unborn if he could do so with decency and honour. Being in the world he will as a general rule stay till he is forced to go; but do you think that he would consent to be born again, and re-live

his life, if he had the offer of doing so? Do not think it. If he could so alter the past as that he should never have come into being at all, do you not think that he would do it very gladly? What was it that one of their own poets meant, if it was not this, when he cried out upon the day in which he was born, and the night in which it was said there is a man child conceived? 'For now,' he says, 'I should have lain still and been quiet, I should have slept; then had I been at rest with kings and counsellors of the earth, which built desolate places for themselves; or with princes that had gold, who filled their houses with silver; or as an hidden untimely birth, I had not been; as infants which never saw light. There the wicked cease from troubling, and the weary are at rest.' Be very sure that the guilt of being born carries this punishment at times to all men; but how can they ask for pity, or complain of any mischief that may befall them, having entered open-eyed into the snare?

17   "One word more and we have done. If any faint remembrance, as of a dream, flit in some puzzled movement across your brain, and you shall feel that the potion which is to be given you shall not have done its work, and the memory of this existence which you are leaving endeavours vainly to return; we say in such a moment, when you clutch at the dream but it eludes your grasp, and you watch it, as Orpheus watched Eurydice, gliding back again into the twilight kingdom, fly—fly—if you can remember the advice—to the haven of your present and immediate duty, taking shelter incessantly in the work which you have in hand.† This much you may perhaps recall; and this, if you will imprint it deeply upon your every faculty, will be most likely to bring you safely and honourably home through the trials that are before you."

18   This is the fashion in which they reason with those who would be for leaving them, but it is seldom that they do much good, for none but the unquiet and unreasonable ever think of being born, and those who are foolish enough to think of it are generally foolish enough to do it. Finding therefore that they can do no more, the friends follow weeping to the courthouse of the chief magistrate, where the one who wishes to be born declares solemnly and openly that he accepts the conditions attached to his decision. On this he is presented with the potion, which immediately destroys his memory and sense of identity, and dissipates the thin gaseous tenement which he has inhabited: he becomes a bare vital principle, not to be perceived by human senses, nor to be by any chemical test appreciated. He has but one instinct, which is that he is to go to such and such a place, where he will find two persons whom he is to importune till they consent to undertake him; but whether he is to find these persons among the race of Chowbok or the Erewhonians themselves is not for him to choose.

---

† The myth above alluded to exists in Erewhon with changed names, and considerable modifications. I have taken the liberty of referring to the story as familiar to ourselves.

CRITICAL READING

1. The chapter begins with Erewhonian reflections on the experience of time. Do you detect satirical intent here? Are there clues that Butler (if not Higgs) might find these reflections specious or absurd? How are they relevant to what follows?

2. Butler comes from a culture professing a belief in an afterlife. Is this what he is satirizing in his account of beliefs about a *before*life? Are there clear correspondences? Are there suggestions that Butler is up to something more—or other—than religious satire in this chapter?

3. Just as much of Woolf's piece was devoted to stories about the Angel in the House and the swimming imagination, much of this chapter is devoted to a long lecture to those contemplating birth. What are the characteristics of this narration within a narration? What is it like in terms of tone and content? What clues does it provide to Butler's purpose in the chapter as a whole?

4. The unborn who would be born are asked to consider a variety of reasons opposing the step they contemplate. How are these ordered? Which seem most important from the lecturer's perspective? Which seem most relevant to Butler's purpose?

5. A favorite device of Butler's is the paradox—the seeming contradiction that nevertheless is true. Which among these paradoxes (including the idea that being born is a capital crime or that we are fettered by free will) seem truest? Do some seem false paradoxes—absurdities rather than truths? Is there a pattern to Butler's use of paradoxes?

6. Remember that Higgs is the narrator, Butler the author. Can you tell the two apart? Are there points where Higgs seems to endorse something Butler might wish to distance himself from, where the narrator's uncritical regard may mask the author's irony? If you think that what Higgs says is not exactly what Butler means, what are your reasons? If you identify the two, what are your reasons for equating Higgs' remarks with Butler's intentions?

CHAPTER EIGHT

DEVELOPING A PERSONAL RESPONSE TO A TEXT

In the previous chapter, the author held center stage, with the attention focused not just on what the author said but on how and why. Now, however, it's time for the reader to step up to the lights—and to play a bigger part than is sometimes thought. The reader's role almost never stops with understanding or even analysis. Instead, reading is inescapably interpretation: *making* something of a text rather than simply *getting* it. Think about it. When you read, your understanding of what you read is almost always a *responsive* understanding. You form an opinion about what you've read. Is it true? Do you agree? Do you think it's significant? Can you relate to it? You ponder these questions even when they aren't asked of you (and in college they often *are* asked of you.) Truth to tell, there really is no such thing as mere comprehension—at least not with more complex and challenging texts. If it were just a matter of "getting it," every competent reader would get the same thing, and that obviously doesn't happen.

To provide concrete demonstration of what we mean by making something of text, we have chosen "The 'Banking' Concept of Education" by Paulo Freire. We admit that we chose it partly because students tend to find it difficult. Mikhael Yanko, a case in point, has nevertheless done an exemplary job of responding to Freire in his essay "Education of the Fittest." We also have two other texts you might choose to respond to: Adrienne Rich's "Claiming an Education" and Peter Elbow's "Representing Course Grades Differently: A Proposal." Like Freire's, these are challenging pieces—political, learned, argumentative—yet they also bear directly on students' experiences.

As a means of getting a handle on such texts, this chapter recommends the double-entry reading journal. It also considers (rather differently than Chapter 7 did) the relationship between what's said in class discussion of a text and what's said in an individual student's paper. In particular, when writing about an assigned reading, focusing on student-teacher relationships as author-audience relationships becomes vital. We have tried to heighten the focus by choosing texts by academics who are criticizing the academy, texts that challenge received wisdom about a university education (and, by implication, any passive acceptance of established ideas). These texts make the great vice of responsive writing—mere recapitulation—doubly inappropriate, just as they make the great virtue—critical reflection—doubly necessary.

WRITING ASSIGNMENT

Write an essay in which you respond to one of the two readings at the end of this chapter (or, on your instructor's advice, any other reading in this book). Throughout your thinking about this assignment, keep in mind two things:

1. Your response has to be a genuine response, not a recapitulation.
2. Your response should be a distinctive response, one that is uniquely yours—not attributable to some hypothetical "average reader," nor to the comments and responses of others made during discussion of the text in class.

READING THE WRITING ASSIGNMENT

What you most want to avoid in this assignment is "knowledge-telling": not thinking critically about the material, not assessing it or questioning it, but just retelling it, giving a rehash, a summary, a digest (and a highly selective one at that). Knowledge-telling, of course, results from just the kind of *retentive* reading that years of school have trained you for: skim for the main points, get the gist, glean information, remember for the exam. But, increasingly, students are asked not just to absorb what they've read but to think about it, question it, even challenge it. It's as if, having been held in the role of passive listeners for so long, students are at last invited—indeed, expected—to join the conversation. They are asked to become active, thoughtful, critical, *responsive* readers. In your own mind, you have to make the move from the sort of reading that allows you to summarize what you've read to the sort of reading that allows you to respond to it—and to do so impressively.

The difference between retentive and responsive reading is something you can't simply be told about; you have to experience it. We can tell you what *not* to do: don't turn your written response into an exercise in knowledge-telling. But no one can tell you what to do because no one can tell you what response to have. What's more, you want to do something that's distinctive, even outstanding, and those very words underscore the fact that there's no standard recipe for that. Still, we can offer some help. That's what the rest of the chapter is all about.

DISCOVERING IDEAS

Analyze Your Text

When we urge you not to engage in knowledge-telling, we are also inviting you to distinguish your purpose from that of the author you're responding to. This means you need to have a sense of the author's purpose, and material from Chapter 7 (devoted to analyzing authorial purpose and technique) may be of some use here. At the very least, ask yourself some key questions. Why is the author writing? Who is the author's audience? What is the author's perspective?

It is of course impossible to identify the author's purpose (and thus to distinguish your own purpose) without first reading the text. Given a choice of texts, Mikhael Yanko took on Paulo Freire's "The 'Banking' Concept of Education," choosing it upon learning Freire was a Brazilian Marxist and educator. An Israeli recently arrived in the States, Mikhael felt he might have some affinity for someone his classmates might think of as a foreigner.

Mikhael was given no more introduction to Paulo Freire and "The 'Banking' Concept of Education" than you have just been given, except to learn that the essay came from a book called *Pedagogy of the Oppressed,* first published (in Portuguese, the language of Brazilians) in 1971. Here is the essay.

THE "BANKING" CONCEPT OF EDUCATION

Paulo Freire

1   A careful analysis of the teacher-student relationship at any level, inside or outside the school, reveals its fundamentally *narrative* character. This relationship involves a narrating Subject (the teacher) and patient, listening objects (the students). The contents, whether values or empirical dimensions or reality, tend in the process of being narrated to become lifeless and petrified. Education is suffering from narration sickness.

2   The teacher talks about reality as if it were motionless, static, compartmentalized, and predictable. Or else he expounds on a topic completely alien to the existential experience of the students. His task is to "fill" the students with the contents of his narration—contents which are detached from reality, disconnected from the totality that engendered them and could give them significance. Words are emptied of their concreteness and become a hollow, alienated, and alienating verbosity.

3   The outstanding characteristic of this narrative education, then, is the sonority or words, not their transforming power. "Four times four is sixteen; the capital of Pará is Belém." The student records, memorizes, and repeats these phrases without perceiving what four times four really means, or realizing the true significance of "capital" in the affirmation "the capital of Pará is Belém," that is, what Belém means for Pará and what Pará means for Brazil.

4   Narration (with the teacher as narrator) leads the students to memorize mechanically the narrated content. Worse yet, it turns them into "containers," into "receptacles" to be "filled" by the teacher. The more completely he fills the receptacles, the better a teacher he is. The more meekly the receptacles permit themselves to be filled, the better students they are.

5   Education thus becomes an act of depositing, in which the students are the depositories and the teacher is the depositor. Instead of communicating, the teacher issues communiqués and makes deposits which the students patiently receive, memorize, and repeat. This is the "banking" concept of education, in which the scope of the action allowed to the students extends only as far as receiving, filing, and storing the deposits. They do, it is true, have the opportunity to become collectors or cataloguers of the things they store. But in the last analysis, it is men themselves who are filed away through the lack of creativity, transformation, and knowledge in this (at best) misguided system. For apart from inquiry, apart from the praxis, men cannot be truly human. Knowledge emerges only through invention and reinvention, through the restless, impatient, continuing, hopeful inquiry men pursue in the world, with the world, and with each other.

6   In the banking concept of education, knowledge is a gift bestowed by those who consider themselves knowledgeable upon those whom they consider to know nothing. Projecting an absolute ignorance onto others, a characteristic of the ideology of oppression, negates education and knowledge as processes of inquiry. The teacher presents himself to his students as their necessary opposite; by considering their ignorance absolute, he justifies his own existence. The students, alienated like the slave in the Hegelian dialectic, accept their ignorance as justifying the teacher's existence—but, unlike the slave, they never discover that they educate the teacher.

7   The *raison d'être* of libertarian education, on the other hand, lies in its drive towards reconciliation. Education must begin with the solution of the teacher-student contradiction, by reconciling the poles of the contradiction so that both are simultaneously teachers *and* students.

8   This solution is not (nor can it be) found in the banking concept. On the contrary, banking education maintains and even stimulates the contradiction through the following attitudes and practices, which mirror oppressive society as a whole:

a. the teacher teaches and the students are taught;

b. the teacher knows everything and the students know nothing;

c. the teacher thinks and the students are thought about;

d. the teacher talks and the students listen—meekly;

e. the teacher disciplines and the students are disciplined;

f. the teacher chooses and enforces his choice, and the students comply;

g. the teacher acts and the students have the illusion of acting through the action of the teacher;

h. the teacher chooses the program content, and the students (who were not consulted) adapt to it;

i. the teacher confuses the·authority of knowledge with his own professional authority, which he sets in opposition to the freedom of the students;

j. the teacher is the Subject of the learning process, while the pupils are mere objects.

9   It is not surprising that the banking concept of education regards men as adaptable, manageable beings. The more students work at storing the deposits entrusted to them, the less they develop the critical consciousness which would result from their intervention in the world as transformers of that world. The more completely they accept the passive role imposed on them, the more they tend simply to adapt to the world as it is and to the fragmented view of reality deposited in them.

10   The capability of banking education to minimize or annul the students' creative power and to stimulate their credulity serves the interests of the oppressors, who care neither to have the world revealed nor to see it transformed. The oppressors use their "humanitarianism" to preserve a profitable situation. Thus they react almost instinctively against any experiment in education which stimulates the critical faculties and is not content with a partial view of reality but always seeks out the ties which link one point to another and one problem to another.

11   Indeed, the interests of the oppressors lie in "changing the consciousness of the oppressed, not the situation which oppresses them";[1] for the more the oppressed can be led to adapt to that situation, the more easily they can be dominated. To achieve this end, the oppressors use the banking concept of education in conjunction with a paternalistic social action apparatus, within which the oppressed receive the euphemistic title of "welfare recipients." They are treated as individual cases, as marginal men who deviate from the general configuration of a "good, organized, and just" society. The oppressed are regarded as the pathology of the healthy society, which must therefore adjust these "incompetent and lazy" folk to its own patterns by changing their mentality. These marginals need to be "integrated," "incorporated" into the healthy society that they have "foresaken."

12   The truth is, however, that the oppressed are not "marginals," are not men living "outside" society. They have always been "inside"—inside the structure which made them "beings for others." The solution is not to "integrate" them into the structure of oppression, but to transform that structure so that they can become "beings for themselves." Such transformation, of course, would undermine the oppressors' purposes; hence their

[1] Simone de Beauvoir, *La Pensée de Droite, Aujord'hui* (Paris); ST, *El Pensamiento político de la Derecha* (Buenos Aires, 1963), p. 34.

utilization of the banking concept of education to avoid the threat of student *conscientização.**

13   The banking approach to adult education, for example, will never propose to students that they critically consider reality. It will deal instead with such vital questions as whether Roger gave green grass to the goat, and insist upon the importance of learning that, on the contrary, Roger gave green grass to the *rabbit.* The "humanism" of the banking approach masks the effort to turn men into automatons—the very negation of their ontological vocation to be more fully human.

14   Those who use the banking approach, knowingly or unknowingly (for there are innumerable well-intentioned bank-clerk teachers who do not realize that they are serving only to dehumanize), fail to perceive that the deposits themselves contain contradictions about reality. But, sooner or later, these contradictions may lead formerly passive students to turn against their domestication and the attempt to domesticate reality. They may discover through existential experience that their present way of life is irreconcilable with their vocation to become fully human. They may perceive through their relations with reality that reality is really a *process,* undergoing constant transformation. If men are searchers and their ontological vocation is humanization, sooner or later they may perceive the contradiction in which banking education seeks to maintain them, and then engage themselves in the struggle for their liberation.

15   But the humanist, revolutionary educator cannot wait for this possibility to materialize. From the outset, his efforts must coincide with those of the students to engage in critical thinking and the quest for mutual humanization. His efforts must be imbued with a profound trust in men and their creative power. To achieve this, he must be a partner of the students in his relations with them.

16   The banking concept does not admit to such partnership—and necessarily so. To resolve the teacher-student contradiction, to exchange the role of depositor, prescriber, domesticator, for the role of student among students would be to undermine the power of oppression and serve the cause of liberation.

17   Implicit in the banking concept is the assumption of a dichotomy between man and the world: man is merely *in* the world, not *with* the world or with others; man is spectator, not re-creator. In this view, man is not a conscious being (*corpo consciente*); he is rather the possessor of *a* consciousness: an empty "mind" passively open to the reception of deposits of reality from the world outside. For example, my desk, my books, my coffee cup, all the objects before me—as bits of the world which surrounds me—would be "inside" me, exactly as I am inside my study right now. This view makes no distinction between being accessible to consciousness and entering consciousness. The distinction, however, is essential: the objects

* **conscientização** According to Freire's translator, "The term *conscientização* refers to learning to perceive social, political, and economic contradictions, and to take action against the oppressive elements of reality."

which surround me are simply accessible to my consciousness, not located within it. I am aware of them, but they are not inside me.

18   It follows logically from the banking notion of consciousness that the educator's role is to regulate the way the world "enters into" the students. His task is to organize a process which already occurs spontaneously, to "fill" the students by making deposits of information which he considers to constitute true knowledge.[2] And since men "receive" the world as passive entities, education should make them more passive still, and adapt them to the world. The educated man is the adapted man, because he is better "fit" for the world. Translated into practice, this concept is well suited to the purposes of the oppressors, whose tranquility rests on how well men fit the world the oppressors have created, and how little they question it.

19   The more completely the majority adapt to the purposes which the dominant minority prescribe for them (thereby depriving them of the right to their own purposes), the more easily the minority can continue to prescribe. The theory and practice of banking education serve this end quite efficiently. Verbalistic lessons, reading requirements,[3] the method for evaluating "knowledge," the distance between the teacher and the taught, the criteria for promotion: everything in this ready-to-wear approach serves to obviate thinking.

20   The bank-clerk educator does not realize that there is no true security in his hypertrophied role, that one must seek to live *with* others in solidarity. One cannot impose oneself, nor even merely co-exist with one's students. Solidarity requires true communication, and the concept by which such an educator is guided fears and proscribes communication.

21   Yet only through communication can human life hold meaning. The teacher's thinking is authenticated only by the authenticity of the students' thinking. The teacher cannot think for his students, nor can he impose his thought on them. Authentic thinking, thinking that is concerned about *reality,* does not take place in ivory tower isolation, but only in communication. If it is true that thought has meaning only when generated by action upon the world, the subordination of students to teachers becomes impossible.

22   Because banking education begins with a false understanding of men as objects, it cannot promote the development of what Fromm calls "biophily," but instead produces its opposite: "necrophily."

> While life is characterized by growth in a structured, functional manner, the necrophilous person loves all that does not grow, all that is mechanical. The necrophilous person is driven by the desire to transform the organic into the inorganic, to approach life mechanically, as if all living persons were things.... Memory, rather than experience; having rather than being, is what counts.

[2] This concept corresponds to what Sartre calles the "digestive" or "nutritive" concept of education, in which knowledge is "fed" by the teacher to the students to "fill them out." See Jean-Paul Sartre, "Une idée fundamentale de la phénoménologie de Husserl: L'intentionalité," *Situations I* (Paris, 1947).

[3] For example, some professors specify in their reading lists that a book should be read from pages 10 to 15—and do this to "help" their students!

> The necrophilous person can relate to an object—a flower or a person—only if he possesses it; hence a threat to his possession is a threat to himself; if he loses possession he loses contact with the world.... He loves control, and in the act of controlling he kills life.[4]

23   Oppression—overwhelming control—is necrophilic; it is nourished by love of death, not life. The banking concept of education, which serves the interests of oppression, is also necrophilic. Based on a mechanistic, static, naturalistic, spatialized view of consciousness, it transforms students into receiving objects. It attempts to control thinking and action, leads men to adjust to the world, and inhibits their creative power.

24   When their efforts to act responsibly are frustrated, when they find themselves unable to use their faculties, men suffer. "The suffering due to impotence is rooted in the very fact that the human equilibrium has been disturbed."[5] But the inability to act which causes men's anguish also causes them to reject their impotence, by attempting

> ...to restore [their] capacity to act. But can [they], and how? One way is to submit to and identify with a person or group having power. By this symbolic participation in another person's life, [men have] the illusion of acting, when in reality [they] only submit to and become part of those who act.[6]

25   Populist manifestations perhaps best exemplify this type of behavior by the oppressed, who, by identifying with charismatic leaders, come to feel that they themselves are active and effective. The rebellion they express as they emerge in the historical process is motivated by that desire to act effectively. The dominant elites consider the remedy to be more domination and repression, carried out in the name of freedom, order, and social peace (that is, the peace of the elites). Thus they can condemn—logically, from their point of view—"the violence of a strike by workers and [can] call upon the state in the same breath to use violence in putting down the strike."[7]

26   Education as the exercise of domination stimulates the credulity of students, with the ideological intent (often not perceived by educators) of indoctrinating them to adapt to the world of oppression. This accusation is not made in the naïve hope that the dominant elites will thereby simply abandon the practice. Its objective is to call the attention of true humanists to the fact that they cannot use banking educational methods in the pursuit of liberation, for they would only negate that very pursuit. Nor may a revolutionary society inherit these methods from an oppressor society. The revolutionary society which practices banking education is either misguided or mistrusting of men. In either event, it is threatened by the specter of reaction.

[4] Eric Fromm, *The Heart of Man* (New York, 1966), p. 41.
[5] *Ibid.*, p. 31.
[6] *Ibid.*
[7] Reinhold Niebuhr, *Moral Man and Immoral Society* (New York, 1960), p. 130.

27   Unfortunately, those who espouse the cause of liberation are themselves surrounded and influenced by the climate which generates the banking concept, and often do not perceive its true significance or its dehumanizing power. Paradoxically, then, they utilize this same instrument of alienation in what they consider an effort to liberate. Indeed, some "revolutionaries" brand as "innocents," "dreamers," or even "reactionaries" those who would challenge this educational practice. But one does not liberate men by alienating them. Authentic liberation—the process of humanization—is not another deposit to be made in men. Liberation is a praxis: the action and reflection of men upon their world in order to transform it. Those truly committed to the cause of liberation can accept neither the mechanistic concept of consciousness as an empty vessel to be filled, nor the use of banking methods of domination (propaganda, slogans—deposits) in the name of the liberation.

28   Those truly committed to liberation must reject the banking concept in its entirety, adopting instead a concept of men as conscious beings, and consciousness as consciousness intent upon the world. They must abandon the educational goal of deposit-making and replace it with the posing of the problems of men in their relations with the world. "Problem-posing" education, responding to the essence of consciousness—*intentionality*—rejects communiqués and embodies communications. It epitomizes the special characteristic of consciousness: being *conscious of,* not only as intent on objects but as turned in upon itself in a Jasperian "split"—consciousness as consciousness *of* consciousness.

29   Liberating education consists in acts of cognition, not transferrals of information. It is a learning situation in which the cognizable object (far from being the end of the cognitive act) intermediates the cognitive actors—teacher on the one hand and students on the other. Accordingly, the practice of problem-posing education entails at the outset that the teacher-student contradiction be resolved. Dialogical relations—indispensable to the capacity of cognitive actors to cooperate in perceiving the same cognizable object—are otherwise impossible.

30   Indeed, problem-posing education, which breaks with the vertical patterns characteristic of banking education, can fulfill its function as the practice of freedom only if it can overcome the above contradiction. Through dialogue, the teacher-of-the-students and the students-of-the-teacher cease to exist and a new term emerges: teacher-student with students-teacher. The teacher is no longer merely the-one-who-teaches, but one who is himself taught in dialogue with the students, who in turn while being taught also teach. They become jointly responsible for a process in which all grow. In this process, arguments based on "authority" are no longer valid; in order to function, authority must be *on the side of* freedom, not *against* it. Here, no one teaches another, nor is anyone self-taught. Men teach each other, mediated by the world, by the cognizable objects which in banking education are "owned" by the teacher.

31   The banking concept (with its tendency to dichotomize everything) distinguishes two stages in the action of the educator. During the first he cognizes a cognizable object while he prepares his lessons in his study or his laboratory; during the second, he expounds to his students about that object. The students are not called upon to know, but to memorize the contents narrated by the teacher. Nor do the students practice any act of cognition, since the object towards which that act should be directed is the property of the teacher rather than a medium evoking the critical reflection of both teacher and students. Hence in the name of the "preservation of culture and knowledge" we have a system which achieves neither true knowledge nor true culture.

32   The problem-posing method does not dichotomize the activity of the teacher-student: he is not "cognitive" at one point and "narrative" at another. He is always "cognitive," whether preparing a project or engaging in dialogue with the students. He does not regard cognizable objects as his private property, but as the object of reflection by himself and the students. In this way, the problem-posing educator constantly re-forms his reflections in the reflection of the students. The students—no longer docile listeners—are now critical co-investigators in dialogue with the teacher. The teacher presents the material to the students for their consideration, and re-considers his earlier considerations as the students express their own. The role of the problem-posing educator is to create, together with the students, the conditions under which knowledge at the level of the *doxa* is superseded by true knowledge, at the level of the *logos*.

33   Whereas banking education anesthetizes and inhibits creative power, problem-posing education involves a constant unveiling of reality. The former attempts to maintain the *submersion* of consciousness; the latter strives for the *emergence* of consciousness and *critical intervention* in reality.

34   Students, as they are increasingly posed with problems relating to themselves in the world and with the world, will feel increasingly challenged and obliged to respond to that challenge. Because they apprehend the challenge as interrelated to other problems within a total context, not as a theoretical question, the resulting comprehension tends to be increasingly critical and thus constantly less alienated. Their response to the challenge evokes new challenges, followed by new understandings; and gradually the students come to regard themselves as committed.

35   Education as the practice of freedom—as opposed to education as the practice of domination—denies that man is abstract, isolated, independent, and unattached to the world; it also denies that the world exists as a reality apart from men. Authentic reflection considers neither abstract man nor the world without men, but men in their relations with the world. In these relations consciousness and world are simultaneous: consciousness neither precedes the world nor follows it.

La conscience et le monde sont donnés d'un même coup:
extérieur par essence à la conscience, le monde est, par essence
relatif à elle.[8]

In one of our culture circles in Chile, the group was discussing...the
anthropological concept of culture. In the midst of the discussion, a peasant
who by banking standards was completely ignorant said: "Now I see that
without man there is no world." When the educator responded: "Let's say,
for the sake of argument, that all the men on earth were to die, but that the
earth itself remained, together with trees, birds, animals, rivers, seas, the
stars . . . wouldn't all this be a world?"

36   "Oh, no," the peasant replied emphatically. "There would be no one to
say: 'This is a world'."

37   The peasant wished to express the idea that there would be lacking the
consciousness of the world which necessarily implies the world of consciousness. *I* cannot exist without a *not-I*. In turn, the *not-I* depends on that
existence. The world which brings consciousness into existence becomes
the world of that consciousness. Hence, the previously cited affirmation of
Sartre: *"La conscience et le monde sont donnés d'un même coup."*

38   As men, simultaneously reflecting on themselves and on the world,
increase the scope of their perception, they begin to direct their observations towards previously inconspicuous phenomena:

> In perception properly so-called, as an explicit awareness
> [*Gewahren*], I am turned toward the object, to the paper, for
> instance. I apprehend it as being this here and now. The appre-
> hension is a singling out, every object having a background in
> experience. Around and about the paper lie books, pencils, ink-
> well, and so forth, and these in a certain sense are also "per-
> ceived," perceptually there, in the "field of intuition"; but whilst I
> was turned towards the paper there was no turning in their
> direction, nor any apprehending of them, not even in a secondary
> sense. They appeared and yet were not singled out, were not
> posited on their own account. Every perception of a thing has
> such a zone of background intuitions or background awareness, if
> "intuiting" already includes the state of being turned towards, and
> this also is "conscious experience," or more briefly a "conscious-
> ness of" all indeed that in point of fact lies in the co-perceived
> objective background.[9]

That which has existed objectively but had not been perceived in its
deeper implications (if indeed it was perceived at all) begins to "stand out,"
assuming the character of a problem and therefore of challenge. Thus, men
begin to single out elements from their "background awarenesses" and to
reflect upon them. These elements are now objects of men's consideration,
and, as such, objects of their action and cognition.

---

[8] Sartre, *op. cit.,* p. 32. ["Consciousness and the world are simultaneous givens: the external world enters consciousness relative to consciousness of it."]

[9] Edmund Husserl, *Ideas—General Introduction to Pure Phenomenology* (London, 1969), pp. 105–106.

39   In problem-posing education, men develop their power to perceive critically *the way they exist* in the world *with which* and *in which* they find
themselves; they come to see the world not as a static reality, but as a
reality in process, in transformation. Although the dialectical relations are
perceived (or whether or not they are perceived at all), it is also true that
the form of action men adopt is to a large extent a function of how they
perceive themselves in the world. Hence, the teacher-student and the
students-teachers reflect simultaneously on themselves and the world without dichotomizing this reflection from action, and thus establish an authentic form of thought and action.

40   Once again, the two educational concepts and practices under analysis
come into conflict. Banking education (for obvious reasons) attempts, by
mythicizing reality, to conceal certain facts which explain the way men
exist in the world; problem-posing education sets itself the task of demythol-
ogizing. Banking education resists dialogue; problem-posing education
regards dialogue as indispensable to the act of cognition which unveils
reality. Banking education treats students as objects of assistance; problem-
posing education makes them critical thinkers. Banking education inhibits
creativity and domesticates (although it cannot completely destroy) the
intentionality of consciousness by isolating consciousness from the world,
thereby denying men their ontological and historical vocation of becoming
more fully human. Problem-posing education bases itself on creativity and
stimulates true reflection and action upon reality, thereby responding to the
vocation of men as beings who are authentic only when engaged in inquiry
and creative transformation. In sum: banking theory and practice, as
immobilizing and fixating forces, fail to acknowledge men as historical
beings; problem-posing theory and practice take man's historicity as their
starting point.

41   Problem-posing education affirms men as beings in the process of
becoming—as unfinished, uncompleted beings in and with a likewise unfinished reality. Indeed, in contrast to other animals who are unfinished, but
not historical, men know themselves to be unfinished; they are aware of
their incompletion. In this incompletion and this awareness lie the very
roots of education as an exclusively human manifestation. The unfinished
character of men and the transformational character of reality necessitate
that education be an ongoing activity.

42   Education is thus constantly remade in the praxis. In order to *be,* it must
become. Its "duration" (in the Bergsonian meaning of the word) is found in
the interplay of the opposites *permanence* and *change.* The banking
method emphasizes permanence and becomes reactionary; problem-
posing education—which accepts neither a "well-behaved" present nor a
predetermined future—roots itself in the dynamic present and becomes
revolutionary.

43   Problem-posing education is revolutionary futurity. Hence it is prophetic
(and, as such, hopeful). Hence, it corresponds to the historical nature of
man. Hence, it affirms men as beings who transcend themselves, who move

forward and look ahead, for whom immobility represents a fatal threat, for whom looking at the past must only be a means of understanding more clearly what and who they are so that they can more wisely build a future. Hence, it identifies with the movement which engages men as beings aware of their incompletion—an historical movement which has its point of departure, its Subjects and its objective.

44   The point of departure of the movement lies in men themselves. But since men do not exist apart from the world, apart from reality, the movement must begin with the men-world relationship. Accordingly, the point of departure must always be with men in the "here and now," which constitutes the situation within which they are submerged, from which they emerge, and in which they intervene. Only by starting from this situation—which determines their perception of it—can they begin to move. To do this authentically they must perceive their state not as fated and unalterable, but merely as limiting—and therefore challenging.

45   Whereas the banking method directly or indirectly reinforces men's fatalistic perception of their situation, the problem-posing method presents this very situation to them as a problem. As the situation becomes the object of their cognition, the naïve or magical perception which produced their fatalism gives way to perception which is able to perceive itself even as it perceives reality, and can thus be critically objective about that reality.

46   A deepened consciousness of their situation leads men to apprehend that situation as an historical reality susceptible of transformation. Resignation gives way to the drive for transformation and inquiry, over which men feel themselves to be in control. If men, as historical beings necessarily engaged with other men in a movement or inquiry, did not control that movement, it would be (and is) a violation of men's humanity. Any situation in which some men prevent others from engaging in the process of inquiry is one of violence. The means used are not important; to alienate men from their own decision-making is to change them into objects.

47   This movement of inquiry must be directed towards humanization—man's historical vocation. The pursuit of full humanity, however, cannot be carried out in isolation or individualism but only in fellowship and solidarity; therefore it cannot unfold in the antagonistic relations between oppressors and oppressed. No one can be authentically human while he prevents others from being so. Attempting *to be more* human, individualistically, leads to *having more,* egotistically: a form of dehumanization. Not that it is not fundamental to *have* in order *to be* human. Precisely because it *is* necessary, some men's *having* must not be allowed to constitute an obstacle to others' *having,* must not consolidate the power of the former to crush the latter.

48   Problem-posing education, as a humanist and liberating praxis, posits as fundamental that men subjected to domination must fight for their emancipation. To that end, it enables teachers and students to become Subjects of the educational process by overcoming authoritarianism and an alienating intellectualism; it also enables men to overcome their false perception of

reality. The world—no longer something to be described with deceptive words—becomes the object of that transforming action by men which results in their humanization.

49   Problem-posing education does not and cannot serve the interests of the oppressor. No oppressive order could permit the oppressed to begin to question: Why? While only a revolutionary society can carry out this education in systematic terms, the revolutionary leaders need not take full power before they can employ the method. In the revolutionary process, the leaders cannot utilize the banking method as an interim measure, justified on grounds of expediency, with the intention of *later* behaving in a genuinely revolutionary fashion. They must be revolutionary—that is to say, dialogical—from the outset.

Record Your Reading Experience in a Double-Entry Journal

We said earlier that the difference, in reading, between getting it (comprehension) and making something of it (response) was something you couldn't simply be told about, something you have to experience for yourself. Ann E. Berthoff has devised a way to heighten the experience. She calls it the double-entry notebook, and here is her own description of how it works:

> I ask my students (all of them: freshmen, upper-classmen, teachers in graduate seminars) to furnish themselves with a notebook, spiralbound at the side, small enough to be easily carried around but not so small that writing is cramped . . . . What makes this notebook different from most, perhaps, is the notion of the double entry: on the right side reading notes, direct quotations, observational notes, fragments, lists, images—verbal and visual—are recorded; on the other (facing) side, notes about those notes, summaries, formulations, aphorisms, editorial suggestions, revisions, comment on comment are written. The reason for the double-entry format is that it provides a way for the student to conduct that "continuing audit or meaning" [a phrase from the work of I. A. Richards] that is at the heart of learning to read and write critically. The facing pages are in dialogue with each other. (*The Making of Meaning,* p. 45)

As Berthoff goes on to point out, such a notebook has a host of specific uses. We are interested in three. First, you can use the double-entry journal as a way of experiencing the difference between reading for sense and forming a response, between comprehension and interpretation. Second, double entries help you to anchor your response to details in the text—and this is vital when it comes time to explain your response in writing. Finally, reading, like writing, is a process, and a double-entry journal helps you to see the way your understanding of the text or your response to it evolves. This, too, can be most helpful to you in explaining why your response took the form that it did.

TRIAL RUN

In Mikhael's case, the instructor recommended that students simply draw vertical lines down the center of regular sheets of paper, heading the lefthand column (the equivalent of Berthoff's righthand page) "Freire" and the righthand column "My Thoughts." You do what seems best for you—or what your instructor advises. It will be instructive to compare your journal to Mikhael's and also to those of your classmates—but only if yours is done as a record of *your* thoughts. Seeming distinctive is all the more challenging when others are responding to the same text. Ideally, every reaction should be registered; any one may be key to making your essay distinctive, impressive, uniquely yours.

CHECKLIST: WRITING A DOUBLE-ENTRY JOURNAL

- Are you keeping remarks dealing with comprehension of the text (what seem difficult or crucial passages, for instance) distinct from those dealing with your responses (such as reasons you agree or disagree)?

- Are you trying for a fair measure of both kinds of remarks, a balance of analysis and opinion?

- Are you trying for as full an account of your reading experience as possible?

Here, typed up, are Mikhael's double entries on Freire's text:

FREIRE	MY THOUGHTS
The problem with the "banking" concept: "Projecting an absolute ignorance onto others, a characteristic of the ideology of oppression, negates education and knowledge as processes of inquiry."	Freire's material is very difficult to read. If he wants to present his ideas for people to consider, why does he alienate them by using language that is so difficult to understand?
F gives a list (a-j) of "attitudes and practices," but where are examples?	I guess I will have to come up with my own. "Four times four is sixteen" makes me think of that math class in 7th grade.

FREIRE	MY THOUGHTS
"Banking" education makes students passive.	Recognizing the "banking" concept people can make people more critically aware.
F says the teacher "must be a partner of the students in his relations with them."	Is it really possible for teachers and students to act as equals? Is F talking to teachers? What can students do?
	*Students must not let their teachers oppress them.
	*Students should question constantly.
	*Students should think independently.
	*Students should find a variety of ways to learn and study.
"The teacher cannot think for the students, nor can he impose his thoughts on them."	F _is_ talking to teachers. But students can question what the teacher does. Even if I disagree with everything my teacher says, I am discovering new things about myself, my relationship with the world, and my intentions.
"Problem-posing" education is the alternative to the "banking" concept.	
"In problem-posing education men develop their power to perceive <u>the way they exist</u> in the world." This is clearly important to F.	

FREIRE	MY THOUGHTS
"A deepened consciousness leads men to apprehend that situation as an historical reality susceptible to transformation." What comes before this is esp. difficult. (I am not sure what "that situation" is.) But it is clear that F wants change, social change, revolution.	F said earlier that he might be thought a dreamer. Is he? He _is_ a revolutionary. He says that. How much do _I_ want the world to change? How much do I believe the world _will_ change?
F says "problem-solving education does not and cannot serve interests of the oppressor."	Do I get problem-solving education? My teachers ask questions all the time. How liberating is this?

When Mikhael finished his last journal entry, he looked over what he had written with a certain satisfaction. Skimming the piece before he wrote any entries, he had felt quite intimidated, even though he seemed to concur with almost everything Freire said (at least as far as Mikhael understood it). But the text seemed so hard and so long, and Mikhael was by no means sure what he was expected to do with it. Now he realized that the point was not to follow and register every turn of Freire's argument; it was to find something to say about it. His journal made that possible—and even had the effect of making Freire seem a lot more manageable than he had seemed on that first skim-through.

Buoyed by this confidence, Mikhael decided to knock out a draft right away. Unfortunately, the result—which we'll get to in a moment—is an example of what _not_ to do in drafting a response to a text. There are two reasons for this. First, Mikhael did not actually use the journal writing he did, work rich in possibilities for a draft; he did the journal because he was asked to, then left it behind—until the need for ideas while revising sent him back to it. The second problem was that Mikhael had not decided on a purpose before drafting his response. That's a mistake you won't want to make.

Decide on a Purpose

We obviously can't know what your purpose will be since we don't know what text you're responding to, but we can be confident that it will follow one of four general tactics—maybe more than one, for these four are by no means mutually exclusive.

Exemplification. You can tap your own experience to illustrate one or more of the ideas in the text. Mikhael found that exemplifying the banking concept in his draft helped to personalize his response. He was by no means alone in being able to tell a story from his own life that spoke to Freire's point; still, no one had precisely the same personal account of the banking concept as he. Furthermore, applying Freire's ideas to his own experience helped to demonstrate his understanding of Freire, and it may have helped to make Freire (whose text tends to be quite abstract) come alive for his reader.

Contradiction. Some of Mikhael's classmates (but not Mikhael himself) argued against one of Freire's main contentions. Freire had argued that absorbing information induced chronic passivity, an inability to think for oneself. Those disagreeing argued that absorbing information was a necessary precondition for being able to think about it—and so to think for oneself. (One student used the example of the law: one must know what the law is before one can interpret it.) Disagreeing with a forceful contender like Freire can be intimidating, but it does guarantee that the resulting response will not be mere knowledge-telling.

Qualification. Qualifications tend to be reservations rather than outright disagreements: following an argument, but not all the way; accepting a line of reasoning, but not necessarily the conclusion drawn from it. In Mikhael's case, he noticed that words like "regrettably" and "unfortunately" in his draft implied that agreeing with Freire left him seriously depressed. He was told, after all, that he was caught in an oppressive system—helpless, hopeless, trapped. Yet he didn't feel that way. Closer examination of his feelings (especially as noted in his reading journal) revealed that he felt teachers had more ways of teaching and students more ways of coping than Freire acknowledged. And he said so in his final version, though he still endorsed the change Freire called for. Like Mikhael's response to Freire, qualifications of arguments do not invalidate those arguments, but they do demand that at least part of them be reconsidered.

Extension. While some responses suggest that authors go too far, others suggest that they don't go far enough. In Freire's case, for instance, someone who is quite persuaded by his indictment of the banking concept may wonder why he restricts his discussion to professional educators and does not consider parents. Such a response could then go on to suggest that parents should also try "problem-solving" as an alternative to the banking (or "because I say so") approach to child-rearing. The point of this limited example is that virtually all arguments are limited in focus—and can be extended beyond those limits. Thinking things through may often mean taking things further.

Note that nowhere above have we identified simple agreement as an option. Simple agreement is knowledge-telling, mere recapitulation what the author has already said, and it leaves you with nothing to say—nothing, at least, that comes from you.

 **T**RIAL RUN

Choose one of the four tactics and use it to direct a ten-minute bout of freewriting in response to the text you've been assigned. (Remember that freewriting means you turn the editor in your head off and just let the words and ideas flow.) Once you've generated some material (ideally, about a page), "nutshell" what you've said in a single sentence. Let's consider this a very tentative thesis for your draft. Evaluate it according to the following checklist, and edit it until the answers to these questions are ones you're comfortable with.

CHECKLIST: TESTING THE VIABILITY OF YOUR THESIS

- Does it give you a purpose distinct from the author of the text you're responding to?
- Does it promise to engage a reader—specifically a reader who has already read this text?
- Is it a statement you can substantiate, either from the text or from your own experience and knowledge?

COMPOSING THE FIRST DRAFT

Use Your Journal

Mikhael did in fact glance over his double-entry journal before writing his first draft, but he didn't study his entries to see if they revealed a general direction his response might take. Had he done so, he would have discovered that his reading of Freire was a good deal more critical and thoughtful than his draft was to suggest. Like so many shortcuts students take in writing, this one cost time rather than saved it.

Take the time to think about the notes you made to yourself while reading. Do specific responses connect up in a general way? Do you find yourself making significant departures from the text, either by disagreeing or by allowing your thoughts to take you where the author doesn't? (Part of Mikhael's journal, for example, departs from Freire's preoccupation with what teachers do to wonder what students can do.) If you find comments or responses worthy of becoming elements of your paper, sketch out a very brief outline of how these elements might be organized.

Give Your Draft a Structure

Whatever point a response makes, it usually follows the same general pattern: the starting point is some concise indication of the argument responded to, followed by the exemplification, contradiction, qualification, or extension of that argument. Even though, as in this case, your reader may have already read what you're responding to, you must still delineate what the author has said. But your task is less to inform your reader of what the author says than to show that you *understand* what the author says— and that you are being fair and reasonable by not oversimplifying or otherwise misrepresenting it.

Once past that introductory part, your sense of purpose should suffice to guide you, though you might sketch a brief plan. For example, you might list some of the evidence (textual or experiential) that you plan to bring into play in the body of the paper. You might also develop a tentative concluding statement, thereby giving your paper a destination to head toward (rather than to search for). A plan like this will help keep you from getting sidetracked or lost in the text you're responding to while you're trying to write your own.

Try Opening with a Hook

An interesting exception to the advice just given is the possibility of opening with what is called a "hook": involving the reader in a particular scene or incident, and only then blossoming out to the general ramifications. Exemplification is one tactic compatible with all the others available to you, and it allows you to demonstrate your understanding of the text by showing its application in specific detail.

In both his draft and final version, Mikhael did not begin with Freire but with Mikhael. Using an anecdotal opening—a short narrative at the outset to engage the reader's interest—is always an alternative to the often cumbersome "Here is what this paper is about" introduction. It's an especially attractive alternative whenever everyone is writing about the same thing or the reader is already familiar with what is being written about, and this in an assignment that meets both of those conditions. Still, the anecdotal opening is not risk-free. If you want to begin with a short personal account, it must be genuinely interesting, relevant, purposeful, and integral. The anecdotal opening that doesn't interest the reader misses the point of beginning anecdotally. The anecdotal opening that isn't relevant misdirects the reader and undermines the author's authority. Like all openings, an anecdotal opening must not simply begin a paper but must lead somewhere; it must be purposeful. And it must be an integral part of the paper, not just a gambit left behind.

 # **T**RIAL RUN

Drawing on your own store of knowledge and experience, tell a story that exemplifies (or perhaps contradicts) something the author you're responding to is talking about. Hold this to a single paragraph. Even if you don't decide to use it as an opening, you may be able to use it—or ideas you get from it—elsewhere in your paper. If you do decide to use it, test it against those four criteria: interest, relevance, purposefulness, and integration. Remember that you can't be certain that it meets all these criteria (and especially the last two) until you turn a critical eye on the whole of your draft.

Mikhael is a case in point. He wasn't sure where he was headed, but yet the very abstractness of Freire's text had forced him to try to anchor the points in his own experience, and a math class long ago sprang to mind. He would start by remarking on that and see where his writing went from there. Here's his draft.

PRESENTING MIKHAEL'S FIRST DRAFT

1   "Let's just assume that the volume of a sphere is equal to pi $\underline{R}$ squared. Now turn to page 127 and do the first 30 problems." This is a typical example of the statements we used to hear in math class in the seventh grade. Most of the pupils would go ahead and do exactly as the teacher instructed without any questions. I was frustrated by these situations because I wanted to understand the formula before I used it. I remember telling my teacher that if she wasn't prepared to explain it to me, I wasn't prepared to use it. So she chose to ignore me and as a result I failed in that area of math, while my classmates who automatically obeyed her instructions were successful.

2   Who was to blame for my failure? For years I used to think that my teacher just didn't want to spend extra time with me. Now I realize that she was probably a product of the education system that Freire describes as the "banking" concept of education, which expects "students to memorize mechanically the narrated content. Worse yet, it turns them into 'containers,' into 'receptacles' to be filled by the teacher. The more completely he [the teacher] fills the receptacles, the better a teacher he is. The more meekly the receptacles permit themselves to be filled, the better students they are." I'm sure that my teacher was a great "receptacle" for her teacher's "deposits," but her education left her totally unequipped to deal with independent-thinking students who asked questions.

3   The experience I mentioned earlier happened in the seventh grade. If it had happened later in my education, it could have limited my career choices enormously, even to the extent of preventing me from pursuing my chosen career. For example, if I had wanted to study medicine and failed math, I could never have done so.

4   Regrettably, I agree with Freire when he says that, in our society, "the educator's role is to . . . 'fill' the students by making deposits of information which he considers to constitute true knowledge. And since men 'receive' the world as passive entities, education should make them more passive still, and adapt them to the world." Unfortunately, our education encourages students not to think, just to accept. Those who are willing to follow this prescription are considered the better students.

5   What makes this reality even sadder is that our education system is merely a reflection of our society, which

encourages everyone to just "fit in." Don't ask questions, don't make waves, just fit in! "The educated man is the adapted man, because he is better 'fit' for the world."

Thinking Critically about Mikhael's First Draft

1. How well does Mikhael's opening meet the criteria of interest, relevance, purposefulness, and integration? If you find any deficiencies along these lines, can you envision ways of correcting them?

2. You have before you, not just Mikhael's response to Freire, but his reading notes. Are there things he says in his draft that you can trace back to the double-entry journal? Are there things he said in the journal that he didn't use in the draft?

3. Where and how does Mikhael differ from Freire? Does he disagree with him at any point? Does he qualify what Freire says? Distance himself from it? Look at the issue from another angle? How different do they seem from each other finally?

4. The primary audience for this paper was Mikhael's instructor. How do you think this paper went over with that audience? Where do you see Mikhael exercising tact—or failing to exercise it—given the intended audience?

5. Tact is one thing and honesty another. How honest do you find this paper, particularly in its conclusion? Can you ground your answers one way or another in evidence offered by Mikhael's text and his reading journal?

RETHINKING AND REVISING

Avail Yourself of What Happens in Class

Precisely because you're putting together a personal response, you need to make use of the thoughts of others. Your goal, remember, is to make your response distinctive, and you can't be at all sure that it is until you know what others are thinking and doing.

Consider what happened to Mikhael. Just as he had when he finished his journal, Mikhael felt good when he reached the end of his draft. But this feeling of confident self-satisfaction did not outlive his next writing class. The class began with a look at the double-entry journals. The students were asked to have the journals out while the instructor walked up and down the rows of desks, seeing what the students had come up with. Looking around, Mikhael could see that his was clearly one of the shorter journals—and the instructor had actually said that quantity was a real measure of success in this particular assignment. It was some consolation that the instructor also said that the two columns should be balanced—that the column of notes and paraphrases should not be much more or much less filled than the column of responses. Mikhael noticed that the student on his immediate left had seemed to transcribe every tenth sentence of Freire's but had very little in the response column. Still, he felt a good deal less sure of his success with the journal than he had when he first surveyed what he had done.

He was in some ways more unsettled by the class discussion of Freire. Mikhael had felt confident that his story about seventh-grade math would make his paper distinctive, but it seemed that everyone in the class had some story from their school days illustrating the "banking" concept. What surprised him even more was that many people seemed to disagree with Freire. Some suggested that "banking" knowledge was appropriate at least for students at the lower levels. (For some this meant elementary school; for others, all instruction before college.) And some students argued that the sort of education Freire criticized was entirely appropriate for certain kinds of classes or disciplines, even at the college level. "Of course four times four is sixteen," said one student. "It would be a waste of time to question that. Using it as an example of the 'banking' concept just shows Freire isn't thinking things through."

Mikhael realized that he partly agreed with the students who disagreed with Freire. Still, he felt the urge to defend Freire. "It's not the form of knowledge Freire is criticizing," he said. "It's the form of instruction. Freire doesn't want students to be passive because passive students become passive citizens." The instructor praised Mikhael for noting Freire's insistence on the connection between the educational system and the entire social system. Better yet, other students chimed in to defend Freire. It soon seemed that more were for him than against him.

But Mikhael was to have his balloon punctured yet again. At the end of the discussion the instructor wondered if those who agreed with Freire weren't simply "banking" what Freire said—accepting it uncritically, not really questioning it—and what would Freire think about that? Mikhael wasn't sure this was a fair characterization of what had been said in the discussion, but he suspected it would become the comment on his paper if he turned in his draft unrevised. He would have to work on it.

Thinking Critically about the Class Discussion

1. Now that you have a sense of the comments made in his class's discussion of Freire, put yourself in Mikhael's shoes. Which of the options—exemplification, contradiction, extension, qualification—would look most attractive to you now? Why?

2. How might you use comments you agreed or disagreed with? Would you attribute them to specific classmates? Why or why not?

3. Class discussion complicated Freire for Mikhael, making neither outright agreement or disagreement real options. But if you can neither agree nor disagree outright, how do you keep from waffling and seeming uncertain?

Strive for Originality

What proved decisive in Mikhael's revision came to him partly as the discovery that others had responded to Freire differently, mostly as a response to the instructor's challenge not to "bank" what Freire said. That's essentially the challenge all writing instructors give their students: the challenge to be "original." It's worth pondering what that challenge means.

Originality eludes definition, but one way of getting at it is to consider the relationship between what's said in class discussions and what's said in individual students' papers. Class discussions are forums of thought, collective enterprises with essentially two purposes. One is to reach a limited sort of consensus on the nature of the subject being discussed, an agreement at the level of basic comprehension—for example, a consensus on what the text is about. Depending on the difficulty of the text, this can be reached quickly or slowly. Then the discussion can turn to its other purpose: exposing the range of thoughts about the subject under discussion. Here general agreement is unlikely—except as agreement on what to disagree on (controversial points in the text, premises accepted by some but not others, questions that seem crucial though answers to them differ). Still, discussion establishes the parameters for responses: one gets a sense of which comments are moderate and which ones are extreme, which ones are tangential and which ones go to the core of the discussion.

The thoughtful participant can capitalize on what is said—and left unsaid—in this emerging spectrum of ideas. Though it didn't strike him at the time, Mikhael did see with the help of hindsight that all of his classmates' comments tried to confirm or disprove what Freire said from a student's point of view. No one wondered if a student's perspective, instead of being used to support or refute Freire, could be used to look at the whole matter differently, to think more about the individual and less about the system. When he turned to his notes, Mikhael found himself feeling that he wasn't Freire's intended audience, that he wondered what someone advising students would say. He found himself parting ways with Freire without actually disagreeing with him. These seeds, overlooked until a discussion showed them to be seeds of distinction, blossomed into an original, insightful paper.

As for your own paper, whatever you do, remember that you are the final arbiter, the key to the puzzle of what originality is. Your own originality is what you bring to an assignment that no one else could: the examples you can draw on, the experiences that have shaped you and your thinking, the reactions you have while reading, the standpoint you have, the viewpoint you take. Originality is finally your contribution to what might be said. As we suggested at the beginning of this chapter, it's as if a conversation is going on; now it's time for you to speak, to make a real contribution, to say what only you can say. The difference is that writing gives you the time to take your time, to pool your resources, to sketch and rethink and revise. This gives you the opportunity to hone a statement you can call your own as actual conversation never could. And that's what writing, specially revision, is all about.

CHECKLIST: REVISING YOUR DRAFT

- Have I availed myself of all that my notes and plans—and my class's discussion—might offer?
- Have I demonstrated a clear understanding of the author I am responding to?
- Have I followed a logical scheme—my own and not my author's—in presenting my response?
- Do I have a distinctive purpose, one that distinguishes what I have to say from my author and my peers as well?

PRESENTING MIKHAEL'S FINAL DRAFT

Education of the Fittest

Mikhael Yanko

Mikhael opens with an anecdote.

1 "Let's just assume that the volume of a sphere is equal to pi R squared. Now turn to page 127 and do the first 30 problems." This is a typical example of the statements we heard in math class in the seventh grade. Most of the pupils, without any questions, would go ahead and do exactly as the teacher instructed. I resisted such passive obedience, frustrated because I wanted to understand the formula before I used it. I remember telling my teacher that if she wasn't prepared to explain it to me, I wasn't prepared to use it. So she chose to ignore me and as a result I failed in that area of math, while my classmates who automatically obeyed her instructions were successful.

The story becomes an illustration of what Freire thinks is wrong with the educational process—a view further fleshed out with a quotation from Freire.

2 Who was to blame for my failure? For years I thought that my teacher just didn't want to spend extra time with me. Now I realize that she was probably a product of the education system that Freire describes as the "banking" concept of education, which expects "students to memorize mechanically the narrated content. Worse yet, it turns them into 'containers,' into 'receptacles' to be filled by the teacher. The more

completely he [the teacher] fills the receptacles, the better a teacher he is. The more meekly the receptacles permit themselves to be filled, the better students they are." I'm sure that my teacher was a great "receptacle" for her teacher's "deposits," but her education left her totally unequipped to deal with independent-thinking students who asked questions.

3

Mikhael allows that the "banking" concept has its uses, but he stresses the counterbalancing importance of the "problem-solving" approach.

I suppose she may also have been surprised that there were any such students left by the seventh grade. I am not completely opposed to the "banking" concept of education in the very early school years, when children are, for example, first learning the alphabet or building their vocabularies. But even then it must be used in combination with a "problem-solving" approach to learning. Children's natural curiosity should always be encouraged, and the "banking" method can only be of value at this stage if the results it produces help to fuel the children's inquiries. Otherwise it only stifles their curiosity and oppresses them, conditioning them to do as they are told and believe what they are told.

4

Referring back to the opening anecdote, Mikhael notes the double danger of the banking system: it not only numbs those who accept it, but punishes those who resist.

For those like me, whose curiosity is still alive, whose conditioning is incomplete, the "banking" system poses another danger. It punishes those who resist it. The experience I mentioned earlier happened in the seventh grade. If it had happened later in my education, it could have limited my career choices enormously, even to the extent of preventing me from pursuing my chosen career. For example, if I had wanted to study medicine, I could never have done so if I had failed math.

5

Mikhael, then, is in fundamental agreement with Freire, whom he cites again.

Regrettably, I agree with Freire when he says that, in our society, "the educator's role is to . . . 'fill' the students by making deposits of information which he considers to constitute true knowledge." Because the "banking" concept teaches students to accept, without question, what the teacher thinks, it doesn't provide the opportunity for students to practice the skills necessary to solve problems for themselves. Of course, the ability to solve problems is essential in our society if one is to work as anything other than what Freire calls an "automaton" (which seems to be the career goal encouraged by the "banking" system).

6

He even endorses Freire's far-reaching solution, though he is not confident it can be achieved.

Freire's solution is to ask teachers to ensure that students are educated to ask questions and solve problems, to examine their relationship in and with the world. Such education can only result in greater awareness and even social change. As Freire admits, this means it will face resistance and take time. I believe it requires some optimism to believe it will happen at all.

7   Even so, students may not be quite as passive or as helpless as Freire thinks. He seems preoccupied with what teachers do, or should do. But students have minds of their own, even when teachers don't admit it. I have found myself disagreeing with teachers who never encouraged me to disagree, and I have found myself learning from that experience. It is also true that not all teachers are alike. Some pose questions; others just lecture. Any student is exposed to a variety of educators, not just one uniform system, and the student learns to make adjustments. Unfortunately, students like me also learn not to make waves, not to question the system out loud; doing that can be dangerous.

Shifting to the students' perspective, Mikhael suggests that Freire's view of education is too uniformly bleak.

8   So I agree with Freire that there must be far-reaching change, change that takes time and thought and struggle. But just as every student who reads Freire's essay should not simply accept his opinion unquestioned, so too should each student wonder how much to subscribe to the bleakness of his view. Until the ideal transformation Freire hopes for takes place, the strongest message we will continue to receive from our society is that "the educated man is the adapted man, because he is better 'fit' for the world." But that is only for those who are completely conditioned. For the others, those who still think and question and adjust, there is another message. The truly educated man is the <u>adaptable</u> man, because he will be able to decide <u>how</u> to fit in the world.

Holding that students shouldn't simply "bank" Freire's views, Mikhael suggests that those who can question but still endure the system that supposedly turns them into automatons may be the ideal problem-solvers.

Commentary on Mikhael's Final Draft

Mikhael's first draft response to Freire ranged all the way from exemplification to unqualified agreement. It began by using Mikhael's own experience to confirm Freire's diagnosis and concluded with a reiteration of that diagnosis—in Freire's own words. Where Freire had moved beyond that diagnosis to a prescription, Mikhael had come to rest with just the diagnosis.

If this sounds too critical, it nevertheless helps to drive home a point that must not be missed. Mikhael was proud of his first draft—and not without reason—but he did not see how it was fundamentally flawed as a response to reading in a college course. What he was doing in that draft was not much more than knowledge-telling. In other words, Mikhael's drafted response to Freire was not a response at all. (He may have been more conditioned by the banking system than he allowed.)

Mikhael's revision, on the other hand, is a fine response: reasoned and reasonable, particular and general, reserved in its agreement and generous in its divergence. What's fascinating is the roots for this response reach back past the knowledge-telling draft to the double-entry journal, where

Mikhael was enjoined to do more than knowledge-telling. And the catalyst for the revised response was the class discussion, which effectively challenged Mikhael to show that he *could* think critically about Freire, and not simply by disagreeing with him.

The result, the revised version, begins more or less as the draft did, by grounding what Freire says in Mikhael's own experience. This is not the only possible means—but certainly one means—of showing that he understands Freire, at least up to a point. Mikhael must show that he follows Freire to some extent (or begin contradicting him straightaway), but that only lays the foundation for his next move.

That next move—after a paragraph recounting his experience and another interpreting it in light of Freire's argument—is to suggest that the banking concept may have a place in education, if only at the earliest stages and even then in conjunction with the problem-solving approach. This is Mikhael's first suggestion that he is distancing himself from Freire. It may seem a slight distance, but Mikhael does not engage in the same blanket indictment of the banking concept that Freire gives.

What's more, the next paragraph shows that the two differ in perspective as well as opinion. Freire's is essentially the perspective of a teacher—more specifically, a teacher of teachers; the consequence of the banking concept he stresses is that teachers thereby render students passive. Students who are not rendered passive have no place in his account. Mikhael looks at things from the student's perspective—more specifically, from the student who has suffered from being insufficiently passive and unquestioning—and thereby establishes his credentials for later comments on both Freire's argument and the system itself. (Note that the roots of this perspective are there in the draft, but Mikhael uses his experience there only to confirm Freire, not to distinguish his own angle of approach.)

The paragraph beginning "Regrettably" might be too easily dismissed as mere knowledge-telling, Mikhael's confirmation of and concurrence with Freire's diagnosis. If you're inclined to look at it that way, you might compare it with its counterpart in the draft, which was just paraphrase and quotation of Freire, followed hard upon by the conclusion (more mere quotation and paraphrase of Freire.) In the revised version, Mikhael interprets the consequences of the banking concept rather differently from Freire. Freire argues that the educational system is horribly efficient as a mechanism for turning out just the sort of mindless followers an oppressive society needs and wants. Mikhael suggests that society is actually now well-served by such products of education—and, crucially, he leaves the door open to the possibility that not all students are such products. This revised paragraph gives him the hinge to swing his new conclusion from, a conclusion comprising three paragraphs of some length and complexity rather than one of three short sentences.

The first paragraph of the revised conclusion returns us to the difference between Freire's and Mikhael's perspectives, now quite an explicit difference. Freire is interested in teacher-initiated changes for a better future. Mikhael does not dismiss this prospect, but he does suggest that it is far-off, maybe even far-flung in its optimism.

In the next paragraph, the penultimate one, Mikhael spotlights his own perspective and its consequences. Even if Freire is not too optimistic in his revolutionary hopes, he does seem to Mikhael too pessimistic in his sense of what is being done to the students. Focusing on teachers, he makes them seem more powerful and pernicious than they actually are. Students have always questioned and criticized their teachers; they just are careful not to do it openly—for reasons Mikhael has already rooted in his own experience. And teachers are not all so many identical cogs in the mechanism. They vary, and their variety forces their students to be adaptable.

This sets Mikhael up for his final stroke. While he endorses Freire's distant goal (to be effected by right-minded teachers), his own focus on students in the here and now gives him a hope that is less far away and less out of his hands: Freire sees the educational system as coercing adaptation and passivity, but Mikhael suggests it is also capable of encouraging adaptability and shrewdness.

All of this is by no means to say that Freire is wrong and Mikhael is right. The difference is not a matter of "correctness" but of purpose and perspective. It is part of Freire's purpose to show the system (and the teachers that carry out its designs) as especially pernicious; after all, it is his purpose to show that changes must be made. Mikhael, potentially (and to some extent actually) a victim of the system, is interested in showing that he is not wholly victimized, duped, conditioned. It is also a part of his purpose, of course, to show that he can understand Freire and yet think for himself. We think he does this admirably. We are also confident you can do no less.

Questions for Further Thought

1. We seem to be assuming that all argumentative essays, even those as long and complex as Freire's, are somehow limited so that they can be extended or qualified—if not contradicted outright—in some way. Is this a cynical assumption, one that does in fact hit at some sort of "recipe" for originality?

2. Freire's essay is indeed long and complex, and Mikhael Yanko's response to it is necessarily selective. How do you know when you're being too selective? Can you proclaim a text's limitations when you yourself are taking a limited view of it?

3. What's to prevent a personal response from being too personal, too exclusively a matter of one's own personal opinion or experience?

PROFESSIONAL ESSAYS

Adrienne Rich

CLAIMING AN EDUCATION

"Responsibility to yourself means refusing to let others do your thinking, talking, and naming for you; it means learning to respect and use your own brains and instincts...."

ADRIENNE RICH, POET, CRITIC, AND TRANSLAtor, was born in 1929 in Baltimore, Maryland. She graduated from Radcliffe College in 1951, the year in which she won the prestigious Yale Younger Poets Award for her first book, A Change of World. *Since then she has received many fellowships and prizes, including two Guggenheim fellowships, the National Book Award in 1974 (for* Diving into the Wreck*), and the 1991 Commonwealth Award. As a leading feminist activist and scholar with a deep moral sense, Rich has written extensively on women's issues; notable among such writings is* Of Woman Born: Motherhood as Experience and Institution *(1976). In her works, Rich uses her own life and personal experiences to reveal general and communal truths, making writing both a private and public act.*

"Claiming an Education" was delivered as the convocation address at Douglass College of Rutgers University in 1977. At the time, Douglass College was a women's college, and so Rich's speech is addressed to the female students who came to Douglass to receive an education. But Rich tells them that "you cannot afford to think of yourself as being here to receive an education; you will do much better to think of yourselves as being here to claim one." The entire talk—we should remember it was written to be spoken, not read—turns on this distinction between receiving and claiming, between passive acceptance and active engagement.

ON THE WAY INTO THE READING

1. Rich's speech was primarily for an audience of women at a particular moment in women's struggle for equality. Do you expect this will limit its relevance for you? Why or why not?

2. If Rich is arguing against receiving ideas passively, do you suppose this will have some bearing on the way she communicates her own ideas? How might this speech be like and unlike the process of education it holds up to critical scrutiny?

3. Whether you see yourself as passively or actively taking in your education, you no doubt see education as a means of achieving certain goals. What are those goals? How much do you expect them to resemble Rich's goals for education?

1   For this convocation, I planned to separate my remarks into two parts: some thoughts about you, the women students here, and some thoughts about us who teach in a women's college. But ultimately, those two parts are indivisible. If university education means anything beyond the processing of human beings into expected roles, through credit hours, tests, and grades (and I believe that in a women's college especially it *might* mean much more), it implies an ethical and intellectual contract between teacher and student. This contract must remain intuitive, dynamic, unwritten; but we must turn to it again and again if learning is to be reclaimed from the depersonalizing and cheapening pressures of the present-day academic scene.

2   The first thing I want to say to you who are students, is that you cannot afford to think of being here to *receive* an education; you will do much better to think of yourselves as being here to *claim* one. One of the dictionary definitions of the verb "to claim" is: *to take as the rightful owner; to assert in the face of possible contradiction.* "To receive" is *to come into possession of; to act as receptacle or container for; to accept as authoritative or true.* The difference is that between acting and being acted-upon, and for women it can literally mean the difference between life and death.

3   One of the devastating weaknesses of university learning, of the store of knowledge and opinion that has been handed down through academic training, has been its almost total erasure of women's experience and thought from the curriculum, and its exclusion of women as members of the academic community. Today, with increasing numbers of women students in nearly every branch of higher learning, we still see very few women in the upper levels of faculty and administration in most institutions. Douglass College itself is a women's college in a university administered overwhelmingly by men, who in turn are answerable to the state legislature, again composed predominantly of men. But the most significant fact for you is that what you learn here, the very texts you read, the lectures you hear, the way your studies are divided into categories and fragmented one from the other—all this reflects, to a very large degree, neither objective reality, nor an accurate picture of the past, nor a group of rigorously tested observations about human behavior. What you can learn here (and I mean not only at Douglass but any college in any university) is how *men* have perceived and organized their experience, their history, their ideas of social relationships, good and evil, sickness and health, etc. When you read or hear about "great issues," "major texts," "the mainstream of Western thought," you are hearing about what men, above all white men, in their male subjectivity, have decided is important.

4   Black and other minority peoples have for some time recognized that their racial and ethnic experience was not accounted for in the studies broadly labeled human; and that even the sciences can be racist. For many reasons, it has been more difficult for women to comprehend our exclusion, and to realize that even the sciences can be sexist. For one thing, it is only

within the last hundred years that higher education has grudgingly been opened up to women at all, even to white, middle-class women. And many of us have found ourselves poring eagerly over books with titles like: *The Descent of Man; Man and His Symbols; Irrational Man; The Phenomenon of Man; The Future of Man; Man and the Machine; From Man to Man; May Man Prevail?; Man, Science and Society;* or *One-Dimensional Man*—books pretending to describe a "human" reality that does not include over one-half the human species.

5   Less than a decade ago, with the rebirth of a feminist movement in this country, women students and teachers in a number of universities began to demand and set up women's studies courses—to *claim* a woman-directed education. And, despite the inevitable accusations of "unscholarly," "group therapy," "faddism," etc., despite backlash and budget cuts, women's studies are still growing, offering to more and more women a new intellectual grasp on their lives, new understanding of our history, a fresh vision of the human experience, and also a critical basis for evaluating what they hear and read in other courses, and in the society at large.

6   But my talk is not really about women's studies, much as I believe in their scholarly, scientific, and human necessity. While I think that any Douglass student has everything to gain by investigating and enrolling in women's studies courses, I want to suggest that there is a more essential experience that you owe yourselves, one which courses in women's studies can greatly enrich, but which finally depends on you, in all your interactions with yourself and your world. This is the experience of *taking responsibility toward yourselves.* Our upbringing as women has so often told us that this should come second to our relationships and responsibilities to other people. We have been offered ethical models of the self-denying wife and mother; intellectual models of the brilliant but slapdash dilettante who never commits herself to anything the whole way, or the intelligent woman who denies her intelligence in order to seem more "feminine," or who sits in passive silence even when she disagrees inwardly with everything that is being said around her.

7   Responsibility to yourself means refusing to let others do your thinking, talking, and naming for you; it means learning to respect and use your own brains and instincts; hence, grappling with hard work. It means that you do not treat your body as a commodity with which to purchase superficial intimacy or economic security; for our bodies and minds are inseparable in this life, and when we allow our bodies to be treated as objects, our minds are in mortal danger. It means insisting that those to whom you give your friendship and love are able to respect your mind. It means being able to say, with Charlotte Brontë's *Jane Eyre:* "I have an inward treasure born with me, which can keep me alive if all the extraneous delights should be withheld or offered only at a price I cannot afford to give."

8   Responsibility to yourself means that you don't fall for shallow and easy solutions—predigested books and ideas, weekend encounters guaranteed to change your life, taking "gut" courses instead of ones you know will chal-

lenge you, bluffing at school and life instead of doing solid work, marrying early as an escape from real decisions, getting pregnant as an evasion of already existing problems. It means that you refuse to sell your talents and aspirations short, simply to avoid conflict and confrontation. And this, in turn, means resisting the forces in society which say that women should be nice, play safe, have low professional expectations, drown in love and forget about work, live through others, and stay in the places assigned to us. It means that we insist on a life of meaningful work, insist that work be as meaningful as love and friendship in our lives. It means, therefore, the courage to be "different"; not to be continuously available to others when we need time for ourselves and our work; to be able to demand of others— parents, friends, roommates, teachers, lovers, husbands, children—that they respect our sense of purpose and our integrity as persons. Women everywhere are finding the courage to do this, more and more, and we are finding that courage both in our study of women in the past who possessed it, and in each other as we look to other women for comradeship, community, and challenge. The difference between a life lived actively, and a life of passive drifting and dispersal of energies, is an immense difference. Once we begin to feel committed to our lives, responsible to ourselves, we can never again be satisfied with the old, passive way.

9   Now comes the second part of the contract. I believe that in a women's college you have the right to expect your faculty to take you seriously. The education of women has been a matter of debate for centuries, and old, negative attitudes about women's role, women's ability to think and take leadership, are still rife both in and outside the university. Many male professors (and I don't mean only at Douglass) still feel that teaching in a women's college is a second-rate career. Many tend to eroticize their women students—to treat them as sexual objects—instead of demanding the best of their minds. (At Yale a legal suit [*Alexander v. Yale*] has been brought against the university by a group of women students demanding a stated policy against sexual advances toward female students by male professors.) Many teachers, both men and women, trained in the male-centered tradition, are still handing the ideas and texts of that tradition on to students without teaching them to criticize its antiwoman attitudes, its omission of women as part of the species. Too often, all of us fail to teach the most important thing, which is that clear thinking, active discussion, and excellent writing are all necessary for intellectual freedom, and that these require *hard work*. Sometimes, perhaps in discouragement with a culture which is both antiintellectual and antiwoman, we may resign ourselves to low expectations for our students before we have given them half a chance to become more thoughtful, expressive human beings. We need to take to heart the words of Elizabeth Barrett Browning, a poet, a thinking woman, and a feminist, who write in 1845 of her impatience with studies which cultivate a "passive recipiency" in the mind, and asserted that "women want to be made to *think actively*: their apprehension is quicker than that of men, but their defect lies for the most part in the logical faculty

and in the higher mental activities." Note that she implies a defect which can be remedied by intellectual training; *not* an inborn lack of ability.

10   I have said that the contract on the student's part involves that you demand to be taken seriously so that you can also go on taking yourself seriously. This means seeking out criticism, recognizing that the most affirming thing anyone can do for you is demand that you push yourself further, show you the range of what you *can* do. It means rejecting attitudes of "take-it-easy," "why-be-so-serious," "why-worry-you'll-probably-get-married-anyway." It means assuming your share of responsibility for what happens in the classroom, because that affects the quality of your daily life here. It means that the student sees herself engaged *with* her teachers in an active, ongoing struggle for a real education. But for her to do this, her teachers must be committed to the belief that women's minds and experience are intrinsically valuable and indispensable to any civilization worthy the name; that there is no more exhilarating and intellectually fertile place in the academic world today than a women's college—*if* both students and teachers in large enough numbers are trying to fulfill this contract. The contract is really a pledge of mutual seriousness about women, about language, ideas, methods, and values. It is our shared commitment toward a world in which the inborn potentialities of so many women's minds will no longer be wasted, raveled-away, paralyzed, or denied.

CRITICAL READING

1. How does Rich differentiate between receiving and claiming an education? How much do her ideas and methods resemble Freire's distinction between "banking" and "problem-solving"?

2. Criticizing "the male-centered tradition," Rich also speaks of efforts to foster "a woman-directed education." Does she think that education can be neutral? Do you? Why or why not?

3. Rich speaks of a "contract" between educators and the educated. What are this word's associations? Why do you suppose Rich chose to use it? How negotiable is the "contract"?

4. Rich refers repeatedly to "hard work." What does hard work involve, and why is it necessary? How does it bear on *claiming* an education?

5. In paragraphs 7 and 8 Rich talks about what she calls "responsibility to yourself." Do you agree with the way she defines what this phrase means? How do you measure up—particularly in terms of what you actually do in your academic life?

6. Members of the faculty were also in Rich's audience. How do you think they responded to what Rich had to say? Do you think, for instance, they might have felt their authority undermined? How much authority should teachers have?

7. Mikhael Yanko, in response to Friere's banking concept, suggests that Friere may be too pessimistic about the state of education. What do you

think would be his response to Rich's idea that unless students, particularly women students, demand to be taken seriously by their mostly male teachers, they will not learn to take themselves seriously? What is your response?

Peter Elbow

REPRESENTING COURSE
GRADES DIFFERENTLY:
A PROPOSAL

"When colleges, employers, or graduate and professional schools see a B, they don't know whether it means that the student who got it was a dutiful striver or erratically brilliant."

IN SOME WAYS, PETER ELBOW SEEMS THE ultimate academic. Educated at four colleges and universities (Williams College, Oxford University, Harvard, and Brandeis), he has taught at even more (Franconia College, Massachusetts Institute of Technology, Evergreen State College, the State University of New York at Stony Brook, and the University of Massachusetts at Amherst). But there is a maverick streak in Elbow, evidenced by the title of his first book Writing Without Teachers *(1973), a book that addresses most of its preface to teachers. They're invited to use the book, but only if they agree to function in a "teacherless writing class," surrendering their accustomed authority. After all, says Elbow, only a few teachers really know how to exercise that authority properly, and "they are exceedingly rare."*

*It says something about writing teachers as well as Elbow that he became an important figure in the profession of English with this book and those that followed it—*Writing with Power *(1981) and* Embracing Contraries *(1986). He was invited to write a book on the 1987 English Coalition Conference, and the result was* What Is English? *(1990). Our selection comes from an appendix in which Elbow proposes the elimination of grades that reduce the evaluation of a student's term-long performance to a single letter or number. As you read it, keep in mind some advice from* Writing Without Teachers:

> *There are two basic games you can use, the doubting game and the believing game.*
>
> *The doubting game seeks truth by indirection—by seeking an error. Doubting an assertion is the best way to find the error in it. You must assume it is untrue if you want to find its weakness. The truer it seems, the harder you have to doubt it.* Non credo ut intelligam: *in order to understand what's wrong, I must doubt....*
>
> *In the believing game the first rule is to refrain from doubting the assertions, and for this reason you take them one at a time and in each case try to put the others out of your head. You don't want them to fight each other. This is not the adversary method.*

In the believing game we return to Tertullian's original formulation: credo ut intelligam: *I believe in order to understand. We are trying to find not errors but truths, and for this it helps to believe. (147–48)*

ON THE WAY INTO THE READING

1. Which of these, the doubting game or the believing game, is the game you usually play as you consider the arguments of others? Which game has served you best in developing your own ideas and truths? Which game would be best to play in developing your response? Or would it be best to play both?

2. Again, our selection comes from a book on the 1987 English Coalition Conference. Who do you figure Elbow sees as his audience? Do you think that, like Mikhael's reading of Freire, your reading of Elbow might find him focusing too little on the student's perspective?

3. What are your own attitudes towards grades and the purposes they serve? Is the big issue for you the thoroughness of the evaluation, or is it the fairness? What about grading would you like to see changed?

1   When a freshman protests, "That C– you gave me will keep me from getting into medical school!" we are tempted to laugh. But the ludicrousness of some students' grade grubbing makes it too easy for us to laugh. Course grades are often far from trivial in their consequences for students—especially grades in their upperclass or major courses. Just one or two important grades can determine whether someone gets a scholarship or gets into a certain college or graduate program. But, if we look at the principles I've been exploring about trustworthiness, stakes, and costs of evaluaton, it turns out that we can see a low-cost way to make course grades much more trustworthy and clear in meaning and at the same time reduce the mystery and the stakes.

2   The problem with course grades is not evaluation itself but how we represent our evaluations. That is, the teacher's evaluative process in most courses has a great deal to recommend it. Though teachers are only single observers, they can usually base their evaluation on multiple observations over a long period of time of students doing multiple kinds of activity: not just performance under test conditions on a single day. Richard Lloyd-Jones was the original author of this perceptive passage in the coalition report on testing:

> Lest we fall into thinking that assessment always necessitates the use of large, formal instruments, we should remember that the most trustworthy assessment is usually conducted by the individual teacher in his or her own classroom as an integral part of the teaching process. After all, a reliable and valid test is more likely to be possible when the activities or materials to be covered are discrete and sharply defined, as in a classroom. Sometimes one can test performance quite directly; in fact, most classroom activities test student skills and knowledge as part of the continuing efforts to improve. When any single measure is ineffective or insufficient at showing what the student really knows or can do, the ongoing teaching situation demands and inevitably brings forth a more successful measure in another mode. (Lloyd-Jones and Lunsford 43)

3   But notice what this passage is describing: the various observations and evaluations made by teachers—not the representation of them into a single letter or number grade. All those valuable perceptions and data are rendered less trustworthy and less useful when they are reduced to a single number. That is, the conventional grading system traps teachers into the key mistake of mass testing: producing a single letter grade that tells us nothing about what the student knows or doesn't know, can or can't do—and, in doing so, heightening bias by keeping hidden or tacit the value system that has permitted all those data to be reduced to a single number. (And if the teacher grades with any degree of "curve," it creates that artificial and needlessly "scarce good" that Astin spoke of in chapter 9.)

4   Most teachers in school and college know a great deal about their student's learning and ability, but the single letter or number grade doesn't permit them to communicate that knowledge to readers. Students get preoccupied and sometimes even obsessed with grades not only because they are sometimes very important but also because their meaning is so mysterious. No one quite knows what that B– or D really means, and people get more hypnotized or cathected to what seems ambiguous, mysterious, or magical.

5   But most students and teachers take conventional grading so much for granted that they feel hopeless that evaluation could ever be more accurate and less vexed—as it is with those report cards given by early elementary teachers, where students get English grades on particular criteria such as comprehension, word recognition skills, oral expression, and written expression. Indeed the main argument for "regular grades" in upper elementary school is usually something like this: "Everything would be better if we didn't have to, but the kids have got to get used to regular grading to be ready for high school." But in fact the typical report card for early elementary grades provides the key to a simple and major improvement. If teachers simply graded by means of a grid of multiple criteria, they would provide much more accurate, trustworthy, and useful information to other teachers and to colleges, employers, and graduate and professional schools. What I

am suggesting, then, is not a different process or amount of evaluation but a different means of representing evaluation.

6   There are various ways this general principle might be fleshed out. Course grades in high school and college could consist of teacher ratings on a short, simple list of criteria such as memory of important information, understanding (or the ability to apply central ideas), effectiveness of writing, and effort (or conscientiousness). Teachers might check off the student's level of accomplishment from three or four or even five boxes for each criterion, using mere numbers or else words (such as weak/satisfactory/strong or poor/fair/good/excellent).

7   I am not arguing for the particular criteria I use above as illustrations. Teachers would have to work out which skill or areas of knowledge are most important and discriminable, given the nature of their course. Other criteria that come to mind, also by way of illustration: critical thinking, creative thinking, effectiveness in speaking, or improvement over the semester. Literature teachers might use more specifically literary criteria, for example, close literal interpretation, imaginative or creative interpretation, or understanding of theoretical and critical issues. Writing teachers might use criteria more specifically geared to composition, for example, clarity of language, rhetorical sophistication, skill at exploratory writing, skill at revising, and skill at giving feedback to others. Even in huge lecture courses where evaluation is accomplished wholly by machine-graded exams, such exams could easily be designed and graded to yield scores on at least two or three criteria (for example, skill criteria like memory, interpretive skill, and problem-solving skill or content criteria like understanding of poetry and of prose). Some teachers would scorn criteria like effort of conscientiousness or improvement, but others would value the chance to use them since they point out things that readers of grades often want to know about. At first glance, this approach might seem much more difficult than regular grading, but it wouldn't take much more time for teachers to check off three to six boxes than to figure out a grade, and many would find it psychologically easier.

8   The crucial principle I insist on here is that the system for representing evaluations must be flexible enough to fit the data—as opposed to the conventional approach, where the system of representation is inflexible and the data must be distorted to fit it (and all for the sake, it seems, of being able to distinguish between someone with a 3.15 and 3.16 grade point average). Interesting consequences follow from this decision to give priority to the evaluative data rather than to the system of representation. That is, there is no necessity that a teacher use all of his or her criteria on every student. A teacher might not be in a position to evaluate one student's speaking skill or effort, but that is no reason to hold back the crucial information that another student was very strong on both counts. Similarly, there is no necessity that all teachers use the same criteria: different teachers, because of what they teach and how they teach it, will have

different evaluative information that they need to communicate. The simple fact is that it can be communicated without much trouble.

9   The logistics of this approach would not be difficult, especially in the age of computers. (Certain experimental colleges such as Hampshire College and the Evergreen State College produce much more unwieldy evaluations—transcripts of many pages of narrative evaluative prose—yet their students are accepted at the full range of graduate and professional schools, and they get all kinds of jobs.) No doubt many registrars might lobby against the idea or might prefer to have a whole department or school agree on a master list of a dozen or a score of criteria—and of course that would be possible and perhaps even desirable. But the reason for evaluation systems is to serve learning and the communication of accurate evaluative information—not the other way around. A high school or college transcript of little grids would be bulkier than at present, but it would still fit on just a few pages. The added bulk would be gratefully received by students, parents, colleges, and employers because the transcript would communicate much more useful information: a record of different teachers' assessments of a student on particular abilities or skills. This system would decrease the need for letters of recommendation—a nontrivial burden on high school teachers who often have to write more than fifty or seventy-five a year. The need for letters of recommendation comes from the widespread and justifiable distrust of grades because of how little they say and how easily they are inflated. When colleges, employers, or graduate and professional schools see a B, they don't know whether it means that the student who got it was a dutiful striver or erratically brilliant. Even if the grade is an A, readers have no way of knowing whether the student was a truly good thinker or a conscientious memorizer—a good writer or a poor one.

10   If we communicated our evaluation of students in this more accurate way, students couldn't sum up their high school or college performance in a single misleading number (grade point average or rank in class). This would vastly improve the climate of learning since students would have to think about specific strengths and weaknesses in their learning process—instead of just about the misleading question of where they fall on a scale or ranking. It tends to feel as though life couldn't go on without a GPA, but my nine years at Evergreen showed me that we all continued to live and breathe—and better.

11   Of course one department cannot unilaterally change the official system for recording and communicating course grades. (On second thought, what if an English department decided to refuse on professional grounds to give conventional uninformative grades and insisted on providing a superior but bulkier set of evaluative information? I don't see what the rest of the institution could do but accept and transmit this more accurate evaluative information—and perhaps learn from it.) But, granting for the moment that we are stuck for a while with regular grades, it would be a vast improvement if we in English provided to students and colleagues the

kind of criterion-based grids or reports I am talking about in addition to regular grades. This would show other departments how much is gained and how little lost by the new procedure. High school teachers could save these evaluative grids for each student and provide them to colleges in addition to or in lieu of recommendation letters. College English departments could save them for each student major and provide them to graduate and professional schools and even employers.

12   These criterion-based course evaluations would still be based on only single observers and thus would be less trustworthy than if based on two or more observers, but that is no cause for concern because of one very important consequence of the system: by replacing a single quantitative grade with multiple ratings or judgments about abilities, we would in one stroke lower the stakes. That is, these new course evaluations could no longer be used to rank students with fine gradations along a single dimension—except in the most general way. If one student has lots of "strongs" and another has lots of "weaks," it will be obvious to anyone that the first one has a better transcript—and that's as it should be, But for many or most students—those with many mixed or middling verdicts—comparative holistic ranking among them would be almost impossible. If one student has strong marks in memory and weak ones in understanding and creative thinking and another student has the opposite verdicts, which has a "better" report card? Colleges, employers, and parents will often disagree among themselves about which criteria are most important and correctly so: their judgments would depend on what qualities they are looking for. And students would have to be more thoughtful in trying to assess how they are doing. It is true that people might have a lamentable impulse to count "strongs" or compute averages, but the results would clearly have little value since different students would have ratings on different criteria, and different students would have different numbers of ratings—sometimes even in the same course.

13   But of course the stakes cannot always remain low. Sometimes we need to make a more definite and global verdict about quality—for example, as to whether someone is doing genuinely unsatisfactory work and should not get credit for a course or should even be flunked out of school. We don't have unlimited space in our classes or colleges, so we need to make these judgments. As for excellence, we may not have such a pressing pragmatic need to identify it, but learning and teaching probably benefit from designating excellent work as an illustration and an incentive. Thus we might have two global or holistic boxes on an evaluation grid to check, *fail* and *honors*. (The system would help to restrain grade inflation. Teachers would be less likely to overuse "honors" if they had a way to say that someone was terrific at certain particular abilities.)

14   These global verdicts of *fail* and *honors* would be given by single observers and thus would be less trustworthy than we could wish, but they would still be far more clear, communicative, and helpful than the F's and A's we now give, since the accompanying grids would communicate the

grounds for the verdicts—as our present grades do not. In so doing, the grids would also communicate the teacher's values or priorities, which also remain hidden with our present grades. For example, suppose one teacher fails a student who is poor in memory of important information but good on all other criteria, and another teacher doesn't call the same situation a failure. This might seem like a problem with the system: a discrepancy in standards. But of course this is exactly what happens all the time with conventional grading, only the discrepancy is disguised: one teacher gives a failing grade and another gives a passing grade, and the reader has no idea that these two contrasting verdicts represent exactly the same student performance!

CRITICAL READING

1. When Elbow says that "the ludicrousness of some students' grade grubbing makes it too easy for us to laugh" he is obviously addressing an audience of teachers. Yet he also stresses "consequences for students." Do you think he does a good job of arguing on behalf of students? How might this argument need to differ if he were making the case to (as well as for) students?

2. Lest his proposal seem too radical, Elbow says what he's suggesting "is not a different process or amount of evaluation but a different means of representing evaluation." Is Elbow going far enough? Does it seem to you that changes need to be made in the process and amount of evaluation as well as the means of representing it? Could it be that the very idea of evaluation seems troublesome to you? Can you envision alternatives?

3. Maybe Elbow's proposal *is* quite radical despite such disclaimers as the one above. He also says that the recommended multi-criteria evaluations could be applied differently to two students in the same class and could differ from teacher to teacher as well as from course to course. Does *this* seem troublesome to you? On the other hand, does it seem that different from what goes on now?

4. Elbow argues that more thorough and complex evaluations would be "gratefully received by students, parents, colleges, and employers." Do you agree?

5. If his proposal were adopted, Elbow says it "would vastly improve the climate of learning since students would have to think about specific strengths and weaknesses in their learning process...." Do you think adopting his proposal would indeed have this effect? How much do you think the current system of evaluation by grades has on the learning process?

6. At the end, Elbow admits there are times when teachers need to designate a student as a failure or a success. He also acknowledges that what one teacher calls a failure another may not but says this happens "all the time with conventional grading." Here and elsewhere Elbow invites

readers to measure his proposal against the way things are now. Do you see the status quo as he does? How reductive are course grades? How good or bad is the system at motivating learning? How much do you feel the people involved want or need more information than such grades provide? Why do you think the current system exists? What supports its continuance besides resistance to change? How much would the system Elbow recommends improve matters?

CHAPTER NINE

WRITING AN EVALUATIVE COMPARISON OF TWO TEXTS

"Who shall decide when doctors disagree?" asked the eighteenth-century poet Alexander Pope—meaning who can say what's right when even experts argue among themselves? You. (Who else?) The academic world and the larger world beyond it constantly confront us with unresolved controversies. People of expertise and principle range themselves on opposing sides. You can't look to them to decide the issue for you; you must weigh their arguments, then decide for yourself. Sometimes what's at issue is a specific point, perhaps reconciling or choosing between conflicting sources in a research project. At other times, working your way through a controversy may ultimately form or transform values that may affect your entire life, determining your choices of lifestyle, political affiliation, career, and so on. Whether the stakes are high or low, your task is to hear the opposing sides out: you should resist snap judgments and come to your own conclusions after weighing the evidence and opinions from both sides.

There are other sorts of evaluative comparisons you could make, of course: you could look at two texts as stages in a development or as different styles of presentation, for instance. We're focusing on evaluative comparisons that weigh opposing arguments because such comparisons tend to be more common as well as more crucial, whether we're defining our philosophies or casting our votes. Do you agree to opt for one side or the other—or do you develop a third position with respect to those two? You must examine each argument in terms of intention and effect, but you must also realize that there is no neutral or objective position to take, that your position will necessarily be determined by who you are, why you read the arguments the way you do, and how the issues they treat bear on you.

Our featured example is Hideaki Kazeno's evaluation of two arguments about whether English ought to be made the official language of the United States. Hideaki does an exemplary job of weighing the arguments of Walter Darlington Huddleston (a United States senator) and Alice Roy (an English professor), and he does so partly because of his perspective as a Japanese immigrant who came to this country only recently. As Hideaki demonstrates—and as we hope you will find in your own comparison (either of the texts by Huddleston and Roy or one of the two other pairs of opposing arguments we provide at the end of this chapter)—writing an evaluative comparison is not a matter of making the right choice; it's a matter of making the choice that's right for you. Doing this means analyzing not just the texts but yourself, for you must scrutinize your own motives as well as those of the authors you're comparing. For everyone concerned—the authors you're evaluating, yourself, your audience—the key thing is not just what is being said but why.

WRITING ASSIGNMENT

Your task is just what this chapter's title specifies: writing an evaluative comparison of two texts (those texts being one of the two pairs at the end of this chapter, the pair treated at length within the chapter, or some other texts chosen by your instructor). You are to weigh the merits of the two texts and come to your own conclusions. You may consider your instructor or your classmates as your audience. In either case, assume your audience is acquainted with the texts you're evaluating.

READING THE WRITING ASSIGNMENT

There's a certain (necessary) vagueness in the sentence that defines the assignment's objective: "You are to weigh the merits of the two texts and come to your own conclusions." Why not a more specific directive like "You are to determine which of the two texts is better"? Well, think about it for a moment. If we said one text in each pair is better than the other, and that we know which one it is, the object of the assignment then becomes to see if you can get the "right" answer, the answer we already know. That would be a narrow and petty assignment, wouldn't it?

So we're not reducing your objective to choosing one of two options. Later on in the chapter, we'll spell out no less than seven distinct options you can choose from in your evaluative comparison. At this point, we want you to reflect on what those options all have in common: each pair of readings will have two articulate people stating intelligent, opposing positions. In understanding these positions, and your position, reasoning things through becomes all-important. What premises underlie the statements in either argument? What strategies are used to sway you, the reader? What motivates your (qualified or unqualified) acceptance or rejection of the statements made?

The lessons of analysis and response (covered in Chapters 7 and 8) will serve you well here. But the challenge now is to transcend one-on-one analysis or response, to rise to the level of examining not just a text but a controversy. Once you see that you are joining a larger argument (between arguments), you will also see that your task presents you with a whole array of options beyond opting for one text or the other. In joining the controversy both texts participate in, you may resolve it, redirect it, extend it, qualify the way either text addresses it, and so on.

Such an evaluative comparison takes a combination of ambition and humility, gall and tact. You have to be fair to both authors and also bold enough to go beyond them. You will be able to do that by scrupulously examining your own motives as well as theirs. If you can see (and show) the reasons behind the reasoning, you will be looking at what will make your answer the "right" answer—at least, right for you.

DISCOVERING IDEAS

Take a Measure of the Texts—and the Context

If you can see that the arguments you are looking at are part of a larger argument, you can see that you need to look beyond both to the context in which they occur. And you need to locate yourself in the context—not just as a spectator but as a participant. What this means specifically will vary depending on what the subject of the controversy is, what text and authors you're looking at, and who you are and where you're coming from.

Consider the case of Hideaki Kazeno. We'll begin with his own context. He was enrolled in a experimental college writing class that fulfilled the requirements of the regular college writing class but that was tailored to students for whom English was a second language. All in good academic standing, these students did as much work as in any section of the course, but instruction in this class attempted to help them capitalize on their bilingualism and cultural distinctiveness. As part of that attempt, the instructor asked the students to write an evaluative comparison of arguments for and against making English the official language of the United States.

Some of the students—Hideaki was one—expressed surprise that this was a matter of controversy: wasn't English already the official language of Americans? The instructor resisted responding at length (and thus, perhaps, hinting at a "right" stand on the issue), saying only that the students would have to read both the "for" and the "against" arguments carefully.

The case for making English the official language was the text of Walter Darlington Huddleston's speech before the US Senate in 1983. Then a senator from Kentucky, Huddleston argued (unsuccessfully) that English should be made this country's official language by means of a constitutional amendment.

Alice Roy, not addressing Huddleston directly, presented her opposing view a few years later, after English had been made the official language of the state of California, a state in which she taught English at the university level. Her original audience consisted mostly of fellow teachers of English.

Before we get to their texts, we should tell you more about Hideaki Kazeno, the third participant we are considering in this controversy. A native of Japan, Hideaki was one of the older students in the class—in his early thirties. Though he had arrived in the United States only a few years before, he already had a job on Wall Street as well as a wife and family. His position in his firm made his fluency in both Japanese and English an important asset. He was also aware that there were various ways of perceiving fluency. His English was better than that of any Japanese person in his circle of acquaintances, but it wasn't good enough to spare him a semester of remediation when he first enrolled in an American college. In short, he had firsthand experience of the issues Huddleston and Roy were treating.

Here, then, are the arguments of Huddleston and Roy.

SPEECH ON BEHALF OF A CONSTITUTIONAL AMENDMENT TO MAKE ENGLISH THE OFFICIAL LANGUAGE OF THE UNITED STATES

Walter Darlington Huddleston

1   Mr. President, the remarks I am about to make will be readily understood by my distinguished colleagues in the Congress. They will be understood by my constituents in Kentucky. They will be understood by the journalists in the press gallery, and by most of their readers across the country.

2   No simultaneous interpreters will be needed for those in this chamber, and no translators will be needed for most of those who will be reading these words in the *Congressional Record.*

3   In order to guarantee that this current state of affairs endures, as it has for over two hundred years, I am introducing today a constitutional amendment to make English the official language of the United States.

4   The amendment addresses something so basic, so very fundamental to our sense of identity as Americans, that some, who are in full agreement with the objectives of this amendment, will nevertheless question the necessity for it. So widely held is the assumption that English already is our national language, that the notion of stating this in our national charter may seem like restating the obvious. However, I can assure my colleagues that this is not the case and that the need for a constitutional amendment grows stronger every day.

5   Almost alone among the world's very large and populous nations, the United States enjoys the blessings of one primary language, spoken and understood by most of its citizens. The previously unquestioned acceptance of this language by immigrants from every linguistic and cultural background has enabled us to come together as one people. It has allowed us to discuss our differences, to argue about our problems and to compromise on solutions. It has allowed us to develop a stable and cohesive society that is the envy of many fractured ones, without imposing any strict standards of

homogeneity, or even bothering to designate the language, which is ours by custom, as the Nation's official one.

6   As a nation of immigrants, our great strength has been drawn from our ability to assimilate vast numbers of people from many different cultures and ethnic groups into a nation of people that can work together with cooperation and understanding. This process was often referred to as the melting pot and in the past it has been seen as an almost magical concept that helped to make the United States the greatest nation on Earth.

7   But for the last fifteen years, we have experienced a growing resistance to the acceptance of our historic language, an antagonistic questioning of the melting pot philosophy that has traditionally helped speed newcomers into the American mainstream.

8   Initially, the demands to make things easier for the newcomers seemed modest enough; and a generous people, appreciative of cultural diversity, was willing to make some allowances. For example, the English language requirements for naturalization were removed for elderly immigrants living here for twenty years who were still unable to meet them; and the use of a child's home language in the school setting was encouraged, in a well-intentioned attempt to soften the pain of adjustment from the home to the English-speaking society that school represents.

9   However, the demands have sharply escalated, and so has the tone in which they are presented. Bilingual education has gradually lost its role as a transitional way of teaching English, and now mandates a bicultural component. This mandate has been primarily shaped and promoted by the federal government. The unfortunate result is that thousands of immigrant and nonimmigrant children are languishing in near-permanent bilingual/bicultural programs, kept in a state of prolonged confusion suspended between two worlds, and not understanding what is expected of them. They and their parents are given false hopes that their cultural traditions can be fully maintained in this country, and that the mastery of English is not so important, after all.

10   This change in attitude was aptly described by Theodore H. White in his book *America in Search of Itself* wherein he stated:

> Some Hispanics have, however, made a demand never voiced by immigrants before: that the United States, in effect, officially recognize itself as a bicultural, bilingual nation.... [They] demand that the United States become a bilingual country, with all children entitled to be taught in the language of their heritage, at public expense. No better hymn to the American tradition has ever been written than *The Education of Hyman Kaplan,* by Leo Rosten, which describes with tears and laughter the efforts of the earlier immigrants...to learn the language of the country in which they wished to live. In New York today, forty years later, Hispanic entitlement has created a college. Hostos Community College— supported by public taxes—which is officially bilingual; half its students receive instruction primarily in Spanish, as they strive to

escape from the subculture of the Spanish ghetto. Bilingualism is an awkward word—but it has torn apart communities from Canada to Brittany, from Belgium to India. It expresses not a sense of tolerance but a demand for divisions.

11 This misdirected public policy of bilingualism has been created primarily by the federal government, at the insistence of special interest groups, and it continues today because elected officials do not want to run the risk of taking a position that could, in some way, offend these groups. An example of how far this special interest influence reaches can be seen by President Reagan's reversal on the issue. At the beginning of his administration he attempted to kill the bilingual program; now he is embracing the concept.

12 Over the last few years the federal government has spent approximately $1 billion on the bilingual education program and this year alone it cost $139 million. What we have bought with this money is a program that strives to keep separate cultural identities rather than a program that strives to teach English. It is a program which ignores the basic fact that in order to learn another language the student must talk, read and use that language on a regular basis.

13 The failure of bilingual education programs to teach children how to speak English in the shortest time has been documented by a study done at the U.S. Department of Education and by the recent report of the Twentieth Century Fund Task Force on Federal Elementary and Secondary Education Policy. The latter report stated unequivocally that:

> The Task Force recommends that the federal government clearly state that the most important objective of elementary and secondary education in the United States is the development of literacy in the English language....
>
> The Task Force recommends that federal funds now going to the bilingual program be used to teach non-English-speaking children how to speak, read, and write English.

14 Even though the bilingual education program has received failing marks by many reputable educators, it still survives because it is a political issue rather than an educational issue. What this means is that we will continue to finance an expensive bilingual program that does more to preserve cultural identities than it does to teach children to speak English.

15 In the area of voting rights we have also formulated a national policy that encourages voting citizens not to learn to speak English. The Voting Rights Act, which was reauthorized in 1982, requires bilingual ballots if more than 5 percent of the citizens of voting age in a jurisdiction are members of specified language minority groups and the illiteracy rate is higher than the national rate. As a result bilingual ballots are required by federal law to be provided in 30 states—even if there is no demand for them.

16 In essence, we have gone far beyond providing a necessary service on a temporary basis; and, we are now engaged in actively encouraging the use of

bilingual ballots, even though in many cases they may not be needed. The wisdom of this policy is clearly lacking when you consider that the vast bulk of political debate, whether it is in the printed press or the electronic media, is conducted in English. By failing to provide a positive incentive for voting citizens to learn English, we are actually denying them full participation in the political process. Instead, we are making them dependent upon a few interpreters or go-betweens for information as to how they should vote. Although this process helps to preserve minority voting blocks, it seriously undercuts the democratic concept that every voting individual should be as fully informed as possible about the issues and the candidates.

17   In many parts of the country foreign language ballots are under attack. In San Francisco, a local initiative petition has been filed urging that local governments be allowed to print ballots in English only. In that area ballots are now printed in English, Spanish, Chinese, and because of the new census figures, Tagalog ballots will probably be printed in the future.

18   There are other less prominent provisions of federal law which now require the use of foreign languages. For example, 28 U.S.C. 1827 requires the Director of the Administrative Office of the U.S. courts to establish a program for the use of foreign language interpreters in federal civil and criminal proceedings for parties whose primary language is other than English; 42 U.S.C. 254 requires the use of foreign language personnel in connection with federally funded migrant and community health centers; and 42 U.S.C. 4577 requires the use of foreign language personnel in the alcohol abuse and treatment programs. Although I can understand that this kind of assistance is helpful, the fact that it must be legislated strongly indicates that we are failing miserably in our efforts to teach immigrants and many of our native born how to speak, read and write English.

19   The federal laws requiring the use of interpreters and foreign languages are merely the tip of the iceberg. I recently sent a request to all of the state governors and the major federal agencies asking for information regarding non-English forms and publications that their offices produce, which are intended for use in this country. Although my staff is still in the process of reviewing the data, and I have not yet received responses to all of my letters, we know that hundreds of different non-English forms and publications are now being printed and distributed on a wide scale throughout the United States. These publications cover a broad spectrum and range from White House press releases in Spanish to National Labor Relations Board notices in thirty-two different languages. The non-English materials which I have received are in a stack that is about 3 feet high, and we are adding to it almost daily. However, even when all the responses are in we still will not have a complete picture of the use of official, non-English publications. Many of the states are only sending a few samples of what they produce, and I am told that if copies of all bilingual educational materials were sent we could fill a large room. While distribution of these materials may be seen as providing just another government service, it can also be seen as reducing the incentive to learn English and demonstrates a growing nationwide problem.

20   At the nongovernment level there is a great deal of emphasis being placed on the use of non-English languages. In some major metropolitan areas English is the second language; minorities, who speak only English, are being told that they must learn a foreign language in order to be eligible for a job in parts of this country; and, in many stores non-English languages are the only ones used to conduct business. It is not uncommon to find areas in this country where an individual can live all of his or her life having all of his social, commercial, and intellectual needs met without the use of English.

21   Statistics show a disconcerting trend away from the common use of English. In 1975 the Bureau of the Census reported that about 8 million people in this country used a language other than English in their households. When the census was conducted in 1980 the number of people who spoke a language other than English at home was found to be over 22 million. Although these numbers are subject to many interpretations, to me they indicate—very strongly—that the melting pot is not working as it once did.

22   My assumption is confirmed by a recent population bulletin, "U.S. Hispanics; Changing the Face of America," which concluded that because of their common language and large numbers, Hispanics will take longer than other immigrant groups to assimilate into the American society.

23   If this situation were static and merely a reflection of the large scale legal and illegal immigration the United States has been experiencing over the last few years—in 1980 more immigrants entered the United States than at any time other than the peak years at the turn of the century—there would not be cause for concern. However, what we are seeing is a decrease in the use of English and a widely accepted attitude that it is not necessary to learn English.

24   There is a new philosophy taking hold, and it is gaining more and more acceptance. In the June 13, 1983, *Time* magazine an article stated in regard to this new philosophy, that:

> Now, however, a new bilingualism and biculturalism is being promulgated that would deliberately fragment the Nation into separate, unassimilated groups . . . [*sic*] The new metaphor is not the melting pot but the salad bowl, with each element distinct. The biculturalists seek to use public services, particularly schools, not to Americanize the young but to heighten their consciousness of belonging to another heritage.

25   The United States is presently at a crucial juncture. We can either continue down the same path we have walked for the last two hundred years, using the melting pot philosophy to forge a strong and united nation, or we can take the new path that leads in the direction of another Tower of Babel.

26   There are many nations in the world today that would give a great deal to have the kind of internal social and political stability that a single primary language (English) has afforded us. For us to consciously make the decision to throw away this stabilizing force would be seen as foolish and stupid in

countries that have paid a high price for not having a universally accepted language.

27   We have to look no further than the nation which is closest to us geographically and culturally—Canada. They have had a long-running experience with bilingualism and biculturalism, and it is an experience that still generates divisiveness and still threatens to shatter the nation's unity. The key cause of Canada's internal conflict is language. According to the Annual Report, 1981, of the Commissioner of Official Languages, the total cost so far in implementing the Canadian Official Languages Act "is on the order of $4 billion spread over the 12 years. The question of cost-effectiveness is more problematical. Measured against the goals of relieving English-French tensions and fostering a common pride in the value of our national languages, the results may be more questionable."

28   Belgium is another nation that has suffered severe internal dissent, much of which has been caused by language differences. In the last thirty-nine years the political coalitions that are necessary to govern that country have been broken apart over thirty times by the fights between the French-speaking Walloons and the Dutch-speaking Flemish. This political squabbling has had serious consequences for Belgium, and it is not the kind of situation to which any nation should voluntarily subject itself.

29   This type of political instability has been repeated throughout history, and is still occurring in many countries today. In countless places, differences in language have either caused or contributed significantly to political, social, and economic instability. While the absence of language differences does not guarantee that these problems will not occur, I believe that it does significantly reduce the chances that they will occur.

30   The constitutional amendment which I am proposing is not unusual, and in fact, many nations have one official language. According to the Library of Congress these include, but are not limited to, Austria, Bulgaria, Denmark, France, the German Democratic Republic, the Federal Republic of Germany, Greece, Hungary, Italy, the Netherlands, Norway, Poland, Romania, and Sweden.

31   Within the United States there is ample tradition and legislation to justify this approach. According to the Library of Congress:

> Several Federal statutes and numerous State laws do require the use of English in a variety of areas.
>
> Thus, the Nationality Act of 1940 (8 U.S.C. 423) requires that—
>
> "No person...shall be naturalized as a citizen of the United States upon his own petition who cannot demonstrate—
>
> "(1) an understanding of the English language, including an ability to read, write and speak words in ordinary usage in the English language" (with provisos).
>
> Secondly, 28 U.S.C. 865 requires that in determining whether a person is qualified for jury service, the chief judge of a district court "shall deem any person qualified to serve on grand and petit juries in the district court unless he (the prospective juror)—

"(2) is unable to read, write, and understand the English language with a degree of proficiency sufficient to fill out satisfactorily the juror qualification form;

"(3) is unable to speak the English language...."

At the state level, most states have statutes requiring the use of English as the language of instruction in the public schools. Some states also statutorily require English as the language of legal proceedings and legal notices, of business regulation, etc.

32   More recently, the U.S. Senate has spoken out very strongly in favor of establishing English as the official language. On August 13, 1982, Senator Hayakawa introduced an amendment to the Immigration Reform and Control Act declaring that "the English language is the official language of the United States." On a rollcall vote seventy-eight senators voted for this amendment and it was included in the bill. When this same bill was again reported out of the Judiciary Committee on April 21, 1983, it again contained this language, and the report of the full committee stated:

If immigration is continued at a high level, yet a substantial portion of these new persons and their descendants do not assimilate into the society, they have the potential to create in America a measure of the same social, political, and economic problems which exist in the countries from which they have chosen to depart. Furthermore, if language and cultural separatism rise above a certain level, the unity and political stability of the nation will—in time—be seriously diminished. Pluralism, within a united American nation, has been the single greatest strength of this country. This unity comes from a common language and a core public culture of certain shared values, beliefs, and customs which make us distinctly "Americans."

33   The concerns that were expressed by the Senate Judiciary Committee are reflected in the concerns of thousands of citizens throughout this country. In fact, a new national organization has recently been created called U.S. English. The honorary chairman of this organization is former U.S. Senator S. I. Hayakawa, who speaks with a great deal of authority on this issue because he is an immigrant and distinguished scholar of semantics and languages.

34   U.S. English refers to itself as "a national, non-profit, non-partisan organization...founded to defend the public interest in the growing debate on bilingualism and biculturalism."

35   If we continue along the path we now follow, I believe that we will do irreparable damage to the fragile unity that our common language has helped us preserve for over two hundred years. Cultural pluralism is an established value in our national life, and one which we greatly cherish. Paradoxically, cultural pluralism can only continue if we retain our common meeting ground; namely, the English language. If we allow this bond to erode, we will no longer enjoy the benefits of cultural diversity, but rather, we will suffer the bitterness of ethnic confrontations and cultural separatism.

36   The constitutional language I am proposing is simple and straightforward: It would serve to establish a principle that would strengthen us as a nation. However, I am aware that adding to the Constitution takes us into uncharted waters, and that there will be many misleading allegations about the extent of the problem and the proposed remedy. This is one of the reasons I have chosen to propose a constitutional amendment in order to address this issue. It will focus national attention on the problem, and subject it to the type of thorough national debate which is necessary.

37   During this constitutional process, all parties, sides, and interests will have the opportunity to present their respective points of view. This will guarantee that the final version submitted to the states for ratification will accomplish only what is needed to be accomplished and that basic individual rights are not interfered with.

38   Even though I believe that the constitutional language I am proposing will work, I am open to all recommendations and I will carefully consider any proposed improvements or modifications. However, regardless of the final language, to a large extent it is the legislative history which determines how the language will be interpreted.

39   Accordingly, it is my intent that the amendment I am proposing would not do a number of things.

40   First. It would not prohibit or discourage the use of foreign languages and cultures in private contexts, such as in homes, churches, communities, private organizations, commerce, and private schools. The United States is rich in ethnic cultures and they would continue to survive as they have in the past.

41   Second. It would not prohibit the teaching of foreign languages in the Nation's public schools or colleges, nor will it prohibit foreign language requirements in academic institutions.

42   Third. It will not prevent the use of second languages for the purpose of public convenience and safety in limited circumstances.

43   On the other hand the amendment would accomplish a number of objectives.

44   First. It would bring national recognition to the proposition that a common language is necessary to preserve the basic internal unity that is required for a stable and growing nation.

45   Second. It would establish English as the official language of federal, state, and local governments throughout the United States.

46   Third. Since voting by citizens is the method of choosing the representatives of these governments and is the first step in the official process of governing, it would prevent the printing of ballots in foreign languages.

47   Fourth. It would permit bilingual education where it could be clearly demonstrated that the primary objective and practical result is the teaching of English to students as rapidly as possible, and not cultural maintenance. It would not affect the use of total immersion in English, which is a proven method of teaching English.

48   Fifth. It would discourage discrimination and exploitation by making it clear to immigrant parents and children that learning English is indispensable for full participation in the American society and economy and by speeding them into the mainstream of our society and economy as rapidly as possible.

49   Sixth. It would reaffirm that we are truly "one Nation…indivisible…."

50   Mr. President, national unity is not a subject to be taken lightly, for without it we would lose much of the strength which sets us apart as a great nation. I believe that history has taught us that one of the vital ingredients for obtaining national unity is a commonly accepted language. This has been confirmed by our own past experience in this country, and it has been proven by other countries that have been divided and weakened by their internal arguments centering around language differences.

51   National unity does not require that each person think and act like everyone else. However, it does require that there be some common threads that run throughout our society and hold us together. One of these threads is our common belief and support of a democratic form of government, and the right of every person to fully participate in it. Unfortunately, this right of full articipation means very little if each individual does not possess the means of exercising it. This participation requires the ability to obtain information and to communicate our beliefs and concerns to others. Undoubtedly this process is greatly hindered without the existence of a commonly accepted and used language.

52   In essence, what a policy of bilingualism/biculturalism does is to segregate minorities from the mainstream of our politics, economy, and society because we are not making it possible for them to freely enter into that mainstream. We are pushing them aside into their own communities, and denying them the tools with which to break out. I have always been against segregation of any kind, and by not assuring that every person in this country can speak and understand English we are still practicing segregation. It was wrong when we segregated blacks because of color and it is just as wrong when we create a system which segregates any group of people by language.

53   As Americans we are a unique people and one of the things that makes us uniquely American is our common language—English. My proposed constitutional amendment would assure that anyone in this country can fully take part in the American dream and that future generations also will have this privilege.

54   Mr. President, I ask unanimous consent that the joint resolution be printed in the *Record*.

55   There being no objection, the joint resolution was ordered to be printed in the *Record,* as follows:

S.J. Res. 167

Resolved by the Senate and House of Representatives of the United States of America in Congress assembled, (two-thirds of each House concurring therein), That the following article is proposed as an amendment to the Constitution of the United States, which shall be valid to all intents and purposes as part of the Constitution if ratified by the legislatures of three-fourths of the several States within seven years after its submission to the States for ratification:

ARTICLE

"SEC. 1. The English language shall be the official language of the United States."

"SEC. 2. The Congress shall have the power to enforce this article by appropriate legislation."

THE ENGLISH ONLY MOVEMENT

Alice Roy

1   In 1986, California became the first state in the country to adopt an amendment to the state constitution declaring English the official language. This was accomplished through a voter initiative sponsored by "U.S. English," founded by S. I. Hayakawa in 1983. The initiative was Proposition 63, called "English Only," and it passed by a wide margin, 73% for, 27% against. U.S. English and another group known as "English First," led by former Virginia legislator Larry Pratt, are working throughout the country to make English the official language. Many people have adopted "English Only" as the cover label for all such groups and legislative actions; others use "official English" for the purpose.

2   Membership in official-English groups appears to be increasing. U.S. English nearly doubled its membership from 150,000 in 1983 to 275,000 in 1986. English First has enrolled 200,000 members just since its beginning in 1986. It may be that this growth spurt is over, that is, that all who are going to join such groups have done so. However, leaders of the two groups and opponents as well predict increasing membership and activity in the 1990s and extending into the 21st century (Orenstein 1).

3   What do official-English acts and amendments do? Most, like California's, declare English to be the state's official language. Others say the state shall not require use of any other language. Some explicitly permit bilingual education; however, only a few have this feature, and none except for Arizona are in the West or Southwest. Some require all official proceedings and publications to be in English. Some, in the form of legislative resolutions, urge passage of federal official-English laws or amendments. A few, among them California's, empower citizens and businesses of the state to sue to enforce official-English laws. Several declare English to be the basic language in public schools. Such acts and amendments may also forbid state legislatures from passing any law which diminishes or ignores the official status of English (Orenstein 3).

4   Thirty-one state legislatures have considered or are considering actions to make English the official state or national language. These proposals take

varying forms, sometimes as voter initiatives on the ballot, more often as state legislative bills. Twelve have passed: Illinois and Nebraska in the 1920s; Arkansas, Mississippi, North Dakota, California, Georgia, Virginia, Nevada, Indiana, Kentucky, and Tennessee since 1984. (Hawaii's state constitutional amendment, passed in 1978, declares English and Hawaiian to be the state's official languages.) In a few other states bills or initiatives are pending but are not predicted to succeed. In 1981, Hayakawa proposed an amendment to the U.S. Constitution to make English the official language. Similar bills have been introduced every year since then, but none have been voted out of committee (Orenstein 1, 2).

5   In strictly numerical terms, official English has not had much legislative success. And, in practical terms, a survey of official-English states found no changes in education or government policy resulting from official-English legislation (Orenstein 2). However, at another level of activity, a lot is going on. For example, in a small town in California, the mayor vowed that election information and "other things" would only come out in English. In Whittier, California, there are plans for legislation calling for state services to be available in English, including driver's tests, welfare applications, and state university financial aid forms. Leaders of official-English groups are reviewing laws and regulations to see which ones do not comply with legislation or amendments already passed. Members of official-English groups work to ensure that school notices will not be sent home in any language other than English. Furthermore, members of some city councils campaign and are elected to office based on a platform supporting English Only. In an administrative action that was later ruled illegal, three judges in a municipal court imposed an English Only order on Latino employees during their work hours in the courthouse. There are efforts to remove non-English business signs, to stop the translations of city newsletters, and to cut bilingual education funds (Chen and Calderone 8). Indeed, two of the explicitly cited goals in the solicitation letter from English First are to make sure that states can "limit bilingual programs *without having the anti-English coalitions overturn them in the courts*" [emphasis theirs]; and to work for "passage at the Constitutional level, which will end the bilingual ballot" (Pratt 4).

6   What is the cause of this apparent linguistic chauvinism? The English Only movement appeals to a fairly simple sentiment—that everyone should speak English. Underneath this, however, are anti-immigrant and divisive sentiments that rest on economic fears. The U.S. economy is currently in a period of slow growth, the annual budget deficit is not reducing, and agriculture and some industries are in a depressed state. At such times, competition for limited resources pits segments of the population against each other. Proposals for national legislation reflect or exacerbate people's fears that immigrant workers may take jobs from U.S. citizens, that the state of the economy is to be blamed on foreign imports, and that bilingual education allows non-English-speaking groups to increase their political power. Angry taxpayers blame immigrants for depleting an already tight

budget with the use of social services such as education, literacy, health, and jobs programs. Funding of bilingual education and misconceptions about the quality and goals of bilingual education increase fears and distrust (Chen and Calderone 7).

7   Seeing the sorts of things that English Only groups do *not* have as goals helps to substantiate this economic interpretation. For example, there have been fears in California that the courts might be able to prohibit foreign language advertising. Analysis of an issue of *Business and Community Impact,* a publication of the Chamber of Commerce in a Los Angeles community with a large Asian population, shows a full-page ad for a realty and insurance agency, mostly in English with a few lines in Chinese; a column of English, advertising a bank, paralleled by a column with the same information in Chinese; and a page giving a Chinese-language summary of the sixteen-page magazine. The head of the U.S. English California office says there is no danger of such economic nonsense as interfering with advertising (Orenstein 2). Translation: bilingual is all right if it makes money.

8   The English Only movement rests on a few myths or misconceptions, some of which we all learned overtly in grade school social studies, some we acquired more implicitly, and some that we as English teachers directly participate in.

9   The first myth is that earlier immigrant populations all learned English. The solicitation letter for the group English First, signed by Jim Horn, Representative to the Texas Legislature, begins:

> I don't know about your forefathers but when mine came to America, the first thing they did was learn English.
> They wanted to be part of the American dream, and they knew that learning English wasn't just a practical necessity. It was a moral obligation.
> Tragically, many immigrants these days refuse to learn English!

Similarly, Larry Pratt, head of English First, says that it is "something that generations of immigrants have taken for granted: when coming to the U.S. one learns English. In fact, those immigrants were proud to have learned English" (4). But in actual fact it wasn't taken for granted. From the beginning of our history, linguistic difference has been an issue. Benjamin Franklin worried about the Germans—they had little knowledge of English, they had their own German press, and Franklin was afraid they would need translators to tell one half of Congress what the other half was saying (Pinon 4). Three-quarters of a century later, the first California state constitution was written in both English and Spanish.

10   The myth that all immigrants learned English right away is closely related to the second myth, that of the "melting pot" as a description of ethnic relations in the U.S. The melting pot metaphor encodes the widely held belief that previous immigrant groups arrived, jumped into the

common cauldron, and came out homogenized. That kind of assimilation was possible for white Northern Protestant Europeans, for linguistic, cultural, racial, and religious reasons. However, we have inherited a "sanitized romanticism" about our immigration history (Janken 4). Certainly the immigrant experience is a deep-running theme in our country's history. Immigrants came to improve their condition, not so much for themselves as for their children and grandchildren. There was a strong sense that this would take a couple of generations to accomplish. The upward mobility that characterizes this immigrant experience must be seen in a context of persecution—not just the persecution being fled from, but the persecution experienced here as well. Immigrants made up the largest proportion of membership in social protest movements in the U.S. in the first thirty years of the 20th century. Was this because they came from places where they experienced persecution and exploitation? Or was it because they perceived inequity and exploitation here in the midst of the American dream? We have just recently celebrated the Statue of Liberty Centennial. In 1882, shortly before the Statue of Liberty was placed in the New York harbor, the Chinese Exclusion Act was passed by Congress. This act was connected to the economic crisis then, for which Chinese were partly blamed. We know that after World War I, immigration restrictions were imposed on eastern and southern Europeans, including Jews who were denied refuge from Nazism. Our "nation of immigrants" legend is largely that of white Europeans. It ignores Blacks, Chicanos, and Native Americans in American history. These groups had no choice of residence: Blacks were brought, Chicanos and Native Americans were displaced—these were not the "huddled masses yearning to breathe free" (Janken 4, 5).

11   The community of Monterey Park in Los Angeles is a modern example of the melting pot myth. It is a suburb of Los Angeles, technically, but quite close to the center of town, well within the metropolitan area. It is now being called the first suburban Chinatown (Arax 1). In the past ten years, a rapid increase in Asian population has occurred—the proportion is now 40% Asian, 37% Latino, 22% Anglo, and 1% Black. Longtime Anglo and Latino residents remember it before the Asian influx. Some Anglos remember the community before the Chicano influx.

12   A few years ago, Monterey Park was euphorically designated an all-American city because of its apparent racial harmony. The sixteen-page *Monterey Park Living,* a community activities publication with articles in the Fall 1986 issue of the Monterey Park Golf Course, the Senior Citizens' Center, medical emergency services, and the recreation schedule, has a single page fully in Chinese, summarizing the information contained in the magazine. Now, however, that community is racially polarized. One night in June of 1986, at 1:30 A.M., when most residents who attend such meetings had gone home, the Monterey Park City Council passed a resolution urging control of U.S. borders, denouncing cities that provide sanctuary to refugees, instructing local police to cooperate vigorously with immigration authorities, and endorsing legislation to make English the official language

of the United States (Ono and Calderon 6). Clearly the English Only movement is part of a larger reaction—it is not just linguistic.

13   At the 1986 convention, the National Council of Teachers of English passed a resolution urging rejection of the tenets of official-English groups. NCTE president Nancy McHugh has received many letters attacking her personally or attacking the NCTE stand generally.[1] These letters make frequent reference to the melting pot:

> Dear "Nancy,"
>   How could you be elected president of NCTE with the grossly narrow view you hold on English? Now a retired English instructor of 50 years, I am *shocked* to learn of your position. We are ONE nation of the most ethnic people in the world who've become U.S. citizens.

Or, as another letter-writer said:

> I'm horrified at the position of your organization—Glad *I'm* not a member! The *melting pot* is our greatest strength—The immigrant groups which succeed are those who learn the language!

14   Along with the melting pot myth, this writer raises the issue of the relationship between language and upward mobility. The third myth that the official-English movement rests on is that language exists and can be learned out of social context. Leaders of the movement often reject bilingual education in favor of holding children who speak limited or no English separate from regular schooling until they have learned enough English to cope in English-speaking classes:

> It is clear that an intensive period of instruction, perhaps as much as a year, should be provided so that a student can study English full time during that period. Then the student is ready to study the other courses in the curriculum—in English (Pratt 4).

Research shows, however, that children who study academic content in their early grade school years, using their native language and developing native language literacy, do as well as native speakers in the long run, and better than those students who are held back from beginning their education until they can do so in English. Theory and research in language acquisition tell us that language does not respond to a head-on assault, that rather we learn a language best when we use it to learn or do something else (for example, see Krashen; Swain and Lapkin; and Brumfit and Johnson). Another letter to McHugh echoes the previous writer's belief that knowing English will get the knower a job:

> We . . . strongly object to those who seek to deny recent immigrants the social and economic opportunities that are only available to those knowing English.

Yet it is more likely that once people have jobs they will learn English than it is that people will earn English before they get jobs. In earlier waves of immigration, men who went out to work learned English, though it was described as "broken English," while the women who stayed at home taking care of children and aged parents did not.

15   The fourth myth on which the official-English movement relies is that language can be controlled and preserved against change. Other letter writers to Nancy McHugh say:

> (1) I think it incredible that you could oppose such a movement as the one pushing for the legal protection of the English language. You may want to pay taxes so *some* can use bilingual voting ballots, etc., but I don't. It's your money. U.S. ENGLISH ALL THE WAY!
>
> (2) In my opinion, I believe there should be a National Academy of English Language Standards to which *ALL* teachers and public speakers should belong.
>
> (3) As a retired teacher of English, I can't believe the National Council of English Teachers would pass an official resolution opposing the movement for the legal protection of the English language in America! All one has to do is read any newspaper in the country or visit any legislature to discover the deplorable lack of the use of standard English in our country.

But language can be neither controlled nor preserved against change. The French Academy has not succeeded in keeping English words out of French. The Spanish Academy has not succeeded in getting all Spanish-speaking people—even in Spain—to speak Castilian Spanish. And two hundred years of English teachers' exhortations and imprecations to get students to stop saying *lay* for *lie* and to stop using *they* for indefinite singular reference have not succeeded.

16   What needs to be done? What can we do?

17   One local group in Los Angeles has a tutorial program called Building Rainbows. Its goals are to help students learn about each others' cultures and to stay in school, to get parents involved in their children's education, and to build parents' leadership in community institutions (Ono and Calderon 7).

18   A recent *ERIC/CLL* (Clearinghouse on Languages and Linguistics) *News Bulletin* describes programs designed to bring parents of children identified as Limited-English Speaking into tutoring relationships with school classes (Simich-Dudgeon 3).

19   Our professional organizations provide leadership and information—the NCTE and the Linguistic Society of America have both passed resolutions opposing English Only legislation. We can work for greater funding of programs to help non-English speakers learn English. For example, in the Los Angeles School District, 192,000 adult students study English in adult education programs; 40,000 are on waiting lists (May 16).

20   Remembering that money talks, we can inform students and the public that we can enrich our resources, industry, tax collection, and consumerism through immigrant populations. At a time when Pacific Rim commer-

cial activity in particular and worldwide exchange in general is increasing, the restriction of use of languages is a particularly parochial aim. We speak for the economic usefulness of a multilingual population.

21   Most especially, as teachers of English at all levels, we can teach our students to respect and enjoy cultural and linguistic diversity. This means relinquishing a value-laden approach to teaching English that makes the use of a certain kind of English a moral or ethical virtue—where correctness replaces cleanliness right up there next to godliness. We must relinquish as well the purity of the received canon of English literature in order to draw on the richness of minor and minority writing. We as English teachers have inherited an elitist view of English, but we don't have to perpetuate it. Although community action is important, we can do our work in our workplace by refusing to collude in the myths and by learning and teaching how language and society interact.

NOTES

[1]I thank Nancy McHugh for making copies of some of these letters available to me for this study.

WORKS CITED

Arax, Mark. "Monterey Park: Nation's 1st Suburban Chinatown." *Los Angeles Times.* 6 April 1987, sec I:1+.

Brumfit, C. J., and K. Johnson, eds. *The Communicative Approach to Language Teaching.* Oxford: Oxford University Press, 1979.

Business and Community Impact. November 1986.

Chen, W., and J. Calderone. "Language Rights and Structural Change." *NDM National Bulletin,* Spring 1987:5–13.

Horn, Jim. "English First" solicitation letter, no date (mailed 1986).

Janken, Kenneth. "The Forgotten 'Immigrant Experience'." *The New Democrat.* August 1986:4–5.

Krashen, Stephen D. *Principles and Practice in Second Language Acquisition.* Oxford/New York: Pergamon Press, 1982.

May, Lee. "Alien Law Puts Strain on English Classes." *Los Angeles Times.* 25 February 1987, sec I:16.

Monterey Park Living. September–November 1986.

Ono, Carol, and Jose Calderon. "No Torch of Liberty in the All-American City." *The New Democrat.* August 1986:6–7.

Orenstein, Mike. "'Official English' Battle Widens." *Hispanic Link Weekly Report.* 20 April 1987:4.

Pinon, Fernando. "The Case for Language Equity." *Hispanic Link Weekly Report.* 20 April 1987:4.

Pratt, Larry. "The Case for English First." *Hispanic Link Weekly Report.* 20 April 1987:4.

Simich-Dudgeon, Carmen. "Involving Limited-English-Proficient Parents as Tutors in Their Children's Education." *ERIC/CLL News Bulletin.* March 1987:3–4, 7.

Swain, Merrill, and Sharon Lapkin. *Evaluating Bilingual Education: A Canadian Case Study.* Clevedon, Avon, England: Multilingual Matters Ltd., n.d.

TRIAL RUN

Thoughtful, thorough, responsive reading is always helped by some kind of writing. This may involve highlighting or annotating key passages in the text; it may involve writing notes as elaborate as the double-entry journal discussed in Chapter 8. Even without a writing implement in hand, your thoughts about the texts are taking shape. You might as well make them a matter of record so that you have something to draw on in the drafting process. At the very least, you might write out answers to the following questions:

CHECKLIST: GAUGING YOUR INITIAL RESPONSE

- **Can you sum up your response to either text?** Try to express your basic response in a sentence or two.

- **Can you identify a particular passage or feature of the text that helps to explain your response?** Try to anchor your response to the text in a specific statement it makes.

- **Can you sum up your response to either text in comparative terms?** Try to couch your reaction in a sentence that compares one author to the other—for example, "I prefer X's politics or tone to Y's."

- **Can you identify something about you that helps to explain your response?** Try to sum up what it is about you—your values, experience, attitudes—that informs your response.

Relate the Texts to One Another

Class discussion of the pieces by Huddleston and Roy began with a quick survey of the students. How many were mainly in agreement with Huddleston? How many were mainly in agreement with Roy? How many felt in agreement with neither? It turned out the class was almost evenly split three ways. (Hideaki included himself in that last group.)

The instructor didn't ask the students to elaborate on why they had responded one way or the other. Instead, the discussion turned to what Huddleston and Roy had in common, since (said the instructor) there wouldn't be adequate grounds for comparison without certain similarities (of topic or subject, of strategy, of premises and principles). The subject—whether English should be made the official language—was mentioned first. Then one of the students said that both Huddleston and Roy seemed to have (or wanted to be seen as having) the best interests of the country (and recent immigrants to it) at heart. Another noted that, though their interpretations differed, both discussed the "melting pot" and used the past to explain the present.

Precisely because they are addressing a common issue, though from differing viewpoints, even opposing authors will likely share certain interests—for example, concern about the conditions that gave rise to the issue, or about its past causes and future ramifications, or about the way it is perceived. As you look at specific debates, you are likely to find telling resemblances beyond these general patterns. Hideaki, for instance, noticed that, while Huddleston and Roy both made much of their concern for the immigrant who came from another language background, neither could speak from the perspective of such an immigrant. Hideaki could, and realizing as much gave him a place from which to pitch his argument.

Discovering shared concerns and strategies also helps to highlight significant differences that occur, not simply in the arguments themselves, but also in their animating motives. Consider how the debating authors differ in terms of social position, political affiliation, moral outlook, ethnicity or race, age, gender. What do they stand to gain by taking the stand they take? And don't just think about them; think about the differences in their constituencies—the people they speak to or for. How do their audiences differ? Whom are they advocates of? Consider differences in their contexts. Does *when* they are arguing make a difference? (Is it significant, for instance, that Huddleston's argument precedes Roy's by several years?)

 # **T**RIAL RUN

We've hardly exhausted the points that Huddleston and Roy might be seen to have in common. Either with classmates or on your own, see if you can't list more—or list similarities between other paired arguments you'll be evaluating. Once you have developed your list, interrogate those similarities for the ways they may clarify differences. Perhaps the two authors share certain principles but arrange their priorities differently. Perhaps they share goals but endorse different means of achieving them. If you can identify an especially crucial difference emerging from this review of similarities, you may have found the key statement your evaluative comparison will make.

Use Burke's Pentad

As similarities between Huddleston and Roy proliferated during class discussion, the instructor noted that these made identifying the whys and wherefores of the opposing perspectives vital. The class was given one scheme for doing so: taken from Kenneth Burke's *A Grammar of Motives* (1945), they are "the five key terms of dramatism": **act, scene, agent, agency,** and **purpose.** Burke explains that, "Although, over the centuries men have shown great enterprise and inventiveness in pondering matters of human motivation, one can simplify the subject by this pentad of key terms, which are understandable almost at a glance."

Bearing some resemblance to the pattern of item analysis introduced in Chapter 6 as well as the procedures for rhetorical reading in Chapter 7, Burke's pentad (*pentad* means a grouping of five) provides a starting point for analysis that is especially interested in motive. Why does a particular author make a particular case? What are the reasons behind the reasoning? What assumptions are made, what interests pursued, what gains or changes sought? Are the motives that animate the argument explicitly stated, or are they only partially disclosed, perhaps even deliberately obscured? If authors are not advancing their own interests, are they advancing those of some party on whose behalf they speak? You can at least begin to develop answers to such challenging questions by using Burke's pentad.

In Hideaki's class, the instructor distributed a sheet using the terms to frame key questions and passed on Burke's claim that "any complete statement about motives will offer *some kind* of answers to these five questions." Students were asked to interrogate each position, including their own (to the extent they knew what it was at that point).

TRIAL RUN

Before you look at what Hideaki came up with, give responses of your own to these questions—one for each text in the pair, and maybe one for the text beginning to take shape in your head.

Questionnaire Derived from Burke's Pentad

Act: What is being proposed?

Scene: What is the context in which it is being proposed?

Agent: Who is doing this—and on whose behalf?

Agency: How is this being done?

Purpose: Why is this being done?

Figure 9-1 shows Hideaki's responses to those questions.

Thinking Critically about Hideaki's Responses

1. Do you find yourself strongly disagreeing with any part of Hideaki's analysis of Huddleston or Roy? Are these questions to which there can only be one generally right answer? Why or why not?

2. Does anything about Hideaki's answers suggest that he has a favorable or unfavorable response to Huddleston? To Roy? Does his resolve in the self-analysis to prove "both are wrong" come as a surprise after looking through his analysis of each?

3. In the cases of Huddleston and Roy, the analysis is of fully elaborated positions. Hideaki's analysis of himself is only the analysis of a prospective

---

Figure 9-1

Burke's Pentad

(Keyed to Huddleston)

ACT: What is being proposed? a constitutional amendment to make English the official language of the United States

SCENE: What is the context in which it is being proposed? in the Congress after a wave of immigrants who don't speak English or are slow in learning English

AGENT: Who is doing this--and on whose behalf? a senator who thinks his culture and heritage are about to be threatened by alien thoughts and languages is proposing this legislation on behalf of his peer group

AGENCY: How is this being done? by means of a speech, using incoherent rhetoric that says he wants this bill, which will harm a lot of immigrants, because he wants to help those immigrants assimilate into American life

PURPOSE: Why is it being done?
to keep the United States united as a nation
to keep immigrants from politics

(Keyed to Roy)

ACT: What is being proposed? multi-cultural education, tolerance toward foreign cultures and their effects on the English language

SCENE: What is the context in which it is being proposed? after arguing that the motives behind the English-only movement are not to preserve the language but to exclude immigrants for economical reasons

AGENT: Who is doing this--and on whose behalf? an English teacher, for immigrants

AGENCY: How is this being done? by arguing that language can be neither controlled nor preserved against change

PURPOSE: Why is it being done?
to make immigrants' assimilation easier

(Keyed to Your Argument)

ACT: What are you arguing? proving that both are wrong, and that there has to be a middle point

SCENE: What is the context in which you are making your argument?
in comparing the two essays

AGENT: Who are you to argue as you do--and on whose behalf?
for struggling students to master English

AGENCY: How are you making your argument?
by pointing out the flaws in their logics

PURPOSE: Why are you making your argument? because I don't like either of their arguments, so I want to prove my point position. Has he said enough to allow you to imagine how he will proceed and why he will argue as he does? If you were in a position to advise Hideaki before he begins drafting his paper, what, if anything, would you tell him he still needed to clarify or resolve?

Hideaki found Huddleston the easiest to analyze in terms of means and motives, for he had not just the help of Burke's pentad but of Roy as well. Though Roy didn't take Huddleston on personally, she did analyze the means and motives of people like him, if only from her own perspective. Roy herself was more difficult for Hideaki to analyze precisely because she seemed more sympathetic to recent immigrants like himself. It was tempting to look upon her essay as primarily an analysis of people like Huddleston, but she was also making a proposal of her own. How well did it jibe with her analysis of her opposition? Hideaki wasn't sure, but he found himself finally resisting her argument almost as much as he resisted Huddleston's. The hardest person to analyze for Hideaki was Hideaki. He had decided he would try to hammer out a third position, but he wasn't sure what that was exactly. For that, he needed a clearer definition of where he came in.

Define Your Purpose: Where Do You Come In?

Let's say that, like Hideaki, you've analyzed the texts, and you've given some thought to how they relate to one another. Now's the time to consider your response and the angle you want to take. This requires making yourself the subject of some analysis. We recommend that you do what Hideaki did: fill out, however briefly and tentatively, the questionnaire derived from Burke's pentad for yourself. What are your motives? Why do you read and respond as you do? What premises do you operate from? Whose interests are you championing? Where do you stand in the struggle between opposing views? Considerations of how you situate yourself with respect to the authors you're evaluating are particularly important as you begin to write. Here, basically, are your options—those seven options we mentioned earlier:

1. **Endorse one author over the other.** We really can't recommend simple endorsement. One purpose of an exercise like this is to show you that you have a mind of your own, and simply jumping on someone else's wagon doesn't do much to suggest that. But you don't have to do that. If you wholeheartedly accept one position and reject another, delving into *your* reasons for doing so—as opposed to parroting the views of the author you favor—could make for a good paper.

2. **Travel with one author only part of the way.** A more attractive alternative to simple endorsement is qualified endorsement. You can cast the views of the author you prefer as rather extreme in certain respects, so that you can follow that road only so far.

3. **Take things further than your preferred author did.** A logical variant of the endorsement-with-reservations is the sort of endorsement that extends the author's argument or its implications, that goes down roads the author did not take or fully explore.

4. **Make such reservations or extensions grounds for rejection rather than endorsement.** This became the route Hideaki took. If he wasn't inclined to endorse Huddleston's and Roy's positions, he was willing to suggest that they made sense—up to a point. But he concluded that they both went "too far." Of course, one could also reject both positions for not going far enough.

5. **Opt for one author as the lesser of two evils.** This is the choice voters often have to make between political candidates, only because one of those candidates presumably must hold the contested office. However, when you're considering viewpoints rather than candidates, your choice isn't usually restricted in just two options, and so the lesser-evil option is a less justifiable resort.

6. **Reject both author's viewpoints, and develop your own as an alternative.** Who says you have to opt for one author or the other? You have a mind of your own. But controversies are complex things; otherwise, intelligent and well-meaning individuals wouldn't be ranged on opposite sides of them. One standard ploy is to accuse one's opponents—people who have presumably thought long and hard about an issue—of oversimplifying. Such an accusation can't very well be succeeded by a simplistic alternative. You'll need to think long and hard yourself.

7. **Resolve the dispute.** Suppose sustained analysis reveals that the antagonists really aren't so antagonistic after all, that their differences can be resolved by adjusting perceptions. Can you use one position to moderate the other? Can opponents meet halfway? The answers naturally depend on the dispute—and the disputants.

We've hardly exhausted the possibilities, but there's a limit to the usefulness of multiplying options in the abstract. What really matters is the option you choose as you address two specific texts—and, of course, *why* you choose it.

 # **T**RIAL RUN

Return to those questions you were asked to consider under the first Trial Run in this chapter (p. 314)—the questions that invited you to sketch out your initial responses to the texts you're comparing. Do you still find that those responses hold true? Do they conform to one of the seven options above? Try summing up your responses in a statement you could use as a tentative thesis. Think about which of the above strategies would work best in elaborating that thesis.

Adopt a Constituency

In the questionnaire derived from Burke's pentad, in the section keyed to Hideaki himself, the question that followed the key word AGENT was "Who are you to argue as you do—and on whose behalf?" Hideaki's answer: "For struggling students to master English." His syntax slipped a bit there, but his heart was in the right place: he was willing to suppose that his response might have ramifications beyond himself. Similarly, as we saw in Chapter 8, Mikhael Yanko discovered that Freire's address to teachers pointed to questions students generally (and not just Mikhael) might be inclined to raise.

Very few of us—and only very rarely—need to feel ourselves isolated in our thoughts and feelings, utterly without solidarity or support. Far more often, we feel, speak, and respond as members of certain groups, and thus find that we do not simply speak out of self-interest but also out of fellow-feeling. As the example of Alice Roy reminds us, we may also speak for those with whom we share identification if not identity; we may adopt a constituency of others who are emphatically other than us but may still command our sympathetic concern. Allying our personal viewpoints with those of others, or at least taking those other viewpoints into account, gives our writing more motive force, more depth of concern, more power. Think, then, as you prepare to draft your evaluation, not just who you are but also on whose behalf you will be speaking.

COMPOSING THE FIRST DRAFT

Select Some Point(s) of Focus

In Chapters 7 and 8, we warned against blow-by-blow accounts of single texts you are analyzing or responding to. Think, then, how much more important it is not to get bogged down in rehash when you have two texts to weigh. And it's not just more important; it's also easier. Comparing texts inevitably makes certain features or portions of both relatively insignificant because they are not crucial to the comparison. You might say that the texts being compared help to bring each other into focus.

Seeing this is really just taking stock of the work you've already done. You've come up with a bottom-line analysis of each text, one that zeroes in on what motivates what's being said, and you've considered the important similarities and differences of the texts. If you've done this thoughtfully and carefully, you may still have more material than you need for your paper. So how do you zero in still further? Here are some possibilities:

1. **Note what an author identifies as crucial.** You can't always take an author at his or her word, but don't look the other way when one says, "This is my most important statement." If an author singles out a part of

the whole argument as the heart of the matter, you have a pretty good excuse for focusing on that.

2. **Look for key points of contact or divergence between the authors you're comparing.** Do your authors agree on a few points so that the disagreement really boils down to one or two points of contention? Does a point of focus in one suggest a neglect of attention in another? Does one seem to know more or see further than the other on a specific point?

3. **Look for chinks in the armor.** If you find yourself not buying what an author is saying, can you say why? Supposedly little things—matters of tone, examples, apparent contradictions—may loom large from this angle. In his final draft, Hideaki keyed in on one small part of Huddleston's speech: his argument against the bilingual ballot. Hideaki didn't need to insist that the statement was the crux of Huddleston's whole text; he justified zeroing in on it by suggesting that the senator's pronouncement belied his professed motive: concern for the enfranchisement of immigrants.

4. **Consider your purpose.** You ultimately determine the direction your evaluation of the two texts takes. If you favor one author over the other, center your discussion on what you find favorable in that author's argument and unfavorable in the other's. If you take a dim view of both viewpoints, zero in on what puts you off—and why. If you have a counter-argument to offer, attend to deficiencies of the other arguments that you can correct or virtues of theirs you can enhance.

Organize Your Evaluative Comparison

The pattern for comparison/contrast is really two patterns, both introduced in Chapter 3. One is to consider, alternatively, the things you are comparing (in this case, two texts). The other is to discuss them both together as you pursue certain points of comparison (like central concerns in both texts).

Hideaki took the former approach, discussing Huddleston, then discussing Roy. Had he taken the latter approach, he might have discussed Huddleston and Roy on the matter of their concern for immigrants in one paragraph, those two authors on the matter of changing patterns of immigration in the next, and so on.

One pattern is no better than the other, though you are likely to organize your comparison around a discussion of one text and then the other if, like Hideaki, those discussions are well-focused and not over-elaborated. (You must not allow the discussion of one text to postpone for too long the discussion of the other.) If you have a number of points to cover, the point-by-point comparison may seem more suitable.

Follow the Rules of Argumentative Etiquette

It is indeed your paper, but written communication is always a social transaction, so there are always rules of etiquette to follow. Briefly, they are these:

1. **Provide an informative overview at the outset.** You do yourself and your reader a favor when you do a little stage-setting. Your audience has read the texts, but relating them to each other is your job, and part of that job is giving a sense of the general circumstances or set of concerns both texts address.

2. **Give some sense of where you are heading.** This paper is an evaluation—that is, an expression of your opinion—and your reader shouldn't have to read through most of it without an inkling of what your opinion is. An inkling will suffice, however. Hideaki's final draft, for instance, begins by noting his authors' common ground, then pronounces Huddleston too uncaring toward immigrants and Roy too sympathetic. Why he says this and what he will conclude from it are matters the reader must wait for—but assured that the paper was written by someone who knew where he was going with it.

3. **Give the authors equal time.** This isn't an absolute rule, but you do need a good reason for breaking it. Too great an attention to one, too little to the other may raise questions about your fairness as an evaluator.

4. **Give yourself away.** The ultimate purpose of an evaluative paper is to deliver yourself of your opinion. What, finally, is your evaluation? If you think Author A is indeed more right-minded than Author B, say so—and tell why. Have both authors missed the point? Say so, and tell what that point is. Whatever you conclude, remember that every author is actuated by motives that must be scrutinized. This includes you. Why do you conclude what you do? However you answer, resist conclusions couched in universals—the "As any idiot can see" sort of conclusion. "Giving yourself away" means rendering, not the absolutely right opinion, but the opinion that's specifically right for you—and saying why.

RETHINKING AND REVISING

Review Your Conversational Etiquette

We spoke before of "rules of argumentative etiquette." Now we're interested in finer points than any "rules" can describe, matters of tone and nuance that you can check yourself on only as you revise a completed draft. These finer points are not icing on the cake; they are crucial to your success in this assignment. In an evaluative comparison, you are basically arbitrating a dispute. That requires considerable tact and discretion. So we invite you to think, for the moment, of writing as conversation: something that happens, not at your desk, but in a social situation.

Kenneth Burke has a charming metaphor for the universe of learned discourse: a vast room where people are talking. It may look and sound like a chaotic din at first. But certain patterns and significant features emerge. Some people talk to large rapt audiences, while others seem to be talking to themselves. Some have been talking for some time; others need to listen and get the gist of the conversation before they can join in.

You're joining in the conversation now, and that should help to explain the importance of certain features of academic writing that may otherwise seem merely arbitrary. Conversation—for instance, the sort conducted at dinner parties—is not exactly rule-bound behavior, but it does conform to certain conventions and expectations. People make an effort to take turns speaking, to attend to other speakers, to stay with a subject as long as it's of interest. It's easy to concoct a list of social blunders for such a context: belches, profanity, outright rudeness, telling jokes and forgetting the punchline, and so on. Similarly, your evaluation of the work of other writers is subject to certain conventions and expectations. You can't simply dismiss them without discussion, meet their moral seriousness with flippancy, respond to their formal diction with street slang, counter their thoughtful arguments with namecalling.

However, a good writer, like a good conversationalist, is distinguished by subtler things than not committing blunders. You can attend to such subtleties because writing is not, after all, conversation. And it differs from conversation chiefly in the opportunity to revise. It's as if you had the chance to play back your part in a conversation, retract some things and recast others, playing the tape in public only after fine-tuning every part of your contribution to the conversation. Particularly in this assignment, you have delicate balances to strike, balances sure to need adjusting once a draft is done. Here are three balancing acts to be especially attentive to as you revise:

1. **Balance courtesy to your authors with courtesy to your reader.** You don't want an author you're discussing to seem to be getting the short shrift, but you don't want such a full account of that author's argument as to weary your reader. Remember that your reader has also read your texts; take out anything that doesn't add to the argument you're building. But you should also be wary of saying too little; your reader, acquainted with your texts, will know what you are leaving out—and perhaps feel you're leaving out too much.

2. **Balance praise and censure.** You want to seem neither uncritical nor hypercritical of the authors you're evaluating. If you agree, do you seem something more than a fan and a follower? If you disagree, do you show how your position builds on the foundations laid by your texts? As a general rule, agree with reservations, and make any disagreement something short of utter. Agreeing only up to a point helps to suggest you have

a mind of your own. Disagreeing only up to a point helps to make you seem reasonable.

3. **Balance what your authors have to say with what you have to say.** When the assignment is evaluating two texts, the most important balancing act is built right into the assignment: it's striking a balance not between the two texts but between your opinion and the opinions of others. Occasionally, students are so eager to give their own opinions that the texts serve as little more than a pretext. But more often summaries of the texts and quotations from them dominate the paper, with the students' evaluations delivered quickly, belatedly, rather timidly. Evaluation is not the special province of the concluding paragraph. It is the task of the paper as a whole. Keep that in mind as you revise.

Above all, keep in mind that you have every right to join the conversation. Don't be intimidated or overwhelmed by the arguments of others. As we shall see in reviewing his final draft, Hideaki is an interesting case in point: though cowed at first to be an immigrant responding to a U.S. senator and an English teacher, he found his experience as a non-native speaker of English gave him a special perspective on their arguments about the role of the English language in the United States. Similarly, you have your own mind to make up, your own expertise and authority, your own opinions. Stand and deliver.

CHECKLIST: REVISING YOUR DRAFT

- Do you begin with an informative overview, one that goes beyond summarizing texts to giving an inkling of your evaluation of them?
- Are you careful to relate the two texts so that your paper seems one evaluative comparison rather than two separate discussions?
- Are you careful to select parts of the texts to discuss that are somehow characteristic or representative of those texts?
- Do you make your own position clear, balancing it against the positions of the authors you're treating?
- Are you careful to make your reasoning clear and consistent, your tone tactful and reasonable?

PRESENTING HIDEAKI'S FINAL DRAFT

A Response to Huddleston and Roy

Hideaki Kazeno

1   We are frequently told that we are living in a "melting pot." And it is true that a lot of immigrants have come to this country and assimilated into the mainstream culture, which

Hideaki begins with historical perspective rather than a statement of his position.

derived much of its character from the English heritage. But the development of this country was not the result of a planned and controlled experiment of migration from the old continent to the new by the British empire. The United States today is made up of people who came for many different reasons from many different cultures. Still, in the pre-revolutionary era, Britain was the predominant power and had easy access to this continent. Therefore, English became the language most widely spoken here, and the American heritage was born with this language as its center.

2

Focusing on the metaphor of the "melting pot," Hideaki uses it to crystallize the authors' positions—and also to begin criticizing them.

Even now it is evident that one has to be able to speak and understand English to succeed economically, politically, or in any other way in America. Both Walter Darlington Huddleston and Alice Roy seem to agree on this point. But Huddleston's assumption is that once one resolves to learn English one's English definitely improves in due time, whereas Roy's experience as an English teacher tells her that it is no easy task for immigrants to learn English. This disparity leads to different opinions of the "melting pot." Huddleston believes that the "melting pot" worked well, at least formerly, because he ignores the strife of immigrants trying to master English. Roy's position makes her perhaps too lenient toward new arrivals, perhaps too distrustful of the "myth" of the "melting pot," which, she says, has worked only for "white Northern Protestant Europeans." This difference of opinion about the "melting pot" makes Roy and Huddleston run on the same track in opposite directions, even though both claim their proposals will benefit immigrants in the long run.

3

Hideaki notes that each author attacks as well as advocates something; in Huddleston's case, what he attacks seems to belie his advocacy of "full participation in the political process."

It is important to see that both arguments are attacks as well as proposals. Huddleston attacks bilingual education, arguing that immigrants, or the children of immigrants, should learn English before they learn anything. And his attack on bilingual ballots is even more revealing. He argues that not giving immigrants political information in their native languages increases the incentive to learn English; therefore, this withholding of information will help them fully participate in the political process the way they are supposed to--in English. But what if people can't communicate well enough even after lots of effort? Will they, even though tax-paying and law-abiding citizens, be ostracized from the political process? Huddleston says, "By failing to provide a positive incentive, we are actually denying them full participation in the political process." To Huddleston, giving information to speakers of languages other than English seems a form of "failing" and "denying." What is "positive" in his view is shutting them out completely-- until they learn English.

Hideaki feels, then, that Huddleston's position denies the rights of immigrants.

4 Preoccupied with the English language's central role in American culture, Huddleston goes too far, forgetting about other aspects of American culture just as central--democracy, tolerance, resistance to discrimination. In pursuing his goal of making English the official language, Huddleston seems too willing to deny the rights of non-English-speaking residents.

Hideaki argues that Roy's attack on "linguistic chauvinism" is an attack on something she cannot control—but might make immigrants less prepared to face.

Roy's position, then, might also result in increased discrimination on the basis of language (at least in the business world).

5 Roy, on the other hand, is too lenient toward immigrants. She attacks the "linguistic chauvinism" that demands they speak English--and do it correctly. In her last paragraph, she argues against "a value-laden approach to teaching English that makes the use of a certain kind of English a moral or ethical virtue--where correctness replaces cleanliness right up there next to godliness. . . . We as English teachers have inherited an elitist view of English, but we don't have to perpetuate it." But what does this really mean? Even if not just Roy but all the English teachers in this country decided to adopt this view, that would not make it the view of the people of the United States. If there is an "elitist view" of English, immigrants will still have to deal with it in the world beyond the classrooms. Roy herself says that "language can be neither controlled nor preserved against change," yet she calls for a change--at least a change of attitude. And such changes happen not in a lifetime but in generations.

Holding that both authors oversimplify, arguing in different ways for control of what cannot be controlled, Hideaki speaks from an immigrant's perspective, arguing for a means of coping with a problem that cannot be easily solved.

6 Someone like Huddleston might worry that Roy, in pursuing her goals, might sacrifice the integrity and heritage of the English language. I am more worried that she might mislead the people she is teaching, suggesting that English is a language without exacting standards. Even now students get away with mistakes on English papers they would never get away with in business letters. Correctness is important, whether English teachers decide to say it is or not.

7 Both Huddleston and Roy go too far. They don't realize that nobody can dictate which and what kind of language people should speak in a democracy. Huddleston worries that current changes threaten the unity of the nation. His anxieties may come true. But we can't preset the course of history for the benefit of the present majority. When people change, the processes they participate in, political, educational, economic, have to adjust. But for the time being English is clearly the language to master to succeed in the United States. As an immigrant, it's my desire to master it in the standard "value-laden" form because only that form gets the full respect of the people I have to communicate with to be a success in this country.

Commentary on Hideaki's Final Draft

Hideaki opens his paper with some stage-setting. His evaluation of Huddleston and Roy mentions neither one of them directly at first. Instead, he writes of how a twist of history centuries past—the same sort of development that determined all of Mexico should be Spanish-speaking or much of Canada French-speaking—made English the predominant language in the United States. His opening remarks on the weight of history are not so much hemming-and-hawing or throat-clearing. They bear directly on the conclusion he finally comes to, as we shall see. Moreover, unlike an earlier draft (which began with the words "Huddleston and Roy go too far"), Hideaki's paper opens in a way that makes him seem neutral and dispassionate. (We said a neutral reading of two opposing texts is impossible. We did not say the initial appearance of neutrality couldn't be strategically useful.)

Cultivating some semblance of neutrality, the first paragraph also ties in well with the next. The conclusion of that first paragraph turns out, in the second, to be the common ground between Huddleston and Roy—at least for the purposes of Hideaki's argument. And that first paragraph began with the noncommittal statement, "We are frequently told that we are living in a 'melting pot.'" Differing perceptions of the "melting pot" as metaphor and historical reality turn out, for Hideaki, to be the crux of the opposition between Huddleston and Roy. These perceptions lead him to characterize the fundamental weakness of each: Huddleston is unsympathetic, the sort who "ignores the strife of immigrants"; Roy is all too sympathetic, "too lenient to new arrivals." Before we leave the second paragraph, we have been given, with remarkable economy, the historical background for a complicated controversy as well as both the common ground and the crucial points of difference for two opposing positions on it.

Hideaki's next paragraph, devoted to Huddleston, is so economical a summary it risks giving Huddleston's long and multi-faceted argument the short shrift. But look at how he does this. His first sentence in this third paragraph—"It is important to see that both arguments are attacks as well as proposals"—gives his key strategy for much of his paper. It justifies homing in on particulars, testing how well what is argued for meshes with what is argued against. Hideaki scrutinizes Huddleston's opposition to both bilingual education and the bilingual ballot in light of the senator's professed concern for the full enfranchisement of immigrants—and he sees an essential contradiction. In a separate paragraph that highlights his conclusion, he goes so far as to say Huddleston "seems too willing to deny the rights of non-English-speaking residents."

Roy gets the same sort of treatment. She advocates moving away from "an elitist view of English," especially among her fellow English teachers. But Roy earlier said that "language can neither be controlled or preserved against change." Hideaki feels that Roy's proposed change of attitude could be harmful if it doesn't correspond to a change in society as a whole. If

English teachers become tolerant of certain types of language usage for which society has no tolerance, this, says Hideaki, could do more harm than good to students by misleading them.

Significantly, Hideaki's conclusions about Roy's argument cause him to speak in his own person, distinguishing his concerns from Huddleston's, tapping his knowledge of the world of business as well as the academic world in doing so. He continues to personalize his remarks in his general conclusion. Perhaps partly motivated by the consciousness that he, like Roy, was addressing an English-teacher audience, Hideaki endorses the sort of "value-laden" instruction in English that Roy rejected, and he does so by speaking for himself: "As an immigrant, it's my desire...." In the paper as a whole, we can see Hideaki uses his experience as an immigrant to identify lack or excess of sympathy for immigrants in the arguments of Huddleston and Roy. He uses his own experience as a source of expertise that allows him to evaluate such "experts" as a U.S. Senator and an English teacher. If he does not solve the problem Huddleston and Roy address, it is largely because he has attempted to show that their solutions oversimplify a complex problem created by twists and turns in the historical process, a problem he believes only further twists and turns in that process can solve.

Hideaki's position as an immigrant may seem to make him a uniquely advantaged respondent to Huddleston and Roy. Actually, he exemplifies a kind of expertise almost anyone can bring to bear on the evaluation of almost any texts. The key to going beyond an uncritical endorsement (or rejection) of a text to a thoughtful, probing evaluation is not knowing more or thinking better than the author; it is knowing other things and thinking differently. Odds are that you fit that bill with respect to any texts you'll be asked to evaluate. You just need to see how to use your store of knowledge and way of thinking to your best advantage.

Questions for Further Thought

1. Are arguments made determined largely by the circumstances of those making the arguments? If so, doesn't this make such arguments inescapably limited and relative? If not, what considerations or values transcend differing circumstances and personal interests?

2. Another way of looking at the same issue: can you imagine someone in Hideaki's situation opposing his argument? What might motivate a different perspective in similar circumstances? Can you imagine someone in your situation disagreeing with the stand you took in this assignment? Why or why not?

3. The views of an expert are not necessarily wiser or more "right" than yours, though a recognized authority is better positioned to get his or her views circulated and implemented. Does realizing this make it easier or harder for you to argue with such authorities? What might it take to get your ideas disseminated and acted upon?

PROFESSIONAL ESSAYS

Just for this chapter (the last chapter that concludes with professional examples), we are going to give introductions to and then questions about pairs of readings rather than individual essays.

The first pair—Charles Krauthammer's "At Stanford, a Setback to Western Civilization" and Ellen Goodman's "Stanford Tries to Expand the Core of Knowledge"—offers two editorial columnists' differing viewpoints on the changes made at Stanford a few years ago in an attempt to reflect greater cultural diversity in the core curriculum.

The second pair—Jesse Jackson's "Why Blacks Need Affirmative Action" and Thomas Sowell's "The Dangers of Preferential Programs"—offers the different positions held by two black political figures on what are usually called affirmative action programs; in both cases, the specific focus is on college admissions.

In both pairings, the piece with the earlier publication date is printed first.

Charles Krauthammer

AT STANFORD, A SETBACK
TO WESTERN CIVILIZATION

"There is everything to be said for having students learn about non-Western cultures, but not as a substitute for one's Western heritage."

Ellen Goodman

STANFORD TRIES
TO EXPAND THE CORE
OF KNOWLEDGE

"In an era of specialization, can we identify a common wisdom without retreating to a narrow mind?"

Both editorial columns speak to a specific time and context, but Krauthammer and Goodman say enough to make their general audience aware of the facts. In both cases, these writers (whose columns appear on what are called "opinion pages") cite facts to support their opinions. It is also true that what happened at Stanford in the late eighties was simply the first widely publicized case of many curricular changes—and controversies about them—centered on the same issue. If we were to boil the issue down to a word (always a dangerous thing to do), that word would be "multiculturalism."

Krauthammer, a doctor of psychiatry turned social commentator, is known as a contributor to the New Republic, a weekly that has gone from liberal to conservative in the past decade (as has Krauthammer). His column opposes the change at Stanford.

Goodman's column, which won a Pulitzer Prize in 1980, is based with the Boston Globe but is syndicated nationally. Writing on a variety of topics, Goodman is especially identified with women's issues. Her piece, appearing two days after Krauthammer's (not in response to his, but just because Stanford's curricular change was a hot topic in April of 1988), applauds the change.

Both columnists address a general audience, and they do so from no particular position of authority beyond their positions as editorial columnists with established points of view.

ON THE WAY INTO THE READINGS

1. How would you characterize your political views? Do they dispose you to favor one or the other columnist, just on the evidence of their titles and what is said about each in the headnote? Do you think this might create a problem for your comparison? Or do you think having pre-established views will help you in making an evaluation?

2. How do you feel about editorial columnists? Do you read any on a fairly regular basis? What effect do you think they have in voicing or shaping public opinion? Why do you think they have national readerships? What motivates people to read their columns?

3. What is your experience with curricular reform? Are there changes going on at your school? Do you have some exposure to some of the controversies Krauthammer and Goodman are discussing? How important do you think issues like diversity or tradition are in your (and your peers') expectations for education?

AT STANFORD, A SETBACK TO WESTERN CIVILIZATION

Charles Krauthammer

1   WASHINGTON—Western civilization has suffered a setback at Stanford University. Civilization will recover. Whether Stanford will is another question.

2   At issue is the core curriculum in Western civilization instituted in the early 1980s at Stanford and elsewhere. At Stanford, it consisted of 15 required and 18 "strongly recommended" political and philosophical classics.

3   It was one of the most popular courses at Stanford, but two years ago a campaign was launched by minority and feminist groups, which denounced it as a racist, sexist compendium of "European-Western and male bias."

4   Last month the faculty capitulated. It did not quite abolish, but it emasculated the program. Fifteen required works became six. Eighteen "strongly recommended" are recommended no more.

5   The slack will be taken up with works that emphasize "cultural diversity and the processes of cultural interaction." A less oblique instruction to the faculty is to include a substantial number of "works by women, minorities, and persons of color."

6   Even the term "Western civilization"—"anachronistic and inappropriate," explains history professor Judith Brown—will have to go. The new name for the program is "Culture, Ideas, and Values."

7   There is everything to be said for having students learn about non-Western cultures, but not as a substitute for one's Western heritage.

8   In pursuit of intercultural understanding, the Stanford faculty could find neither the nerve nor the will nor the arguments to insist that Homer, Dante and Darwin be read. Or to "strongly recommend" Locke and Mill, to say nothing of Jefferson, Madison, Hamilton and Jay.

9   In fact, it had trouble defending the very idea of Western civilization, which is what the protest was about.

10   The protestors oppose the core curriculum on the grounds that white male authors are overrepresented and the groups to which these critics owe their allegiance—women, blacks, Native Americans, Hispanics, etc.—are missing.

11   Bill King, a student leader of the protest, not only accused Stanford of "crushing the psyche of those others to whom Locke, Hume and Plato are not speaking" but of suppressing facts such as that "the Iroquois Indians in America had a representative democracy that served as a model for the American System."

12   It is unfortunate that the Iroquois left no written language. It is a crime that blacks were excluded from intellectual life (and much else, of course) during centuries of slavery. It is a great injustice that women were denied opportunity and education until very recently.

13   But these are historical facts. And they explain why the corpus of great works, of which these excluded people were obviously capable, were either lost or never created. It does no good to pretend otherwise and to invent or exaggerate historical influences (such as the Iroquois on the Federalist Papers) as a gesture of historical restitution.

14   Affirmative action for people is problematic but, on the whole, a good thing: It gives those who were denied opportunity an extra chance to compete. Affirmative action for great books is an embarrassment.

15   The critics further charge that the core curriculum not only denies American ethnics their due. It denies the "global culture" its due. In today's global village, the idea of a Western culture is seen as narrow, biased and ethnocentric.

16   (The aversion to ethnocentricity does not, however, prevent the critics from demanding great works that come from the right ethnic, racial and gender groups.)

17   There is nothing wrong with believing in a world culture and wanting students to gain familiarity with it. But before approaching the larger world, it is essential to have a sense of self, to know who you are and where your ideas come from.

18   One has to know one's own culture first. Without understanding it, how can one be intelligently critical of it?

19   It makes no sense to recommend a dab of East Asian history, a few semester hours of African art, and a bit of American Indian architecture for 17-year-olds, the majority of whom don't know when the Civil War was, what the Magna Carta was, or who wrote "The Canterbury Tales."

20   The first obligation of a university is to help a student fulfill the injunction: Know thyself. Or is that too Western an idea?

21   A pastiche of "global culture" for a population utterly ungrounded in its own culture produces the most haphazard jumble of knowledge. It guarantees intellectual disorientation and perpetuates in college the cultural illiteracy produced by high school.

22   To say that a Western core exists and that it is valuable is not to say that it is immutable. For the foreseeable centuries, the Bible and Plato will not become less relevant to the West.

23   One should, however, always be prepared to add to the core as history requires—but on the basis of the genius and the influence of a book, not on the basis of the race or sex of the author.

24   The declared project of the anti-Western-culture forces is to eliminate not just the course or the books but the concept. Last year 500 demonstrators (led by—who else?—Jesse Jackson) celebrated Stanford's acquiescence to a new ideologically correct history course with the chant, "Hey hey, ho ho, Western culture's got to go!"

25   At Stanford, they won. If they win elsewhere, we will be firmly embarked on another round of cultural deconstruction.

STANFORD TRIES TO EXPAND THE CORE OF KNOWLEDGE

Ellen Goodman

1   There was a time when people believed they could know it all. An educated person could read every book ever written, learn every equation ever devised. Knowledge was seen as a kind of pie. You could keep slicing away at it until you had eaten the whole thing.

2   We have no such illusions anymore. Education in the information age is something quite different. Every time we find an answer, it leads exponentially to lists of new questions. It's rather like mapping the universe as it keeps expanding. We know more than our ancestors, and yet we know a much, much smaller percentage of the sum total of what is known.

3   Once you get beyond the three R's, learning today becomes a process of specializing. Those who want to know a great deal study deeply rather than broadly. The best and the brightest of one field may be ignorant of another, unable to communicate. In the explosion of information, the center doesn't hold.

4   This is why we have such raging debates right now on college campuses about what every graduate should know. It's an argument about creating a core, about reconstituting common wisdom.

5   There is much agreement that we need something to hold onto in this centrifuge. There is the belief that people who inhabit the same country or community need to share some body of knowledge the way they need to share a body of laws.

6   But it's much harder to agree on what to put in that core. We are, after all, arguing about what is most important in our culture, struggling for intellectual power.

7   One small piece of this struggle has gone on at Stanford University this year over the content of a required course on Western civilization. For eight years, this class focused on 15 books, classics of Western philosophy and literature. Not surprisingly, the authors were all white men.

8   To many in the university community, the subjects had a subtext that said our civilization was at root a white male civilization, and the body of knowledge worth knowing then and now was European and male. It passed along this tradition with the other values in those texts.

9   After much debate, sometimes heated, sometimes thoughtful, the Stanford Faculty Senate voted at the end of March to open up this hard core a bit. They renamed the course "Cultures, Ideas and Values," and added "works by women, minorities, and persons of color." They added the study of one non-European culture and of race, gender and class.

10   Into this situation walked Secretary William Bennett the other day. Bennett has honed the skills of reverse negotiation over these years. He is an expert at "getting to no." He contended that the faculty had been intimidated into lowering their standards and, in effect, letting down the side. The side being Western civilization.

11   Bennett seems to regard the inclusion of women and minorities, of non-Western cultures, in the inner circle of learning the way many like him regard affirmative-action programs. It means an automatic sacrifice of excellence to political pressure.

12   He was surely one of the few who thought that civilization was actually threatened by a Stanford student chant last fall: "Hey, hey, ho, ho, Western culture's got to go!"

13   But the debate raised in California is not just about the West or the Great Books (by White European Men) Tradition. It's about agreeing on a central core of knowledge in a society that is pluralistic in its information as well as its population.

14   We need shared texts to communicate across the information explosion. But cries for unity, whether they are for family unity or national unity, can often be a call to silence diversity into one traditional voice. In an era of specialization, can we identify a common wisdom without retreating to a narrow mind?

15   Like many other institutions, Stanford is trying to do something quite difficult: to pass on tradition without perpetuating it as an exclusive club. Going back to basics doesn't mean going back in time. A core curriculum that left only a European male spine would, with apologies to Allan Bloom, close the American mind.

CRITICAL READING

1. Krauthammer announces his position in his very first sentence. Goodman doesn't even broach hers till she's seven paragraphs into a piece no longer than Krauthammer's. Why the postponement? Which strategy do you find more effective?

2. Krauthammer gives more specific examples than Goodman, names more names, more texts, more participants in the debate. In your eyes, does he gain or lose by giving more details than Goodman? If Goodman is less focused on details, is she more focused on something else?

3. Do Krauthammer and Goodman have common ground? Do they share, for example, what Goodman calls "the belief that people who inhabit the same country or community need to share some body of knowledge"? Or are apparent agreements really illusory because the differences go too deep?

4. Both authors address a debate. Imagine them debating between themselves, perhaps even negotiating a compromise. What could either bargain away and what would either refuse to give up? Why?

5. If your reaction to one of the texts is more favorable, can you put your finger on what it is that decides you in favor of that text? If they both put you off, can you explain why?

6. In an article titled "The Cult of Multiculturalism," published in the *New Republic* in mid-February 1991, Fred Siegel quotes an unnamed "Stanford student who, when asked about studying important non-Western trends such as Islamic fundamentalism and Japanese capitalism, responded, 'Who gives a damn about those things? I want to study myself.'" What about you? How does your perspective on your own need or desire for knowledge (and perhaps particular kinds of knowledge) affect your response to Krauthammer and Goodman?

Jesse Jackson

WHY BLACKS NEED
AFFIRMATIVE ACTION

"The only thing whites are giving up because of affirmative action is unfair advantage—something that was unnecessary in the first place."

SINCE THE CIVIL RIGHTS ACT OF 1964, "affirmative action" has been a feature of the political landscape, as has the controversy generated by programs so named, programs designed to redress minority underrepresentation in colleges and the workforce. One debate centered on the Bakke vs. University of California *lawsuit of 1978. Allan Bakke, a white applicant to law school, charged that he was denied admission because of preferential treatment given to minority applicants. (The verdict went against him.)*

Jesse Jackson's piece, published in the government watchdog journal Regulation *in late 1978, is*

An Interview with Thomas Sowell
THE DANGERS OF PREFERENTIAL PROGRAMS

"There is a tremendous amount of recurring violence over these preferential policies."

a response to the Bakke case. Jackson's position, evident from his title, is consistent with his long involvement in civil rights. A follower of (and in some ways a successor to) Martin Luther King, Jr., he has directed the Poor People's Campaign, People United to Save Humanity, Project Breadbasket, and the Rainbow Coalition. He was also twice a candidate for the Democratic presidential nomination.

Like Clarence Thomas, a recent Supreme Court appointee, Thomas Sowell is proof that not all blacks support affirmative action programs. A senior fellow at the Hoover Institution, Sowell is an influential black conservative. His books include Civil Rights: Rhetoric or Reality? *(1985).* "The Dangers of Preferential Programs," *published in the politically conservative journal* Public Interest, *is an interview with Sowell following the publication of his book* Choosing a College *(1989).*

ON THE WAY INTO THE READINGS

1. The headnote, needing to characterize the two figures in a few broad strokes, connects Jackson with Martin Luther King, Jr., and Sowell with Clarence Thomas. Do you find yourself coming to conclusions about which you will prefer before you do the reading? Can you be conscious of any predisposition as you read? Will you duly note whether your expectations are met?

2. Have you already developed views on means of achieving racial equality? Can you identify what it is about you—your upbringing, your experiences, your racial or ethnic background—that has been most responsible in forming your opinions on such issues? What would it take to get you to think otherwise? How open do you think most people are to changing their pre-existing views on racial equality and other social concerns?

3. Do you have any experience with what Jackson calls "affirmative action" and Sowell calls "preferential programs"? Have you benefited or known others who benefited? Do you feel these programs might result in injustice as well as corrections of injustice? Since the existence of inequalities in college admissions and the labor force is undeniable, how do you think they might ideally be addressed?

WHY BLACKS NEED AFFIRMATIVE ACTION

Jesse Jackson

1   According to a recent publication of the Equal Employment Opportunity Commission, at the present rate of "progress" it will take forty-three years to end job discrimination—hardly a reasonable timetable.

2   If our goal is educational and economic equity and parity—and it is—then we need affirmative action to catch up. We are behind as a result of discrimination and denial of opportunity. There is one white attorney for every 680 whites, but only one black attorney for every 4,000 blacks; one white physician for every 659 whites, but only one black physician for every 5,000 blacks; and one white dentist for every 1,900 whites, but only one black dentist for every 8,400 blacks. Less than 1 percent of all engineers—or of all practicing chemists—is black. Cruel and uncompassionate injustice created gaps like these. We need creative justice and compassion to help us close them.

3   Actually, in the U.S. context, "reverse discrimination" is illogical and a contradiction in terms. Never in the history of mankind has a majority, with power, engaged in programs and written laws that discriminate against itself. The only thing whites are giving up because of affirmative action is unfair advantage—something that was unnecessary in the first place.

4   Blacks are not making progress at the expense of whites, as news accounts make it seem. There are 49 percent more whites in medical school today and 64 percent more whites in law school than there were when affirmative action programs began some eight years ago.

5   In a recent column, William Raspberry raised an interesting question. Commenting on the *Bakke* case, he asked, "What if, instead of setting aside 16 of 100 slots, we added 16 slots to the 100?" That, he suggested, would allow blacks to make progress and would not interfere with what whites already have. He then went on to point out that this, in fact, is exactly what has happened in law and medical schools. In 1968, the year before affirmative action programs began to get under way, 9,571 whites and 282 members of minority groups entered U.S. medical schools. In 1976, the figures were 14,213 and 1,400 respectively. Thus, under affirmation action, the number of "white places" actually rose by 49 percent: white access to medical training was not diminished, but substantially increased. The trend was even more marked in law schools. In 1969, the first year for which reliable figures are available, 2,933 minority-group members were enrolled; in 1976, the number was up to 8,484. But during the same period, law school enrollment for whites rose from 65,453 to 107,064—an increase of 64 percent. In short, it is a myth that blacks are making progress at white expense.

6   Allan Bakke did not really challenge preferential treatment in general, for he made no challenge to the preferential treatment accorded to the children of the rich, the alumni and the faculty, or to athletes or the very talented—only to minorities.

THE DANGERS OF PREFERENTIAL PROGRAMS

Thomas Sowell

1   *Question:* One of the things that you talk about in your book is the mismatch between the student and the school. There have been so many incidents of overt racism on campus these days; do you think that contributes to it?

2   *Sowell:* Absolutely. I am convinced of it for a number of reasons. One is the pattern of these violent outbreaks of racism on campus. The conventional wisdom is that this is all due to the Reagan administration. To the conservative mood in the country. There are institutions that keep track of these things, and their statistics showed that there were more of these outbreaks in Massachusetts alone than in the entire South. You find them at places like Berkeley and the University of Massachusetts and Wellesley much more than you're likely to find them at conservative campuses like Hillsdale, or Whitman, or Davidson.

3   There is also international evidence. I'm working on a book on preferential policy internationally and wherever those policies are put in, there is this backlash. The longer the policies have been in place, the worse the backlash. The worst places are India and Sri Lanka, which have had these policies for several decades. Sri Lanka is an especially sad case because they began with what were regarded as model race relations—far better, let's say, than they've been in the United States. Within a decade people were burning each other alive in the streets. The civil war got so bad that some political groups began to have a vested interest in the polarization, as such, quite aside from the substantive divisions.

4   The notion that we seem to have in all our foreign policy—that no matter what the strife is about, you can always come in with some nice compromise that you've worked out back in the State Department and give it to both sides and they'll say, "Hey, why didn't we think of this?"—is naive. No, there are people in Sri Lanka who have a vested interest in the continuation of the strife because that serves their power; on both sides, among the Tamils and the Sinhalese, there are factions who are killing numerous members of their own group because these members want to compromise. This is not one of the happier examples.

5   India has gone this route as well. There is a tremendous amount of recurring violence over these preferential policies. In the state of Gujarat alone as many as two hundred people have been killed in riots set off by medical-school quotas. Ironically, in a recent year, there were only six places set aside in the quotas—and forty-two people died in riots over those six places.

6   Some people have argued that the objection is that one group is losing something to another group and that this is the fundamental reason for the backlash, but that doesn't stand up to the evidence either. There are many programs that provide special benefits to many groups, in India as in other countries. But it is the programs that take the specific form of pre-

ferences and set-asides that cause most of the violence and most of the litigation.

7   In the United States as well, there are campuses where the Asian students take far more places than the blacks or the Hispanics, or sometimes the blacks and Hispanics put together, and yet there is not the same degree of backlash against them because of the manner in which they took those places. There's an old song that says, "It ain't what you do, it's the way that you do it." There are whites who have no problem with Bill Cosby making tens of millions of dollars a year, but who would soar through the roof if a black kid is brought in under a preferential program at a minimum wage to be an assistant apprentice.

8   You could go through the whole list everywhere. Anyone who watches basketball knows that basketball teams are not ethnically representative of the United States.

9   It's not even true by position. That is, if you look at baseball, an absolute majority of all outfielders are black. It's hard even to think of a black third baseman. The last one I can remember was Jackie Robinson. At the end of his career as second baseman they shifted him over to third.

10   **Question:** In the process of researching *Choosing a College*, did you have occasion to look at the effect of any of these quotas or special standards on the military academies?

11   **Sowell:** Only in a minor way. Actually, I looked this up some years ago, or rather it came to me through a leak from the Air Force Academy, which did not cooperate in my research. The Air Force Academy had an internal memorandum marked "Confidential—for your eyes only," which came to my eyes; it gave different cut-off scores for blacks, whites, Asians, and Hispanics for admission to the Air Force Academy. The Asians had to meet the same standards as the whites, by the way.

12   There was also a note at the bottom that those who are athletes may be admitted with scores that did not meet these standards. I don't remember what the standards were exactly, but they were not impressive standards. You could get in hundreds of points below the average of the U.S. Air Force Academy if you belonged to the right group.

13   I never saw any data on how many of each of these different groups had survived the rigors of the academy. Even those data, which are usually unavailable, are becoming less and less reliable as you get what someone called "affirmative grading," which is also a worldwide phenomenon. In Soviet Central Asia the professors are under pressure to pass more central Asians. In Israel, at one time at least, there was a ruling that you could not leave back in the public schools a disproportionate number of Sephardic Jews as compared to the Ashkenazi.

14   One of the many illusions of these policies is that we have such total control over them that we can say that this will be a transitory policy for this period, and then we'll do this, or we will have it at the stage of search but not at the stage of admission, or at the stage of admission but not at the

stage of judging and graduating and so forth. And in country after country this has proved to be an illusion.

15   I think I'll leave you with the classic example of Pakistan, which back in the 1940s instituted preferential programs for the East Pakistanis because they were greatly underrepresented in all sorts of occupations. But like so many other preferential policies, they began to spread from the East Pakistanis to other groups, further and further removed from the original rationale. The preferences were supposed to last five or ten years, but they kept on being extended; this all started in the forties and back in 1984 the late president Zia extended them until 1994—even though by 1984 East Pakistan had become a separate country called Bangladesh. The people who were the original beneficiaries of this program were no longer part of Pakistan, but so many other groups had piggy-backed on them that now it became politically impossible to get rid of the preferential programs.

CRITICAL READING

1. The act of naming your subject is crucial because words are almost never entirely neutral. Note that Jackson speaks of "affirmative action," Sowell of "preferential programs." Those terms did not originate with those authors—they were there to choose from—but they represent important choices. How do these different labels invite different responses? How do they bespeak the differences in Jackson's and Sowell's viewpoints?

2. Both Jackson and Sowell stress the importance of locating issues and incidents in a historical context. Do they do this differently? How and why?

3. Jackson cites positive and Sowell negative consequences of the programs at issue. Whose evidence seems to you more persuasive? Why?

4. Unlike Jackson, Sowell says a great deal about other countries' programs and their results. How applicable do you find such analogies? Does his analysis make Jackson's seem more limited? Or does Jackson seem more focused on what is clearly relevant?

5. Sowell is actually speaking in response to an interviewer's questions, but Jackson's written piece also has a "voice." How do you respond to each man with respect to matters of tone and style and approach to the subject?

6. In Jackson's emphasis on fairness and potential good, Sowell's emphasis on feasibility and potential harm, we see different strategies at work, but also different fundamental concerns. When you decide whose position you prefer, can you identify concerns of your own that one or the other has more effectively addressed?

SECTION **FOUR**

GENERAL APPROACHES TO RESEARCHED WRITING

I t would have been so much easier to have one chapter instead of three here, to say of the research paper that everyone follows essentially the same procedures and winds up with essentially the same results. But we don't subscribe to the myth of the generic research paper, so we can't ask you to. In our experience, students do not merely write different kinds of research papers but write them from different kinds of motivation; the results involve fundamentally different relations between the writer and the subject as well as the writer and the reader.

Chapter 10 treats what we call the **inductive** paper, the sort of paper explaining, on the basis of gathered examples and evidence, the way things were, are, or will be. Such papers tend to be written by students with special authority in their topic area, or at least special interest in investigating it. Evidence is crucial to success here, but so is the ability to show how the evidence supports whatever claim about the nature of things is being advanced.

In Chapter 11, we have what we call the **deductive** paper, the paper proceeding from philosophical or moral principles and delivering a judgment or opinion rather than the inferential conclusion of the inductive paper. Here, though evidence certainly counts, the concern is less with the way things are than the way they should be, and what is especially crucial is the persuasive power such a paper exerts on a reader.

Chapter 12 presents a variant of the deductive paper we call the **dialectical** (or **dialogic**) paper, one that, in advancing its judgment or opinion, does not merely recognize opposing opinions but adjusts the argument to meet them halfway. For this paper, the opposition becomes not just a problem to contend with but a resource to use.

The differences between these general approaches have much more to do with motivation than procedure or structure. But basic differences in goals give rise to other basic differences. Writers relying chiefly on evidence need to see that evidence can't just be presented, that it must be interpreted. Writers delivering judgments need to see that being convinced of an opinion is not the same as making that opinion convincing; the reasoning must be elaborated. Writers confronting opposing reasons need to see that they have choices besides ridiculing them or succumbing to them; argument can also be negotiation.

As always, details of the process as well as the product make all the difference, so each student's sample research paper is accompanied by its biography, its story of how it came to be. Each also involves primary sources in the form of surveys or interviews as well as secondary (or library) sources.

CHAPTER TEN

THE INDUCTIVE RESEARCH PAPER

Speaking from experience—that is, speaking inductively, generalizing from observations and examples—we could say that students write essentially two kinds of research papers (though we also have a third chapter on a tactical twist to the second). The first, the one treated in this chapter, is the paper about the way things *are* (or will be, or have been). The other is the paper about the way things *ought to be* (or ought to have been). That first kind is fundamentally fact-based or descriptive; it stands or falls by its evidence. The second is evaluative and value-based; it rests on premises about how life (or some aspect of it) should be arranged. What is especially interesting to us—again, we are speaking from experience—is that students tend to prefer the second kind to the first.

It's not hard to guess why. We live in a society of experts and specializations. Students tend to think anything that can be demonstrated chiefly by means of facts already has been demonstrated. So they turn their attention from the way things are to what should be done about them: what should be done about world hunger or violent crime or teenage pregnancy or whatever. Evidence is relevant in those cases as well, but ultimately conclusions are matters of opinion, and one opinion is presumably as good as another. Evidence, by contrast, is non-negotiable stuff, hard-and-fast, cut-and-dried, pre-empted by experts.

Actually, that's not true. Facts, or the inferences drawn from them, can be as slippery as opinions. And just as opinions need to be accompanied by evidence, facts need to be fleshed out by reasoning. Moreover, specialists and experts haven't claimed all the territory open to exploration. That will never happen. And we hope you've been given reason to think you have your own areas of expertise, your own grounds for authority.

Induction works primarily by observations and examples, so we'll begin by making some observations about our sustained example, a research paper on "Koreans and Abortion" by Kooheon Chung, or Harry (as he prefers to be called). As Harry reasons through the effects of cultural background and generational difference on individual thinking, we think you'll see just how ambitious and complex an inductive research paper can be. We expect that you'll also sense how a paper defining a situation can often be more successful—more informative, more convincing, more useful—than a paper giving an opinion on what ought to be done about it. Yet whether the claim is fact-based or value-based, it is in fact a claim, something the reader needs to be talked into accepting. Harry's paper is no mere report. To establish his claim about Koreans and abortion, he needs persuasive skill and careful reasoning as well as evidence. The key, as Harry found, is to realize that you needn't look too far from your own door for significance. What makes a topic rich or big is the extent of your interest in it, your curiosity about it, your willingness to pursue it through the gathering of evidence to the drawing of conclusions.

WRITING ASSIGNMENT

Tackle an issue or a situation about which you are more curious than morally incensed: changes in fashion, economic trends, shifting political winds, the rising incidence of drug use, changing dietary or viewing habits, rollerblading, whatever. Write a cause-and-effect paper about your topic using primary and/or secondary sources. Basically, you have two options. You can explain why something is happening (or did happen). Or you can predict what will happen as a consequence of past and present circumstances.

READING THE WRITING ASSIGNMENT

Like Harry, writing about abortion, you may be writing about a moral or legal issue or some other matter of opinion, but your own remarks about it will be fact-based rather than value-based, inferential rather than judgmental. Your assignment is to make a claim about the way things are (or have been or will be), not about the way things should be (or should have been). This is worth stressing because people tend to jump to conclusions, and what they usually jump past is the crucial fact-gathering and reasoning that would give them a firm basis for concluding.

Let's say you're interested in some aspect of the **status quo** (Latin for the *state in which* we find ourselves, our current conditions): you're concerned about local pollution problems, rising tuition costs, drug use in your peer group, limited jobs in your chosen career. The tendency is to start with the assumption that something ought to be done. But what? Shouldn't we first make sure that the problem is indeed a problem—and is perceived as such? Shouldn't we begin by investigating why a problem exists and to what extent it exists?

If you're tempted to answer such questions with another question—"Why stop there?"—we might respond, "How long do you want your paper to be?" But there are other reasons for sticking to facts and not moving on to calls for change. An antonym for *anxiety* is *certainty*: sometimes acquiring more knowledge about what you perceive as a problem might be the best way of addressing it. You might be impressed with local drug rehabilitation programs or recycling efforts, maybe even satisfied with your campus's job placement record or its attempts to keep tuition costs down. Even if you're not, you might find yourself weighing the wisdom of proposed solutions like those you yourself might have proposed.

But it's also worth stressing that we're not necessarily talking about problems (and solutions). Harry didn't look at abortion exclusively as a "problem": he was more interested in charting a trend in changing attitudes toward it. You probably don't need to be told that the ability to chart trends and make predictions is a useful one in today's society; here's your chance to test yours by putting your finger on the pulse in music, dress, buying patterns, or the like. You might even write a fact-based paper on opinions and how they change, as Harry did.

DISCOVERING IDEAS

Find a Subject

Maybe you've already found a subject. That was Harry's case. When the instructor first mentioned the research paper, and that was the first day of class, the students were warned to be wary of the done-to-death topics: abortion, capital punishment, gun control, etc. Even as he was being discouraged from writing on abortion, Harry realized that abortion was the topic he wanted to pursue. He met with the instructor after class and explained that, for personal reasons (which he alludes to in his research paper), he was interested in the topic of abortion, specifically as it's viewed in Korean culture. The instructor granted that the cultural angle could prove interesting but warned that issues like abortion tended to be discussed in terms of rooted moral principles rather than empirical or factual evidence. If Harry really wanted to test and not simply assert a claim about the topic, he would need to be open to opposing viewpoints; if he wanted to say something new, he would be more likely to say it with newly discovered evidence than with long-rehearsed opinions. Harry agreed, and when assigned to do a survey, he seized the chance to initiate the research part of his research paper by surveying Korean-American women on the subject of abortion.

Like Harry, you may already have a subject that came to mind as soon as the opportunity for research came up. Maybe you have even done a survey report that represents unfinished business, or at least something you can pursue further. The survey report (as discussed in Chapter 5) is, after all, essentially an exercise in inferential or inductive reasoning.

If you're starting from scratch, the most important thing about finding a subject is to be guided by your curiosity, your interest in finding out more about a subject (and, of course, passing that on). This might seem to be apt advice for any assignment, but it's especially important given the task at hand. We are not, after all, talking about a mere matter of opinion here, but a conclusion that is drawn from data. You will have to work with the evidence you have, and dig for the evidence you don't have but need. If you're not interested in your topic, this won't be much fun.

TRIAL RUN

The object of the assigned research project is to explain why or how something is happening or has happened or will happen. Harry, sensing Koreans' attitudes toward abortion were changing, wanted to know why and how they were changing. When trying on a subject, turn that subject into some "why" and "how" questions you will need to answer. Write these out, and scrutinize them to ensure that they are questions asking for explanations, not for value-based opinions. For instance, "Why are attitudes toward abortion changing?" is fine. "Why must we change our attitudes toward abortion?" is not. Watch out for words like *must* or *should* or *ought to;* they signal a shift from fact-based argument to argument based on principles or values.

CHECKLIST: TESTING A TOPIC'S VIABILITY

If you are interested in a topic, but not yet committed to it, try these questions on for size:

- **What do you already know about the topic?** You don't need to have all of the answers, but you need to have interesting questions.

- **Why are you interested in your topic?** Asking and answering that question is one way of determining your topic's significance, not just for you, but also for your reader—so long as the answer transcends purely personal interest.

- **Where are you going to get your evidence?** Again, some uncertainty is fine, so long as you know of places to start and ways to proceed. For one, see immediately below.

Consider Yourself a Resource

During a library tour, Harry stumped a very resourceful reference librarian by asking about access to up-to-date *Korean* sources about Korea. He had to rely on his own devices to a considerable extent, drawing on his knowledge of Korean government policies, the Korean Attitude Movement, and so on.

We may expect Harry, as a Korean-American student, to be knowledge-able about Korean society, but the knowledge he had to bring to his topic is really just a particular manifestation of a general principle: everyone with a powerful interest in a topic is a potential resource on that topic, and that tends to be increasingly true the more powerful the interest. As teachers, we have had compelling papers on addiction written by students who were recovering alcoholics or anorexics; shrewd business projections written by students who were watchers of certain products or markets; unsparing analyses of college recruitment practices by athletes who had an insider's perspective—and the list could go on and on. What special knowledge do you have to draw on? What special interest do you have to pursue?

Also keep in mind that you are invited to use primary sources (surveys, interviews, and the like) as well as secondary sources (of the sort found in the library). Thus, your peculiar advantage may be not just what you know but whom you know. Do you have access to special interest groups, unusual sources of opinion or knowledge, unexamined files or other sources of data? If you're investigating attitudes in your peer group or circumstances in your school or neighborhood, you may be ideally positioned to exploit sources no one else—not even so-called experts—has seen fit to tap.

Form a Purpose

Be led by your evidence. Preliminary research is vital. You're not simply delivering yourself of an opinion about some situation. You're writing about how things got the way they are and where they're going. You need to speak from knowledge.

Harry began with a loose sense that attitudes toward abortion among Korean-Americans (and perhaps Koreans as well) were changing. Preliminary research confirmed his guess that the shift was generational—that younger Korean-Americans were more tolerant of abortion than their parents; further research confirmed that this change of attitudes was characteristic of Koreans as well as Korean-Americans. He ascribed the change to the Americanization of the Korean-Americans and the modernization of Korea. Eventually, this entailed specifying what words like "Americaniza-tion" and "modernization" meant and what the relationship between them might be, a heady task that turned out to be the crux of his argument.

TRIAL RUN

In a sense you are your audience—not the you who eventually acquires the evidence and makes sense of it, but the you who began with curiosity and interest. What needs to be said to such a curious, interested person? Give yourself a list of questions to answer before you really begin investigating your topic. What are the likely causes of the effect you are investigating? Or what future effects do you see springing from present causes? What is obvious? What might be less apparent but still important? What is especially intriguing? What might be the crux of your investigation? As in so many other situations, two heads may be better than one: ideally, develop such questions with some help from a friend or classmate or tutor.

Expand Your Thinking by Analogy

Harry's argument, as it turned out, wasn't entirely bound by cause-and-effect connections. The great link between the results of his surveys of Korean-American women and his discussion of Korean society is **analogy**. Derived from the Greek word for proportion, analogy is a special kind of similarity, one in which two things known to be similar in some respects can be assumed to be similar in other respects. Thus you can infer that something may be true of one thing when you know it's true of the other. "The younger women I surveyed are similar to the younger people in Korea," Harry says halfway through his paper, and at the end he says that "those younger women seem to come closer to defining the Korea of the future." Harry is inferring that a trend he has verified among Korean-Americans in this country will correspond to a presumed trend among Koreans who still live in their native land. Similarity is not identity; the conditions that helped shape those younger women's formative years in this country are not the same as for the younger generation in Korea. But the causal chains seem similar, so connections can still be made, analogies rather than causal links: *A* is to *B* as *C* is to *D*—living in this country is to the younger women Harry surveyed as living in an increasingly Westernized Korea is to the younger people in that country; what's more, those younger women are to the older women as the Korea of the future is to the Korea of the past.

Arguments by analogy require some imagination; that is their virtue and their danger. They can open up new avenues for applying evidence and exploring significance, as they did for Harry. Taken too far, though, they may also devolve into mere figures of speech or stretches of the imagination. But the risk is worth running, especially at the prewriting stage.

TRIAL RUN

Are you investigating circumstances (drug use, date rape, political preferences) in your school or community that have been explored by others in other contexts? Often specifically focused research can be developed with reference to more general studies. Do you discern the beginnings of a trend in, say, product sales or viewers' preferences that is similar to some other trend that has already played itself out? Sometimes analogies with past patterns can help you extrapolate from present circumstances. And there are times when pondering an analogy between your cause-and-effect relation and another will open your eyes to possibilities for research or argument you might not have considered otherwise. One way of developing your topic is to complete statements like "The effect (or cause) I am investigating is to this presumed cause (or effect) as _____ is to _____." Try it. It may take you places.

COMPOSING THE FIRST DRAFT

Research Your Subject

We have already made some suggestions about how to begin. We might also put in a word for reference librarians. We noted how Harry stumped one, but most students, of course, are not asking for Korean sources, so most reference librarians tend to be quite helpful when asked concrete questions about where to get what. If you're stuck, or even if you just want the research path made smooth, go spend some time with a reference librarian.

Remember, too, that you have been encouraged to tap primary as well as secondary sources—to get stuff straight from the source's mouth as well as from library books and periodicals. Harry's surveys, presented as a part of his report, were based on the discussion of informal surveying techniques in Chapter 5. You might also avail yourself of on-site data and interviews—both discussed in Chapter 12. The important thing is not to follow some step-by-step methodology, though; it's to go out and get what you think you need, then to begin thinking enough about the argument you're planning to determine if it *is* what you need.

Draft *as* You Research

Don't suppose that research stops after the initial acquisition of sources. Nothing will serve you so well as the sort of experience Harry had with his survey report—which showed him how he had to modify his research process to achieve his purposes. Even if you don't do an assignment like that and get an instructor's feedback on it, the most efficient way to proceed, *once you have done some preliminary research,* is to try a very rough draft—one that represents a first-go rather than a near-final shot at the final version. What you want is an opportunity to identify the gaps in your knowledge, the facts and connections that need to be filled in. This is much more efficient than researching a subject at length, calling a halt to that stage of the process, and then trying to decide what to say.

Let's take Harry's survey report as an example. The survey part of it began when he took a table in a Korean restaurant near his home in Queens (a borough of New York City), politely asking women who came in if they would spare a few minutes to answer questions for a study he was doing. One thing he found out right off was that Korean-American women were reticent on the issue of abortion. They were more likely to say no than yes to his request. Once he had surveyed twenty (and been turned down by at least that many), he felt he had done a representative sampling of Korean-American women—in his neck of the woods, anyway.

But when he began tabulating the responses, he noticed a problem: eighteen of his twenty respondents were under 35 and all were under 45. He was sure that older Korean-American women were more likely to be opposed to abortion—his grandmother certainly was—but he had no hard evidence for that. So he interviewed his grandmother. She and her views on abortion figured prominently in his paper as the voice of "old Korea," the Korea of fading customs and beliefs and traditions. Most of the younger women whom he interviewed were in favor of the women's right to choose an abortion; he cast them as representatives of the "new Korea," more modern, more liberal, more similar in many ways to America.

Here is the instructor's comment on Harry's paper:

> Yours was not the most extensive survey in the class, but it does offer the most solid sample since your target population is something fairly specific (Korean women living in this country). You also have interesting things to say (or suggest) about the relations between their opinions about abortion and the larger context of Korean governmental policy and the Korean culture. But you need to remember that your survey was conducted in the U.S. and that any connections between those responses and what is happening in Korea need to be placed on firmer ground. You should also be aware that, though you stress the "generation gap," the only older woman you mention who is clearly identified as being anti-abortion is your grandmother. She's a great example, but she's a lousy statistic (as any party of one would be in a survey on any issue). The beginning of one sentence—"My research compared with my grandmother's opinion"—neatly sums up the lopsidedness that results. Still, you've done a good job of developing a specific angle on a complex general issue, and this of course bodes well for your research paper.

Thinking Critically about Harry's Survey Report

That's just the teacher's comment, which is largely a matter of opinion, but it's an expert opinion—and from the same source that would decide the grade on Harry's research paper. You don't have to read Harry's survey report to sense that his use of his grandmother is what logicians call an inadequate sampling. What may be less clear, but no less important, is that Harry's exclusive reliance on opinions gathered in this country to chart a change of attitudes in Korea represented a similar problem with evidence. What needs to be done? That's a big question. Answering some more specific questions might help answer it:

1. Most people share Harry's almost unsubstantiated assumption that older women tend to be more anti-abortion than younger women. Why? Does

your answer point to a way out of Harry's problem with evidence in this regard?

2. Similarly, most people are likely to find a term like Americanization semi-synonymous with a term like modernization. Why? Does your answer help you to see how to remedy Harry's lack of evidence on this head?

3. If statements seem fairly reasonable, do they still need to be supported by evidence? How much evidence is needed?

Be(a)ware of the Fuzziness of Facts

Those just-posed questions seem both simple and hard because of the complexities Harry was wrestling with. His was from first to last a fact-based project, but it was also, from first to last, an excellent demonstration of the inescapable fuzziness of some fact-based conclusions. For one thing, he had to be interested, not just in what people believed (or said they believed), but also why. And who knows at all precisely what goes on in people's heads? Sorting through the evidence, Harry posited a "generation gap": younger women, whom he had sampled fairly extensively, seemed to be more likely to accept the idea of abortions than older women, whom he had sampled really only in the person of his grandmother. Let's suppose the pattern holds—and it did when Harry actually surveyed older Korean-American women. The question remains: why the difference?

Harry's answer—and here things get complicated—is that the changes between the older and younger women are symptomatic of changes between the more traditional Korea of the first half of the century and the more modern Korea of today. But he also suggested that the younger women he talked to, inhabitants of this country and not of Korea, were more tolerant of abortions because they were more Americanized, more Western-ized. Could they actually be compared to citizens of Korea? Talking with Harry, his instructor said that the answer was a qualified yes. Harry could draw a connection between the Americanization of the women he surveyed and the Westernization of Korea, a connection that would be an analogy rather than a direct causal link.

This is tricky stuff. How can we measure the effect of a culture on an individual? (And remember that, in Harry's survey, he was in a sense measuring the effect of two different cultures.) To what extent could an individual's—or a culture's—position on a complex issue like abortion serve as a sort of litmus test of a complex phenomenon like Westernization? Harry's paper was indeed fact-based, but there could be nothing like absolutely conclusive proof, however many facts Harry gathered. Careful reasoning would necessarily be crucial to his success. He would have to resist glib certainties in matters where there was no real certainty, but he would also have to be careful not to qualify his points into oblivion.

TRIAL RUN

Think for a while about the parts of our argument that aren't susceptible to conclusive proof. You might want to return to work you did in the prewriting stage listing "how" and "why" questions or questions you felt you needed or wanted to answer. Make another list now, one of statements that you cannot decisively demonstrate but still want to make. How are they likely to strike your reader? Where do facts leave off so that reasoning must take over? If you are speaking of opinions, you may not be able to read minds, but you can supply reasonable explanations. If you are predicting trends or events, you may not be able to see into the future, but you can show how past and present circumstances warrant your conclusions.

RETHINKING AND REVISING

Test for Coherence

Harry's paper titled "Koreans and Abortion," though only a little over eight pages long (discounting appendices), was the longest he had ever written. Increasingly, Harry's case seems to be the rule rather than the exception: the research paper written for a composition course, even when it is of only moderate length, tends to be the longest the student has written thus far. Small wonder, then, that most students find the great task of revision in such projects is to make sure this unusually long composition coheres— holds together. As we have recommended elsewhere—in Chapter 6, for instance—it is often useful to do an outline of the draft *after* it has been written; turning each paragraph into a topic statement and then examining how those interrelate can be very helpful in charting the paper's logical consistency and flow. Because a fleshed-out argument is not just its skeleton, here are a couple of other recommendations:

1. **Don't drop a stitch; make every transition count.** Right after arguing, in his final version, that the older women he surveyed find "it difficult to accept change because they are accustomed to traditional ways," Harry tells us that "Korean society is rapidly changing." In a sense, we have a major change of focus as Harry turns from his survey results to Korea's technological advances, but he has also forged an important connection, one that is in fact vital to his argument. Sustained researched arguments don't cohere of themselves; you need to take care in ensuring that ideas link up.

2. **Don't interpose attitudes and opinions.** Harry twice alludes to his own attitude toward the abortion debate in his final version, but he does so in ways that make his paper seem purposeful, not polemical. Even if he didn't cast himself as being someone who really hadn't made up his mind, endorsing his argument wouldn't mean endorsing his opinion on

the issue. This is an inductive argument: in order to accept his conclusions, we need to agree with what he does with his evidence, not with his position on abortion. Remember the inferential paper is grounded in evidence, not opinions; it builds to fact-based inferences, not value-based judgments.

Test for Common Sense and Probability

Some inferences are more solid than others. Strictly speaking, the prediction of anything that hasn't happened yet is an inference. But it's a pretty safe bet that the sun will rise tomorrow. Harry's task was to make inferences about why people are thinking the way they do about abortion in Korean culture—and where this thinking is headed. That's something you can't take a black-and-white picture of. But readers of his paper tend to find it quite persuasive. Why? Well, he has evidence that birth control practices and illegal abortions are dramatically on the rise in modern Korea. There seem to be pretty clear trends there, and there's no reason to suppose they won't continue. His survey finds that younger Korean women in this country, many of them college students, are more likely to be tolerant of abortion than older women—no great surprise there—and he suggests that those older women may be less tolerant of change generally. Now, obviously, a greater resistance to change among the elderly is hardly unique to Korean culture.

We are not saying Harry's argument is a cakewalk. It's true that we would be inclined to believe some of his statements even if they weren't reasoned through or supported by evidence—like his claim that little old ladies from Korea are more resistant to change than women half their age. Yet some parts of the argument, notably the connection between Westernization and support for abortion, are dauntingly complex. Harry tells us plenty of things we didn't know or might even be skeptical about, but he does so by blending new insights with received wisdom, evidence with speculation, disparate facts with careful reasoning about possible connections. If his paper as a whole is persuasive, in other words, it is because he is attentive to precisely those three things you must be attentive to in revision if you want to give your argument the air of common sense and probability:

1. **Make sure every important statement is supported by evidence.** Remember that Harry actually thought, back in the survey report, that he could get away with using his grandmother as a survey of one. In his research paper, no such shortcuts are taken. We presumably know that Korea has undergone radical industrialization—we see Hyundais everywhere—but Harry supplies evidence to drive the point home. We may suppose that older women are more opposed to abortion and more resistant to change than their younger counterparts, but Harry makes sure we don't have to suppose; he has the data to support the contention.

2. **Blend the unknown with the familiar.** When you take your reader into unfamiliar territory, see if you can point out similarities to and connections with things closer to home. We may not be familiar with Korean attitudes toward abortion, but comparing recent developments with what has happened in our own culture can enlighten us considerably, especially when that point of comparison is also cast as a line of influence.

3. **Don't go beyond what your evidence will support.** Taking the "inferential leap" doesn't mean jumping to conclusions. It means inferring what you can't possibly know for certain, but this doesn't give you a license to violate common sense. And common sense is just what the term implies—a sense that you have in common with others. Do you seem too speculative? Are you taking off on a tangent? Are you preaching when you should be content with predicting? How can you tell? The best way is to stop being yourself for a while, to look at your writing with your reader's eyes. As is always the case when you write, you must think of your audience.

CHECKLIST: REVISING YOUR DRAFT

- Have you been clear about just what causal situation your paper seeks to explain?
- Have you determined that your paper is logically and rhetorically coherent?
- Are all of your important statements supported by evidence?
- For statements that must be speculative or inferential, have you made your reasoning and the grounds for your speculation clear?
- Have you made causal or comparative (especially analogical) connections between what is fairly obvious and what is less apparent?
- Are all your claims, not least of all those you conclude on, supported by your evidence and reasoning?

PRESENTING HARRY'S FINAL DRAFT

Koreans and Abortion

Kooheon Chung

Harry begins with a personal anecdote about what motivated his research. Note

1   Two years ago my friend Christine (not her real name) got an abortion. She was nineteen years old at the time. Her family had immigrated to America from Korea eleven years before. Christine's abortion caused many arguments in her family. Her parents, who had lived in Korea for most of their lives,

that everything about it (cultural context, generational difference) is relevant to his argument. He concludes the paragraph by broaching his position.

2

Harry gives background briefly but in some historical depth.

3

He notes changing attitudes in the not-too-distant past.

4

Defining abortion, Harry focuses specifically on the incidence of abortions in Korea in recent years.

thought that abortion was morally wrong. Unlike her parents, Christine, who had spent most of her life in the United States, believed abortion was a morally acceptable choice. Why did Christine think differently than her parents? I decided to find out if more young Korean women felt the same way Christine did about the issue of abortion, and if so, why. I conducted two surveys and gathered information from books and articles. I discovered that there are many young Korean women who are in favor of abortion, and I believe their opinions have been shaped by the influence of Western culture.

In Korea, there was for a long time a social system similar to the caste system in India. Marriages between members of different social classes were prohibited. If a relationship between members of two different social classes did occur, then, and only then, the woman would have the unborn child terminated. Only when the woman had a relationship with a man of the same social status would Korean society accept the relationship and encourage the woman to have as many children as she desired. For many centuries, the social system in monarchical Korea controlled the country's population.

However, since World War II, Koreans' attitudes toward inter-class relationships have slowly but significantly changed. Social status has become less important and more and more inter-class relationships have occurred. Such new social attitudes have increased the country's population dramatically. To slow down the increasing population, the Korean government has encouraged the use of birth control devices or contraceptives. However, the government's policies do not include legalized abortion. Even though many sexual partners practice the government-endorsed birth control, many women are having abortions illegally.

The term "abortion," generally stated, is "the termination of a pregnancy before the fetus is viable, or capable of living outside the womb" (Academic American Encyclopedia 60). During the 1960s, according to the New York Korean Journal, approximately 100,000 illegal abortions were performed each year in Korea, yet 87% of Koreans surveyed did not feel that abortion should be legalized (Yoo 16). By the 1970s, however, illegal abortions increased by 50% and a pro-abortion movement was formed in Korea (Yoo 17). Such changes in social attitudes in an increasingly Westernized as well as industrialized Korea may be greatly influenced by concurring events in the United States, where abortion is legal and survey after survey has shown that the majority of Americans support legalized abortion.

5

Bringing us up to the present state of affairs, Harry explains the motives and methods of his investigation.

Currently, more than 300,000 abortions are performed yearly in Korea, and members of the pro-abortion organization have proposed an amendment which would make abortion legal (Yoo 17). Even though I think I am traditional in many ways, I find myself becoming more open-minded towards those who are pro-abortion. Interested in how other Koreans feel about the abortion issue, I surveyed two different groups of Korean women here in America. One group was made up of women between the ages of twenty and forty-five. The other group was made up of women of the ages sixty to eighty. The women in the first group were 70% pro-abortion (see Appendix A); those in the second group were more than 90% opposed to abortion (see Appendix B). The younger women who supported abortion most commonly gave financial difficulties and rape as reasons for having an abortion. The older women cited family traditions and cultural backgrounds as their chief reasons for opposing abortion.

6

Harry reviews his survey results.

A slightly larger number of the younger women had stayed slightly longer in this country than was true for the group of older women, but a more important difference may be that the majority of the younger women were college students whereas a majority of the older women were housewives. Time in this country is not the only reason to realize that the younger women were more exposed to Western ideas. The clearest difference between the two groups, the difference in age, could be the most important. The younger women, in dress and hair styles and manner, seemed more able to blend their own culture with Western culture. Those surveyed who were more than forty-five seemed less able to adapt to changes or situations that conflict with their beliefs, and they have held those beliefs for many years. They found it difficult to accept change because they are accustomed to traditional ways.

7

Having noted resistance to change in the old, acceptance of it in the young, Harry turns his attention to changes in Korea.

In fact, Korean society is rapidly changing. The New York Times states, "In little more than 30 years, an agrarian society has become industrial, a society of country dwellers has become urban, and people who once struggled to put enough food on the table now enjoy television sets, refrigerators and stereos" (Chira A1). Indeed, from 1965 to 1985, the urban population in Korea increased from slightly more than one-third of the general population to nearly two-thirds (Chira A1), and the basis of trade switched from the exporting of rice to the exporting of cars (Chira A6). Such changes indicate how Korea is becoming Westernized and also challenging Western countries in traditionally Western markets.

8

The younger women I surveyed are similar to the younger people in Korea. After the Korean War, social attitudes

Harry connects his survey results with the changing cultural scene in Korea.

changed significantly. The American military bases such as the one in Itaewon have greatly influenced the attitudes of the younger generation. According to the <u>Korean Times</u>, "...Itaewon, a section of Seoul, is becoming a big hang out place for younger Koreans for the past two decades...." (Kim 3). In addition, being exposed to Western mass media (particularly television shows), more and more young Koreans have adopted the American style of living, adopting Western fashions, modern music, pop art, and other means of entertainment. This in effect conflicts with Korean traditions because Western culture emphasizes the individual instead of the group. Western culture encourages the individual to be liberated, more open-minded and more independent. Such exposure to Western ideals has to have a significant effect on the attitudes of young Koreans who are increasingly likely to be pro-abortion as they decide to support the right of the individual woman to choose whether to abort or not.

9

Harry also notes an exception to the general trend of Westernization but he casts it as an exception that proves the rule.

Despite changing social attitudes and the influence of Western ideals, or maybe because of them, some young Koreans are espousing conservative ways, clinging to traditional beliefs and values. The Korean Attitude Movement, a fairly small but vocal and so widely known group of college students, is an example of growing groups of young people who insist upon holding to the old traditional ways. They fear that otherwise young Koreans will lose their heritage and the essence of their history. However, this fear some Koreans have that they will actually lose their culture and identity to social changes and Western influences is, in a sense, just more evidence of how radical the changes in modern Korean society have been.

10

He notes that the key is not "acceptance of abortion" itself, but the reasons for it—especially in a country that urges birth control.

Acceptance of abortion is not necessarily a sign of modernization. As I said earlier, abortion is a time-honored practice in Korea, once resorted to because of social prejudices that are now breaking down. What is actually newer to Korean society is the acceptance of birth control throughout the population. The government policies promote the use of condoms, birth control pills, I.U.D.'s, sponges, gels, and other means of preventing conception. Since Korea's population rate is increasing and hurting the country economically, the Korean government recommends that its citizens have no more than two children per family. Such policies may provide strong support for abortion. They certainly conflict with Korean traditional values promoting large, tightly-knit families. In the meantime, the number of illegal abortions keeps rising. So does the number of Koreans supporting legalized abortion.

Harry singles 11
out "individual
choice" as the
consideration
uniting such dis-
parate and com-
plex phenomena
as Westernization
and attitudes
toward 12
abortion.

Social conditions and Western influences make individual choice more important in Korea than it ever was before. The government, by promoting birth control, asks the people to choose to have fewer children, and to choose when to have them carefully. Western influences stress individuality and variety, so much, in fact, that some young Koreans like those in the Korean Attitude Movement choose to cling to old values. In the midst of all this change, hundreds of thousands each year choose the illegal option of abortion.

The new empha-
sis on individual
choice gives Harry
grounds for hope
precisely because
abortion is not
perceived as an
easy choice.

One hopeful sign is that choice seems to require reasoning. The younger Korean women I surveyed who favored abortion did so only in certain circumstances. They gave as acceptable reasons the financial burden a child can be, the suffering caused a rape victim who carries the rapist's child, and the possible dangers to the mother's life. However, the older women who opposed abortion did not consider special cases. All abortions were wrong because they conflicted with family values and cultural or religious beliefs. For better or worse, those younger women seem to come closer to defining the Korea of the future. Nothing will be done just because that is the way it has always been done. Issues like abortion will have to be reasoned through. There is no turning back.

Citations are 13
done MLA style.
(The encyclopedia
entry is insuffi-
cient. Can you tell
what's missing?)
Note how much
Harry relied on
personal knowl-
edge and primary
sources (his
surveys).

Works Cited

"Abortion." <u>Academic American Encyclopedia.</u> 1986 ed.

Chira, Susan. "Boom Time in South Korea: An Era of Dizzying Change." <u>New York Times</u> 7 Apr. 1987:A1, A6.

Chung, Kooheon. Survey #1. 14 June 1991.

-----. Survey #2. 20 June 1991.

Kim, Shungshin. "Itaewon Today." <u>Korean Times</u> 23 Sept. 1989:A3.

Yoo, Kyungil. "Abortion Boom." <u>New York Korean Journal</u> March 1990:15-17.

Appendix A

(Survey #1)

Material you've 14
generated in your
research—tabula-
tions of survey

Number of respondents: 20
Target population: Korean females between 20 and 45
<u>RESPONSES</u>
Age
   20-25 (12)   26-35 (6)   36-45 (2)

results, question-
naires you used,
transcripts of
interviews—may
be presented as
appendices.

```
Occupation:
    Housewife  (2)     Employed  (6)     Student  (12)
How long have you been living in the United States?
    Less than 1 yr  (2)      1 yr–5 yrs  (2)
    6 yrs–10 yrs  (11)       Over 10 yrs  (5)
Are you pro-abortion or anti-abortion?
    Pro-abortion  (14)     Anti-abortion  (6)
What would you consider an important reason for having an
abortion?
    Financial difficulties  (6)     Rape victim  (8)
    Family conflicts  (2)           Mother's health  (3)
```

In his tabulation,
Harry identifies
the target popula-
tion (the group
he's researching),
the number of   15
respondents (the
people from that
group he actually
talked to), and
their responses to
specific questions
(with the number
of respondents for
each response in
parentheses).

Appendix B

(Survey #2)

```
Number of respondents: 15
Target population: Korean females over 45
RESPONSES
Age:
    46–60  (4)      61–70  (5)      71–75  (5)      76–80  (1)
Occupation:
    Housewife  (12)     Employed  (3)
How long have you been living in the United States?
    Less than 1 yr  (2)      1 yr–5 yrs  (2)
    6 yrs–10 yrs  (11)       Over 10 yrs  (5)
Are you pro-abortion or anti-abortion?
    Pro-abortion  (1)     Anti-abortion  (14)
Why are you opposed to abortions?
    Family values  (6)     Cultural background  (5)
    Religion  (3)
```

Commentary on Harry's Final Draft

Harry's research paper is basically a cause-and-effect argument. But we should say right away that it investigates a topic that offers no clear and simple causal relations. Harry himself notes as much by saying things like "Acceptance of abortion is not necessarily a sign of modernization." But we should also say that some things about his paper are quite clear: the way the responses in his two groups of respondents sort out, the Korean government's policies to promote birth control, the extent to which the Korea of today is radically different from the Korea that existed before the Second World War, the fact that abortions in Korea are on the rise, and so on. Still, gathering such facts is only the first step. Harry must supply the reasoning that explains the relations between them. His great challenge is to establish connections among these bits of data, to draw for his readers, not just a picture of what is happening, but why. Though he does work from facts, his is no easy task. He has to proceed carefully.

One of his strategies, and we think it is a good one, is to show, explicitly, that he is resisting the oversimplification of a complex set of relationships. How do attitudes about abortions, generational differences, social and cultural changes, technological advances, government policies, and population growth all link up? Where does one begin in such a tangled web of relations?

Harry begins with his own motivation for pursuing the topic in the first place. He mentions his friend Christine, like him the child of Korean immigrants, who did what her mother would apparently have regarded as unthinkable: she had an abortion. And Harry's reaction—we learn later (in paragraph 5) that his mind was not made up on the issue—was to want to find out if Christine's choice was typical of a general, generational shift away from traditional values toward abortion among Koreans. He doesn't leave us in suspense long. Before we leave that first paragraph, we know that he has concluded younger Korean women are indeed predominantly pro-choice, and that he attributes this to "the influence of Western culture."

Ambitious claims these, but the next paragraph signals that still more is at stake. Here the focus broadens to Korea generally. This is general background, but it is also focused, purposeful background. If Harry is going to ascribe Western influence as a cause, he needs a counterpoint: what an un-Westernized Korea was like. The second paragraph, in a few bold strokes, paints a social system that has faded from the historical scene. Here, and even more in the third paragraph, Harry focuses on relations between the sexes, noting that less rigid social stratification has resulted in population growth and attempts to curb it. The fourth paragraph returns us specifically to abortion, illegal but very much on the rise in Korea; this paragraph concludes with Harry once again broaching the importance of Western influence: "Such changes in social attitudes in an increasingly Westernized as well as industrialized Korea *may be* greatly influenced by concurring events in the United States, where abortion is legal and survey after survey has shown that the majority of Americans support legalized abortion." But that's as it *may be* at this point. Harry needs to do all that he can to firm up this complex connection.

It is at this point that he introduces his two surveys (the one on which he based his survey report and the other he did to give substance to the position his grandmother represented in that paper). The first of the two paragraphs (5 and 6) devoted to the surveys gives the bottom line for each: most of the older women were opposed to abortion; most of the younger ones were not. The second of these paragraphs offers reasons for the results. Without suggesting either is a sufficient cause, Harry notes differences between the two groups with respect to occupations held and time spent in the U.S. Then he suggests that the most important difference is generational: the younger women are more open to change; the older women, more resistant to it.

Is this really the reason? A moment's thought is enough to suggest that there probably can't be a single reason we can call *the* reason. The difference between the two groups on the abortion issue, construed as an effect, is the result of so many causes that they could never be adequately investigated or tabulated. The individual beliefs and experiences of each one of the women, what they didn't say as well as what they said when they talked to Harry, the varying degrees to which they actually had their minds made up on the issue—somehow all of this would have to be taken into account. And that's impossible. Harry does what he can, noting several patterns of difference and wondering about the connections between them before suggesting (not insisting) that the generational difference is the one that best explains the different attitudes toward abortion. Since there can be no absolute certainty here, Harry must only meet the test of reasonableness. We think he does.

It doesn't hurt that the reason he hits upon also makes for an effective transition and link in his chain of reasoning. Had he in fact determined that time spent in America made all the difference, he would have been hard-pressed to connect his surveys and what he concluded from them with statements about Korean society. But instead he proposes that resistance to change is the big difference between the two groups—and then goes on to show that change, change that can also be cast as Westernization, is what modern Korea is all about.

The general remarks about this Western-flavored change in the seventh paragraph give way to more specific remarks in the eighth, the paragraph we see as the real linchpin of Harry's argument. This paragraph begins by comparing the attitudes of the younger women surveyed with "the younger people in Korea." And Westernization is here given its most specific guise: not change, not industrialization, not democratization, but above all concern for the individual—and individual choice. Looking at this paragraph after having read Harry's whole paper, we realize how crucial this paragraph is to his argument, and especially his conclusion.

It may seem strange, then, to find that he seems to undercut it in the paragraph that immediately follows it. Here he notes that there is a conservative backlash to change, and that it seems to be concentrated in "the younger people of Korea"—the same general group he had just placed in the vanguard of change. Should Harry have admitted as much? We think he indeed should have for three reasons. First, not admitting this social phenomenon would have been suppressing evidence. It's not hard to give a uniform picture of the way things are if you are willing to make your paper like the Procrustean bed of Greek mythology, lopping off or stretching the truth to make it fit your sense of things. But there are better ways of being convincing than being dishonest. Harry realizes as much, which brings us to our second reason for approving his potentially damaging admission: he has made it part of his plan to resist oversimplifying things; this is one of the ways he meets the test of reasonableness, one of the reasons he earns our provisional assent as he draws connections among complex phenomena. He may not be right about something no one can be absolutely certain about, but at least he keeps giving us reason to believe that he's not being simplistic. Third—and this is Harry's real coup—he actually turns the existence of groups like the Korean Attitude Movement to his advantage, noting that such resistance to change "is, in a sense, just more evidence of how radical the changes in modern Korean society have been."

Harry can now begin winding up. As he does so, starting with the tenth paragraph, he again resists the easy way out, explicitly rejecting a facile connection between abortion and modernization. Instead, he sets up a complex causal chain: the democratization of relations between the sexes in Korea has increased the population; this, in turn, has produced an official policy of encouraging birth control; this, in its turn, counters time-honored traditions and promotes the importance of individual choice about when to have children, including the choice to abort.

Choice is the keynote of the eleventh, the penultimate paragraph. Harry ties it to Western influence and concern for the individual; he finds it reflected, not only in government-sanctioned birth control, but in the creation of groups like the Korean Attitude Movement, groups that consciously resist changes the old Korea never knew. He also finds it reflected in the fact that "hundreds of thousands each year choose the illegal option of abortion."

But Harry does not end there. He notes that a corollary of having options is the need to weigh them. He returns to his survey, noting that the older women rejected abortion out of principle while the younger ones specified conditions, cases, reasons for allowing it. When Harry says that "those younger women seem to come closer to defining the Korea of the future," he is stressing their willingness to think things through, not their stand on abortion—though he is also implying a connection between the two. This may seem tactful to some readers and slippery to others. To us, it seems an effective way of concluding the discussion of a complex and controversial issue that admits of no easy resolution. Harry is not fence-straddling here. There is nothing wishy-washy about his parting shot, "There is no turning back." He, too, has made his choice. And he has shown us a line of reasoning characterized by thoughtful deliberation and a resistance to oversimplification. He has demonstrated that, though they rest on facts, inferences have at least this much in common with the opinions he considers here: they "have to be reasoned through."

Questions for Further Thought

1. Basing your argument on facts is supposed to be good, but manipulating facts is supposed to be bad. How can we tell when this business of "reasoning through" shifts from the former to the latter, when the process of reasoning becomes a process of rationalization?

2. Most claims have to confront some evidence to the contrary. In Harry's case, for instance, there's the Korean Attitude Movement, a campaign against Westernization whose very existence he uses to underline the extent of Westernization. This is, as the saying goes, an exception that proves the rule—but how do we know it doesn't disprove it? How can you tell when opposing evidence does not simply oppose your claim but invalidate it?

3. Harry's conclusion is, in part, an endorsement of individual choice. How firm can the distinction between fact-based arguments and value-based ones be? Is it possible to have a value-free argument, one that doesn't rest on philosophical principles or moral judgments of any kind?

CHAPTER ELEVEN

THE DEDUCTIVE RESEARCH PAPER

It may have struck you as odd that the scientific progress that has taken us to the moon, the learning that has filled vast libraries, the educational institutions that have made for mass literacy have all done so little to resolve disagreements among people. The more we know, it seems, the more we argue. If that were in fact a sound statement—that knowledge breeds argument—we could *deduce* that knowledge alone is not enough to resolve all arguments. Why might this **deductive** conclusion be true? That would take further reasoning. Take the example of scientific progress. We can think of plenty of instances of such progress creating dangers as well as comforts—Chernobyl, the depletion of the ozone layer, acid rain, chemical and nuclear weapons—and thereby arrive at the **inductive** conclusion that what we can do is not always what we should do.

And what should we do? That's the sort of question we will always argue about, never finally resolve. An inductive conclusion—one resting on facts, observations, examples, probabilities—can only be overturned through a better use of evidence. But there are vast realms of human endeavor—politics, morality, aesthetics—where the crucial claims are judgments rather than inferences, value-based rather than fact-based claims. What is the right thing to do in our foreign policy? What are the rights of an individual or the duties of a parent? What makes Leonardo da Vinci's *Mona Lisa* a masterpiece? Evidence can be used to address such questions, but ultimately the answers will be derived from premises, priorities, principles—to some extent shared yet always contestable.

This is where deduction comes in. Inductive arguments derive their conclusions from observations; deductive arguments draw theirs from fundamental principles. Evidence is not irrelevant to such arguments, but the focus is on the soundness of the logical relationship between statements. And it is that relationship of links throughout the argument, not just the fundamental premise, that must strike the reader as logical. We are interested in persuasion in today's complex world, where few claims and beliefs are indisputable beginning points.

The great challenge, then, is not simply to argue from a premise (about what is right or good or desirable) but to make that premise—and all that you conclude from it—seem acceptable to your reader. Simply stating your position won't do. A persuasive deductive argument needs to explore the chosen issue, canvass opinions on it, weigh alternative positions. That sort of argument can shape the thinking of the reader evaluating the argument, and that's just the sort of argument Ruby Huang presents in her paper "Rape: Should the Press Publish the Victims' Names?" Her way of making her answer seem the best of all possible answers is the time-honored way: by testing it against other answers, other viewpoints.

WRITING ASSIGNMENT

Think for a moment about the way things should be. Does your mind quickly light on an issue that matters deeply to you, one that others—perhaps public figures or people in positions of power—don't see the same way you do? Do you have a sense of what their arguments are, what means you might have of countering them, what your own reasons are for leaning the way you do? Make a case for your position on the issue while taking other positions into account.

READING THE WRITING ASSIGNMENT

Remember that deductive argument is argument from premises or principles. You do not simply say how you think things ought to be; you give your reasons for holding such a position. Don't suppose, by the way, that you must argue for a change. (In her paper, Ruby resisted a change in the media's unofficial policy not to give the names of victims in rape cases.) The important thing is that you oppose your sense of what's right or desirable with someone else's. Because a **researched** argument is called for, it is also important that you don't simply speculate on what the opposition might be; you must actually find out what the people you disagree with are saying and incorporate that into your argument. And you must uncover their reasons or premises just as you must explore your own. Ultimately, a deductive argument weighs not just opposing positions but also the motives for holding them.

What does this mean concretely? A simple, diagrammatic way of reasoning from premises is the **syllogism.** Greek for "reckoning together," it proceeds through two premises which, if valid, lead inevitably to a valid conclusion. We could say, for instance, that Ruby's paper fleshed out this syllogism:

Major premise: The rights of the individual have priority over other rights.

Minor premise:	The rape victim's right to privacy is such a right.
Conclusion:	It has priority over the public's right to know.

Actually, as you'll see, Ruby's paper is much more complicated than that. It involves wondering how seriously to take "the public's right to know" when that right is advanced by the head of a news organization (for one must gauge motives as well as reasons). What's more, Ruby considers not just rights but interests. She contends with the argument—again from the press—that revealing victims' names is in the public's best interest since it denies the crime of rape any cloak of secrecy. Ruby wonders if such revelations might work against the general interest, cloaking rape further by making victims reluctant to come forward. In support, she cites opinions she has canvassed. Evidence is clearly important, but in such an argument as Ruby's it cannot be conclusive. Too much is a matter of speculation or judgment. The reader is most likely to be swayed by thorough reasoning—a careful weighing of arguments and counterarguments—and that can never be contained in a tidy syllogism. Hard (or dubious) as it is to boil things down to a neat bottom line, such reasoning does come to rest on trust rather than verification, principle rather than proof. You had better know the *why* behind *what* you are arguing.

DISCOVERING IDEAS

Find a Subject

When it came to finding a subject, Ruby Huang was both pressed and blessed. She was pressed because she was taking Expository Writing in the summer session. Though, like the regular version of the course, the summer version culminated with a research paper, the six-week session clearly wasn't going to give Ruby the time for decision-making and library legwork that students had during the regular fourteen-week term. The instructor stressed the point the first day: efficiency, not time and effort, would be the secret of success in this summer course. The sooner each student settled on a potentially rich but focused research topic and got cracking, the better.

Ruby was blessed because she had decided on a topic even before she was encouraged to. She felt it had been handed to her on a platter. There was no doubt about what the hot story was that summer: down in Palm Beach, William Kennedy Smith, nephew of Senator Edward Kennedy of Massachusetts, had been charged with rape. The story seemed inexhaustible in the number of angles it offered the press. There was the senator, Ted Kennedy, a high-profile figure, apparently scandal-prone: caught drinking heavily again, trouserless at the scene of the alleged crime, curt with both investigators and the press. There was the nephew, William Kennedy Smith, the latest manifestation of what some journalists were calling the "Kennedy curse," and the press reported that this was not the first rape he had been accused of. But nothing seemed to feed the press's fascination with the story like the release of the alleged victim's name by NBC News. Other news agencies had to decide whether to pass on the name or not. The issue became the subject of countless debates in editorial pages and TV news commentaries across the country. This, Ruby decided, was just the topic for her.

She was interested in the topic for other reasons. She was a freshman, commuting for the first time from her quiet neighborhood to busy downtown Manhattan. Her mother, reacting to another rape case that became a nationwide story—the rape and brutal beating of a Central Park jogger by teenage boys—had forbidden Ruby to take night classes, saying, "It isn't safe." And two women in Ruby's circle of friends had been the victims of sexual assault—and had never reported these attacks to the police.

Your personal circumstances are no doubt different from Ruby's, and the case that caught her (and the nation's) attention is old news now, but you may find it just as easy to hit upon a topic of prepossessing interest. After all, we're surrounded by controversies. Whether you're interested in sports or space, the newborn or the elderly, physical attractiveness or fiscal policy, individual rights or social responsibilities, crime or punishment, you really can't think of an area of interest without almost immediately hitting upon a topic of contention. The challenge, then, is not finding a controversy; it's selecting one that you can actually contribute to.

TRIAL RUN

With the help of friends or classmates, make a list of current controversies. Remember that they don't have to be knotty national issues like what to do about the federal deficit. Most of Ruby's classmates found their topics close to home: the use of metal detectors or the distribution of condoms in local high schools, issues of crowd control posed by a recent concert and recent student demonstrations against a tuition hike, proposals for the placement and counseling of ESL (English as a Second Language) students. Keep your list going till you have at least half a dozen items. Once you do, see if one or two in particular seem to catch and hold your interest. To help you make your choice, you might consider—perhaps even give written responses to—the following questions.

CHECKLIST: TESTING A TOPIC'S VIABILITY

- **Does the issue have some bearing on you personally?** For all that might be said in favor of disinterested speculation, you probably need some stake in the argument you will be constructing in order to realize fully what is at stake.

- **Do you think you have something to say besides what you might already have heard said?** Your task is to reason the issue through guided chiefly but not exclusively by your own lights—not to parrot someone else's position.

- **Do you have some respect for those whose arguments you will be opposing?** If they seem like moral cretins or mental midgets to you, you may say so—and that's name-calling, not arguing. If they have so little of your respect, they may get no more from your reader, who may not think much of your attempt to counter arguments scarcely worth intelligent consideration.

- **Can the topic of controversy sustain interest and further thought?** Be wary of topics that have given rise to entrenched attitudes, fruitless divisiveness, perhaps weariness at the mere mention of the subject. You cannot choose your reader's opinions, but you can choose a topic that still offers opportunities for new insights rather than standard lines, new persuasive strategies rather than well-worn tactics.

Sample Opinions on Your Subject

Because the way people (above all your reader) respond to your chosen topic is so vital in determining your strategy, you would do well to get some sense of people's responses by doing a formal or informal survey. Your options are many: you may have access to professional surveys or opinion polls on the issue; you may, equipped with just a clipboard and some courage, go to the nearest shopping mall and poll passers-by; you may just chat the matter up among friends and acquaintances.

Given the compressed time frame of her summer-session course, Ruby made her assigned survey report a first stab at her research-paper topic. She did a survey of her friends on the issue she had decided to investigate: should the press publish the names of rape victims? Of the ten friends she interviewed, all female college students like herself (including those two friends who had been sexually assaulted but had not reported it), seven said yes, the media could go public with the names only if the victim gave permission; two said no; and one said she didn't know. No one chose the option "Yes, with no limitations" Ruby had written on her interview sheet. Asked, "If you had been raped and knew your name would be released by the press, would you be less inclined to report the rape?" seven said yes; three, no. When Ruby asked if rape victims whose names were published were likely to experience further victimization, all but one of her respondents said yes. Asked to elaborate, most of the respondents (no less than seven) said they thought victims would be shunned, taunted, and quite possibly molested. The only question for which Ruby did not get a clear majority decision was her last: she asked if publishing the names of rape victims would make rape seem more "normal" and less heinous a crime. Five said no, three said yes, and two said they didn't know.

Writing her survey report, Ruby had good reason to be glad she had conducted her survey by interviewing each individual rather than by simply distributing a questionnaire. She had asked not just what her respondents thought but invited them to say why. She could report with confidence, then, that "The main reason why my friends were against the media giving victims' names was that it is an invasion of privacy. Rape is a traumatic experience, and they felt the victim should not be exposed to the additional strain of public attention." Inviting her respondents to explore their feelings on the issue made her report much richer than it would have been had she simply tabulated yes or no answers to questions. For instance, Ruby noted that a thoughtful minority, putting themselves in the position of rape victims, "thought publicity would prolong their anguish by making it impossible for them to forget the rape. They said they thought the emotional wounds would heal more easily if they were spared questions and reminders. Two said that even sympathy would upset them." Here's how Ruby concluded her survey report:

> Overall, my survey results were quite close to my own opinions. Most of my friends agreed that although victims should be allowed to give their names if they wish, the media should not reveal their identity without their consent. The uniquely personal nature of the crime makes it especially important to respect the privacy of the victim.

Her instructor called the paper

> . . . thoughtful, detailed, to-the-point, topical. Its great strength is the way it offers, in addition to the answers you received, the thoughts and principles and reasoning informing those answers. Rich in that sense, it's a bit thin from another perspective. You propose to find out what "young people" think about this issue, but the survey is actually of ten of "my friends," and (as tends to be the case with friends) you find they tend to agree with you. What about the people who don't think the way you do? Perhaps that's a question your research paper will answer.

Thinking Critically about Ruby's Survey Report

1. Why is disagreement so important? Can't it be enough just to have one side of an argument well fleshed out?

2. Can you think of a way Ruby's survey might have developed a wider range of opinion but taken about the same amount of time? Would a broader range of opinion be worth the loss of some depth in reasons given for holding an opinion?

3. Could Ruby have developed—can you extrapolate—some sense of what opposing opinions might be from the responses she did get? Why or why not?

TRIAL RUN

Take an informal poll of opinions on your topic, even if you just follow Ruby's example of finding out what friends think. Like Ruby, you may well find that your friends—typically people at your own age and stage in life—will feel much as you do about an issue. If they don't, that's certainly useful to know. Even if they do, they are likely to identify points of interest and perspectives that wouldn't have occurred to you on your own.

Better yet, seek people outside of your mental set and age group. See if you can't reach some who represent significant differences of opinions. And see if you can't go beyond asking one or two yes-or-no questions. Remember that you are best served by polling practices that give you some sense, not just of different opinions, but also of reasons those opinions are held.

CHECKLIST: SURVEYING OPINIONS

- **Are you making a point of getting disparate points of view?** You need to "randomize your sample" (as statisticians say): poll different age groups, income groups, etc. Your topic may require you to go out of your way to get certain people in your sampling. A poll on what ought to be done about date rape should reach out to both genders, for instance.

- **Are you allowing respondents to elaborate on their reasons?** If Ruby's survey lacked range, it did have depth—and remember that the reasoning behind opinions is absolutely crucial for a deductive argument.

- **Have you planned your sampling of opinion to ensure the sort of results you need?** Ruby conducted interviews so as to explore the opinions of her respondents—and she thought a series of questions through ahead of time. Think about developing a questionnaire or an interview script so that you can ask, not just the big question, but the other questions it brings to mind.

Research Your Subject

By the time she had her survey report behind her, Ruby was three weeks into the six-week intensive term. It was high time to begin research in earnest. With some help from a reference librarian, she already had two articles from the *New York Times* (a newspaper that does its own index). Her instructor had told the class that people researching current events should pretty much stick to periodical literature anyway, that books spent so much time in publication that even those recently published contained fairly dated information, useful chiefly as background. Asking her instructor after class if there was a useful background book on her topic, Ruby was told that Susan Brownmiller's *Against Our Will* (1985) might be good.

Ruby went straight to the library and typed the name *Brownmiller, Susan* into the one of the terminals of the library's new computerized catalog. Several books were listed, including the one her instructor had mentioned. When she called it up on the screen, however, she saw the notation MISSING: ASK LIBRARIAN FOR ASSISTANCE. When she did just that, she learned that the two forms of assistance were ordering a new copy and borrowing a copy from another library on interlibrary loan. Either option would almost certainly get the book to her after her research paper had to be done. Ruby went back to the terminal screen and wrote down the catalog number, then went to take a look in that part of the stacks. If the library didn't have that particular book, it might have others in that same area she could use. After looking the shelves over, she decided to check out two. One, with a 1980 copyright, was rather dated, but it had the promising title *Rape and Woman's Identity.* The other, titled simply *Rape* and with a 1986 copyright, was a collection of scholarly articles, including one called "Rape and the Silencing of the Feminine." Then, working with two microfilm indexes—the Newspaper Index and the Magazine Index—for about an hour, Ruby came up with the titles of half a dozen newspaper and magazine articles. It felt like a good day's work.

The next day Ruby had the day off from classes, so she looked over the two books. She was disappointed. That scholarly piece about silencing the feminine was written by an anthropologist who wrote on tribal societies in Polynesia, South America, Africa, New Guinea, and Sumatra; the conclusion was that rape occurred more frequently in societies that emphasized "silencing the feminine" in *men.* Other pieces in the book were about Australia, New Zealand, and especially England; for the first time Ruby noticed the book had a British publisher. The other book, *Rape and Woman's Identity,* turned out to be using "identity" in a psychological sense, not in terms of revealing someone's "identity," but she earmarked a couple of pages with passages that might be worth quoting.

Thinking Critically about Ruby's Research Process

1. Ruby's instructor had told her that, especially for people researching current topics, books would be useful chiefly as sources of background information. What kind of background information would you want to have as the reader of a paper on Ruby's topic?

2. Suppose that Ruby's lack of books was not due chiefly to a lack of time on her part, that there really wasn't much of anything in the way of book-length treatments of her subject (as there wasn't, say, of AIDS in the early eighties). Can you think of how you might use the fact of a lack of sources on your subject in your argument?

3. Ruby found out the hard way that the focus of a source is crucial, and that titles can be misleading. If the sources you find originate in other countries or approach your topic from angles quite unlike your own, can this, too, be somehow turned to your advantage?

TRIAL RUN

Take an exploratory first stab at getting your hands on some sources on your topic (editorials might be especially useful at this preliminary point) and see how positions are being laid out. A single article may have, quite literally, a good dozen positions for you to consider. They will be sketched out all too briefly perhaps, but they will be enough to suggest what you have to contend with. Perhaps it would be a good idea to do a double-entry journal (as discussed in Chapter 8), a journal in which you could record what others have said on one side and how you respond on the other.

Use your library and all that it offers: indexes, reference librarians, tours or workshops or computer searches (if they're offered). You might want to consult Chapter 17, which offers detailed advice on locating and keeping track of sources. However you proceed, you're likely to find that doing research is a thing of fits and starts, bursts of energy and quirks of luck. Like Ruby, you may find a touted source is not to be had, that another that looks useful really isn't, that a single article may give you half the statements you need to sketch out the opposition. Things work that way in real life. So we won't prescribe a list of procedures for you, but we will give you a few questions to keep in mind.

CHECKLIST: RESEARCHING A TOPIC

- **Are you giving yourself enough time?** Research can be a quirky business, as we said. A corollary of Murphy's Law ("If something can go wrong, it will") is "Whatever it is, it will take longer than you think."

- **Are you letting sources lead you to sources?** Let's say one source puts you on to two more sources (for a total of three), and those two give you four more (for a total of seven), and those four give you eight more (for a total of fifteen). But the best of them all may be the fifteenth—another reason to give yourself time.

- **Are you considering your sources?** When working with opinions, you need to ponder the reasons for holding them. (Why do you suppose the positions Ruby contended with were held by important people in the media?) As you review the opinions held by others, consider their contexts, their interests, their stakes in the matter.

COMPOSING THE FIRST DRAFT

Keep Track of Positions and Not Just Sources

Drafting and research tend to run almost concurrently, so it's hard to tell when one leaves off and the other begins. We were just speaking of considering your sources, for instance. Once you begin not just checking sources out of the library but checking them out in the sense of looking at what they have to say, you're well into the drafting process. And one of the things you need to see, as you check out those sources, is that a single source almost always represents a variety of positions.

One of the subjects covered by Ruby's class was identifying points of view or positions or voices in a source. The instructor noted that an article may be the expression of a viewpoint, but it is likely to contain a host of viewpoints—opponents cited, allies enlisted, expert testimony called on. The class went over a brief newspaper editorial suggesting that educational standards were declining; students identified more than a dozen "subject positions" (as the instructor called them).

Again, Ruby went straight to the library after class. She got her hands on those articles she had found in the indexes, copied them, and headed home. Using green and yellow markers, she began identifying statements in each that were either *for* (yellow) or *against* (green) the publishing of the names of rape victims. In a notebook, she began noting who held what position and why. Two positions seemed to her especially important, both of them opposed to Ruby's own position of not making rape victims' names public. One was that of Michael Gartner, who took responsibility for releasing the name of the victim in the Palm Beach rape case; he held that releasing the name was justified by the public's right to know. The other was that of newspaper editor Geneva Overholser, who held that making the names of victims public might more effectively combat rape by getting all the facts about the all-too-common crime out in the open.

TRIAL RUN

Once you have a few articles on hand, do a tabulation of "subject positions." (Everyone quoted or even alluded to in a piece represents a "subject position," as do viewpoints sketched but not ascribed to specific individuals.) You might begin by using colored highlighters as Ruby did, but don't neglect to come up with discriminations more fine-tuned than simply "for" and "against." Note not just differences in positions but other (possibly motivating) relevant differences: gender, age, social circumstances, religion, and so on. (Ruby, for instance, had assumed that women, especially feminists, would incline to her position, and so found Overholser's position more of a challenge to her own than Gartner's, though both were "media people.")

Contend with the Opposition

It may be helpful to keep in mind that the word *opposition* has the word *position* in it: it's the position you want to keep your focus on. Your job is emphatically not to behave like a sleazy politician and attack your opponent. Logicians call that an *ad hominem* ("at the person") attack and note, quite properly, that is not a way of advancing an argument but a way of avoiding real argument, taking the spotlight off a position on an issue and putting it on the individual who holds that position. Still, you need to consider your source because vested interests and personal stakes do bear on the reasons a person takes a position. And you do need to attend to the reasons, if not the person. How do you examine your opponents' reasoning? Here are some basic ways, exemplified by the strategies Ruby used in her paper:

1. **Uncover premises—stated and unstated.** You need to "unpack" statements, taking inventory of motivations and implications. Take the public's-right-to-know argument advanced by Gartner. You don't say the public has a right to know unless you believe that it's good for the public to know. What's more, this right has some bearing on other rights like freedom of speech and the press. Further, asserting this right in a world of contending rights also means giving it priority over other rights, notably someone's right to privacy. Finally, asserting this right in the context of an argument over whether the press should release the names of rape victims carries the obvious implication that it is germane to the argument. Ruby does not reject all of these premises; she does not propose to infringe on the freedom of the press. But she does question others, noting, for instance, that courts have held that the "public's right to know" can get in the way of a fair trial (that, in other words, it's not always a good thing).

2. **Search out contradictions.** The first thing Ruby does with Gartner's assertion is to suggest that it does not so much address the issue as dodge it. "The more we tell our viewers," he says, "the better informed they will be in making up their own minds." But, as Ruby points out, "Once the public has been 'informed' of the victim's name, their minds, at least on this issue, have already been made up for them...." It is hard to object to what Gartner says, but Ruby finds it easy to say that it's not really relevant to the discussion. Like Ruby, you may find that an opponent makes high-sounding claims about the virtues of, say, Mom, the flag, and apple pie, when Mom, the flag, and apple pie really have nothing to do with the issue at hand.

3. **Pursue consequences.** Anytime anyone says something should happen, one (typically unstated) premise is that it won't have unfortunate consequences that will make us wish that it hadn't happened. Supporting the idea that rape victims' names can and should be reported, Gartner and Overholser imply that this practice will be largely positive in its effects; Overholser says this explicitly. Ruby challenges this assumption, noting that victims who have gone public have regretted it, that her survey respondents tell her such a practice would make them reluctant to report rapes, and so on. If someone proposes a change you resist—or resists a change you advocate—on the basis of one scenario, you need to do some scenario painting yourself.

4. **Think through choices.** We don't want to suggest that arguing over principles is a good-guys/bad-guys thing. Often the argument is over choices that are hard to make. Let's face it: in a perfect world, we wouldn't have to argue over what to do with the names of rape victims because there wouldn't be any. In "our far from perfect society," as Ruby calls it, we have uncomfortable decisions to make. Either limits are imposed on the public's right to know or incursions are made on the victim's right to privacy. You have to weigh those choices and give your reasons for the choice you make. But don't suppose they're always either/or, black-or-white, "you're-either-for-me-or-against-me" decisions. Ruby didn't. Looking at some of the arguments for and against publishing victims' names, she might have been led to think that the press either should or shouldn't. What she realized, however, was that the choice could be made on an individual basis, by the individual most immediately concerned: the victim. Choices don't always come in pairs; there is often another option, another angle.

Establish Your Own Position

You can't just berate the opposition; you have to make your own stand. But this is by no mean utterly distinct from checking out what others—especially others you disagree with—have said. You don't oppose a position without envisioning an alternative, and you don't envision an alternative without trying to address the problems of that other position and things the proponents of that position have forgotten or suppressed.

As you'll see, for instance, Ruby was the only "subject position" in her paper raising the issue of real risk to the victim. This potential disadvantage of publishing victims' names is an important part of her argument—not least of all because no one else seems to be thinking of it (though Ruby herself got some prompting from her survey respondents). When she does find herself sharing a premise with an opponent (believing with Geneva Overholser, for instance, that the public needs a heightened awareness of rape), Ruby is able to see other means of realizing shared goals and priorities. (In this instance, she proposes public education and safety campaigns.) Faced with a choice she feels neither she nor the press has the right to make, she offers the alternative of letting the victims themselves decide.

What you do with sources will have much to do with your own topic, your own points of contention, your own lines of thought. But remember that the operative word here is "your": it's your paper, however much it is built around what others think and say. Ultimately, what tips the balances as you test premises and extrapolate consequences and come to conclusions is your sense of what should be. You make choices on the basis of your priorities. That's what makes the paper yours, despite all the other voices or positions it contains. Keep that in mind.

RETHINKING AND REVISING

Make Sure Your Presentation Is Balanced

Pressed for time, Ruby went right from work on identifying various positions to doing a draft, the whole of it written in two long days over a weekend. Reading it over when she was done, Ruby saw that it had one major problem: she had become so caught up in charting the positions of the various parties that she hadn't presented her position until the last two paragraphs. For other assignments, Ruby had found it difficult to see what about a draft needed work, at least until her instructor or a classmate had pointed it out to her. This time, she didn't need another reader to tell her that she was waiting too long to present her own "subject position." The position she was taking mattered to her, and looking at opposing viewpoints had only made her think it through still further, answering objections, fleshing out her reasoning, pondering more deeply. It was a good position, one she could present with conviction, in what was, after all, *her* paper. She resolved to give it priority in her final version.

Ruby's predicament represents one of the two unfortunate tendencies you want to be wary of: the tendency to give accounts of who's saying or thinking what for pages, finally giving the author's position only at the end. Don't bury yourself in your own paper. The other tendency is the opposite: scarcely acknowledging opposing viewpoints in the process of sketching out your own—or giving them cognizance but no real substance by leaving out the reasoning that makes them points you have to grapple with. It's not enough to reject an opposing viewpoint; you must say why. And it's difficult to do that without giving some substance to why someone else might hold it in the first place.

Do Unto Yourself What You've Done Unto Others

We keep urging you to look at your writing with a reader's eyes. Much of this chapter is about being an especially demanding reader, one who unpacks statements and looks for hidden premises; one who questions relevance and seeks out contradictions; one who thinks through unforeseen or unacknowledged consequences; one who weighs hard choices but resists false dilemmas. Now it's time to turn that scrutinizing gaze on your draft. Do you seem honest and up-front in your reasoning? Have you explained yourself thoroughly? Do you seem fair and honorable in your handling of the opposition? Are you careful to be consistent in your logic? If you set up hypothetical situations or make predictions, do you explore them thoroughly? Do you show yourself careful to resist oversimplifications? What do you need to do? Do it.

CHECKLIST: REVISING YOUR DRAFT

- **Are you clear about your subject and purpose from the outset?** The analysis of an issue and positions on it won't be nearly as clear if you don't give some preliminary sense of your specific focus and viewpoint.
- **Have you researched your subject thoroughly and made the best possible use of that research?** Sometimes last-minute research might be needed to plug a gap; sometimes just more thought may allow you to get more out of what you have on hand.
- **Are the positions discussed explored in some depth?** Remember that you need to dig all the way to premises and motives—and to seem fair in so doing.
- **Have you fairly represented your own position as well?** Keep in mind that this is not a report but an argument—and that your position in your argument should be a pervading presence in your paper, not an afterthought.

PRESENTING RUBY'S FINAL DRAFT

Rape: Should the Press Publish the Victims' Names?

Ruby Huang

1

Ruby gets right to the point: what the debate is about and what her own position is.

The question of whether the media should reveal the names of rape victims is highly controversial and has provoked intense debate, particularly among journalists and feminists. The answers bear not just on the victims but on the public's perception of rape as a crime. Here I will review the arguments on both sides and present my own position, which, stated simply, is that the decision to go public should rest with the individual woman concerned.

2

Background is briefly presented, including specific impetus for the debate.

Before the 1970s it was not unusual for the media to publish names of rape victims, but since then editors have maintained a voluntary silence due to pressure from women who think publicity will discourage victims from reporting rapes ("Editors Debate" 6). This, and a reluctance to cause the victims further pain, kept names out of the media for a long time, but recently there has been renewed interest in the subject after the name of the victim was revealed in the William Kennedy Smith case in Palm Beach. Although NBC justified airing the name on the grounds that it was already well-known who the woman was, the incident has sparked a new, intensified discussion of the ethical and legal questions surrounding the issue.

3

Ruby introduces one of the two major challenges to her position. She questions its validity even as she introduces it, drawing support from another journalist who stresses the complexity of the issue.

Among journalists, two opinions seem to prevail. One is that news is news, and the press has a right to print anything that will be of interest to readers. Michael G. Gartner, president of NBC News, has said, "The more we tell our viewers, the better informed they will be in making up their own minds" ("Naming Names" 29). However, this may be just an attempt to evade the ethical dilemma involved, taking the burden off those who report the news by leaving everything up to those who listen to broadcasts and read the newspapers. Once the public has been "informed" of the victim's name, their minds, at least on this issue, have already been made up for them; the question of the victim's right to privacy or anonymity has already been answered by the media. I am more inclined to agree with Frank A. Daniels III, who said, "It's a problem that has no right answer. . . . It goes to the heart of male-female relations, the power of sex, the invasive nature of the crime of rape and how society has stigmatized it" ("Editors Debate" 6).

4

Ruby introduces the other major challenge to her position.

Stigmatization is a key issue in this controversy. Most people engaged in the debate agree that it is wrong to stigmatize the victims, but they disagree about whether identifying the victims will make things better or worse. Those who are in favor of naming names argue that greater publicity will reduce the shame attached to being a rape victim. Geneva Overholser, editor of the <u>Des Moines Register</u>, said "As long as rape is deemed unspeakable, public outrage will be muted as well" ("Breaking Silence" 20).

5

She questions its validity in a separate paragraph. She does so because she has two arguments to counter it with, each accompanied by supporting evidence.

I myself find the contrary argument more persuasive. If the media routinely publish victims' names, I think women will be more, not less, reluctant to report rape. Reducing the stigma attached to rape and increasing public awareness are surely desirable goals, but I do not think that many women want to be pioneers, especially when that means suffering the unwanted attention that rape victims still attract in our far from perfect society. One woman who did go public later regretted it. She said, "When people know you have been raped, they know or think they know something sexual about you. It makes people uncomfortable" ("Different Kind" D3). It is also arguable that it is not necessary to publish names in order to provoke public sympathy and outrage. The identity of the Central Park jogger was never revealed, but the case attracted a lot of attention and generated much sympathy and concern for the victim, not just here in New York but nationwide.

6

Ruby once again stresses the complexity of the

Publishing the names of rape victims is not the only way to change people's attitudes about rape, and, as Frank Daniels said, the problem of rape reflects deeper questions concerning relations between men and women in our society. The recent

issue. Problems stem from deep-rooted attitudes. There can be no quick fixes.

debate about "date rape" in American universities is part of a reassessment of the relationship between the sexes. Women are increasingly rejecting traditional attitudes that define certain ways of dressing and behaving as "provocative" so that men may feel justified in assuming the sexual activity they initiate is actually invited. As women become more confident in fighting discrimination and sexual harassment, they will probably also become more willing to speak openly about their experiences of rape. But, in the meantime, it seems counterproductive to try to coerce them to do so by revealing their identities and denying them privacy.

7

Since Overholser argues for treating rape like other crimes, Ruby argues that it is a special case, a crime that places special burdens on the victim.

Rape is not the same as other crimes. It is a harrowing experience that may leave lasting emotional scars. As the sociologist William B. Sanders has noted, the way women are socially defined puts them in a double bind when they become rape victims: "When women are raped, their integrity is questioned on the basis of not resisting sufficiently even though the social role of women is mandated to do otherwise-- namely, to be passively dependent" (Rape and Women's Identity 141). In this sense, too, I do not think it is right to make rape victims reveal their identities unless they are sure they want to. In the course of a rape trial, a lot of personal information about the accuser's past sexual behavior is likely to be brought up by the defense in an attempt to undermine her reputation and make the charge of rape seem less plausible. No matter whether the victim wins the case or not, the public exposure of this personal information could put an additional strain on women who are already under great emotional strain. It is as if the women are presumed guilty until proven innocent so their assailants may be presumed innocent until proven guilty.

8

Ruby's concern for the victims of rape is borne out by interviewees who identify with such victims.

Recently I interviewed ten women at this college to see whether they had anything to add to the debate. I found that the majority of them felt the victims' privacy should be respected and they should not be forced to reveal their identities to the public. These women I interviewed admired women who had the courage to discuss their experience openly and endure the risk of being stigmatized, but they thought that this must be a painful process that most women, and certainly they themselves, would be unwilling to go through.

9

Ruby notes not just her interviewees' position on the issue, but also their reasons for

In general, the women felt that publishing victims' names would not be much help in combatting rape, and that it was more important to urge women to report the crime in the first place, regardless of whether they allowed their names to be published. Overall, the interviewees agreed with the editorial that said, "The stigma on rape victims is fading, but

taking such a
position.

10

Ruby holds that
concern for the
victims of rape
should have
precedence over
other concerns.

11

She explicitly
identifies "the
central concern"
as "the individ-
ual's right to
privacy" and
explains why.

Noting that the 12
right she holds
central conflicts
with the right
asserted by some
in the media,
Ruby expresses
some concern
about the possible
consequences of
that latter
position. 13

Returning to "the
complexities of
the issue," Ruby
opts for letting

it's still there, and the publication of these people's names--often against their wishes--would seem to us to be a cruel and not particularly effective way of combatting it" ("Rape: Naming Names" A22).

There are more serious issues at stake here than the issue of effective strategy in combatting rape. Another issue is safety for the victims. If victims' names and addresses are published in the newspapers and broadcast on the air, it will be easy for their attackers or possibly other criminals to find them. Admittedly, this would not happen in every case, not even in most cases, but it should never happen at all. Even if publicized victims were not physically assaulted, they could become the recipients of obscene phone calls or hate mail. Surely it would be preferable to spare them this.

A review of the arguments against revealing the victims' names shows that the central concern is the individual's right to privacy. In my opinion, it is healthier to allow women to decide for themselves whether they wish to give their names out to the public. People's attitudes about rape are changing, but this is a gradual process, and it is not fair to force women who have already suffered so much to bear the additional pressure of publicity. Even Nancy Ziegenmeyer, who won the Pulitzer Prize for her account of her own rape, did not want to have her identity revealed immediately after she was raped. It was seven months before she went public. I would imagine that many women would feel and act similarly, prefer-ring to choose their own time and their own words to discuss their experience, rather than being at the mercy of the whims of the often insensitive and sensationalist media.

Michael G. Gartner's policy for NBC News and the media gen-erally, "The more we tell, the better," is founded on the public's right to know, but it conflicts with the victims' right to privacy. People do have a right to make up their own minds, as Gartner insists, but information released by the press is never entirely neutral in its effects. The William Kennedy Smith case shows this by the way Smith's lawyers now argue that he cannot receive a fair trial because of all the advance publicity. If we are concerned that the press may prejudice the public against an alleged rapist, surely we must show the same concern for the victim.

Given the complexities of the issue, I think the best policy for the media is a case-by-case policy that takes the wishes of the victim into consideration. Of course women who are willing to reveal their identity should not be prevented from doing so, but I do not think the press should publish the names of rape victims without their consent. Those who believe,

victims them-
selves decide the
issue in individual
cases. She notes
that her position
can accommodate
the expressed
objectives of the
two major oppos-
ing positions to
some extent.

with Geneva Overholser, that "public outrage will be muted" if the names of rape victims are not released can do what they can to fuel public outrage against rape without doing so at the victims' expense. They can fight rape and sexual discrimination by putting their energies into public education, campaigns to make the streets safe for women, and so on. It is not important for the public to know the name of every rape victim, but it is important for both young people and adults to be reminded that rape is a brutal crime for which the man, not the woman, should be blamed.

List of Sources

Citations are
done MLA Style.
Note the reliance
on (then current)
newspapers and
news magazines.

"Breaking Silence." <u>The Economist</u> 28 July 1990:20.

Greenfield, Meg. "Palm Beach Runaround." <u>Washington Post</u> 22 April 1991:A9.

Huang, Ruby. Personal survey. June 1991.

Jones, Alex. "Editors Debate Rules on Rape Victims." <u>New York Times</u> 13 April 1991:A6.

Kantrowitz, Barbara. "Naming Names." <u>Newsweek</u> 29 April 1991:26-32.

Mann, Judy. "A Different Kind of Rape." <u>Washington Post</u> 24 April 1991:D3.

Overholser, Geneva. "Why Hide Rapes?" <u>New York Times</u> 11 July 1991:A19.

"Rape: Naming Names." <u>Washington Post</u> 19 April 1991:A22.

Sanders, William B. <u>Rape and Woman's Identity</u>. Beverly Hills: Sage, 1980.

Commentary on Ruby's Final Draft

We have a confession to make. Like many instructors we know, we have a pronounced distaste for any "The purpose of this paper is to..." opening. It seems to lack grace, subtlety, charm. It makes us want to say something like "Don't say what you're going to do; just do it." Ruby's introductory paragraph, then, is rubbing up against one of our pet peeves. "Here," she writes (where else? we wonder), "I will review the arguments on both sides and present my own position, which, stated simply, is that the decision to go public should rest with the individual woman concerned." We might wish that Ruby had broached the matter at hand a little less stiffly, but we might look beyond our own preferences for a moment to something more important. Two things, actually. First, Ruby gets right to the matter at hand; there is no beating around the bush. And that's important. Still more important, she gives her reader a sense of direction and even destination. This is especially important in a paper of this length. Research papers are relatively long rides for a reader; it's nice to know where you are going.

Since you've already been told that Ruby's draft saved the statement of her position till the last two paragraphs, you may think that her revised introductory paragraph (and particularly its last sentence) served as her quick fix. In fact, if you were to read her paper without the benefit of that first paragraph, it wouldn't take you long to figure out her position. Her strategy is not simply to state it at the outset, but to restate it and elaborate it throughout her paper. After she notes Gartner's position, for instance, she says, "I am more inclined to agree with Frank A. Daniels III...." Similarly, she follows a quotation from Geneva Overholser with the statement, "I myself find the contrary argument more persuasive." And so it goes throughout her paper.

But what actually is Ruby doing? Is she really just citing the opposition and then saying she doesn't agree? Hardly. For one thing, simple citations won't do; she has to define positions as economically as possible while taking care not to seem to oversimplify. Then—and this is the key—she has to unpack those positions. Are they wrapped in sound reasoning? Do they hide ulterior motives? Are they tied up all too neatly?

Ruby begins making her case even as she seems to be simply placing it in context. Her second paragraph deftly justifies her lack of background by pointing to a particular historical moment and even a particular case as the impetus for a new consideration of the issue. And the way she describes that case suggests, subtly but still clearly enough, that the impetus is a story rich in temptations for the press to publicize, sensationalize, dig for dirt. The revelation that, in this case, this had included the temptation to publicize the alleged victim's name, and that NBC News succumbed to that temptation, sets up Ruby for her first encounter with the opposition, here in the person of Michael G. Gartner, (now former) president of NBC News. She makes due note of the public's-right-to-know argument, suggests that it is more of a way of dodging the issue than addressing it, and presents an alternative position she can endorse. This in fact establishes her pattern for dealing with opposing viewpoints. Sketched out graphically, it might look something like this:

Opposing viewpoint	Ruby's critique of it	The alternative
the public has a right to know/decide	the public isn't given a choice of knowing	recognize how complex the issue of rape is; leave the choice to victim
publishing names will increase sympathy for victims, outrage against the crime	this will increase reluctance to report rapes and also suffering of the victims	realize attitudes are changing slowly; don't make victims take the lead; there are other ways

It isn't a very extensive chart, but then addressing the opposition is only a part—about a third—of Ruby's whole paper. Basically, the opposition has two arguments Ruby needs to counter. One, centering on the public's right to know, is attributed to Gartner. The other, suggesting that naming victim's names will make rape seem less shrouded in mystery, more likely to be reported, more open to public attention and outrage, is attributed to Geneva Overholser.

Ruby finds Gartner's is the easier position to respond to. As she presents his position, Ruby simply needs to note that the public's right to know is advanced without what she feels is adequate concern for the victim's right to privacy. Overholser's position, as Ruby presents it, is more difficult. Both she and Overholser have to be speculative about the effects of "naming names," though Ruby does have some anecdotal evidence about a victim who released her name and regretted it, and also about a victim (the Central Park jogger) who remained anonymous yet was the focus of "much sympathy and concern." (Anecdotal evidence is the sort of evidence that gives examples in support of your point, but without statistics or other, wider samplings of the phenomenon that would show those examples to be representative. As one of our own teachers used to say, "Examples only exemplify; they don't prove anything.")

With the sixth paragraph, Ruby is no longer addressing Overholser's position explicitly, but she has broadened her focus—as Overholser does—to consider, in general terms, the status of rape as a crime and the public's perception of it. She notes that attitudes are changing, citing a new attention to "date rape" and an increased resistance to sexual harassment and sexual discrimination. If Overholser is suggesting that names be named for the sake of such social progress, Ruby implies, the policy really doesn't seem necessary, especially considering the cost to the victim.

It is precisely that cost she turns to next. She has said that "Stigmatization is a key issue," and now she grounds that issue in evidence and reasoning, citing Sanders on typical perceptions of the victims and noting the strategy of defense counsel in rape trials. She might have brought more evidence to bear on this point, but she is focusing on the public's perception, and so she turns to her survey results. She is not just speculating on women's reactions to having their identities revealed if and when they become rape victims; she has data. It isn't a wealth of data, not much more than anecdotal evidence, really—she notes she is drawing on interviews with "ten women at this college"—but it does help to develop her projections about the effects naming names would have on important matters like willingness to report a rape in the first place.

Her tenth paragraph raises an issue that came up in her survey, though Ruby doesn't mention the survey here. She suggests that revealing identities might put victims at further risk. Here, interestingly, she doesn't provide any evidence at all, just the posing of a possibility. But does she need to substantiate the likelihood of further victimization, especially since she is careful to qualify it, saying that "this would not happen in every case, not even in most cases, but it should never happen at all"? Like Gartner and Overholser, she is focusing on persuasive reasoning, not hard data. She is trying to sway her readers, not convince them. It's worth noting that, at this point, she is not responding to Gartner or Overholser at all. At least in the pared down versions of their positions Ruby has provided, neither considers the issue of further risk to the victim. Ruby is not just arguing against their reasons for releasing victims' names; she is also considering other reasons *not* to release names. All this helps to make her case.

She's just about done making it. She begins her summation, like a lawyer making concluding remarks to a jury. "A review of the arguments against revealing the victims' names shows that the central concern is the individual's right to privacy." Lest we should begin to feel a can't-see-the-forest-for-the-trees effect at this point, she focuses our attention on a single principle. It doesn't really give us a reductive sense of what she is saying (whether the violation of privacy causes anxiety or a real risk to life, it remains a violation), and so we have a point to focus on. It's a good thing, because Ruby's strategy as she winds up is to stress complexity—changing attitudes, a woman's right to choose not just whether to go public but when and how, the effect of publicity on the possibility of a fair trial.

"Given the complexities of the issue," Ruby says in her last paragraph (having just accentuated the complexities), "I think the best policy for the media is a case-by-case policy that takes the wishes of the victim into consideration." It is essentially the same position she broached in her opening paragraph, but we are fully apprised of why she holds it at this point. We may be so appreciative of "the complexities of the issue," thanks to Ruby, that we may be glad she has spared us the need to make or endorse any way of resolving them once and for all. If we're especially attentive, we may even notice that Ruby's proposal has a little something in it for the noble opposition. For Gartner, there is the possibility of publishing the victim's names, if only "with their consent." For Overholser, for whom a policy of publishing names was a means of addressing the public's perception of rape, Ruby proposes other means of doing this, notably education. This does not mean that Ruby is willing to be accommodating at the expense of her convictions. Her concluding sentence makes her uncompromising position clear and forceful. But she has given her opponents' positions thoughtful attention and reasoned response. That's just the sort of balance a good deductive argument should strive for.

Questions for Further Thought

1. How clear is the distinction between inductive arguments and deductive ones? For example, one argument here is that reporting rape victims' names will make victims more reluctant to report rapes. Isn't that a kind of inference or inductive point made on the basis of limited evidence?

2. That question raises another one. It looks as if a fairly complex argument, even one as short as Ruby's, is actually a collection of arguments (here arguments about consequences, about rights, about priorities).

How varied and involved can or should such collections of arguments get? What makes them unified rather than miscellaneous collections?

3. When you "unpack" a statement, how do you know you're uncovering what's actually there—and not ascribing premises or motives or implications that aren't really a part of the "package"?

4. If matters of opinion must rest on premises and principles, this presumably includes notions of what, in argumentation, passes for fairness or coherence or reasonableness or persuasiveness. How would you "unpack" these concepts? What principles or premises do they rest on?

CHAPTER TWELVE

THE DIALECTICAL RESEARCH PAPER

We often imagine written arguments on the model of a court of law: lawyers argue their cases before a judge or jury, whose verdict determines whether they argued persuasively. But how are laws made in the first place? Legislators representing a variety of interests debate a bill sponsored by one of their members. Lobbying goes on; alliances are formed; amendments are made. The successful bill is not just a triumph of persuasion; it is the result of compromise. The same is true of much "real-world" writing. Imagine working out a contract with a client, recommending a change in office procedures, proposing a new marketing strategy. You would need to sound out the parties involved, balance interests and abilities, come up with something workable as well as desirable—and pitch it tactfully. In short, you would need to negotiate. This is an important means of working things out in the working world. It is also a good way to write a college research paper.

As you've seen in other parts of this book, writing is a collaborative activity in any number of ways (from getting input to getting feedback). Even working in apparent isolation, a writer must gauge the reader's expectations, other authors' contributions, opposing arguments. Just in the last chapter, for instance, we stressed how much depends on your premises when you argue, how your reader might respond to them, how opponents might respond. The difference here is that you don't simply imagine possible opposition, you meet with it—hear the other side out, seek common ground, negotiate a compromise. If other arguments can be seen as debates against unseen opponents, the dialectical or dialogic argument can be seen as a conversation, a process of reaching agreement rather than winning a contest. The "other side" becomes a resource instead of an obstacle. And your own point of view is not simply presented; it's challenged, tested, tempered by the resistance it meets with. The result of this process is what any good argument for change should be: not just the airing of your opinion, but the presentation of a workable plan.

As an example of this process and its result, we have the story of Jennifer Leung's paper "Giving Freshmen Access to a Freshman Course," a paper treating a local issue and so relying primarily on local (or on-site) sources. The problem Jennifer chose to treat was that the introductory course in her major was always closed out by the time freshmen and most sophomores were scheduled to register. As she tried to propose a remedy to what she saw as a problem, she found herself confronting, not just institutional inertia, but opposition from within that academic department. She persevered in her project, not by speaking out against the opposition, but by taking it into account: she heard and addressed objections, solicited support, modified her reasoning. Her eventual success is not a victory that is someone else's defeat, but a triumph of mediation. That's the way it is with the dialectical research paper.

WRITING ASSIGNMENT

Tackle an issue that's been bugging you—not something that would take an act of Congress or a Supreme Court decision, but something closer to home, more pressing, more manageable. Once you've decided what you want changed—and how you can make a case for making others want the same—actively seek out those who could be doing something about the situation but aren't. What's the story at their end? Are there difficulties you weren't aware of, resistances you can quell, demands you can meet? Make addressing objections and resistances an important part of your paper.

READING THE WRITING ASSIGNMENT

Staking out a topic represents precisely that point in the research-paper process where communication between teacher and student is most likely to break down. The teacher wants the topic to be both "narrow" and "significant." " 'Narrow' and 'significant'?" thinks the student. "Aren't those contradictory terms?" Deciding that if the topic is "narrow" it can't be truly "significant" (and vice versa), the student too often decides on something big and important (and sure to figure in a wealth of sources), while the teacher jokes with colleagues about the students who, despite all remonstrations to the contrary, are determined to solve the problem of world hunger or the plight of the homeless in six to eight pages.

The student who wants to tackle something important is right. No one should be committed to a topic that will make the research paper an exercise in triviality. But a big, burning issue is often intractable, and writing on one is too often done without real hope of making any difference, actually effecting any change—which makes the research paper just an exercise in doing something the teacher requires. "Narrowness" is a bad term: what you want is focus, particularity, and ideally the sort of scope within which you can make a real difference.

Having that sort of scope is doubly important in this case, because this writing assignment isn't an invitation to take a pet peeve out for a walk. You must confront (and even contend with) opposition to your views. Maybe you don't like the way registration works each term. Maybe you (and others) have problems with parking on campus. Maybe you want to resist a looming tuition hike. Or maybe there's something that needs changing in your neighborhood: an eyesore that should be removed, a roadway that needs bikepaths, an intersection that ought to have a traffic light. Pursuing any such possibility means not just getting the relevant data but contacting the parties involved, especially any party that might obstruct the change you'll be pushing for. This can mean using your interpersonal skills more than another kind of research paper might require, but it can also mean using the library less. And if talking things through and working them out is a bit intimidating as a prospect, it can be enormously satisfying once done.

DISCOVERING IDEAS

Take Inventory

Before you begin casting about for a suitable subject, you might ask yourself if you haven't already done some work on one. Maybe an earlier paper, especially something you did for Section Two, could feed into this project. That's what happened in Jennifer Leung's case. It's a long story—since her paper can be traced back through not one but two assignments—but it's worth going into, above all for the way it shows how research papers are not always born in flashes of inspiration; at least as often they begin with missteps and thwarted expectations.

Jennifer's Leung's work on her research paper actually began with her survey paper (her response to the sort of assignment outlined in Chapter 5). She had determined to write about a very specific population: students who were like her in being Chinese-American, female, and interested in majoring in accounting. She herself had decided to major in accounting without knowing very much about it either as a career or as an academic major, and she wanted to know what other students like her might know. Jennifer just knew that she was good with numbers and that accountants tended to be well-paid. To her dismay, though she found and interviewed fifteen female Chinese-American students who planned to major in accounting, she didn't find a single one who seemed to know much more about accounting than she did. Yes, they had a knack for math; yes, they understood that accounting was an honorable and lucrative profession; no, they didn't know what courses in the major were like; no, they didn't know about the different kinds of accounting called for in the business world. "Not one of them,"

Jennifer wrote in her paper, "can explain what it is exactly that an accountant (or an accounting major) does. To be honest, neither can I."

It was some small consolation that Jennifer's survey at least turned up the apparent cause of her respondents' ignorance about accounting: eleven were freshmen (like Jennifer), four were sophomores, and none had taken Accounting 1101: Introduction to Accounting—the course that was the basis for the accounting major. They had all wanted to, but accounting was a popular major, and so ACC 1101 was a popular course. Seniors and juniors registered first; as sophomores and freshmen registered, they learned that the available sections were all filled. This always happened, they were told.

Jennifer was frustrated by her survey results—she had been looking for something she didn't find—but her instructor assured her that the results were truly edifying, that surveys were often used to demonstrate a need or a problem. Jennifer accepted the invitation to use her survey as the basis for the short argument she was assigned (the sort of assignment outlined in Chapter 6). Here is how that paper began:

> The college bulletin states that courses numbered 1000 are courses for first-year students, so presumably freshmen and sophomores can take Accounting 1101. But many accounting and business majors who already have upper sophomore status are denied this privilege because of the insufficient number of ACC 1101 sections that are offered. These victims face a catastrophic consequence: they may not graduate in four years as they expected.

Words like "victims" and "catastrophic" give it away: though it was earnest and even impassioned at points, Jennifer's argument was not so much an attempt at persuasion as a railing against injustice. Her instructor, in commenting on it, wondered if it might not be recast:

> I'm impressed—especially by the strength of your feelings. It's clear that you feel something is terribly wrong, and I'm sure there are others who feel as you do. But what can be done? You say, "It's about time for the Accountancy Department to do something to solve the problem." What, exactly, would that "something" be? What more would you need to find out about the problem before proposing a solution? What would you then propose? How much thought would you need to give to implementation? What would be the likelihood that your recommendation would be acted on? What do you think about turning this into a research project?

Jennifer was not surprised by that last question. The instructor had billed the short argument as a possible first run at the researched argument. And the prospect suited her. She had ideas. The changes she had in mind seemed to be commonsensical. She had already done some preliminary research—her survey, for instance. True, a conference with her instructor clarified the need to do further research, not just into the solution, but also in defining the problem. She has spoken of "many" students without specifying *how* many, for instance, and she had alluded to "catastrophic consequences" without clarifying whether these would be financial, emotional, academic, or all of the above. But these hardly seemed insuperable difficulties. The important thing was that she was genuinely interested in the matter, and her instructor had endorsed her interest, saying (at the end of the comment on her argument), "Local problems are not little problems; they're precisely the problems that tend to loom largest—and to seem most responsive to the kind of careful thinking you show yourself capable of here." So Jennifer was decided, and two papers she felt rather disappointed with formed the basis for what turned out to be a very fine research paper.

TRIAL RUN

Look back over the writing you've done. Is there a line of thinking you want to pursue further (or perhaps turn the corner on)? Try extending some part of your work thus far. Even if it was only a sidelight before, it might deserve the spotlight now.

CHECKLIST: REASONS FOR EXTENDING WORK ALREADY DONE

1. **Save yourself time.** We're talking about extending work, not recycling it; still, such extensions tend to economize effort. Has your writing tapped into your experience or your circumstances in a way that might save you time on research (or at least indicate the directions research ought to pursue)?

2. **Get early access to second thoughts.** Too often we realize the best way to perform a task only when it's finished. Perhaps you've done work for which you could now avail yourself of such second thoughts. Or perhaps, like Jennifer, you got feedback on a paper pointing the way to a better, more ambitious project.

3. **Take care of unfinished business.** Was there a question you raised but didn't answer, a claim you made but didn't have the evidence to substantiate? Now's the time to follow through.

Test Your Subject

Whether you cast about for it or found it (or at least the seeds of it) in writing you've already done, let's suppose you have a point to argue, a change to advocate. Now, there are always reasons why things are the way they are; they may not be good ones, but their existence means you'll need to do some serious thinking. Your criticisms will have to be constructive, your suggestions sensible, your entire approach tactful. After all, you're not being asked just to dream up an improvement on the status quo; you're being asked to motivate that improvement, to be resourceful enough to outmanuever reluctance, maybe even real resistance.

TRIAL RUN

We recommend some controlled brainstorming. Make your general proposal a "should be" statement: Thus-and-such should be changed. (In Jennifer Leung's case, the statement would be "There should be more sections of ACC 1101.") Now change the "should be" statement into a "won't be" statement: Thus-and-such *won't* be changed. And come up with a list of reasons why it won't. (In Jennifer's case, the reasons why "there *won't* be more sections of ACC 1101" included concerns about costs, limited classroom space, and so on.)

Once you've come up with a list of reasons why what you want to see happen *won't* happen, take a good long look at it, considering it in light of the following two questions.

CHECKLIST: TESTING A TOPIC'S VIABILITY

1. Does that list of obstacles to your proposal make you feel defeated, awash in difficulties that make you think you'll never get beyond the wishful-thinking stage? If so, perhaps you had better try the exercise with some other topic, though there's the very real possibility you can salvage your basic idea by refining your focus, taking on a little less.

2. Do you instead feel energized, full of ideas about how objections can be met with, resistances can be overcome? If so, you've found your subject, and the best way to begin work on it may well be to jot down these good ideas while you have them in mind.

Form a Purpose

We should stress that the best way to develop a dialectical research paper is not to go picking a fight. You're not looking for a confrontation; you're looking for a change. You're also prepared to find that not everyone is looking at things the way you do. In a sense, this means what you're doing is quite the opposite of picking a fight: in a world of conflicting interests, you are looking for conflict resolution. The standard model for this is labor arbitration. The unions want as much in the way of money and benefits as they can get. Management wants to give as little as possible. Mediation means trying to satisfy both parties by moderating and balancing their demands.

TRIAL RUN

You've already done some thinking (in the previous Trial Run section) about resistance your proposal might meet with. Now try to imagine how you might cope with that. Are there concessions you can make without doing violence to your desired goals? Are there certain points on which you can expect flexibility from the other side? In a scenario of give-and-take, what might you give, and what might you take? Even at this early point, it might not be a bad idea to imagine the balancing act you might eventually perform.

At the initial stages of your project, of course, you can't know exactly what that will entail in your case. You're one of the parties, and you know what you want. You've also tried to imagine what stands in the way of getting what you want—and how you might deal with such obstructions. Going further means getting out there and doing research. As you prepare to do that, you need to keep in mind that your response is not to bully the opposition into submission. Nor is it to go on and on about what you think should happen, never really duly acknowledging the other parties and interests involved. Your purpose is neither to debate nor orate; it is to engage in dialogue. That means going out there, setting up interviews, doing research.

THE RESEARCH PROCESS

Before we say anything else, we want to stress that the research process is not a discrete stage of writing the research paper. You don't just find a subject, go out and research it, then sit down to write. Almost every careful writer finds, while drafting a research paper, that more research is needed. It's less obvious but no less true that, in a sense, research began before a subject was even chosen. Any writer is going to be wary of staking out a subject in an area of utter ignorance. So realize even as you "begin" to research that the research has already begun, that you come to this project with some useful resources already at the ready. And the research won't stop till you turn the paper in—stopping only then, not because you will have exhausted the process, but because an arbitrary deadline must be met.

Give Some Thought to On-Site Data

You may be struck, in examining Jennifer Leung's research paper, by the dearth of library sources. Learning to use the library and the rich array of sources it houses is a useful skill, without a doubt, but the use of sources close at hand (as in Jennifer's paper) is also valid. In fact, when the focus is on local concerns, local sources have a greater validity; library sources can't contribute much more than background. Most writing in the so-called real world relies on what is called "on-site data": material in the office files, a marketing study done by the folks in the marketing research department, sales figures for the past fiscal year.

Teachers often make a distinction between primary sources and secondary sources. Library sources are secondary sources; from them you get material second-hand: data gathered by others, experts as quoted by others. A primary source is straight-from-the-horse's-mouth stuff: you know what So-and-so thinks about something because you went and asked So-and-so. You can't do that with the president of the United States, but you can do it with your school's registrar or the head of campus security. And if what you're writing about is extending registration hours for evening students, the registrar or security chief is going to be more helpful than the president anyway.

As you plan your research, give some thought to resources besides the library. Are you looking into career possibilities for people who share your academic major? Then your campus's placement service will probably be your most useful source of data. Are you concerned about the incidence of crimes during after-dark hours in a poorly lit area? Your best source would be the local precinct's police records—or someone who has access to them. Does a local corporation seem to you to be ecologically irresponsible? You can contact that firm's public relations office for its side of the story. We can't presume to know what you're inclined to investigate, but we can assume that there will be relevant stores of information and opinions besides the library—and that, as you tap them, you'll feel yourself piecing together a story no one else but you can tell.

RIAL RUN

Take the time to make as comprehensive a list as you can of local, primary sources. Remember that the place to begin is with your envisioned opposition. Whatever individuals or institutional entities might resist your proposal can at the very least be asked to say why. Beyond that, remember that most firms and institutions typically have their own offices of records or research, sometimes even their own libraries. Local governments and politicians keep records on their functions and their constituencies; local newspapers typically have certain journalists and editors assigned to certain areas; and any college or university is an especially rich concentration of experts on a wide variety of subjects.

Use People as Sources

Important input for a dialogic (our other term for dialectical) research paper is obviously going to be dialogue. Jennifer's interviews with the two accounting professors were absolutely crucial. You'll see from her list of sources that they were also easy exercises in documentation: no page numbers, no publishing house, no other complications—just name and date.

Actually setting up and conducting an interview is more complicated than documenting it, so here's some advice.

CHECKLIST: PLANNING INTERVIEWS

- An arranged interview is better for everyone: you have time to prepare, and the interviewee is expecting you. If possible, then, call ahead and set it up.

- Do prepare. Think, not just about the questions you want to ask, but also the possible answers and where they might lead. Rare is the interviewee who will be delighted to meet with you again because there are some follow-up questions you neglected to ask the first time.

- Get as complete a transcript as you possibly can. If your interviewee doesn't mind, you might want to record the conversation. If your interviewee does mind, take extensive notes. If your interviewee minds even note-taking, write out an account of the interview as soon as it's over. However you keep track of what's said, consider it a courtesy to the interviewee to ask for confirmation or clarification of any remark that seems strange. Think how much difference failing to write down a little word like "not" might mean to a statement's meaning.

- Don't suppose interviews must be face-to-face confrontations, especially with hard-to-see people. Interviewing someone over the phone is, as the phone company would say, the next best thing to being there. Letters of inquiry are also useful, but the time span for a research paper means you will have to count on prompt replies—and you can't always.

- Like other sources, interviews can point you to still more sources; for instance, Jennifer was told something like her plan had been tried elsewhere. Give yourself time to track down such leads by scheduling interviews as early as possible in the research process.

COMPOSING THE FIRST DRAFT

Define the Problem

The standard term for the sort of paper you are working on is the problem-to-solution paper. The general organization takes you from the definition of the problem you have chosen to address to the solution you propose. You should be careful not to consider defining the problem and proposing the solution as two utterly separate tasks; any thought given to one must be thought given to the other as well. You are trying to argue not just *what* (the general change you advocate) should happen but *why* (your definition of the problem) and *how* (your solution). Looked at that way, your proposed solution (whatever it is) should suggest that defining the problem, for your purposes, is not just one task but two. You must make a change seem desirable, but you must also make it seem feasible. If you succeed in making a state of affairs seem just awful, so awful that there's no hope of real improvement, then your paper is a form of lamentation, not argumentation.

If, on the other hand, you take on a problem so amenable to your solution that it requires little thought and less effort, you force the reader to wonder how bad the problem could be in the first place.

As always, then, you must somehow see the paper whole just to make a beginning—and you must see it with your reader's eyes and not just your own. A few questions should help you do that.

CHECKLIST: DEFINING THE PROBLEM

- How much background does your reader need? (A little scene-setting is always in order, but it should always be just a little—never more than a fifth of your paper and usually more like a tenth.)
- How far-reaching is the problem you're addressing? (What time span are you treating? How many people are affected? Can you describe the effects in qualitative as well as quantitative terms—invoking, say, a sense of justice and fair play as well as giving a head count?)
- Who or what is responsible for the problem's existence—and its elimination or amelioration? (Remember that your paper is an attempt to solve a problem, not to assign blame for it. Especially in the case of a dialectical paper, the very people who seem to stand in the way of a solution should, if at all possible, be drawn into the solution.)

Interestingly enough, defining the problem was the hardest task Jennifer faced even though it was a problem she had experienced. She hadn't been able to register for ACC 1101 when she wanted to. Left at that, the problem could just be a matter of personal inconvenience, hardly something that might call for a restructuring of the status quo. Then she discovered that others had had the same experience, and she began to wonder about the implications. What did it mean that freshmen and sophomores couldn't register for ACC 1101? Could what individuals experienced as a temporary setback turn out to have generally significant, long-term effects?

The answer to her was an obvious Yes. But would it seem so to her reader? The question is important because Jennifer ultimately failed to get the kind of information that would have allowed her to demonstrate, conclusively, that accounting majors were graduating later because they couldn't begin work on a "credit-heavy" major till they were juniors. She found out from the Office of the Registrar that no one had any way of knowing how many students were turned away from closed courses. No records were kept on that. Similarly, the Office of Institutional Research, the college's center for collecting data on students' backgrounds and academic progress, could only tell her how many students had graduated after a certain time, how many were still registered, and how many were no longer registered. When Jennifer asked the director how much the postponement of ACC 1101 might postpone graduation, she was told, "We don't keep data on that."

Thinking Critically about Jennifer's Research Process

What do you do when you don't get the data you need to clinch a point? If your research project is typical, that's a question you'll be asking yourself about some part of it. When you do, here are some other questions that might help you. See if you can answer them on Jennifer's behalf—or on your own.

1. If you don't have the sort of evidence that constitutes absolute proof, do you have (or can you get) evidence that will seem persuasive—evidence that may not prove you're right but can at least suggest you're on track?

2. When the data won't serve, can you use reasoning instead? (For instance, proponents of safety measures, unable to establish how many lives an advocated measure might save, often argue from the premise that a single life saved would make the measure worthwhile.)

3. Think about both your topic and your reader. How crucial do they make evidence on a particular point seem? If your claims are radical or your reader antagonistic, you may need plenty of substantiation, but more often, as in the case of more moderate claims or a reader disposed to entertain your ideas, you need only meet the test of reasonableness.

Propose—and Test—Your Solution

Defining the problem is indeed half the battle. Though we invite you to think of the dialectical research paper as something more like a dialogue than a debate, one rule of formal debate does apply: the assumption rests with the status quo. If there isn't a pressing need to change, let's let things go on as they are. If you've suggested that this assumption isn't a fair one in your case—if you've defined a problem that does indeed seem pressing—then your solution will seem desirable as long as you make it seem workable.

That's the tall order here: making your proposal seem workable. And the dialectical research paper forces you to confront it by confronting the other parties involved. What happened when Jennifer did that was initially terrifying but ultimately quite productive. Things had been going swimmingly, especially after she got her hands on the Annual Freshman Survey (put out by the Office of the Dean of Students), a rich resource for her purposes. Then one day, a few weeks before the research paper was due, she came up to her instructor after class.

"I have to change my research paper topic."

"Why?"

"It won't work."

"But why, Jennifer? It seems to me very workable."

"You don't understand. I talked to professors in the Accountancy Department. I told them my basic idea. They say it won't work."

Jennifer had gone to the Accountancy Department, equipped with hard numbers and ready to get an answer to that question her instructor had posed: "What would be the likelihood that your recommendation would be acted on?" She had not exactly expected instant applause, but she hadn't expected to be stonewalled either. When she tried the first professor who taught ACC 1101 and happened to be in his office, he quickly dismissed her suggestion that there be more sections: "Can't be done. We don't have the faculty to staff them." Jennifer was ready for that. What about hiring more faculty? "Can't be done. We don't have the budget." Jennifer was even ready for that. What about increasing the class size? That way, more students could be taught by the same number of teachers. "Large classes destroy a teacher's effectiveness. You lose intimacy, contact. The faculty would never go for it." When another professor confirmed that opinion, Jennifer felt utterly defeated. She would have to change her topic.

"But what makes you think teachers have all the answers—even and especially about how classes should be taught?" her instructor asked. "I appreciate their objections, but they're not the final word. Can't you think of a solution that might address those professors' concerns as well as yours? Otherwise, think of all the wasted time a change of topic would mean at this point."

Thinking Critically about Jennifer's Meeting with the Opposition

Resistance to change—not least of all from people who would be affected by it or even asked to implement it—is only to be expected. But how do you cope with it? Can you think your way out of the quandary Jennifer found herself in? Here are some questions that you might address as you do so:

1. Jennifer supposed that the professors' authority was so much more consequential than hers that the issue was closed because they closed it; Jennifer's instructor suggested otherwise. How can you balance issues like authority and self-interest in cases like this? What might Jennifer do to lend her position more authority? What reasoning might make the professors' authority seem less intimidating?

2. Jennifer's instructor asked her to see if she couldn't somehow address the professors' objections in her proposal. Do you see a way she might do this?

3. Accommodation is one strategy, but not the only one. Can some of the objections made be argued against rather than accommodated?

Whatever your answers might be, they suggest three strategies worth stressing. First, you can consider (and perhaps even adjust) the authority invested in the parties involved—including yourself. Second, you can qualify or counter those objections. Third—and, in a paper based on negotiation, most important—you can do your best to address those objections, to accommodate them somehow. An objection is only rarely a stonewall, a flat-out No. More often than not, it poses a condition that must be met before your demands can be met. Does what you want take money that isn't currently available? Perhaps you can discover or propose a source of funds. Does it seem to require stretching available resources too far? Perhaps you can see how those resources may be used more efficiently. Does a party with a crucial role lack the motivation to get involved? Perhaps you can suggest an incentive, a trade-off, something in it for them.

The details of each particular case will make an enormous difference, of course, but one thing never changes from one dialectical research paper to the next: the operative principle is being realistic rather than utopian. As in the example of unions versus management, the goal is not to make the dream of either side come true, but to balance the wishes of both; it is to propose a plan that promises, not just something that is desirable, but something that can be done. Even with that qualification, don't be afraid to dream a little; if people gave up on things because others said they couldn't be done, walking would still be the only means of transportation.

RETHINKING AND REVISING

Turn the Process into a Paper

The product of a research-paper process is only the topmost tip of the iceberg. You can never include all the information you gather nor all the thinking you've gone through. Everyone realizes this, but not everyone follows through with that realization. Often the result is disproportion: some parts of the paper are marvels of economy, but here (say, the introductory background) things get bloated and there (say, the conclusion) things get the short shrift. Strive for a balance of detail and economy, remembering that thinking about your reader determines when more specificity or less elaboration is needed.

The other tendency shared by drafts of research papers—especially those that carry you beyond the library—is that they become not so much arguments based on research as accounts of the research process. In her draft, Jennifer presented her plan, then the professors' objections to it. Why? For no better reason than this: first she concocted her plan; then she obtained their feedback. Only in revision did she see that the order in which things came to her was definitely not the ideal order in which to present them to her reader.

The crucial insights into organization tend to occur after a draft has been written. If you feel you need an outline before drafting, by all means sketch one, but entertain the possibility that the ideal time for outlining is once your ideas have been fleshed out. You may have been lucky enough to discover the ideal structure in the initial articulation, but more often than not you'll see reasons to rearticulate your points. The post-draft outline is the X-ray that will let you see your paper's skeleton—and whether you've joined its head to its hip.

RIAL RUN

If you've done a draft, distill the contents of each paragraph to a single sentence. (If this is a problem for you with any one paragraph, you may want to check that paragraph's organization: you may be asking it to express and develop more than one idea.) Once you have your series of sentences, read through them. Does the ordering of points seem to make sense? Are you building your argument logically? Does anything seem out of sequence, underdeveloped, or blown out of proportion?

Do Some Reality (and Desirability) Testing

We could say that proof (or persuasiveness) is in the eye of the beholder, but you need to realize that it's not your eye we're talking about. Speaking with conviction does not always amount to being convincing; you need a second opinion, someone to perform in the role of the reader—and, especially in this case, the other (perhaps recalcitrant) participants in your scenario. If you're getting objections from interviewees, see if you can get back to them as Jennifer did with hers so that you can try out your ideas for accommodating their thinking. If not, solicit help from your peers. Invite them to do a little role-playing for your sake, taking the parts of the people you are trying to persuade, motivate, meet halfway.

You've received many invitations to work with your peers in this text, perhaps enough to feel a change that collaborative thinking and learning can bring about: you find you can "inhabit" another person's point of vantage, understand their interests, almost think their thoughts. We never become mind readers, but conscious consideration can sometimes make us seem so. Sympathy plays an important role here, but so does self-interest: we need a sense of others' needs so that we can function as writers for readers—and also, of course, as people among people.

CHECKLIST REVISING YOUR DRAFT

- Have you carefully defined your problem, gauging its causes and extent?
- Have you presented evidence whenever necessary? Have you presented no more than what is necessary?
- When evidence is lacking, have you used careful and persuasive reasoning to suggest what you cannot prove?
- Have you tested your proposal's desirability and workability with other parties involved?

- If objections have been raised, have you countered them or met them?
- Have you double-checked the effectiveness of your organization?

PRESENTING JENNIFER'S FINAL DRAFT

Giving Freshmen Access to a Freshman Course

Jennifer Leung

1

Jennifer does not begin by immediately decrying a problem. Instead, she establishes a context in which that problem can be appreciated.

The City University of New York, led by Baruch College, has surpassed Harvard and Yale as the country's top source of business executives. The Gourman Report ranks Baruch sixteenth out of 1000 colleges in the nation for its business programs. The National Association of State Boards of Accounting has ranked Baruch's graduate school number one for having the highest passing rate on the most recent CPA examination. The most recent survey of Baruch alumni reports, on its first page, "Of the five most popular business majors, the highest median salary was reported by graduates in Accounting ($32,000)...."

She identifies a **2** large population potentially affected by the problem she treats.

It is no wonder that students interested in business careers, and especially careers in accounting, come to Baruch College. According to the Annual Freshman Survey for Fall 1989, 1,570 students entered Baruch in that semester. The survey indicates that 37% of these freshmen identified accounting as their expected major field of study.

3

Jennifer's specific problem (limited access to a course) is connected to a larger problem: delayed graduation.

It's interesting to find how optimistic these new students are about their aspirations and expectations. As the Annual Freshman Survey reports, "Sixty-nine percent of the 1989 freshmen rated themselves as having a 'very good chance' of graduating in four years..." (15). But how many actually do? When I asked this question of Dr. Susan Morgulas, Director of Institutional Research, she said that on average only a quarter of any freshman class at Baruch graduates after just four years. Another quarter of these students continue their studies, and the remainder have taken time off from college, dropped out, or transferred to other schools.

Jennifer defines **4** her specific problem, not as *the* cause, but as *a* cause of delayed graduation.

Dr. Morgulas stressed that the reasons why more students do not graduate in four years are complicated, and I'm sure she is right. But one reason seems clear to me. More than a third of any class of freshmen want to major in accounting, and we become juniors before we can take the basic prerequisite for our major--ACC 1101. That's because all the sections are already closed by the time the sophomores begin their registration.

She gets more   5
specific about the
specific problem
of limited access
to ACC 1101: the
number of
people who need
it as opposed to
the number of   6
people who can
actually take it.

We learn what,
specifically, the
difficulties are for
accounting stu-
dents who can't
take ACC 1101
until their junior
years.

Jennifer looks   7
beyond the aca-
demic context for
further ramifica-
tions of her prob-
lem: missed
opportunities for
income and
employment.

The problem-   8
definition part of
her paper over,
Jennifer turns   9
from the problem
to her proposed
solution.

She introduces
the accounting
professors she   10
contacted.

It's not just accounting majors who have to take ACC 1101. It is one of the "business base" courses, meaning all BBA (Bachelor of Business Administration) students are required to take this course. There are more than 10,000 business majors at Baruch. Yet only 14 sections of ACC 1101 were offered this semester; each holds about 50 students, for a total of 700 students. Fourteen sections are not even enough to hold just the students majoring in accounting.

This section shortage poses a real problem for accounting majors. The accounting courses they must take amount to 30 credits, and the recommended sequence for students in public accountancy includes more than 30 credits in other courses--mathematics, statistics, law, finance, business organization, business policy, management, and computer information systems. In this recommended sequence, only the math courses may precede ACC 1101. So we have a program of about 60 credits that an accounting major really can't get started on till the junior year. At fifteen credits a semester, the student has no room for any other courses, any course-load reduction, any chance to finish up base requirements that might remain from the first two years.

So some students are forced to postpone graduation. These students have to spend more money and more time on their education than they had originally planned. Furthermore, the delay may cost students golden opportunities. For one, it may be a chance to earn some money. For another, it could be a chance to secure a job in an internship program. The delay could be justified if the students chose to stay in college willingly, but not if they are compelled to stay because of the school's failure to supply a sufficient number of ACC 1101 sections to meet the students' demands.

It is about time for Baruch to do something to resolve the existing problem. The only way I see this can happen is to implement certain reforms.

In the process of developing a workable proposal, I interviewed two of our accounting professors: Professor Joseph Kerstein and Professor Thomas Verghese. I hoped through the interviews I could help them to recognize how seriously the problem has affected the students. Perhaps through their influence the school will take some action to remedy the present situation.

I understand that the simple solution of adding more sections (which would need to be taught by more professors) is just not feasible for budgetary reasons. Still, there are

After discounting one possible solution as unworkable, Jennifer introduces the basis for her solution: increasing 11 access by increasing class size.

She notes the professors' objection to increased class size—but she also wonders how serious an objection it really is.

less expensive measures that may be no less effective. For instance, a number of lecture halls exist on campus, with seating capacities ranging from 200 to 500. Using the lecture hall that can seat 500 students, three lecture classes of ACC 1101 could accommodate up to 1500 students--more than twice as many as the 700 students now in 14 sections of ACC 1101.

In response to this idea, both professors I interviewed contended that large lecture classes tend to create a dissociation between the teacher and students. I am inclined to agree, and it is true that students will have less interaction with their teacher in a large lecture class. But how much interaction do students now have in ACC 1101 anyway? I am now taking two courses with enrollments of about 50 students, and more than two-thirds of the students in these classes do not interact with the teacher at all. How much difference would it really make to most students whether they are in a large lecture class or a smaller class? Moreover, ACC 1101 is an introductory course, a course intended to communicate basic, general information. Interaction between teacher and student may be vital in an advanced course with complex content, but it may not be in an introductory course.

Besides, there is no need to eliminate interaction. The school can recruit and train qualified juniors, seniors, and perhaps graduate students as recitation teachers. We can have 38 recitation sections meeting once a week, each with 40 students, attached to the large lecture classes of ACC 1101 I have proposed. The school could give the students who lead these sections hourly wages.

12

Jennifer, attempts to meet the professors halfway by proposing recitation sections with student leaders.

13

Jennifer notes the professors' objection to this part of her proposal— but, once again, she doesn't simply note the objection: she wonders how valid it really is.

The professors I interviewed expressed concern about having students act as recitation teachers. They pointed out that students, however bright, do not have the same credentials and experience that professors do. Therefore, the students' inadequacies might cause more harm than good. Until the idea is actually tested, such an objection is a matter of opinion. It is my opinion that students might in some ways be more helpful than professors. I am not talking about just any students, of course, but students who have shown themselves to be outstanding in ACC 1101 and the accounting courses beyond it. I think such students might be particularly helpful in dealing with other students' questions about the course material. For one thing, they might be more understanding of difficulties the students have than a professor would be because they would have the students' perspective.

14

If training in teaching is important, a course could be established to provide that. Why would qualified students be willing to take it? Well, we have students already willing to

Once again, she tries to accommodate the professors' concern, this time by guaranteeing careful screening and training.

Jennifer notes the benefits that would accrue to the student 15 **teachers.**

She stresses the benefits to the students who want to take ACC 1101.

16

She notes an important point of agreement with both professors— and a kind of endorsement of her plan from one of them.

17

Jennifer concludes by stressing the advantages of her plan for all concerned.

settle for $6 an hour as math tutors. Let's say we give these students, once they have completed the course, $10 an hour; figuring an hour for the recitation and another hour for preparation, that would come to $300 apiece, only about $10,000 for everyone involved. That's much less than it would cost to hire one professor. And the students involved would get much more than just the hourly wage. Teaching would give them an opportunity to develop and evaluate their leadership potential, and also to improve their communication skills. This training would definitely come in handy once they are outside in the real world. And the experience would look good on their resume.

The people who would benefit most, of course, would be the students who could now take ACC 1101 when they couldn't before. Giving students greater access to ACC 1101 would mean that even freshmen could take what is supposedly a first-year course. This would give them a chance to explore whether they have a real interest in this field or not. Although taking one course would not teach them all there is to know about accounting, at least they could decide if they want to continue with the major. If not, they can easily switch to something else without having to wait till their junior year to realize that they have no real interest or ability in the field.

I am pleased to note that the two professors I interviewed have no opposition to the idea of freshmen taking ACC 1101. This would be possible, of course, only if we were to change the present system by implementing something like the above proposal. And I was encouraged to think it might really be workable. Professor Kerstein once taught at a school in Pennsylvania where they used graduate students as section leaders and it seemed to work out fine. If other schools can do it, so can Baruch.

If the proposal I have made is implemented, not only will the students benefit from it, but the school will as well. The school will not have to spend a lot of money hiring accounting professors, who seem to be scarce anyway, and yet Baruch will be able to let more Baruch students take a course they want when they want. Greater access to ACC 1101 will ease students' anxiety about not being able to register for a course so crucial to so many academic careers. ACC 1101 professors, released from the need to staff multiple sections of the same introductory course, will be able to devote their energies to more advanced accounting courses. And the experience as recitation teachers might inspire some of the best students to consider teaching as their profession, thus alleviating the nation's present shortage of accounting professors. If a bargain benefits all parties, I don't see why we shouldn't have it!

Sources

Baruch College Directory of Classes, Spring 1990. Baruch College, 1989.
Baruch College Undergraduate Bulletin 1990/92. The City University of New York, 1990.
Gourman Jack. *The Gourman Report: A Rating of Undergraduate Programs in American and International Universities, 7th Edition.* National Education Standards, 1989.
Kerstein, Joseph. Interviews. April 19, 1990, and May 2, 1990.
Morgulas, Susan. Interview. April 12, 1990.
Teilman, Shebal. *Annual Freshman Survey, Fall 1989.* Baruch College, 1989.
-----. *Alumni Survey: Class of 1986.* Baruch College, 1989.
Verghese, Thomas. Interviews. April 18, 1990, and May 2, 1990.

Sources are done according to the MLA style of documentation. Note the reliance on local sources.

Commentary on Jennifer's Final Draft

Again, Jennifer Leung's research paper is basically a problem-to-solution paper. The term is useful because it has the built-in reminder that, if you plan on presenting a solution to a problem, you have to define what that problem is first.

And defining the problem was a problem for Jennifer. She could speak of her own personal problem with taking ACC 1101 when she wanted to, but she had trouble getting evidence to establish more wide-ranging and long-term effects. How many people who tried to register for the course were turned away? How many ultimately had the completion of their degrees delayed in consequence? Despite contacting the offices of the Registrar and Institutional Research, Jennifer could not get the data to answer those questions conclusively. In fact, she learned that no one was even keeping track of such things.

What Jennifer was experiencing was what many people experience when they research a problem: the limits of research. "Proving" something is not just a matter of looking long enough and hard enough. In this case, in retrospect, we might see how Jennifer could have designed a very ambitious survey of seniors, juniors, and alumni in accounting that might have given her the sort of data she needed. But she didn't have the time for that. Even if she had, would she have obtained "proof"? She was looking at an extremely complex cause-and-effect relation: the relation between the postponement of one crucial three-credit course and the time it took to accumulate the 120 credits for the degree. Think of all the other factors that might come into play. How could Jennifer prove that this one factor was decisive in postponing graduation for a specific number of people?

Happily, she didn't have to. As we have suggested, "proof"—or at least persuasive demonstration—is in the eye of the beholder. Jennifer had to use the information she *could* get to persuade the reader that, given the limited access to ACC 1101, students in significant numbers experienced significant delay—with significant consequences. Did she do that? We think she did, but your answer is as good as any.

Let's look at her strategy. She began by setting up the entering students' expectations: why most of them came to her college, how many of them planned to major in accounting, how soon they expected to graduate. With all this established—and we're still on the first page—she contrasts expectations with reality: just over a third of those who expect to graduate in four years *do* graduate. Why? Without denying the existence of other reasons, Jennifer offers ACC 1101 as one, and then she homes in on that reason, developing it in terms of how many students must take the course, how many students can actually register for it, how crucial it is to an accounting curriculum that amounts to two years of course work.

In an earlier draft, she stopped there, at least as far as defining the problem went. But she also quoted one of the professors as saying, "It doesn't matter whether it will take even six or seven years for accounting majors to graduate because what they are doing in these few years in college will have an enormous effect on their future." Well, thought Jennifer, that was one way of looking at it. As a student en route to a career, she couldn't help thinking of all the missed opportunities the extra year or three of college might mean. And so her final draft devotes a paragraph to what the delay might mean to students, suggesting that it's one thing if they really want to hang around, quite another if they're eager to move on.

The upshot of this exercise in problem definition is the sense that Jennifer's college might logically, justly, humanely do better by its accounting students than it is doing now, especially since all that is asked for is greater access to one course. A skeptic wanting to know the precise number of affected students might demand more, but we have a sense that a problem exists and are disposed to ponder a proffered solution. Jennifer has our attention.

At this point, poised on the verge of presenting her solution, she also brings in the two accounting professors. The interviews with them are presented as part of "developing a workable proposal." Jennifer also expresses her hopes that they might use their influence to effect the sort of changes she proposes. Yet they are soon revealed to be much more like adversaries than allies, and Jennifer's use of them is the other great challenge her paper addresses. It is not as formidable a challenge as it first seemed to Jennifer because, just as defining the problem is not so much "proving" it as persuading the reader that it exists, confronting the opposition is not so much routing or refuting its objections as showing them consideration. In an earlier draft, she saved the professors and their objections for the end. This created the effect of presenting a proposal and then letting others take potshots at it. In her final version, she acknowledges the objection to each part of her proposal and resolves it, at least to her satisfaction, before moving on to the next step. Were we to chart her progress, it would look something like this:

Jennifer proposes...	The professors object...	Jennifer responds...
larger classes	too little interaction between teachers and students	how much interaction goes on now? besides, we'll have recitation sections
student leaders for recitation sections	students lack professors' experience and training	students offer a different, useful perspective—besides, they'll get training

The list doesn't show Jennifer's whole argument, just the coping-with-objections part, but it's worth pausing over to see Jennifer's strategy for coping with objections. Note that each time an objection is raised, Jennifer does two things: 1) she weakens the force of the objection, suggesting that its validity is limited; 2) then she shows, to the extent it *is* valid, that something will be done to address it, and this something becomes the next step in her argument.

But Jennifer's strongest suit is what happens once the professors' objections have been met with. She began with a problem; then she handled problems others had with her solution; now she focuses on advantages. The first, unmentioned at the outset, is not the peril of preventing freshmen from taking ACC 1101, but the virtue of allowing them to take it: they'll be exposed to accounting as a potential major and career early on, getting to know what they're getting into. This happens to be a point of agreement between Jennifer and the professors: no objections here. Then she notes one professor even has evidence to offer in support of her plan. Finally, she stresses how her plan will benefit everyone: students taking the course, students teaching the recitation sections, accounting professors, the school, even the nation (at least in so far as it's short of accounting professors). It's a wonderful array of positives, such an upbeat crescendo to end on that we don't even object to Jennifer's use of the exclamation point (not our favorite punctuation mark).

Good papers can always be made better. In the case of research papers, improvements tend to take the form of further support and substantiation. For instance, one of the two professors pointed Jennifer down a road not taken: there are precedents for her plan at other colleges and universities, and they would have been well worth looking into. But any good paper is, more than anything else, an effective exercise in communication, and Jennifer's paper communicates well. It is thoughtful, tactful, determined, shrewd. It begins with a problem, meets with resistance, makes adjustments, finds common ground and even outright agreement, and ends by offering potential rewards all around. Rhetorically, it's a fine piece of work.

Questions for Further Thought

1. If even something like defining the problem can be a matter of persuasion rather than proof—if everything is ultimately a matter of opinion—how do you know when you've done enough? How can someone else say that you haven't?

2. So much about the dialectical research paper is a matter of strategy. Are there places where your strategy would differ from Jennifer's? Do you think, for instance, that she should have pushed harder for students' rights and worried less about faculty objections? Is the opposition or resistance you are contending with leading you to be more or less accommodating than Jennifer was? Why?

3. Who is Jennifer's audience? Obviously, this is a research paper that must be submitted to the instructor who assigned it, but should it have been pitched to another specific audience—say, by addressing the accounting professors directly or agitating students to push for more ACC 1101 sections? What would be the consequences of such a recasting in terms of tone, presentation, organization?

4. Is the ultimate test of a proposal like Jennifer's whether it gets implemented or not? If it doesn't, has she failed? How else can we gauge success in exercises like this?

SECTION FIVE

"DISCIPLINED" APPROACHES TO RESEARCHED WRITING

Section Five introduces you to library research in the disciplines—the exciting, challenging, frustrating, and often intimidating world of scholarship. In place of the rhetorical and process guidelines in the earlier chapters, we concentrate on the writing conventions in the academic disciplines to provide principles of research strategy, evolution of the outline, writing the researched paper, and editing. We do not claim to be experts in all the subjects discussed in this section nor do we expect you to become authorities. Our purpose is to expose you to some of their basic concepts and concentrate on the general problem-solving approaches they represent that may serve as orientation to college courses. For example, before you actually take a literature course, Chapter 13, "Writing a Literature Paper," may give you some ideas about the discipline itself, its principle modes of investigation, and research procedures.

The writing assignments require you to go beyond your immediate surroundings and experiences to opinions of authorities in the field for supportive evidence. The formal and conventional aspects of researched writing, as the student papers illustrate, need not necessarily hamper your own creativity. Your research reflects your choices of sources as well as your capacity to sift through and evaluate the source material to best serve your needs. So "disciplined" approaches to research refer both to the various disciplines or academic subjects and a more controlled and formal research procedure.

If you write in a composition class about courses you may take in the humanities, social sciences, or natural sciences, you may see immediate and practical connections between the conventions of writing well in general and the writing demands of the larger academic community. As a college student, you have to make constant adjustments to different kinds of intellectual challenges and demands. In one class you may be required to examine cells under a microscope, and in the next you may analyze Lincoln's Gettysburg Address. You do not have the time to realize that in spite of the differences, there are certain operative principles of thought and analysis that are shared by all disciplines. A literary critic and a biologist both define terms, ask why and how things happen, examine similarities and differences, make evaluations. Understanding these connections may help you comprehend the ideas in these subjects and become better writers in college. While we acknowledge the general principles shared by all good writing, we also stress the characteristic situations, ideas, and the language of individual disciplines. We hope the research procedures will encourage your involvement with other thinkers who have specific knowledge so that you may intertwine some of their ideas with your own.

CHAPTER THIRTEEN

WRITING A LITERATURE PAPER

How do we write about a story, a novel, a poem, or a play? Does writing about fiction and nonfiction require a different approach? Both fiction and nonfiction use language to express the writer's ideas, attitudes, beliefs, desires, and values, real or imagined. While these are expressed directly in a more straightforward way in expository writing, a story may use imagined situations and attitudes to convey ideas that have to be discovered by the reader. Writers of literary works do not deliberately conceal meaning from readers. Instead, they reveal meaning through characters, plot, setting, pattern, themes, and imagery. It may seem as though the meaning is concealed, but this may be because we may not be familiar with the ways or the literary techniques used to express meaning. The following two descriptions, both related to maps, exemplify the characteristics of literary and expository prose:

> a) "But there was in it one river especially, a mighty river, that you could see on the map, resembling an immense snake uncoiled, with its head in the sea, its body at rest curving afar over a vast country, and its tail lost in the depths of the land. And as I looked at the map of it in a shop window, it fascinated me as a snake would a bird—a silly little bird." (Joseph Conrad, *Heart of Darkness*).

> b) "Early maps were designed to show the spatial relationship between local geographical features, territorial boundaries, and routes. The early use of maps for finding the way has persisted, first for travellers on land, later for mariners, and more recently for airmen and space travellers." (*The New York Times Atlas of the World*).

A poet or a fiction writer does not merely inform us about a place or a person but rather conveys to us an experience of what it is like to be a particular imaginary person in a representatively human situation with which we can identify. Conrad's description of the map tells us less about "spatial relationships between local geographical features," for example, and more about the character who is awed by the river and feels very small when he looks at it. Literary writers use techniques such as presenting characters, settings, and images (like the river) to suggest certain ideas and experiences. Therefore, writing about literature—fiction, poetry, drama—requires us to read in a different way. We are required to interpret the literature in order to understand and write about it. We have a personal response to a story or a poem, we use what we know about the elements of literature to analyze the text, and we research background material and critical articles by others, all in an attempt to find out what the work means and write about it. Even without knowing it, we approach a literary work like a detective does a mystery, as something to be "figured out" and interpreted.

There are some basic questions we need to ask before we decide on an interpretation. How do we go about this detective work? Is there a "right" way to interpret a literary work? In this list of statements about interpreting literature, which ones make sense to you?

- The "right" interpretation of the text is what teachers and critics say about the text.
- A "right" interpretation is whatever any individual decides about the text.
- There is one "right" interpretation of the text which was intended by the author.
- There are several interpretations of a text which are possible or probable, some of which the author may or may not have intended.
- No one interpretation is better than any other.
- A "good" interpretation must be supported by referring to the text.
- There are objective standards to measure good and bad literature.

If you are unclear about the "rightness" of the above statements, the following guidelines for interpreting literature may help you:

- The best "authority" you have as a reader and interpreter is the text itself—the words on the page in front of you. The author's life and his worldview may help in understanding the work, but you are the detective and the interpreter. The instructor might offer an interpretation or analysis of the literary work, but it is also up to you to offer your own.
- There is no absolutely "right" way to interpret a literary work, no expert to tell you what exactly it means the way a biologist can tell you, for example, how blood circulates through the body. On the other hand, some interpretations are more convincing than others.
- Writers of literature use language to create characters, actions, situations that the readers can visualize and identify with. So writing about literature requires us to pay special attention to the language used by the authors.

Interpretation involves using our intuitive abilities to understand and express our personal feelings about a story, our intellectual abilities to broaden our understanding by using literary terminology to describe evidence from the text, and our research abilities to support our position with the opinions of others. In this chapter we will see how Alexandra Cruz responded to a writing about literature assignment treating William Faulkner's "A Rose for Emily." We will see how Alexandra used her own intuition to determine her feelings about the story, extended her initial impressions by making use of literary terminology, and supported her position with evidence from other sources.

WRITING ASSIGNMENT

Write a paper in which you describe your personal responses to a short story. Read the story carefully to become engaged with the imagination, emotions, experience, knowledge, and values. Support your position with evidence from the text and with critical material.

READING THE WRITING ASSIGNMENT

You may have some general ideas about the story you choose or are assigned, but the writing task often requires you to view it from particular angles that you might not have considered during your earlier readings. So it is important that you understand the assignment in order to look for those elements in the story which are the focus of the assignment. The above assignment seeks your *personal* response. The way you will interpret the story will be uniquely yours, different from the others in your class. So be creative in your approach; don't hold back any response, however impromptu or impulsive. You will have many opportunities to weed out those you do not like during the writing and rewriting process.

Literary works reflect life in its myriad aspects, so as you read, look for parallels in your own life—things that may have happened to you or to people you know, ideas you may have had, or emotions you may have felt. Making these connections between the characters and events in the story and those in your own life or lives of people you know may help you to get "into" the story and become more involved with it.

As you read the story, taking your cues from the assignment, you should keep in mind that literary language is seldom one dimensional; it often involves layer upon layer of meaning. Even seasoned readers have to read a literary work a few times before arriving at a confident interpretation. As important as the storyline is in a good short story, a literary work is seldom read only to find out what happens next. **What** the authors say is at least as important as **how** they say it and sometimes even more. For example, if you read the famous French novel, *Madame Bovary,* by Gustav Flaubert, one of the masters of nineteenth-century fiction, just for the story, you might be pretty disappointed. What is so dynamic in a story about the wife of a country doctor who turns to an adulterous relationship to escape her boredom and is driven to suicide? Certainly not much. Yet after more than a hundred years, Flaubert is read for his exquisite craft—the authenticity of details, the impersonal narrative method, language intensely precise and disarmingly simple at the same time. Because literary works speak to us indirectly, often suggesting meaning through images and symbols, each new reading adds to the readers' comprehension and pleasure by yielding small surprises and discoveries. So sit yourself down in a quiet place and concentrate on the story you will be writing about.

No matter how many times and how well you read a story before actually writing your paper, you will need to refer to it often during the writing process. You cannot shelve the book and sit down to write your paper. You may remember the story line, but it is impossible to remember all the rich details. So have the book handy while you write. In addition to supportive evidence from the text itself, the assignment calls for critical support, most of which you will have to gather before writing the paper. But as you write, you may find that another trip to the library is necessary to support a new insight. All these things may take place almost simultaneously as you compose the first draft of your writing assignment. So get a good start by a thorough reading of the story. That's what Alexandra did when she received her assignment on "A Rose for Emily."

Here is William Faulkner's "A Rose for Emily" for your careful reading.

A ROSE FOR EMILY

William Faulkner

I

1   When Miss Emily Grierson died, our whole town went to her funeral: the men through a sort of respectful affection for a fallen monument, the women mostly out of curiosity to see the inside of her house, which no one save an old manservant—a combined gardener and cook—had seen in at least ten years.

2   It was a big, squarish frame house that had once been white, decorated with cupolas and spires and scrolled balconies in the heavily lightsome style of the seventies, set on what had once been our most select street. But garages and cotton gins had encroached and obliterated even the august names of that neighborhood; only Miss Emily's house was left, lifting its stubborn and coquettish decay above the cotton wagons and the gasoline pumps—an eyesore among eyesores. And now Miss Emily had gone to join the representatives of those august names where they lay in the cedar-bemused cemetery among the ranked and anonymous graves of Union and Confederate soldiers who fell at the battle of Jefferson.

and Miss Emily sat in it, the light behind her, and her upright torso motionless as that of an idol. They crept quietly across the lawn and into the shadow of the locusts that lined the street. After a week or two the smell went away.

25   That was when people had begun to feel really sorry for her. People in our town, remembering how old lady Wyatt, her great-aunt, had gone completely crazy at last, believed that the Griersons held themselves a little too high for what they really were. None of the young men were quite good enough for Miss Emily and such. We had long thought of them as a tableau, Miss Emily a slender figure in white in the background, her father a spraddled silhouette in the foreground, his back to her and clutching a horsewhip, the two of them framed by the back-flung front door. So when she got to be thirty and was still single, we were not pleased exactly, but vindicated; even with insanity in the family she wouldn't have turned down all of her chances if they had really materialized.

26   When her father died, it got about that the house was all that was left to her; and in a way, people were glad. At last they could pity Miss Emily. Being left alone, and a pauper, she had become humanized. Now she too would know the old thrill and the old despair of a penny more or less.

27   The day after his death all the ladies prepared to call at the house and offer condolence and aid, as is our custom. Miss Emily met them at the door, dressed as usual and with no trace of grief on her face. She told them that her father was not dead. She did that for three days, with the ministers calling on her, and the doctors, trying to persuade her to let them dispose of the body. Just as they were about to resort to law and force, she broke down, and they buried her father quickly.

28   We did not say she was crazy then. We believed she had to do that. We remembered all the young men her father had driven away, and we knew that with nothing left, she would have to cling to that which had robbed her, as people will.

III

29   She was sick for a long time. When we saw her again, her hair was cut short, making her look like a girl, with a vague resemblance to those angels in colored church windows—sort of tragic and serene.

30   The town had just let the contracts for paving the sidewalks, and in the summer after her father's death they began to work. The construction company came with niggers and mules and machinery, and a foreman named Homer Barron, a Yankee—a big, dark, ready man, with a big voice and eyes lighter than his face. The little boys would follow in groups to hear him cuss the niggers, and the niggers singing in time to the rise and fall of picks. Pretty soon he knew everybody in town. Whenever you heard a lot of laughing anywhere about the square, Homer Barron would be in the center of the group. Presently we began to see him and Miss Emily on Sunday afternoons driving in the yellow-wheeled buggy and the matched team of bays from the livery stable.

31   At first we were glad that Miss Emily would have an interest, because the ladies all said, "Of course a Grierson would not think seriously of a Northerner, a day laborer." But there were still others, older people, who said that even grief could not cause a real lady to forget *noblesse oblige*—without calling it *noblesse oblige*. They just said, "Poor Emily. Her kinsfolk should come to her." She had some kin in Alabama; but years ago her father had fallen out with them over the estate of old lady Wyatt, the crazy woman, and there was no communication between the two families. They had not even been represented at the funeral.

32   And as soon as the old people said, "Poor Emily," the whispering began. "Do you suppose it's really so?" they said to one another. "Of course it is. What else could..." This behind their hands; rustling of craned silk and satin behind jalousies closed upon the sun of Sunday afternoon as the thin, swift clop-clop-clop of the matched team passed: "Poor Emily."

33   She carried her head high enough—even when we believed that she was fallen. It was as if she demanded more than ever the recognition of her dignity as the last Grierson; as if it had wanted that touch of earthiness to reaffirm her imperviousness. Like when she bought the rat poison, the arsenic. That was over a year after they had begun to say "Poor Emily," and while the two female cousins were visiting her.

34   "I want some poison," she said to the druggist. She was over thirty then, still a slight woman, though thinner than usual, with cold, haughty black eyes in a face the flesh of which was strained across the temples and about the eye-sockets as you imagine a light-house-keeper's face ought to look. "I want some poison," she said.

35   "Yes, Miss Emily. What kind? For rats and such? I'd recom—"

36   "I want the best you have. I don't care what kind."

37   The druggist named several. "They'll kill anything up to an elephant. But what you want is—"

38   "Arsenic," Miss Emily said. "Is that a good one?"

39   "Is...arsenic? Yes, ma'am. But what you want..."

40   "I want arsenic."

41   The druggist looked down at her. She looked back at him, erect, her face like a strained flag. "Why, of course," the druggist said. "If that's what you want. But the law requires you to tell what you are going to use it for."

42   Miss Emily just stared at him, her head tilted back in order to look him eye for eye, until he looked away and went and got the arsenic and wrapped it up. The Negro delivery boy brought her the package; the druggist didn't come back. When she opened the package at home there was written on the box, under the skull and bones: "For rats."

IV

43   So the next day we all said, "She will kill herself"; and we said it would be the best thing. When she had first begun to be seen with Homer Barron, we had said, "She will marry him." Then we said, "She will persuade him yet," because Homer himself had remarked—he liked men, and it was known

that he drank with the younger men in the Elks' Club—that he was not a marrying man. Later we said, "Poor Emily" behind the jalousies as they passed on Sunday afternoon in the glittering buggy, Miss Emily with her head high and Homer Barron with his hat cocked and a cigar in his teeth, reins and whip in a yellow glove.

44   Then some of the ladies began to say that it was a disgrace to the town and a bad example to the young people. The men did not want to interfere, but at last the ladies forced the Baptist minister—Miss Emily's people were Episcopal—to call upon her. He would never divulge what happened during that interview, but he refused to go back again. The next Sunday they again drove about the streets, and the following day the minister's wife wrote to Miss Emily's relations in Alabama.

45   So she had blood-kin under her roof again and we sat back to watch developments. At first nothing happened. Then we were sure that they were to be married. We learned that Miss Emily had been to the jeweler's and ordered a man's toilet set in silver, with the letters H. B. on each piece. Two days later we learned that she had bought a complete outfit of men's clothing, including a nightshirt, and we said, "They are married." We were really glad. We were glad because the two female cousins were even more Grierson than Miss Emily had ever been.

46   So we were not surprised when Homer Barron—the streets had been finished some time since—was gone. We were a little disappointed that there was not a public blowing-off, but we believed that he had gone on to prepare for Miss Emily's coming, or to give her a chance to get rid of the cousins. (By that time it was a cabal, and we were all Miss Emily's allies to help circumvent the cousins.) Sure enough, after another week they departed. And, as we had expected all along, within three days Homer Barron was back in town. A neighbor saw the Negro man admit him at the kitchen door at dusk one evening.

47   And that was the last we saw of Homer Barron. And of Miss Emily for some time. The Negro man went in and out with the market basket, but the front door remained closed. Now and then we would see her at a window for a moment, as the men did that night when they sprinkled the lime, but for almost six months she did not appear on the streets. Then we knew that this was to be expected too; as if that quality of her father which had thwarted her woman's life so many times had been too virulent and too furious to die.

48   When we next saw Miss Emily, she had grown fat and her hair was turning gray. During the next few years it grew grayer and grayer until it attained an even pepper-and-salt-iron-gray, when it ceased turning. Up to the day of her death at seventy-four it was still that vigorous iron-gray, like the hair of an active man.

49   From that time on her front door remained closed, save for a period of six or seven years, when she was about forty, during which she gave lessons in china-painting. She fitted up a studio in one of the downstairs rooms, where the daughters and grand-daughters of Colonel Sartoris' contemporaries were sent to her with the same regularity and in the same spirit that they

were sent to church on Sundays with a twenty-five-cent piece for the collection plate. Meanwhile her taxes had been remitted.

50   Then the newer generation became the backbone and the spirit of the town, and the painting pupils grew up and fell away and did not send their children to her with boxes of color and tedious brushes and pictures cut from the ladies' magazines. The front door closed upon the last one and remained closed for good. When the town got free postal delivery, Miss Emily alone refused to let them fasten the metal numbers above her door and attach a mailbox to it. She would not listen to them.

51   Daily, monthly, yearly we watched the Negro grow grayer and more stooped, going in and out with the market basket. Each December we sent her a tax notice, which would be returned by the post office a week later, unclaimed. Now and then we would see her in one of the downstairs windows—she had evidently shut up the top floor of the house—like the carven torso of an idol in a niche, looking or not looking at us, we could never tell which. Thus she passed from generation to generation—dear, inescapable, impervious, tranquil, and perverse.

52   And so she died. Fell ill in the house filled with dust and shadows, with only a doddering Negro man to wait on her. We did not even know she was sick; we had long since given up trying to get any information from the Negro. He talked to no one, probably not even to her, for his voice had grown harsh and rusty, as if from disuse.

53   She died in one of the downstairs rooms, in a heavy walnut bed with a curtain, her gray head propped on a pillow yellow and moldy with age and lack of sunlight.

V

54   The Negro met the first of the ladies at the front door and let them in, with their hushed, sibilant voices and their quick, curious glances, and then he disappeared. He walked right through the house and out the back and was not seen again.

55   The two female cousins came at once. They held the funeral on the second day, with the town coming to look at Miss Emily beneath a mass of bought flowers, with the crayon face of her father musing profoundly above the bier and the ladies sibilant and macabre; and the very old men—some in their brushed Confederate uniforms—on the porch and the lawn, talking of Miss Emily as if she had been a contemporary of theirs, believing that they had danced with her and courted her perhaps, confusing time with its mathematical progression, as the old do, to whom all the past is not a diminishing road but, instead, a huge meadow which no winter ever quite touches, divided from them now by the narrow bottleneck of the most recent decade of years.

56   Already we knew that there was one room in that region above stairs which no one had seen in forty years, and which would have to be forced. They waited until Miss Emily was decently in the ground before they opened it.

57 The violence of breaking down the door seemed to fill this room with pervading dust. A thin, acrid pall as of the tomb seemed to lie everywhere upon this room decked and furnished as for a bridal: upon the valance curtains of faded rose color, upon the rose-shaded lights, upon the dressing table, upon the delicate array of crystal and the man's toilet things backed with tarnished silver, silver so tarnished that the monogram was obscured. Among them lay a collar and tie, as if they had just been removed, which, lifted, left upon the surface a pale crescent in the dust. Upon a chair hung the suit, carefully folded; beneath it the two mute shoes and the discarded socks.

58 The man himself lay in the bed.

59 For a long while we just stood there, looking down at the profound and fleshless grin. The body had apparently once lain in the attitude of an embrace, but now the long sleep that outlasts love, that conquers even the grimace of love, had cuckolded him. What was left of him, rotted beneath what was left of the nightshirt, had become inextricable from the bed in which he lay; and upon him and upon the pillow beside him lay that even coating of the patient and biding dust.

60 Then we noticed that in the second pillow was the indentation of a head. One of us lifted something from it, and leaning forward, that faint and invisible dust dry and acrid in the nostrils, we saw a long strand of iron-gray hair.

DISCOVERING IDEAS

Use Your Own Intuition as You Read

An immense help in writing about literature is keeping a **reading response journal** when writing about a story, a poem, or a play. Following are some suggestions to get you started:

a) Soon after reading a literary work, put your thoughts down on paper. You may begin your responses by "I thought...," "I felt that...," "I didn't realize...."

b) Make a note of what seemed easy to understand and what proved difficult: "I understood..." or "I was utterly confused by...," "I can't really understand why...."

c) Try to predict the writer's purpose—Why is the story narrated in a certain way? Why does the writer go back and forth between events?

d) Write down the issues the literary work raises and your own thoughts about them. Is there a deeper meaning underneath the story line? "I can't believe the author is just telling us...," "Could the moral of the story be...?"

e) Write down how the story, poem, or the play relates to your own life and experiences. Does it bring back memories for you? Does the association cause you pain or comfort? Your responses may begin with "The character of...reminds me of...," or "Now that I look at it, it makes me think about...," "If she were my friend...."

f) Observe how writers use words. Copy any nice turn of phrase, descriptions, dialogue, a striking image that might have especially appealed to you. They may help you to improve your own style and word power. Most writers keep journals to store words and ideas that they can draw upon when needed.

Alexandra read "A Rose for Emily" quickly the first time, and recalled later her initial understanding of the text. Here is what she wrote:

> Understanding "A Rose for Miss Emily," by William Faulkner, was not an easy task. First I carefully read the story like I read other stories for school. I read half of it in bed before I fell asleep and the other half on the bus on my way to school. When I finished, the first thought on my mind was, "I am dead."
>
> There I was, not far from the moment when I would have to stand in front of my class and try to carry on a detailed discussion on what the story means, and I had no idea what it meant. I was under a lot of pressure to get started, and because I work best under pressure, I slowly began the story again. I sat down on my bedroom floor and high-lighted every word that I thought would be helpful in either understanding Emily or Faulkner.
>
> The first time I read the story, I was in a state of total confusion. The story seemed so jumbled up. The sequences of the story seemed disorganized. Then during the second reading I came upon the idea that Faulkner was not writing chronologically. He jumped around on purpose. Faulkner began "A Rose for Emily" with Emily's death. Then he jumped from that point of her life cycle to after her father's death. I was also confused about the storyteller. The person telling the story kept saying "We" saw this, and we heard that. But I was not sure who this was because to me it sounded like one person. There were a lot of things I had to figure out. It made the reading of the story more exciting. Faulkner's way of writing is confusing. I had no idea of what was coming next. It was like a mystery and I was the detective. At the end, when I put all the pieces together, read some books on Faulkner and figured out the order of events, I felt like I just had a great accomplishment.

TRIAL RUN

Read the short story you have chosen or have been assigned. Then write your first impressions down in a few paragraphs. What were the toughest obstacles to understanding the story? What helped you to understand it? What stood out in your mind?

We mentioned earlier that interpreting literature is **intuitive** and **intellectual.** Our instincts and our mind are both at work. Alexandra Cruz's first response to "A Rose for Emily" exemplifies this adequately. It is full of her intellectual curiosity about the text and her emotional frustration at not being able to answer the questions that were coming to her mind.

We have also said that the first step in writing about a literary work is to read it very carefully. Alexandra's initial response to the text was, "I'm dead." This confusion was partially the result of the nature of her reading—she read half of it in bed before falling asleep and the other half on the bus on her way to campus. Alexandra was obviously aware of this because, to clear the confusion in her mind, she read the story carefully a few times. Only then did certain patterns and ideas begin to emerge out of the story that she had not noticed after the first cursory reading.

Annotate to Improve Your Reading

As Alexandra reread the text, she wrote down her feelings and thoughts about characters, setting, plot, structure, imagery as they came to her mind. She underlined words that seemed important to the text's meaning or which the author repeated. She looked for word clusters, words identifying sensory details—colors, shapes, consistency, sounds, smells. Then she tried to find out if these clusters formed patterns that might lead to her understanding of the story. Her annotation of Section I of "A Rose for Emily" looked like this:

A ROSE FOR EMILY

Is Emily the rose? Does someone give her a rose?

William Faulkner

I

When Miss Emily Grierson died, our whole town went to her funeral: the men through a sort of respectful affection for a <u>fallen monument</u>, the women mostly out of curiosity to see the inside of her house, <u>which no one save an old manservant—a combined gardener and cook—had seen in at least ten</u> years.

Why is she a fallen monument What is her importance?

It was a big, squarish frame house that had once been white, decorated with cupolas and spires and scrolled balconies in the heavily lightsome <u>style of the seventies</u>, set on what had once been our <u>most select street</u>. But <u>garages and cotton gins</u> had encroached and obliterated even the august

She must have been someone important

a strange woman

built in 1870s? New + not so nice changes

names of that neighborhood; only Miss Emily's house was left, lifting its stubborn and coquettish decay above the cotton wagons and the gasoline pumps—an eyesore among eyesores. And now Miss Emily had gone to join the representatives of those august names where they lay in the cedar-bemused cemetery among the ranked and anonymous graves of Union and Confederate soldiers who fell at the battle of Jefferson.

Could be used to describe the woman + not the house. Are they similar?

Civil War reference

Alive, Miss Emily had been a tradition, a duty, and a care; a sort of hereditary obligation upon the town, dating from that day in 1894 when Colonel Sartoris, the mayor—he who fathered the edict that no Negro woman should appear on the streets without an apron—remitted her taxes, the dispensation dating from the death of her father on into perpetuity. Not that Miss Emily would have accepted charity. Colonel Sartoris invented an involved tale to the effect that Miss Emily's father had loaned money to the town, which the town, as a matter of business, preferred this way of repaying. Only a man of Colonel Sartoris' generation and thought could have invented it, and only a woman could have believed it.

She stands for the old way. How times have changed

No woman today would believe it!

When the next generation, with its more modern ideas, became mayors and aldermen, this arrangement created some little dissatisfaction. On the first of the year they mailed her a tax notice. February came, and there was no reply. They wrote her a formal letter, asking her to call at the sheriff's office at her convenience. A week later the mayor wrote her himself, offering to call or to send his car for her, and received in reply a note on paper of an archaic shape, in a thin, flowing calligraphy in faded ink, to the effect that she no longer went out at all. The tax notice was also enclosed, without comment.

Everything about her is old fashioned

They called a special meeting of the Board of Aldermen. A deputation waited upon her, knocked at the door through which no visitor had passed since she ceased giving china-painting lessons eight or ten years earlier. They were admitted by the old Negro into a dim hall from which a stairway mounted into still more shadow. It smelled of dust and disuse—a close, dank smell. The Negro led them into the parlor. It was furnished in heavy, leather-covered furniture. When the Negro opened the blinds of one window, they could see that the leather was cracked; and when they sat down, a faint dust rose sluggishly about their thighs, spinning with slow motes in the single sun-ray. On a tarnished gilt easel before the fireplace stood a crayon portrait of Miss Emily's father.

no one came to visit for 8-10 years

The interior of the house is dusty + moldy

A second reading led to some important revelations for Alexandra. This was her response after the first reading: "The story seemed so jumbled up. Then during the second reading I came upon the idea that Faulkner was not writing chronologically. He jumped around on purpose." At this stage, she discovered some major clues to understanding literature:

1. Events in stories, unlike steps in a scientific experiment, do not necessarily have to be told in the order in which they happened.

2. If the author "jumps around," it is often for a purpose. This knowledge lifted a major barrier to her comprehending and enjoying the story.

Alexandra's few thorough readings gave her the confidence to interpret the meaning of the story as she found it. This also made her trust her own instincts before reading what others have had to say.

TRIAL RUN

As you read your story carefully for a second or third time, annotate the pages the same way Alexandra did for "A Rose for Emily." React and respond to the text as you write your impressions in the margin. You may raise questions and look for answers to them later when you read the critical material.

Extend Your Understanding: Use Literary Terms

A work of literature is a unit or a whole piece with individual elements that relate to one another. Close reading of a story in the exercises above revealed to Alexandra some patterns in Faulkner that helped her understand the story. However, we can learn to understand stories better and write more interesting papers about them if we understand some literary terms and concepts. Not only does learning about literary terminology help us understand our reading better, it also gives us new vocabulary with which to write about literature. The more we are able to connect these separate elements in a literary work, the better our understanding of it. We might think of separate parts, described in literary terms, as our basic tools for examining the connections or doing the detective work involved in understanding literature.

Narration and Narrators

Fictional works are narrated or "told" by someone referred to as the **narrator** from a perspective known as **point of view.** The narrator has the choice of several points of view or vantage points from which to observe and tell the story.

1. The first-person point of view uses the "I" as the eye that sees and tells the reader what is going on. The "I" may be a character who participates in the action or someone who stands aside and observes. Authors use the first-person point of view when they want the meaning of the story to be confined to what one person can see in a limited but realistic way.

2. The third-person point of view employs one character, referred to by name, who is usually involved in the action, and through whose eyes the reader views action.

3. The omniscient or "all-knowing" narrator presents the inner thoughts and feelings of his characters, the past and the future of action, as if he or she had god-like vision. The voice may belong to a character who appears in the work or the reader may hear the voice but never "see" the possessor of the voice. Omniscient narration is used by authors who want the widest perspective possible.

In "A Rose For Emily" by William Faulkner, the narrator is not an "I" nor "he" or "she." It is a "we" that represents the citizens of Jefferson. The "we" is the collective consciousness of the townspeople in the same way the chorus of men and women was the voice of the people in Greek tragedies. The townspeople in "A Rose for Emily" do not take part in the action directly but comment on it. "So *we* were not surprised when Homer Barron—the streets had been finished some time since—was gone. *We* were a little disappointed that there was not a public blowing-off, but *we* believed that he had gone on to prepare for Miss Emily's coming, or to give her a chance to get rid of the cousins." Only in the last paragraph does one person step out of the group to pick up the long strand of iron gray hair from the pillow next to Homer Barron. At this point of the story, it was necessary to have a single individual to perform this particular act. "Then *we* noticed that in the second pillow was the indentation of a head. *One* of us lifted something from it, and leaning forward, that faint and invisible dust dry and acrid in the nostrils, *we* saw a long strand of iron-gray hair." Faulkner could have shifted the point of view from "we" to "I" in this instance. But that would have interfered with the anonymity of the group that was maintained throughout the story. So he settled for the more general "one." What is intriguing about Faulkner's use of the narrative voice in this story is that even though the narrating voice is nameless, at the end we may want to believe that the narrator may be the citizen of Jefferson who steps out of the group to pick the strand of hair and who wishes to remain anonymous.

Narratives may use a strictly **chronological** order—the order in which the events take place. For example, a story may begin with the birth of the main character and follow the events of his life until his death. Or it may begin at the end, as does "A Rose for Emily," with Emily's death. The story makes a complete circle and goes back to the scene of Emily's death and the shocking discovery by the townspeople of Homer Barron's decayed body. In between these events, Faulkner sets the details of Emily's life. Fiction writing has no set way of telling a story, which adds to the excitement of reading. Writers may begin at the beginning, move swiftly to the end, and then get to middle details. They may also use flashbacks or a quick look at the past, a technique often used in movies, which breaks up the flow of events.

When reading a story, we have to pay special attention to how it is told, who tells the story, from what angle the narrator is looking at events, how much does he or she know, how much is deliberately being withheld from the reader, or should we trust everything the narrator says? Sometimes, depending on his or her character, a narrator cannot be fully trusted, and the reader has to be extra cautious when presented with an unreliable narrator. What we should look for is how the story is shaped by the narrator.

CHECKLIST: DETERMINING POINT OF VIEW

Question	Alexandra's question	Your question for your story
Is the narrator a character in the story?	Who is the "we" in "A Rose for Emily"?	
Does the action take place in the mind of the character?	Can the people in "A Rose" see the past? Can they enter Emily's head?	
Does the story affect the narrator?	How does the discovery of Homer Barron's body affect the townsfolk?	
Can we trust the narrator all the time?	Can we trust the townspeople's observations of Emily all the time?	

Plot

This term refers to the arranged sequence of events in a literary work, usually linked by a cause-and-effect relationship and frequently involving conflict and resolution. Events in a plot usually have a rational explanation unless they are fantastic or supernatural.

CHECKLIST: CONSIDERING PLOT

Question	Alexandra's question	Your question for your story
What events have major consequences in the story?	What effects do the arrival of Homer, the buying of rat poison, the smell and discovery of the putrid body have on the story?	
What are the main character's objectives?	Does Emily wish to avenge her own pride, her family's pride, preserve Southern tradition, teach the town a lesson?	
What does the character do to achieve the objectives?	What does Emily do to get what she wants?	

What are the results of the events?	Does Emily retain her pride in death? Do the townspeople see her in a new light?
Does the author, through action, make a comment on life?	Is the story about Emily or a way of life? Is it worth clinging to old ways?

Character

A character is a person who is often described by the author as talking, feeling, thinking, acting, and looking like a real person, or in the case of science fiction or fables, a non-human being or animal who displays human traits and complexities. Character reveals action and is itself revealed mainly through action, physical appearance, and dialogue. Before writing about character, it may be helpful to take extensive notes, guided by the following Checklist.

CHECKLIST: CONSIDERING CHARACTER

Question	Alexandra's question	Your question for your story
Who is/are the most important character(s)? (protagonists)	Who are main characters—Emily, Homer, the townspeople, the town of Jefferson?	
Who acts against important characters? (antagonists) When does the character begin to sense his or her predicament?	Who acts against Emily, Homer, the townspeople? When does Emily feel that her life values are in jeopardy? (When industrial growth chokes her neighborhood, when tax people demand money, when Homer threatens to leave her?)	
When does his or her conflict within or with the outside world begin to intensify?	What happens when Homer jilts Emily or when the townspeople pry into her life?	

| When is the character's fate decided? Are the conditions predisposed or do characters have control over destiny? | Was Emily's fate decided when the South lost the war, when her father died, when she killed Homer, or was she herself the instrument of action? |

Setting

The time and location in which action takes place in a literary work provide us with clues to understanding the story's meaning. It is much more than just scenery or a backdrop. A New England village, a frontier town, the mean streets of inner cities, or an old house can reveal important information about the physical surroundings, geographical location, and the historical period in which the story is set.

CHECKLIST: EXAMINING SETTING

Question	Alexandra's question	Your question for your story
Where does the action take place?	Does it take place in Emily's house, in town, or in people's minds?	
Does the setting remain constant or does it shift locale?	What are the differences between Emily's neighborhood when she was young and as it is now? What happens when the scene changes from Emily's old house to the town?	
Does the setting evoke particular emotions?	Does the old house evoke melancholy, fear, despair, or evil? Do the changes in the setting in town stand for rejuvenation or doom?	
What is the time, season, or weather like when action takes place?	What is the significance of the time (1870s) when Emily's house was built? What are differences between then and 1920s? What do the old men at Emily's funeral represent?	

Irony

Words used ironically often mean the opposite of what they mean on the surface. They suggest a tacit understanding between the author and the reader that words don't always mean what they say. A friend of ours, saying that he was eager to get back to Los Angeles, said, "I miss the smog terribly." We knew he was being ironic.

CHECKLIST: EXAMINING IRONY

Question	Alexandra's question	Your question for your story
What words and images express the author's attitudes to the main character?	What do words used to describe Emily say about the writer's attitude toward her?	
What words and language express the author's beliefs and temperament?	What does Emily's pride stand for? What does she have to be proud of?	
Does irony help in understanding the emotion of the work?	Does the image of death separating Homer and Emily reveal anything about Faulkner's own attitudes toward the South and the North?	

Structure

Structure is the organization of the story—the way it opens, foreshadows incidents, presents conflicts, sustains suspense, and leads to a climax. It refers to the work as a whole, comprising of the various parts intricately related to one another.

CHECKLIST: CONSIDERING STRUCTURE

Question	Alexandra's question	Your question for your story
What are the main parts—chapters, sections, stanzas?	Why the five sections in "A Rose"? What purpose do they serve to advance the story?	

Question	Alexandra's question	Your question for your story
How are the parts linked? (by chronology, reversal, flashback) and to what end?	Why do events in "A Rose" sometimes break chronology? When does the smell of the body appear first? What is the effect of such arrangement?	
Do short stories often end in dramatic reversal of fortunes or emotions?	Is the end of "A Rose" dramatic? Does it take the reader by surprise?	

Symbol

The Statue of Liberty, as a symbol of America, stands at the entrance to the New York harbor. Lady Liberty's flaming torch signifies a warm welcome for the immigrants from distant shores. The book in her hand stands for knowledge as opposed to darkness and ignorance. The fact that she is a woman symbolizes mercy and compassion for the "huddled masses." In literature, things, people, action, places, when used as symbols, are capable of multiple meanings that stimulate both our intellect and emotions.

CHECKLIST: LOOKING FOR SYMBOLIC MEANING

Question	Alexandra's question	Your question for your story
Does a particular object suggest something else?	What does Emily's house stand for? And the gas station?	
Does an object stand for an emotion?	What does Emily's ebony cane with its tarnished gold head evoke?	
Does the work represent its author's values?	Does Emily's story reveal anything about Faulkner's own feelings and attitudes?	
Can action be symbolic?	What does Emily's ultimate triumph over Homer symbolize?	

Theme

The theme song or theme music of a movie is heard, off and on, throughout its length. Likewise, the theme in a literary work is not located in any one character, action, setting, or symbol though all of them contribute to expressing the theme. It is, in fact, the unifying factor that ties the various elements of the story together. It expresses the author's attitudes and personal values that may have prompted him or her to create the work.

CHECKLIST: DETERMINING THEME

Question	Alexandra's question	Your question for your story
What are the possible subjects of the work?	What lies beneath the surface story of Emily's life?	
Does the story do more than entertain? Do we learn anything?	What do we learn from Emily's unhappy life about pride or resistance to change?	
Is the special meaning focused in one area or is it spread over the story?	What do the different segments tell us? Is one more important than others? How do they connect? Could any one be eliminated without affecting the story?	
What concrete details suggest and support the main ideas?	Emily's house, the old neighborhood, the people, Homer, the old servant—how do they suggest the main idea of the story?	

USING RESEARCH IN YOUR WRITING

Writing about literature generally involves two key steps: an **interpretation** of the work as we discussed earlier and **textual evidence** to support the reasoning of the interpretation. **Researched** writing about literature adds a third step. In addition to the above, it uses sources *outside* the text itself to support and strengthen claims.

A research paper in literature has the following characteristics:

1. It is written for a well-informed and demanding audience.

2. It has a clear purpose or thesis.

3. In addition to the text itself, it uses other scholarly writings as evidence of support, following its own rules of documentation.

Audience Consideration

Alexandra's first response was intended for herself. But before actually embarking on writing her research paper, one of her major considerations was the audience for whom the paper was intended. If her audience knew the story well, she would not have to re-tell every detail. Long plot summaries will only bore a knowledgeable audience. So before getting started, Alexandra decided to sketch a audience portrait. She referred to the following Checklist:

CHECKLIST: CONSIDERING YOUR AUDIENCE

- How old are the readers?
- Are they mostly men or women?
- What is their educational background?
- What else do I (or should I) know about their background?
- Do they know the subject?
- Do they like the subject?

Based on the information she obtained, she devised a portrait of the people for whom her writing was intended:

Most of the people who will read my paper will be my classmates, who are about as old as I am, with a few exceptions, and all of them have high school diplomas. All are enrolled in college. The teacher, for example, who is also a reader, is definitely older than most of us and has more degrees and diplomas than the students do. About half of these are men and many of the students hold part-time jobs. All of them are supposed to have read the story, and I believe most have. From the class discussions, I gathered that some people did not approve of certain characters and actions in the story. They are heavily divided on Emily. While many feel sorry for her and try to understand her, others think she is some kind of an evil being.

For such an audience, Alexandra realized she did not have to review the entire plot. In general, the audience is more interested in your interpretation than in what they already know. A paper that declares a thesis (what we intend to say) and then lapses into a summary fails to fulfill the promise it made to the audience. Alexandra decided to use as much textual evidence as she would need to convince her audience of the point she was trying to make.

▐RIAL RUN

Using the Checklist above, consider the audience for your paper. Then write a paragraph describing them.

The Thesis Statement: Declaring Your Purpose

A thesis statement is the window through which you allow your readers to view a literary work. Though the thesis grows out of your understanding of the different elements of the story—character, plot, setting, theme, structure, symbolism—your angle of vision and your purpose for writing expressed in the thesis will probably be different from that of anyone else writing about the same story. Your readers are likely to be familiar with the story and will be more interested in what you have to say about it. By announcing what follows, an effective thesis often succeeds in capturing the readers' interest. Your angle of vision also narrows the range of possibilities and limits the scope of your paper. So the thesis provides a freshness of approach to a work and keeps the discussion within the reasonable limit of the assigned paper. While affording you an opportunity to be creative in your approach, the thesis, however, requires you to return to the text frequently for concrete details to support your ideas. If you find no textual evidence for your claims, then it is a signal that you may need to re-examine your thesis.

The more evidence you gather, the more important it becomes to organize the information around your major intent. Alexandra turned to her original responses for help to pull together her ideas. She liked what she had said about detective work in understanding "A Rose for Emily." "It was like it was a mystery and I was the detective." She decided to focus on the signs or symbols that held clues for her in solving the mystery. She felt it might interest her readers to know how she had gone about this, with some help from the scholarly writings. Though she had decided on the central theme, she was not sure of where to place it. Should her paper begin with the thesis statement? Does the thesis have to be one long statement in the first place? Could she break it down into a few statements? She felt she was getting bogged down with these possibilities, and so she decided to forge ahead with the writing.

It is no doubt important to achieve focus through a thesis. But at the same time it is not worth allowing the thesis to become a straitjacket. You should have control over the thesis, not let the thesis control you. Papers are not stamped out; they evolve. Often, in the course of your writing, you might find that you are drifting away from the thesis, but what you are saying sounds good. In that case, you have the freedom to go back and modify the thesis to fit the content of the paper. Though the logical place for the thesis, as the guide for the paper, is somewhere early in the paper, there is no rule that tells us where exactly it should be. Again the writer is the best judge.

In addition to starting the essay with the thesis, you can return to it to provide an effective ending. Such a return brings the progression of ideas in the paper to their logical conclusion.

▌RIAL RUN

Try out several thesis statements as different approaches to your paper. Though your aim is to have a precise thesis, avoid getting fixed on one at this stage in the process. Look at the thesis as a tentative declaration of your intent that may change later as you get into your paper. Once you find one you like, get some feedback from your classmates or the instructor. Your purpose is not to find out whether they agree or disagree with what you have to say. They might tell you if it is a workable thesis that gives the reader a clear idea of what's to come in the paper, if it shows your approach to the story, and if its scope is limited for a writing assignment in your class.

Scholarly Writings as Evidence of Support

We are often led to believe that if our literature paper is generously sprinkled with quotations from important literary critics, we will be able to impress our readers. While this is a false notion, scholarly and critical opinions, used for a purpose, often can extend and strengthen our own ideas. For example, we may disagree with a critic's opinion and refute his or her ideas in our paper. We may find some thoughts to which we may add our own to extend them. Or we may compare two or more critical opinions in interpreting a literary work. When you do use critical material, however, it is important to cue your readers so they see where you have inserted the borrowed material to differentiate it from your own. If you quote a critic's words exactly, use quotation marks or a block quotation, depending on the length of the quote. Even if you do not use the exact words of a critic but paraphrase some of his ideas, make sure you let your readers know that. Failure to acknowledge the use of others' ideas is a serious offense. Unauthorized borrowing, **plagiarism,** is like any other form of stealing and is punishable by law. So exercise great caution when incorporating the researched material into your paper.

When you use critical and scholarly opinions, you should remember that your readers are primarily interested in what *you* have to say in *your* paper rather than what *other people* have said in *their* papers, articles, and books. Alexandra kept this in mind when she struggled to follow Faulkner's complex narrative voice. She was, in a way, pleased that she had not done much critical reading before studying the text because it forced her to wrestle with the story and eventually trust her own instincts. For her final draft, however, Alexandra realized that some of her comments would only gain strength with supportive evidence from experts. In addition, her familiarity with some of the major scholarly writings on the author would make her own voice more convincing. So she read some authorities on Faulkner in the library. She also referred to the style manual published by the Modern Language Association (MLA) for documenting her research. (For details on library research procedure and documenting following the MLA style, refer to Chapter 17.)

CHECKLIST: USING SCHOLARLY WRITINGS

- Does the critical material support my own ideas?
- Does the critical material challenge what I have to say?
- Am I comparing two or more critical opinions—and for what purpose?
- Am I focusing too much on what others have had to say and not enough on my own ideas? Have I maintained a balance between the two?
- Have I used quotation marks when using the exact words of a critic? Have I identified the critic to my readers?
- If the critical material consists of a long paragraph or more than a paragraph, have I used the block quotation method to set it off from the rest of my paper?
- Have I acknowledged paraphrased critical material in the body of the paper as well as in the work-cited section?

Before turning in her final draft, Alexandra **proofread** her paper carefully. Working as her own editor, in collaboration with her instructor, Alexandra fine-tuned her paper to be the best that she could create by using the following Checklist:

CHECKLIST: EDITING THE FINAL DRAFT

- Does my opening clearly tell the reader what I am writing about and my attitude toward my topic? Is my purpose clear? Do I sound too dogmatic or self-effacing? Do I sound too pompous or too chatty? Will I make a positive impression in some way on my readers?
- Does my paper have some original ideas? Is my topic stimulating? Does my paper have something to say that might interest the reader?
- Do I use enough details and examples to make my point? Do I provide textual support for what I say? Do I use too much or too little critical opinion?
- Do I have a strong ending paragraph? Does it relate to the purpose of my essay? Do I leave the readers with something to think about?
- Have I used transitional words to tie my sentences and paragraphs together? Are the individual paragraphs unified, coherent, and well developed? In other words, is my paper easy to follow?

• As an interpretation exercise, has my paper used both my thinking abilities and my intuitive feelings? Have I avoided too much of either feeling or the intellect?

PRESENTING ALEXANDRA'S FINAL DRAFT

My Own Understanding of "A Rose for Emily"

Alexandra Cruz

Alexandra uses critical opinion as the framework for her paper.

1   In a book called <u>William Faulkner of Yoknapatawpha County,</u> the author, Lewis Leary, says of Faulkner's writing, "...Faulkner's writing can seem unnecessarily roundabout and obscure. He often withholds information which it is necessary for a reader to have in order to understand a person or a situation. He moves backward and forward in time so that a reader has difficulty in determining exactly where he is. Rather than telling a story simply and directly, from its beginning to its end, he often proceeds in circles. For life is fluid, and what man does often moves in circles" (24). Leary further states about Faulkner's writing style, "In life, he seems to say, no story is ever finished. Lovers die, but not love. The secrets of no person are ever completely revealed" (24).

Alexandra begins to understand the sequence of events, which had confused her earlier.

Thesis limits the topic.

2   I do not think any other words would explain Faulkner's writings better. I think Faulkner withholds information often necessary to understand a person or situation. And he sees life as a cycle. No matter where one starts on the circle, one always winds up in the same place. To Faulkner, it did not matter if he started at the end of Emily's life. The cycle would still be completed. These two statements by Lewis Leary on Faulkner's writing style certainly helped my understanding of "A Rose for Emily."

Alexandra uses quotes and paraphrased text as supportive evidence. She does not give long summaries for her readers.

3   In keeping with his belief that the secrets of a person are never completely revealed, Faulkner, in "A Rose for Emily," revealed very little directly about Emily. Throughout the story we get vague descriptions of Emily. We know that she is fat from the description of her when she is talking to the men about her taxes. Her personality is briefly touched upon when she is described as someone who carried her head high even in her fallen state. We are also told that "she passed from generation to generation--dear inescapable, impervious, tranquil, and perverse" (79). But do these descriptions really tell us much about Emily? I do not think so. Most of

Alexandra uses her voice to tell the reader her own interpretation.

Alexandra uses researched information to interpret the story.

what is said about Emily are the impressions the townspeople have about her. We meet Emily through the eyes of the town. But I don't think Emily is only what the town thinks of her. We never go into her head to find out what she is thinking or feeling. There is more to Emily than what Faulkner lets us know. However, that's what makes his story so intriguing. Faulkner thought that people were mysterious, and he believed that no one knew everything about anyone else. He believed that people had secrets that they never revealed. This makes Emily in the story close to a real person because there are so many mysteries about Emily that are never revealed. We never find out everything about Emily because the townspeople who tell us about her do not know much themselves.

4   Lewis Leary's comment about Faulkner's writings that lovers die but love doesn't can be applied to "A Rose for Emily." Homer Barron not only dies but is killed by his lover in the story. However, Emily's love for him does not die. This is evident by the way she preserves their bedroom. Everything in it remains perfect for the perfectly happy couple. Emily was starved for love. I feel she kills the person she loves so much in order never to lose him. After her father dies, Homer Barron is the only person who can give her the love she craves for.

Alexandra's own interpretations are supported by critical and textual evidence.

5   Many who read this story believe that Emily slept with the corpse of Homer Barron. However, in an article on "A Rose for Emily," the critic John V. Hogopian suggests that the hair found on the second pillow was left there on purpose. "The act of cutting off one's hair (or locks of it) was among the ancient Greeks a ritual gesture of grief and farewell or remembrance at the corpse or grave of a beloved person. Since Emily's lover is named Homer, something Greek about the action involving him would seem to be suggested" (68). Of course, this is only a theory; however, Emily comes from an aristocratic Southern family and is most likely to have read Homer, who mentions this ritual in his writings. Emily may have taken her knowledge of this ritual and used it to show her love for Homer Barron.

Alexandra uses critical evidence to support her opinion.

6   While reading the story, I found other symbols like the hair that Faulkner uses to tell the reader about Emily. For example, at the very beginning of the story, she is described as a "fallen monument." Later, he sees her as "those fallen angels in colored church windows." He also says "her face is like a strained flag." He further describes her presence in the old house "like the carven torso of an idol in a niche." In all of these descriptions, Emily is seen in terms of inani-

Here Alexandra extends critical opinion to include her own interpretation.

mate objects, all objects for which people have reverence, however. I believe these do not describe Emily herself but are a symbol of what she represents in the story. Emily represents something bigger, beyond her person. She represents the time when she was young. She represents the old South.

7   A passage in the <u>Academic American Encyclopedia</u> states that "In his lifetime and in his works, Faulkner bore witness to great political, economic, and social changes on the life of the South" (36). I believe "A Rose for Emily" is one of his works in which he focuses on the changes in Southern society. The new South, represented by the tax collectors, intrudes into Emily's old ways. When Emily dies, what she stands for dies with her.

8   The title "A Rose for Emily" itself is suggestive and symbolic. Where is the rose? There is no mention of the flower in the whole story. There may be several explanations about why Faulkner gives the story this particular title. The title may imply that Emily deserves a rose or that she stands for a rose, the treasured memory of old Confederate veterans. A further suggestion may be that the rose stands for lovers.

9   My own theory, however, is altogether different. I see the rose as a symbol for saying good-bye to someone who has died. When Emily died, I could see a rose being put on her coffin. In the story, however, I see the rose as a symbol of saying good-bye to what Emily stands for--the old aristocratic South.

Alexandra uses her own voice to interpret the title of the story.

10   Faulkner, one of America's best-known novelists, "often considered his books failures because they did not measure up to his expectations" (<u>Encyclopedia</u>, 36). However, the world disagreed with him because he received the Nobel Prize for literature in 1949. I also think he underestimated his abilities. If you read ''A Rose for Emily'' as I did the first time, read it again. As a matter of fact, scrutinize it as I did. Then you will see the ingenuity of the structure and how the hints, suggestions, and symbols throughout the story let you piece the whole story together like a jigsaw puzzle.

Works Cited

"Faulkner." <u>Academic American Encyclopedia</u>, 1987 ed.

Hogopian, John V. "Faulkner's 'A Rose for Emily,'" <u>Explicator</u> vol. XXII (1964):68.

Leary, Lewis. <u>William Faulkner of Yoknapatawpha County</u>. New York: Thomas Y. Crowell, 1973.

Commentary on Alexandra's Final Draft

In this paper, Alexandra Cruz deftly succeeds in preserving her own "reading" even while incorporating critical views into her writing. By doing this, she is able to overcome one of the most difficult challenges faced by the researcher—becoming overwhelmed by authoritative opinions to the point of losing one's own voice. As we discussed earlier in this chapter, writing about literature uses **interpretation**, which involves our critical thinking abilities as well as our own feelings and emotions. From that point of view, this paper is Alexandra's own interpretation of "A Rose for Emily," supported by the text itself and established critical opinions. It is, as the title suggests, her own understanding of the story, supported by two critical views on Faulkner's writings—the way he withholds information and his feelings about life in general. The last sentence of the introduction, "These two statements by Faulkner certainly helped my understanding of "A Rose for Emily," limits her topic and lets the reader know the focus of her paper.

When Alexandra was planning her paper, she had prepared a sketch of her audience. Because she knew that most of her readers will have read the story, she was able to avoid weighing down the paper with detailed summaries and concentrate on her purpose, which was to show the reader how she read and understood the story. Yet throughout the paper, she uses textual evidence to support her ideas. For example, her statement in paragraph 3, "Faulkner revealed very little directly about Emily," is consistently supported by textual evidence to make it quite convincing, her main argument being that the readers see Emily through the eyes of the townspeople who did not really know Emily.

In addition to the text, some critical writings on William Faulkner enhanced Alexandra's own understanding of the story. In fact, what the critics said helped in removing two major obstacles in her enjoyment of Faulkner. First, Alexandra was completely perplexed by the way Faulkner "jumped around on purpose." She was vaguely aware of a purpose but was not quite sure what it was. She was equally puzzled by the paucity of information the author provided about the characters. Her research on Faulkner helped her understand both Faulkner's major ideas and how those ideas translated into his writings. In fact, she uses the critical opinion as a framework for her paper to which she adds her own thoughts. For example, when she discussed how the reader has to look for clues in the text for comprehension, she refers to a critical reading that uses Greek mythology. Following that interpretation, Alexandra offers her own when she shows, through textual evidence, that Faulkner created Emily's character to represent something bigger and beyond herself, an object of reverence and respect.

Another distinctive feature of Alexandra's paper is the strong narrative "I." Not all research papers in literature use a personal voice as Alexandra's does, but there is no rule that says one cannot use one's own voice in research papers as long as one adheres to the basic guidelines of writing about literature: not to bore the reader with a summary but to use the text to uphold opinions, not to use critical opinion as embellishment, not to use only the head or the heart but to use both intellect and intuition in interpreting literature. Alexandra's use of the personal "I" does not violate these basic guidelines but helps her establish a close bond between her and her reader. Her own self-expression may encourage her readers to trust their own voice. Since self-expressive writing is somewhat relaxing and informal, we have to know if the audience will be able to relate to it. Alexandra's own assessment of her audience assured her that they would be able to identify with her use of the first person point of view as long as she used the text and critical writings to support her own voice.

Questions for Further Thought

1. How do the two statements about Faulkner help Alexandra lead into her part? How does she weave the critic's opinion into her own purpose? Does a reading of the first paragraph give you an idea what her paper is going to be about?

2. Alexandra counters, supports, or extends the critical opinions with her own. What does this juxtaposition of opinions do for the paper? Does she convince the reader of the validity of her own critical insights? How?

3. Throughout her paper, Alexandra uses the first person point of view. For example, in paragraph 8 she says, "My own theory, however, is altogether different. I see the rose as a symbol for saying goodbye to someone who has died." What effect does this voice have on the paper?

4. According to Alexandra, Emily is close to a real person because there are so many mysteries about Emily that are never told. Do you agree with this statement? Is it possible to know someone completely in real life? Would you have wanted Faulkner to tell you more about Emily?

5. In spite of the scant information, Alexandra is able to piece together Emily's life quite adequately. What are some of the clues in the story that she uses?

6. Was it difficult for you to follow the paper because Alexandra does not retell the story? What do you think prompted her decision?

7. Interpreting literature, as discussed earlier, is an activity that is both intellectual and intuitive, involving both the head and the heart. Where would you place Alexandra's paper? Is it too intellectual or too intuitive? Support your response with evidence from the paper.

READING AND WRITING ABOUT POETRY

We have presented the process of writing a literature paper by using a short story. However, you may also be asked to write about poetry or drama.

While plays and poems can certainly be analyzed and understood using the techniques used above with the short story, they also have special characteristics that you should consider.

Poetry is, Emily Dickinson said, "what takes the top of your head off." If it is capable of doing that, it must be powerful stuff. It is language compressed in a relatively short space with force, elegance, rhyme, and meter that has gained for poetry its reputation as the most intense of all writings. To understand a poem, its language has to be "unpacked" to manifest its latent meaning. Each beguiling and elusive word has to be read slowly to feel the power of the language. This is a challenging task in our complex technological society. According to Mark Strand, the former poet laureate of the United States, "In poetry the power of language is most palpable. But in a culture that favors speed reading, fast food, 10-second news bites and other abbreviated forms of ingestion, who wants something that encourages a slowdown?" (*The New York Times Book Review,* September 15, 1991, p. 36). If we do take the time, the pleasures well compensate for the effort.

It is hard to define or describe poetry. The critic Walter Pater said that all art aspires to music. The difference between poetry and prose is that poetry aspires to music more intensely. Like the short story, a poem may have a plot, setting, characters, theme, symbols, and irony. However, poets also use rhyme and meter to communicate their meaning. An example of poetry contrasted with prose may help illustrate this. Consider a poem by Emily Dickinson and its prose summary.

I gave myself to Him–

I gave myself to Him–
And took Himself, for Pay,
The solemn contract of a Life
Was ratified, this way–

The Wealth might disappoint–
Myself a poorer prove
Than this great Purchaser suspect,
The Daily Own–of Love

Depreciate the Vision–
But till the Merchant buy–
Still Fable–in the Isles of Spice–
The subtle Cargoes–lie–

At least–'tis Mutual–Risk–
Some–found it–Mutual Gain–
Sweet Debt of Life–Each Night to owe–
Insolvent–every Noon–

A possible **paraphrase** of the poem is:

I gave myself to him in marriage and took him as a payment. This was how we worked out this serious contract. He might be disappointing to me, but I was also a worse bargain for him than he had anticipated. Each day the value of what we have purchased from each other goes down. But until one buys, one doesn't know the value. At least the disappointment in marriage is the same for both. Every night we owe each other the sweet payment of love only to find each other bankrupt (insolvent) every noon.

The more accessible language of the paraphrase makes it easier to understand the poem but it also does away with the special features that make it a poem. To begin with, it completely obliterates its shape. Each short paragraph or **stanza** gives the poem its special form, intrinsically, verbally, and visually. The stanzas with their **rhyme** (pay/way, prove/love, buy/lie) and **meter**, a system of stressed ´ and unstressed ˘ syllables to create rhythm, (Ĭ gáve m̆ysélf t̆o hím,/ănd tóok m̆ysélf fŏr páy) help the poem skip along lithely. Poems are best read aloud, which makes it possible for one to hear the "music," mostly created by rhyme and meter, though not all poetry, particularly modern poetry, uses rhyme. In the process of bringing the deeper meaning of the poem to the surface, the paraphrase not only destroys the shape but also the subtlety, elegance, and rhythm, and dilutes the force of the language. The use of mercantile and legalistic **images** (contract, ratified, merchant, debt, risk, gain, purchase, depreciate, cargoes, insolvent) brings out the commercial and contractual nature of marriage. Poets write in images because by creating word pictures, images have the capacity to say a lot in a short space. Through the use of powerful images, the poet suggests that marriage is a form of mutual debt that the husband and wife owe each other. It is as risky as gambling in the stock market, foreshadowing the alienation implicit in marriage in a society dominated by materialistic values. If Dickinson had directly stated that marriage is like gambling, she would have used a **simile**, which compares one item to another, using the sign of comparison such as *like* or *as*. But she uses **metaphors** which are implied comparisons without the *like* or *as*, for example, "the solemn contract of life." In fact, the whole poem is an extended metaphor, comparing marriage to a contractual commercial agreement.

Here is a poem by Diane Burns for your own interpretation:

Sure You Can Ask Me a Personal Question

How do you do?
No, I am not Chinese.
No, not Spanish.
No, I am American Indi-uh, Native American.
No, not from India.
No, not Apache.
No, not Navajo.
No, not Sioux.

No, we are not extinct.
    Yes, Indin.
Oh?
    So that's where you got those high cheekbones.
Your great grandmother, huh?
    An Indian Princess, huh?
Hair down to there?
    Let me guess. Cherokee?
Oh, so you've had an Indian friend?
    That close?
Oh, so you've had an Indian lover?
    That tight?
Oh, so you've had an Indian servant?
    That much?
Yeah, it was awful what you guys did to us.
    It's real decent of you to apologize.
No, I don't know where you can get peyote.
    No, I don't know where you can get Navajo rugs real cheap.
No, I didn't make this. I bought it at Bloomingdales.
    Thank you. I like your hair too.
I don't know if anyone knows whether or not Cher is really Indian.
    No, I didn't make it rain tonight.
Yeah. Uh-huh. Spirituality.
    Uh-huh. Yeah. Spirituality. Uh-huh. Mother
Earth. Yeah. Uh'huh. Uh-huh. Spirituality.
    No, I didn't major in archery.
Yeah, a lot of us drink too much.
    Some of us can't drink enough.
This ain't no stoic look.
    This is my face.

▋RIAL RUN

Paraphrase "Sure You Can Ask Me a Personal Question." First answer the following questions, which may help you to understand the poem; then write your paraphrase and interpretation.

CRITICAL READING

1. How would you characterize your first impression of the poem?

2. Who is the speaker? What does the poem reveal about the speaker's character?

3. With whom is the speaker talking, in what situation?

4. Can you figure out the statements of the other person?

5. If the speaker is talking about a specific situation, from what perspective (akin to point of view in prose) is she doing so? What significance does it have for the speaker?

6. The reader can only hear the voice of the speaker, so the poem is a **monologue.** It would be a **dialogue** if the reader could hear both the speaker and the person being spoken to. Can you make the poem into a dialogue by providing the other speaking voice? What is gained or lost?

7. Do you know anything about the other person's attitude? How do you know it?

8. How does the speaker respond to the other person's comments and questions?

9. Can you point to some of the imagery in the poem? Emily Dickinson's poem, "I Gave Myself to Him," uses images predominantly from the legal world. How would you characterize the images in this poem? Why does the poet use them? Is the language formal or straightforward and informal? Why? How would you compare it with Dickinson's language?

10. The last two lines are crucial to the understanding of the poem. Can you explain their meaning and significance?

11. Is the central idea of the poem stated directly or indirectly? Where would you find it?

12. After a careful study, have you altered your first impression? If so, how and why?

READING AND WRITING ABOUT DRAMA

Drama is the most familiar literary genre to the generations raised on movies and television. A sitcom is often a one-act play, and television commercials, too, depict dramatic situations. Drama has all the elements of the story such as setting (commonly referred to as scenes in drama), characters, plot, theme, and so on. But two most essential elements of drama are **action** leading to **conflict** followed by **resolution** often referred to as **denouement,** and **dialogue.** A television commercial that lasts a few seconds is often intensely dramatic. It may show action in the form of two characters choosing two different brands of cereal. Conflict ensues when they disagree over the amount of essential nutrients in the two brands. The conflict is resolved when one character presents "evidence" that claims superiority of one brand of cereal over the other.

Dialogue is perhaps what distinguishes drama from the other literary genres. The audience learns what is on the characters' minds by listening to the words they speak. In a novel or a story, however, an omniscient narrator, through often long descriptive passages, enables the reader to enter the characters' mind and learn about their thoughts and feelings. This is one of the reasons why movie versions of great novels are often so disappointing. Dialogue and facial expressions of the characters often do not capture the richness of the novelists' contemplative ideas. Playwrights, on the other hand, allow the characters to speak their minds, often through monologues and asides, so it may not be necessary to enter their minds.

Because people "talk" to each other, the language of drama comes close to the language of real life, hence more easily understood. We are familiar with the way people talk in Woody Allen's *Death Knocks* (following); we hear similar language spoken around us. You may say, "But what about Shakespeare's *King Lear*?" Precisely because we do not hear Elizabethan English spoken around us, we find the language difficult. Most people in Shakespeare's time probably did not find the language opaque as Shakespeare was one of the most popular and prolific playwrights in his country. Yet the vision in both *Death Knocks* and *King Lear* is shaped by characters, scenes, action, and dialogue that essentialize certain human conditions.

Because drama portrays characters who often speak and act like real people, readers and viewers can identify with them. We get involved with the lives of the characters, share their joys and sorrows, want to warn or caution them, especially if we know something that they do not know. How many times have we watched a play or a movie and wished to warn the characters about something that we, the audience, knew would happen to them that they were completely unaware of? This is **dramatic irony,** a device used by playwrights to let the audience to know more than the characters do, that ensures a total involvement by the audience.

Plays are written to be performed. So the best way to "read" a play is to see it performed. If you cannot go to see it, read the play in class, with different people playing the characters. Read Woody Allen's short play *Death Knocks* in the classroom. Those of you familiar with Allen's films know of his obsession with death. Allen's treatment of this solemn theme is funny and particularly contemporary because death, like life, often does not make much sense. The play amuses us because we are surprised by the absurd and fantastic turn of events and are willing to submit ourselves to the author's imagination.

DEATH KNOCKS

Woody Allen

The play takes place in the bedroom of the Nat Ackermans' two-story house, somewhere in Kew Gardens. The carpeting is wall-to-wall. There is a big double bed and a large vanity. The room is elaborately furnished and curtained, and on the walls there are several paintings and a not really attractive barometer. Soft theme music as the curtain rises. Nat Ackerman, a bald, paunchy fifty-seven-year-old dress manufacturer is lying on the bed finishing off tomorrow's Daily News. *He wears a bathrobe and slippers, and reads by a bed light clipped to the white headboard of the bed. The time is near midnight. Suddenly we hear a noise, and Nat sits up and looks at the window.*

Nat: What the hell is that?

(Climbing awkwardly through the window is a sombre, caped figure. The intruder wears a black hood and skintight black clothes. The hood covers his head but not his face, which is middle-aged and stark white. He is something like Nat in appearance. He huffs audibly and then trips over the windowsill and falls into the room.)

Death   *(for it is no one else)*:   Jesus Christ. I nearly broke my neck.

Nat   *(watching with bewilderment)*:   Who are you?

Death: Death.

Nat: Who?

Death: Death. Listen—can I sit down? I nearly broke my neck. I'm shaking like a leaf.

Nat: Who *are* you?

Death: *Death.* You got a glass of water?

Nat: Death? What do you mean, Death?

Death: What is wrong with you? You see the black costume and the whitened face?

Nat: Yeah.

Death: Is it Halloween?

Nat: No.

Death: Then I'm Death. Now can I get a glass of water—or a Fresca?

Nat: If this is some joke—

Death: What kind of joke? You're fifty-seven? Nat Ackerman? One eighteen Pacific Street? Unless I blew it—where's that call sheet? *(He fumbles through pocket, finally producing a card with an address on it. It seems to check.)*

Nat: What do you want with me?

Death: What do I want? What do you think I want?

Nat: You must be kidding. I'm in perfect health.

Death   *(unimpressed)*:   Uh-huh. *(Looking around)* This is a nice place. You do it yourself?

Nat: We had a decorator, but we worked with her.

Death   *(looking at picture on the wall)*:   I love those kids with the big eyes.

Nat: I don't want to go yet.

Death: *You* don't want to go? Please don't start in. As it is, I'm nauseous from the climb.

Nat: What climb?

Death: I climbed up the drainpipe. I was trying to make a dramatic entrance. I see the big windows and you're awake reading. I figure it's worth a shot. I'll climb up and enter with a little—you know...(*Snaps fingers*) Meanwhile, I get my heel caught on some vines, the drainpipe breaks, and I'm hanging by a thread. Then my cape begins to tear. Look, let's just go. It's been a rough night.

Nat: You broke my drainpipe?

Death: Broke. It didn't break. It's a little bent. Didn't you hear anything? I slammed into the ground.

Nat: I was reading.

Death: You must have really been engrossed. (*Lifting newspaper Nat was reading*) "NAB COEDS IN POT ORGY." Can I borrow this?

Nat: I'm not finished.

Death: Er—I don't know how to put this to you, pal....

Nat: Why didn't you just ring downstairs?

Death: I'm telling you, I could have, but how does it look? This way I get a little drama going. Something. Did you read "Faust"?

Nat: What?

Death: And what if you had company? You're sitting there with important people. I'm Death—I should ring the bell and traipse right in the front? Where's your thinking?

Nat: Listen, Mister, it's very late.

Death: Yeah. Well, you want to go?

Nat: Go where?

Death: Death. It. The Thing. The Happy Hunting Grounds. (*Looking at his own knee*) Y'know, that's a pretty bad cut. My first job, I'm liable to get gangrene yet.

Nat: Now, wait a minute. I need time. I'm not ready to go.

Death: I'm sorry. I can't help you. I'd like to, but it's the moment.

Nat: How can it be the moment? I just merged with Modiste Originals.

Death: What's the difference, a couple of bucks more or less.

Nat: Sure, what do you care? You guys probably have all your expenses paid.

Death: You want to come along now?

Nat (*studying him*): I'm sorry, but I cannot believe you're Death.

Death:	Why? What'd you expect—Rock Hudson?
Nat:	No, it's not that.
Death:	I'm sorry if I disappointed you.
Nat:	Don't get upset. I don't know, I always thought you'd be...uh ...taller.
Death:	I'm five seven. It's average for my weight.
Nat:	You look a little like me.
Death:	Who should I look like? I'm your death.
Nat:	Give me some time. Another day.
Death:	I can't. What do you want me to say?
Nat:	One more day. Twenty-four hours.
Death:	What do you need it for? The radio said rain tomorrow.
Nat:	Can't we work out something?
Death:	Like what?
Nat:	You play chess?
Death:	No, I don't.
Nat:	I once saw a picture of you playing chess.
Death:	Couldn't be me, because I don't play chess. Gin rummy, maybe.
Nat:	You play gin rummy?
Death:	Do I play gin rummy? Is Paris a city?
Nat:	You're good, huh?
Death:	Very good.
Nat:	I'll tell you what I'll do—
Death:	Don't make any deals with me.
Nat:	I'll play you gin rummy. If you win, I'll go immediately. If I win, give me some more time. A little bit—one more day.
Death:	Who's got time to play gin rummy?
Nat:	Come on. If you're so good.
Death:	Although I feel like a game....
Nat:	Come on. Be a sport. We'll shoot for a half hour.
Death:	I really shouldn't.
Nat:	I got the cards right here. Don't make a production.
Death:	All right, come on. We'll play a little. It'll relax me.
Nat	(*getting cards, pad, and pencil*): You won't regret this.
Death:	Don't give me a sales talk. Get the cards and give me a Fresca and put out something. For God's sake, a stranger drops in, you don't have potato chips or pretzels.
Nat:	There's M&M's downstairs in a dish.

Death: M&M's. What if the President came? He'd get M&M's, too?

Nat: You're not the President.

Death: Deal.

(*Nat deals, turns up a five.*)

Nat: You want to play a tenth of a cent a point to make it interesting?

Death: It's not interesting enough for you?

Nat: I play better when money's at stake.

Death: Whatever you say, Newt.

Nat: Nat. Nat Ackerman. You don't know my name?

Death: Newt, Nat—I got such a headache.

Nat: You want that five?

Death: No.

Nat: So pick.

Death   (*surveying his hand as he picks*):   Jesus, I got nothing here.

Nat: What's it like?

Death: What's what like?

(*Throughout the following, they pick and discard.*)

Nat: Death.

Death: What should it be like? You lay there.

Nat: Is there anything after?

Death: Aha, you're saving twos.

Nat: I'm asking. Is there anything after?

Death   (*absently*):   You'll see.

Nat: Oh, then I will actually see something?

Death: Well, maybe I shouldn't have put it that way. Throw.

Nat: To get an answer from you is a big deal.

Death: I'm playing cards.

Nat: All right, play, play.

Death: Meanwhile, I'm giving you one card after another.

Nat: Don't look through the discards.

Death: I'm not looking. I'm straightening them up. What was the knock card?

Nat: Four. You ready to knock already?

Death: Who said I'm ready to knock? All I asked was what was the knock card.

Nat: And all I asked was is there anything for me to look forward to.

Death:	Play.
Nat:	Can't you tell me anything? Where do we go?
Death:	We? To tell you the truth, *you* fall in a crumpled heap on the floor.
Nat:	Oh, I can't wait for that! Is it going to hurt?
Death:	Be over in a second.
Nat:	Terrific. (*Sighs*) I needed this. A man merges with Modiste Originals....
Death:	How's four points?
Nat:	You're knocking?
Death:	Four points is good?
Nat:	No, I got two.
Death:	You're kidding.
Nat:	No, you lose.
Death:	Holy Christ, and I thought you were saving sixes.
Nat:	No. Your deal. Twenty points and two boxes. Shoot. (*Death deals*) I must fall on the floor, eh? I can't be standing over the sofa when it happens?
Death:	No. Play.
Nat:	Why not?
Death:	Because you fall on the floor! Leave me alone. I'm trying to concentrate.
Nat:	Why must it be on the floor? That's all I'm saying! Why can't the whole thing happen and I'll stand next to the sofa?
Death:	I'll try my best. Now can we play?
Nat:	That's all I'm saying. You remind me of Moe Lefkowitz. He's also stubborn.
Death:	I remind him of Moe Lefkowitz. I'm one of the most terrifying figures you could possibly imagine, and him I remind of Moe Lefkowitz. What is he, a furrier?
Nat:	You should be such a furrier. He's good for eighty thousand a year. Passementeries. He's got his own factory. Two points.
Death:	What?
Nat:	Two points. I'm knocking. What have you got?
Death:	My hand is like a basketball score.
Nat:	And it's spades.
Death:	If you didn't talk so much.

(*They redeal and play on.*)

Nat: What'd you mean before when you said this was your first job?

Death: What does it sound like?

Nat: What are you telling me—that nobody ever went before?

Death: Sure they went. But I didn't take them.

Nat: So who did?

Death: Others.

Nat: There's others?

Death: Sure. Each one has his own personal way of going.

Nat: I never knew that.

Death: Why should you know? Who are you?

Nat: What do you mean who am I? Why—I'm nothing?

Death: Not nothing. You're a dress manufacturer. Where do you come to knowledge of the eternal mysteries?

Nat: What are you talking about? I make a beautiful dollar. I sent two kids through college. One is in advertising, the other's married. I got my own home. I drive a Chrysler. My wife has whatever she wants. Maids, mink coat, vacations. Right now she's at the Eden Roc. Fifty dollars a day because she wants to be near her sister. I'm supposed to join her next week, so what do you think I am—some guy off the street?

Death: All right. Don't be so touchy.

Nat: Who's touchy?

Death: How would you like it if I got insulted quickly?

Nat: Did I insult you?

Death: You didn't say you were disappointed in me?

Nat: What do you expect? You want me to throw you a block party?

Death: I'm not talking about that. I mean me personally. I'm too short, I'm this, I'm that.

Nat: I said you looked like me. It's like a reflection.

Death: All right, deal, deal.

   (*They continue to play as music steals in and the lights dim until all is in total darkness. The lights slowly come up again, and now it is later and their game is over. Nat tallies.*)

Nat: Sixty-eight...one-fifty...Well, you lose.

Death   (*dejectedly looking through the deck*):   I knew I shouldn't have thrown that nine. Damn it.

Nat: So I'll see you tomorrow.

Death: What do you mean you'll see me tomorrow?

Nat:	I won the extra day. Leave me alone.
Death:	You were serious?
Nat:	We made a deal.
Death:	Yeah, but—
Nat:	Don't "but" me. I won twenty-four hours. Come back tomorrow.
Death:	I didn't know we were actually playing for time.
Nat:	That's too bad about you. You should pay attention.
Death:	Where am I going to go for twenty-four hours?
Nat:	What's the difference? The main thing is I won an extra day.
Death:	What do you want me to do—walk the streets?
Nat:	Check into a hotel and go to a movie. Take a *schvitz*.[1] Don't make a federal case.
Death:	Add the score again.
Nat:	Plus you owe me twenty-eight dollars.
Death:	*What?*
Nat:	That's right, Buster. Here it is—read it.
Death	(*going through pockets*): I have a few singles—not twenty-eight dollars.
Nat:	I'll take a check.
Death:	From what account?
Nat:	Look who I'm dealing with.
Death:	Sue me. Where do I keep my checking account?
Nat:	All right, gimme what you got and we'll call it square.
Death:	Listen, I need that money.
Nat:	Why should you need money?
Death:	What are you talking about? You're going to the Beyond.
Nat:	So?
Death:	So—you know how far that is?
Nat:	So?
Death:	So, where's gas? Where's tolls?
Nat:	We're going by car!
Death:	You'll find out. (*Agitatedly*) Look—I'll be back tomorrow, and you'll give me a chance to win the money back. Otherwise I'm in definite trouble.
Nat:	Anything you want. Double or nothing we'll play. I'm liable to win an extra week or a month. The way you play, maybe years.
Death:	Meantime I'm stranded.

[1]*schvitz:* steam bath.

Nat: See you tomorrow.

Death (*being edged to the doorway*): Where's a good hotel? What am I talking about hotel, I got no money. I'll go sit in Bickford's.[2] (*He picks up the* News.)

Nat: Out. Out. That's my paper. (*He takes it back.*)

Death (*exiting*): I couldn't just take him and go. I had to get involved in rummy.

Nat (*calling after him*): And be careful going downstairs. On one of the steps the rug is loose.

(*And, on cue, we hear a terrific crash. Nat sighs, then crosses to the bedside table and makes a phone call.*)

Nat: Hello, Moe? Me. Listen, I don't know if somebody's playing a joke, or what, but Death was just here. We played a little gin....No, *Death.* In person. Or somebody who claims to be Death. But, Moe, he's such a *schlep!*[3]

Curtain

CRITICAL READING

1. The play begins abruptly, without exposition, that is without telling the viewer or reader much about the past or present context. What effect is achieved by this beginning? Because we do not have much information, does it affect our understanding of the play?

2. Discuss the use of dramatic irony. For example, because we know who the intruder is, what nuances in the language are we able to capture that escape Nat Ackerman?

3. The setting of the play, as in most of Allen's works, is New York City. The locale of this play is Kew Gardens, a residential neighborhood in Queens, one of the five boroughs of New York. Point out the objects that make it a particularly New York setting? What elements in the setting add to the humor?

4. Of the two characters, is one more important than the other? Is one major and the other minor? How do they each contribute to the overall theme of the play?

5. The dialogue moves fast and is full of examples of local color. Can you point them out? What do they add to the play? Does the dialogue amuse you? Why?

6. What is the central conflict in the play? Is it resolved to our satisfaction?

[2]*Bickford's:* a now defunct chain of coffee shops in New York City.
[3]*schlep:* a jerk or nerd.

7. Plays are meant to be performed. Imagine yourself as the director of *Death Knocks*. How would you want the action staged? How would you cast and coach the actors? Are there points in the play that pose special interpretive challenges to you from this angle?

 **RIAL RUN**

Focus on any one of the literary elements in *Death Knocks* or any other play you may have been assigned (character, plot, setting, symbol). Create a thesis statement that relates your analysis of the literary element you select to the overall theme of the play.

A BASIC GUIDE TO RESEARCH IN LITERATURE

The Book Review Digest, New York: The H. W. Wilson Company.

Gibaldi, Joseph, and Walter S. Achtert, eds. *MLA Handbook for Writers of Research Papers.* 3rd ed. New York: Modern Language Association, 1985.

The MLA Directory of Periodicals: A Guide to Journals and Series in Languages and Literature, New York: Modern Language Association.

The MLA International Bibliography of Books and Articles on Modern Languages, New York: Modern Language Association.

Readers' Guide to Periodical Literature: An Author and Subject Index to Selected General Interest Periodicals, New York: The H. W. Wilson Company.

CHAPTER FOURTEEN

WRITING A SOCIOLOGY PAPER

As an academic discipline, sociology is the systematic study of people living together and interacting with each other within an organization or entity called society. But sociology is not only a subject studied in college. It is a part of our everyday lives because, as people living in society, we interact with other people, follow rules of conduct and behavior, and try to bring about changes in our surroundings and in the way we live. Sociology investigates how people come together as a social entity, what skills and values they acquire and how, what kind of behavior is acceptable or unacceptable, and what roles people play as members of society.

The first person to study society in a systematic way was the French philosopher Auguste Comte, who used the term "sociology" to describe his writings (published between 1830 and 1842) about the collective behavior of people living in society. He felt that philosophy, psychology, political science, and economics—disciplines that dealt primarily with selected aspects of life—did not sufficiently deal with relationships between human behaviors. Sociology, therefore, grew out of a need to identify patterns of behavior among people and provide explanations for such patterns. It became a major academic discipline in the early twentieth century.

As a behavioral science, sociology often uses organized and systematic methods of investigation and formulates theories to explain the findings. But we do not have be social scientists to read and write about sociology as it covers a wide range of topics and uses different modes of investigation, from the more systematic that rely on experiments, charts, and graphs to those that use readings and observation. We advance our understanding of society when, for instance, we observe and write about group behavior of children in a day-care center. We may notice patterns of behavior that may prove or disprove accepted notions of child behavior. While we may not all be sociologists, sociology is very much a part of our lives.

WRITING ASSIGNMENT

Select a social issue that you feel strongly about. For example, in general, women are paid less than men for the same jobs. Or children are growing up with too much violence around them, especially on TV and in the movies. Write a paper in which you investigate the issue, discuss causes, provide observed and researched evidence, and recommend changes that you would like to see.

READING THE WRITING ASSIGNMENT

The assignment calls for you to select and investigate a social issue. What is a social issue? Since we know that society is made up of many different individuals, a social issue must, therefore, touch a large number of people. If you become too focused on what affects only you or someone you know, your paper will be more personal than sociological. For example, a conclusion that there are no inequities in women's earnings based on your own personal situation will not be a sociological investigation. An important requirement of this assignment is, therefore, using researched evidence, in addition to your own observation, to speculate about causes and provide solutions.

The selection of a topic that you feel strongly about is key to a successful paper. Your own observations, opinions, and enthusiasm about a particular issue, supported by some published research, are your best assets. Try to avoid topics that you think are very current but that may not appeal to you personally. Your selection should also be guided by the scope of the topic. If it is too broad, it needs to be narrowed to fit your purpose. For example, a paper on the inequities in women's salaries may best be limited by expertise, age, and location of the population discussed. Your instructor or classmates may let you know if your topic is too far-flung and help you to make it fit your purpose. Another guide to topic selection should be the availability of library resources and observable information. You may be hard-pressed to come up with research material on, for example, the different attitudes among the Sioux toward raising male and female children, if you are not able to observe their behavior or find enough information in your library.

For whom you write is almost as important as what you write, especially when discussing sociological issues, because of the many possible ways of approaching a problem and the many answers that can be gleaned. Who is your target audience? If you wish to argue that children do learn violent behavior from watching violent television programs and movies, some of your readers may not be regular TV viewers or moviegoers. Or they may believe the source of violence lies elsewhere than in television shows. In order to change their opinions, you have to provide data (always plural)—

factual information gathered through research and observation—as the basis for your reasoning. When you use sociological terms and ideas that you may come across in your research, make sure you define abstract terms and use your own concrete examples to illustrate them. Though your audience is likely to be intellectually curious, with some knowledge about the topic, they may not know everything and may be eager to hear what you have to say.

Your purpose is not to provide an either/or solution when there may not be one to begin with. For example, violent behavior on TV and in the movies affecting children's behavior is a controversial issue which may not have a clear-cut answer. Some might argue that the behavior of the adults around them has the greatest influence on children's behavior. Sensitive writers pay attention to other people's opinions even if they are in conflict with their own, especially when dealing with controversial and emotional questions. So make sure you include opposing ideas to show how yours may be different from those of others. Too aggressive an approach and a refusal to acknowledge opposing ideas may put your audience on the defensive. You will promote your cause better if you are less threatening to the audience and more willing to compromise.

DISCOVERING IDEAS

Ask Questions

Interesting and stimulating research in sociology often begins with imaginative questions. The sociologist C. Wright Mills used the term the "sociological imagination" to describe the creative thinking process sociologists use to link the individual and the personal to a collective or group experience. Why do the Japanese students study so hard in school? Why are multiple-choice exams not necessarily effective ways to test knowledge? Sociologists often do not have all the answers, but the questions themselves set the thinking in motion. The focus of your sociologically motivated questions should be groups rather than individuals. Your personal experiences of alienation or cohesion with certain aspects of the society remain just that, personal and autobiographical. In order to be considered sociological, they must have some connections with the larger society. For example, if you recall in Section Two, Chapter 4, Guneet Kaur wrote poignantly about feeling alienated in a new society in her essay, "Being an Indian Student in an American College." Guneet's essay was mostly about people like herself. Had she been interested in a sociological inquiry, she would need to look beyond her immediate circumstances. Her study would then have moved from the personal to the sociological, from the restricted to a wider perspective.

Missole Louizaire, who came to the United States from Haiti, heard people on television and on campus discuss the country she had come from.

Many television reports and newspaper stories were about the increasing population and the pressure it put on the scarce resources in Haiti. There was not enough food, medical care, or opportunity for education available to many families. Though large families, especially for the poor, caused considerable hardship, women still preferred to have a large number of children. The most frequently stated reason was that, because of the existence of child labor in Haiti, poor people had more children to add to the family income.

But Missole was not completely satisfied with this explanation. If money were the only reason, most of these families would have noticed that they were not getting any richer by adding numbers of people. Surely there must be other reasons for this attitude than just to add to their own hardship! This doubt or questioning was the core of Missole's research, questioning which led her to the library in search of answers. Because of her familiarity with Haitian society, she combined researched information with her own observations (which she had put down in her journal) in writing her paper.

When looking for some answers, Missole made sure that the material she needed could be found through research and observation, and could be documented. Her questions were, "Do Haitian women have more children to please their men? If so, why?" She used research as well as observation to support her claim that the large families may be the result of social and sexual exploitation of women.

An excellent source of ideas for sociological topics is an **observation journal.** Since much of sociology is about what you see around you, it is worth your time to write down your feelings, ideas, thoughts, questions, and possible sources of support. The questions you raise may lead you to gather more information to develop your ideas.

▐RIAL RUN

Start an observation journal in which you write down your observations, thoughts, questions, and responses to what's happening around you and what you read. It may also be a good place to provide answers to some of the questions, however brief and tentative. But do not hold back questions if you feel you may not have possible answers right away. A close look at these questions may help you to focus on a topic for your paper.

CHECKLIST: FORMULATING QUESTIONS

1. Do my questions focus on one person or individuals in groups? Biographical questions about an individual may not be applicable to group situations.

2. Do my questions ask for yes/no answers or do they require several possible answers for a wider range of possibility and flexibility?

3. Do my questions look for similarities and differences between groups and individuals in society?

4. Do my questions focus on more than one society, for example, comparing women in Japan with women in the United States?

Formulate a Hypothesis

By observing how individuals interact in society, you may learn about the way people behave in different situations. For example, by observing the way people buy toys for their children, you might ask questions that would lead to a study of social class and juvenile behavior. In addition to observation, you might be stimulated by something you have read. The starting point of your research may be agreeing or disagreeing with what other people have written or said. A disagreement may be energizing, especially if it leads to a positive challenge leading to new insights. If you agree with a previously stated answer, the purpose of your research would be to acquire information to test its accuracy. If, on the other hand, you disagree with a previously stated position, you may collect information to come up with your own **hypothesis** or assumption. As the basis of research, the hypothesis is similar to the thesis statement. The research may prove the hypothesis or the researcher's hunch to be valid or invalid. When it fails to do either, the researcher may have to start all over again. In general, sociologists collect data or information to test a pre-existing hypothesis or to create their own.

Even before Missole started the research for her paper, she had often heard or read that the economic conditions in the lower-income families in Haiti were responsible for the large families. Her own readings on the topic basically confirmed what she had already known. But she was not completely satisfied by the economic explanation that poor people had more children only because the children added to the family income. Most of the research, she felt, ignored a major segment of the population, namely women. Having lived in Haiti and having had direct contact with many mothers with large families, she felt that the women in Haiti played a significant role in the population growth and there were sociological reasons that were as important as economic ones.

Examining the population question from a woman's point of view, Missole collected data through research and observation to create her own hypothesis, the basis of her argument that the social and sexual exploitation of women also contributed to the large families. By creating her own hypothesis through observation and research, Missole tested the validity of an accepted idea. This limited her research and gave focus to the writing. The validity of her hypothesis depended on data or information she acquired as evidence.

TRIAL RUN

Based on your observations, questions, and readings, formulate a tentative thesis or hypothesis about a topic that interests you and that relates to people living in society. Remember that your hypothesis is only a basic assumption about your topic that may be proven true or untrue by the findings of your research. For example, you may begin with the assumption that males do better than females in math and science because of the different gender roles assigned to men and women in our society. Your ultimate goal is to prove that assumption by research and observation.

Collect Data to Support Your Hypothesis

The main sources of data in sociological research are historical information, statistical information, and field research and observation.

Historical information is necessary when writing about societies in the past. For example, in order to write about the sexual behavior and marriage patterns among the late nineteenth-century slave population in the rural South, you will need to read books, articles, examine documents such as marriage records in courts and churches that date back to that period in history. You will need to look into the sexual behavioral patterns of both the slaves and the slave owners, how they acted sexually within the group and how the groups interacted with each other.

Statistics or numbers add credibility to research and give it focus. People, in general, are often more willing to accept statements as valid if they are accompanied by numbers. You must, however, make sure the numbers are accurate. The difference between the statements that "SAT scores have declined since 1985," and "SAT scores have declined by 29 percent since 1985," is the statistical support that makes the second statement seem more convincing. Numbers also have the power to shock people into accepting a statement. An alarming 29 percent decline in the SAT scores often shakes people out of their complacency to pay attention to the situation. Careful writers avoid manipulating numbers to influence their readers. For example, a majority may be 51 percent or 85 percent. It is only fair to let your reader know that.

Collecting original information through observation helps, especially when you are not convinced by the existing explanations. Missole's observation of some Haitian women led to findings that she had not come across in her research. For example, in the library, Missole found a number of historical, statistical, and economic explanations for the population explosion in Haiti, some of which she decided would be useful for her paper. But she felt that they were from a male perspective and lacked a female point of view. When she searched for material from a woman's perspective, she did not come across much. In order to find out how the women felt about large families, she had to rely on her own observations. How you go about acquiring information, therefore, depends, to a great extent, on your need and availability of sources. But before embarking on research, you should have some idea about why you are collecting information and what you intend to do with it as Missole did.

CHECKLIST: COLLECTING DATA

1. Do I have some background information (historical or political) that may help in understanding a current situation? How does the past relate to the present, or how has the past created the present?

2. Do I have some statistical information—numbers that make quick impressions on the audience? Have I checked the accuracy of figures and numbers? Have I used them honestly, or have I manipulated numbers to affect my readers' attitude? For example, have I made a distinction between a 51-percent majority and 85-percent majority?

3. Have I observed the world around me as a potential source of information? In what ways are my observations different from those in books and articles? Do I have something new to add?

Analyze and Interpret Your Data

"Analyze" and "interpret" may sound more complicated than they really are. When you analyze, you first break up the collected information into smaller pieces to examine them closely, to compare them, to find causal links among them, or to clarify their meanings by defining them. Interpretation is the fun part because it requires you to use your own judgment and opinions in conjunction with researched information. For example, you may read about an experiment in which two groups of children were shown two television programs, one full of violence and one without. Children who had watched the violent show acted violently with each other while the other group did not behave violently. How you interpret this information is up to you. You may conclude, given the evidence, that watching violence on television leads to violence in social behavior. Or you may decide, based on your own observation and reading, that there are other factors that contribute to violent behavior among children.

After she collected the researched and observed information, Missole's main task was to analyze it. She used the following strategies to sift through and organize her data in order to arrive at her own evaluation.

Classification

Missole made a list of her observations, or *classified* her data. **Classification** is an essential part of sociological inquiry because it helps the researcher separate facts and see connections between them. Missole found that the women, especially the poorly educated ones from the lower-income families, had certain characteristic attitudes towards children and childbearing:

1. They were bound by tradition, which placed a great deal of emphasis on fertility and procreation.

2. They were plagued by their husbands' "chronic infidelity," which was not condemned by society. While the men indulged in extra-marital sex, their wives found solace and comfort in their children.

3. Their children were also one of the few sources of diversion for these women whose lives were dull and monotonous.

4. Most of these women had little education or job training and were not able to work alongside their husbands.

5. The women used their children as a shield to prevent their marriages from breaking up. If there were children involved, the men were less inclined to abandon their wives.

6. The high rate of infant mortality made women want larger families.

While classifying her information, Missole made sure that there was a common and consistent element between the different categories. She had to keep her focus strictly on the women's feelings. In addition, she had to see that the categories did not overlap, since that might make the list fuzzy. The list, which contained most of her observed information, enabled her to see the connections between the separate elements and how they related to her original idea that poverty was not the only explanation for the large families.

TRIAL RUN

Make a list of your ideas related to your topic that are supported by observed and researched data. Focus only on the essential for precision and brevity. Group together the categories that relate to each other and look for similarities and differences between the groups. Look also for relationships between the data and your tentative thesis about your topic.

Cause and Effect

Interpretation of data often involves a cause and effect relationship, a tool often used by sociologists. One of the well known studies of cause and effect relationship in sociology is that by the French sociologist, Emile Durkheim, on the causal connection between the rate of suicide and the degree of cohesiveness or closeness among people in society. Durkheim's pioneering study states that melancholy, alienation, and exasperated weariness pervasive in a society affect individuals and often cause them to commit suicide. (If you want to know more about Durkheim's law of suicide, you may want to read *Suicide: A Study in Sociology* [trans. John A. Spalding and George Simpson, Glencoe: The Free Press, 1951].)

Sociological inquiries often recommend changes based on cause-and-effect relationships. For example you may want to examine why a large number of college students admitted on athletic scholarships end up as dropouts with menial jobs? This may involve a cause and effect analysis that may lead to suggestions for changes in the admission policies. Missole's study makes careful causal connections between society's attitudes towards the women and their desire for large families to reach her own conclusion that children were more than a source of income in the low-income Haitian families. A large family with eight to ten children, instead of causing only misery, gave the women the much needed comfort, support, and security. This was not a widely accepted or obvious cause but rather a hidden one as she did not find it clearly stated in her researched material. When using causal analysis in the social sciences, it is prudent to use "mostly," "generally," or "often" in reporting results to avoid faulty generalizations or statements that may not apply to all situations.

TRIAL RUN

List the causal evidence that supports your hypothesis or tentative assumption about your topic. Are the causal links obvious or hidden? If you do not find much in your researched material to support your own findings, do not assume you are wrong, but make sure that you are not confusing cause and effect relationships with trends or fads that may not have specific causes. Then write a paragraph summing up the causal evidence. What assumptions do you think your readers will have about your findings? Will you sound convincing to them?

Definition

As a science of human behavior, sociology uses particular terms and language that may not be easily understood by people outside the discipline. Therefore it is important for you to **define** or make clear the words that have special sociological significance. We often hear of "subcultures" within the dominant culture in society. What does a sociologist mean by "subculture"? A concrete example always helps to illuminate an abstract concept such as "subculture," which can be defined as an alternate culture for people outside of mainstream culture, for example, gay men and women. Members of the subculture tend to associate and identify more with the people within the subculture. A subculture, like the main culture, has its own history, rules, and traditions, but it only operates on a smaller scale.

Sometimes you have your own reasons for using a word that may vary from its general usage. You are entitled to your own usage as long you make it clear to the reader what the word means to you in addition to its traditional meaning. For example, to some, definition of incest may not be limited to intercourse between people with close blood ties. Incestuous behavior can take place even when the victim is not touched physically, as when an adult derives pleasure from watching a child undress. One of the important observations in Missole's paper that had been overlooked by the general society was the promiscuous sexual behavior among some Haitian men. Missole used the sociological term "deviant" to explain this behavior and she defined "deviant" behavior as behavior outside the norms of society, such as crime and prostitution. Her definition of "deviant" behavior as a sociological concept within the Haitian society enabled her to emphasize the magnitude of the problem.

TRIAL RUN

Define key terms and concepts in your researched material that you think may not be easily understood by your readers. An unabridged dictionary is a good place to find definitions. You may need to provide concrete examples when defining abstract terms. Some words or concepts may require conventional or standard definitions. But if you use a word in an unconventional way, you may need an extended definition to explain your particular usage.

COMPOSING THE FIRST DRAFT

Arrange Details

The first draft is your first opportunity to introduce your topic, state your hypothesis or tentative thesis, and use evidence that supports or challenges your assumptions. Your goal is to show your readers that your assumptions are plausible, and therefore acceptable. Your first attempt may not prove your hypothesis to be more plausible than other explanations, as Missole's draft indicates.

Missole's initial response to the question of overpopulation among lower economic groups in Haiti was not conventional. Her own observations had convinced her that the economists, statisticians, and demographers had, in general, ignored women's role in reproductive issues. But this was a research paper in which her own observations had to be supported by researched evidence. Missole did not find much that would directly support her assumption. In fact, she had to challenge or add to some of the existing views in order to make her own point.

Missole's challenge was how to arrange the details. Should she divide her paper into two halves, one devoted to her own ideas about population growth and the other to existing opinions? Should she intertwine the two? Examining her researched and observed information and finding the details not too numerous, she decided to state the existing opinions as a **block** before stating her own tentative thesis or hypothesis. This method would not have been feasible had she gathered a large amount of information, which might have required her to arrange the ideas **point by point,** that is, each general opinion followed by her own question or addition to that opinion. The **block-by-block** arrangement, she felt, would give the readers information necessary to better understand and appreciate her angle of approach. The overall structure of her paper looked like this:

- important general information on the causes of overpopulation in Haiti
- support for these generalizations
- her own claim about the causes of overpopulation in Haiti
- support for her own claim
- acknowledgement of some improvement and statements of recommendations

The arrangement of your details would depend on their nature and quantity. If you have a great number of details, it would be easier for your readers to view smaller portions at a time than to be overwhelmed by them at one time. Break them into sections and juxtapose them with opposing or additional ideas that you may have, making sure you cue your readers by using transition words—*in addition, furthermore, nevertheless, however, so, too*—between ideas. Whatever the amount of researched or observed evidence, be sure you know your reason for using it. It is not your readers' responsibility to guess their significance. The order in which you arrange details will depend on their importance relative to your hypothesis. Missole begins with the economic causes for large families in Haiti because they are cited most frequently; she later attempts to show that they are not as important as they are made out to be. By no means arrange your details in the order you came upon them, discussing the early ones first and so on. The point is not to show your readers how much information you have gathered and in what sequence but how well you have selected and arranged the information.

CHECKLIST: ARRANGING DETAILS

- Have I used block-by-block or point-by-point arrangement? What would facilitate my readers' understanding?
- Have I provided some general information before introducing my own thoughts on the topic?
- Have I included enough details about opposing ideas?
- Have I used transition words or phrases between ideas to signal my readers?
- Have I restated the original purpose of my research at the end of the paper?

• Have I presented my findings in plausible terms, avoiding faulty generalizations?

PRESENTING MISSOLE'S FIRST DRAFT

1   As I was searching in the library for information on my paper on the population problem in Haiti, I came across several explanations for the large families among both the rural and urban poor in Haiti. Many Haitian people, especially those among the lower economic classes, have more than ten children. The children's economic value is high in the rural areas among low income families. Children, especially the male children in these families, are a source of income. The girls mostly stay home with their mothers and help out with the domestic chores because the poor women cannot afford to hire help. The boys, on the other hand, often go to their fathers' workplace and do menial jobs to add to the income. So the birth of a boy is more desirable in these families than a girl.

2   Though these explanations have some validity, I feel they fail to take into consideration some other reasons which I feel are very important. During my several visits to Haiti, I often talked to women, in both rural and urban areas about many things, not just reproductive issues. These women were intrigued by my life as a student in the United States as I was with their lives. Many of the younger women whom I talked with were already mothers of several children and seemed to be quite content with the situation though they lived in very poor conditions. This was somewhat puzzling to me. So when I asked them cautiously if they would rather have fewer children, many of them answered in the negative. They felt comfortable enough with me to tell me that a large family often prevented their husbands from abandoning them. For many of these women, sharing their husbands with mistresses was a common situation. They told me of their lonely lives when their husbands spent time away from home with other women. Their children were a source of comfort and company for them. So why should they not have children?

3   Talking to these women made it clear to me that there was more to the population problem in Haiti than what we heard or read in the media. In my paper I will incorporate the economic and other reasons but stress the women's points.

4   Procreation, the ability to bring new life into the world, is an activity that is held in very high esteem in Haiti. Traditionally, Haitian people have preferred large

families. The average family size ranges from 8 to 10 people according to official estimates. Family, in this context, includes father, mother, and children. In rural areas where about 70% of the population live, according to the <u>World Book Encyclopedia</u>, the number of children in most families exceeds 10. This number is true in almost all low-income families throughout the country.

5   Several other factors explain the people's desire to have large families. Children's economic value is well known in rural areas and the urban low-income families that cannot afford domestic help. There are no available statistics about child labor in Haiti, but children typically perform useful tasks from an early age in these families. Children contribute to domestic labor beginning as early as 5 or 6 years old. Gender plays an important role in the allocation of duties. Girls, for example, devote more time to household chores such as cooking and taking care of younger children while boys help in agriculture, construction and maintenance work. Children are also considered security in old age when the parents can no longer work and help themselves. Children are their assets and savings. As there is no state sponsored social security system in Haiti, their children represent the only source of support in old age.

6   A major cause of large families from the woman's point of view and one which is seldom discussed is their husbands' chronic infidelity. Because the subject of male infidelity is a taboo in Haitian society, no accurate statistics are available as evidence. But it is a widely known and accepted practice. In general, the Haitian male is polygamous or has more than one sexual partner. Throughout my observation, it may not be an exaggeration to affirm that at least 90% of the men have extramarital liaisons and children. Sometimes they have more children outside their marriage than with their wives. Many sociologists would call this form of behavior as deviant behavior that differs from the norm or accepted social practice in most societies, such as crime, prostitution, and vagrancy. But in certain segments of Haitian society, polygamy seems to be an accepted form of behavior, and not deviant. This may be one of the most difficult situations the women have to deal with. One woman said her situation was that of a puppet on a string. Her life was guided by the whim and desire of her husband. Children in these circumstances help the women bear their frustration and monotony that is a constant part of their lives.

7   Another long-standing belief in the Haitian culture, mostly held by women, is that children keep the family

together and prevent it from breaking easily. The women believe that their husbands are less likely to abandon them because of the children. Having more children thus becomes a way of keeping their husbands. Many believe that unstable unions are associated with low fertility rate among the women. In addition, they believe that children are their "reason of being." The high rate of infant mortality also leads women towards large families because they know not all their children will survive infancy.

8   However, though children fulfill certain social and emotional needs, especially for the women, it is a myth and misconception that having more children provides solution to major social and economic problems among the low-income families. Permanent problems such as despair, loneliness, abandonment, and divorce undermine family life. In fact, having many children, instead of providing a solution, further complicates the situation by undermining the economic and sociological wellbeing in the long run. The economy of the country is largely based on agriculture. According to Robert Maguire, in 1971, the average size of the family farm was 3.5 acres. This size became smaller from year to year because every year the small plot had to be divided among several children. As the division continued, the small parcel of land inherited was not enough to feed a single family. Ironically, parents, by having more children for their satisfaction and security, deprived these same children of financial security in the long run. After 187 years of independence, the situation is catastrophic.

9   Fortunately the last two decades have witnessed an awakening of national conscience and a sensitivity toward some fundamental issues such overpopulation, food, health, and education. With a better communication system, parents, even in the low-income families, have access to information with regard to their well-being. Now they have an opportunity to compare their way of life with people in other countries. Though most Haitian people still think it is important to have relatively large families, they are gradually changing their views on the children's role in society. They realize that children cannot provide support for them unless the children themselves are provided for adequately. They are beginning to realize that with children comes the responsibility of providing for them, especially if they are to be an asset in the future. For example, in the past, it was customary to send only the few younger children in the large families to school so that they could act as the "eyes" of the family in situations involving reading and writing. But now they want to educate all their children.

10 Some improvement in the situation is indicated by the 1987 statistics that show a decline in birth rate among the low-income people due to better family planning centers, sex education, and the availability of contraception. But much more needs to be done to change society's attitude towards women and children. The male dominated society makes particularly the less-educated lower-income women feel helpless and insecure. So they desire more children to hold on to their marriage and to get solace and comfort from them when they feel abandoned. Unless these deep-rooted sociological attitudes are changed through education and more opportunities for women outside the home, they will continue to view themselves only as wives and mothers and do everything to cling on to their marriages.

Thinking Critically about Missole's First Draft

1. Missole begins her first draft with her own observations. Why do you think she does this? Do you think this was a good writing decision? Give reasons for your answers.

2. What is Missole's basis for her research or her hypothesis? Where does she state it? Comment on its location. What alternative locations can you suggest and why?

3. Missole's research found that though both men and women preferred larger families, it was for different reasons. How did she arrive at this conclusion? How much was she helped by the opinions of experts in the field?

4. Paragraph 5 states that gender plays an important role in the allocation of duties. What does Missole mean by "gender role?" Has she defined the word clearly? Have you noticed the influence of gender in the allocation of duties in our society? Give examples.

5. Does the draft use any comparison? If you find any, look for the basis of the comparison. Do you think Missole's use of comparison is appropriate and effective? Could you suggest more comparisons that might help her conclusion?

6. Take a close look at each reason Missole presents and the supportive evidence. Is her reasoning logical and the evidence plausible? Where is she most convincing or most vulnerable? What advice would you have for improvement?

7. Examine the draft for balance in presenting information and evidence. Is there too little or too much background information? Adequate or too little evidence? Should some ideas be more emphasized than they are? What would you recommend?

Figure 14-1

1. DEVELOPMENT: Are you exploring your ideas or just broaching them? Your draft would improve with some background information about the topic. When you state the women's point of view, make sure you present some opposing ideas. The contrast may add strength to your own argument.

2. DETAIL: Are you being specific--giving enough examples as evidence? Your paper gains strength when you combine outside sources of information with your own observations. Your personal observations are crucial to this paper. They are also credible because of your own background. So focus more on them as you do in the draft, but keep in mind that you need other supportive details of the existing conditions in Haiti for your paper to be credible.

3. ECONOMY: Are you being concise and keeping proportion? I was impressed by your own keen observations and the way you bring together some of the different and complex sets of reasons why some people in Haiti want to have large families. In your final draft, be conscious about using only information and statistics that serve a purpose in your paper. For example, you may collect a lot of data with regard to birth rate and death rate in Haiti and may want to include them all in your paper, thinking that you may impress the reader with your scholarship. Be aware that numbers, figures, and other researched information; used haphazardly, only detract from your paper.

4. ORIGINALITY: Are you thinking for yourself? Going beyond the obvious? This is one of the strong points of the paper, which goes beyond the accepted beliefs to the ones overlooked by society, namely, the sexual behavior of Haitian men in the lower economic groups. Stay focused on this.

5. COHERENCE: Does your paper hold together? Do ideas link up? As your reader, I did not have difficulty understanding you, though I realized that you would add outside sources to your final draft to strengthen your paper. However, some critique and concrete suggestions to improve the situation at the end would make it a stronger paper. Have things improved over the years? What would you like to see done with regard to the population problem in Haiti? Do you see a positive or a negative step in this direction?

RETHINKING AND REVISING

Her instructor commented on Missole's excitement and enthusiasm about her topic, which was quite apparent in her first draft. But the instructor also pointed out that in her eagerness to report her findings, Missole had omitted the background information that her readers might not have about her topic and the area of the world she was discussing. In your own writing make sure you provide some cultural, sociological, historical, or geographical background information, especially if you feel your reader may not be familiar with your subject.

On her instructor's advice, Missole made a few more structural changes following a review checklist containing the instructor's comments (Figure 14-1).

By now you know that a research paper includes both the information obtained from library research and the researcher's own observations and conclusions. No one can tell you exactly the proportion or how much of each to include in your paper. It is important to remember that researched material is used only as supportive evidence for your hypothesis and conclusions. A research paper is not a compilation of opinions by experts. Following her instructor's recommendations, Missole expanded her initial thoughts into the final draft, making sure that she had established her own hypothesis that could be supported by researched evidence.

It is not an easy task to incorporate researched material into the core of ideas in a draft. To begin with, you should select material that is relevant to your discussion and find appropriate locations for it in your paper. A common method is to state your own position and follow it with supportive evidence or evidence that your own opinion challenges. The juxtaposition allows readers to evaluate your ideas in conjunction with those of others. You may quote authorities directly or you may paraphrase their ideas, which means you use your own words to convey the condensed meaning of a passage. In both instances, you must cite sources to acknowledge the contribution of others to your paper. This is simple academic courtesy. You would not borrow something belonging to someone else without permission. So it is with words and ideas. You let the readers know that all the ideas in your paper are not exclusively yours. For documentation, writings in the social sciences use the American Psychology Association (APA) style described in Chapter 17 under Bibliographic Form.

PRESENTING MISSOLE'S FINAL DRAFT

Role of Women and Children
in Family Relationships in Haiti

Missole Louizaire

1   Haiti is a country with certain highly distinctive features. Besides being the first country to free itself from

slavery, it is by far the poorest country in the Western Hemisphere. According to the Encyclopedia Britannica, it has also the highest birth rate: 34.0 per 1000 people in 1987 with the world average at 27.1. Although emigration of about 15% of the population helps to relieve the pressure of population, the density is still very high. While the numbers may vary, a 1989 census revealed 200 to 250 people per square kilometer (630).

New opening paragraphs are added to the final draft to provide background information. The revised essay does not begin by stating the problem.

2   The population, according to the Encyclopedia Britannica, is estimated at 6 million. At that speed of growth, despite a high death rate of 13.0, a demographic explosion threatens the country in the coming years. Moreover, due to the essentially mountainous nature of the terrain, there is a scarcity of land that can be used for agriculture (630). Therefore, people tend to crowd in areas where they can farm for food. This puts pressure on the available land and creates food shortages that increase the country's dependence on imported food and international aid. However, these problems are not about to be solved, given the high birth rate, which is based on the belief, especially among the women, that more children satisfy immediate and future needs of the family.

Here Missole defines her target population—their numbers, geographic location, and economic background.

3   Procreation, the ability to bring new life into the world, is an activity that is held in very high esteem in Haiti. Traditionally, Haitian people have preferred large families. The average family size ranges from 8 to 10 people according to official estimates. Family, in this context, includes father, mother, and children. In rural areas where about 70% of the population live, according to the Britannica Micropedia Ready Reference, the number of children in most families exceeds 10. This number is true in almost all low-income families throughout the country (622–623).

When providing reasons for large families, Missole states the generally accepted beliefs first.

4   Several other factors explain the people's desire to have large families. Children's economic value is well known in rural areas and the urban low-income families that cannot afford domestic help. There are no available statistics about child labor in Haiti, but children typically perform useful tasks from an early age in these families. Children contribute to domestic labor beginning as early as 5 or 6 years old. Gender plays an important role in the allocation of duties. Girls, for example, devote more time to household chores such as cooking and taking care of younger children while boys help in agriculture, construction and maintenance work. Children are also considered security in old age when the parents can no longer work and help themselves. Children are their assets and savings. As there is no state sponsored

social security system in Haiti, their children represent the only source of support in old age.

5

Here she moves from conventional reasons for population growth to her own hypothesis that the women in Haiti may have their own reasons, other than economic ones, for wanting larger families.

But there are other important reasons that are often overlooked that make Haitian women desire large families. When asked why they have so many children, one of the most common responses is that the women want to let their men know that they are fertile and capable of bearing many children. This is important in a society that puts a lot of value on procreation. An infertile woman is held in low esteem by Haitian people. They also claim that children bring love and closeness in a family. They play an important role in providing companionship and distraction, especially for the women, who are often neglected by their husbands and are excluded from the male sphere of activities. In a society where the educational opportunities are scarce to begin with, the women have less of a chance to get an education than men. There are very few job opportunities for the low-income woman except to work as a domestic.

6

Missole begins to provide specific support for her hypothesis.

A major cause of large families from the woman's point of view and one which is seldom discussed is their husbands' chronic infidelity. Because the subject of male infidelity is a taboo in Haitian society, no accurate statistics are available as evidence. But it is a widely known and accepted practice. In general, the Haitian male is polygamous or has more than one sexual partner. Throughout my observation, it may not be an exaggeration to affirm that at least 90% of the men have extramarital liaisons and children. Sometimes they have more children outside their marriage than with their wives. Many sociologists would call this form of behavior deviant: behavior that differs from the norm or accepted social practice in most societies, such as crime, prostitution, and vagrancy. But in certain segments of Haitian society, polygamy seems to be an accepted form of behavior, and not deviant. This may be one of the most difficult situations the women have to deal with. One woman said her situation was that of a puppet on a string. Her life was guided by the whim and desire of her husband. Children in these circumstances help the women bear their frustration and monotony that is a constant part of their lives.

Missole defines a sociological term.

7

Missole provides further evidence to support her hypothesis.

Another long-standing belief in the Haitian culture, mostly held by women, is that children keep the family together and prevent it from breaking easily. The women believe that their husbands are less likely to abandon them because of the children. Having more children thus becomes a way of keeping their husbands. Many believe that unstable unions are associated with low fertility rate among the women. In addition, they believe that children are their "reason of being." The high rate of infant mortality also leads women towards large families because they know not all their children will survive infancy.

8

After stating the women's reasons for desiring large families, Missole introduces the consequences of their decisions. She moves from supportive evidence to reporting results.

However, though children fulfill certain social and emotional needs, especially for the women, it is a myth and misconception that having more children provides solution to major social and economic problems among the low-income families. Permanent problems such as despair, loneliness, abandonment, and divorce undermine family life. In fact, having many children, instead of providing solution, further complicates the situation by undermining the economic and sociological well-being in the long run. The economy of the country is largely based on agriculture. According to Robert Maguire, in 1971, the average size of the family farm was 3.5 acres. This size became smaller from year to year because every year the small plot had to be divided among several children. As the division continued, the small parcel of land inherited was not enough to feed a single family. Ironically, parents, by having more children for their satisfaction and security, deprived these same children of financial security in the long run. After 187 years of independence, the situation is catastrophic (9–12).

Here she states her conclusion.

9

Though her conclusion about population growth is pessimistic, she adds specific information to indicate changes in attitudes toward population growth.

Fortunately the last two decades have witnessed an awakening of national conscience and a sensitivity toward some fundamental issues such as overpopulation, food, health, and education. With a better communication system, parents, even in the low-income families, have access to information with regard to their well-being. Now they have an opportunity to compare their way of life with people in other countries. Though most Haitian people still think it is important to have relatively large families, they are gradually changing their views on the children's role in society. They realize that children cannot provide support for them unless the children themselves are provided for adequately. They are beginning to realize that with children comes the responsibility of providing for them, especially if they are to be an asset in the future. According to the International Encyclopedia of Education, in the past, it was customary to send only the few younger children in the large families to school so that they could act as the "eyes" of the family in situations involving reading and writing. But now they want to educate all their children (2130).

10

But the parents alone cannot alter their lives. The government provides very little assistance for such basics as food, health, and education. For example, with the average size

Missole adds this
paragraph in the
final draft, giving
researched data
to show the fail-
ure of government
to control popula-
tion growth. This
adds strength
to her own
observation.

of 8 people per family and a per capita income of US $360.00
per year, according to the 1990 <u>Encyclopedia Britannica</u>,
it is virtually impossible for the families to provide for
the basic needs without some help from the government.
Health conditions are poor and are characterized by a chronic
shortage of doctors and medical facilities, especially
in the rural areas. For example, in 1985, one physician was
available for 6539 persons. The death rate, 13.0, is among
the highest in the region. Life expectancy is around 55–60
years. The infant mortality rate is 100 among 1000. Though
education is free for children between the ages of 6 and 12,
only 48% attend school. Of those who attend, only 10% finish
primary school and 5% enter secondary school. The numbers
are even lower in the rural areas where only 26% of all 6–12
year olds attend school. When there is no food at home,
parents would rather send their children out to earn money
than to school. So even a free education does not help unless
other social and economic needs are met. The different attitudes towards childbearing among the higher-income, educated urban women and the poor, mostly rural women proves
this point. The higher-income educated women have an average
of 2–3 children as opposed to the 10–12 in the low-income
families (630).

11

Missole returns
to her own hypo-
thesis involving
women and popu-
lation growth.

In addition, the <u>Britannica Micropedia Ready Reference</u>
reports that in 1987, only about 48% of the population was
actively involved in economic productivity (623). Such a
precarious socioeconomic situation touches all aspects of
life, particularly population control. For the people of
Haiti, particularly the women, this is a vicious cycle. They
want to have smaller families and provide a decent life for
their children. But without any help from the government,
they fall back on the large families for emotional support and
child labor to make ends meet.

12

Missole concludes
by stressing the
results of her
findings, that
society ignores
women's points of
view in discussing
population
problems.

Some improvement in the situation is indicated by a slow
decline in birth rate among the low-income people due to better family planning centers, sex education, and the availability of contraception. But much more needs to be done to
change society's attitude towards women and children. The
male-dominated society makes particularly the less-
educated, lower-income women feel helpless and insecure. So
they desire more children to hold on to their marriage and to
get solace and comfort from them when they feel abandoned.
Unless these deep-rooted sociological attitudes are changed
through education and more opportunities for women outside
the home, they will continue to view themselves only as wives
and mothers and do everything to cling on to their marriages.

References

"Haiti." <u>Britannica Book of the Year</u> (1990). Chicago: Encyclopedia Britannica Inc. 630-31.

"Haiti." <u>Britannica Micropedia Ready Reference</u> (1988).
London: Encyclopedia Britannica Inc. Vol. 5. 622-23.

"Haiti: System of Education." <u>The International Encyclopedia of Education</u> (1987). New York: Pergamon Press. Vol. 4.
2129-32

Maguire, R. (1979). <u>Bottom-up development in Haiti</u>. Chicago:
Inter-American Foundation.

Commentary on Missole's Final Draft

Aware that she is writing a paper with a sociological focus, Missole begins by raising some sociologically relevant questions, relating to groups rather than to individuals. Her major question is why Haitian women, in general, prefer large families. Had she focused on one woman's life, her paper would have been biographical, not sociological. Sociologists are often concerned with situations and interactions among people whose significance may be overlooked or not easily understood. In this sense, Missole's concern about the feelings and attitudes of women in Haiti, often ignored by the dominant male society, is sociological. She asks questions that involve people, keeping in mind that sociology is the study primarily of people living in society. If she needs to use numbers, statistical or economic analysis, she has to make sure that she relates them to people and groups. One of the reasons Missole's paper captures our attention is that her questions center on those most involved in childrearing, the women of Haiti, and she cites numbers and other sources of information to strengthen her opinion.

Paragraphs 1 through 3 are added to the final draft to provide background information absent in the first draft. Her opening sentence in paragraph 1 now reads, "Haiti is a country with certain distinctive features." The following two paragraphs elaborate on these distinctive features. The second paragraph talks about the population problem in general and provides some statistics. The third paragraph moves Missole closer to the focus of her paper, the woman's angle from which to view the population problem in Haiti. This provides a good lead to paragraph 6, with its focus on the causes of large families from a woman's point of view. The new introduction is more informative, focused, and less rambling than the one in the first draft.

A further examination of the draft convinces Missole that she is making too sudden a leap from the general information in paragraph 4 to her main idea in paragraph 6 that the woman's point of view is ignored when discussing population problems in Haiti. She includes paragraph 5 in the final draft to make the transition smoother. It begins, "But there are other important reasons that are often overlooked that make Haitian women desire larger families." The new paragraph, while acknowledging the existing general information, points to what has been left out, namely the women's point of view.

Most of the questions Missole asks may have more than one answer. This can be viewed in two ways. First, sociological concepts, unlike those in the natural world, are seldom seen as absolutes. For example, one can explain with certainty why an apple falls to the ground by referring to the law of gravity, but it is not always possible to provide accurate explanations why violence on television affects some children and not others. So she frames her questions in terms of probabilities rather than absolutes and makes sure that her responses take this into consideration. When she states that one cannot contest that women in Haiti believe that children bring a lot of satisfaction, she adds that children also make their lives more complex and problematic. Secondly, the questions have the depth and complexity to demand more than one answer that can be developed into supportive evidence for the paper's argument. Missole's paper never loses sight of this because she never tries to give simple yes or no answers to complicated questions such as why the Haitian women want to have large families when they cannot provide some basic necessities for their children. Though her paper approaches the population problem more from a woman's and socio-logical perspectives, she reminds the reader that the country's economic situation is to a large extent responsible for the population explosion.

In order to be more credible sociologically, Missole focuses on two or more groups, ideas, or concepts. For example, while discussing women's attitudes towards childbearing in Haiti, Missole makes the distinction between the poor and the more affluent women. Her question is: Do all women in Haiti feel the same way about having large families? Do the poor women feel a greater need for larger families than the more educated middle-class women? If so, why? Her comments on the sexual promiscuity among many Haitian men, particularly among the lower-income men, is based, as she states, primarily on observation. But her observation is credible to her reader because of her intimate and firsthand knowledge of the society as a native-born Haitian.

Because her topic is complex and her questions may have several possible answers, Missole has to make sure that they can be answered within the time and space she has. She avoids embarking on a research project that would require more time than she may have, and concentrates on the socioeconomic aspects of her topic, steering clear of issues involving moral-ity and judgment. She does not try to establish whether the women are right or wrong in feeling the way they do. She relies mostly on the visible and tangible evidence. But she makes her readers aware that the powerlessness of the women—economic, social, and political—is at the root of much of the population problem in Haiti. She illustrates this by referring to the expres-sion, "puppet on a string," used by one woman to describe her complete dependence on her husband. This analogy helps the reader understand the seriousness of the situation and see the need for empowering women to deal with population problems.

Throughout her paper, Missole uses numbers as supportive evidence, beginning with paragraph 1, in which she compares the birthrate of Haiti at 34.0 per 1000 people in 1987 as opposed to the world average of 27.1. She cites a 1989 statistic of 200–250 people per square kilometer, which is considerably less in area than a square mile. Such numbers immediately rivet the reader's attention to the seriousness of the population problem in Haiti. The use of death-rate figures may seem superfluous at the first glance, but it helps the reader see another aspect of the population problem. While it is desirable to have a lower death rate, it also adds to overpopulation.

In the concluding paragraph, Missole reiterates her main point. But she adds two new paragraphs, 10 and 11, to the final draft that serve a particular purpose. While acknowledging some changes among the Haitian people toward childbearing, Missole feels that the government has not done enough to improve the economic situation that has a direct bearing on population growth. Paragraphs 10 and 11 conclude that without help from the government, the people alone cannot be expected to control the population. Paragraph 12 returns to her main point that unless society's attitudes toward women change considerably, the population question will continue to plague Haiti. As the most important agents in reproductive issues, Missole concludes that women have to be empowered through education and equal job opportunities for a satisfactory solution to the population problem.

Questions for Further Thought

1. If you are able to prove that your opponents' ideas are wrong, is that enough to prove that your ideas are right? How far can a writer challenge and refute opposing views? How effective a writing strategy is it?

2. Missole does not mention the names of the women whose opinions she includes in her paper. What do you think are her reasons? Does every writing situation demand naming the informant or the source of information? Would she have strengthened her position if she identified the women? What would you have done in a similar situation?

3. If the goal of most writers is to affect the audience, who do you think has a better chance of convincing the readers—a very confident writer expecting and demanding complete agreement from readers or a cautious writer suggesting that the reader, too, use caution in judging a situation? Would the latter technique be perceived as a way of covering up a weak argument?

For more information on library research and documentation using the guidelines of the American Psychology Association (APA), refer to Bibliographic Form in Chapter 17. The list on the next page is a brief guide to sociology journals:

American Journal of Sociology, Chicago University Press
American Sociological Review, American Sociological Association
Contemporary Sociology, American Sociological Association
Journal of Health and Social Behavior, American Sociological Association
Journal of Marriage and the Family, National Council on Family Relations
Social Problems, Society for the Study of Social Problems
Rural Sociology, Rural Sociological Society
Urban Life

WRITING A SCIENCE PAPER

Writing about science often conjures up images of graphs, statistics, and unintelligible technical language, leading people to think that only scientists can comprehend the language of science. This may be true of writing on highly specialized and technical topics. But it should put us at some ease knowing that until the end of the nineteenth century, major scientific works were written to be understood and enjoyed by the lay reader. The English physician William Harvey's epoch-making work on blood circulation, *On the Motion of the Heart and Blood in Animals* (1628), or naturalist Charles Darwin's *Journals of Researches into the Geology and Natural History of the Various Countries Visited by H.M.S. Beagle* (1839) and his great work *On the Origin of Species by Means of Natural Selection* (1859) are immensely readable books that can be enjoyed by both scientists and general readers. Among our contemporary scientists, the writings of Oliver Sachs, a physician, or Stephen Jay Gould, a biologist, are read avidly by people from both scientific and nonscientific communities.

WRITING ASSIGNMENT

Write an essay examining a natural phenomenon. It may be something you have observed or experienced yourself, heard or read about in the media or a book, or learned about in a course you are taking. Explain to your readers why the phenomenon or occurrence takes place with plausible evidence from your readings and observations.

READING THE WRITING ASSIGNMENT

This is a challenging assignment that requires a clear understanding of the topic. You are being asked to select a phenomenon or occurrence. What does this mean? Is any incident or happening a phenomenon? One of the meanings of "phenomenon" (plural "phenomena") in Webster's *New Collegiate Dictionary* is "a fact or event of scientific interest, susceptible of scientific description and explanation." That may give you some idea, but you need a more precise understanding before you embark on your assignment.

Let's begin with what a phenomenon is not. It is not a temporary fad nor a one-time event. Last year it was cool to dress a certain way, but this year it is not. If you want to keep up with fashion trends, you have to be up to date with the frequent and seasonal changes in clothing or hairstyle. Roller skates are out; roller blades are in. Fads come and go, often without leaving a lasting impression. In addition, it is generally difficult to point to a reason or a combination of reasons to satisfactorily explain a fad. Why was black last summer's hottest color and this summer it is orange or yellow?

A phenomenon, on the other hand, has a more lasting implication. For it to establish itself, it needs to have taken place over a long time with a certain degree of regularity. It is never a one-time event. The salmons' remarkable journey upstream to spawn, with some variations in their path or time, is a natural phenomenon. A repeated occurrence of something over a period of time that sets a pattern could be construed as a phenomenon. A decline in math and science scores among American students in recent years or the number of women entering politics comes close to a phenomenon that can be explained. In addition, these topics leave room for argument and discussion in reference to their causes, whereas why the sun rises every morning is not arguable. Most natural phenomena have indisputable evidence while most social, political, or economic ones have plausible or possible ones. Topic choice is an important part of this assignment. You may check with your instructor to see if you are on the right track.

In order to explain why something happens you have to speculate about possible causes and form tentative assumptions or hypotheses which you have to support by researched and/or observed evidence. In addition, you may need to provide some background information describing and explaining the phenomenon and indicate what kind of evidence you will use to support your explanation.

Since your purpose is to prove your point to your audience and influence them to accept your point of view, you have to be attuned to your audience's feelings in reference to the topic. Riding roughshod over them will not win you points. Show your readers that you are aware of differing opinions and have examined views other than those you propose. Try to anticipate how much your reader may know about the topic and how much you need to say in order to establish that the phenomenon does exist. Keep an open mind about your topic. As long as you do not make your readers feel that you are the only authority they should be listening to and regularly refer to alternative approaches and sources, you will reduce the risk of alienating them.

DISCOVERING IDEAS USING THE SCIENTIFIC METHOD
Select a Topic: Observe and Ask Questions

Scientists, like other researchers, begin by asking questions. How well a science paper is written depends, to a great extent, on the nature of the questions, the thoroughness of the investigation, and the clarity of the answers. Valentina Fedorovsky, the student writer in this chapter, emigrated from the Soviet Union six years ago. Growing up as a woman belonging to the Jewish faith in Russia, she was almost forced into being a keen observer of society. The less than fair treatment of Jewish people in the Soviet Union often made her wonder if she would have access to higher education, particularly to the field of her interest, medicine.

Fortunately for Valentina, her family immigrated to the United States and settled in the New York area. This move, while affording her wonderful new opportunities, also presented challenges and situations that she would never have anticipated in her native Russia. She revelled in the differences—new language, new food, new friends, and above all, the new freedom to do and achieve whatever she wanted. School work, in general, did not pose much problem; her training in Russia served her adequately. What stumped her, though, were the batteries of computerized tests that the American students were expected to pass. She was thrown by such cryptic terms as SAT (Scholastic Aptitude Test), GRE (Graduate Record Examination), and, above all, the IQ (Intelligence Quotient) test. Can people's intelligence be judged by having them provide quick answers to long lists of questions that may or may not have anything to do with their lives? The idea of placing so much faith in computerized tests so as to declare a person intelligent or not gnawed at her brain. She soon found out she was not alone in her doubt. The debate over the validity of the IQ tests seemed endless, on television reports, talk shows, in newspaper or magazine articles. Were the observations made by the tests fair? Was the population targeted adequate? Were the methods of testing valid? Were the results accurate and reliable? Were the results applicable to all situations? The core of Valentina's research was her observation of a "mentally retarded" artist in an art school that she had attended. This observation led her to questions for which she had to look for some answers. With her writing assignment due in a couple of weeks, Valentina launched into her preliminary investigation and wrote down the questions that came to her mind as the groundwork for her paper.

Not everyone's experiences are as special as Valentina's. Her topic is strengthened by the intensity and uniqueness of her situation and observation. But we all have the capacity to observe life around us, and often overlook many things or take them for granted. Develop your critical eye and be alert to life around you. You may be surprised by your own observations.

Several years ago at an art school Valentina had attended, an artist visited her class every week to show his paintings. He was not an ordinary artist. What was extraordinary about him was that he was retarded, with the mental capabilities of a young child. Furthermore, he was legally blind with serious visual impairment. Yet, in spite of his handicaps, his paintings exhibited a beauty and artistry that would be far beyond the capabilities of most people with "normal" intelligence.

Observing him and his work ignited Valentina's curiosity about measuring human intelligence. What did the term "intelligence" really mean? It seemed to her that it could have several definitions. So she decided to investigate to see if she could find some clues to the most reasonable and crucial components of the term "intelligence."

TRIAL RUN

Try to determine if your chosen topic is a bona fide phenomenon. Generate interesting and significant questions that would test your topic and distinguish it from fads and one-time events. Your choice may be based on what topic generated the most interesting questions and came closest to meeting the criteria for a phenomenon.

CHECKLIST: SELECTING A TOPIC

- Is my topic about a one-time event or something that has occurred regularly over some time?
- Can my topic be explained by logical reasoning?
- Are the causes apparent and obvious to my readers?
- Are the causes hidden so that they need to be explained to the readers?
- Is my topic debatable and controversial? Will some of my readers agree with me to some degree?
- As I look for possible explanations, do I take into consideration opinions that support my views and those that challenge them?

Formulate a Hypothesis: Look for Possible Answers

The way researchers arrive at answers to their questions may vary. They may observe several occurrences, examples, or instances of a particular phenomenon or situation and arrive at a general conclusion. For example, researchers may want to examine the effectiveness of a pesticide against Dutch elm disease afflicting the elm trees in their area. By examining the records of tree damage before and after the use of pesticides both in their own area and elsewhere, they may be able to comment, with some degree of certainty, on the effectiveness of the pesticide to combat Dutch elm disease.

Another situation may require researchers to guess or have a hunch about a possible answer to form a *hypothesis* prior to looking for all the answers. The word **hypothesis,** which in its original Greek means a base or foundation, is often used in scientific research to mean the basis for an argument. This foundation or position taken by the researchers enables them to explore unknown territories where their questions may lead to one or several possible answers. The hypothesis or a hunch may or may not lead to the result the researcher anticipates, so the experiment may have to be conducted again with an altered hypothesis. Your purpose is not necessarily to prove or disprove a hypothesis but to support or discredit it in arriving at a conclusion. Valentina began her research with her own hunch that perhaps IQ tests were not all that they were made out to be.

Before reading the specialists on the topic of testing human intelligence, Valentina decided to sample the opinions of ten people, six of whom were immigrants from Russia. They were from similar economic and educational backgrounds, with degrees in economics or accounting. Half of those interviewed said that the major component of intelligence was the ability to solve problems. People who can reason logically, identify problems, and provide solutions are more intelligent than those who fail in these areas. The majority of the interviewees felt that verbal skills played an important part in measuring a person's intelligence. The effective use of language to communicate successfully with others was deemed by most to be a key element in testing intelligence. Valentina particularly agreed with this point because beyond communication, language skills are closely tied to the ways people think about and understand the world around them.

Another interesting opinion that came out of this investigation was that social compatibility and social competence were necessary parts of intelligence. The ability to show an interest in others' views, interact effectively with them, and offer help when needed was considered to be a sign of intelligence. In a sharp departure from the earlier views, quite a few of the interviewees felt that a close to accurate measure of intelligence could not and should not overlook the racial, social, and cultural backgrounds of people. To prehistoric humans, intelligence might have been measured by their hunting or other survival skills. In the concrete jungle of New York City, however, survival skills may include success in business, academia, or other professional areas of life. In other words, an intelligent person, as opposed to an unintelligent person, is able to utilize the resources available to him or her to better oneself.

Valentina was confused by so many ways to determine intelligence. By speaking with several people on the subject, she came to realize that there was no single factor underlying intelligence. The question still was whether intelligence was made up of certain accepted patterns of behavior and performance or was it manifested by a person's individual skills? The mentally retarded artist did not conform to the generally accepted definition of intelligence. He could not communicate "effectively" or think "logically." But he did interact effectively with people through the beauty of his paintings. Valentina believed that while there were several components to intelligence, the absence of one or some of these components need not necessarily make a person not intelligent. Armed with this knowledge,

Valentina arrived at a possible answer, her hypothesis, that since there was no single way to **define** intelligence, there could not be a single way to **measure** and **test** intelligence.

In order to investigate the occurrence of your choice, you would need to know the possible causes that you may support or discredit through research and observation. You have two ways to approach this. You may arrive at a general answer by several observances. Or you may guess a general answer that you would need to support with research and observation.

TRIAL RUN

Using any one of the approaches discussed above, try to arrive at a hypothesis about your topic that you will be able to support or challenge by plausible reasons.

CHECKLIST: FORMULATING A HYPOTHESIS

- How much do I already know about my topic?
- How much more do I need to know to form a hypothesis about my topic?
- Have I been cautious not to state my observations and opinions as facts?
- What are my expectations or my reasons for investigating the topic—to show I am right about my own hunches, to show there are other causes, or to discredit existing causes by providing counter causes.
- What ideas might my readers have about my approach to the topic? Will we share some common thoughts and approaches? How confident am I about convincing them?

Support Your Findings with Researched Evidence

The opinion sample helped, to an extent, provide a few definitions of human intelligence for Valentina. But it also confirmed that there could be no one definition. And still there was the nagging question of the mentally retarded artist whose works she admired so much and who, by most standards, would be considered not intelligent. It was time, she felt, to look for opinions of experts in the field of human intelligence and intelligence testing. Her instructor and the librarian guided her to some authorities in the area of her investigation. In her readings she came across many opinions that challenged her own hypothesis that there was no clear cut and sure way to test human intelligence, and she made note of these comments. At the same time, she was excited to find that so many of the authorities on the topic of intelligence testing agreed with her. Having read some of the works by authors including Alfred Binet, Gerald Bracey, and Stephen Jay Gould, she felt somewhat confident to formulate her hypothesis. Because there was no clear-cut definition of intelligence, there could be no clear-cut ways of testing intelligence either. So what about the IQ tests, which claim to test and rate numerically the level of people's intelligence? Her library research buoyed Valentina with confidence that she was on the right track. She felt ready to write the first version of her paper.

Where does one begin to look for support and evidence for a topic? The library is certainly a main source, but it is not the only source. Looking through your own collection of books and periodicals may be a good place to start because you might have marked some passages that might come in handy now. For a basic guide to science books and periodicals, turn to the back of this chapter. Your librarian and instructor are also valuable sources of information. Once you locate books and articles, read them carefully to understand the authors' ideas before taking notes. This will enable you to focus on only what is relevant to your discussion. A preliminary reading may save you time from taking notes if an article or a book does not relate to your topic. Also try to use your own words when noting ideas from your research material; this will prevent any inadvertent plagiarism when you refer to the notes later. It does not matter whether you use note cards or a notebook. What is important is that you have the title of the work, the edition, name of the author, name of the publisher, year of publication, page numbers, and the call number, if any, to help you go back to the source. Nothing is more frustrating than not being able to go back to a source that you have used in your paper.

▐ RIAL RUN

Before taking notes, read through the collected books and articles quickly to make sure they relate to your topic. Then write down all pertinent information and short summaries of large chunks of information that you can return to later. Make sure you note the necessary information that will enable you to go back to the source material if you need to.

CHECKLIST: COLLECTING AND EVALUATING SUPPORTIVE EVIDENCE

- Why am I collecting the information? How would it help me to support my point?
- Am I focusing only on the information that would make my ideas look more plausible?
- Am I looking for opposing and counter arguments that may challenge my own beliefs?
- Am I making a clear distinction between my own opinions and those of others for my readers?
- Have I taken care to cite my sources so as not to mislead my readers into thinking that the opinions of experts included in my paper are my own?

• Does the researched material serve a clear purpose, that is, support or challenge my own views or present alternative views? Or am I simply using names of authorities to impress my readers?

COMPOSING THE FIRST DRAFT
Organize Notes

The first step in composing the draft is to read all notes from your research and observations. This is the time to sift through those that are relevant to your topic and reject facts and ideas that do not belong. A temptation may be to include more than you really need for all the long hours you put in collecting the information. It is a temptation that ought to be scrupulously avoided. Remember your audience includes your instructor, who may be familiar with the major research in the area of your interest and will not benefit by unnecessary information. Using more than you need may lead your audience to believe that you are attempting to add bulk to your paper without saying much yourself. You may use the researched information to support your hypothesis, you may challenge the authorities as Valentina often does in her paper, or you may use their argument to extend your own. Your reader is more interested in your approach and what motivated you to investigate your topic. There are hundreds of studies supporting or challenging IQ tests, but Valentina's motive for enquiry is different from most people's and her approach is also her own. She uses the strong authorial voices of some well known biologists and natural scientists as support for her hypothesis, while questioning the opinions of others with whom she disagrees.

Arrange Details

The arrangement of your notes should help you to progress toward supporting your stated hypothesis. State early what you hope to achieve and why. The "how" segment of the paper is where most of the researched evidence is necessary. It is enough to provide summaries simply to let your readers know what an authority has to say. Your purpose is to compare and contrast the researched evidence with your own or other experts', to define ideas, establish causal links, analyze, and discuss evidence as they relate to your topic. Valentina used the French scientist Alfred Binet's work to show how his ideas relating to intelligence testing were unscientific and unreliable. In contrast, Stephen Jay Gould provided the support that Valentina needed to establish that the earlier tests were unreliable and there was no perfectly objective way to measure human intelligence. Both sources helped Valentina advance her own hypothesis that since there was no one way to define human intelligence, there cannot be a correct method to test it. For more on analyzing evidence, go to Chapter 14, "Writing a Sociology Paper."

PRESENTING VALENTINA'S FIRST DRAFT

1   When Alfred Binet, a scientist at the Sorbonne, first decided to study measurement of intelligence, he turned naturally to "the favored method of a waning century" and to the work of his great countryman, Paul Broca (Gould 146). He set out in short to measure skulls, never doubting at first the basic conclusion of Broca's school: "The relationship between the intelligence of subject and the volume of the head is very real . . ." (Gould 146). He might not have been very convinced by his findings, having derived most of his ideas from Broca, and abandoned his project for a couple of years.

2   When Binet returned to the measurement of intelligence after 2 years, he remembered his previous frustration and switched to other techniques, and constructed a set of tasks that might assess various aspects of reasoning more directly. The first intelligence tests followed a simple premise: if performance on certain tasks or tests items improved with age, then performance could be used to distinguish more intelligent people from the less intelligent ones within a particular age group. Using this principle, Alfred Binet devised the first formal intelligence test to identify those children, whose lack of success in normal classrooms suggested the need for some form of special education. He decided to bring together a large series of short tasks, related to everyday problems of life, for example, counting coins or assessing whose face is "prettier." Binet began by presenting tasks to same-age students who had been labeled "bright" or "dull" by their teachers. If a task could be completed by the bright students but not by the dull ones, he retained the task as a proper test item. At the end he came up with a test that distinguished between the bright and dull groups. This method was further developed to distinguish intelligence among children in different age groups (Gould 158).

3   The first intelligence test was called "intelligent quotient" or IQ. The 1908 version established the criterion used in measuring intelligence even now. At the very beginning Binet meant his test simply as an educational tool. The modern version of IQ tests are fairly straightforward. The Westchester Adult Intelligence Scale exam, for example, is given in a personal interview. It consists of eleven subscribers that ask examinees to do such things as define words, solve math problems, recall strings of digits in forward or reverse order, and arrange blocks according to a specific design (McKean). IQ tests are used to identify children who

are slow or speedy learners, to evaluate job candidates as part of a psychological exam, and to help draw a picture of a person's mental strengths and weaknesses.

4   An Intelligent Quotient is calculated by dividing a subject's mental age by his physical age and multiplying by 100. Thus a 6 year old performing at the 6-year-old-level would have an IQ of 100; if he performed at the 9-year-old-level, his IQ would be 150.

5   How come it is so easy to measure human intelligence? Is it really so simple? I'm sure that it is not simple at all. The assumption that test scores represent a single scalable thing in the head called general intelligence, biologist and author Stephen Jay Gould refers to as just a 20th-century version of craniometry, the 19th-century "science" that claimed a man's intelligence could be determined by measuring his head (155). Why should intelligence be measured at all? A simple answer is because intelligence is the principal ability that separates man from other creatures. If so, are the IQ tests a fair and accurate way to measure intelligence? I believe they are not.

6   The importance of devising fair intelligence tests that measure knowledge unrelated to cultural and family background and experience would be minor if it were not for one important and persistent finding; members of certain racial and cultural groups consistently score lower than members of other groups (Weinberg 99). For example, as a group, Blacks tend to average 15 IQ points lower than whites, according to a survey at Yale University (McKean 28). Does this reflect a true difference in intelligence? The point is that biological intelligence is meaningless when separated from its cultural roots. The higher IQ scores are not necessarily an indication that whites are more intelligent than non-whites. In fact, there is reason to believe that some standardized IQ tests contain elements that discriminate against minority group members whose experience differs from those of the white majority (Sternberg 696).

7   Another important point is that tests should measure consequential kinds of behavior. That is, they should bear close links to the real world. Even creators of the artificial kinds of tasks found in most intelligence tests have often defined intelligence in terms of adaptation to a real-world environment (Gould 198). According to this view, intelligent performance in the real world centers on the ability to capitalize on one's strengths and to compensate for one's weakness and on the ability to modify the environment so that it will better fit one's adaptive skills. But what is adaptive

differs at least somewhat from person to person and situation to situation. Intelligence cannot be quite the same thing for different people and in different situations. The skills of capitalizing on the strengths and compensating for the weakness may be the same, but what is capitalized on and what is compensated for will vary.

8   The next argument about failure of IQ tests is the assumption that people who are more intelligent process information more rapidly which underlies the majority of IQ and aptitude tests. It is a rare test that is not timed; rare, too, is the test that virtually all examinees can finish by working at a comfortable rate. The assumption that faster is smarter is true for some people but not for all. Almost everyone knows people who, though often slow in performing tasks, perform the tasks better. In a study of the role of planning behavior in problem solving, Robert J. Stenberg found that persons who are more intelligent tend to spend relatively more time than do less intelligent persons on global (up-front) planning and relatively less time on local (problem-specific, lower-level) planning (697).

9   In addition, the anxiety experienced during the test may influence the result. Few situations in life are as stressful as facing a standardized test. Most test takers know that the results of these tests are crucial to their future and that a few hours of testing may have more impact on their future than years of school performance. Moreover, because anxiety is common to standardized test situations, anxiety-related errors in measurement resulting from a single testing situation will be compounded by errors stemming from other testing situations (Stenberg 698). According to this view, a bright but test-anxious person with repeated low scores, may appear to be stupid. From my own observation, students do much better on different kinds of tests during regular class time than during scheduled exams.

10   Intelligence tests should be based on a validated theory of the nature of intelligence because only through a sound theory can people have a clear idea of just what intelligence means. Definitions such as "intelligence is whatever IQ tests measure," are conceptually vacuous and tell nothing about intelligence as a characteristic of human wisdom. Measurement should proceed from theory, not vice versa. Because there are so many definitions and theories of intelligence, the validity of IQ tests based on them should be questioned.

11   With so many different variables, no one intelligence test could claim to have a general applicability. We all have known people with low IQ scores who do well in the world, and others

with high IQ's who never amount to much. The IQ scores are overrated partly because of their mystique; the vagueness that makes them questionable also makes them strangely unquestionable. People tend to be impressed by technically accurate-sounding information almost without regard to its validity. Everyone knows people who have been denied access to their goal or advancement because of low test scores. But prior grades should be the best predictor of future grades, prior job performance the best indicator of future performance. When such information is available and its quality known, then it is certainly more useful than IQ test scores. So new standards for measuring intelligence should be designed and instituted to prevent people from being denied opportunities because of low IQ test scores.

Thinking Critically about Valentina's First Draft

1. Comment on the location of the first two paragraphs. What purpose do they serve? Do they get the reader directly involved with the topic?

2. Consider the appropriateness of the outside sources Valentina uses as evidence to build her argument, from the nineteenth-century Binet to the contemporary scientists. Does she have too much or too little researched evidence? What criteria would you use in judging how much is enough for the writer's purpose?

3. Why does Valentina present the researched historical information in reference to IQ tests? How do they advance her own hypothesis? Do you think she places enough emphasis on her own observations?

4. What are Valentina's conclusions with regard to the validity of the IQ tests? Which paragraph begins to point toward the conclusions of her findings? How plausible are they?

RETHINKING AND REVISING

The library research took longer than Valentina had expected. With some help from the librarian, she came across so many interesting and provocative ideas that she felt she had more information than she could use in her paper. With all the new ideas fresh on her mind, Valentina put down her thoughts in the first draft quite quickly and decided to return to it for a review before she turned it in.

Thinking back to what the instructor had said about choosing a phenomenon and defining it clearly, Valentina felt that her beginning did not quite let her readers know what her paper was about. Beginning with Alfred Binet's experiments to measure human intelligence might mislead her readers to believe that she concurred with his views while, in reality, she held them in question later on in the paper. So she decided to open her final draft with paragraph 4, which clearly defined IQ tests, and followed it with paragraph 5, which declared her own position with regard to the validity of IQ tests. These changes, she felt, made clear to the readers what her topic was and where she stood in reference to it. Valentina was aware of the importance of the historical information for the progression of her ideas. So she retained the information but presented them later in the final draft, following the two opening paragraphs. Make sure the researched material does what you intend it to do in your paper and does not detract from it.

The second area that Valentina felt needed improvement was the use of examples to illustrate some of the ideas. This sent her back into the researched material to come up with some more appropriate examples. To illustrate the point that IQ tests are not necessarily an indication that whites are more intelligent than non-whites, she includes paragraphs 7 and 8, and 10 containing valuable supportive evidence from her research, in the final draft.

Finally, during the revision process, Valentina felt more confident about her own knowledge of the subject to put emphasis on her own voice. For example, paragraph 8 in the first draft, which is paragraph 11 in the final draft, ends with Valentina's own assertion about the questionable fact that speed in processing information is a factor in measuring intelligence: "The point is that," Valentina states, "brighter people spend more time encoding and understanding the terms of a problem than do less bright ones." The same confidence prompted her to include paragraph 14 in the final draft to add to her suggestions about what needs to be done to bring about fairness in testing intelligence. Do not hesitate to voice your own opinion even if it challenges the authorities in the field.

The first draft captures and shapes your ideas, making them visible for you to add, rearrange, alter, or delete. It is often easier to revise someone else's writing than your own. Try to have another inquisitive and interested reader comment on your draft for content, clarity, and smooth flow of ideas. When you revise, give yourself some distance from the time of writing and then go back to it for a more critical reading.

Most science papers use the APA (American Psychology Association) style for documentation. For information on APA style, refer to Bibliographic Form in Chapter 17.

CHECKLIST: REVISING YOUR DRAFT

- Have I selected my topic carefully? Have I made a distinction between a fad and a phenomenon or an occurrence?
- Have I defined my topic clearly so that my readers understand my selection of the phenomenon?
- Do I have a hypothesis or a tentative thesis that is examined and tested in the course of the paper?

- Does my researched information show a range of opinion on my topic? Have I included opinion that challenges my own or have I stayed mostly with those whose views I share?

- Have I made sure that I state my own point of view and not merely summarize the experts' opinions?

- To what purpose do I use the researched material? Do I use opinions of authorities in the field to strengthen my own views?

- Have I used the APA style for documenting my research?

PRESENTING VALENTINA'S FINAL DRAFT

IQ Tests: Are They Fair?

Valentina Fedorovsky

Unlike the first draft, the final draft begins by defining IQ to make the concept clear for the reader.

1   An Intelligence Quotient is calculated by dividing a subject's mental age by his physical age and multiplying that by 100. Thus a 6 year old performing at the 6-year-old level would have an IQ at 100; if he performed at the 9-year-old level, his IQ would be 150.

Paragraph 5 in the first draft is paragraph 2 in the final draft. It adds immediacy by raising questions central to Valentina's research.

2   How come it is so easy to measure human intelligence? Is it really so simple? I am inclined to believe it is not simple at all. The assumption that test scores represent a single scalable thing in the head called general intelligence, biologist and author Stephen Jay Gould refers to as just a 20th-century version of craniometry, the 19th-century "science" that claimed a man's intelligence could be determined by measuring his head (155). Because it is the humans' intelligence that separates them from other animals, researchers have gone to great lengths, trying to measure intelligence. But do IQ tests accurately and fairly measure human intelligence? I tend to think they do not.

Valentina formulates her hypothesis.

3   When Alfred Binet, a scientist at the Sorbonne, first decided to study measurement of intelligence, he turned naturally to "the favored method of a waning century" and to the work of his great countryman, Paul Broca (Gould 146). He set out in short to measure skulls, never doubting at first the basic conclusion of Broca's school: "The relationship between the intelligence of subject and the volume of the head is very real..." (Gould 146). He might not have been very convinced by his findings, having derived most of his ideas from Broca, and abandoned his project for a couple of years.

Paragraph 1 in the first draft is paragraph 3 in the final draft. Valentina begins the final draft with her own questions and includes researched material later.

4   When Binet returned to the measurement of intelligence after 2 years, he remembered his previous frustration and

Valentina reports
researched
findings to ad-
vance her own
hypothesis.

switched to other techniques, and constructed a set of tasks that might assess various aspects of reasoning more directly. The first intelligence tests followed a simple premise: if performance on certain tasks or test items improved with age, then performance could be used to distinguish more intelligent people from the less intelligent ones within a particular age group. Using this principle, Alfred Binet devised the first formal intelligence test to identify those children, whose lack of success in normal classrooms suggested the need for some form of special education. He decided to bring together a large series of short tasks, related to everyday problems of life, for example, counting coins, or assessing whose face is "prettier." Binet began by presenting tasks to same-age students who had been labeled "bright" or "dull" by their teachers. If a task could be completed by the bright students but not by the dull ones, he retained the task as a proper test item. At the end he came up with a test that distinguished between the bright and dull groups. This method was further developed to distinguish intelligence among children in different age groups (Gould 158).

5

Valentina reports
researched
material.

The 1908 version of this test, known as "intelligent quotient," established the criterion used in measuring intelligence even today. At the beginning Binet meant his test simply as an educational tool. The modern versions of IQ tests are fairly straightforward. The Westchester Adult Intelligence Scale exam, for example, is given in personal interviews. It consists of 11 subsections that ask examinees to define words, solve math problems, recall strings of digits in forward or reverse order, and arrange blocks according to a specific design (McKean 27). IQ tests are used to identify children who are slow or speedy learners, to evaluate job candidates as part of psychological or psychiatric exams, and to provide a picture of a person's mental strengths and weaknesses.

6

Here Valentina
questions some
authorities she
had mentioned
earlier in the
paper by citing
further evidence.

The importance of devising fair intelligence tests that measure knowledge unrelated to cultural and family background and experience would be minor if it were not for one important and persistent finding: members of certain racial and cultural groups consistently score lower than members of other groups (Weinberg 99). For example, as a group, Blacks tend to average 15 IQ points lower than whites, according to a survey conducted by Yale University (McKean 28). Does this reflect a true difference in intelligence? The point is that biological intelligence is meaningless when separated from its cultural roots. The higher IQ scores are not necessarily an indication that whites are more intelligent than members of other groups.

7 In fact, there is reason to believe that some standardized IQ tests contain elements that discriminate against members of minority groups, whose experiences differ from those of the white majority (Sternberg 696). According to a survey conducted by the Institute of Child Development, children from different backgrounds had different answers to the question, "What would you do if another child grabbed your hat and ran with it?" Most white middle-class children answered that they would tell an adult, and this response was scored as "correct." On the other hand, a reasonable response might be to chase the person and fight to get the hat back, the answer that was chosen by many urban Black children and scored as "incorrect." The possibility of bias and discrimination against minority group members in traditional IQ tests suggests that they should be banned. For example, the state of California does not permit public schools to give Black students IQ tests to decide whether they should be placed in special education classes.

Valentina provides researched evidence to support her hypothesis.

8 Kevin McKean gives a classic example that proves that tests designed for people from one cultural and ethnic background are faulty when applied to another. That example is the study by Joseph Glick of Liberia's Kpelle tribesmen. Glick, a professor and researcher at New York University, asked the tribesmen to sort a series of objects in a sensible order. To his dismay, they insisted on grouping them by function, placing potato with a hoe, for example, rather than putting the potato with other foods. By Western standards, it was an inferior style of sorting. But when Glick demonstrated the "right" way to sort the items, one of the tribesmen retorted that only a stupid person would sort things that way. Thereafter, when Glick asked tribesmen to sort the items the way a stupid person would, they sorted them taxonomically, without any difficulty (McKean 36).

Valentina presents further researched evidence to support her hypothesis.

9 Another important point is that tests should measure consequential kinds of behavior. That is, they should bear close links to the real world. Even creators of the artificial kinds of tasks found in most intelligence tests have often defined intelligence in terms of adaptation to a real-world environment (Gould 196). According to this view, intelligent performance in the real world centers on the ability to capitalize on one's strength and to compensate for one's weakness and on the ability to modify the environment so that it will better fit one's adaptive skills. But what is adaptive differs at least somewhat from person to person and situation

Valentina adds more researched evidence to strengthen her hypothesis.

to situation. Intelligence cannot be quite the same thing for different people and in different situations. The skills of capitalizing on strengths and compensating for weakness may be the same, but what is capitalized on and what is compensated for will vary.

10

More examples support the hypothesis.

The best evidence to support this comes from an experiment conducted by the psychiatrist Seymour Sarason in 1942 on the mentally retarded (Stenberg 695). When he arrived at the school for the mentally retarded, some students had managed to elude the security and escape from the school premises. When the escapees were caught, Sarason was left to do his job: to give them the "Proteus Maze Test." The students who plotted and executed the successful escape were totally unable to complete even the first problem on the test. Obviously, the question is, which is the better measure of intelligence, the problem of escape or the "Proteus Maze Test"?

11

Valentina continues to question existing opinions by providing counter-opinions through researched evidence.

The next argument about failure of IQ tests is the assumption that people who are more intelligent process information rapidly, which underlies a majority of IQ and aptitude tests. It is a rare test which is not timed; rare, too, is the test that virtually all examinees can finish by working at a comfortable rate. The assumption that faster is smarter is true for some people but not for all. Almost everyone knows people who, though often slow in performing tasks, perform them better. In a study of the role of planning behavior in problem solving, Robert Stenberg found that people who are more intelligent tend to spend relatively more time than do less intelligent people on global (up-front) planning and relatively less time on local (problem-specific, lower-level) planning (697). The point is that brighter people spend more time encoding and understanding the terms of a problem than do less bright ones. Sometimes speed is desirable; sometimes it is not. Whether it is desirable or not depends on the task, the components of information processing involved in solving problems, and a person's own style of problem solving.

12

Valentina gives more supportive evidence.

In addition, the anxiety experienced during the test may influence the result. Few situations in life are as stressful as facing a standardized test. Most test takers know that the results of these tests are crucial to their future and that a few hours of testing may have more impact on their future than years of school performance. Moreover, because anxiety is common to standardized test situations, anxiety-related errors in measurement resulting from a single testing situation will be compounded by errors stemming from other testing situations (Stenberg 698). According to this view, a bright but test-anxious person with repeated low scores, may appear to be stupid. From my own observation, students do much better on different kinds of tests during regular class-time than during scheduled exams.

Valentina provides a plausible explanation for her hypothesis.

13 Intelligence tests should be based on a validated theory of the nature of intelligence because only through a sound theory can people have a clear idea of just what intelligence means. Definitions such as "intelligence is whatever IQ tests measure," are conceptually vacuous and tell nothing about intelligence as a characteristic of human wisdom. Measurement should proceed from theory, not vice versa. Because there are so many definitions and theories of intelligence, the validity of IQ tests based on them should be questioned.

Valentina recommends changes to improve testing.

14 Intelligence tests, no doubt, must be missing something. Most importantly, they overlook the personality or motivational factors, but IQ tests should not measure these factors in the first place. I believe there should be new standards for measuring intelligence. IQ tests should consider motives for speed selection rather than speed itself. In addition, the examiner should do everything to allay test anxiety rather than create it. The tests should be conducted in a supportive and cooperative environment, with an examiner willing to offer help to the examinees rather than impassively observe their success or failure. And finally, the procedure for measuring intelligence should require measuring skills relating to the cultural, social, and economic environment of the test takers. In other words, all measures must be relevant to the experience and real-world coping skills of the person being assessed (Sternberg 698).

She questions IQ tests and their applicability.

15 With so many different variables, no one intelligence test could claim to have a general applicability. We all have known people with low IQ scores who do well in the world, and others with high IQ's who never amount to much. The IQ scores are overrated partly because of their mystique; the vagueness that makes them questionable also makes them strangely unquestionable. People tend to be impressed by technically accurate sounding information almost without regard to its validity. Everyone knows people who have been denied access to their goal or advancement because of low test scores. But prior grades should be the best predictor of future grades, prior job performance the best indicator of future performance. When such information is available and its quality known, then it is certainly more useful than IQ test scores. So new standards for measuring intelligence should be designed and instituted to prevent people from being denied opportunities because of low IQ test scores.

Valentina recommends improved methods of testing prior to using IQ tests to measure intelligence.

Works Cited

Bracey, G. (1990). Whole lotta whole language. <u>Phi Delta Kappan, 35</u>, 81–82.

Gould, S.J. (1981). <u>The mismeasure of man</u>. New York: Norton Press.

McKean, K. (1985). Intelligence: New ways to measure the wisdom of man. <u>Discover, 35</u>, 24–41.

Stenberg, R. (1984). Testing intelligence without IQ tests. <u>Phi Delta Kappan, 65</u>, 694–698.

Weinberg, R. (1989). Intelligence and IQ: Landmark issues and great debates. <u>American Psychologist, 44</u>, 98–104.

Commentary on Valentina's Final Draft

Valentina is one step ahead when her instructor assigns a paper based on the scientific method on a science topic. Her own initial dissatisfaction with the timed tests that require quick answers and her observation of the creative capability of the mentally retarded man have often made her wonder about the nature and definition of intelligence and the efficacy and validity of intelligence testing. She has a problem that interests her, which is one of the keys to an effective paper. A topic that does not interest or arouse the curiosity of the writer ultimately becomes a drudgery to both the writer and the reader. In addition, the problems relating to testing that intrigue Valentina are specific and circumscribed, neither trivial nor highly improbable. Their discussion can be limited to a short essay, yet the issues raised have meaningful relations to those in the larger world. Furthermore, they are significant propositions about which there are wide differences of opinion. This affords Valentina the opportunity to test the merits of her own assumptions by juxtaposing them with the opinions of experts in the field.

The first paragraph is unlike most opening paragraphs that tell the reader where the writer intends to go. Though it does not yet tell us the writer's intent, the observation in the short paragraph with its disarming simplicity sets the writer's stance. It subtly but effectively points to the elementary nature of the IQ test, thus setting the stage for her argument that its application in measuring an enormously complex phenomenon, namely human intelligence, may be questionable. So when in paragraph 2 she raises the two major questions—1) How come it is so easy to measure human intelligence, and 2) Do IQ tests accurately and fairly measure human intelligence—the reader is willing to hear her argument. The basis of her research rests on the answers to these questions: "I am inclined to believe it is not simple at all," and at the end of the paragraph, "I tend to think they do not." She organizes her paper first to prove the methods are unreliable and then to show that their results, too, cannot be accurate. With the burden of proof on her, Valentina proceeds to support her opinions with researched evidence and her own observations.

The opening sentence in paragraph 5 firmly confirms the outdated and "unscientific" nature of the tests themselves. "The 1908 version of this test, known as 'intelligent quotient,' established the criterion in measuring intelligence even today." This is a startling piece of information. With the advancement in science and technology, the mechanisms for measuring human intelligence are basically the same today, almost the twenty-first century, as they were in the very early years of the twentieth century. Valentina builds up to this conclusion by summing up the works of the pioneering scientists in this field, Paul Broca and Alfred Binet. Her own mistrust of these tests is supported by the writings of other contemporary scientists, whose works are cited throughout the paper as evidence. The kind of originality that Valentina is working toward is a matter of synthesizing—taking something from A, something from B, adding her own ideas, and creating Z, something that cannot be found anywhere else.

Having established that the methods in these tests are questionable, Valentina proceeds to suggest that the results they arrive at cannot be accurate. The series of evidence from paragraphs 6 through 11 not only supports her assumption but also enlightens and entertains the reader through appropriate and convincing researched information. For example, to show that some aspects of the IQ tests are unfair to certain cultural and racial groups, Valentina cites a research conducted at Yale that proves children from different backgrounds may provide different answers to the same question, which may be right or wrong, depending on the circumstances. Another fascinating example of cultural difference is described in paragraph 8. The experiment conducted by Joseph Glick with the Kpelle tribesmen of Liberia clearly shows that there may not be one "right" way of approaching problems. The differences may even point to a superior intelligence rather than the lack of it these test results often suggest.

Paragraph 9 introduces the complex idea of testing to measure consequential kinds of behavior. Since Valentina never loses sight of the fact that she is not writing as a scientist for a scientific community, she takes care to define terms that may not be intelligible to the general reader and follow them with appropriate examples. For instance, to define "measure of consequential kinds of behavior," Valentina relies on Stephen Jay Gould: "That is they should bear close links to the real world. Even creators of artificial kinds of tasks found in most intelligence tests have often defined intelligence in terms of adaptation to a real-world environment." The experiment that supports this idea is the one conducted by Seymour Sarason on the mentally retarded escapees, a fascinating story that immediately captivates the reader's attention while providing convincing evidence.

With paragraph 12, Valentina begins to pull together the researched information to arrive at the conclusions that would prove her earlier assumptions about the nature and accuracy of intelligence testing. Her first major claim in the conclusion is that measurement should proceed from theory, not vice versa. If people cannot come to a consensus with regard to the nature of intelligence, then the validity of tests based on them should be questioned.

Though the last two paragraphs offer suggestions to improve the current IQ tests, they do so in quite different ways. Paragraph 13 basically reiterates some of the problems discussed earlier and recommends ways to take care of them, for example, "IQ tests should consider motives for speed selection rather than speed itself." Paragraph 14, on the other hand, expresses personal observations. Statements such as, "We all have known people with low IQ scores who do well in the world, and others with high IQ's who never amount to much," and "Everyone knows people who have been denied access to their goal or advancement because of low test scores," bring the realm of intelligence testing close to our own lives. All writers, including science writers, wish their readers to identify with their ideas and opinions. And any writing is more convincing when it touches our own lives. Science and technology are in so many ways a part of our daily lives, which Valentina's paper illustrates so well. Has her paper allayed some of your fears about writing on topics relating to science and technology? We hope so, and we encourage you to write one of your own—or at least to feel comfortable and confident should you have an instructor in a writing or a science class who asks you to write one.

Questions for Further Thought

1. Most science writing accepts, rejects, or extends prior thinking. What are some of the methods a writer can use to do this? Does one have to be an expert in the field to challenge prior thinking? What should student writers do if they wish to question prior thinking?

2. If science writing is based on objectivity, how appropriate or inappropriate is it to use personal voices and experiences? Are impersonal writings, on the other hand, always objective? How would you define objectivity that ensures fairness?

3. The purpose of most writings, including writing about science, is to convince the readers. In science writing, in particular, does this mean that writers must prove their point conclusively? Do all scientific investigations lead to absolute truths or does it suffice to say that the causes of a phenomenon are plausible? How would you define plausible causes? Why do you think they will appeal to your readers?

The following short general guide to preliminary science research may give you a start.

Annual review of information science and technology. 1966 to date. Washington: American Society for Information Science.

Applied sciences and technology index. 1933 to date. New York: Wilson.

Asimov, Isaac. 1982. *Asimov's biographical encyclopedia of science and technology.* Garden City: Doubleday.

Dictionary of scientific biography. 1980. 15 vols. New York: Scribner's.

Encyclopaedia Americana

Encyclopedia Britannica

Rider, K. J. 1970. *History of science and technology: A select bibliography for students.* 2nd ed. New York: International Publications Service.

Van Nostrand's scientific encyclopedia. 1982. 6th ed. New York: Van Nostrand.

Review Journals

American Scientist

Natural History

Science Progress

Scientific American

SECTION SIX

SPECIAL APPLICATIONS AND MATTERS OF CONVENTION

n a book that is essentially a series of stories about papers, about how and why they get written, there comes a point when we need to say that certain important kinds of writing are omitted from such accounts, as is a sustained look at conventions that matter mightily in the academic context. This section is that point. We almost hesitate to call the sections within this section chapters; they are more like collections of thoughts that didn't fit in chapters elsewhere, but we'll call them chapters anyway, just for convenience and consistency's sake.

Chapter 16, then, is a collection of remarks on kinds of writing that aren't really standard papers but are certainly standard assignments and means of handling coursework: note-taking, journal-keeping, essay exams, book reviews. Most students finally find their own way of dealing with any or all of these by trial and error, but that may not be the most efficient way to handle things with no little bearing on your grade for a course. Here you'll find examples of what works and explanations of why.

Chapter 17 treats the sometimes scary business of dealing with library sources: tracking them down, keeping track of them once you have, quoting from them, giving them due credit, doing bibliographic entries properly. We could go on about the procedures and proprieties at great length—others certainly have—but this is a short guide to using sources because it focuses on the reasons for having such conventions in the first place, and it deals in specific examples rather than long exhortations.

Chapter 18 is a discussion of errors and especially why they matter. We use a survey of attitudes toward errors to exemplify which errors bother people and why some bother people more than others. This means giving a lot of short history and sociology (and maybe also psychology) lessons, so the least we could do is spare you any exercises or quizzes or rules phrased in the imperative. Instead, we give three general points of advice. You take it from there.

The principle unifying what might otherwise seem a hodgepodge of a section is that here we are foregrounding what is kept in the background throughout the rest of the book: elsewhere we would like to keep the stress on what you can do, on what range of possibilities awaits decisions from you to make the possible real in your own case, in your own way; here we have to focus on what is expected of you, on what established practices require some degree of conformity, some knowledge of the ropes, some modicum of writerly etiquette. Other parts of the book may be more liberating, but this section, too, is about your getting welcomed into a community, the academic community.

CHAPTER SIXTEEN

SPECIAL APPLICATIONS: IN-CLASS WRITING AND BOOK REVIEWS

The preceding sections concentrated on writing essays and papers, some shorter and more spontaneous, others longer and researched. Your audience was primarily your teacher or your classmates. Though you had limited time for these assignments and were pushed by deadlines, still you were able to consult your friends and teachers, acquire information in the library, and work on several drafts before the final one. The writing situations in this section are somewhat different from the point of view of both time and audience. For example, your audience may not always be your teacher. You may take an in-class exam, which will be read by your teacher, but the journal notes and entries in a course or from a book are primarily for yourself. While the essay exam is intended for the teacher, the short amount of time you are allowed to complete this essay makes it a much more pressured situation than writing the kinds of essays discussed in the earlier sections. This chapter guides you through reading and note-taking, prepares you to stay cool while writing under the fire of exams, and provides some general advice about reviewing books and articles.

TAKING CLASS NOTES

The way you take notes is mostly your own. No one can tell you exactly what to do. What you can do, however, is learn ways to organize your notes so they can help you in your writing. Disorganized and jumbled notes are more of a hindrance than a help. You may organize information by writing notes about your reading in the book itself, referred to as annotation. Or you may take down lecture notes in the classroom in a notebook or journal.

Annotating

You generate certain ideas or feelings as you read a textbook, a reference book, or an article in a course. These ideas may seem unformed, fragments of personal memories stimulated by the reading, and may even seem unrelated directly to the book. These small rumblings are, however, important as a fuller response to your reading begins with these fragmented ones. The first effort you can make toward writing about a particular topic is to take note of these early responses. The easiest way to record them is to annotate your book. This means writing in the margins and making your mark on the text. There is nothing sacred about a published book and you have the right to make it your own, if of course the book belongs to you and not to the library.

CHECKLIST: ANNOTATING TEXT

- Underline all new words and write their meanings in the margin. In addition to improving your vocabulary, this will help you to understand the book.
- Underline all important words, generalizations, and important points the author makes.
- Write short summaries of important passages in the margin.
- Write your own short responses to the ideas in the paragraphs; do you agree or disagree with the author's views?

Try to be familiar with the assigned readings before going to class. If you read and annotate the text before it is discussed in class, you will be able to follow the class lecture better and also get answers to questions you may have had while reading the assignment for the first time. When you review the book for the final exam, these comments and markings will help you recapitulate the information. Figure 16-1 shows an annotated page from a history text. Note how the student underlines unfamiliar words and events and writes brief explanations in the margin.

 **T**RIAL RUN

1. Summarize the paragraphs below.
2. Do you detect a clear point of view? Is the writer supporting or condemning Brown?
3. Use the above guidelines to read books in any course and start a notebook to record your thoughts.

Besides writing in the text itself, another form of annotation is a double-column or dialectical notebook (treated in Chapter 8), which is basically a dialogue with yourself about your responses to a reading. By raising questions about the reading and attempting to provide answers, you move from simple understanding to interpretation and analysis. More important, these

Figure 16-1

Sample of Annotated Text

Religions Orthodoxy that imposed the fear of hellfire in next life and punishment in this life

John Brown was born in Connecticut, the son of a tanner, in 1800. His father imbued him with a passionate Calvinistic obsession with evil and the need not only to resist sin, but to battle it. Two hundred years earlier, Brown would have been a doughty Massachusetts pioneer, a maker of towns against all the odds of wilderness. In the twentieth century he would have warred against whiskey or sexual immorality. In the mid-nineteenth century, like many Americans of evangelical bent, his ardor fastened on the national sin of slavery.

(annotations: Brown's ideas were shaped by the time he lived in; early settlers; Christians with militant + crusading zeal)

Brown failed at business—several businesses. It is not clear, when he joined his sons in Kansas in 1855, if he was at all interested in having a go at a homestead on the plains. He may well have been attracted to Kansas only by the fact that there the debate over slavery had been transformed into violent confrontation. Proslavery "Jayhawkers" and "Border Ruffians" from western Missouri, seeing that they were simply out-voted, bullied and terrorized the growing antislavery majority. Much more ominous, and accounting for the fact that abolitionists who called themselves pacifists would support Brown, the administrations of presidents Franklin Pierce and James Buchanan positively abetted winning Kansas for slavery by horsewhip and gun.

(annotations: Those who rode across the state line to vote illegally in Kansas; Kansas native anti-slavery guerrillas; 1853-57; 1857-61)

As early as 1851, Brown had said that if blacks had any sense of "manhood," they would kill anyone who tried to enforce the Fugitive Slave Act. By 1854, prominent abolitionists were no longer responding with frowns of disapproval. In August 1856, he reacted to a proslavery raid on Lawrence, Kansas, by riding to a cabin on Pottawatomie Creek and hacking to death five proslavery settlers (who had nothing to do with the Lawrence raid).

(annotations: Great deal of violence on question of slavery; 1850 law against helping fugitive slaves; look up on a map)

Brown was now a fugitive, wanted for murder. Incredibly, however, he toured New York and New England more or less openly. He addressed public meetings, was cordially received by prominent citizens, and given money by six well-to-do abolitionists. The fruit of the Kansas-Nebraska Act and the Dred Scott Decision was not to protect slavery, as too many southerners foolishly believed, but to turn otherwise conservative moralists into exponents of holy war

(annotations: 1854 allowed settlers in Kan/Neb to decide whether or not they wanted slavery; 1857 Supreme Court ruling that denied the Negro the right to freedom)

and retribution against men guilty of nothing more than the fact that they approved of the institution of slavery.

Brown may have kept the specifics of his plans from the "Secret Six," but all knew that he intended violence. Among other things, he ordered a thousand pikes from a forge in Connecticut. When the raid at Harper's Ferry failed and Brown was arrested, tried, and sentenced to hang, all but one of the six went into hiding. They had savored Brown's tales when they were told in parlors but, like Brown in that faltering moment in the arsenal, they were not willing to face up to the consequences when revolutionary reveries were translated into action.

(annotation: look on map)

The one backer who stood his ground, Thomas W. Higginson, frankly stated that Brown's execution would do more good than if he were pardoned or even if his raid had succeeded. Higginson was correct and prophetic. In jail, Brown himself grasped the point and deported himself not as an avenging angel or field marshall of the holy war, but as a calmly dedicated Christian awaiting his destiny and salvation. His perception was brilliant — "I am worth inconceivably more to hang than for any other purpose" — his actions, really for the first time, were indisputably rational and selfless.

(annotations: Unitarian minister-pro-abolitionist)

In the long run, John Brown's significance was indeed to make the war against slavery a mass movement—in the form of the blue-coated thousands of the Union Army. In the short run, his raid revealed just how unsure white southerners were of their contented darkies. There had been no slave revolt in the South since Nat Turner's Rebellion a generation earlier. White southerners pointed to that fact in defense of their institution. But John Brown, for all his failures, laid bare the fact that they did not really believe their own boasts.

(annotations: What Brown's movement revealed; 1831 Slave rebellion in Virginia led by Turner)

Southerners joined hands with Brown and Higginson in looking forward to Brown's execution. But they were acting out of fear and vengeance rather than on the basis of reasoned calculation. The same might be said of the secession movement that began almost exactly a year after the hanging in December 1859.

(annotations: grew in 1850's and ended with Civil War)

Figure 16-2

Sample of Double-Column Notebook

Thoughts and Questions	Answers and Suggestions
1. What is Calvinistic obsession?	It refers to the ideas of the French Protestant philosopher John Calvin (1509–64), who influenced the Protestants in America. It is interesting that Calvin's ideas denies the concept of free will. If God chooses the individuals He wishes to save, man can do nothing about it. Now I can see how Brown must have felt duty bound to God to end slavery even if it meant using violence.
I can see how Brown must have been obsessed with the idea of freedom for the slaves to blow up innocent people. But what is <u>Calvinistic</u> obsession?	
2. Another religious word, evangelical bent	This, too, refers to the Protestant faith. It means a strong personal faith — more to do with preaching than ritual. The kind of person I would expect Brown to be.

(cont.)

Figure 16-2, cont.

3. Jayhawkers and border ruffians — The words referred to the robbers and bandits — guerrillas in Kansas and Missouri during the Mexican border dispute in 1857.

4. Abolitionists — These were the people wanted to end slavery. John Brown was among them. The first anti-slavery society was formed in Philadelphia in 1775. So more than 300 years ago there were people who wanted to end slavery.

5. Fugitive Slave Act — This act of 1850 required the return of all runaway slaves. If people gave shelter to them they were punished with fines and imprisonment. Reminds me of what the Nazis did during World War II to people who hid the Jews or helped them to escape.

(cont.)

Figure 16-2, cont.

6. Pottawatomie Creek, Lawrence, Kansas

Site of a big massacre. John Brown and his six followers murdered five pro-slavery men in May 1856. The massacre led to all-out guerrilla war in Kansas. Shows Brown as a real fanatic.

entries help you visualize the abstract and philosophical reading process. If you can "see" the way you read, you can improve upon it by paying more attention to details or explaining your own responses. Figure 16-2 is a sample of dialectical notebook entries on the textbook excerpt from the life of John Brown.

Taking Good Notes from Lectures

Most class lectures relate to textbooks. Therefore, a familiarity with the assigned reading is the first step in taking good lecture notes. If you know the chapters, you will be less inclined to take down every word the instructor says in class and concentrate more on the information that enhances your understanding of the book. Be alert to any particular sections that the instructor may emphasize, because quizzes and exams may be based on them. You may also disagree with some of the instructor's interpretations by writing those questions in the margin of your notes. Class notes are not a substitute for the text but an aid to enriching your understanding of the text. Figure 16-3 shows original class notes from a lecture, before they have been reorganized and rewritten as in Figure 16-4.

CHECKLIST: TAKING NOTES

- Begin notes with the date and with the names of corresponding chapters in the book.
- Write clearly and leave space between words and lines.

Figure 16-3

Sample of Disorganized Class Notes

"The New Woman"
Suffrage
home + the work place in the 20's

Women in the 1920's

—19th Amendment ratified in 1920 culminated decades of struggle for the vote. Again progressives' legislation reflects issues that have existed for a long time but only with progressives does ~~federal~~ legislation pass (ex. immigration prohibition)

—~~1848~~— Seneca Falls "rewrote" declaration of independence—men are the oppressors in this rewrite, women list grievances against men, call for unalienable rights—freedom in wages property, vote.

After 1848 women put energy behind abolition. Abolition movement gave women experience in organizing and speaking. Some resistance to women speakers—'women don't belong on stage."

Controversy within movement over 14th Amendment. Split into National Womens Suffrage Assoc
and American Womens Suffrage Assoc

—Still women's movement only represents a limited number of women in America!
Women's Christian Temp Union was largest women's organization and temperance was biggest movement.
Why the resistance to suffrage as an issue?
Seen as radical by men and women—potential to change society. Traditional indoctrinated view of woman as subordinate

Temperance is backed by church—attempt to reform society. Suffrage is not so much backed by church and is seen as attempt to achieve equality. Equality is a troubling notion for Americans and arguments against it claim that by changing the relationship between men and women you will change and possibly imperil the sanctity of the American family. Suffragists want women to take a place of (cont.)

Figure 16-3, cont.

power in society, they want to affect the decisions of the government. Many women resisted suffrage movement —they feared change in the social = family relationships. Suffragists changed their rhetoric to appease the uneasiness. Mount campaign to pass more suffrage legislation at federal rather than state level. National Amer Womens suffrage Assoc. — joining of two older groups.

— New argument — women are different than men but their influence could help to harmonize society, promote peace and sanctify domestic life in society. Suffrage passes in part because the rhetoric has become more conservative.

After suffrage passes movement begins to achieve equal rights for women as reflected in the more radical rhetoric á la Seneca Falls.

—Realization of women's vote — Women are expected to make a big change in politics but they don't — they vote in much the same way as their families — their place in society — women vote but they vote much like the nation voted before them.

by 1920 23% of labor force are women mostly in gender seperated occupations, clerical, garment, etc. Social workers, teachers, nurses, telephone operator, domestic help. Majority of women workers are foreign born or black. Statistics don't include women on the farm. Women are not included in labor organization APL rhetoric is patronizing but ambiguous.

1917 Gompers allow women in unions but their representation is slight, almost "token"

Figure 16-4

Sample of Revised, Rewritten Class Notes

U. S. History
Professor B. Cole
10/28/90

Terms
the new woman
suffrage
home and the work place in the 20s

1. Why the changes in the 1920s?
   The Amendment to the Constitution was ratified in 1920. It was a culmination of a long struggle started in the 1848 Seneca Falls Convention when women
listed grievances and called for economic, social, and political independence.
Controversy within the movement over the 19th Amendment caused the group to
split into two: National Women's Suffrage Association and American Women's
Suffrage Association--one group supported amendment while the other felt it
was Black America's issue, not theirs. Still these two groups represented a
limited number while the bigger movement was Temperance, with 5000 Temperance
societies in 1835.

2. Why the resistance to Suffrage?
   It was seen as trying to achieve "equality" between men and women, a troubling notion not backed by church and seen as a threat to the American family.

3. Why did they change their argument in 1920?
   Suffragists changed their argument and their rhetoric--the new argument:
women are different from men (no longer earlier equality) and their influence
would bring harmony to society. Suffrage passed in part because the rhetoric
had become more conservative. Movement now began to achieve equal rights for
women as reflected in the more radical rhetoric of Seneca Falls.

4. What was the effect of the vote?
   Women were expected to make big changes in politics but they didn't. Why?
They voted much the same way as their families and their husbands because of
their still inferior status in society. This was vote without accompanying
social changes such as education and power.

5. Home and the workplace in the 1920s.
   23% of labor force were women, majority in gender segregated occupations
such as clerical, garment workers, social workers, teachers, nurses, telephone
operators, and domestic help. Majority of them were Black or foreign born.
Women were not included in the labor organizations--AFL rhetoric was
patronizing but ambiguous. In 1917 Gompers allowed women in unions but
representation was token.

- Do not try to write every word. Your notes should reflect the basic outline of the general discussion. Pay particular attention to any new information not so evident in the text.

- Class notes invariably tend to be disorganized. For best results, reorganize and rewrite them after class. This is also the best way to review the lesson.

Figure 16-4 shows the same class notes reorganized by questions and answers, which probably indicate the instructor's emphasis on the various aspects of the topic. Segment 5 summarizes the condition of working women in the 1920s. Notes in this clear form are an immense help for fast review without having to go through the whole text again.

WRITING UNDER PRESSURE: SHORT EXAM QUESTIONS

Writing well under time pressure takes more than just knowledge of the subject. Your instructor may require you to write two short essays in an hour. You may know a lot about the topic, but your success in the exam will not depend on your knowledge alone but on your ability to zero in on exactly what is being asked, to select relevant details, and present them in an organized essay. The following *do's* and *don'ts* may help you to get better at taking short essay exams:

1. Read the question carefully to figure out what exactly is being asked. Plan your answer briefly before you plunge into the writing. Saving time is important while taking an exam, but you may end up losing time if you do not focus on the question.

2. On a separate sheet of paper, write down your random thoughts on the subject and shape them into a brief outline. Do not plunge into the final version immediately after reading the question.

3. Make sure your essay states its purpose clearly at the beginning and has enough evidence to support your claim.

4. Remember neatness counts. Do not aggravate the examiner by making your handwriting impossible to read.

5. Do not keep writing until the last minute. The last few minutes to review for content, organization, and mechanics can make a big difference in the grade.

6. Try to get some practice before the exam in thinking and writing under pressure.

The two sample student essays following illustrate a good exam (A) and a poor exam (B) in a freshman urban studies course.

QUESTION: Discuss the urbanization of the United States in the last half of the nineteenth century with reference to the following: immigration, transportation, settlement houses, Jacob Riis, the boss system, tenements, and sweatshops.

(A)   Many factors contributed to the growth of American cities. Industrialization helped provide a workplace for the growing number of people. Technology made it possible through transportation and housing to accommodate the larger numbers. And a surge of immigration provided a cheap source of labor.

   Industrialization blossomed in the urban setting. Cities were located at strategic points for transportation by rail and water. They also were financial centers to attract capital investment. And as population centers, they contained a labor force and a market. Advances in technology helped establish the large urban areas. Streetcar transportation expanded the physical size of the cities. They eliminated the problems of horsedrawn carriages and allowed people to commute to work. Advances in architecture created high apartment buildings with elevators and these accommodated more people and changed the city skyline. Immigrants were drawn to America by a combination of problems at home in Europe and visions of success in America. Often they arrived with no capital to travel further than the big Eastern cities. Also these cities contained ethnic neighborhoods that offered a degree of network and solidarity to immigrants from similar ethnic backgrounds.

Urbanization, however, presented America with a new set of problems. Immigrants were often packed into tenements, sometimes several families into one apartment. These tenements were crude structures with few windows and no running water or indoor toilets. The immigrants were often preyed upon by a host of traders and merchants who cheated them through phony deals. Also, in the workplace, the immigrants were paid less than other workers because they were willing to work for meager wages. Work was often done indoors by women and children, and whole families worked in the garment industry, in cigar factories and various other jobs. These sweatshops, often located in basements of buildings, employed immigrants who rarely saw the sunlight.

The immigrant population threatened the old city workforce. This gave rise to strong anti-immigrant and pro-native-son sentiment. This was often expressed as anti-Catholic, anti-Semitic, and pro-Anglo-Saxon rhetoric and often became a political issue. The resultant rise of the urban political machine, the boss system, is one of the controversial issues in American history. It created a strong network of power base in individual neighborhoods. Through patronage, parades, beer parties, shoes for children and other gifts, the political bosses could secure the votes of the workers and the new immigrants. These political bosses changed the nature of city services by building projects, parks, roads, bridges, hospitals, and by providing sanitation and emergency relief. But these "philanthropic" acts were also tainted by grafts and large "cuts" for their awards of patronage. This was an expensive government but more responsive to the needs of the immigrants than previous ones.

Reform in the late 1800s in the cities took several forms. Muckrakers like Jacob Riis, Lincoln Steffens, or later, Ida Tarbell tried to expose the problems in the government to the public. Settlement workers ran community oriented houses that focused on education and practical aid within the neighborhoods. "Good government" reformers thought cities should be run like businesses by specialists. They achieved power in few cities but not for too long. They would often cut programs that benefitted the people and so alienate their supporters in the neighborhoods who put them in office.

These new brands of politicians with their reform measures sought to solve the problems of the unsafe sweatshops, overcrowded tenements, and political grafts. But often their well-intentioned laws were difficult to enforce, and the plight of the immigrants did not change very much.

(B)   In the last half of the nineteenth century, immigrants were moving into the urban settings, virtually forcing out original ccity dwellers. They lived in settlement houses with people of their own culture and racial backgrounds. Because there were such large numbers of immigrants who came at this time, they took jobs away from the people who lived in the cities so there was a lot of tension between them. They worked for very long hours in sweatshops for little pay. The boss system was operative in these sweatshops and factories by which an overseer supervised the work and all that was produced went to the boss. The immigrants provided the cheap labor. They worked hard while the boss profited by the fruit of their labor.

The immigrants lived in dark, unhealthy dwellings. But they lived in these cities because there was public transportation and they could move about freely. The politicians built roads and houses for the immigrants who voted for them. The immigrants contributed to the growth of the large urban areas and developed their own brand of political system by ousting the older existing system. The new politicians like Jacob Riis provided more services but they also took bribes.

So basically the lives of the new immigrants remained unchanged in spite of the new laws to improve their lives.

Let us take a look at these two short exams to see how close they come to fulfilling the basic requirements of a well-written answer.

1. **Adequate knowledge of the subject.**

   Paper A shows the writer's confidence stemming from a clear knowledge of the subject. Each of the categories in the question is clearly developed with appropriate examples, dates, and details of time and place. For example, the question on Jacob Riis is completely overlooked in paper B. Paper A, on the other hand, has a whole paragraph on the benefits and failure of the "good government" reformers. The writer takes care to build up to this paragraph by describing the corrupt patronage system that was in bad need of reform.

   Paper B does not address all the points asked in the question. This may lead the examiner to believe that the writer did not have enough information to develop the essay. The paper briefly touches upon immigration, settlement houses, and sweatshops, but does not discuss transportation, Jacob Riis, the boss system, and tenements, and those that are mentioned are not adequately dealt with. For example, one of the topics, settlement houses, is given one brief sentence in paper B while paper A has a whole paragraph on the same topic.

2. **A clear understanding of what is being asked.**

   Paper A illustrates that its writer understands the question, which asks for a discussion of a list of items only as they relate to urbanization of America. The first sentence of the opening paragraph, "Many factors contributed to the growth of American cities," provides the organizing structure as each of the listed items is discussed in terms of a contributing factor. Each paragraph makes a separate point, thus avoiding repetition. The conclusion, too, relates to the question by stating that the lives of the immigrants did not change much in spite of the reforms in the cities.

   The writer of paper B reveals a lack of understanding of the question by not relating the items addressed to the issue of urbanization of America. The introductory sentence does not reveal the writer's point of view or give the essay its focus. What follows is a haphazard discussion of subjects listed in the question, without a main idea holding them together.

3. **A clear knowledge of the points to be covered.**

   The question requires the writer to discuss several aspects in reference to the urbanization of the United States in the last half of the nineteenth century. To maintain a balance in this answer, the writer must address all the issues raised in the question as illustrated by paper A. The list is quite long but the issues are interrelated. Paper A shows an awareness of interconnections between the several conditions set out in the question and weaves them carefully into the answer. It does this effectively by making immigration and industrialization the main focus of the paper and relating the other conditions—for example, transportation, settlement houses, sweatshops, and the boss system—to the main focus. Another virtue of paper A is that it shows an awareness of the nature of the question by not simply presenting a summary of the information. Sometimes an answer may have adequate information, but if it is only a summary, it seldom answers the question. Paper A is an analytical discussion and not a summary because it makes causal connections. For example, paragraph 4 begins with the statement: "Urbanization, however, presented America with a new set of problems." The several items in the question—settlement houses, tenements, sweatshops, the boss system—are then discussed as examples of the problems. Again in paragraph 5, the philanthropy of the politicians is questioned for the awards of patronage.

This understanding and the resultant balance are absent in paper B, which begins and ends with immigrants. The introductory sentence attempts to address the question but the rest of the paper does not adequately discuss the issues raised in the question, which are addressed at random, without any clear pattern. The paper also is a short summary because it describes *what* these conditions were rather than *why*.

4. **Clear sentence structure that connects ideas.**

The sentences in paper A present ideas clearly by defining important terms and making causal connections. In paragraph 5, the boss system is first defined as a political system with examples. Then it is shown as an inadequate system, tainted by graft and patronage. However, paper B does not clearly define the term and does not emphasize its political significance in the lives of the immigrants. It sees the boss system operative only in sweatshops and not as a political machine.

Your instructor, aware of the pressure you are under when taking an exam, does not expect perfection. If you are able to show an adequate knowledge of the subject with an awareness of some of the items discussed above, you will probably do well in an in-class exam.

WRITING BOOK REVIEWS

A common assignment in a college course is a book review, which is a short essay evaluating a book or an article. Though it may briefly summarize the content, a book review is not a summary. Its primary aim is to encourage readers to read the book or article or discourage them from doing so. The reviewer's task is to rate or evaluate the book according to some standards such as its theme, its method of presentation and organization, its language and style, the author's opinions, values, and point of view. The reviewer may judge the book by comparing it to other works on a similar topic. Though a knowledge of the author's life and other works, if any, may enhance your understanding, the main source of evidence for your comments is the book itself. You may frequently have to refer the reader to sections of the book to support your comments, but avoid very long quotations as they detract from the review itself.

Though each review is an individual critical evaluation and there is no clear formula, the following general guidelines may help you in writing reviews.

CHECKLIST: PREPARING A REVIEW

1. Read the book or article thoroughly and make journal entries of your responses.
2. Read reviews in professional and popular journals to make yourself familiar with the format.
3. Clearly identify the book at the beginning of the review with the title, name of the author or editor, publisher, the date and place of publishing, number of pages, and the edition.
4. Describe the subject and range of the book.
5. Support your comments with examples from the book.
6. Briefly summarize the main points of the argument.
7. Say if the author's argument is convincing or not.
8. Show how the ideas and arguments in the book relate to the world in general, to other studies on the same subject, and to your particular course.
9. Try not to praise or criticize a book based only on personal reactions. A book on the effects of divorce on children should be meaningful to someone who is neither divorced nor a parent.

The following review is by a student. The book appeals to the reviewer particularly because she can identify with some of the situations the author discusses.

Student review of How to Break Your Addiction to a Person by Howard M. Halpern, N.Y. Bantam Books, 1982, 289 pp.

My decision to read a book is guided by whether or not the book would help me in some way. When I began to read How to Break Your Addiction to a Person, I realized the author was describing me and the techniques I have used to deal with my relationships. Could my experiences and disappointments be so common?

One of the main points made in the book is finding the basis of your addiction to a person. The author states that there are three "levels of linkage" that can influence your decisions about staying in a relationship. At the top of the levels are "Practical Considerations for Not Leaving a Relationship." These are the most observable and understandable of the three levels. One example is the difficulty a couple faces in ending a marriage when there are children involved. At the next level are the "Beliefs You Hold about Relationships and about yourself." An example of a belief that many people have is that being alone is humiliating. The most significant level is the third level. This is "Attachment Hunger," which is the basis of being addicted to a person. To understand "Attachment Hunger," the author makes you examine your childhood experiences. The extent to which "Attachment Hunger" will affect your relationships as an adult depends on your relationships as a child.

While reading this book, I realized how many of my childhood experiences had in fact affected my relationships. My father left when I was 5 years old and my only memory of him is the day he left. I sat on the bed while he packed his things and asked him why he was leaving. He told me he had to live close to where he worked. At age 5 I could not understand this. Why was he really leaving? Was it because of me? My mother was very depressed. Here she was, 29 years old, with two children, and her husband leaving. This scenario made me stop and think why I have such a strong "Attachment Hunger" in my own relationships. I was trying to mend what went wrong when I was a child without really understanding what I was doing. I tried so hard to stay with someone emotionally removed from me because I could not deal with his leaving. I wanted him to stay so I could mend the hurt that I felt when my dad left. Throughout this book, with each case study, the author points out what long-term effects your childhood experiences can have on you.

Another way this book helps you is by exercises to make you decide whether or not to end a relationship. One which I found interesting is the benefit/cost analysis. If the benefits of the relationship outweigh the costs, then one should work at maintaining it. These questions and exercises help you to locate areas that are strong and areas that are lacking.

My response to this book is that everyone, whether in a strong or devastating relationship, should read this book. It has helped me to examine my past and understand my present.

Commentary

The aim of a book review is to inform the reader about the author, give some idea of the book's contents, and suggest whether the book is worth reading.

The student review of *How to Break Your Addiction to a Person* begins on a personal note. Though it does not provide any background information about the author, we may guess from the title that the author is probably a sociologist or a psychologist. It presents the key ideas and supports them with examples from the book. The personal anecdotes are acceptable in this review because they relate directly to the content of the book. Since the reviewer makes it clear that she reads a book only if it helps her in some way, this book certainly fits into her reading plan. So when she shows the reader how she has been helped by this book, she is not completely off the track, especially because her personal comments are made general by being closely related to the ideas in the book itself. Professional reviewers, too, sometimes bring their personal experiences to a book review. It is important to remember that comments, however personal, must have close ties with the subject of the book. What matters is that your readers get an idea about the book through your comments and recommendations, which this student review accomplishes quite effectively.

CHAPTER SEVENTEEN

A GUIDE TO USING SOURCES

The point of this short guide is to help you manage the sometimes complicated business of gathering and citing secondary sources—the sort you find in a library. One whole section of the book, Section Two, shows you how to use primary sources like surveys and interviews, and such primary sources figure in all three of the research papers discussed in Section Four, so we won't treat them here. The fact is that they're actually easier to document, if not actually easier to gather in the first place. Citing secondary sources is trickier because it is more convention-bound, more hemmed in by rules and regulations for everything from what is legally allowable to what is formally acceptable. With secondary sources, we enter the realm of copyright laws and styles of documentation, styles that often vary from one discipline or type of writing to another.

The legalities and procedural niceties can seem intimidating, so it's good to keep in mind that their great reason for existing is to keep things fair and convenient. They provide established ways of legally borrowing from others because the unacceptable alternative would be literary theft—the precise term for which is **plagiarism.** Thanks to the general agreement to follow these established procedures, the sources you use leave their own documented trails of research, just as your documentation marks whatever trail you blaze as you explore some area of knowledge and opinion and information.

It's still more important to realize that you are never just exploring a topic. The very phrase "using sources" suggests, quite properly, that they are but a means to an end. What you get from sources cannot *be* your paper; it can only feed and sustain and support what your paper has to say. You need to begin with an idea. That idea may change and develop—feeding anything, not least of all an idea, does lead to that kind of organized, purposeful change we call growth—but you need to have at least the glimmerings of a point you can call your own. Otherwise, you're just gathering information, going to books and encyclopedias to collect stuff you can package and call "America's Railroads" (or whatever). And why would you do that? What's the point of doing all that work if you don't have a point to make, a purpose to accomplish?

OK. So let's say that you have an idea (or the glimmerings of one). Where do you go? What do you do? You might, of course, go to the library or campus bookstore for one of hundreds of whole books devoted to the subject of gathering, using, and citing sources. But maybe you don't have that kind of time. Maybe you have a strong suspicion that there's something inevitably haphazard and task-specific about research, that no two people do it the same way and no one person does it the same way twice, that a few general guidelines will let you figure the rest out for yourself. If so, read on.

USING THE LIBRARY

Looking into a Subject

The point you have to make will do much—it is impossible to overemphasize how much—to define your subject for you. But you also live in a world of preconstituted topics, ways of defining fields of research, focused ongoing discussions, areas of interest or concern. Your own thinking will inevitably be influenced by a sense of what other people see as a subject and its significance. Knowing how material on a subject you have in mind gets collected and indexed will be useful to you.

Let's say that, like one of our students, you're interested in racial and ethnic tensions between cultural groups living in New York City—specifically, the tensions between West Indian Blacks and the Hasidim (an Orthodox Jewish community) in Crown Heights (a section of Brooklyn), tensions that exploded into riots when, in mid-1991, a car with a Hasidic driver struck two young African-American children and killed one. Let's say you see this essentially as a conflict of cultures, and you want to see if there's some general background you can use to frame your discussion. If you begin looking under "conflict of cultures," you'll find (though the world is sadly full of such conflicts) that nothing is listed—not in the subject listings of the library's card or computer catalog, not in the various indexes to periodicals, not anywhere. So what do you do?

What you do—what you should always do when you're interested in researching a subject—is to look into a two-volume work called the *Library of Congress Subject Headings,* available in any library. There you will find that the heading to look under is "culture conflict" (which includes such cross-listed subheadings as "marginality, social" and "race relations"). Big deal? It is if it saves you hours of wasted time. One of our students once came to us with the incredible news that our library had only two books on the Vietnam War. What had happened is that, once the student typed in "Vietnam War" as the subject to be searched in the computer catalog, the computer search identified only two books in the whole library—two books with the phrase "Vietnam War" in their titles. More might have been found had the student typed "War in Vietnam," but the complete listings are available only to someone who knows, by consulting the *Library of Congress Subject Headings,* that "Vietnamese Conflict" is the way the subject is defined.

Books versus Periodicals

We've been speaking of books more than periodicals up to this point, not because books are more important (the primary secondary sources, so to speak), but because they are good places to begin. If, in fact, you (like so many students) have a research paper somehow focused on current events, books aren't especially helpful as much more than a starting point. What with copy editing, text design, typesetting, etc., it tends to take about a year for a manuscript to become a printed and distributed book. Even with recent copyrights, books tend to be old news. But old news is also called history, which is to say that books are often indispensable sources of background, sources that are typically researched much more thoroughly than periodical articles. They also come with tables of contents and indexes that help you to home in on just the information you need. (Students sometimes avoid books as sources on the mistaken assumption that it will take too much time to wade through them. But you don't need to wade; just dip.)

Like books, articles in journals, magazines, and newspapers (collectively called periodicals because they come out periodically) also have their own virtues and liabilities. They tend to be much more up-to-date than books, more focused on whatever is current about a current event or controversy. This very focus, though, necessarily excludes much historical or contextual background. With the notable exception of popular magazines (which have their own, more general biases), they also tend to be geared to particular, often specialized audiences and interests. As with all sources, you must consider your source: Is important background information left out? Is the vocabulary pitched to a specialized audience? Is the discussion or evidence given a particular slant?

Tracking Things Down

Just what sort of sources will be of use to you depends on just what you are up to in the first place—what kind of topic you are investigating, what kind of point you are arguing. Still, some sources are so generally useful they deserve mention here.

We've already mentioned books as good sources of background information. Still more obvious sources along these lines are encyclopedias and dictionaries. Students often don't imagine such sources will be of much use because they think only of the encyclopedias and dictionaries they've been exposed to since grade school. Actually, you'll find many specialized ency-clopedias and dictionaries with helpful short summary articles (and often bibliographies) on any number of subjects. That student interested in culture conflicts, for instance, might be well served by consulting *A Dictionary of Social Sciences* or *The International Encyclopedia of the Social Sciences.*

Books in the library are usually located by means of a card catalog or a computer catalog, which functions in much the same way as the card cata-log—allowing you to check for books under author, title, or subject. Almost all libraries now classify and file books according to the Library of Congress system—yet another reason for becoming acquainted with that two-volume work *Library of Congress Subject Headings,* since it will determine what subject headings are used. And your search will be conducted (at least initially and often primarily) by subject headings, unless authors and titles in your subject area are familiar to you.

Books may also be found in indexes that list articles in periodicals. The most comprehensive of these are the *Bibliographic Index* (a general resource for finding books and articles), the *Readers' Guide to Periodical Literature* (which indexes popular journals and magazines), the *Humanities Index* (which indexes books and more authoritative, academic journals in humanis-tic disciplines like literature and history), and the *Social Sciences Index* (which indexes books and more authoritative, academic journals in social sciences like anthropology and psychology). Most such indexes (and there are many more) are themselves periodicals, typically coming out once each year and representing a collocation of a year's worth of material. They are orga-nized by subject headings—so we again meet with the importance of knowing how your subject (whatever you yourself call it) is listed.

Newspapers are also indexed, if less extensively and variously. Only three U.S. newspapers index themselves—the *New York Times,* the *Wall Street Journal,* and the *Christian Science Monitor*—but articles in many other newspapers are indexed by *The National Newspaper Index,* which is not a book at all, but a microfilm-projection unit that looks much like a TV set and is available in most libraries.

Deciphering what is said on the cards (or screen) in a card (or computer) catalog and especially in entries in the aforementioned indexes can be a formidable task. Cryptic symbols and abbreviations may throw you, as may finding your way around the library itself. For help in such matters, consult the reference librarian(s) on hand. Of all the resources available in your library none is more valuable: expert, enormously resourceful, above all, human—able to answer questions, to puzzle things out with you, to give you advice on how to conduct your search for sources.

Keeping Track of What You've Tracked Down

Guides to research often go into elaborate descriptions of what procedures to follow in gathering information—what size note cards to use, what corner to write the author's name (if any) in, and so on. We don't see much point to this; whatever system you follow is fine *so long as you keep track of what you need.* "What you need" includes all the bibliographic information you will need for due source attribution (which we'll get to shortly) as well as the exact wording of anything you might want to quote. In our experience, most students balance effective cost-management against effective time-management and do judicious photocopying. This is certainly preferable to marking up or ripping off what your library has (and wants to keep) in the stacks. Whatever you do, keep track of sources and what they say; the alternative is wasting a lot of valuable time rereading what you've already read, maybe even tracking down the same source twice.

CITING AND DOCUMENTING SOURCES

When Do You Give Credit?

You give credit whenever credit is due. You must provide enough information to allow a reader to identify and refer to all the sources you have used. Anything else is plagiarism. (There's that word again.) Plagiarism is using other people's words or ideas without giving them credit, and this form of theft is considered a heinous crime in the academic community (where words and ideas are particularly prized commodities). So you want to avoid outright theft or—what is much more common—inadequate acknowledgment because of an uncertainty about the rules and procedures for due source attribution. We'll get to the procedures shortly. Here we want to concentrate on the rules, the laws, the moral imperatives. Again, the general rule is to provide enough information to allow a reader to identify and refer to all the sources you have used. Here are some specific applications of that general rule:

1. **Anything you quote**—anything you cite word-for-word—**must be acknowledged as coming from a source.** This is just common sense and basic ethics.

2. **Anything you paraphrase**—any opinion or information coming from elsewhere but restated in your own words—**must be acknowledged as coming from a source.** This, too, is common sense. Rewording what someone else said doesn't make it yours.

3. **Any idea or opinion that informs your thinking** and you know you encountered elsewhere **must be acknowledged as coming from a source.** Common sense should be your guide here as well. The idea that there are no new ideas is itself hardly a new idea, but let's say you come across an interesting proposal for dealing with the problem of homelessness in a newspaper editorial. You don't need a guidebook or a lawyer to tell you that representing that idea as your own isn't right.

4. **Any information that is common knowledge** ("Dinosaurs once walked the earth") **or any opinion that is generally held** ("Child abuse is an

appalling crime") need *not* be acknowledged as coming from a source. The problem is not that there are no sources for such statements but that there are so many. You can't cite them all—so you needn't cite any.

5. **When in doubt, acknowledge a source rather than cover your trail of indebtedness.** The best test is a sense of what your reader might be curious about. (It's always a good idea to try to anticipate questions your reader might have about what you have to say.) When reading your writing with your reader in mind, do you at any point imagine that person thinking, "I wonder where the writer got this?" If so, then that's a point where you probably need source attribution.

Kinds and Degrees of Acknowledgment

Consider the following passage, which comes from Ira Shor's *Culture Wars: School and Society in the Conservative Restoration 1969–1984* (Boston: Routledge & Kegan Paul, 1986), 155.

> A society that refuses to direct available resources to education must use tough authority to get students and teachers to perform. Rules and punishment substitute for prosperity and democracy. Instead of merit pay schemes, teachers need big pay increases across-the-board. They should establish their own mechanisms for rewarding peers they admire. Also, there should be mechanisms by which students and the community both reward and challenge teachers, for their devotion and for their lapses. These interactions should be self-organizing and mutual, based in support rather than punishment or unequal rewards.

Using any part of this—or, still more obviously, the whole of it—without indicating in any way that it came from Shor would of course be plagiarism. But because there are kinds and degrees of acknowledgment there can also be kinds and degrees of plagiarism. In each of the following illustrations, the acknowledgment will be *formally* correct—in accordance with established conventions for source attribution—but it will not necessarily be ethically and wholly correct because it may not be entirely fair or adequate acknowledgment.

Consider this instance:

```
According to Ira Shor, "A society that refuses to direct
available resources to education must use tough author-
ity to get students and teachers to perform. Rules and
punishment substitute for prosperity and democracy"
(Culture Wars 155). There are better ways. We could
establish local, self-governing systems in which teach-
ers could identify the best among them as deserving
reward, systems in which students could also identify
their best teachers as deserving reward.
```

Note, first of all, the form of acknowledgment because that much at least is correct. The author of the source is identified in the process of introducing a quotation—and it is always better to do something like this than force your reader to consult your list of sources to see who said what—and the book title and page number are given in the standard form for parenthetical in-text documentation. (The book title is not necessary unless there is more than one work by Shor in the list of sources.) So everything is fine, no? No. Our imaginary author has suggested that his or her debt to Shor ends with the end of the quotation. In effect, Shor is posing a problem for which our imaginary author seems to have the solution—though it is in fact Shor's. This is plagiarism, misrepresentation, outright theft. It wouldn't be hard to fix, though. A little sentence like, "At least that is what Shor recommends" at the end would do the trick.

Let's look at another case.

> In <u>Culture Wars</u>, Ira Shor criticizes society's inclina-
> tion to use rules and punishment rather than prosperity
> and democracy to make teachers and students get the job
> done. He advocates allowing teachers and students to
> devise means of identifying and rewarding good teaching
> and good scholarship. Such reward systems would be self-
> organizing and mutual, based in support rather than pun-
> ishment or unequal rewards (155).

Here, again, the form of attributing the source, though slightly different, is correct. And it would be hard to call the problem—for there is a problem—outright theft. Framed by a mention of the author and title at the beginning and a parenthetical page number at the end, the whole of what we have here is indicated as coming from Shor. But the absence of quotation marks suggests that we are not looking at Shor's words, just his ideas. Is that true? Comparing the text with the original reveals that certain words and phrases have been lifted directly. Perhaps our imaginary author was being lazy—or just forgetful about how closely he or she was following the wording as well as the meaning of the source. Either way, the smaller sin we have before us in this instance is understandable—adequate paraphrase is almost always harder to do than direct quotation—but that doesn't make it right. If you want to quote someone like Shor and you aren't sure just what is meant by a phrase like "self-organizing and mutual," you had better put it in quotation marks or leave it out altogether.

Let's do just one more. We could do dozens (any passage leads itself to at least that many possible ways of citing what it has to say), but this last one will allow us to correct what was wrong in the previous instance and throw in a little something extra for you to think about.

> In <u>Culture Wars</u>, Ira Shor criticizes society's incli-
> nation to use "rules and punishment" rather than "pros-
> perity and democracy" to make teachers and

```
students get the job done. He advocates allowing teach-
ers and students to devise means of identifying and
rewarding good teaching and good scholarship. Such
reward systems would "be self-organizing and mutual,
based in support rather than punishment or unequal
rewards" (155). But this is easier said than done. Such
reward systems would also need built-in safeguards to
prevent them from turning into political or popularity
contests. If they rewarded the teachers with the most
clout or the fewest assignments, education would be made
worse, not better.
```

The point here is that adequate acknowledgment (important as it is) is not enough. Why? The reason is something we began this guide with: the idea is not simply to cite sources, but to *use* them. If you're citing an opinion—as is the case here—you want to extend it, qualify it, refute it, not just parrot it. If you're citing information, you want to interpret its significance, explain its relevance, show how it fits with other data in the picture-puzzle you're putting together. You don't just borrow. You borrow and *use*.

The Formal Proprieties of Quotation

We said, just a little while ago, that direct quotation is usually easier to do than adequate paraphrase. That's true, provided you know how to quote. Showing how means having something to quote, and it might as well be an apt quotation. So here's a paragraph from Lewis Thomas's "Notes on Punctuation," an essay published in *Medusa and the Snail* (New York: Viking Press, 1979), 127:

> Quotation marks should be used honestly and sparingly, when there is a genuine quotation at hand, and it is necessary to be very rigorous about the words enclosed by the marks. If something is to be quoted, the *exact* words must be used. If part of it must be left out because of space limitations, it is good manners to insert three dots to indicate the omission, but it is unethical to do this if it means connecting two thoughts which the original author did not intend to have tied together. Above all, quotation marks should not be used for ideas that you'd like to disown, things in the air so to speak. Nor should they be put in place around cliches; if you want to use a cliche you must take full responsibility for it yourself and not try to job it off on anon., or on society. The most objectionable misuse of quotation marks, but one which illustrates the dangers of misuse in ordinary prose, is seen in advertising, especially in advertisements for small restaurants, for example "just around the corner," or "a good place to eat." No single identifiable, citable person ever really said, for the record, "just around the corner," much less "a good place to eat," least likely of all for restaurants of the type that use this type of prose.

We've already exemplified one convention: if you have a long quotation (typically one of more than two sentences or five lines), you present it as a block quotation, which is to say you indent the whole thing (typically ten spaces). Since the indentation signals that it is a quotation, you don't need quotation marks.

When you do need quotation marks, you need to know how they work with other punctuation marks. One rule—one of the very few in American edited English that has no exceptions—is that commas and periods always go inside. Example:

> Lewis Thomas advocates using quotation marks "hon-
> estly and sparingly." [or] Lewis Thomas advocates using
> quotation marks "honestly and sparingly," and so do we.

If, however, you're following the quotation with a parenthetical page number, this changes everything.

> Lewis Thomas advocates using quotation marks "hon-
> estly and sparingly" (127). [or] Lewis Thomas advocates
> using quotation marks "honestly and sparingly" (127),
> and so do we.

You notice that, though our quotation leaves much out, we do not use the "three dots" or ellipsis Thomas speaks of. You only have to do that when what you're quoting looks like a complete statement—but isn't. Example:

> According to Thomas, "...it is necessary to be very
> rigorous about the words enclosed by the [quotation]
> marks."

Note the space after each dot in the ellipsis. Note, too, the brackets that allow us to insert something into the quotation that wasn't there in the first place. If we actually want to interrupt a quotation to say something (rather than inserting something into it), the result looks like this:

> "If something is to be quoted," observes Thomas, "the
> <u>exact</u> words must be used"; this should go without
> saying.

Note interruptions like this mean closing and reopening quotations, usually by a phrase set off by commas (the first of which goes, as adjacent commas must, inside the quotation marks). Note, however, that the semicolon goes outside the quotation. Semicolons and colons, signaling that you are adding on something of your own, never go inside, just as commas and periods always do.

You might want to ponder those unusual absolutes, but we want to return to such matters as ellipses (the plural form of *ellipsis*) and interpolations (the big word for insertions). An end-ellipsis is actually four dots rather than three because one is a period.

> Thomas insists, "...quotation marks should not be
> used for ideas that you'd like to disown...."

Note that there is no space between the first of the four dots and the terminal letter of the quotation. Once again, though, the addition of a parenthetical page number creates a different situation.

> Thomas insists, "...quotation marks should not be
> used for ideas that you'd like to disown..." (127).

So Thomas insists. But what if there's something about a quotation you're using you would like to disown, something you're not responsible for? Suppose your instructor can't abide abbreviations, but Thomas is using one in a statement you want to quote. You use the Latin word for *thus* to show you're quoting what Thomas wrote exactly (or, to use the Latin, verbatim):

> According to Thomas, "...if you want to use a cliche
> you must take full responsibility for it yourself and not
> try to job it off on anon. [sic], or on society."

We should warn you, though: *sic* is to be used sparingly. Otherwise, it may seem a snide and pedantic way of poking fun at your source.

Finally, there is the business of quotation marks within quotation marks. In American edited English—the British do this quite the opposite—we use double quotation marks for single quotations, single quotation marks (the same key as the apostrophe on most typewriters and word processors) for double quotations. Example:

> Do you suppose Thomas is right in saying, "No single,
> identifiable, citable person ever really said, for the
> record, 'just around the corner,' much less 'a good place
> to eat,' least likely of all for restaurants of the type
> that use this type of prose"?

We threw one more wrinkle in there: a question mark (or an exclamation point, for that matter) doesn't go inside quotation marks—unless it's part of the quotation.

If, after all this, you think that we were wrong, that with so many persnickety rules and niceties quoting can't possibly be easier than paraphrasing, we invite you to return to the original citation of Lewis Thomas and try doing an acceptable paraphrase of the third sentence. The meaning must be the same; the words must be different. Good luck. You'll need it.

Bibliographic Form

Just one more thing remains. You need to know how to list the works you consulted or cited. Even more, you need to know why you need to know this. You may be put off by the fact that there are different styles of source-listing and that each of them is more than a little complicated. What they all have in common is the purpose of providing all of the information someone might need to refer to your source. Sources do come in different editions or translations with different places of publication or pagination schemes; give the matter a little thought, and you'll see that all the information you're asked to provide really is potentially useful.

Just how you proceed is determined by what documentation style you're following. We'll include only the two most common: the MLA (Modern Language Association) style, used for most of the humanities, and the APA (American Psychological Association) style, used for most of the sciences. Let's consider first what the two styles have in common. In both, the bibliographic entry begins with the last name of the author (or, if there is no author, the first main word of the title), and the list of entries is alphabetized according to the first letter of that name or first word. Each part of each entry (author's name, title, publication information, etc.) is followed by a period and two spaces—in other words, punctuated as if it were a complete sentence. Each entry begins flush with the left margin and is indented five spaces to the right for any subsequent lines. Book titles (or the titles of brochures, government documents, monographs, pieces of software, record albums, or any other stand-alone sources—sources that are not inclusions in something else) are underlined.

That's what the MLA and APA styles have in common. The differences are not all that great. MLA calls for the author's full name; following APA, you would give not the first name but just the initial. In the sciences, the currency, the up-to-dateness of sources is very important, so the date follows the author's name in APA style; MLA style places the publication date with other publication information (the place of publication, then a colon, then the press or publishing house, then a comma, then the date—the same as APA except for the inclusion of the date). Finally, titles in APA style have only the initial letter (and, of course, the first letter of any proper nouns or adjectives) capitalized, and the titles of articles are not placed in quotation marks; in MLA, the initial letters of the first and last words and all the major words (all words except prepositions and *a, an,* and *the*) are capitalized, and the titles of articles (as well as poems, lyrics, short stories, and other items that are typically collected rather than stand-alone texts) are placed in quotation marks.

OK. Those are the basic principles. Now let's look at some examples. First, here are the three main kinds of MLA entries. For a book:

```
Litterateur, Jean. The Great American Text. Urbanville:
    Big City Press, 1991.
```

For an essay or article or poem or whatever in a collection:

```
Tractator, Pat. "Something about Something." The Ency-
    clopedic Anthology. Ed. Chris Scribe. Smalltown: Uni-
    versity State Press, 1987, 15-30.
```

For an article in a periodical:

> Free, Lance. "News to You." <u>Moreover Monthly</u> 15 (April
>   1993): 12-20.

If you were paying attention earlier, you should find nothing strange about the first entry. The second has a few new wrinkles. The names of editors (and also people like translators [**Trans.**]) are given after the title of the anthology or collection, and you need to give the inclusive page range for the piece you are citing. As you can see from the third entry, you need to give inclusive pagination for periodical articles as well, but you also need to give, right after the title of the periodical, the volume number (and parenthetically the date) before the colon that precedes the page range.

Now let's look at APA-style entries for the same sources. For a book:

> Litterateur, J. (1991). <u>The great American text</u>. Urban-
>   ville: Big City Press.

For an essay or article or poem or whatever in a collection:

> Tractator, P. (1987). Something about something. In
>   Scribe, C. (Ed.), <u>The encyclopedic anthology</u> (pp. 15-
>   30). Smalltown: University State Press.

For an article in a periodical:

> Free, L. (1993). News to you. <u>Moreover Monthly, 15</u> (1),
>   12-20.

Again, the first entry is simply an example of the basic principles. The second entry indicates that, for a collection, you precede the editor's last name and first initial with "In" and follow it with "(Ed.)" and a comma, then give the anthology title and inclusive pagination for the article, doing that last in parentheses (and after the standard abbreviation for "pages"). The third entry is different from its MLA counterpart not just because of different capitalization and the lack of quotation marks, but because APA asks for the volume number to be underlined and the issue number to be included in parentheses, then followed by a comma and the page range. (Note: The issue number should be left out if there is continuous pagination throughout the volume.)

The complexities of documentation styles can seem confusing even to practiced scholars. The idea is not to memorize the rules, but to refer to them. We have omitted literally hundreds of variants (dual authorship; dual editorship; publications lacking dates, places of publication, or pagination; reprints; unpublished dissertations; etc.). We don't have the time, and we expect you don't have the patience. As in all else about documenting your use of sources, let common sense be your guide. Follow your instructor's advice and instructions. Use references on source documentation that are recommended to you or seem useful to you. Above all, remember that, however knotty or irksome, the conventions of citation and source attribution exist to keep things fair to the sources you're using and convenient and informative for the reader you're addressing. These are pretty good reasons to follow those conventions.

CHAPTER EIGHTEEN

A GUIDE TO ERRORS
(AND HOW TO AVOID MAKING THEM)

What are errors anyway? We can't answer that without asking why so-called errors happen and how we know them to be errors. And if we ask how much they matter, we had better specify a context. After all, what's said between friends on a street corner is one thing, what gets past a newspaper editor's scrutinizing eye is another, and what's appropriate in the eyes of your professors yet another. If you're a typical product of the American educational system, you've already had a fair amount of feedback from teachers on the issue of errors, so let's begin somewhere else: with how people outside the educational system, in the so-called real world, respond to error.

We're going to let Maxine Hairston take care of a lot of this for us. A while back she did a survey of non-academics—lawyers, doctors, business executives, and so on—polling them on how much errors bothered them. The article was published in *College English* (Volume 43, December 1981, pp. 794–806) so you can read it if you like. What we want to look at are the results of the survey.

We should say a few words about the survey's limitations. First, it is flawed by what logicians would call inadequate sampling (especially of female respondents); more extensive polling would need to be done before we could feel sure the opinions sampled are truly representative. Second, the survey can't really be regarded as a sampling of "real-world" attitudes toward error because these errors were not encountered in the real world, but in an itemized survey created by an English teacher (so it looks very like a quiz); responding to an error in a sentence guaranteed to contain an error is not the same thing as responding to an error in the context of a memo. Finally, like all error surveys, Hairston's has its blind spots—notably the intentional exclusion of what other error studies have shown to be the most frequent error: misspelling.

Why use it then? Because it does what other studies of error do not: it gives reactions to error instead of just giving error counts or patterns. As teachers, we know the party line on errors is that they are unfortunate, bothersome distractions to readers, and Hairston's survey gets people to say how much they're bothered by different kinds of errors. Let's look at it then.

We have taken the items of the survey out of the order in which they were presented to the respondents, arranging them instead with the most bothersome first and the least bothersome last. The numbers indicating how many respondents were not bothered, were bothered a little, or were bothered a lot are given for each item. We will stop after each to say a few words about what kind of error we are looking at, why it happens, and why people may find it as bothersome as they do. Here's the first, the most bothersome of all:

1. When Mitchell moved, he brung his secretary with him.

Does not bother me.	Bothers me a little.	Bothers me a lot.
Male: 0	M: 1	M: 57
Female: 0	F: 0	F: 22
Total: 0	T: 1	T: 79

Do people actually say "brung"? The problem is that some indeed do, and writers or listeners like the professionals surveyed know such people to be non-members of the educated elite, all of whom speak Standard English (the dialect of this important group). Dialectical departures from Standard English usually make good sense—*ring, rang, rung,* so why not *bring, brang, brung?*—but they also mark the users of such dialects as speakers of a non-Standard dialect. *Bring* is an irregular verb; unlike regular verbs that form the past by adding *-ed,* it takes a special form for the past: *brought.* There is no rule. You simply have to know the irregular forms—and you probably do. If you don't, just remember that speakers of Standard English, like the members of any "in" group, don't respond well to outsiders. As the saying goes, "When in Rome, do as the Romans do."

2. Him and Richards were the last ones hired.

Does not bother me.	Bothers me a little.	Bothers me a lot.
Male: 0	M: 1	M: 56
Female: 0	F: 0	F: 22
Total: 0	T: 1	T: 78

Pronouns come in three cases: nominative (*I, we, he, they, who,* etc.), objective (*me, us, him, them, whom,* etc.), and possessive (*my/mine, our/ours, his, their/theirs, whose,* etc.). What we have here is a use of the objective where the nominative is called for—since it's called for in the subject position and also as a complement for any form of the verb *to be.* This wasn't always the rule in formal English. In the King James Version of the Bible, Jesus asks, "*Whom* do they say that I the son of man am?" And in informal usage we often use the objective where formal propriety calls for the nominative, as in "It's *me*" rather than "It is *I.*" In certain informal or dialectical uses, the objective form is used in the subject position for emphasis—as a kind of verbal underlining. In this case, the sentence might be a non-Standard (but emphatic) reply to a question like "Who is that guy?" Again, then, it bothers people as much as it does because it is a form that is used—but not by speakers of Standard English.

3. There has never been no one here like that woman.

Does not bother me.	Bothers me a little.	Bothers me a lot.
Male: 0	M: 1	M: 56
Female: 0	F: 0	F: 22
Total: 0	T: 1	T: 78

This is the dreaded "double negative"—a form condemned back in the eighteenth century (the century that saw the first English dictionaries) by those who wanted the English language to be as logical as mathematics (in which two negatives cancel each other out). Before then writers like Shakespeare and Chaucer used double negatives for emphasis (Chaucer even has a quadruple negative in the Prologue to his *Canterbury Tales*). Certain dialects—notably the dialect sociolinguists call Black English Vernacular—still do. The problem, again, is that the usage is non-Standard.

4. Calhoun has went after every prize in the university.

Does not bother me.	Bothers me a little.	Bothers me a lot.
Male: 1	M: 0	M: 55
Female: 0	F: 0	F: 22
Total: 1	T: 0	T: 77

Here we have another irregular verb—and it's a bit irregular even among irregular verbs. Most verbs have the same form for the past and the past participle: in the case of *bring,* we have *brought* and also *has brought;* but in the case of *go,* we have *went* but *has gone.* Consistently, dialectical variations on Standard English are attempts at simplification. The problem is that such simplifications are scorned and stigmatized by users of Standard English.

5. When we was in the planning stages of the project, we underestimated the costs.

Does not bother me.	Bothers me a little.	Bothers me a lot.
Male: 2	M: 0	M: 52
Female: 0	F: 0	F: 22
Total: 2	T: 0	T: 74

Here we have another irregular verb, the most highly irregular one of all: *to be.* It is the only verb that takes different forms for the singular and plural in the past tense: *I was* but *you were; he was* but *they were.* Because forms of the verb *to be* are so complicated—again, it is the only verb to make you worry over subject-verb agreement in the past tense—there have been all sorts of attempts to simplify it, with the best known simplification of all being the present tense contraction *ain't.* Compare formal and informal forms:

Singular	Plural	Singular	Plural
I am not	we are not	I ain't	we ain't
you are not	you are not	you ain't	you ain't
he/she/it is not	they are not	he/she/it ain't	they ain't

Ain't is obviously the simpler form, but, as Will Rogers said, "Most folks that say *ain't* ain't eatin'." They're poor and they're likely to stay that way as long as they talk that way. That's not fair, of course, but language is like life in that respect: it ain't fair.

6. Jones don't think it is acceptable.

Does not bother me.	Bothers me a little.	Bothers me a lot.
Male: 0	M: 1	M: 56
Female: 0	F: 0	F: 22
Total: 0	T: 1	T: 78

Don't is like *ain't* in this instance; saying *Jones don't* instead of *Jones doesn't* marks the speaker's or writer's usage as non-Standard. What's interesting is that *he don't* was perfectly acceptable two hundred years ago. Only one contraction existed for both *does not* and *do not*. Then the legislators of language decided *don't* would do for *do not* but not for *does not*. Consequently, we have an informal Standard contraction *doesn't* that doesn't save us a syllable—and that, after all, is the chief point of having contractions. Standard English doesn't always have logic on its side; what it does have is power. Keep both those things in mind.

7. State employees can't hardly expect a raise this year.

Does not bother me.	Bothers me a little.	Bothers me a lot.
Male: 2	M: 4	M: 49
Female: 0	F: 1	F: 20
Total: 2	T: 5	T: 69

Another double negative—though less striking than "no one/never."

8. Senator javits comes from new york.

Does not bother me.	Bothers me a little.	Bothers me a lot.
Male: 4	M: 4	M: 47
Female: 0	F: 2	F: 20
Total: 4	T: 6	T: 67

Actually, Senator Javits *came* from New York (he's dead now), but the mistake in terms of usage is the failure to capitalize the proper nouns we just capitalized. Capitalizing proper nouns (names of specific people, cities, nations, etc.) is a rule you learned back in elementary school—a rule that is strictly a matter of conventions of *writing*, not speaking. What's interesting is that violating this basic rule is less bothersome to nearly a dozen people than the use of *brung*. Why? The answer has to be speculative, but we strongly suspect that one error conjures up, in the minds of the respondents, someone who is having trouble with the typewriter shift key; the other conjures up someone they don't think belongs in their office.

9. The company is prepared to raise prices. In spite of administrative warnings.

Does not bother me.	Bothers me a little.	Bothers me a lot.
Male: 4	M: 9	M: 44
Female: 0	F: 2	F: 20
Total: 4	T: 11	T: 64

"In spite of administrative warnings" is punctuated as something it isn't: a complete sentence. This bothers a lot of people a lot, but it's more tolerable than the errors that preceded it for two reasons. First, we punctuate not just our writing but also our speech, not with commas and periods but with "suprasegmentals": tone, pitch, stress, and juncture—with juncture (pausing) being the most important of these. (If we were to transcribe a dialogue in which this statement occurred, it might be punctuated this way—with the period representing a significant pause.) The other factor inclining at least some respondents to tolerate this error is print advertising, which, since it likes to try to approximate the spoken rather than the written, is fond of punctuating things this way. (This gives it more flair. More pizzazz. More punch.)

10. Good policemen require three qualities: courage, tolerance, and dedicated.

Does not bother me.	Bothers me a little.	Bothers me a lot.
Male: 5	M: 6	M: 46
Female: 1	F: 3	F: 18
Total: 6	T: 9	T: 64

Here the problem is not a departure from Standard English; it's a departure from a pattern the sentence itself sets up: "(noun): (noun), (noun), and ([whoops!] adjective)." Teachers call this faulty parallelism. This sort of thing happens all the time. Why? Because there are any number of ways of saying the same thing. They compete in the writer's brain, and what gets written may leave the competition unresolved. In addition to a statement that ended with "dedication" rather than "dedicated," this writer may have been thinking of something like "Good policemen need to be courageous, tolerant, and dedicated." Both ways of expressing the thought are fine. It's mixing the constructions together that bothers people.

11. He concentrated on his job he never took vacations.

Does not bother me.	Bothers me a little.	Bothers me a lot.
Male: 5	M: 11	M: 41
Female: 0	F: 2	F: 20
Total: 5	T: 13	T: 61

This is what teachers call a run-on sentence. If you think about what happened the first time you read it, you know why: without any signal that a new clause is beginning with the second "he," you went careening on into it. It only takes a minute to readjust, but that's chiefly because the two clauses are both so short. If they were much longer, think how much more you would be "bothered" by the absence of a period or semicolon. The lesson to be learned here: punctuation marks sort out your words into blocks of meaning. They're useful signals, not decorative marks.

12. Cox cannot predict, that street crime will diminish.

Does not bother me.	Bothers me a little.	Bothers me a lot.
Male: 6	M: 10	M: 42
Female: 0	F: 3	F: 19
Total: 6	T: 13	T: 61

In Francis Bacon's time, this would have been correct. The convention back then was to put a comma before a *that* clause. But we don't do that anymore. This gives us a corollary to the lesson just given above: punctuation marks are not the salt and pepper of writing—something to be sprinkled about whatever you're serving up to your reader. Use them as needed (or as convention dictates); otherwise, you'll "bother" people.

13. The lieutenant treated his men bad.

Does not bother me.	Bothers me a little.	Bothers me a lot.
Male: 1	M: 17	M: 38
Female: 0	F: 4	F: 18
Total: 1	T: 21	T: 56

Something interesting is going on here: almost everyone is bothered by this sentence (or the error in it), but a lot more people are not bothered a lot. Why? The error is the use of the adjective *bad* for the adverb *badly*. Adjectives modify nouns; adverbs, verbs (and adjectives and other adverbs). We're in one of the fuzzier areas of grammar here, not because people can't tell the difference, but because some forms blur the difference. Certain adjectives like *lonely* and *friendly* look like adverbs. The adjective *good* pairs off with the adverb *well* though *bad* pairs off with *badly*. And then there are adjectives that modify subjects by way of linking verbs (they're called predicate adjectives) and so are positioned like adverbs. You feel bad? That means you're sick. You feel badly? That means your sense of touch is off. But people confuse them, partly because "You don't look good" and "You don't look well" are both ways of saying the same thing—since "well" is not just an adverb but an adjective when it's used with reference to health. Confused? Even if you aren't, you probably see why a number of people are forgiving about what just about everyone sees as a somewhat bothersome error.

14. The army moved my husband and I to California last year.

Does not bother me.	Bothers me a little.	Bothers me a lot.
Male: 2	M: 18	M: 38
Female: 1	F: 3	F: 18
Total: 3	T: 21	T: 56

"The army moved my husband and *me*" is the correct form, since something moved (rather than doing the moving) is the object (rather than the subject) and so should be in the objective case. Why is this so much less bothersome than the related error in #2? Well, it's not an error in the lead word. It's also a fairly common mistake and has been for some time. In *The Rudiments of English Grammar* (1761), Joseph Priestly complained that "the nominative case is sometimes found after verbs and prepositions"; citing Priestly in *Unlocking the English Language* (New York: Hill and Wang, 1991), Robert Burchfield mourns, "It is sad to think that after two centuries of condemnation the erroneous use is still very widespread" (35).

15. He went through a long battle. A fight against unscrupulous opponents.

Does not bother me.	Bothers me a little.	Bothers me a lot.
Male: 9	M: 12	M: 38
Female: 1	F: 3	F: 18
Total: 10	T: 15	T: 56

We've finally reached the double digits in the "does not bother me" column. This is essentially the same error we found in #9. Why is this instance less bothersome? We think it's because there we had an adverbial phrase ("In spite...") masquerading as a complete sentence; here we have a noun phrase ("A fight..."). This latter formulation is especially popular in print advertising—and so something our eyes have grown accustomed to. You know: "The Zigzag. A sports car. A family car. A car for all seasons."

16. If Clemens had picked up that option, his family would of been rich.

Does not bother me.	Bothers me a little.	Bothers me a lot.
Male: 6	M: 14	M: 36
Female: 1	F: 2	F: 19
Total: 7	T: 16	T: 55

Hairston calls *would of* a "colloquialism," but it's actually a misspelling (in a survey that was not intended to have any). The correct (but informal) form is *would've,* and *would of* is what teachers call a homophonic (sound-alike) misspelling, just as people occasionally write *to* for *too, their* for *there,* etc. Sound (even when we read silently) contributes so much to sense that this error can slip by some readers, and it is frequent (and understandable) enough to be forgiven by others, but let's not forget that we're still among errors that bother the majority "a lot."

17. I was last employed by texas instruments company.

Does not bother me.	Bothers me a little.	Bothers me a lot.
Male: 3	M: 15	M: 38
Female: 0	F: 4	F: 17
Total: 3	T: 19	T: 55

This is the same sort of error as in #8—but less bothersome probably because company names aren't quite as well established as personal or places names (Javits, New York) as proper nouns.

We've already hit a few semi-redundancies in the survey (with respect to verb forms, double negatives, fragments, pronouns, and now capitalization), and we're only at #17 in a 65-item survey. You may be deeply interested in why one instance of a particular kind of error bothered people more than another instance, but we can't count on it. You'll probably start jumping ahead if we don't, so bear with us, and we'll try to keep to the more helpful and revealing items.

21. The reporter paid attention to officers but ignores enlisted men.

Does not bother me.	Bothers me a little.	Bothers me a lot.
Male: 5	M: 19	M: 30
Female: 0	F: 5	F: 19
Total: 5	T: 24	T: 49

This is a near-relative of what happened back in #10. That was a word-class shift (a switch from nouns to an adjective); this is a tense shift (a switch from past to present). In both cases, there is no rule that one form is right and the other is wrong, just an expectation set up by the sentence.

26. The interruption will not effect my work.

Does not bother me.	Bothers me a little.	Bothers me a lot.
Male: 20	M: 13	M: 26
Female: 4	F: 3	F: 15
Total: 24	T: 16	T: 41

The correct word is *affect:* an interruption that will not *affect* your work will not have an *effect* on it. Like other words that look or sound somewhat similar (*lie/lay, then/than*) and actual homophones or sound-alikes (*to/two/too, there/their/they're*), *affect* and *effect* are often confused. Similarity makes such confusions a little less noticeable than some errors (and a little more forgivable once noticed), but this is something to keep an eye out for when editing.

33. Having argued all morning, a decision was finally reached.

Does not bother me.	Bothers me a little.	Bothers me a lot.
Male: 17	M: 17	M: 23
Female: 3	F: 7	F: 12
Total: 20	T: 24	T: 35

Syntax—the arrangement of words in sentences—needs to be consistent and logical. We have already noted inconsistencies or shifts in sentences #10 and #21. Here we have something different. The rule for noun and adjective phrases—what we have here is a participial phrase (formed from the participle *having*) acting as an adjective—is that they refer to whatever they're closest to. The sentence logic here tells us that the decision argued all morning. The correct form would be "Having argued all morning, we finally reached a decision." This replaces a passive with an active construction—something most instructors are in favor of most of the time—but note that you would have to do the opposite to fix a sentence like "Driving in my car, a dog chased me."

36. Enclosed in his personnel file is his discharge papers and job references.

Does not bother me.	Bothers me a little.	Bothers me a lot.
Male: 8	M: 15	M: 32
Female: 0	F: 2	F: 2
Total: 8	T: 17	T: 34

This is inverted syntax. Invert it back to what is more common, with the subject in the lead position, and the problem is easier to spot: "His discharge papers and job references is enclosed in his personnel file." Now it's obvious that *is* should be *are.* You need to realize, though, that syntax in which the subject is not up front, signaling the need for a singular or plural verb, is quite common itself. Frequently used forms include questions ("Are the results posted?" "What are we going to say?") and constructions following a relative pronoun like *what* ("What I think we need are the proper tools").

41. Sanford inquired whether the loan was overdue?

Does not bother me.	Bothers me a little.	Bothers me a lot.
Male: 5	M: 33	M: 18
Female: 0	F: 7	F: 15
Total: 5	T: 40	T: 33

Many of the survey's middle-range errors are punctuation mistakes. This is one. The problem here is the question mark at the end of a declarative (not an interrogative) statement. Sanford may have asked a question (something like, "Is the loan overdue?"), but this is not it.

44. I have always hoped to work in that field, now I will have the opportunity.

Does not bother me.	Bothers me a little.	Bothers me a lot.
Male: 12	M: 34	M: 10
Female: 6	F: 7	F: 19
Total: 18	T: 41	T: 29

This error is what many English teachers call a comma splice. That's the splicing together of two independent clauses—each of which could stand as a complete sentence—with a comma. A comma can't do that. It takes a semicolon. Still, a comma splice is less bothersome than a run-on (see #11), which would lack any internal punctuation.

50. Its wonderful to have Graham back on the job.

Does not bother me.	Bothers me a little.	Bothers me a lot.
Male: 23	M: 21	M: 10
Female: 3	F: 8	F: 12
Total: 26	T: 29	T: 22

We have another of those sound-alike confusions: *Its* should be *It's.* This one is especially common because *it's,* the contraction for *it is,* looks like a possessive—(Ricardo's), but the possessive pronoun *its* lacks an apostrophe (as do all the other possessive pronouns—*his,* for instance). Since your (there's another possessive pronoun) ear won't help you with this, you need to keep an eye peeled for it.

56. Tact not anger is the best tactic in this case.

Does not bother me.	Bothers me a little.	Bothers me a lot.
Male: 16	M: 25	M: 12
Female: 6	F: 10	F: 6
Total: 22	T: 35	T: 18

Toward the top end of the survey, many of the errors are fairly fine points of punctuation. Here, *not anger,* the noun phrase stuck in between the subject (*tact*) and the verb (*is*), needs to be set off by commas—just as we have set off the noun phrase we stuck between our subject and our verb in this sentence.

Just in case you're wondering what we're skipping past in the survey now that we're up in the fifties, we'll let you in on some of these high-end errors: mistaking *between* (referring to two) for *among* (three or more); comma-splicing (twice); leaving out a comma before the conjunction *and* in a compound sentence; leaving out a comma after an introductory clause; saying "employees *that*" rather than "employees *who*"; and thinking that the word *unique* can be modified by a word like *most* (when there can't be degrees of uniqueness—something is either unique or it's not). Now let's look at the last five, wondering as we do just how important are the errors that don't seem very bothersome, how much, in fact, they are really and clearly errors.

60. The worst situation is when the patient ignores warning symptoms.

Does not bother me.	Bothers me a little.	Bothers me a lot.
Male: 26	M: 24	M: 8
Female: 9	F: 7	F: 6
Total: 35	T: 31	T: 14

In formal Standard Edited English, only two things can follow a form of the verb *to be:* an adjective (or something performing the function of an adjective) or a noun (or something performing the function of a noun); "when the patient ignores warning symptoms" is an adverbial clause—and so illegal. But it also conjures up a "situation" and so functions a little like a noun phrase. To dispense with all the jargon for the moment, it's also the sort of thing people say all the time, and the more people say something, the more likely it is to become "correct," even in writing. Instances of this transformation abound: the eroded distinction between *that* and *which,* the eroding distinction between *who* and *whom,* the increasing use of *hopefully* in the sense "it is to be hoped," etc.

61. The situation is quite different than that of previous years.

Does not bother me.	Bothers me a little.	Bothers me a lot.
Male: 24	M: 25	M: 7
Female: 9	F: 7	F: 6
Total: 33	T: 32	T: 13

Different is an adjective, so this sentence follows the rule the previous sentence broke. The problem is that it should read *different from* and not *different than. Different from* is what is called an idiom: an expression formed by words joined to give a particular meaning, not because of any rules, just because of habit. The problem is that *different* denotes comparison or contrast, and almost all other locutions that do that use *than: greater than, less than,* but *different from. Than* has been worming its way in for some time—especially in the expression *differently than*—so that by the time your children say *different than* you may not feel the need to correct them. Children do that because they learn the rules quickly; only gradually do they see how often "correct" usage breaks them. If Standard English were systematic, the past tense of *catch* would be *catched.* And the correct idiom for something *other than* would be *different than,* not *different from.*

62. Three causes of inflation are: easy credit, costly oil, and consumer demand.

Does not bother me.	Bothers me a little.	Bothers me a lot.
Male: 32	M: 16	M: 6
Female: 10	F: 3	F: 6
Total: 42	T: 19	T: 12

There's no call for a colon after *are.* The verb *to be* is the verbal equivalent of the equals sign; using a colon (the punctuation-mark equivalent of "namely") after it is a form of redundancy. But it's a popular form of redundancy, especially in business writing and print advertising. The colon is a dramatic punctuation mark, a little like saying "I'm about to give you something and—ta-da!—here it is." So people do it for effect, more and more, and the more they do it, the more familiar (and close to correct) it becomes.

63. Almost everyone dislikes her; they say she is careless and insolent.

Does not bother me.	Bothers me a little.	Bothers me a lot.
Male: 31	M: 24	M: 3
Female: 12	F: 5	F: 6
Total: 43	T: 29	T: 9

Though we have skipped to the least bothersome instance, errors in using *everyone* have come up earlier (in items #37, #42, and #47). It crops up often because of the way it is always plural in reference but grammatically singular. Here, following *everyone* with the grammatically correct *he* (instead of *they*) is sexist and conflicts with the meaning of the sentence. The use of the grammatically correct *she* for *they* also might be sexist (and confusing, since we already have a *she,* or rather a *her*)—and it also conflicts with the meaning of the sentence. The use of the grammatically correct *he or she* for *they* is not sexist, but it is clumsy—and it, too, conflicts with the meaning of the sentence. So what do you do? According to the official pronouncement on sexism and language developed by the National Council of Teachers of English, you leave the sentence just as it is—except in the most formal situations. We would add that it's easy to recast the sentence so that it reads something like "Almost all the people in the office dislike her; they say she is careless and insolent."

64. The data supports her hypothesis.

Does not bother me.	Bothers me a little.	Bothers me a lot.
Male: 38	M: 16	M: 5
Female: 12	F: 5	F: 3
Total: 50	T: 21	T: 8

Certain nouns in English are borrowed from the Latin so directly that they come complete with the Latin plural forms. In some cases, we don't know which to use, the Latin plural or the English. Is it *syllabuses* or *syllabi*? *Cactuses* or *cacti*? It's even trickier in cases where the plural is as common as the singular: *criteria* as the plural of *criterion, media* as the plural of *medium;* folks will often construe the plural form as singular. It's trickiest of all when the plural is far more common than the singular—and people don't always realize the plural is plural. *Data* is the plural of *datum,* but who uses the singular? And the plural is often construed as meaning "body of data." So educated people say "data supports" rather than "data support" all the time. After reading through the survey and our comments, you don't need to be told what happens when educated people say something often enough. You know that it becomes just fine to say it that way. You know, in fact, that the data support(s) that hypothesis.

That's the survey. In case wading through it makes you wonder if you can see the forest for the trees, we should stress a few overarching points. First, the most stigmatizing errors are those that mark the people making them as users of dialects other than Standard English, dialect of the educated elite. At the other end of the scale are errors that are scarcely bothersome because they're the sorts of things members of the educated elite write and say all the time. It's worth noting, though, that a small core of respondents (especially from the small sample of females) were consistently bothered by errors of any kind. These are people in the professions, women in particular, who know that it's the little things that matter, that seem to betray your intelligence when all they betray is your social roots or your familiarity with conventions or your inclination to proofread.

What should you do about errors? We suggest three things.

1. You should realize that some errors are shifts away from standardized forms and conventions. These are all codified to some extent. Spelling is the most thoroughly codified, and the codification is called a dictionary.

Make sure you have one, and use it. If you don't know irregular verb forms, get a list and memorize them. Other especially regularized, academic conventions such as the rules for quotation you'll find in this section of this text. But the way you learn the conventions of writing is, for the most part, not by way of lists and rules; you learn them by seeing them in action. In short, you learn them by reading. So read.

2. Most other errors are shifts away from forms and expectations you yourself set up as you write: these are tense shifts, cases of faulty parallelism or mixed constructions, misplaced modifiers, pronoun reference problems. In addition to needing to be consistent with the established conventions of the language, you need to be consistent with yourself: make sure your sentence logic is indeed logical, and you'll spare your reader a lot of bother. Of course, this can happen only if you make sure that what you meant to say is actually what you said, and that's possible only if you proofread carefully.

3. The idea is not to learn all the rules and all the exceptions thereto. It's to know only what you need to know. You are at a level where your language proficiency, both in speaking and writing, is at a very advanced level. You're fine-tuning. Reading will help you more than anything—this is what expands your repertoire, your range, your reach—but you may need to work on your language production (writing/editing as output) as well as extend your language acquisition (reading/learning as input). If you're making errors, work on the errors *you* make. We've generalized about kinds of errors here: how much they matter, why they happen. Now you have to identify what your specific patterns and problems are, why they happen, how much they matter. You need to work with your instructor on this, but you also need to realize that you, ultimately, are responsible for your own language use.

COPYRIGHT ACKNOWLEDGMENTS

INDEX